International Film Guide

2011

the definitive annual review of world cinema

edited by Ian Haydn Smith

47th edition

now online! www.internationalfilmguide.com

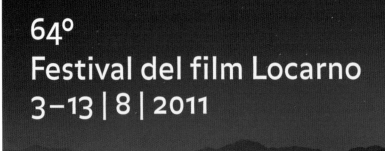

64°
Festival del film Locarno
3–13 | 8 | 2011

Main sponsors:

UBS   æt   MANOR°   swisscom

www.pardo.ch

Credits

International Film Guide
4 Eastern Terrace Mews
Brighton
BN2 1EP
tel: +44 (0)1349 854931
saraifg@aol.com
www.internationalfilmguide.com

ISBN 978-1-908215-00-0

A catalogue record for this book is
available from the British Library

Copyright
© 2011 International Film Guide

Printed and bound in Poland
by Hussar Books & POZKAL

For information on sales and distribution in all territories worldwide,
please contact the International Film
Guide on saraifg@aol.com

Editor
Ian Haydn Smith

Publisher
Yoram Allon

Founding Editor
Peter Cowie

Consultant Editor
Daniel Rosenthal

Editorial Assistant
Anne Hudson

Selected Contributors
Laurence Boyce, Alfredo Friedlander,
Siobahn Griffin, Hannah Patterson,
Michael Pierce, Ben Walters,
Helen de Witt, Jason Wood

Designer
Elsa Mathern

Production Manager
Tom Cabot

Photo Consultants
The Kobal Collection
www.picturedesk.com

International Business Manager
Sara Tyler
Europe, Film Festivals
tel: +44 (0)1349 854931
saraifg@aol.com

International Consultants
Sherif Awad
Egypt, Iran, Turkey
mobile: +20 12 0827398
sherif_awad@link.net

Scott Bayer and Beth Ann Holderman
North America
Tel: +1 917 365 0999
indiefilmreport@gmail.com

Voula Georgakakou
Cyprus, Greece
Tel: +30 694 439 0510
voulageorg@yahoo.gr

Anita Lewton
Belgium, France, Republic of Ireland,
United Kingdom
Tel: +44 (0)7866 294766
anita.lewton@googlemail.com

Lisa Ray
India, Italy, Middle East, South East
Asia, South Africa
Tel: +44 (0)7798 662955
l.ray@hotmail.co.uk

Front Cover
Natalie Portman plays the troubled ballerina in Darren Aronofsky's **Black Swan** (courtesy of Fox Searchlight Pictures).

Contents

International Liaison 6
Notes from the Editor 7

Directors of the Year
Darren Aronofsky 11
Juan José Campanella 15
Alejandro González Iñárritu 19
Kim Longinotto 23
Apichatpong Weerasethakul 28

Industry Spotlight:
Film i Väst 33
Education Spotlight:
Whistling Woods International 38
DVD Focus 41

World Survey
Algeria 63
Argentina 65
Armenia 68
Australia 70
Austria 75
Belgium 78
Bolivia 82
Bosnia & Herzegovina 85
Bulgaria 87
Canada 89
Chile 93
China 95
Colombia 99
Croatia 101
Cuba 104
Cyprus 106
Czech Republic 108
Denmark 112
Ecuador 116
Egypt 118
Estonia 123
Finland 126
France 129

Georgia 136
Germany 138
Greece 142
Hong Kong 145
Hungary 149
Iceland 152
India 155
Iran 159
Ireland 163
Israel 166
Italy 169
Japan 173
Kazakhstan 177
Latvia 179
Lithuania 181
Luxembourg 183
Malta 185
Mexico 187
Morocco 190
Mozambique 192
Netherlands 194
New Zealand 198
Nigeria 201
Norway 203
Poland 206
Portugal 210
Romania 213
Russia 216
Serbia 220
Singapore 223
Slovakia 225
Slovenia 227
South Africa 229
South Korea 233
Spain 237
Sweden 242
Switzerland 245
Taiwan 245
Thailand 252
Tunisia 255

Turkey 257
Ukraine 260
United Kingdom 262
United States 269
Uruguay 278
Vietnam 282

Additional Countries
Burkina Faso 283
Cambodia 283
Cameroon 284
Chad 284
Costa Rica 285
Gabon 286
Ghana 286
Guatemala 287
Guinea 287
Iraq 288
Ivory Coast 288
Kyrgyzstan 288
Lebanon 289
Mali 290
Mauritania 291
Montenegro 291
Nepal 292
Pakistan 292
Palestine 293
Peru 294
Senegal 295
Syria 296
Uzbekistan 297

Festival News 299
Digital Festival Report 305
IFG Inspiration Award Winners 307
Festival Director Profile 310
Film Festivals Calendar 314
Leading Festivals 317
Festivals and Markets of Note 391

Index to Advertisers 411

International Liaison

Algeria: Maryam Touzani
Argentina: Alfredo Friedlander
Armenia: Susana Harutyunyan
Australia: Peter Thompson
Austria: Gunnar Landsgesell
Belgium: Erik Martens
Bolivia: José Sanchez-H.
Bosnia and Herzegovina: Rada Sesić
Bulgaria: Pavlina Jeleva
Burkina Faso: Honoré Essoh
Cambodia: Michelle Vachon
Cameroon: Honoré Essoh
Canada: Tom McSorely
Chad: Agnes Thomasi
Chile: Hugo Díaz Gutierrez
China: Luna Lin
Colombia: Jaime E. Manrique and
   Pedro Adrián Zuluaga
Costa Rica: Maria Lourdes Cortés
Croatia: Tomislav Kurulec
Cuba: Jorge Yglesias
Cyprus: Ninos Fenek-Mikelidis
Czech Republic: Rudolf Schimera
and Michal Kriz
Denmark: Christian Monggaard
Ecuador: Gabriela Alemán
Egypt: Sherif Awad
Estonia: Jaan Ruus
Finland: Antti Selkokari
France: Michel Ciment
Gabon: Agnes Thomasi
Georgia: Nino Ekvtimishvili

Germany: Andrea Dittgen
Ghana: Steve Ayorinde
Greece: Ninos Fenek-Mikelidis
Guatemala: Maria Lourdes Cortés
Guinea: Agnes Thomasi
Hong Kong: Tim Youngs
Hungary: John Cunningham
Iceland: Eddie Cockrell
India: Uma Da Cunha
Iran: Kamyar Mohsenin
Iraq: Sherif Awad
Ireland: Donald Clarke
Israel: Dan Fainaru
Italy: Lorenzo Codelli
Ivory Coast: Honoré Essoh
Japan: Katsuta Tomomi
Kazakhstan: Gulnara Abikeyeva
Kyrgyzstan: Gulnara Abikeyeva
Latvia: Toms Treibergs
Lebanon: Sherif Awad
Lithuania: Ilona Jurkonytė
Luxembourg: Boyd van Hoeij
Mali: Honoré Essoh
Malta: Daniel Rosenthal
Mauritania: Agnes Thomasi
Mexico: Carlos Bonfil
Montenegro: Goran Gocic
Morocco: Maryam Touzani
Mozambique: Guido Convents
Netherlands: Leo Bankersen
Nepal: Prabesh Subedi

New Zealand: Peter Calder
Nigeria: Steve Ayorinde
Norway: Trond Olav Svendsen
Pakistan: Aijaz Gul
Palestine: Sherif Awad
Peru: Isaac León Frías
Poland: Barbara Hollender
Portugal: Martin Dale
Romania: Cristina Corciovescu
Russia: Kirill Razglov
Senegal: Honoré Essoh
Serbia: Goran Gocic
Singapore: Yvonne Ng
Slovakia: Miro Ulman
Slovenia: Ziva Emersic
South Africa: Martin P. Botha
South Korea: Nikki J. Y. Lee
Spain: Jonathan Holland
Sweden: Gunnar Rehlin
Switzerland: Marcy Goldberg
Syria: Sherif Awad
Taiwan: David Frazier
Thailand: Anchalee Chaiworaporn
Tunisia: Maryam Touzani
Turkey: Atilla Dorsay
Ukraine: Volodymyr Voytenko
United Kingdom: Jason Wood
United States: Tom Charity
Uruguay: Jorge Jellinek
Uzbekistan: Gulnara Abikeyeva
Vietnam: Sylvie Blum-Reid

Notes from the Editor

Since founding editor Peter Cowie published the first edition of the International Film Guide in 1963, it has become an indispensable overview of the shifting trends in world cinema. Championing filmmakers and their films, the guide has also focused on new voices and forms, often in difficult climates, from economic and cultural to political.

I mentioned in my introduction to the 2010 guide that the global financial meltdown placed severe stress on many national film industries, as evidenced in the number of countries featured. The last 12 months have done little to ease the situation. However, there are signs that activity is beginning to return, and the next edition of the guide will reflect the increased vitality of cinema around the world.

It is not only smaller countries that have been affected by the drastic economic measures taken by governments to ensure their stability. Bulgaria, Denmark, Estonia, Greece and Hungary have all experienced problems with state funding of films, a lack of private resources to make them or a general malaise on the part of local audiences. Problems also exist in exhibition, with Colombia, Iran and Pakistan all suffering from a dearth of cinemas.

However, a number of countries have seen a significant increase in market share. China and India are both branching out into the world, as well as witnessing radical changes in domestic production, although, as Luna Lin points out, China's approach to censorship is desperately in need of the overhaul that the authorities promised, but have been resistant in making.

Australia, Ecuador, Norway and Turkey all witnessed a strong year, both commercially and artistically. Hong Kong is also in a

Ian Haydn Smith

period of positive transition. As filmmakers understand the need to respond to changing tastes – recognising the desire to see a culture represented accurately rather than through the filter of lazy, overused genres – local audiences are once again willing to watch domestic releases. Germany, by contrast, has experienced something of a revival in genre filmmaking. Andrea Dittgen reports on a number of impressive films that adopt original approaches to familiar genres.

In Portugal, filmmaker João Botelho not only self-distributed his latest feature, *Film of Disquiet*, by screening it at ad-hoc venues around the country, he saw its returns far outstrip what it would have made through more traditional distribution. As Hannah Patterson writes in her report on the influential Power to the Pixel conference at the BFI London Film Festival, new modes of production, distribution and exhibition are likely to increase in their impact on the global film industry.

The In Memoriam section is now solely on the IFG website (www.internationalfilmguide. com) and although the DVD Focus continues to highlight the year's best releases in this edition, an extended version of the section appears online.

The website also expands on the partnerships and relationships discussed in this guide, both on an industry and festival front. Film I Väst, whose impressive work in developing a strong film community in Western Sweden is examined in the Industry Spotlight, will also be featured on the website throughout the year. Their work, like that of other companies, such as Filmgate, has transformed Sweden into a major player for international productions.

Our Education Focus looks at Whistling Woods, in India, which has made a name for itself as one of the world's leading international film schools, offering a vital role in encouraging and training future generations of filmmakers.

We have introduced the Festival Director Profile, which this year focuses on Olivier Père of Locarno, who took over in 2010, and Luciano Barrisone, the new Director of Nyon's Visions du Réel.

Visions du Réel is also one of our festival partners, and the IFG will once again cover the event with daily online reports, highlighting its role as one of Europe's most prominent platforms for non-fiction and documentary film. In addition, we will be covering other festivals throughout the year, from Fantasporto in Portugal and Era New Horizons in Poland, to Cottbus in Germany and Black Nights in Tallinn, the latter rounding-off a year celebrating that city's role as the 2011 European Capital of Culture.

The IFG Inspiration Award also increased its presence at festivals over the last year. The prize is given to up-and-coming filmmakers, with the winners becoming part of a network of directors from around the world whose progress the IFG will follow. Ultimately, it is

hoped that these filmmakers will develop into the new voices of future generations and may one day become one of the guide's Directors of the Year.

These directors' films are just a small number of the many impressive releases from the last year. Filmmakers such as Michelangelo Frammartino and Pedro Gonzáles-Rubio, with *Le quattro volte* and the exquisite *Alamar*, focus on our place in the greater scheme of things. There have also been films that convey the precariousness of the human condition, more often than not the result of our own devices. Xavier Beauvois' *Of Gods and Men* and Patricio Guzman's *Nostalgia for the Light* detail the search for hope in the face of violence and oppression.

However, the year ended on a bleak note, with news that Iranian filmmaker Jafar Panahi had been jailed for six years and prevented from making films, writing screenplays, travelling abroad or being interviewed by the media for twenty. He has been accused of 'assembly and collusion and propagation against the regime'. Another filmmaker, Mohammad Rasoulof, was also sentenced to six years on the same charges. At the time of this book's publication, both men are still in prison. However, there has been an increasing groundswell of international protest against the sentencing, including a petition organised by the Cannes Film Festival. To be a filmmaker, like any other artist, is to have a unique voice that can both question and inspire. Jafar Panahi and Mohammad Rasoulof embody the fight for every artist's right to freedom of expression without persecution.

Films of the Year – Editor's Choice
Nostalgia for the Light (Patricio Guzman)
Of Gods and Men (Xavier Beauvois)
Alamar (Pedro Gonzáles-Rubio)
Le quattro volte (Michelangelo Frammartino)
The Social Network (David Fincher)

Cinematographic reflexology

english français italiano español

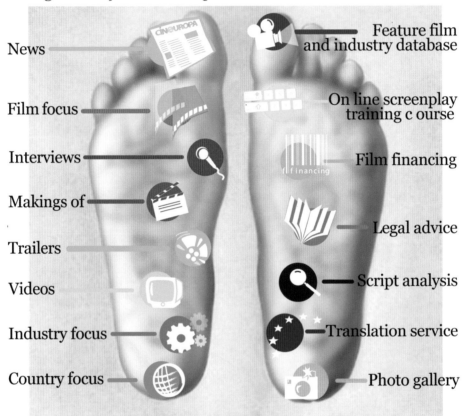

News

Film focus

Interviews

Makings of

Trailers

Videos

Industry focus

Country focus

Feature film and industry database

On line screenplay training c ourse

Film financing

Legal advice

Script analysis

Translation service

Photo gallery

● THE SITE FOR EUROPEAN CINEMA

cineUROPA.org

film's most relevant reflex points

MEDIA
A programme of the European Union

CINEUROPA.ORG IS THE ONLY PORTAL DEDICATED TO
THE EUROPEAN FILM INDUSTRY IN FOUR LANGUAGES

Cineuropa.org is an initiative co-financed by the MEDIA Programme of the European Commission, the Italian Ministry of Culture, Cinema Centre of the Ministry of French Community of Belgium, Swiss Films, Federal Cinema Office of Switzerland, Centre National de la Cinématographie, ICAA - Institute of Cinematography and Audiovisual Arts, German Films, Luxembourg Film Fund, Filmunio, Czech Film Centre, Slovenian Film Fund, Malta Film Commission, the Irish Film Board

Directors of the Year

Darren Aronofsky by Michael Pierce

Once heralded as the leading light of American independent cinema, Darren Aronofsky has emerged as a daring, ambitious and intensely practical filmmaker, working within a focused team of highly creative artists, both in front of and behind the camera. Turning the auteur theory on its head, it is his collaborative efforts with these writers, actors, musicians and producers that have created uniquely cinematic narratives and enduring, iconic characters. Whilst most of his films tend to forgo political statements and contemporary commentary, it is the spiritual, the universal and the physicality of the body that are prioritised, revealing anxieties at the heart of Western society. Like his characters, Aronofsky's obsessive quest for perfection as both a writer and director drives him to continually adapt in order to challenge expectations and progress as an artist. On the verge of his biggest achievement, as *Black Swan* arouses salivation from critics and

audiences alike, and as he prepares for his first foray into mainstream cinema with Marvel Comics' *The Wolverine*, now more than ever it is important to analyse Aronofsky's career as signposting the future development of American cinema.

The Story of π

Born out of a determination not to waste a Harvard and AFI education in filmmaking, in 1997 Aronofsky employed a crew of friends to produce his first feature, the enigmatically named π. Turning 'no-budget filmmaking' to his advantage, with a monochrome, lo-fi, cyberpunk aesthetic in the vein of Shinya Tsukamoto's *Tetsuo*, Aronofsky created a modern chase thriller that would reveal his talent for stylised filmmaking and individualistic writing. The film enters the subjective inner world of Max Cohen, a prodigiously gifted mathematician who has become obsessed with uncovering the hidden formula behind the stock market. Encountering a Kaballah-devotee who believes the Hebrew name of God is also a mathematical code, Max's mission hurtles him into a treacherous world as external forces vie for his research. Skilfully blending the two prescient worlds of stock-market forecasting and religious apocalypticism, Aronofsky's debut showed a flair for the entrepreneurial as he implemented a guerrilla marketing campaign based on the peculiarity of the film's titular mathematical symbol. Accepted into competition at Sundance, where it was awarded the Best Director prize, π would eventually secure worldwide distribution. A huge financial and critical success, with his first feature Aronofsky was propelled to the forefront of the American indie scene.

Requiem for a Dream

Adaptation of a Dream

Hugely influenced by the works of Hubert Selby Jr, Aronofsky and his producing partner Eric Watson acquired the rights to the author's 1978 novel *Requiem for a Dream*. Working directly with Selby on the script, Aronofsky's approach to the adaptation was to add personal touches, transposing action from the Bronx to his hometown of Coney Island, replicating incidents from his own youth and removing period detail, giving the film a timeless quality. Following four narratives, the film cuts across the lives of heroin addict Harry, his girlfriend Marion, best friend Tyrone and mother Sara. Whilst Harry enlists his friends in a get-rich-quick scheme that has tragic consequences, it is Sara's obsession with appearing on television that becomes the crux of the film, revealing addictions of the legal kind to be just as damaging as narcotics. With distinctive visual flair and editing to an iconic score by long-term collaborator Clint Mansell, it was the fine performances from a young cast, all playing against type, and Ellen Burstyn's gut-wrenching, Oscar nominated role that marked Aronofsky as a talented director of actors. In interviews, Aronofsky often compares the writing process to tapestry weaving, and in π and *Requiem for a Dream*, his main thread begins to take shape; he is fascinated by the obsession that drives his characters past their body's tolerance levels as they attempt to realise their heart's desire, culminating in a sense of inner peace or clarity of vision.

Death and Rebirth

This same obsession would personally affect Aronofsky on his next project, *The Fountain*, the final part of a self-professed trilogy. Developed with his friend Ari Handel, *The Fountain* was to be a modern legend dealing with man's eternal struggle against death, told across three timelines. In 2002, backed by Warner Bros with an epic budget and Brad Pitt attached as lead, the stage was set for Aronofsky's progression as a major Hollywood artist. However, when Pitt stepped down from the role, the studio decided to pull the plug. Aronofsky accepted defeat until a chance to turn his original script into a graphic novel reignited his determination to realise his pet project. Rewriting the story on a more manageable budget, in 2004 the refinanced film began shooting with new leads, Hugh Jackman and Aronofsky's then-partner Rachel Weisz.

The Fountain

Traversing three eras, *The Fountain* centres on the present-day struggle of Tom Creo, a scientist whose work attempting to halt the ageing process is exacerbated by the terminal cancer of his wife, Izzi. As she accepts her fate, it is her unpublished story of a sixteenth century conquistador seeking the Tree of Life that forms the second part of the narrative. Both parts are bookended by a seemingly future version of Creo, unable to come to terms with the loss of his wife, travelling through outer space with the extinguishing Tree of Life. As all three narratives come together, the future Creo ultimately sacrifices himself in a supernova to restore the tree, just as Tom finds inner peace after Izzi's death in the present. *The Fountain* is a visually sumptuous film whose science-fiction trappings retain an organic quality by eschewing CGI for digitally photographed microscopic organisms. Premiering at the Venice Film Festival, its ambitious narrative would result in contrasting reviews, but it was ultimately the poor box-office returns that saw it condemned as a financial blot on Aronofsky's CV.

The Comeback Kids

Aronofsky's next venture, *The Wrestler*, would see a new, stripped-down approach, using Super 16mm handheld cameras and replacing his trademark subjectivity with the style of an objective documentary. Inspired by a love of the art of wrestling and a fascination with what happened to wrestlers once they retired from the professional circuit, Aronofsky originally lined up Nicolas Cage to play the lead. However, it became clear that Aronofsky's first choice, Mickey Rourke, would be a closer fit for the story of a washed-up celebrity wrestler. Rourke conceded that this was a chance to get back in the ring and so, in 2008, he began an intense physical regime in preparation for the role of Randy 'The Ram' Robinson. The film begins with 'The Ram' resigned to appearing in a series of brutal, un-televised matches. When a heart attack forces him to re-evaluate his life, his attempts to find love with a stripper and a reunion with his estranged daughter are ultimately not enough for him to resist the ring. A major comeback for both director and star, *The Wrestler* won Aronofsky the Golden Lion at Venice and an Academy Award nomination for Rourke.

The Wrestler

Black Swan

The Ultimate Performance

A companion piece to *The Wrestler* in theme and style, *Black Swan* also focuses on a performer driving their body to extremes to achieve the ultimate response from their audience. Natalie Portman revels in the performance of her career as Nina Sayers, a young ballerina given an opportunity to dance the lead in *Swan Lake*. Faced with the daunting prospect of playing both the innocent White Swan and the sensual Black Swan, Nina's crisis of confidence is intensified by her rivalry with a new dancer, her attraction to her director and a loosening grip on the world around her. Tightly scripted, tautly edited and with fine support from Vincent Cassel, Mila Kunis and Barbara Hershey, *Black Swan* is a masterpiece of paranoid horror as Nina begins to question her own identity and struggles to unleash her inner turmoil, ending in a epically cathartic final section. Rightly attracting favourable comparisons to Polanski's early films and awards buzz, *Black Swan* looks set to cement Aronofsky's reputation as provocateur and is the crowning achievement in his career thus far.

Future

A firm believer in the power of classical narrative structures, Aronofsky's flirtation with mainstream Hollywood cinema is well documented, having worked on treatments for the *Batman* and *Robocop* franchises. Now set to take on *The Wolverine*, can Aronofsky bring his personal threads of obsession and spirituality into the story of an iconic character? It is his ability to mix the fantastical with personally motivated agendas that has become Aronofsky's cause of inspiration; the paranoia in π evoked his memories upon moving to LA, whilst *The Fountain* began as a direct response to his parents' own cancer scares. It is this personableness that has earned him the respect of cineastes and peers alike, with his candid diaries and interviews allowing the process of filmmaking to be comprehended and respected. His later films have addressed an understanding of the demands of an audience, whose oversaturation with images means that, to succeed in a genre led business, conventions must be challenged in order to capture the public's attention. By examining themes across his work, it is not hard to divine Darren Aronofsky's personal investment in his cinema. However, a closer inspection of his films reveals that it is his selfless determination to make cinema a collaborative enterprise that has seen his success transfer to those he works with, whether it be Clint Mansell, Matthew Libatique, Ellen Burstyn, Mickey Rourke or Natalie Portman – all have benefited from the Aronofsky effect.

MICHAEL PIERCE is currently studying Film Curating in London, is programmer of Midnight Movie events at Curzon Cinemas and is deputy editor of *Little Joe* magazine.

Darren Aronofsky filmography

[feature film directing credits only]

1998
π
Script: Darren Aronofsky, Eric Watson and Sean Gullette. Photography: Matthew Libatique. Production Design: Matthew Maraffi. Editing: Oren Sarch. Music: Clint Mansell. Players: Sean Gullette (Max Cohen), Mark Margolis (Sol Robeson), Ben Shenkman (Lenny Meyer), Pamela Hart (Marcy Dawson), Samia Shoaib (Devi), Stephen Pearlman (Rabbi Cohen). Produced by Eric Watson. 84 mins.

2000
REQUIEM FOR A DREAM
Script: Darren Aronofsky and Hubert Selby Jr, based on the novel by Hubert Selby Jr. Photography: Matthew Libatique. Production Design: James Chinlund. Editing: Jay Rabinowitz. Music: Clint Mansell. Players: Ellen Burstyn (Sara Goldfarb), Jared Leto (Harry Goldfarb), Jennifer Connelly

(Marion Silver), Marlon Wayans (Tyrone C. Love), Christopher McDonald (Tappy Tibbons). Produced by Eric Watson and Palmer West. 102 mins.

2006
THE FOUNTAIN
Script: Darren Aronofsky and Ari Handel. Photography: Matthew Libatique. Production Design: James Chinlund. Editing: Jay Rabinowitz. Music: Clint Mansell. Players: Hugh Jackman (Tomas/ Tom Creo), Rachel Weisz (Isabel/Izzi Creo), Ellen Burstyn (Dr Lillian Guzetti), Sean Patrick Thomas (Antonio), Donna Murphy (Betty), Ethan Suplee (Manny), Mark Margolis (Father Avila), Stephen McHattie (Grand Inquisitor Silecio), Fernando Hernandez (Lord of Xibalba), Cliff Curtis (Captain Ariel). Produced by Eric Watson, Iain Smith and Arnon Milchan. 96 mins.

2008
THE WRESTLER
Script: Darren Aronofsky and Robert

D. Siegel. Photography: Maryse Alberti. Production Design: Tim Grimes. Editing: Andrew Weisblum. Music: Clint Mansell. Players: Mickey Rourke (Randy), Marisa Tomei (Cassidy/Pam), Evan Rachel Wood (Stephanie), Mark Margolis (Lenny), Todd Barry (Wayne), Wass Stevens (Nick Volpe), Judah Friedlander (Scott Brumberg), Ernest Miller (The Ayatollah). Produced by Darren Aronofsky and Scott Franklin. 109 mins.

2010
BLACK SWAN
Script: Mark Heyman, Andres Heinz and John J. McLaughlin. Photography: Matthew Libatique. Production Design: Thérèse DePrez. Editing: Andrew Weisblum. Music: Clint Mansell. Players: Natalie Portman (Nina Sayers), Vincent Cassel (Thomas Leroy), Mila Kunis (Lily), Barbara Hershey (Erica Sayers), Winona Ryder (Beth Macintyre), Benjamin Millepied (David), Ksenia Solo (Veronica). Produced by Scott Franklin. 107 mins.

Juan José Campanella by Alfredo Friedlander

Film director Juan José Campanella was born in Argentina, on July 19th 1959. He spent his youth in Vicente López, a traditional neighbourhood of Buenos Aires, where he recalls going to the cinema two or three times a week, often with two films screening back-to-back. During the sixties, cinemas such as the one he attended (the Roxy in Vicente López) programmed mainly English-language films. He used to go with friends, but, for him, films were more important than playing soccer or other popular sporting activities.

He began a degree in electronic engineering, but decided to give up his studies, moving instead into a film career. In 1979, he began his attendance at two of the few institutions in Argentina that taught film and, over the next few years, would study under Aída Bortnik, Aníbal Di Salvo and José Martínez Suárez, now the octogenarian President of the Mar del Plata Film Festival.

Before emigrating to the US in 1983, where he took a masters degree in Fine Arts at New York University, he directed *National Priority* (*Prioridad Nacional*), his first short film, which has since been lost. It was inspired by *Singin' in the Rain* and was made with a very basic camera. The film was produced during a time when Argentina and Chile were on the verge of starting a war over border disagreements. He has said that, at that moment, he felt very patriotic and the main character of the short film was similar to him, trying first to enlist in the army but soon discovering he is afraid and attempting to escape. The film was never shown commercially but was projected in bars and cine-clubs. Three years later, when the Falklands War began, he screened it to a class he was giving.

When asked about the films and directors that most influenced him, he mentions Billy Wilder, Ernst Lubitsch and Frank Capra. He admits to having seen *It's a Wonderful Life* almost a hundred times.

Campanella's first feature, *Victoria 392*, co-directed and co-produced by Fernando Castets, a frequent collaborator on future scripts, began filming in 1981 and took a year to complete. It was shot on Super-8 and displays the influence of *Airplane*, with its absurdist humour. It also features Eduardo Blanco, one of the director's closest friends, who has participated in almost all of his other films. The story of two young guys involved in a crime, it was not released commercially but received a number of individual screenings.

Campanella's first commercial feature, *The Boy Who Cried Bitch*, was shot in the United States and received a limited international release. Juan Carlos Frugone, a former critic at a popular Argentine newspaper, included it at the Valladolid Film Festival, where Harley Cross won the Best Actor prize. It is now memorable for its featuring Jesse Bradford, Moira Kelly, Jason Biggs and a young Adrien Brody.

Love Walked In, Campanella's first film to be given a commercial release in Argentina, was also an American production. Based on the book Ni el tiro del final, by the Argentinean writer José Pablo Feinman, it featured an international cast that included Terence Stamp, Denis Leary, J.K. Simmons, Michael Badalucco, Danny Nucci, Moira Kelly and Spanish actress Aitana Sánchez-Gijón. Unfortunately, Campanella had several problems with Columbia Pictures, who controlled the film's final cut. Shortly after, the director returned to Argentina, dissatisfied with the studio's decisions.

Campanella broke through commercially in Argentina with his third film, *The Same Love, the Same Rain* (*El mismo amor, la misma lluvia*), a romantic comedy involving two lovers across twenty years of their lives. It opens in the early 1980s, a period of political upheavals, with the military regime still in power. Jorge (Ricardo Darin) meets Laura (Soledad Villamil) on a rainy day. He is a second-rate journalist working for *Cosas*, a yellow-press magazine. She earns her living as a waitress, although she wants to become an artist. They fall in love immediately, but their relationship will be tested over two decades, as Argentina's political face changes, from military occupation, through the Falklands War, to democracy.

Son of the Bride

Son of the Bride (*El hijo de la novia*) not only marked Campanella's biggest success to date in Argentina, it received a nomination for Best Foreign Film at the Academy Awards. Partly inspired by his parents' relationship, it tells the story of Rafael Belvedere (Ricardo Darín), a man whose mother (Norma Aleandro) suffers from Alzheimer's disease and whose father (Héctor Alterio) berates him for not visiting her. His ex-wife is no less happy, complaining about his tardiness in collecting their daughter from school, while his young girlfriend considers leaving him because of his lack of emotion. Eduardo Blanco again appears in this film as a very inconvenient friend.

Avellaneda Moon

In 2004, Campanella had another big hit with *Avellaneda Moon* (*Luna de Avellaneda*), also starring Darín and Blanco, as well as Mercedes Morán, Valeria Bertucelli and Silvia Kutica. The title refers to a popular sports club in the 1950s that faces a crisis and the possibility of closure. When an associate (Daniel Fanego) appears with a proposal to sell the club and build a casino, opinions are divided between those who want to preserve it and others who believe a new venue is the only possible answer. The decline of the club has been seen by some critics as a symbol of Argentina's changing circumstances.

Campanella's most recent film, *The Secret in their Eyes* (*El secreto de sus ojos*), was released locally in August 2009 and went on to win the Academy Award for Best Foreign Film, an achievement that only one other

The Secret in their Eyes

Argentinean film (*The Official Story*) could boast. Ricardo Darín, in his fourth collaboration with the director, plays Benjamín Espósito, a lowly employee in the penal court of justice. On his retirement, he decides to fill his empty hours by writing a book based on an unsolved case, the rape and assassination of a young and beautiful woman. The film then returns, in flashback, to the original investigation. Espósito is helped by Ricardo Morales (Pablo Rago), the husband of the victim, and by his alcoholic colleague, Sandoval (a stunning performance by Guillermo Francella). The arrival of a new prosecutor, Irene Martínez Hastings (Soledad Villamil), creates an emotional turmoil for Espósito, one that is not fully resolved for over three decades. *The Secret in their Eyes* is a powerful political thriller whose original story unfolds in 1974, when violence was rife in Argentina, with Peron returned as President, a mere two years before the military coup. Over two million people watched the film domestically, with overseas audiences, particularly Spain, France, the UK and the United States, making it a huge success.

On the set of The Secret in their Eyes

Campanella, together with Ricardo Freixá, Jorge Estrada Mora and Eduardo Blanco, set up the production company 100 Bares in 2003. Its first project was the 13-part television series, *Winds of Water* (*Vientos del agua*). The project was the outcome of several meetings and discussions with Eduardo Blanco, whose parents, like Campanella's grandparents, were Spanish. It portrays two stories: one takes place in Spain, during the Civil War, while the other unfolds in Argentina at the beginning of this century. The main characters are played by Ernesto Alterio in the Spanish story and Hector Alterio (Ernesto's father in real life) in modern times, together with Eduardo Blanco as his Argentinean son. The drama's framing device is the emigration of characters, from Spain to Argentina in the 1940s and back to Spain during Argentina's recent economic collapse. Seven of the episodes were directed by Campanella. Italian actress Julia Michelini played an emigrant who meets her future husband on a ship, played by newcomer Pablo Rago. His performance in the series prompted Campanella to cast him as Ricardo Morales in *The Secret in their Eyes*. Many other noteworthy actors participated in the series, such as Valeria Bertucelli who had already gained some popularity with her role in *Avellaneda Moon*.

Campanella has also been prolific in directing numerous TV series in the US, including *House M.D.*, *Law & Order*, *30 Rock* and *Strangers with Candy*. When asked about his opinion of television there, Campanella has asserted that, all too often, it is superior to the country's cinema, in particular because of the quality of the writing.

Campanella was recently appointed President of the Art and Cinematographic Science Academy of Argentina.

ALFREDO FRIEDLANDER is a member of the Asociación de Cronistas Cinematográficos de Argentina. He writes regularly for www.leedor.com and presents movies at the 56-year-old Cine Club Núcleo.

Juan José Campanella filmography

[feature film directing credits only]

1983

VICTORIA 392

Script, Editing and Direction: Fernando Castets, Juan José Campanella. Photography: Fernando Castets (FC), Hugo Colace. Sound: Marcelo Céspedes. Players: Eduardo Blanco, Osvaldo Peluffo, Omar Pini, Daniel Asayag, Osvaldo Belli, Horacio Heredia, Fernando Castets, Juan José Campanella, Gabriel and Sonia Palermo. 92 mins.

1991

THE BOY WHO CRIED BITCH

Script: Catherine May Levin. Photography: Daniel Shulman. Editing: Darren Kloomok. Music: Wendy Blackstone. Players: Harley Cross (Dan Love), Karen Young (Candice Love), Jesse Bradford (Mike Love), J.D. Daniels (Nick Love), Gene Canfield (Jim Cutler), Moira Kelly (Jessica), Adrien Brody (Eddie), Dennis Boursikaris (Orin Fell), Jason Biggs (Robert). Produced by Louis Tancredi for Pilgrims 3 Corp. 105 mins.

1997

LOVE WALKED IN

Script: Lynn Geller, Larry Golin and Juan José Campanella. Photography: Daniel Shulman. Editing: Darren Kloomok. Music: Wendy Blackstone. Players: Denis Leary (Jack Hannaway), Terence Stamp (Fred Moore), Aitana Sánchez-Gijón (Vicky Rivas), Danny Nucci (Cousin Matt), Moira Kelly (Vera), Michael Badalucco (Eddie Blanco), Gene Canfield (Joey), Marj Dusay (Judith Moore), J.K. Simmons (Mr Shulman). Produced by Jorge Estrada Mora and Ricardo Freixá for Jempsa and Apostle Pictures. 90 mins.

1999

THE SAME LOVE, THE SAME RAIN

Script: Fernando Castets and Juan José Campanella. Photography: Daniel Shulman. Editing: Camilo Antonini. Music: Emilio Kauderer. Players: Ricardo Darín (Jorge), Soledad Villamil (Laura), Ulises Dumont (Márquez), Alfonso de Grazia (Mastronardi), Alicia Zanca (Sonia), Eduardo Blanco (Roberto), Graciela Tenenbaum (Marita), Mabel Zanotta (Mauge). Produced by Jorge Estrada Mora for Jempsa. 120 mins.

2001

SON OF THE BRIDE

Script: Fernando Castets and Juan José Campanella. Photography: Daniel Shulman. Editing: Camilo Antonini. Music: Ángel Illaramendi. Players: Ricardo Darín (Rafael Belvedere), Héctor Alterio (Nino), Norma Aleandro (Norma), Eduardo Blanco (Juan Carlos), Natalia Verbeke (Naty), Claudia Fontán (Sandra), Salo Pasik (Daniel), Adrián Suar (Dodi), Alfredo Alcón (himself), Atilio Pozzobón (Francesco). Produced by Pol-ka Producciones, Jempsa, Tornasol Films (Spain). 123 mins.

2004

AVELLANEDA MOON

Script: Fernando Castets, Juan Pablo Doménech and Juan José Campanella. Photography: Daniel Shulman. Editing: Camilo Antonini. Players: Ricardo Darín (Román Maldonado), Mercedes Morán (Graciela), Eduardo Blanco (Amadeo), Valeria Bertucelli (Cristina), Silvia Kutica (Verónica), José Luis Lopez Vázquez (Don Aquiles), Daniel Fanego (Alejandro), Atilio Pozzobón (Emilio). Produced by Pol-ka Producciones, 100 Bares Producciones, Tornasol Films (Spain). 142 mins.

2009

THE SECRET IN THEIR EYES

Script: Eduardo Sacheri and Juan José Campanella. Photography: Félix Monti. Editing: Juan José Campanella. Music: Federico Jusid. Players: Ricardo Darín (Benjamín Espósito), Soledad Villamil (Irene Menéndez Hastings), Guillermo Francella (Sandoval), Pablo Rago (Morales), Javier Godino (Isidoro), José Luís Gioia (Báez), Mario Alarcón (Judge Fortuna Lacalle), Mariano Argento (Romano). Produced by Haddock Film, 100 Bares, Tornasol Films (Spain). 124 mins.

Alejandro González Iñárritu by Jason Wood

A former DJ and commercials director born in Mexico City, Alejandro González Iñárritu's first feature, *Amores Perros*, world-premiered at the 2000 Cannes International Film Festival, winning the Grand Prix in the Critics' Week. The film would go on to accumulate numerous other international prizes, including a BAFTA for Best Foreign-Language Film, and swept the Mexican Academy of Cinematographic Arts and Sciences' Silver Ariel Awards (Mexico's equivalent of the Oscars) with 13 wins. The film, amongst the most widely decorated Mexican features of all time, is generally credited with kick-starting a critical and commercial renaissance in Mexican cinema that reverberates to this day.

An anomaly in that it received no financial support from the government-funded Mexican Film Institute (IMCINE), *Amores Perros* arrived entirely unannounced, bestowing upon Iñárritu outsider standing for its independent production status, uniqueness of vision and the fact that its autodidact director had not attended any of the country's first-rate film schools. Set in a teeming Mexico City, where it was shot on location during a scarcely believable 10-week period, three separate but overlapping stories unfold. The tripartite

narrative structure was to become a major element of the director's first three features, prompting debate regarding the extent of the input of Iñárritu's writer, Guillermo Arriaga.

Roughly translated as *Love's a Bitch*, *Amores Perros* starts with the story of Octavio (Gael García Bernal) and Susana (Vanessa Bauche), two youngsters from the wrong side of the tracks. Susana is married to Octavio's older, brutal brother (Marco Pérez), but Octavio is determined to rescue her. Across town, a successful businessman (Alvaro Guerrero) is in the process of leaving his wife to move into his dream apartment with his beautiful supermodel girlfriend (Goya Toledo); and, finally, a disenfranchised ex-political activist (Emilio Echevarría) is hired as an assassin to resolve a case of professional jealousy between two brothers.

Filmed with passion, style and energy, the film effectively captured the international limelight as well as the aspirations and sensibilities of Modern Mexicans. It also launched the career of Gael García Bernal, whose on-screen magnetism and good looks saw him become the new icon of Mexican cinema. Iñárritu offered a very simple explanation for the

Amores Perros

domination of handheld in the film. 'You and I and every human being sees the world in handheld. In other words, we look and move our heads. My head and eyes have never been mounted on a crane, a dolly or a tripod. Those things are stylish and unnatural to our relationship with the world. The approach is both more intimate and more real.'

After a notable contribution to the post-September 11 portmanteau picture, *11'09'01*, with co-directors including Sean Penn, Youssef Chahine, Amos Gitai, Shohei Imamura, Claude Lelouch, Ken Loach and Samira Makhmalbaf, Iñárritu's second feature was *21 Grams*. Set in Memphis, the film retained the director's key technical collaborators (described as 'family'), most prominently Arriaga, cinematographer Rodrigo Prieto, production designer Brigitte Broch, sound designer Martín Hernández and composer Gustavo Santaolalla, for a piercing tale revolving around an ongoing fascination with family, grief, tragedy and atonement.

21 Grams

Cristina (Naomi Watts) is a recovered drug addict, happily married to an architect, with two beautiful children. Paul (Sean Penn) is a mathematician with a critical heart ailment, trapped in a spent relationship. Jack (Benicio Del Toro) is an ex-convict desperately trying to keep himself pure. Three souls in isolation from one another until a terrible incident enmeshes them together. Moving freely through time, before and after the fatal moment when the characters' lives collide, the film, whose title is a reference to the supposed weight of the human soul, also considers human fragility.

Securing final cut from Focus Features, the film drew criticism before a single frame was shot for Iñárritu's decision to work outside of his native Mexico (the project was originally to be made in Spanish). Alfonso Cuarón and Guillermo del Toro, Iñárritu's co-Mexican filmmaking figureheads, have faced similar censure, responding that as artists they have the right to work wherever they wish and that a broadening of artistic horizons should not be viewed as a betrayal of their roots. Iñárritu was clear on the issue: 'The main reason I relocated was that I wanted another challenge and this gave me the opportunity to go to new territories. This really excited me and got me focused. I always focus more clearly when my adrenalin is running high. I think that you can know your idiosyncrasies much better and your *Mexicanidad* from the outside rather than just by living in the inside in your own little ranch of fear and prejudice.' Admired, if not universally acclaimed, *21 Grams* was similarly rewarded at numerous awards ceremonies and took Iñárritu's reputation as a supreme visual stylist with a humanitarian bent to new heights.

Arguably the director's most ambitious project to date, *Babel* found Iñárritu spinning another intricately constructed tale of consequence and intertwined fate. When two boys fire a rifle at a tourist bus in Morocco, the lives of four groups of people, across three continents, collide. Richard (Brad Pitt) and Susan (Cate Blanchett) are a holidaying American couple aboard the bus; Amelia (Adriana Barraza) is

Babel

their Mexican nanny who decides to take their kids with her across the border so she can attend her son's wedding; her hot-headed nephew Santiago (Gael García Bernal) will drive them; and in Tokyo a rebellious deaf-mute student Chieko (Rinko Kikuchi) is grappling with the loss of her mother and the frustrations of adolescence.

A final collaboration with Arriaga (the pair would part under acrimonious circumstances), *Babel* premiered at the 2006 Cannes Film Festival, earning González Iñárritu the Best Director prize. Linking personal stories and global politics, the film completes a trilogy and is again concerned with the consequences of apparently random acts. The title originates from the biblical reference to people being scattered around the world, speaking different languages and unable to communicate. The ensemble cast, well known and less so, give expressive, naturalistic performances, which add to the film's sense of immediacy and authenticity. Combining intimate stories

Babel

with epic scale, *Babel* is a bold, confident and largely successful cinematic assertion that assumptions and prejudices are more divisive than language barriers or borders. Winning the Best Drama Golden Globe, the film also earned numerous Academy Award nominations – including Best Director (with González Iñárritu being the first Mexican to be nominated for the accolade), Best Picture and Best Original Screenplay.

Returning to Cannes in 2007 with his contribution to the ambitious *Chacun son cinéma*, a project in which 33 of the world's leading directors express their feelings about cinema, Iñárritu has also used his position and influence to foster emerging Latin American filmmaking talent: 'Some people have described it as a responsibility but I think it's more of a privilege to be involved with filmmakers such as Carlos Reygadas and projects such as Carlos Armella and Pedro González-Rubio's *Toro Negro*. It is an absolute honour to help, mention and perhaps force open the door a little for these people.'

Biutiful

After a hiatus of four years, Alejandro González Iñárritu's fourth feature is *Biutiful*, the director's first Spanish-language project since his incendiary debut. Adopting a significantly stripped-down approach to narrative, *Biutiful* is an intimate and heartbreaking tale whose relative simplicity heralds a more cohesive clarity of vision. Winning the Best Actor prize at Cannes for his performance, Javier Bardem is mesmerising as the conflicted Uxbal, a son, father, lover and former drug dealer, eking out a meagre living in the dangerous underworld of contemporary Barcelona. Working as a shady businessman, Uxbal helps Chinese immigrants find illegal jobs, treating them with dignity and respect despite accepting his role in their exploitation. A single parent whose love for his children knows no bounds (his wife is mired in her own personal hell), Uxbal's life takes an even darker turn when he is confronted first by the diagnosis of a terminal illness, and then by a childhood friend now working as a police officer.

Offering an astute, finely observed and sobering critique of modern society, *Biutiful* is characteristically fraught with compassion and technical ambition (Rodrigo Prieto excels himself and Stephen Mirrione's editing is sublime). A police street raid, shown in extended detail, is thrillingly executed and resides in the memory as the film's standout sequence. Sombre and almost resolutely downbeat in tone, *Biutiful* is far from easy viewing, but it is impassioned, intense and heartfelt. Iñárritu once again made his attraction to the narrative clear: 'The stories that I am interested in are to do with emotions. For me, the objective of making films and in fact the objective of every artistic expression is catharsis. My work is always focused on how we make sure that there is transference of empathy between the characters and an audience. I have to be able to show them pure and naked in terms of emotion. Sadness and fear are understandable in any language, and the face, the most interesting map of the world.'

JASON WOOD is a film programmer and contributor to *Sight and Sound* and the *Guardian*. He has also published several books on cinema.

Alejandro González Iñárritu filmography

[feature film directing credits only]

2000
AMORES PERROS
Script: Guillermo Arriaga. Photography: Rodrigo Prieto. Production design: Brigitte Broch. Editing: Luis Carballar, Alejandro González Iñárritu and Fernandez Pérez Unda. Players: Gael García Bernal (Octavio), Vanessa Bauche (Susanna), Marco Pérez (Ramirez), Goya Toledo (Valeria), Alvaro Guerrero (Daniel), Emilio Echevarría (El Chivo). Produced by Alejandro González Iñárritu. 154 mins.

2003
21 GRAMS
Script: Guillermo Arriaga. Photography: Rodrigo Prieto. Production Design: Brigitte Broch. Editing: Stephen Mirrione. Players: Sean Penn (Paul Rivers), Naomi Watts (Cristina Peck), Danny Huston (Michael), Benicio Del Toro (Jack Jordan). Produced by Alejandro González Iñárritu and Robert Salerno. 124 mins.*

2006
BABEL
Script: Guillermo Arriaga, from an idea by Alejandro González Iñárritu Photography: Rodrigo Prieto. Production Design: Brigitte Broch. Editing: Stephen Mirrione and Douglas Crise. Players: Brad Pitt (Richard Jones), Cate Blanchett (Susan Jones), Gael García Bernal (Santiago), Adriana Barraza (Amelia), Rinko Kikuchi (Chieko). Produced by Steve Golin, Alejandro González Iñárritu and Jon Kilik. 143 mins.

2010
BIUTIFUL
Script: Alejandro González Iñárritu, Armando Bo, Nicolás Giacobone. Photography: Rodrigo Prieto. Production Design: Brigitte Broch. Editing: Stephen Mirrione. Players: Javier Bardem (Uxbal), Maricel Álvarez (Marambra), Eduard Fernández (Tito). Produced by Fernando Bovaira, Alejandro González Iñárritu and Jon Kilik. 147 mins.*

Kim Longinotto by Helen de Witt

'Every time I go to make a film, I meet wonderful, wonderful people that I, sort of, fall in love with. It makes me feel good about being alive and about being a human being.'

Pink Saris, Kim Longinotto's latest film, has garnered praise and awards from around the world. In many ways, the evocation of its protagonist, Sanpat Pal, 'If you're shy, you die', could be the mantra of Longinotto herself. Her films have screened around the world at festivals and been seen theatrically as well as on television. They have also been vital components for education and activism via distribution outlets such as Women Make Movies in the US and formally through Cinenova in the UK.

Like the majority of Longinotto's films, made over the course of 30 years, *Pink Saris* exposes societal injustice towards women and the bold and sometimes extreme measures that are taken up by brave women who confront these wrongs. Sanpat is the leader of the Gulabi Gang, or Pink Saris, named after their distinctive colourful dress. For the past 20 years Sanpat has been fighting for women's rights in Northern India, where the caste

system is still rigidly enforced in a way that can often have catastrophic and sometimes murderous consequences for young women from the lowest, or 'Untouchable', caste. Sanpat's method is to vigorously expose these injustices by creating a huge furore, and the consequent media attention means the police have to take her complaints seriously. She also uses her pink-saried gang of followers to attract attention in public, by staging demonstrations at local ceremonies such as weddings.

Exposing the issue of violence and abuse towards Untouchable women is only one part of what Longinotto achieves with this film. She also presents a fascinating character study of Sanpat herself. By following her subject relentlessly, Sanpat's own story is gradually revealed, including her past as a victim of abuse – the motivation for her activism. Longinotto shows her vulnerability but also her character flaws, as her celebrity status increasingly has a detrimental effect on her own marriage. She achieves this intimate and moving portrait not through a 'Broomfield-esque' hectoring approach, but through a closeness to, almost love for, her subjects, despite their inadequacies. What we see in Longinotto's documentaries is more than the

Pink Saris

investigation of an issue or a character study. They are actually about building relationships between people.

What has distinguished Longinotto's approach to her subjects across all her films is her technique of being ever present, right in the middle of their lives. In the case of *Pink Saris* it means that Sanpat's story tells itself. She is able to create the impression that the viewer is actually present to witness the events. In this way, her films are able to make you forget, as fiction films do, that you are actually watching a film.

Longinotto made her first film, *Pride of Place* (1978), while studying camera and directing at the National Film and Television School in the late 1970s. It was co-directed with Dorothea Gazidis and is a semi-autobiographical work that looked at the strict treatment and punishment regime of girls in the boarding school that she had attended. A year later, the school was closed down. This experience set the tenor for Longinotto's future work. She would make films that exposed the personal suffering caused by injustice and prejudice, fiercely supporting those who sought to put an end to it.

She spent some time working as a director of photography on television reportage. Her second film, 1979's *Theatre Girls*, was co-directed with Claire Pollak. It was filmed over several months in a hostel for homeless women in London. Together, these early films showed a filmmaker who was both

Theatre Girls

compassionate and uncompromising, her style created through living in the same places and sharing the same experiences as her subjects.

Throughout her career, Longinotto has often worked with co-directors in order to gain access and insights into other cultures. She is never prying eyes looking in, but an invitee, there to witness and tell. Her discreet method of long shoots, working with a tiny crew and – sometimes literally – lying low, makes her as unobtrusive to the process of filmmaking as possible. Then, in the editing room, she builds her characters and creates her stories.

Divorce Iranian Style

Longinotto's work has rightly won the highest acclaim. Among many accolades, she received a BAFTA in 1998 for *Divorce Iranian Style*, co-directed with Ziba Mir-Hosseini. It is a ground-breaking film that follows the complex operation of a Tehran divorce court. Always seeking to break with universal clichés and assumptions, Longinotto and Mir-Hosseini reveal not only the human consequences of Islamic law for women, but the struggle for solutions to difficult relationships within the judicial system of such a restricted society. She made one more film in Iran, *Runaway* (2001), again with Mir-Hosseini. It shows how young women in a Tehran women's shelter give each other mutual support and create a community amongst themselves, despite having fled from violent family situations in a society designed to keep women apart from one another.

Sisters in Law

Longinotto was also awarded the Cannes Prix Art et Essai Award for *Sisters in Law* (2008), co-directed with Florence Ayisi. This film also investigated the legal system from a woman's point of view, but this time in Cameroon where two formidable women, Prosecutor Vera Ngassa and Judge Beatrice Ntuba, fight to bring men responsible for spousal abuse to justice.

Japan is another country that has long fascinated Longinotto, due to its highly ritualised gendered performances. Her first film made there was *Eat the Kimono* (1989), co-directed by Claire Hunt, with whom she set up the production company, Twentieth Century Vixen. The film's title refers to a saying by its subject, feminist avant-garde dancer Hanayagi Genshu, who urges Japanese women not to be dominated by the restrictive values symbolised by traditional costume, but instead confront them. *The Good Wife of Tokyo* came next, again made with Hunt. The film follows punk singer Kazuko Hohki's return to Japan with her band, The Frank Chickens, after living in England for 15 years. Accompanied by her British boyfriend, Hohki visits traditional families and a priest to compare her emancipated Western lifestyle with the constrained options available to Japanese women at the time.

Longinotto went on to make *Dream Girls* (1993), this time with Jano Williams, about the women-only Takarazuka Revue musical theatre company, where girls go to study both male and female roles, which result in spectacular shows. The performers of both parts are famous celebrities with a large and fanatical female following. After *Dream Girls*, Longinotto made *Shinjuku Boys* (1995), another collaboration with Williams, which looks into the lives of 'onnabes', women who live as men and have 'straight' girlfriends. The women cite the kindness and warmth of the onnabe boys, rather than any attraction to gender-bending women, as the reason they choose them over traditional Japanese men. Longinotto and Williams returned to Japan again in 2000 to make *Gaea Girls*. Once more, its subject is women who lead traditionally masculine lives, this time as wrestlers.

Dream Girls

As well as *Sisters in Law*, Longinotto has made three other films in very different parts of Africa. Her first, *Hidden Faces*, made in 1990, with Claire Hunt, depicts Safaa Fathay, a Paris-based Egyptian returning to Egypt to interview the celebrated feminist activist Nawal El Saadawi. Readings from her work accompany Fathay's investigation into the lives of contemporary Egyptian women.

The Day I will Never Forget

The Day I will Never Forget (2002) is possibly Longinotto's most harrowing film. With great sensitivity, but being no less honest for it, the film deals with female genital mutilation in Kenya. The sad irony of the situation is that other women, often the mothers, are complicit in this extreme violence. The film's main focus is Nurse Fardhosa, a strong woman who tirelessly engages in community education projects in an attempt to eradicate the practice.

Confronting abuse was central to *Rough Aunties* (2009), which won the Grand Jury Prize at the Sundance Film Festival. Made in South Africa, the 'aunties' in question are a group of multi-racial Durban women who have set up Bobbi Bear, a child welfare organisation to investigate and protect children from violence and sexual assault. The aunties, many of whom have come from poor and abusive backgrounds, have to fight corrupt authorities

Rough Aunties

to ensure that perpetrators are brought to court. Once again, Longinotto puts a human face on universal issues, showing that in order to make a difference you don't have to be perfect; it is more a question of will.

In 2007, Longinotto returned to Britain to make *Hold Me Tight, Let Me Go*. She spent a year inside the Mulberry Bush School in Oxfordshire, which cares for children suffering from severe emotional trauma. The film follows the emotionally traumatic process disturbed children go through, with support from the school's long-suffering staff, in their journey towards recovery. It's a film about distress, certainly, but a message of hope dominates.

Hold Me Tight, Let Me Go

Kim Longinotto's career has been devoted to speaking out, to telling the stories of those who are allowed no voice of their own, and of those who are toiling tirelessly to support them. Never shy of confronting authority or courting controversy, it is the death of injustice and intolerance that her work seeks.

HELEN DE WITT is producer of the London Film Festival and the London Lesbian and Gay Film Festival at the BFI and teaches Film Studies at Birkbeck College, University of London.

Kim Longinotto filmography

[feature film directing credits only]

1976
PRIDE OF PLACE
Director: Dorothea Gazidis and Kim Longinotto. Photography: Kim Longinotto. Editor: Dorothea Gazidis.

1979
THEATRE GIRLS
Director: Kim Longinotto and Claire Pollak. Photography: Kim Longinotto.

EAT THE KIMONO
Director: Kim Longinotto. Photography: Kim Longinotto. Produced by Kim Longinotto.

1991
HIDDEN FACES
Director: Kim Longinotto and Claire Hunt. Photography: Kim Longinotto. Editing: John Mister. Music: Anne Dudley/Jaz Coleman. Produced by Claire Hunt.

1992
THE GOOD WIFE OF TOKYO
Director: Kim Longinotto and Claire Hunt. Photography: Kim Longinotto. Editing: John Mister. Music: The Frank Chickens. Produced by Claire Hunt and Kim Longinotto.

1994
DREAM GIRLS
Director: Kim Longinotto and Jano Williams. Photography: Kim Longinotto. Sound: Claire Hunt. Editing: John Mister. Music: Takarazuka and Carl Dante. Produced by Kim Longinotto, Alan Bookbinder.

1995
SHINJUKU BOYS
Director: Kim Longinotto and Jano Williams. Photography: Kim Longinotto. Editing: John Mister. Music: Nigel Hawks. Produced by Kim Longinotto, Alan Bookbinder.

1996
ROCK WIVES
Produced by Helen Terry.

1998
DIVORCE IRANIAN STYLE
Director: Kim Longinotto and Ziba Mir-Hosseini. Writer: Ziba Mir-Hosseini. Photography: Kim Longinotto. Editing: Barrie Vince. Sound: Christine Felce. Produced by Kim Longinotto and Ziba Mir-Hosseini.

2000
GAEA GIRLS
Director: Kim Longinotto and Jano Williams. Writer: Kim Longinotto and Jano Williams. Photography: Kim Longinotto. Editing: Brian Tagg. Sound: Mary Milton. Produced by Kim Longinotto and Michael Poole.

2001
RUNAWAY
Director: Kim Longinotto and Ziba Mir-Hosseini. Writer: Kim Longinotto and Ziba Mir-Hosseini. Photography: Kim Longinotto. Editing: Oliver Huddleston. Sound: Mary Milton.

2002
THE DAY I WILL NEVER FORGET
Photography: Kim Longinotto. Editing: Andrew Willsmore. Sound: Mary Milton. Music: Charlie Winston. Produced by Kim Longinotto, Paul Hamann, Richard McKerron.

2005
SISTERS IN LAW
Director: Kim Longinotto and Florence Ayisi. Photography: Kim Longinotto. Editing: Oliver Huddleston. Sound: Mary Milton. Music: D'Gary and Ernest Randrianasolo. Produced by Kim Longinotto, Peter Dale.

2007
HOLD ME TIGHT, LET ME GO
Photography: Kim Longinotto. Editing: Oliver Huddleston. Sound: Mary Milton. Produced by Kim Longinotto, Roger Graef, Richard Klein.

2008
ROUGH AUNTIES
Photography: Kim Longinotto. Editing: Oliver Huddleston. Sound: Mary Milton. Produced by Peter Dale, Teddy Leifer, Paul Taylor.

2010
PINK SARIS
Photography: Kim Longinotto. Editing: Oliver Huddleston. Music: Midival Punditz. Produced by Amber Latiff and Claire Bailey

Apichatpong Weerasethakul by Ben Walters

The pronunciation of his name is not the only way in which Apichatpong Weerasethakul has provoked uncertainty. In fact, as James Quandt notes in the monograph he edited for the Austrian Film Museum about the singular young Thai filmmaker's work, it has already become something of a cliché to throw one's hands in the air in response to his work – to say something along the lines of: 'I love it; it's like a dream; don't try to understand; submit.' It's an understandable reaction. Apichatpong's movies are resistant to both easy comprehension on conventional narrative and formal terms and straightforward categorisation according to established experimental approaches. And yet, taken as they come, they offer myriad pleasures, at once unfathomably withholding and ecstatically simple. Is critical abdication, then, the proper response? Is any attempt to unpack these works doomed to fail, even a kind of violence? 'Not at all,' Apichatpong told Quandt. 'I find it refreshing to read what others think my films mean. It helps me think about my next film.'

Apichatpong was born to doctor parents in Bangkok in 1970 and grew up in the northeastern town of Khon Kaen. (The northeast of Thailand, formerly part of the Khmer empire, holds a special place in his imagination.) After studying architecture in Khon Kaen – precautionary training, he has said, for a proper career, and also a way of thinking about space in a disciplined way – Apichatpong went to the School of the Art Institute in Chicago to take an MFA in experimental filmmaking. The professors there were impressed with him but his name kept tripping people up so he began calling himself Joe. He had already begun making experimental films and videos and helping coordinate the distribution and exhibition of such work in Thailand.

Apichatpong's first feature, 2000's *Mysterious Object at Noon*, sets out much of what is formally distinctive about his filmmaking: his cinema baffles the conventional distinctions between fiction and documentary, performer and role, the story and its telling. In a sense, his films are records of their own creation, none more so than this debut. Inspired by the surrealist 'exquisite corpse' game, in which a drawing is passed from one hand to the next with only the end of a line visible to suggest what came before, Apichatpong travelled Thailand for three years encouraging a range of people – some, he has said, unfamiliar with the concept of fiction, let alone filmmaking practice – to enlarge upon a story about a crippled boy, his carer and the space-child somehow born to her. Elephants, jealousy, boxing, witch-tigers, schoolchildren, soldiers, cityscapes come and go. Post-modern primitivism? Perhaps. *Mysterious Object* is a mood piece, a paean to collaboration, a 16mm record of cinema's limitations – it's a shape-shifting miscellany yet within its rich clutter there are discernible tectonic movements. 'The mood shifts,' Apichatpong has said. 'The second half of the film is totally slower. It seems like the film stops because I'm so sick of looking for stories and I enjoy more looking at locations and people.'

Blissfully Yours

This willingness to have a film start as one thing and become another was again evident in *Blissfully Yours* (2002), the film that established Apichatpong on the global stage, taking a prize at Cannes. Inspired by witnessing the arrest of illegal Burmese immigrants at the zoo while making *Mysterious Object*, the filmmaker found himself pondering 'moments of happiness existing in an oppressive environment'. At the town doctor's, two women, one younger, one older, are seeking treatment for a young man with a skin complaint – an illegal Burmese immigrant, we learn, seemingly mute and pliable. Subtle jealousies and resentments play out for a time among these three and a couple of other characters; then we are driving into the forest and, nearly halfway through the film, its title credits appear. Now we enter a kind of idyll, the characters suspended in a beautiful natural world into which human affairs still intrude. There are sudden sexual irruptions – urgent fucking, a cock stroked to life in loving close-up – and long, still, rhapsodic shots of the sun in the leaves. The film's makers invented ways of floating the camera on water and stopped work for ten weeks after consulting a tree spirit.

Apichatpong's propensity to diptych and recapitulation deepened in his next two features. *Tropical Malady* (2004, also a Cannes prize-winner) presents a couple of courtships, one between men, the other between man and spirit. Its first half is an impossibly endearing naturalistic romance between a soldier and a village boy, the former's cockiness gradually creaking under the suggestion of something more profoundly wild inside the latter. There's hand-holding, sweet nothings, trashy pop. The film's second half – a continuation or a retelling in a different register? – is all wildness. The soldier is in the night jungle, tracked by a shape-shifting spirit, a ghost-man-tiger who loves him to death. Suspense compounds to a crescendo of ecstatic submission. The sounds of the jungle were recorded illegally. A wise baboon is subtitled.

Tropical Malady

Syndromes and a Century (2006) tells twice a story much like that of Apichatpong's parents' courtship, first time round set in a rural hospital, focusing on a woman doctor, then in a city, with more attention to the man. Some scenes are repeated more or less verbatim but the narratives ramble and detour; in the first part we follow an orchid salesman and a dentist-singer with a crush on a monk; in the second, we explore a clinical subterranean realm of false limbs that hold hooch and eerie plumbing. 'Look at the roots,' says the orchid man. 'They're not so pretty, twisting all over. People don't like it. It seems to lack form and order.' But *Syndromes* is perhaps Apichatpong's most precisely calibrated feature, its narrative dualism echoed formally

Syndromes and a Century

by balances of – rather than contrasts between – natural and artificial light, rural and urban settings, male and female subjects, yearnings and acceptances.

The dentist-singer asks the monk if he might have been his dead brother in an earlier life. No, the monk says, he was a horse. *Uncle Boonmee Who Can Remember His Past Lives* (2010, Palme d'Or winner) brings Apichatpong's interest in the supernatural to the centre of a film. (There is, he has said, 'a special association between cinema and reincarnation. Cinema is man's way to create alternate universes, other lives.') At a country house, Boonmee prepares to die. His kidneys don't work. He's attended by his sister-in-law, a nephew from the city and an immigrant worker; his late wife materialises at the dinner table and his son, now a shaggy-coated, red-eyed 'ghost monkey', also appears. There are sequences showing life as a water buffalo, a princess's encounter with a horny catfish, a trip to a cave in the hills. The film plays with light and darkness a lot.

Uncle Boonmee Who Can Remember His Past Lives

These are not, then, easily categorisable films – this is where the difficulty in speaking about them arises. A number of recurring motifs emerge: lengthy takes, some documenting the changing view from moving vehicles, others locked-off records of more-or-less imbalanced social exchanges; medical matters and hospitals; characters assuming the role of storyteller; moments when the filming process becomes part of the scene; the subtle effects on daily life of political pressure; the affectionate use of Thai pop culture; the sun in the leaves. Such motifs can feel like toe-holds in slippery terrain. Yet this seeming slipperiness itself speaks to perhaps a crucial aspect of Apichatpong's work: an abiding and humble attentiveness to fluidity. We see this in the artist's easy movement between cinema, gallery and grindhouse: as well as features, the past decade has seen him make, on the one hand, dozens of fine-art installations – pieces such as 'Haunted Houses', 'Worldly Desires', 'Mobile Men' and the umbrella project 'Primitive' (incorporating *Uncle Boonmee*) that are distinct from, but distinctly in conversation with, his features – and, on the other, a knockabout pastiche drag escapade (*The Adventure of Iron Pussy*, 2003).

The Adventure of Iron Pussy

But fluidity is at the heart of the work itself. Apichatpong's films tell stories, but they are equally interested in the experiences of the performers, the circumstances of their own production, the natural world in which they are found. The way their stories repeat and refine themselves; the way their characters' selves warp and flex; the way the supernatural is an accepted and unknowable part of their life; these all point to a profound acceptance of the contingency and inadequacy of categories, a recognition of ineffability in life and in the art that seeks to represent it, to illuminate it, perhaps to reincarnate it even as it happens. 'Film is a parallel life that keeps intersecting with real life,' Apichatpong has said. 'I wonder if it's possible to merge it with real life.

Maybe in the future there will be a tool to facilitate this idea, to a point where you cannot differentiate the two.'

BEN WALTERS is the author of books about Orson Welles, *The Office*, and (with JM Tyree) *The Big Lebowski*, and contributes regularly to *Film Quaterly*, the *Guardian*, *Sight & Sound* and *Time Out*.

Apichatpong Weerasethakul filmography

[feature film directing credits only]

2000

MYSTERIOUS OBJECT AT NOON

Script: Apichatpong Weerasethakul. Photography: Prasong Klimborron and Sayombhu Mukdeeprom. Editing: Tony Morias and Apichatpong Weerasethakul. 83 mins.

2002

BLISSFULLY YOURS

Script: Apichatpong Weerasethakul. Photography: Sayombhu Mukdeeprom. Production Design: Akekarat Homlaor. Editing: Lee Chatametikool. Players: Kanokporn Tongaram (Roong), Min Oo (Min), Jenjira Jansuda (Orn). Produced by Eric Chan and Charles de Meaux. 125 mins.

2003

THE ADVENTURES OF IRON PUSSY

Co-directed with Michael Shaowanasai. Script: Apichatpong Weerasethakul and Michael Shaowanasai. Photography: Surachet Thongmee. Costume Design: prae Pakmis. Players: Michael Shaowanasai (Iron Pussy), Siriyakorn Pukkavesh (Rungranee), Krissada Terrence (Tang), Theerawat Thongjitti (Pew). 90 mins.

2004

TROPICAL MALADY

Script: Apichatpong Weerasethakul. Photography: Jarin Pengpanitch, Vichit Tanapanitch and Jean-Louis Vialard. Editing: Lee Chatametikool and Jacopo Quadri. Players: Banlop Lomni (Keng), Sakda Kaewbuadee (Tong), huai Dessom, Sirivech Jareonchon, Udom Promma. Produced by Charles de Meaux. 118 mins.

2006

SYNDROMES AND A CENTURY

Script: Apichatpong Weerasethakul. Photography: Sayombhu Mukdeeprom. Art Direction: Akekarat Homlaor. Editing: Lee Chatametikool. Players: Arkanae Cherkam (ple), Jaruchai Imaram (Dr Nohng), Sakda Kaewbuadee (Sakda),

Sin Kaewpakpin (Old Monk), Nu Nimsonboom (Toa), Jenjira Pongpas (Pa Jane), Sophon Pukanok (Noom), Nantarat Sawaddikul (Dr Tei), Wanna Wattanajinda (Dr Wan). Produced by Charles de Meaux and Apichatpong Weerasethakul. 105 mins.

2010

UNCLE BOONMEE WHO CAN RECALL HIS PAST LIVES

Script: Apichatpong Weerasethakul. Photography: Sayombhu Mukdeeprom and Yukontorn Mingmongkon. Production Design: Akekarat Homlaor. Editing: Lee Chatametikool. Players: Sakda Kaewbuadee (Tong), Jenjira Pongpas (Jen), Thanapat Saisaymar (Boonmee). Produced by Simon Field, Keith Griffiths and Apichatpong Weerasethakul. 114 mins.

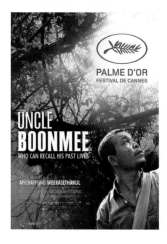

Industry Spotlight: Film i Väst

Film i Väst has put Västra Götaland on the map!

Film i Väst is a regional film fund located on the Swedish west coast in Västra Götaland. It's main headquarters are in Trollhättan, approximately 70km from the region's largest city, Gothenberg, and is the country's leading film city, affectionately referred to by local Swedes as Trollywood.

Film i Väst office and studio

Trollywood

Film i Väst has directly contributed to the growth of the industry, the education of film workers, and the development of new talent in the region. Now involved in 30-40 feature film co-productions each year, it is one of the most significant regional film funds in all of Europe and the most significant source of funding for films in Sweden, after the Swedish Film Institute. It acts as a co-producer, part owner and financier of feature films, short and documentary films, and quality drama for TV, and offers many additional resources for film production.

Founded in 1992 as Västernfilm in Alingsås, the organisation changed its name to Film i Väst in 1993 and moved to Trollhättan in 1996. The first two feature film co-productions to be shot in Trollhättan were Leif Magnusson's *Love Fools* and Hans Åke Gabrielsson's *The Lake*.

Trollhättan quickly began to witness massive growth in film production. 11 feature films were shot in Västra Götaland's region in 1999, including Lars von Trier's Palme d'Or-winning *Dancer in the Dark*. Two years later, Film i Väst co-produced 15 feature films in a single year. In 2004 Film i Väst inaugurated the Studio Fares in Trollhättan, an 1100m² state of the art film studio, which is the largest sound stage in Scandinavia. In 2006 the region was used for Peter Flinth's *Arn* films, the largest and most expensive feature films ever made in Sweden.

Film i Väst's Studio Fares, sound stage and set construction

Film i Väst has participated in over 300 feature film co-productions, in addition to many TV dramas, shorts and documentaries. The facilities in Trollhättan now include production offices, a mix studio, sound studio, foley studio, animation studio, a stage workshop equipped with props and supplies, in addition to make-up, costume and dressing rooms.

Since Film i Väst's inception, Västra Götaland region is now home to many film companies that include VFX, sound and picture edition, lighting, and equipment rentals helping to establish Västra Götaland as the most prominent film region in Sweden.

A Key Factor in Swedish and International Cinema

2010 began with much of the same success for Film i Väst's co-productions as 2009. Daniel Espinosa's *Easy Money* dominated the box-office at the start of the year, outselling every film except *Avatar*. It screened at the Toronto International Film Festival, was sold to the Weinstein brothers for US distribution and also sold the remake rights. Josef Fares's comedy, *Farsan*, was another huge success, becoming one of the top six films at the Swedish box-office for the year.

Joel Kinnaman, Matias Padin and Dragomir Mrsic in **Easy Money**

Film i Väst had three international co-productions premiere in competition at the Berlinale, including Pernilla Fischer Christensen's *A Family*, Florin Serban's *If I Want to Whistle, I Whistle* and Michael Winterbottom's *The Killer Inside Me*, while Ruben Östlund's short film *Incident by a Bank*,

Sebastian Hiort af Ornäs in **Sebbe**

won the Golden Bear for Best Short Film. *A Family* received the Ecumenical Prize of the Jury, and Serban's film earned the Jury Grand Prix- Silver Bear and Alfred Bauer Prize for broadening cinematic horizons. Babak Najafi's *Sebbe* rounded-off the Film i Väst award winners at Berlin by capturing the Best First Feature Award.

The Killer Inside Me was one of three Film i Väst co-productions to screen at the Sundance Film Festival, accompanied by the Estonian film *The Temptation of St Tony*, directed by Veiko Ounpuu and Mads Brügger's Danish Documentary, *The Red Chapel*, which was awarded the Grand Jury Prize for World Documentaries.

At Cannes, Ola Simonsson and Johannes Stjärne Nilsson's *Sound of Noise* screened in Un Certain Regard, winning the Youth Jury Award. Daniel Joseph Borgman's *Berik* picked up the Grand Prix Canal+ for best short film in the Un Certain Regard section.

Susanne Bier's *In a Better World*, which has won numerous international festival prizes, is also nominated for the Best Foreign Language film at the Golden Globe Awards and is Denmark's official entry for Foreign Language Film for the Academy Awards. *If I Want to Whistle, I Whistle*, *Eastern Plays* and *The Temptation of St Tony* are also national submissions for the award.

Film i Väst's international co-productions topped the box office in their own territories in 2010. Mikkel Braenne Sandemosse's *Cold*

Prey III was one of the top five domestic successes in Norway, while *In a Better World* finished third among Danish releases and Dome Karukosi's *Lapland Odyssey* was the top Finnish film of the year. In Bulgaria, Dimitar Mitovski's *Mission London* outperformed *Avatar* and set a new box-office record.

And in 2011?

Film i Väst's 2011 slate is already lined up with an impressive number of co-productions:

David MacKenzie's **Perfect Sense**

- *Perfect Sense* by David MacKenzie, starring Ewan McGregor, Eva Green, Connie Nielsen and Ewen Bremner.
- *Melancholia* by Lars von Trier, starring Kirsten Dunst, Kiefer Sutherland, Charlotte Gainsbourg, Charlotte Rampling, Stellan Skarsgård, Alexander Skarsgård and John Hurt.
- *The Island* by Kamen Kalev starring Thure Lindhart and Laetitia Casta.
- *Loverboy* by Catalin Mitulescu, starring George Pistereanu
- *The Magnificent Eleven*, by Irvine Welsh, starring Sean Bean, Robert Vaughn and Dougray Scott.
- *The Last Furlong*, by Agnes Merlet, starring Rachel Hurd-Wood, Harry Treadaway and Thomas Sangster.
- *Simon and the Oaks* by Lisa Ohlin, starring Bill Skarsgård.
- *Åsa-Nisse – välkommen to Knohult*, by Fredrik Boklund, starring Kjell Bergqvist.

Film i Väst's co-productions so far include partners from England, Scotland, Ireland, France, Germany, Spain, Romania, Bulgaria, Denmark, Norway and the USA.

Film I Väst will be the focus of an IFG Spotlight throughout the year at **www. internationalfilmguide.com**

What are we looking for?

Film i Väst accepts applications for feature film co-productions throughout the year. All co-productions are required to bring elements of production and post-production to Västra Götaland, work with a Swedish production partner, and hire crew and workers from the region. With Film i Väst's growing success, the application process has become increasingly competitive. Projects need to secure the majority of financing in their own territory prior to their application, demonstrate the ability to obtain theatrical distribution in Sweden and show a potential for competitive entry at prestigious international film festivals.

Film i Väst are:
Tomas Eskilsson, Chief Executive Officer
Katarina Krave, Chief Financial Officer
Jessica Ask, Head of Production, Swedish Feature Film and Television Commissioner
Sofie Björklund, Documentary and Short Film Commissioner
Per Nielsen, Co-Production Consultant
Anthony Muir, Senior Executive International Co-Productions

For more information, go to: **www.filmivast.se**

Kjell Bergqvist and Michael Segerström in **Åsa-Nisse**

Timeline

1992 – The county council of Älvsborg funds Film i Väst under the name Västernfilm, with its headquarters in Alingsås.

1993 – Västernfilm changes name to Film i Väst and presents an official proposal for a west Sweden film fund.

1994 – The west Sweden film fund is established. Film i Väst is awarded a Guldbagge for its inspiring work.

1996 – Film i Väst moves to Trollhättan.

1997 – *Love Fools* and *The Lake* become the first two feature film co-productions to shoot in the region.

1998 – Lukas Moodysson's debut feature *Show Me Love* is released, and proceeds to sell 867,576 admission tickets in Sweden, making it the most attended Swedish film ever visited by moviegoers in Sweden at the time.

Rebecka Liljeberg and Alexandra Dahlström in **Show Me Love**

1999 – 11 feature films are shot in Västra Götaland, among them Lars von Trier's *Dancer in the Dark* starring Björk and Catherine Deneuve. *Show Me Love* captures two Awards in Berlin, as well as prizes at Karlovy Vary and Rotterdam, and recieves US Distribution.

2000 – Colin Nutley's *Under the Sun* is nominated for the Best Foreign Language Film at the Academy Awards, Lars von Trier's *Dancer in the Dark* wins the Palme d'Or and

Best Actress prize at Cannes, Ella Lemhagen's *Tstatsiki, morsan och polisen* attracts 400,000 admissions and goes on to win the Crystal Bear and Deutsches Kinderhilfswerk Grand Prix prizes at Berlin, and four Guldbagges. Lukas Moodysson's *Together* premiers in Venice, is nominated European Discovery of the Year at the European Film Awards, Best Foreign Film at the Independent Spirit Awards and draws a local audience of over 850,000 in Sweden, with 187,000 in the US and 400,000 in Italy.

2001 – Film i Väst co-produces 15 features in one year. *Dancer in the Dark* is nominated Best Music, Original Song at the 73rd Academy Awards and surpasses one million admisions in France, 785,000 in the US, and 400,000 in Spain. Anders Nilsson's *Livvakterna* attracts 480,000 admissions. *Jalla! Jalla!* by Josef Fares screens at the Berlinale, and goes on to attract 790,000 admissions domestically. It is also nominated for the European Discovery of the Year.

2002 – Film i Väst celebrates its 10th Anniversay by attracting Lars von Trier and Nicole Kidman to Trollhättan to shoot *Dogville*. It also hosts Thomas Vinterberg's *It's All about Love*, which later premiers at Sundance. Lukas Moodysson's *Lilya 4-Ever* premieres in Venice and receives nominations for two European Film Awards and the Independent Spirit Best Foreign Film award.

2003 – *Dogville* competes for the Palme d'Or in Cannes and wins Best Director and Best Cinematographer at the European Film Awards. *Lilya 4-Ever* wins 5 Guldbagges. Josef

Nicole Kidman in **Dogville**

Farres' *Kopps* is the top Swedish film at the box office and wins Best Film from Europe at the Montreal World Film Festival. Daniel Lind Lagerlöf's *Miffo*, Ulf Malmros' *Slim Susie* and Björn Runge's *Daybreak* are also huge local box-office successes.

2004 – Film i Väst inaugurates its new studio in Trollhättan, Studio Fares, with the largest sound stage in Scandiavia. Fares's *Zozo* is the first production to shoot there. *Daybreak* receives US distribution and wins four Guldbagges, in addition to two awards at the Berlinale and a Golden Bear nomination. Maria Blom's *Masjävlar* (*Dalecarlians*) is the top Swedish film of the year, with 785,716 admissions. Lars von Trier returns to Trollhättan to film *Manderlay*.

2005 – *Manderlay* screens in competition at Cannes, before going on to Karlovy Vary, Toronto and Cairo. *Zozo* also screens in Toronto and Cairo. *Masjävlar* wins three Guldbagges.

2006 – *Arn: The Knight Templar* begins production in Västra Götaland. Jesper Ganslandt's *Falkenberg Farewell* premiers at Venice and becomes Sweden's entry for Best Foreign Language Film at the Academy Awards.

2007 – Anders Nilsson's *When Darkness Falls* wins the Amnesty International Award at the Berlinale. Johan Brisinger's *Suddenly* wins the Audience Award at the Guldbagges. *Arn* tops 1,000,000 admissions at the domestic box office, only the second Swedish film to do so.

2008 – Film i Väst establishes a new animation studio. Manni Maserat-Agah's *Ciao Bella* and Simon Staho's *Heaven's Heart* screen at the Berlinale. Ella Lemhagen's *Patrik 1.5* premieres at Toronto and attracts 330,000 in Sweden. Lance Daly's *Kisses* screens at Locarno and Toronto, and is sold to Focus Features. It also receives a nomination for Best Foreign Film at the Independent Spirit awards and wins two Irish Film and Television Awards. Ruben Östlund's *Involuntary* is selected to screen in Un Certain Regard at the Cannes Film Festival and becomes Sweden's official entry to the Academy Awards.

Ruben Östlund's Involuntary

2009 – Film i Väst is involved as co-producer in four of the six most commercially successful films of the year, including the *Millenium* trilogy and Staffan Lindberg's comedy *Summer with Goran*. Swedish films accounted for more than 30% of the Swedish box-office admissions. *The Girl with the Dragon Tattoo* captured three Guldbagge's. In all, Film i Väst co-productions captured nine out of 11 possible Guldbagge's. Lisa Siwe's *Glowing Stars*, Fredrik Edfeldt's *The Girl*, Henrik Hellström's *Burrowing* and Lukas Moodysson's English-language debut, *Mammoth*, all premiered at the Berlinale. Siwe's film and Ulf Malmros's *The Wedding Photographer* were another two Film i Väst co-productions that did well at the local box office. Lars von Trier's *Antichrist* is the first Film i Väst co-production since 2005 to be nominated for the Palme d'Or at Cannes, with Charlotte Gainsbourg winning the Best Actress award. Kamen Kalev's *Eastern Plays* screened in the Director's Fortnight and won the grand prize at Tokyo and Warsaw.

Noomi Rapace in **The Girl Who Played with Fire**

Education Spotlight: Whistling Woods International

Founded by one of the India's leading filmmakers – Subhash Ghai - and promoted by Mukta Arts Limited & Filmcity Mumbai, **Whistling Woods International** is Asia's largest Film, Television, Animation and Media Arts institute, providing world-class education in all technical and creative aspects of filmmaking and television. The 20 acre Mumbai campus is located inside Mumbai's Film & Television production 'Filmcity' hub, and offers courses that vary in duration from 1 year to 3 years, which are both full-time and part time in nature. All the major specializations of the Media & Entertainment industry are catered to, including *Acting, Animation, Cinematography, Direction, Editing, Producing, Screenwriting, Sound and Media Studies*. Whistling Woods International also launched **India's first MBA in Media & Entertainment**.

The full-time faculty of **Whistling Woods International** (WWI) is a body of academics and industry professionals that include Subhash Ghai, Rajen Kothari, M

Whistling Woods International Film School

Krishhnamurthy, Rob Reece, Anjum Rajabali, Rakesh Ranjan, Ashmaki Acharya, Somnath Sen, Samar Khan, and Dhananjay Khore. Regular guest lectures are provided by leading Indian & International filmmakers, actors & technicians including Ashutosh Gowarikar (Director of Oscar-nominated "Lagaan"), Ashok Amritraj, Shyam Benegal, Naseeruddin Shah, Danny Boyle (academy award winner for "Slumdog Millionaire"), Shelley Page (head of international outreach for Dreamworks SKG), Guillermo Navarro (Academy Award winning DoP), Theo Angelopoulis, Syd Field, Steve Barron, Claude Lelouch, Olivier Assayas, Leonard Goldberg and many more. Hence, students at **Whistling Woods** have the unique benefits of one-on-one interaction with the biggest names of the Indian film industry.

The courses and curricula at WWI are international, English language and a unique hybrid of about thirty percent theoretical and seventy percent practical, with learning

Students using state of the art equipment

Students learning camera work

outcomes focused on enabling student matriculation into their professions. Student studies also include the crucial co-curricular of Film Appreciation, International Art, Literature and Culture, Production Design and Music.

Student exercises of WWI's dynamic film school program have driven its student body expansion over three times in the past three years. Further, WWI's reputation is a global phenomena, with almost 15% of students now international, from the USA, Canada, UK, Germany, Italy, France, Holland, Vietnam and others, choosing WWI over the many leading global film school options.

The Institute's prime learning objective commitment to professional engagement

Video Lab

and advancement naturally leads its students to prime employment options. WWI's graduates are currently working in most leading media organizations. Among them are Excel Entertainment, Fox Star Studios India (20th Century Fox's India operations), Anil Kapoor Productions, BIG Animation, Balaji Telefilms, Channel 31 Australia, Dharma Productions, Technicolor, Mukta Arts Limited, Rhythm & Hues, Prana Studios, Red Chillies Entertainment, Reliance Mediaworks, Spice Entertainment, Walkwater Films and several more.

Students enjoying an Acting Class

In 2010, **Whistling Woods** received two benchmark achievement acknowledgements. In The Hollywood Reporter's August 2010 feature article, WWI is ranked in the top 10 best film schools in the world, along with NYU Tisch, NFTS, FAMU and AFTRS. WWI was the youngest school on the list. Also, in November 2010, WWI was accepted as a full member of CILECT (Centre International de Liaison des Ecoles de Cinéma et de Télévision) – a global association of the world's leading film schools. This high-standards requirement membership is rapidly expanding WWI's already impressive campus partner affiliations of student and faculty exchanges, expanded programs, degrees and co-productions. Some of WWI's several present academic and co-production relationships include those with Deakin University and Griffith University in Australia, Bradford College in UK, Syracuse University in USA and NYU Tisch Asia.

Classical Animation LAb

With the Mumbai campus operational since July 2006 and the student body having grown from 90 to 350 over 3 years, **Whistling Woods International** is currently also expanding both in course verticals and campuses. New course verticals being prepared include an e-learning platform with online courses, Broadcasting and VFX verticals, and a broad range of studies from its Short Courses Unit. Additional WWI campuses being prepared for near future opening are in Alicante, Spain (mid-2011), Haryana (mid-2013) and Hyderabad, India (mid-2013), these projects having been finalized with the respective governments.

Requested by the Government of India, WWI designed and created the groundbreaking Media Studies curricula for the 11th and 12th grade schools. This first-time-ever program began in 2010 for the primary High School Board (the CBSE board), is a major acceptance success and will be significantly expanding in 2011.

In November 2010, Sony signed a landmark agreement to set up a Sony Global Centre of Excellence at WWI. Sony's Media Technology Centre is WWI's additional film school leadership recognition. This SMTC will sustain new and emerging technology equipment and software in the fields of High Def acquisition, 3D filmmaking, digital projection and tapeless HD Broadcast. Apart from setting up the latest technology, Sony is stationing on campus some of their best technology experts from whom WWI faculty and students will receive continuing cutting-edge training.

The above is merely a brief of **Whistling Woods International**'s accomplishments and near future plans to become *the institute of choice for media and entertainment education globally*. For additional information, please visit **www.whistlingwoods.net**.

Sounds Lab

DVD Review

The Criterion Collection
(Region 1)

Started in 1984, the Criterion Collection has become the gold standard of DVD releases, never straying from their mission statement of 'gathering the greatest films from around the world and publishing them in editions that offer the highest technical quality and award-winning, original supplements'.
And as technology has moved on, so has Criterion's willingness to try out new formats, while remaining true to its commitment to 'publishing the defining moments of cinema for a wider and wider audience'.

In addition to the exceptional quality of their releases – much of the work being done in-house with skilled staff and state-of-the-art facilities – Criterion often works with individuals originally involved in a film's production, from the director and cinematographer to editor and writer, or with experts whose knowledge of a film is beyond compare. In doing so, they ensure the film we watch is as close to the original intentions of its creators as it can be. Such high quality is further enhanced by the plethora of extras included with each film, impressive design and packaging, and booklets that place the film in context. The result is a library that anyone interested in cinema could not fail but be stunned by.

Few classical Hollywood-era films released over the last year are as potent or relevant as Leo McCarey's blistering account of America during the depression, **Make Way for Tomorrow** (1937). Jean Renoir once said that no one understood people better than McCarey and his account of an elderly couple forced to move in with their grown children is one of the great masterpieces of depression-era cinema. Beginning with Ma and Pa Cooper's confession to their children that the bank is about to foreclose on their house, resulting in their separation as they move in with different siblings, and the bitterness their presence causes, McCarey's vision of a world caught in the grip of an economic meltdown is best captured in its details. In one of the most moving scenes in the film, Ma and Pa, played by Victor Moore and Beulah Bondi, begin a waltz on a dance floor, only to find the tempo speed up and they are unable to keep time. Adrift in a world they fail to comprehend, both

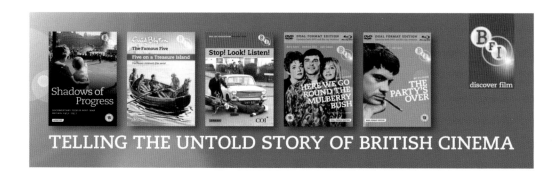

TELLING THE UNTOLD STORY OF BRITISH CINEMA

Make Way for Tomorrow

inside and outside the family hearth, the film ultimately offers a heartfelt plea for tolerance in a time of personal and financial upheaval, sentiments echoed in Ozu's *Tokyo Story*, which was inspired by McCarey's unflinching film. ***Extras:*** a short film featuring an interview with Peter Bogdanovich, discussing Leo McCarey's career and the importance of the film; an interview with critic Gary Giddins; a booklet featuring writing by Bertrand Tavernier, Tag Gallagher and Robin Wood.

Criterion also released three films dealing with different wars, each one unique in its own unique way. Nagisa Oshima's **Merry Christmas Mr. Lawrence** (1983) is the oddest of the three. Loosely based on the wartime memoirs of Laurens van de Post, though channelled through the homoerotic fiction of Yukio Mishima (whose *Patriotism* is one of Criterion's most impressive releases in recent years), it details life in a Japanese prisoner of war camp, where the lives of four men are intertwined. Tom Conti and Ryuichi Sakamoto (who also composed the film's score) are two

Merry Christmas Mr. Lawrence

officers obsessed with the enigmatic Jack Celliers (David Bowie), while Takeshi Kitano's brutish sergeant attempts to maintain discipline amongst the prisoners and his own men.

Central to the film is the conflict between honour and desire – how the structured world of the prison camp contrasts with the rising tensions amongst the men. And for the most part, Oshima excels at sustaining suspense. However, the film often lapses into cliché, particularly in its climactic scenes, although the performances and Sakamoto's beautiful score ensure that it is never less than fascinating to watch. ***Extras:*** a making-of featurette and documentary on Laurens van de Post; interviews with producer Jeremy Thomas, writer Paul Mayersberg, Tom Conti and Ryuichi Sakamoto; a booklet with an essay by Chuck Stephens and interviews with Nagisa Oshima and Takeshi Kitano.

Ride with the Devil

Ride with the Devil (1999) is arguably the most overlooked and underrated of Ang Lee's films. Adapted from Daniel Woodrell's novel 'Woe to Live On', it's a highly original take on the American Civil War, detailing the skirmishes between the Bushwackers and Jayhawkers, renegades on either side of the conflict, on the border between Kansas and Missouri. Following the death of his father, Jake (Tobey Maguire) joins the Southern cause only to find his allegiances and beliefs tested.

A stunning riposte to detractors who had previously questioned Lee's skills as a 'cinematic' filmmaker, whilst once again displaying his ability to draw career-best performances from his actors, *Ride with the Devil* is remarkable for side-stepping issues that normally encumber representations of the Civil War, instead exploring the lives of characters caught up in a conflict where the causes they fight for are not always the ones they believe in. **Extras:** accompanying this director's cut are two commentaries, by Lee and his producer-screenwriter James Schamus, and cinematographer Frederick Elmes, sound designer Drew Kunin and production designer Mark Frieberg; a video interview with Jeffrey Wright; a booklet featuring essays by Godfrey Cheshire and Edward E. Leslie.

The Thin Red Line

Hailed as a masterpiece by some and pretentious by others, Terence Malick's magisterial adaptation of James Jones' **The Thin Red Line** (1998) has only grown in stature since it was first released. If Spielberg's *Saving Private Ryan*, released six-months earlier, presented the horror of battle and the bond between men who fight together, Malick's film adopts a more profound approach, questioning the very act of conflict, both between men, in themselves, and with nature itself. From Jim Caviezel's opening gambit, 'What is this war at the heart of nature,' to his Christ-like sacrifice, *The Thin Red Line* is both a war film and a rare example of Hollywood producing a big-budget art film.

Detailing the battle for the island of Guadalcanal at the turning point of the Second World War, Malick's film moves between the members of a platoon, developing his

voiceover style, away from the 'innocents' of *Badlands* and *Days of Heaven*, instead employing multiple voices as a kaleidoscope of feeling and thought, as the soldiers engage with the Japanese forces. The result is emotionally overwhelming in its treatment of the embattled troops. **Extras:** A wealth of audio commentaries and interviews with cast and crew; archive footage from newsreels; 14 minutes of outtakes; Melanesian chants; a booklet featuring essays by David Sterritt and James Jones.

Eclipse
(Region 1)

The younger sibling of Criterion, the Eclipse series has now asserted itself as a singular collection of works. The idea behind the series was to produce high-quality films that were hard to find and might appeal to a narrower audience range.

Nowhere is the remit of Eclipse best exemplified than by **The Actuality Dramas of Allan King**. The Canadian filmmaker has produced a variety of films and television programmes over the course of five decades, but it is for his verité-style films that he is best known. Or, as he describes them, 'actuality drama – filming the drama of everyday life as it happens, spontaneously without direction, interviews or narrative'. As observer, aiming to 'serve the action as unobtrusively as possible,' King has produced a collection of searing films, often uncomfortable to watch, but remarkable for their bluntness in detailing every aspect of their subjects' lives. This box-set features five of King's most acclaimed works: his feature debut, *Warrendale* (1967), set in a home for troubled youths; a riveting account of domestic life in *A Married Couple* (1969); *Come on Children* (1972), which details life on a farm for a group of visiting children; *Dying at Grace* (2003), which looks at the last days of five terminally ill patients; and *Memory for Max, Claire, Ida and Company* (2005), an affecting portrait of the elderly at a nursing home. King's earliest films are arguably his best known. Like Nick Broomfield's *Juvenile Liaison*, *Warrendale* excels because of its unwillingness to treat the youths as either miscreants or victims of a careless society. Instead, the film attempts to grapple with the kids' problems and the unorthodox methods employed by the institution, aimed at getting them to verbalise their feelings. Likewise, *A Married Couple* is an unflinching portrait of a marriage in crisis. The film also bears the fruits of the director's style, where he spends a significant amount of time with his subjects before filming, believing that 'in order for anything significant to occur in action or drama the subjects must make a huge leap of faith in the filmmaker'.

Most remarkable of all is *Dying at Grace*, which ranks alongside Maurice Pialat's *La Gueule Ouverte* and Kirby Dick's *Sicko: The Life and Death of Bob Flanagan, Supermasochist*, in its portrayal of the last moments of human life. King's approach shows him to be one of the great humanist directors, a filmmaker whose compassion for his subjects and the sensitivity with which he portrays their life (and death) is beyond compare.

Continuing Eclipse's focus on the works of Japanese directors, **Oshima's Outlaw Sixties** features five early films by the renegade filmmaker. The collection, which includes *Pleasures of the Flesh* (1965), *Violence at Noon* (1966), *Sing a Song of Sex* (1967), *Japanese Summer: Double Suicide* (1967) and *Three Ressurected Drunkards* (1968), is an

eclectic mix of titles that follows on from the director's blazing early work.

The influence of Godard can be seen throughout the films, most notably in *Sing a Song of Sex*, but they are far from copies of French New Wave style. Japanese culture and the rigid structures of tradition and discipline are eviscerated by Oshima's focus on rebels, low-life's and habitual criminals, from the rapist in Violence at Noon to the gang in *Japanese Summer: Double Suicide*. And if the films lack the immediacy of early works such as *Cruel Story of Youth*, *The Sun's Burial* and *Night and Fog in Japan*, they remain important examples of the development of a singular, sometimes visionary, filmmaker.

Flicker Alley
(Region 1)

Silent and pre-sound cinema is lovingly brought to life by Flicker Alley (the nickname of Cecil Court, in London, which was the centre of the British film industry during the silent film era). As Jeff Masino, who founded the company in 2002, stated, 'The company was born out of a passion for film history and a desire to bring filmmakers and films from out of the past to new audiences and renewed recognition. Known for projects that are the culmination of hundreds of hours of research, digital restoration, music composition and scoring, collectively, they reflect the expertise and shared passion of many talented collaborators.'

One of the finest DVD releases of recent years, Flicker Alley's sumptuous *Georges Méliès: The First Wizard of Cinema* is now accompanied by **Georges Méliès: Encore**, a collection of 26 films made by the French illusionist and filmmaker, as well as two previously credited to him, directed by Segundo de Chomon. Many of the films, of which a few are the remaining fragments of lost works, were recently discovered and, along with the five-disc set, offer a complete overview of this remarkable filmmaker's career. With interest in Méliès' work likely

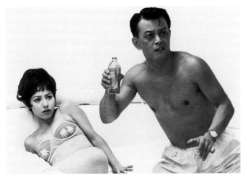

Pleasures of the Flesh

to gain momentum with Martin Scorsese's upcoming *Hugo Cabret*, these two collections highlight how essential the Flicker Alley label has become in reminding audiences of the riches of early cinema.

Another collection, **Chaplin at Keystone**, is an excellent overview of the fruitful relationship between the actor, early in his film career, and Mack Sennnett, whose films were defined by their madcap humour and ingenious set-pieces. Many of the films were in various states of disrepair, so this box-set (also released on Region 2 by the BFI) is a triumph of restoration.

Tillie's Punctured Romance

Although Chaplin was rarely credited in these early films, his star was already on the rise. Within a year, audiences turned out in droves to see the adventures of the likeable, winning Tramp, who first appears in 1914's *Kid Auto Races at Venice, Cal.*, although it was in *Mabel's Strange Predicament* that the Tramp first appeared (the film was not finished until later). What these films show is the development of the tics and eccentricities of his on-screen persona. Aside of the six films made with fatty Arbuckle and Keystone's first feature-length comedy, *Tillie's Punctured Romance*, this set is best taken as a whole, a remarkable document of the rise to prominence of one of Hollywood's greatest icons. ***Extras:*** short documentaries on the restoration and the locations used in Keystone films; an excerpt from *A Thief Catcher*, featuring Chaplin as a Keystone Cop;

an animated film, *Charlie's White Elephant*; a gallery of rare images; an excellent booklet detailing Keystone's history and each of the films included in the box set.

With the release of Frank Urson and an uncredited Cecil B. DeMille's **Chicago** (1927), we can forget Rob Marshall's recent musical adaptation of Roxie Hart's story and enjoy this fabulously scandalous version of Maurine Watkins' 1926 stage play. Phyllis Haver is sublime as the alluring Roxie, imprisoned for murder but placing all her hopes of an early release in the hands of mob lawyer Billy Flynn (Robert Edeson). Sexy and sassy, the film pulls no punches in its attack on the gutter press and the moral hypocrisy of the day. In addition to the main feature, the two-DVD special edition also includes *the Golden Twenties* (1950), a 'March of Time' feature about the period, featuring a wealth of archive footage, and *The Flapper Story* (1985), a retrospective look at the jazz age, with testimonies from those who enjoyed it. ***Extras:*** a documentary, *The Real Roxie Hart*, produced, directed and edited by Jeffrey Massino and Silas Lesnick; a booklet with essays on Maurine Watkins and Chicago in the 1920s.

Chicago

Another stage adaptation, René Clair's **The Italian Straw Hat** (1927) comes from Eugène Labiche and Marc Michel's 1851 stage farce, but Clair chose to move the action to 1895, at the inception of cinema. An homage to the birth of the art form that made his name, Clair's film is a delightful comedy of errors, sparked off by the horse of a groom-to-be eating the hat of a woman indulging in a tryst with her lover. From there, Clair effortlessly draws moments of comic genius from the mayhem of the unfolding events. Like Ernst Lubitsch's silent comedies, *The Italian Straw Hat* highlights the beauty of Clair's directorial style, the movement of the camera playing up each comedy scene and belying the complexity of the choreography in the creation of this near-perfect farce. ***Extras:*** Clair's short *la Tour*; Ferdinand Zecca's farcical *Noce en Goguette*; a copy of the complete 1851 play and its 1916 English version in a DVD-ROM application; a booklet with essays by Lenny Borger and Iris Barry.

The Italian Straw Hat

Microcinema DVD
(Region 1)

One of the most interesting niche labels in the US, Microcinema has created an impressive platform for 'the acquisition, exhibition, and distribution of independently produced moving images of an artistic and socially-relevant nature'.

Two fascinating profiles stood out from Microcinema's releases over the last year. In **Words of Advice: William S. Burroughs On the Road**, Lars Movin and Steen Møller Rasmussen gather together the footage shot of the reclusive author's 1983 tour of the Scandinavian countries and set out on a journey to investigate the inspiration behind his final trilogy, 'The Place of the Dead Roads', 'Cities of the Red Night' and 'The Western Lands'. The result is a fascinating account of the last ten years of Burroughs' life, drawing

William S. Burroughs

on testimonies from friends and admirers, to build a picture of a complex man whose view of the world was often prophetic. ***Extras:*** an almost complete version of Burroughs' reading event in Copenhagen, in 1983; two short tribute films; a statement by Columbia University Professor Ann Douglas.

Robert Snyder's **The World of Buckminster Fuller** (1974) is an impressive portrait of the polymath, whose thoughts on the state of the world and, of increasing relevance, the sustainability of our species, make for fascinating viewing. If the film veers a little towards the hagiographic, it is never less than fascinating. ***Extras:*** Jaime Snyder's short, *Modelling Universe*.

BFI
(Region 2)

From a general strategy of releasing popular world cinema titles, BFI DVD has transformed into a platform for an exceptionally wide range of films that cover the length and breadth of British cinema. In 2009, the label created another branch, BFI Flipside, featuring little-known or overlooked works from the 1960s and 70s. But the label's vision of remapping the history of British film is now best seen not in each individual strand, but as one endeavour.

Over the last year, BFI DVD brought out 40 new releases, comprised of 297 titles (features/shorts/documentaries). Of these, 249 were mastered from materials preserved in the BFI National Archive, with 245 having never previously been released on any format in any region. A number of the titles were released in the dual format edition.

The BFI's aim to encompass all areas of cinema now extends to younger ages. As well as a selection of *Famous Five* features, they released Ken Loach's little-seen foray into children's film, **Black Jack** (1979). Adapted from a novel by Leon Garfield and set in the 18th century, it tells the story of Tolly Pickering, a young lad forced to go on the run with the nefarious Black Jack. On their journeys they encounter the underbelly of English society and Tolly understands the meaning of true friendship. Like Terry Gilliam's earlier *Jabberwocky*, Loach's film is steeped in the dirt and grime of the times, all beautifully captured by Chris Menges camerawork (interiors were shot on 35mm while the exteriors were all filmed on 16mm, further emphasising the murky world). Although it is ostensibly a children's film, *Black Jack*'s dark themes and unsettling moments are probably best enjoyed by a slightly older age group. But to a wider audience, this film is a fascinating entry from one of the UK's most consistently engaging filmmakers. The film features both the English and French language versions. ***Extras:*** a superb feature-length commentary by Loach; original trailer and deleted scenes; a booklet featuring an essay and biographies.

The story behind the making of **Bronco Bullfrog** (1969) is as fascinating as the film itself. Frustrated by the gang violence and intimidation suffered by her actors and audiences at Stratford East's Theatre Royal, Joan Littlewood, her assistant Peter Rankin and ex-Small Faces keyboard player Jimmy Winston, who grew up in the area, encouraged local boys to work together creatively, first in theatre workshops and then, with the help of west London filmmaker Barney Platt-Mills, on a documentary. When that was completed, they embarked on a feature that reflected the boy's lives, centred around the seemingly hopeless situation of Del Quint (Del Walker)

Bronco Bullfrog

and the charismatic ex-con Jo Saville, aka Bronco Bullfrog (Sam Shepherd). The resulting film cost a mere €17,000. Platt-Mills was heavily influenced by the Italian Neorealists and draws fine performances from his cast. But the film's lasting impression is its vivid snapshot of life in the less salubrious areas of London and the surrounding countryside at the end of the 1960s. ***Extras:*** Platt-Mills' original documentary with the boys, *Everybody's an Actor, Shakespeare Said* (1968); an interview with Joan Littlewood; Eric Marquis' short film, *Seven Green Bottles* (1975); a booklet featuring essays and images from the film.

A more decadent view of the 1960s can be found in **The Party's Over** (1965). A stark contrast to Guy Hamilton's previous film, *Goldfinger* (although the chorus of Annie Ross's theme song recalls the classic Bond themes of the time), it attracted the ire of the censors, who so enraged Hamilton and his producer with the cuts imposed on the film,

The Party's Over

they removed their names from the credits. This BFI release includes both the original version and the BBFC's cut. Hamilton's vision of London's beat culture is a fascinating artefact of 60s chic. At its heart is Oliver Reed's magnificently malevolent gang leader, pushing the amorality of the kingpin he played in Joseph Losey's *The Damned* to its limits.

When the American fiancée of a young socialite turns up in London to look for her, he becomes enmeshed in the beat's alternative lifestyle, before discovering the awful truth. Like the film's evocative opening credit sequence, with the gang roaming west London's empty streets, *The Party's Over* is a stylish, surprisingly shocking portrait of lives with no consequence or meaning. **Extras:** theatrical trailers; the short films *Emma* (1964) and (*The Party*); a booklet featuring essays and Guy Hamilton recalling the making of the film.

Running in parallel to the BFI and Flipside's rediscovery and restoration of lost or forgotten British features is the release of official documentaries, covering the entire century and running the gamut, from sex education and the country's rich industrial past to coping during wartime and government information films.

Shadows of Progress, like its predecessor, *Land of Promise*, which looked at the British documentary movement from 1930-50, is a remarkable collection of documentaries. This time the focus covers the post-war period, beginning in 1951 with Paul Dickson's affectionate portrait of the Welsh poet D.R. Griffiths, *David*, and ending with Derek Williams' *The Shetland Experience*, chronicling life at Britain's northernmost point. Between them are 30 films that chart over two decades of British society. Beyond their role as a document of life in the UK, the films are collected together under four separate headings, each presenting an aspect of Britishness or a view on the times in which they were made. 'The Island', 'Return to Life', 'The Shadow of Progress' and 'Today in Britain'

capture a society in flux, from the austerity of the post-war period, through thee Swinging Sixties and into the depression of the 1970s, which was also marked by the increase of violence, both on the streets and in the increased tensions in Northern Ireland.

Shadows of Progress

The collection highlights the work of filmmakers who followed on from John Grierson, often in stark contrast to his style, presenting a harsher account of life on Britain's streets and in its workplaces, although films such as Jill Craigie's *To Be a Woman* (1951) and Lindsay Anderson's *Three Installations* (1952) still feature a lyricism in the way they capture their subjects. **Extras:** As with *Land of Promise*, the collection includes a booklet with essays and extensive notes on each film. A companion book, with longer essays on the films included in the collection has also been published.

Those in search of a more novel approach to the BFI's vast swathes of archive documentary material need go no further than **Misinformation**. Following the release of four volumes of COI (Central Office of Information) films, this last disc remixes some of the better-known titles with a new soundtrack, which blends the voiceovers of the original films with an ambient, occasionally discordant score. The result is not dissimilar to the excellent score Yo La Tengo composed for the BFI's release of the Jean Painlevé collection, allowing audiences to look at material afresh and outside the context of their original presentation.

Masters of Cinema
(Region 2)

Masters of Cinema began as a website in 2001 with its four co-founders spread around the world. In 2004 it joined forces with Eureka Entertainment Ltd, the leading UK distributor of silent and early films. Since then, the Masters of Cinema Series (MoC) has gone from strength to strength. In addition to new releases, Masters of Cinema are in the process of releasing a number of earlier titles on Blu-ray. They have also released films exclusively on this format (*The World*, *Will Success Spoil Rock Hunter*, *City Girl* and *Make Way for Tomorrow*, the latter featuring the same extras as the Criterion release), although some are now being released on DVD.

Of the year's DVD releases, **Metropolis** (1927) easily counts as one of the best. Following the discovery of footage in a small museum in Buenos Aires in 2008, archivists have reconstructed the film, finally presenting a version as close as it is possible to get to Fritz Lang's 1927 original. The result is stunning, presenting a more potent view of Lang's futuristic vision. Gone are the narrative jumps that made earlier versions of the film disjointed (although as Jonathan Rosenbaum points out in his excellent essay in the accompanying booklet, it 'has one of the lamest endings of any great film I can think of'). Instead, there is more convincing characterisation, particularly in Maria's journey. However, it is the scale of Lang's

Metropolis

world that leaves the greatest impression; one that dwarfs the imaginations of most contemporary filmmakers. **Extras:** Audio commentary by David Kalat and Jonathan Rosenbaum; a documentary about the film; the 2010 trailer; a booklet featuring a wealth of articles, including Rosenbaum's essay and a 1927 review by Luis Buñuel.

No less impressive is Lang's 1931 masterwork, *M*. Peter Lorre is chilling as the child killer, but Lang takes the film beyond a simple cat-and-mouse thriller, showing how the crimes impact the very fabric of an ostensibly civilised society. A key influence over so many films, what surprises most with this restoration is how potent the film remains, 80 years on from its premiere. This version features both the restored original and the shorter (93 minutes, compared to the original 110) British version, released in 1932. Together with *Metropolis*, the film sees Fritz Lang at the height of his considerable powers and adds to the already impressive record of Masters of Cinema's Lang collection, which also includes the *Dr. Mabuse* trilogy. **Extras:** Audio commentaries by film scholars, as well as excerpts from Peter Bogdanovich's interviews with the director; a 1968 documentary on Fritz Lang's German career; a booklet featuring an article by and interview with Lang, details of a missing scene, an overview of the various versions of the film and production drawings.

A nos amours (1983) completes Masters of Cinema's collection of Maurice Pialat's releases. And like the first film in the series, *L'Enface-nue*, it is a powerful portrait of youth, embodied in Sandrine Bonnaire's astonishing screen debut. She plays Suzanne, the object of affection and desire for a number of men, none more so than her father, played by Pialat himself. This pairing is riveting and disturbing, blurring the lines between filmmaker and character, and marks the central relationship of a disintegrating family, which prompts Suzanne to embark on a series of affairs. Often compared to Cassavetes, Pialat's style is more controlled. Even in the film's most famous

A nos amours

sequence, the climactic dinner party that sees the unannounced return of the father (Pialat had apparently not told his cast that he would enter this scene) and a bitter row ensue, feels measured to ensure an exact response from the audience. Elsewhere, the director undercuts the conventions of the family melodrama by limiting information or passing off details with little explanation, preferring mood and expression to navigate our responses. The result is edgy and uncomfortable; a brilliant examination of the family and one of Pialat's best films. ***Extras:*** an interview with Sandrine Bonnaire; a documentary on the film; a 1983 TV interview with Pialat; screentests for the film; trailers for Pialat films; a booklet including essays and interviews.

Arguably Masters of Cinema's most outrageous release of the year, Nobuhiko Obayashi's **House** (1977) is a bizarre, eccentric and near-indescribable mix of melodrama, kung-fu, teen issues, comedy and horror. What plot there is, deals with Ryoko, whose anger at her father's decision to remarry prompts her to travel with her friends to spend the summer with her late mother's aunt, who turns out to

House

be less welcoming a host than the group had originally thought.

House was produced when the Japanese film industry was in the doldrums. Though initially resistant to Obayashi's script, which was mostly based on ideas thought up by his ten-year-old daughter, Toho financed the film, only to relegate it to B-movie status. However, its enduring popularity prompted an international release. Throwing everything but the kitchen sink at the screen, Obayashi's film is a mish-mash of styles, with almost every shot featuring some kind of special effect. The result is a strikingly original film, whose artificiality, like that of Coppola's *One From the Heart*, makes it a unique viewing experience. ***Extras:*** 90 minutes of archive interviews; the original Japanese trailer; a booklet featuring an extended essay and original promotional material.

Second Run
Region 2

One of the outstanding UK-based boutique labels, Second Run has consistently surprised with its output. The label champions 'niche-market films' that 'anyone who seriously cares about cinema would want in their collection – but which, crucially, have never before been available anywhere in the world on DVD'. Extras are normally limited to interviews and a booklet essay, but the choice of films and the care and attention paid in ensuring the best quality transfer make the label essential for serious film lovers. Recent titles include Juraj Herz's *Morgiana* (1972), František Vláčil's *The Valley of the Bees* (1967) and Jan Němec's *Diamonds of the Night* (1964) – directors who have previously had work released by the label (*The Cremator*, *Marketa Lazarová* and *The Party and the Guests* respectively).

Pia Marais' **The Unpolished** (2007) is one of Second Run's few forays into more recent fare, it is the unflinching story of a young girl (the excellent Céci Chuh) whose wayward parents offer her little guidance or lasting affection, seeming more concerned with their drug habit and network of shady friends. What is surprising about the film is the warmth with which Marais presents Stevie's story (it is an interesting companion piece to another Second Run release featuring a young girl adrift in an adult world, Anne Turner's *Celia*). Her compassion for the girl and her predicament, as well as the character's determination to break free and find the life she wants to live makes for compelling viewing. And as a feature debut, *The Unpolished* marks the arrival of a major new talent in European film. ***Extras:*** an interview with Pia Marais; a booklet featuring an essay by author and critic Brad Stevens.

The release of Xie Fei's **Black Snow** (1990) goes some way to filling the void of what happened to Chinese filmmakers between the end of the Cultural Revolution and the arrival of the Fifth Generation in the 1980s. Although his films were made around the same time as

Black Snow

Chen Kaige and Zhang Yimou's, Xie Fei was much older and this film is markedly different from their most famous works of the period; lavish reconstructions of the past, shot through with veiled critiques of the state. Interestingly, *Black Snow* bears closer comparison with Sixth Generation filmmakers such as Jia Zhang-ke and Wang Xiaoshuai, in capturing the reality of contemporary Chinese life. Unfolding in the aftermath of the 1989 demonstrations in Beijing, the film follows a former prisoner in his attempts to fit back into society. However, his path is never easy and in his study of one man's plight through China's underworld, the

film becomes transforms into a dark, politically daring tract. ***Extras:*** an interview with Xie Fei; booklet essay by author and academic Professor Shaoyi Sun.

In recent years, Second Run has taken to championing the work of British documentary filmmakers, such as Kim Longinotto (featured in this year's Directors of the Year section) and Marc Isaacs. **All White in Barking** (2007)/ **Men of the City** (2009) finds Isaacs offering two distinct perspectives on his home city. The first film details life for a variety of individuals living in an area of east London that has seen the rise in popularity of the anti-immigration, far-right British National Party. But rather than vilify all those who agree with the group's beliefs, Isaacs offers a compelling portrait of people who have had change thrust upon them and are floundering in their inability – or unwillingness – to adapt. *Men of the City* was shot as the full impact of the 2008 financial meltdown became apparent. Isaacs presents an account of life in the City of London, from a street worker through to a financial analyst. Constantly challenging our perceptions of these characters and what they stand for, he explores the lives behind the façade of their function in the city, in the process overturning assumptions and stereotypes. Both films are fascinating on their own, but together they create a riveting dialogue about life in a modern city. ***Extras:*** an interview with BBC Storyville producer Nick Fraser; booklet essay by Noel Megahey.

All White in Barking

Artificial Eye
Region 2

Arguably the UK's most prominent first-run release label for mostly European releases, Artificial Eye has built-up an impressive back catalogue of titles from some of the world's greatest directors.

The label bolstered its back catalogue of French directors with three collections from Agnès Varda, Eric Rohmer and Alain Resnais. **The Agnès Varda collection** spans two volumes, each with four films. Volume one includes her feature debut, *La Pointe Courte* (1954), two of her most acclaimed features from the 1960s, *Cleo from 5 to 7* (1961) and *Le Bonheur* (1964), and her wonderful travelogue from 2000, *The Gleaners & I*. Volume two includes her most recent film, *The Beaches of Agnès* (2008), *L'une chante l'autre pas* (1977), one of her most acclaimed films, *Vagabond* (1985), and her tribute to her late husband Jacques Demy, *Jacquot de Nantes* (1991). Together with an excellent array of shorts and documentaries, these collections offer an introduction to one of French cinema's most distinctive and enduring talents. Of the film, the lesser known *Le Bonheur* is something of a revelation. A feminist tract about the subservience of women in relationships, it is shot through with surreal moments and dark humour – a contrast to the soft colour scheme Varda employs – before the film's devastating ending. ***Extras:*** dozens of short

The Beaches of Agnes

films, featurettes and trailers; Jacques Demy's short film *Le Sabotier du Val de Loire* (1956); interviews with Varda; Varda's follow-up to *The Gleaners & I*, *Two Years Later* (2002).

The death this year of Eric Rohmer robbed cinema of one of its greatest directors. Of all his works, **Six Moral Tales**, alongside the wonderful *Tales of the Four Seasons* (previously released by the label) best represents his brilliance as a filmmaker.

Claire's Knee

Together, *The Girl at the Monceau Bakery* (1962), *Suzanne's Career* (1963), *La Collectioneuse* (1967), *My Night at Maud's* (1969), *Claire's Knee* (1970) and *Love in the Afternoon* (1972) are drawn around a common theme that the director described as 'a man meeting a woman at the very moment when he is about to commit himself to someone else'. This theme is best reflected in *My Night at Maud's*, in which Jean-Louis Trintignant's young man finds his moral certitude compromised when an encounter with a divorcée makes him question his belief that a member of a church is actually the woman he is destined to be with. In one of his best performances, Trintignant plays an archetypal Rohmer character, his life taken over by the quandary of his situation, but never short of a pithy line or two. These six films show Rohmer's subtle, restrained style at its best. ***Extra:*** a selection of trailers; Rohmer's short films, *Veronique and Her Dunce*, *The Curve*, *Nadja a Paris*, *Charlotte et son Steak* and the filmed interview *Discussion on Pascal*.

The Alain Resnais Collection is perhaps the weaker of the three sets. The four films included – *Life is a Bed of Roses* (1983), *Love Unto Death* (1984), *Melo* (1986) and *I Want to go Home* (1989) – come from a period of Resnais' long career that has attracted a fair amount of critical ambivalence. Yet there is much to enjoy here and the films offer a link between the experimental earlier films and the director's more playful recent work. Two of the films present an homage of sorts to directors of old. In *I Want to Go Home*, Hollywood songwriter and composer Adolph Green is a cartoonist who uses an exhibition of his work to travel to Paris to mend his relationship with his daughter. Less referential than his other work and featuring a rich score by John Kander, the film playfully highlights the differences between America and France, whilst simultaneously undermining clichés and stereotypes. *Life is a Bed of Roses* is comprised of three different stories, shot in the style of Georges Méliès, Marcel L'Herbier and Eric Rohmer. A precursor to the more successful *On connaît la chanson*, the film has characters break into song, but who rarely finish due to interruptions by other characters, creating a conflict between song and dialogue. The same cast appear in the remaining films in the collection, of which *Love and Death*'s interminable interludes may test the patience of even the hardiest of Renais fans. ***Extras:*** Interviews with Renais, his cast and crew; theatrical trailers.

Axiom
(Region 2)

An excellent distributor, specialising in independent fare from around the world, Axiom has gradually built up an impressive library that spans the best films of Wim Wenders, including a superb box set of his documentaries, and works by John Sayles, Pablo Trapero, Peter Greenaway, Bernard Rose, Ramin Bahrani and Daniel Burman.

Following the release of his more recent 'erotic thrillers', *A l'Aventure* and *The Exterminating Angels*, Axiom have brought out a collection

The Sound and the Fury

of Jean-Claude Brisseau's early work: **A Brutal Game** (1983) and **The Sound and the Fury** (1988). Both films feature a raw central performance by Bruno Cremer as a bullying patriarch. In the earlier film, he is a scientist with a physically disabled daughter, whose anger at the youths who destroyed his lab unhinges him, resulting in his hunting them down. At the same time, his daughter's burgeoning sexuality is awakened by the arrival of a handsome young man. Reminiscent of Michael Haneke's early work, with a callousness to human life that recalls *The Vanishing*, the film is a marked, though no less unsettling, contrast to his more polished later work. *The Sound and the Fury* stands alongside *La Haine* and *Savage Nights* as a portrait of disaffected youth and the callousness of contemporary society on the fringes of Paris. But unlike Kassovitz and Collard's films, it is shot through with moments of surrealism, as it tells the story of Bruno, a young boy who has moved in with his mother in the Banlieue. Like *A Brutal Game*, Brisseau's youth drama is a bleak view of life, but in pulling no punches, he produces a powerful and deeply disturbing portrait of the despondency felt by a generation with no hope for the future. ***Extras:*** both films feature an interview with the director.

Second Sight

Arguably the UK's most eclectic label, Second Sight have amassed an impressive library that runs from children's films and trash culture to middlebrow entertainment and the very best of European art-house. If it lacks a specific identity, the label is to be credited for making available many titles that have never been released, or are released in pristine editions, with a plethora of extras. Such was the case with the wonderful *Berlin Alexanderplatz* box set (released in a similar set in the US by Criterion) and a sterling, multi-disc edition of Peter Weir's *Picnic at Hanging Rock*.

Fassbinder returns once again to the label with the release of his little-seen two-part, 1973 sci-fi drama, **World on a Wire**. Overtly referencing *2001: A Space Odyssey* and Godard's *Alphaville*, Fassbinder's adaptation of Daniel F. Galouye's 'Simulacron-3' also looks forward to *Videodrome* and *The Matrix* in its creation of a word that distorts our consciousness. Its banal corporate design is in keeping with other sci-fi films of the era, but arguably the most unsettling aspect of the film is the cast. Coming off the back of *Effi Briest*, most of the performers who appeared in that film are present here, making for a somewhat surreal viewing experience. However, with its playful tone and the director enjoying the opportunity to indulge in a full-blown genre piece, *World on a Wire* is a fascinating film, if not quite up there with Fassbinder's best work. **Extras:** a documentary on the film, *Fassbinder's World on a Wire*.

Between his critiques of contemporary British society, Joseph Losey also slipped in a genre film, albeit an outrageous parody of the 1960s spy movie. A playful adaptation of Peter O'Donnell's comic strip, **Modesty Blaise** (1966) finds Monica Vitti shaking off the glacial veneer of the characters she played for Antonioni, to portray the sassy secret agent, charged, along with her East End sidekick Willie (Terrence Stamp), with combating the shenanigans of camp villain Gabriel (Dirk Bogarde). Made two years before *Barbarella*, it is as kitsch as Vadim's film, whilst drawing on the excesses of London's 'swinging' atmosphere, as well as locations around Europe. Losey's acceptance of the absurdity of the story allow him to poke fun at caper films whilst having a hoot indulging its excesses.

Modesty Blaise

With the film's eponymous hero exclaiming in his opening gambit, 'What? What? What? What? Man the Lifeboats. Ban the Bomb. The Dam's burst. Is me nighty on fire? Vote Conservative. Keep off the Grass,' it's hard to imagine **Dougal and the Blue Cat** (1970) being made today. The feature offshoot of *The Magic Roundabout*, a television series also directed by Serge Danot, but given new life thanks to Eric Thompson's wonderful re-writes and voiceover, it's the closest children's programming ever came to the 1960s counterculture. In this film version, a new arrival in the Magic Garden threatens life for Dougal, Florence, Zebedee, Dylan and their friends. With the most rudimentary animation, shot through with the era's penchant for psychedelia, it is Thompson's wonderful narration, with his parody of Britishness that makes the film so charming and funny. The DVD also features the French version of the film, with English subtitles, which further underpins Thompson's genius

Dougal and the Blue Cat

for comedy. ***Extras:*** a short documentary featuring contributions by Emma Thompson, Phyllida Law and Fenella Fielding, who voices the Blue Cat; an interview with film critic Mark Kermode, who discusses Thompson's re-invention of the film.

No less mad, but significantly more disturbing, is the release of Andrzej Żuławski's **Possession** (1981). A continuation of the director's bleak view of the world, starring Isabelle Adjani and Sam Neill, it is probably best known in the UK for being caught up in the 'Video Nasties' scandal of the early 1980s. A psychological horror film, replete with the director's usual

Possession

philosophical underpinnings, it details the breakdown in relations between a married couple. However, the husband's belief that his wife is having an affair with another man barely covers the extra-marital relationship she has embarked upon. If Zulawski brilliantly captures the angst of jealousy and betrayal in the film's earlier scenes, the physical and emotional horror that follows, like David Cronenberg's *The Brood*, highlights the destructive forces behind marital discord. ***Extras:*** a making of featurette; an interview with Andrzej Żuławski; a photo gallery.

Park Circus

Formerly known for simplifying rights owners' ability to offer their back catalogue for exhibition, Park Circus now also offer an eclectic collection of releases, ranging from classic features and silent films to a number of acclaimed documentaries.

Two titles stand out. **Henri-Georges Clouzot's Inferno** (2009) might be the best film about a film never made. Directed by Serge Bromberg and Ruxandra Medrea, it details the acclaimed French director's dalliance with a project about an hotel manager's descent into jealousy and self-destruction, which was to feature Romy Schneider. Clouzot was given artistic and financial freedom to pursue his vision, but within three weeks the production had fallen through. What remains of the footage makes up part of this fascinating film, which explores Clouzot's particular genius, the reason's behind the films collapse and an attempt to reconstruct elements of the film. The footage is startling, both in its power and beauty. Schneider's screen tests are an explosion of colour, tempting audiences to wonder what the finished film may have been like. It is possible it would never be quite as special as the vision Bromberg and Medrea present us, in a film that ranks alongside *Burden of Dreams* and *Hearts of Darkness* as a fascinating snapshot into the mind of a truly gifted filmmaker. ***Extras:*** *They Saw the Inferno*, a 57-minute film featuring unseen material; an interview with the directors; theatrical trailer; photo gallery.

A different kind of ecstasy permeates Albert Lewin's rediscovered classic, **Pandora and the Flying Dutchman** (1951), thanks to Jack Cardiff's sumptuous Technicolour™ cinematography and two full-blooded performances. An epic tale of doomed love, featuring the legendary Dutch seafarer, doomed to sail the seas until he finds a woman willing to die for him, it features James

Henri-Georges Clouzot's Inferno

Pandora and the Flying Dutchman

Mason and Ava Gardner, who is stunning in her first appearance, wearing a halterneck dress and crooning after a love she has yet to find. Drawing on German and Greek myth, with references to de Chirico and cultural critic Matthew Arnold, and a palate that frequently explodes with colour (Cardiff's work here ranks alongside his miraculous vision of Nepal in *Black Narcissus*), Lewin's film is a one-off; insane, delirious and compelling, with Gardner in full bloom as the intoxicating enchantress. ***Extras:*** a selection of trailers; the 1946 short film *Death of Manolete*; alternative opening titles; original production documents and a gallery of stills.

Two documentaries blend myth and reality with intriguing results. Maximilian Schell's **Marlene** (1984) began as a straightforward profile of the Hollywood star, who chose the actor to make a film about her. However, as soon as the project starts, Dietrich made it clear that she was unwilling to participate. The result is Schell's intriguing exploration of Marlene's persona and an act of generosity on his part, as he allows himself to be the butt of her vicious quips in order to gain more access to her. Dietrich is an irascible, but engaging guide through her life and her antagonism towards her quarry makes for compelling viewing. ***Extras:*** stills gallery.

No less strange is Anne Feinsilber's attempt to separate legend from truth in **Requiem for Billy the Kid** (2006). Hollywood has only muddied the waters regarding what happened to William H. Bonney, from Paul Newman's young turk to Kris Kristofferson's grizzled interpretation. As Lincoln County's real sheriff decides to re-open the investigation into outlaw's death, always believed to be at the hands of his old friend, Pat Garrett, Feinsilber's fascinating film blends an exploration of Hollywood representations with an attempt to uncover the real history surrounding Billy the Kid's final days. Kristofferson returns to play the role for the first time since he appeared in Peckinpah's 1973 film, his gravely voiceover also helping to blur the lines between fiction and reality. ***Extras:*** stills gallery.

Artefact
(Region 2)

Artefact Films are the only UK-based DVD label to specialise solely in non-fiction and feature films, championing both new releases and classic titles. Though most titles feature few, if any, extras, the variety of titles available is impressive.

On one level, **Hoop Dreams** (1994) is about two young black boys whose dream is to make it to the NBA and enjoy the success of being a professional basketball player. However, Steve James' exceptional film also paints a larger picture, of American society and the aspirations it instils in people, versus the reality of their situation. Rightly regarded as one of the finest documentaries to come out of the US, this epic account (the three-hour film was originally meant to have been a 30-minute short) of the struggle faced by these two boys over six years, where raw talent and the desire for success is never always enough, is more riveting than most fiction films.

Humanity's attempt to change the environment, with devastating results, has rarely been so well documented as it is in Hubert Sauper's **Darwin's Nightmare** (2004). In order to replenish the overfished waters of Lake Victoria, in Africa, some four or five decades ago the Nile perch was introduced.

An aggressive species that dominated all others, it gradually wiped them out, all for a European market whose demands for perch have resulted in both a natural and human disaster in the region. As a metaphor for the voracious appetite of global capitalism, Sauper could not find a better example than the perch, one of nature's most aggressive predators, but the film's power derives from its unflinching account of what has happened to the region in the name of profit.

Injustice is also the subject of **Roman Polanski: Wanted and Desired** (2008), in which two crimes are investigated: the statutory rape charge against the filmmaker and his treatment at the hands of an unfair system. Marina Zenovich's film is an even-handed account of the legal debacle that unfolded following Roman Polanski's arrest in 1977. Although the film refuses to portray the director merely as a victim, it refutes the notion that a criminal should be hounded, at any cost, by the law. Interviewing all surviving members of the case, it is a damning indictment of a system that succumbed to the glamour and celebrity of Hollywood.

DVD Releases of the Year
Make Way for Tomorrow (Criterion)
The Thin Red Line (Criterion)
The Actuality Dramas of Allan King (Eclipse)
Chicago (Flicker Alley)
The Party's Over (BFI)
Shadows of Progress (BFI)
Metropolis (Masters of Cinema)
A nos amours (Masters of Cinema)
Dougal and the Blue Cat (Second Sight)
Henri-Georges Clouzot's Inferno (Park Circus)
Hoop Dreams (Artefact Films)

Key DVD labels

Ian Haydn Smith profiles the essential distributors of world cinema in the English language

Arrow Films
A strong range of films across the spectrum of world cinema, some with a fine array of extras.
www.arrowfilms.co.uk

Artefact Films
A new UK documentary label, featuring an impressive roster of international titles.
www.artefactfilms.tv

Artificial Eye
A major UK label, whose extensive catalogue reflects the best in contemporary and art-house releases.
www.artificial-eye.com

Axiom Films
High quality presentation of new and classic releases, running the gamut of world cinema and the arts.
www.axiomfilms.co.uk

BFI
An essential DVD label, covering world cinema, animation, documentary and archive material, and experimental film.
http://filmstore.bfi.org.uk

Criterion (& Eclipse)
The benchmark of excellence amongst DVD labels, now spearheading the future with the impressive Online Cinematheque.
www.criterion.com

Facets
An eclectic and wide-ranging selection of films from around the world.
www.facets.org

Flicker Alley
Specialising in pre-sound and early film, this label has quickly established itself as one of the best.
www.flickeralley.com

Masters of Cinema
MoC match Criterion, both in transfer quality and the extensive extras and accompanying booklets.
www.eurekavideo.co.uk/moc

Milestone
A US label, whose recent releases are a mark of high quality.
www.milestonefilms.com

Network
The UK's leading label for British television series, but also features a growing roster of quality films and documentaries.
www.networkdvd.net

Park Circus
A relatively new label, with a small, but impressive, collection of titles.
www.optimumreleasing.com

Microcinema
One of the best collections of underground and experimental films from North America.
www.microcinemadvd.com

Second Run DVD
An excellent collection of must-have titles by many directors who have dropped off the cinematic radar.
www.secondrundvd.com

Second Sight
An eclectic collection of films and TV programmes, ranging from classical Hollywood to contemporary world cinema.

Soda Pictures
A diverse catalogue populated with some of the best contemporary world cinema releases.
www.sodapictures.com

World Survey

6 continents | 92 countries | 1,000s of films...

Abu Dhabi Film Commission

ADFC is dedicated to assist the development of the Film and TV industry in Abu Dhabi, nurture new talent, contribute to the promotion of Arab culture through film and promote Abu Dhabi as a key player on the international film scene.

Location Services
ADFC promotes Abu Dhabi as a new filming location to international producers and filmmakers to expose a fantastic variety of potential locations. From the heart of downtown Abu Dhabi, to varied coastlines, desert islands, the garden city of Al Ain, and the breathtaking dunes and oasis of the Western Region.

ADFC Locations and Production Support Team provides assistance in clearing scripts and advice on approvals, scouting for potential locations, granting permits for filming in public locations, advising on local support services and crew, providing support for location filming and offering discounts and special deals with hotels.

Training
ADFC initiatives include a diverse programme of mentorship and internship opportunities,

Yas Island. Abu Dhabi.

professional development, production schemes, scriptwriting competitions, and masterclasses giving emerging filmmakers the opportunity to meet and learn from some of the top creative professionals in the film and television industry.

UAE Talent
While the UAE's film industry is still very young, it is alive! By 2009, 15 feature films had been produced by Emirati filmmakers in the UAE. The first feature film shot in the UAE was *Wayfarer (Abir Sabeel)*, directed by Ali Al Abdoul and was released in 1988. Another significant film was *A Dream (Hulm)* produced in 2005 by Hani Al-Shibani, who directed many shorts in 2001 and a feature film titled *Juma and the Sea* in 2007.

In 2009, three major feature films were produced, including *A Hotel in The Town (Fundq Fil Madina)*, directed by Hani Al Shibani, *City of Life (Dar LLhai)*, directed by Ali Mustafa.; and *The Circle (Al Dairh)*, directed by Nawaf Al Janahi who has recently finished shooting his second feature film *Sea Shadow* funded by Imagenation Abu Dhabi.

In addition to the feature-length productions of 2009, there were more than 50 shorts

---

ADFC Initiatives

- The Circle Conference
- $100,000 Feature Script Development Grant
- Aflam Qaseera Short Film Fund
- New Voices Documentary Series
- Film Location Services
- Production & Training Programmes
- Production Internships
- Emirates Media Skills Training Council

ADFC with UAE filmmakers at Sundance 2010

and documentaries produced by local filmmakers. They included major shorts and documentaries, such as *Al Jazeera Al Hamra*, *In the Eyes of Filmmakers*, directed by Ahmed Zain and Ahmad Arshi. There is an increasing number of talented filmmakers in the UAE including Hani Al-Shibani, Nawaf Al Janahi, Saaed Al Marri, Fadel Al Muhairi, Manal Bin Amro, Nayal Al Khaja, Hanan Al Muhairi, Saeed Al Dhahri, Majid Al Ansari, Khalid Al Mahmood and Abdulla Al Kaabi.

UAE Production

- 15 feature films were produced up to 2009
- Three feature films alone were produced in 2009
- 500 shorts, documentaries and animation were produced during 2000-2009
- More than 50 short films were produced in 2009.

The year 2010 saw a different approach by the emerging filmmakers, many of which partnering with major production investments in Arabic film and with international production companies outside the UAE. *The Philosopher*, a 17-minute production by Abdulla Al Kaabi, starring French/Hollywood actor Jean Reno was an achievement for the film industry in the UAE, bringing interest in international investment to Emarati films. Abdulla Al Kaabi is currently developing another Emarati-French

---

Some Regional Film Initiatives

- Royal Film Commission Jordan
- Doha Film Institute
- Egyptian Association of Film Writers and Critics
- Union of Artist Syndicates - Egypt
- Bahrain Cinema Club
- Bahrain Keraleeya Samajam Cinema Club
- Amman Filmmakers Cooperative -Jordan
- RAWI Screen Writers Lab - Jordan
- Iraq Short Film Festival
- 7th Art - Kingdom of Saudi

---

feature film in association with a French Production Company, again starring Jean Reno

Regional Initiatives

Across the Middle East and North Africa the film industry is growing in countries such as the Kingdom of Saudi Arabia, Bahrain, Qatar, Iraq, Lebanon, Tunisia, Morocco, Egypt and Jordan. More importance is being placed on the Arabic film industry, with each country perfecting their current film resources and creating new media organisations, film development agencies, film festivals, funding programs and support programs for local talent. Each has dedicated talent, funding and support to advance filmmaking in their respective country and the wider Arab film industry. ADFC has been supportive in regional and international film efforts to help promote investments in Arabic film and local talent, and to educate audiences on the rich culture of the Arabic world.

Group photo at the Circle Conference 2010

Algeria Maryam Touzani

Although Algerian film production has not been particularly prolific this year, the country has nonetheless succeeded in marking its place on the cinematic landscape thanks to directors such as Rachid Bouchareb. A number of features made their way to prominent festivals, including Cannes, ensuring that Algeria maintained a high profile as a country that uses cinema to analyse and expose the human stories behind its turbulent past.

Rachid Bouchareb's **Outlaws**

After last year's acclaimed *London River*, Rachid Bouchareb made an explosive return with **Outlaws** (*Hors-la-loi*), which attracted much controversy prior to its world premiere at the Cannes Film Festival. The story, which was exploited by the French media before the screening, unfolds in the aftermath of the Second World War, when demonstrations for Algerian independence were frequent in France. It begins with the massacre that took place in Setif on 8 May 1945 and recounts the history of three brothers and their mother, between the years 1945 and 1962, who are scattered across the world. Messaoud joins the French army fighting in Indochina, Abdelkader becomes a leader of the Algerian independence movement in France and Saïd

moves to Paris to make a living in the crooked clubs and boxing halls of Pigalle. They are eventually reunited in Paris, where freedom for Algeria is their goal, at any cost. Bouchareb had previously faced animosity from the press in 2006, with his award-winning *Days of Glory*, the story of four North Africans who enlist in the French army to liberate France from Nazi oppression in 1943. Many of that cast, who were collectively awarded the Best Actor award at Cannes, were reunited for this French-Algerian co-production, which was budgeted at €20 million and was Algeria's most significant film of the year.

Taxiphone, a Swiss-Algerian co-production directed by Mohammed Soudani, recounts the story of Oliver and Elena, a young Swiss couple crossing the Sahara in a truck heading for Timbuktu, where their client is waiting impatiently to buy the vehicle. But when the truck breaks down at a remote town in the middle of the desert, the couple are forced to stop, a respite that soon turns into an indefinite stay. Solely focused on repairing his truck, Oliver becomes increasingly distant from Elena, who decides to go off on her own to explore the area. She meets Aya at the

Mohammed Soudani's **Taxiphone**

local phone centre, as well as a mysterious clairvoyant in one of the side streets. These encounters reveal a world straight out of the Arabian Night and transform what should have been a simple transit into a life-changing journey.

Amal Kateb's **We Will Not Die**

A few noteworthy shorts were also made in the last year. In Mounès Khamma's **The Last Passenger** (*Le Dernier Passager*), the soul of a young man who has jumped from a cliff pays a visit to his two impossible passions, a woman and a beloved concert hall, before leaving them forever. Yasmine Chouikh's **The Djinn** (*Le Djinn*) tells the story of Amber, a young girl who has three days to escape from the Djinn that haunts her village, but whose encounter with Amel changes everything. In **Brother** (*Khouya*), Yanis Koussim depicts a tragedy that unfolds in a typical Algerian home, where a man beats his three sisters, violence which will only stop with death. Abdenour Zahzah's **Garagouz** has played ay numerous international festivals. It is the story of Mokhtar, a puppeteer assisted by his apprentice son, who together travel in the man's old van between a few schools littering the barren countryside. In Amal Kateb's **We Will Not Die** (*On ne Mourra Pas*), after completing a report in Kaboul, Salim returns to Oran at prayer time to meet the women he loves. He wants to celebrate their reunion with a bottle of wine. But they do not have a corkscrew…

A number of documentaries concerning Algeria were shot this year, but most of them were produced and directed for French national television. Algerian documentaries

that were made include Malek Bensmail's **The Secret War of the FLN in France** (*La Guerre Secrète du FLN en France*), his follow-up to *China is Still Far*. His latest film recounts the role of the FLN in taking a popular revolution and transporting it to the occupying country. Ali Mouzaoui's **Mouloud Feraoun** is a profile of the life and works of the acclaimed writer, whose structure is a patchwork of different timeframes, interviews and archive footage.

It is certainly better to advance gradually than to stagnate and Algeria stands as proof of this. The country continues to produce its own cinema, which mostly engages with its past. Although significant co-productions remained scarce this year, a fact undoubtedly linked to the global economic crisis, the coming year promises to offer a number of rich projects.

The year's best films
Outlaws (Rachid Bouchareb)
Brother (Yanis Koussim)
We Will Not Die (Amal Kateb)

Quote of the year
'I think that in every fight for freedom, there are terrible human tragedies. I wanted the film to have an epic quality. I developed characters who run the revolution in the same way Al Pacino ran business and the family in *The Godfather*. That freed my hands from a historical point of view. My film isn't a documentary. I make movies.' **Outlaws** *director* **RACHID BOUCHAREB.**

Directory
All Tel/Fax numbers begin (+213)
Cinémathèque Algérienne, 49 rue Larbi Ben M'Hidi, Algiers. Tel: (2) 737 548. Fax: (2) 738 246. www.cinematheque.art.dz

---

MARYAM TOUZANI is a freelance journalist based in Morocco and working internationally, specialising in Art and Culture.

Argentina Alfredo Friedlander

The last year saw the best cinema attendance (40 million admissions) in over ten years, as well as an increase in the number of films released domestically (around 310 features). This was mainly due to the fact that the number of local releases, for the first time in history, slightly exceeded 100.

The 12th Buenos Aires International Film Festival (BAFICI) once again screened 400 films across two competing sections. The International competition was won by Pedro González Rubio's **Alamar**, while the National Award went to Gonzalo Castro's **Winter House** (*Invernadero*).

The 25th International Film Festival of Mar del Plata, once again under the direction of veteran filmmaker José Martínez Suárez, included three competition sections. Jerzy Skolimowski was on hand to receive the International Prize for **Essential Killing**. The award for best film in the Latin American contest was shared between **October**, directed by the Peruvian brothers, Daniel and Diego Vera, and **Transit Love** (*Amor en tránsito*), the first feature by Argentine director Lucas Blanco. Finally, the national competition was won by Tamae Garateguy's **Pompeya**.

Mariano Cohn and Gastón Duprat's **The Man Next Door**

Another important event, Ventana Sur, had its first edition during November 2009 and its second one at the beginning of December 2010. This undertaking of the National Institute of Films and Audiovisual Arts (INCAA) from Argentina together with the Cannes Film Festival and its Marché du Film is a market where most new movies from Latin America are screened and sold.

Ricardo Darin and Martina Gusman in Pablo Trapero's **Carancho**

Argentina had a strong presence at both the Berlin and Cannes Film Festivals, screening two and five films respectively. Of the Cannes entries, two screened in Un Certain Regard. One of them, **Carancho**, was also selected by the Academy of Art and Cinematographic Sciences of Argentina to compete for Best Foreign Film at the 2011 Academy Awards. Directed by Pablo Trapero, it has Ricardo Darin, who also appeared in *The Secret in their Eyes*, as Sosa, an ambulance-chasing lawyer. One night he meets Luján (Martina Gusman), who is attempting to save a man's life, whom Sosa sees as a potential client. A love story with tragic consequences follows.

Probably the best Argentine film of 2010, **The Man Next Door** (*El hombre de al lado*), was directed by Mariano Cohn and Gastón Duprat.

It is their second collaboration after *The Artist*. The film is about a small incident between two neighbours, when a window 'the man next door' wants to build will affect the privacy of the neighbour. Thanks to the performances of Daniel Aráoz and Rafael Spegelburg, the film was something of a surprise, which stood out from most domestic films and was rightly put forward as the Argentine entry for the Best Foreign Film prize at the Spanish Goya awards.

Nine out of the ten films that topped the year's box-office statistics came from the United States, including **Toy Story 3**, **Shrek Forever After** and **Avatar** with around three million admissions each. The only Argentine movie to make it to the top ten was Diego Kaplan's **Just Like Me** (*Igualita a mí*), a light comedy featuring popular actor and producer Adrián Suar, which attracted almost one million admissions. *Carancho* came second at the domestic box office, followed by Daniel Burman's **Two Brothers** (*Dos hermanos*), the story of two siblings with very little in common, beautifully portrayed by veterans Graciela Borges and Antonio Gasalla.

Puzzle (*Rompecabezas*) was premiered at the Berlin Film Festival and received a positive reception from critics. Natalia Smirnoff's debut feature, it starred María Onetto (*The Headless Woman*) as a 50-year-old housewife who lives a dull existence on the outskirts of Buenos Aires. She discovers a passion for assembling puzzles and through it meets millionaire Roberto (Arturo Goetz). Together, they share a dream of taking part in the world puzzle championships.

The Lips (*Los labios*) was the other entry in Un Certain Regard at Cannes and was co-directed by Santiago Loza and Iván Fund. It follows three women who are appointed by the National Ministry of Health Care to work in a small community in the Santa Fe province. This semi-documentary details the difficulties they face in taking care of sick people, due to the absence of any supplies at a mostly abandoned hospital.

Che a New Man (*Che un hombre nuevo*), an ambitious and overlong documentary by Tristán Bauer, features new material about Che Guevara that was uncovered by the director and his co-screenwriter, Carolina Scaglione. It presents a more intimate perspective of the political icon, particularly his love for poetry and his family.

Enrique Piñeyro's **The Rati Horror Show**

Several other documentary films were released during the year, although none of them achieved any box-office success. Arguably the best, which screened at the 12th BAFICI, was **The Rati Horror Show**. Directed by Enrique Piñeyro, who is a medical physician, airline pilot and actor, it is a plea for clemency for an ordinary man accused of a murder he did not commit, which has seen him incarcerated for 30 years.

Miguel Cohan's feature film, **No Return** (*Sin retorno*), also refers to an incident, this time a traffic accident, where an innocent man (Leonardo Sbaraglia) is charged with a murder he did not commit. Supported by other fine actors (Federico Luppi, Martín Slipak) it was a box-office hit.

Leonardo Sbaraglia and Bárbara Goenaga in Miguel Cohan's **No Return**

Gabriela David's **A Fly in the Ashes**

A Fly in the Ashes (*La mosca en la ceniza*) was directed by Gabriela David only months before she died. It is the story of two young girls who arrive from the Northeast of Argentina to Buenos Aires, believing a better life is possible in the big city. They become victims of human traffickers and find themselves trapped in a brothel they cannot escape from. A solid film from the director of *Taxi, an Encounter*.

Finally, several other interesting films should be mentioned. They include Diego Lerman's **The Invisible Eye** (*La mirada invisible*), Israel Adrián Caetanos' **France** (*Francia*), Hector Olivera's **The Mural** (*El mural*) and Nestor Montalbano's comedy, **Birds Flying** (*Pájaros volando*).

The year's best films
The Man Next Door (Mariano Cohn & Gastón Duprat)
The Lips (Santiago Loza & Iván Fund)
Carancho (Pablo Trapero)
Puzzle (Natalia Smirnoff)
The Rati Horror Show (Enrique Piñeyro)

Quote of the year
'Until the day of my death I will not forget him. I carry him forever in my heart. With Robert Bresson I learned a lot, he gave me confidence in myself, he chose me and allowed me to survive... the novelty of starting to work in movies. He was the teacher who helped me to find myself.' DOMINIQUE SANDA, *one of the jury members at the 25th International Film Festival of Mar del Plata.*

Directory
All Tel/Fax numbers begin (+54)
Critics Association of Argentina, Maipu 621 Planta Baja, 1006 Buenos Aires. Tel/Fax: 4322 6625. cinecronistas@yahoo.com.
Directors Association of Argentina (DAC), Lavalle 1444, 7° Y, 1048 Buenos Aires. Tel/Fax: 4372 9822. dac1@infovia.com.ar. www.dacdirectoresdecine. com.ar.
Directors of Photography Association, San Lorenzo 3845, Olivos, 1636 Buenos Aires. Tel/Fax: 4790 2633. adf@ba.net. www.adfcine.com.ar.
Exhibitors Federation of Argentina, Ayacucho 457, 1° 13, Buenos Aires. Tel/Fax: 4953 1234. empcinemato@infovia.com.ar.
Film University, Pasaje Guifra 330, 1064 Buenos Aires. Tel: 4300 1413. Fax: 4300 1581. fuc@ucine.edu.ar. www.ucine.edu.ar.
General Producers Association, Lavalle 1860, 1051 Buenos Aires. Tel/Fax: 4371 3430. argentinasonofilm@impsat1.com.ar.
National Cinema Organisation (INCAA), Lima 319, 1073 Buenos Aires. Tel: 6779 0900. Fax: 4383 0029. info@incaa.gov.ar.
Pablo Hicken Museum and Library, Defensa 1220, 1143 Buenos Aires. Tel: 4300 5967. museudelcinedb@yahoo.com.ar.
Producers Guild of Argentina (FAPCA), Godoy Cruz 1540, 1414 Buenos Aires. Tel: 4777 7200. Fax: 4778 0046. recepcion@patagonik.com.ar.
Sindicato de la Industria Cinematográfia de Argentina (SICA), Juncal 2029, 1116 Buenos Aires. Tel: 4806 0208. Fax: 4806 7544. sica@sicacine.com.ar. www.sicacine.com.ar.

ALFREDO FRIEDLANDER is a member of the Asociación de Cronistas Cinematográficos de Argentina. He writes regularly for www. leedor.com and presents movies at the 56-year-old Cine Club Núcleo.

Armenia Susanna Harutyunyan

In 2011, the state budget for the Armenian film industry remained the same as 2010, at approximately US$1.6 million. The amount set aside for film production was US$1.2 million, with US$299,000 for animated films and US$131,575 for documentaries. Sadly, these subsidies are not enough and it remains necessary to find alternative, non-governmental resources for the national film industry's development.

Within this context, success has been attained by co-production initiatives with European states, developing prosperous conditions to follow European models and adopting universally accepted standards within the Armenian film industry. The task has been difficult. Although Armenia is a member of the Council of Europe, it has yet to join European programmes such as MEDIA and EURIMAGE. Finding a solution to these problems has been the primary goal of the Directors Across Borders Regional Co-production Forum (DAB Forum), set up within the framework of the Golden Apricot Yerevan International Film Festival.

DAB Forum is a unique annual film industry event in the Caucasus region and it provides an environment for local, regional and international film industry professionals to meet, and opens access to European and Asian markets. It has also proven vital for the continued development of independent film production in Armenia.

The winning projects from the first DAB Forum in 2007, Inna Sahakyan and Arman Yeritsyan's documentary, **The Last Tightrope in Armenia** (*Hajastani Verjin Larakhaghatze*), was successfully released in 2010 and presented at a number of acclaimed festivals. It received the Main Prize in the Armenian Panorama Competition at the 2010 Golden Apricot Film Festival. Maria Saakyan's **I Am Going to Change My Name** (*Alaverdi*), a winning project at the DAB 2008 Forum, is currently in production. Likewise, Nika Shek's feature-length debut, **My Poor Darling Mother** (*Im Kheghtch Sireli Mayrig*), was presented at the 2009 Forum and received support in 2010 from the Armenian National Cinema Centre.

Mikayel Vatinyan's **Joan and Voices**

At the moment, there are many local features at the post-production stage which will be completed in 2011. One of them is Mikayel Vatinyan's **Joan and Voices** (*Jannan ev Dzajner*), the study of a woman who travels throughout post-war Armenia in the late-90s.

Aram Shahbazyan's long-awaited **Chnchik** (*Chnchik*), whose post-production took an unexpectedly long time due to financial problems, promises to be a unique dramatic account of a small village's everyday life, as seen through the drama of a family and a village-girl named Chnchik, who appears distanced from this image of family life.

Armenian cinema has been beset by a number of problems in recent years, but 2011 looks set to be a promising year, with many new

Edgar Baghdasaryan's **From Ararat to Zion**

releases. The most successful Armenian films of 2010 were feature documentaries. Of those, three stood out. *The Last Tightrope in Armenia*, produced by one of the original and most successful independent production companies in Armenia, BARS Media, explored the ancient folk tradition of tightrope dancing and the few remaining masters who keep this ancient art alive. Edgar Baghdasaryan's **From Ararat to Zion** (*Araratits Sion*) follows the paths taken by Armenian pilgrims travelling from Mount Ararat to Zion. It depicts the spirit of a pilgrimage that nurtured and sustained the sanctuaries and monasteries on the journey to the Holy Land over the centuries.

Finally, Grigor Harutyunyan's **Kayatsum** (*Kayatsum*) offered a photographer's perspective on the 20 years of recent Armenian history and the country's situation today. Despite all the difficulties faced by the country, it is very much a state in progress.

The year's best films

The Last Tightrope in Armenia
(Inna Sahakyan and Aram Yeritsyan)
From Ararat to Zion (Edgar Baghdasaryan)
Kayatsum (Grigor Harutyunyan)

Quotes of the year

'I care very much about platforms like "Directors Across Borders". It is very important to support new directors from the region... This is my first visit to Armenia. I have been curious about Armenia before coming. It is very recent that we started to talk about Armenians in Turkey. As one of the first who signed an apology for the events 1915, it was really important for me to come and try to have a dialogue.' *Turkish director and Golden Apricot 2010 jury member* SEMIH KAPLANOGLU.

'There are wonderful Armenian directors in the Diaspora. And you can see all of this Armenian production in the [Golden Apricot] festival, which creates a place for Armenian directors from the Diaspora and from the past. But the most important thing is that the tradition of Armenian Cinema is alive.' *The Honorable President of Golden Apricot IFF, Canadian-Armenian director* ATOM EGOYAN, *commenting on Armenian cinema today.*

Directory

All Tel/Fax numbers begin (+374)

Armenian Association of Film Critics & Cinema Journalists, #3, Moskovyan Str., 0001 Yerevan. Tel/Fax: 10 52 10 47. aafccj@arminco.com. www.arm-cinema.am.

Armenian National Cinema Centre, 38, Pushkin Str., Yerevan. Tel/Fax: 10 51 82 30 (31). abovyans@yahoo.com.

Golden Apricot Fund for Cinema Development, 3 Moskovyan Str., 0001, Yerevan. Tel/Fax: 10 52 10 42 (62). info@gaiff.am www.gaiff.am.

SUSANNA HARUTYUNYAN graduated in film criticism from Moscow State Cinema Institute in 1987. She has been film-expert of the daily *Respublika Armenia* since 1991 and is president of Armenia's Association of Film Critics and Cinema Journalists (the Armenian National Section of FIPRESCI) and Artistic Director of the Golden Apricot Yerevan International Film Festival.

Arman Yeritsyan's **The Last Tightrope in Armenia**

Australia Peter Thompson

Australians still have the big-screen habit. Cinema attendance was up in 2010 by around eight per cent, at close to AU$950 million. Several locally produced films performed respectably at the box office. And Screen Australia, the federal government's funding and administrative body, proudly announced that investment in local film and television production had risen by two per cent to AU$731 million for 2009/10.

All the good news seemed to reflect the generally positive outlook for a country that has weathered the financial crises of recent years better than other advanced economies, thanks largely to the Chinese appetite for raw materials. But there's plenty of angst and uncertainty about. Julia Gillard's Labor Party only just squeaked back in at the September election, flaunting the conventional wisdom that governments can't be voted out in good times. The housing bubble also appears to have a puncture. And, by year's end, the film-production lobby was howling for more assistance as Hollywood productions disappeared over the horizon, frightened off by Australia's steadily appreciating dollar.

Foreign production has effectively subsidised the local industry for decades (AU$2.27 billion between 2001 and 2008 alone). Relying on overseas help to fuel a national culture is short-sighted at best, but Australia is still locked into an obsolete economic rationalism, which insists that art pays for itself. This cultural malaise, if that's what it is, is reflected in Australian films themselves. Of approximately 20 features released commercially in 2010, at least five are barely recognisable as Australian. Not that one wants kangaroos jumping out of cupboards, but if artists are not working from some authentic base, what's the point? Young Australian filmmakers are increasingly attracted to genre and with dozens of expatriate actors stomping the streets of L.A., enthusiastically spouting American accents, it's a growing trend.

Andrew Lancaster's **Accidents Happen**

A particularly egregious example is Andrew Lancaster's **Accidents Happen**. While American-born Brian Carbee's script has a core of lived experience, the film is a curious hybrid, set in 1980s Connecticut but filmed in a Sydney suburb with a mainly Australian cast. No worse than the average Europudding, perhaps. Its saving grace is a stalwart performance by Geena Davis as the foulmouthed, acerbic mother of an unfortunate family plagued by a never-ending series of tragic accidents. Occasionally funny and even moving at times, *Accidents Happen* never quite overcomes its blighted origins.

But if Andrew Lancaster, clearly ambitious and talented, is comfortable in a kind of mock-American limbo, he's not alone. **Triangle**, an Anglo-Australian co-production shot in Queensland and written and directed by Britain's Christopher Smith, is set literally in just such a limbo, vaguely suggestive of the Bermuda triangle. Jess (horror specialist

Christopher Smith's **Triangle**

Melissa George) and her friends survive a yacht rollover in a freak storm and scramble aboard an apparently deserted cruise-liner. Imagine *The Shining* meets Mary Celeste. The final bloodbath comes as a relief, if not a surprise.

Writer-director Sean Byrne's gory revenge fantasy, **The Loved Ones**, may have Australian accents but in every other respect it too belongs to the stateless netherworld of horror. Student Brent (Xavier Samuel, more recently seen in *The Twilight Saga: Eclipse*) makes the fatal error of rejecting Lola's (Robin McLeavy) invitation to the school dance, the result of which is his kidnapping and torture at the hands of Lola and her father (John Brumpton).

The Horseman by writer-director Steven Kastrissios is equally accomplished in its own fiendish way. Another contemporary revenge fantasy, it merges into serial-killer territory as Christian (Peter Marshall) goes on an escalating rampage to avenge the death of his daughter at the hands of porn merchants. It can be argued that horror is a boon for young filmmakers. Lancaster, Byrne, Kastrissios

Steven Kastrissios' **The Horseman**

and their kin have plenty of local role models and they only have to look over the ditch (as the Tasman Sea is called) to New Zealand to see where splatter movies have taken the great Peter Jackson. And the *Saw* franchise, invented by Queensland pair James Wan and Leigh Whannell, has become the world's most successful horror franchise. Blood and fear have also launched the careers of *Wolf Creek*'s Greg McLean and the Spierig Brothers, Michael and Peter (*The Undead*), most recently enlisted to direct **The Power of the Dark Crystal**, a sequel to Jim Henson's 1982 movie, which should reach our screens next year.

Sean Byrne's **The Loved Ones**

The Spierigs' latest film, **Daybreakers**, looks like any other big-budget, international horror movie. Which is what it is, although it's officially an Australian-American co-production. A virus has turned humans into vampires and the world is running out of blood. Predictably, a small band of uninfected rebels (led by Willem Dafoe) fights to survive and find a cure for the virus. The Spierigs are imaginative and resourceful but they are working well inside

Michael and Peter Spierig's **Daybreakers**

by John Marsden, it is young-adult ,action-adventure with tinges of romance. Foreseeing a ruthless invasion of Australia by an unnamed foreign power, it pitches a group of seven teenagers into a life and death struggle to survive and eventually retaliate.

Beattie is a remarkable Australian success story, another that invites emulation by a younger generation. Positioning himself in Los Angeles in the late 90s, he wrote and pitched films tirelessly, eventually chalking up successes with the *Pirates of the Caribbean* series, *Collateral* and *G.I Joe*. He returned home in 2008 to co-write *Australia* for Baz Luhrmann.

No matter how advantageous the tax regime, an Australian film costing AU$27 million, as *Tomorrow When the War Began* did, has to recoup its costs through commercial channels and simple market economics dictate that the U.S is the primary target. Beattie's film has already grossed AU$13 million domestically, but its success in America will be crucial. Perhaps this explains why the writer-director has dumbed down Marsden's original story, which placed considerable emphasis on the complex internal experience of his characters as they faced the sudden obliteration of their world, the world of their childhood. Beattie's film is a spectacular shoot-em-up with overtones of nationalistic paranoia.

their limits here. Curiously, *Daybreakers* has been far more successful internationally than domestically, grossing over AU$50 million worldwide. Australian audiences appear to have a modest appetite for horror, which doesn't seem to bother the filmmakers, but should concern the funding agencies who administer the Producer Offset.

The Offset, introduced three years ago, has been hailed as a game changer for local pro-duction. 40% of what is defined as 'qualifying Australian production expenditure' (QAPE), which might account in practical terms for 90% of a film's total budget, is paid back out of federal tax revenue – virtually a gift to inves-tors. The problem now for bigger-budget films raising funds overseas is that the appreciating Aussie dollar has wiped out any cost advan-tage Australian producers once enjoyed.

One film to survive unscathed is **Tomorrow, When the War Began**. Directed by Stuart Beattie, who adapted the best-selling book

Co-production has proved a convenient way for larger-budget films that inevitably depend on foreign money to access the Offset. It has

Stuart Beattie's **Tomorrow, When the War Began**

made a film like the AU$80 million **Legend of the Guardians: The Owls of Ga'Hoole** possible. With exceptionally beautiful, cutting-edge 3D CGI animation by Animal Logic, the Australian studio behind George Miller's 2006 Oscar-winning *Happy Feet*, it falls short of that earlier film's popular appeal and emotional payoff. Nevertheless, based on the novels by Kathryn Lasky and under the guidance of Zack Snyder (*300*, *Watchmen*), it packs some dazzling visual artistry. A grab bag of well-tried plot devices, the film follows the young owl Soren (voiced by Jim Sturgess, also the central character in Peter Weir's forthcoming **The Way Back**) on his perilous journey to selfhood. The flying sequences are marvellous.

Jeremy Hartley Sims' **Beneath Hill 60**

Zack Snyder's **Legend of the Guardians: The Owls of Ga'Hoole**

Also reaching for epic status, albeit on a more serious scale, is Jeremy Hartley Sims's **Beneath Hill 60**, written by David Roach (*Young Einstein*) and based on the true story of Captain Oliver Woodward of the 1st Australian Tunnelling Company, who helped dig beneath enemy lines and set off the largest man-made explosion in history, at Messines Ridge, on the Western Front of

Belgium, on 7th June 1917. 10,000 German troops are estimated to have died in minutes, but *Beneath Hill 60* concentrates not on the gargantuan loss of life, nor the tragic futility of war, but on the heroism of the Australians involved. Shot in Queensland on a budget of AU$6 million, it is full of admirable historical detail, but lacks the broader perspective achieved by earlier films such as Bruce Beresford's *Breaker Morant* (1980) and Peter Weir's *Gallipoli* (1981).

Which brings us to David Michod's debut, **Animal Kingdom**, the only recent film to receive unanimous critical acclaim in Australia and favourable reception elsewhere. Premiering at Sundance, where it won the World Cinema Jury Prize, it earned a record 18 nominations at the 2010 Australian Film Institute Awards, the winners of which had yet to be announced at the time of writing. The record was previously held by Cate Shortland's *Somersault* (2004), a comparatively minor film in a lacklustre year (although it did introduce Abbie Cornish and Sam Worthington to the world). *Animal Kingdom* is bigger, beefier and more emotionally harrowing but, like *Somersault*, it belongs totally to its setting. It is a gangster film deeply rooted in a specific social milieu – the criminal underworld of Melbourne. Over the last 13 years, 36 criminals or their partners have been murdered in an unprecedented wave of violence and public interest in their stories is inevitably high. Jackie Weaver, whose career spans more than 40 years and includes many of Australia's cinematic landmarks (*Alvin Purple*, *Picnic at Hanging Rock*, *Caddie* etc) is breathtakingly good as 'Smurf', the matriarch of the Cody clan, doling out death sentences and kisses with an equal amount of insouciance, as the family disintegrates. And veteran Ben Mendelsohn is more deadly than an ice pick as Pope, the psychotic uncle to the central character 'J' (James Frecheville). Guy Pearce and Joel Edgerton add steel to the mix.

Like the lives of its three participants, Gillian Armstrong's unplanned series about adolescent working-class tearaways Kerry, Diana and Josie has matured into a profoundly moving and life-affirming chronicle. **Love, Lust and Lies** revisits the four previous films and involves Armstrong herself more intimately than ever before. This feature-length documentary is arguably her best work, despite her distinguished career as a drama director (*My Brillliant Career*, *Oscar and Lucinda* and, most recently, *Death Defying Acts*).

And what of the others who spearheaded Australia's film revival 40 years ago? Phillip Noyce has climbed back on the Hollywood bus to make **Salt** with Angelina Jolie, but he still has a number of Australian projects on the back burner. Peter Weir ends a seven-year hiatus with *The Way Back*, a deliberately epic tale of endurance based on the true story of four men who escape from a Siberian gulag in 1942. Bruce Beresford has three more films in the pipeline and, perhaps most intriguingly, Fred Schepisi is preparing **Eye of the Storm** for release in 2011. Based on Patrick White's novel about an ageing matriarch orchestrating the circumstances of her own death, it stars Charlotte Rampling, Judy Davis and Geoffrey Rush.

PETER THOMPSON is an award-winning filmmaker and writer. He has also been reviewing and presenting movies on Australian television for 28 years.

David Michod's **Animal Kingdom**

The year's best films
Animal Kingdom (David Michod)
Love, Lust and Lies (Gillian Armstrong)

Quotes of the year
'We're halfway through the deconstruction of the Australian film industry.' TONY CLARK, *chairman of visual effects company Rising Sun.*

'We've crossed the threshold... Now you can literally do anything you want.' GEORGE MILLER *on new 3D CGI technology.*

Directory
All Tel/Fax numbers begin (+61)
Australian Directors Guild (ADG), PO Box 211, Rozelle NSW 2039. Tel: (2) 9555 7045. Fax: (2) 9555 7086. www.adg.org.au.
Australian Entertainment Industry Association (AEIA), 8th Floor, West Tower, 608 St Kilda Road, Melbourne, VIC 3004. Tel: (3) 9521 1900. Fax: (3) 9521 2285. aeia@aeia.org.au.
Film Australia, 101 Eton Rd, Lindfield NSW 2070. Tel: (2) 9413 8777. Fax: (2) 9416 9401. www.filmaust.com.au.
Screen Australia, Level 4, 150 William St, Woolloomooloo NSW 2011. Tel: (2) 8113 5800. Fax: (2) 9357 3737. www.screenaustralia.gov.au.
Screen Producers Association of Australia (SPAA), 34 Fitzroy Street, Surry Hills NSW 2010. Tel: (2) 9360 8988. Fax: (2) 9360 8977. spaa@spaa.org.au www.spaa.org.au.

Austria Gunnar Landsgesell

In 2009, the domestic box office for Austrian films hit an all-time high of 1.2 million visitors. 2010 might reach 700,000, which is a respectable result for a country with a modest film industry. There were around 40 domestic releases in 2010, half of them documentaries.

There was a rush to upgrade projection at mainstream cinemas to digital. However, little funding was available for art-house and independent cinemas to convert. It is hoped funding will be in place in 2011. A number of independent venues have joined together to ensure their demands are heard. In response to longstanding demands from Austrian film producers, the Ministry of Economy has established an additional film fund. 'Filmstandort Austria' works similarly to the German DFFF and is designed to attract international co-productions.

If 2010 lacked the remarkable festival success of the previous year, it was the third consecutive year that Austria, a country with almost no history at the Academy Awards, saw itself in the running. After Stefan Ruzowitzky's Oscar-winning *The Counterfeiters* and Götz Spielmann's nominated *Revanche*, Christoph Waltz was honoured for his role as SS-officer Hans Landa in Quentin Tarantino's *Inglorious Basterds*. Michael Haneke's *The White Ribbon* was shortlisted for Best Foreign Film, with cinematographer Christian Berger also nominated for his work on that film.

One of the outstanding films of the year, Benjamin Heisenberg's **The Robber** (*Der Räuber*), was produced by Geyrhalter Film and featured in the main competition at the Berlinale. Undermining the structure and

Benjamin Heisenberg's **The Robber**

tone of the conventional heist picture, the film details the existential crisis of a bank robber (Andreas Lust), caught between the tension of his work and the banality of his personal life. Based on an actual case that took place in Vienna in the 1980s, the protagonist leads an unobtrusive life, his only passion, outside of crime, being his passion for running marathons. The film suggests that his profession is less about the money he steals than the kick of robbing a bank and challenging the authorities.

This story of unspoken desires, isolation and eccentric mavericks stands alongside the work of other Austrian auteurs, such as Jessica Hausner (*Lourdes*), Ulrich Seidl, Götz Spielmann and Tizza Covi/Rainer Frimmel (*La pivellina*). In fiction, the works of Thomas Glavinic display similar themes. Robert Adrian Pejo has directed a screen version of Glavinic's **The Cameramurderer** (*Der Kameramörder*), which tells the story of two couples spending a weekend in a remote villa who, during their stay, discover a 'snuff movie'. The film is a powerful exploration of trust between friends.

A refreshing attempt at presenting the past can be found Peter Kerekes' documentary, **Cooking History**. It details the role played by army cooks in determining victory and defeat in battle as a result of the way they prepare dishes for the soldiers. It offers an intriguing and visually distinctive take on the art of war.

The national comedy, whose tastes are rarely enjoyed outside a country's borders, was best represented by Andreas Prochaska's affectionate and naively funny **The Unintentional Kidnapping of Mrs Elfriede Ott** (*Die unabsichtliche Entführung der Frau Elfriede Ott*). Adopting a classical Hollywood narrative, the film plays up parochial petty-mindedness and the way the Austrian identity is both presented and perceived.

Peter Tscherkassky's **Coming Attractions**

The long and acclaimed tradition of avant-garde filmmaking in Austria still continues to thrive, as it has since the 1960s. Martin Arnold, Peter Tscherkassky and Siegfried A. Fruhauf are the biggest names in experimental film in Austria today. At the Venice Film Festival, Tscherkassky received the Orizzonti Award for **Coming Attractions**. The avant garde also informed the intricate narrative of Jahannes Hammel's **Follow Me** (*Folge mir*), which is an all-too-common story of lovelessness as it details the breakdown of a woman.

One of the most promising new faces over the last year was Film Academy alumnus, Barbara Eder, who directed the impressively elaborate drama, **Inside America**, which blends documentary and fiction in its portrayal of life in a high school on the Tex-Mex border. It is an astute insight into the realities of life

Michael Glawogger's **Kill Daddy Goodnight**

in this controversial area. The relationship between an African refugee (Clare-Hope Ashitey) and a smuggler (Fritz Karl) is explored in Erwin Wagenhofer's **Black Brown White**. It may be heavy-handed at times, but the film scores through its refusal to present a stereotypical view of a refugee. It is also visually resplendent, offering lush vistas of the Andalusian landscape.

Expectations are also high for another refugee drama, **Spain** (*Spanien*), directed by Anja Salomonowitz. Ulrich Seidl will also return to cinemas with his new film, **Paradise** (*Paradies*). Seidl, a notoriously slow filmmaker, presents a series of fragmented narratives about three women from one family, touching on the clash of cultures, sexual relationships and religious belief.

The year's best films
The Robber (Benjamin Heisenberg)
Inside America (Barbara Eder)
Tranquility (Siegfried A. Fruhauf)
Follow Me (Johannes Hammel)
The Unintentional Kidnapping of Mrs Elfriede Ott (Andreas Prochaska)

Quote of the year
'The purpose of co-productions is to establish good networks. In my mind partners are relevant when they think outside the box to build bridges [and] on those you can form something new.' OSEF AICHHOLZER, *the producer of* **Outbound** *and* **The Counterfeiters**.

ViENNALE
VIENNA INTERNATIONAL FILM FESTIVAL

OCTOBER 20 — NOVEMBER 2, 2011
www.viennale.at

Directory

All Tel/Fax numbers begin (+43)

Austrian Film Museum, Augustinerstr 1, A-1010 Vienna, Tel: (1) 533 7054-0. Fax: (1) 533 7054-25. office@filmmuseum.at. www.filmmuseum.at.

Filmarchiv Austria, Obere Augartenstr 1, A-1020 Vienna. Tel: (1) 216 1300. Fax: (1) 216 1300-100. augarten@filmarchiv.at. www.filmarchiv.at.

Association of Austrian Film Producers, Speisingerstrasse 121, A-1230 Vienna. Tel/Fax: (1) 888 9622. aafp@austrian-film.com. www.austrian-film.com.

Andreas Prochaska's **The Unintentional Kidnapping of Mrs Elfriede Ott**

Association of the Audiovisual & Film Industry, Wiedner Hauptstrasse 53, PO Box 327, A-1045 Vienna. Tel: (1) 5010 53010. Fax: (1) 5010 5276. film@fafo.at. www.fafo.at.

Austrian Film Commission, Stiftgasse 6, A-1070 Vienna. Tel: (1) 526 33 23-0. Fax: (1) 526 6801. office@afc.at. www.afc.at.

Austrian Film Institute (OFI), Spittelberggasse 3, A-1070 Vienna. Tel: (1) 526 9730-400. Fax: (1) 526 9730-440. office@filminstitut.at. www.filminstitut.at.

Location Austria, Opernring 3, A-1010 Vienna. Tel: (1) 588 5836. Fax: (1) 586 8659. office@location-austria.at. www.location-austria.at.

Vienna Film Fund, Stiftgasse 6, A-1070 Vienna. Tel: 526 5088. Fax: 526 5020. office@filmfonds-wien.at. www.filmfonds-wien.at.

GUNNAR LANDSGESELL is a freelance writer for *Blickpunkt: Film*, *Format*, *the gap*, *kolik*, *ray filmmagazin*. Co-Editor of *Spike Lee* (Bertz Verlag Berlin). He has contributed to several books, a.o. on Peter Patzak, Avi Mograbi, Diagonale.

Belgium Erik Martens

Only a few decades ago, political scientists referred to Belgium as the supreme example for the kind of enlightened state in which communities speaking a variety of languages managed to live together in peace and harmony. From time to time, the French- and Dutch-speaking communities quarrelled in public, but thanks to ingenious political engineering, problems were solved without resorting to bloody confrontation. For the last few years, however, the level of disagreement between the communities has never been as intense. Politicians have come to the understanding that the state should be reformed and that the communities should receive a larger piece of the Belgian cake. How the cake should be sliced remains the subject of an ongoing debate.

As far as the filmmaking community is concerned, all is well in Belgium. Business is still booming thanks to tax-shelter measures and more films are being made. On the other hand, the language issue has resulted in various sections of the film community evolving in different directions. Until a few years ago, Belgium had its national 'Plateau' film prizes. Today, the Flemish have their Flemish Film Awards, linked to the recent Ostend Film Festival, while the French community created its 'Magritte' awards, the first of which will be presented in February 2011. Its committee chose veteran filmmaker Jaco Van Dormael as 'godfather' for the initiative.

2011 marks 20 years since Van Dormael surprised both Belgian and international audiences with his first feature film, *Toto the Hero* (1991). The playful tone and the sparkling visual approach were unprecedented in Belgian cinema. Five years later, Van Dormael made *The*

Eighth Day (1995) and then kept silent for 15 years, during which the Dardenne brothers and their social-realist style dominated. Obviously, the return of Van Dormael aroused great curiosity. His new film would be an English-language production with a budget of more than €35 million. When the film was released at the start of the year, its reception was mixed. Formally, the film is an amazing achievement, but, due to the extremely complex narrative, it proved difficult for audiences to identify with the characters. **Mr Nobody** is a highly virtual and multi-layered construction. It tells the story of Nemo (an excellent Jared Leto) and the three loves of his live: Anna (Diane Krüger), Elise (Sarah Polley) and Jeanne (Linh Dan Pham). Nemo's indecision over the women is the film's main thrust and also its failing, as it presents three possibilities simultaneously, at various stages of Nemo's life, ending in the sci-fi world of 2092.

Jaco Van Dormael's **Mr Nobody**

2010 also proved to be Flemish filmmaker Jan Verheyen's year. With a taste for the commercial, his films keep to conventional structures, often remaking existing films. **Dossier K** is Verheyen's follow-up to the 2003 box-office hit, *The Alzheimer Case*, by Eric Van Looy. Again, the film is based on a crime novel by Flemish author Jef Geeraerts. The result is an entertaining popcorn thriller, involving police inspectors Vincke and Verstuyft and their encounters with a gang of Albanian mobsters. The film pokes fun at classical Belgian topics and lingers around familiar Antwerp locations, which endeared it to local audiences.

Jan Verheyen's **Crazy About Ya**

Less than a year later, Verheyen returned to Antwerp with **Crazy About Ya** (*Zot van A*), a remake of the Dutch director Joram Lürsen's film, *Love is all* (2007), based on a script by Kim van Kooten. Amsterdam becomes Antwerp in Verheyen's multi-plotted romantic comedy. There is little to no originality in the film, but it tells its story well and, while critics savaged the film, audiences embraced it.

As Christmas neared, another Flemish romantic comedy was released. Actress-turned-director Hilde Van Mieghem's **Madly in Love** (*Smoorverliefd*) finds four female characters (mother, daughter, sister and aunt) dealing with relationship problems. Again, Antwerp is the central location, its role in the film more pronounced than in *Crazy About Ya*. Audience response was very mixed,

Hilde Van Mieghem's **Madly in Love**

due to a poor script and wildly over-the-top performances.

The only true Christmas film this year was called **Little Baby Jesus of Flandr** (*En waar de sterre bleef stille staan*) by newcomer Gust Van Den Berghe, who transformed his student graduation project into a feature. It references a Christmas-themed play by popular Flemish author Felix Timmermans, about three beggars who encounter Jesus while in the countryside. Van Den Berghe shot the film in black and white and employed disabled actors in the main roles, whose performances are convincing. Although the film is far from flawless, its ambition and visual style proved strong enough to attract acclaim at the Directors' Fortnight in Cannes.

Gust Van Den Berghe's **Little Baby Jesus of Flandr**

Back on more familiar ground, Olivier Masset-Depasse's **Illegal**, which also screened at the Director's Fortnight, is an attack on Belgium's immigration policy and the system of incarcerating illegal immigrants in detention centres. Tania has fled from White-Russia with her son Ivan. She has found a job in Belgium and her son goes to school. But one day she's arrested and put behind bars. Masset-Depasse opts for a militant caméra-vérité style, which suits the subject perfectly, but ultimately can't save the film from its didactic approach.

The same goes for Hans Van Nuffel's feature debut, **Oxygen** (*Adem*), which describes the hardships, both emotional and medical, of young people suffering – as the filmmaker does – from cystic fibrosis. The film has been selected for numerous festivals and was

Hans Van Nuffel's **Oxygen**

awarded both the Grand Prix des Amériques
and the Ecumenical prize at the Montreal
World Film Festival. Coincidentally, in 2007, Nic
Balthasar's similarly themed *Ben X* won exactly
the same awards.

The issues addressed in **Turquaze** by
newcomer Kader Balci are more of the social
kind. Belgians with a Turkish background
have had to face Flemish prejudices. Lovers,
like those played by Kader's brother, Burak
Balci, and Charlotte Vandermeersch, have to
find a way to live with them. Balci's romantic
comedy takes place in Ghent. But, unlike
an earlier Ghent-set production, *Moscow
Belgium* (2008), the film lacks fluency and
remains less compelling, which was reflected
in an underwhelming critical and commercial
response.

Kader Balci's **Turquaze**

In Vanya D'Alcantara's **Beyond the Steppes**,
the idea of the exotic is subverted. A young
Belgian filmmaker retraces her family's past
in other parts of the world. During World War
Two, D'Alcantara's Polish grandmother was
deported to Siberia by the Russian army. The
young director rephrases the story in a purely
visual style. By contrast, Bernard Bellefroid's

approach to narrative is more concrete. In
The Boat Race (*La régate*), young Alex has
a passion for rowing. The sport is also a way
to escape his violent father. *The Boat Race* is
a simple but compelling psychological drama
starring newcomer Joffrey Verbruggen as Alex
and Spanish actor Sergei Lopez as the coach.

Bernard Bellefroid's **The Boat Race**

Three films were produced outside the
conventional production chain. Kris De
Meester's **Four Roses** was shot in one location:
a hotel in Antwerp. It's style and concept are
minimalist. A dozen characters meet, usually
two-by-two, in one of the hotel rooms. Sadness
and loneliness are the pervading tone, leavened
with deadpan humour reminiscent of early Jim
Jarmusch. The performances, by an American
cast, are impressive and, although the script
doesn't always convince, it makes De Meester
a talent to watch.

Johan Grimonprez's **Double Take** is an
extremely referential creative documentary
about the atmosphere of terror and paranoia
that pervaded the world from the 1950s
onwards. Grimonprez employs Alfred
Hitchcock and his double, Ron Burrage, as a
catalyst in the mix, alongside topics ranging
from the Cuban crisis, the appearance of
colour television, and the strange encounters
between Khrushchev and Nixon.

If *Double Take* isn't quite a documentary,
Hélène Cattet and Bruno Forzani's **Amer** is
not really a fiction film. Yet both are extremely
interesting cinematic experiences. It's not very
clear what really happens in *Amer*, since Cattet

and Forzani focus on Anna's morbid and erotic fantasy world. References abound in the film, particularly Italian exploitation cinema from the seventies. It is too long, but the editing and its formal virtuosity highlight two promising filmmakers.

2010 will probably be remembered as a year mostly dominated by newcomers. All of them left their mark, to varying degrees of success. Aside of Van Dormael's return, French-speaking Belgium performed under par. For Flemish Belgium, it was a productive year. Its audience was entertained, even if the critics weren't.

2010 was also a year in which documentary filmmakers focused their attention on Africa and, more specifically, the former Belgian colony of the Democratic Republic of Congo, which celebrated its 50th year of independence in June. In particular, there was Françoise Levie's documentary about Paul Panda Farnana, one of the first Congolese to study in Belgium, and Filip De Boeck's **Cemetary State**, about Kinshasa's Kintambo cemetery, which is inhabited by both the dead and the living.

Next year, Belgian cinema will likely face budgetary cuts. Flemish TV drama, on the other hand, will benefit from extra money and a new funding scheme installed by the Flemish Audiovisual Fund. For the French-speaking community of Belgium, 2011 will bring new films by Luc and Jean-Pierre Dardenne, as well as Joachim Lafosse, which is good news for the Belgian brand.

Johan Grimonprez's **Double Take**

The year's best films
Mr Nobody (Jaco Van Dormael)
Double Take (Johan Grimonprez)
Amer (Hélène Cattet & Bruno Forzani)
Little Baby Jesus of Flandr
(Gust Van Den Berghe)
The Boat Race (Bernard Bellefroid)

Quote of the year
'Growing older means I have more doubts and fewer certainties. I have more questions, fewer answers. In a story everything has a reason, there is cause and effect. Everything is controlled, and comes together in the third act. Exactly the opposite of real life.' JACO VAN DORMAEL *commenting on the complexity of his film,* **Mr Nobody**.

Directory
All Tel/Fax numbers begin (32)
Royal Belgian Film Archive, 3 rue Ravenstein, 1000 Brussels. Tel: (2) 551 19 00. Fax: (2) 551 19. info@cinematek.be. www.cinematek.be
Communauté Française de Belgique. Le Centre du Cinéma et de l'Audiovisuel, Boulevard Léopold II 44, 1080 Bruxelles. Tel: (2) 413 35 01. Fax: (2) 413 20 68. www.cfwb.be/av
Wallonie Bruxelles Images (WBI), Place Flagey 18, 1050 Bruxelles. Tel: (2) 223 23 04. Fax: (2) 218 34 24. info@wbimages.be. www.wbimages.be
Wallimage, Rue du Onze Novembre 6, 7000 Mons. Tel: (6) 540 40 33. Fax: (6) 540 40 39. info@wallimage.be. www.wallimage.be
Ministry of the Flemish Community. Media & Film, Arenbergstraat 9, 1000 Brussels. Tel: (2) 553 45 50. Fax: (2) 553 45 79. film@vlaanderen.be. www.flanders.be
Flemish Audiovisual Fund (VAF), Bischoffsheimlaan 38, 1000 Brussel. Tel: (2) 226 06 30. Fax: (2) 219 19 36. info@vaf.be. www.vaf.be
Flanders Image, Bischoffsheimlaan 38, 1000 Brussels. Tel: (2) 226 06 30. Fax: (2) 219 19 36. flandersimage@vaf.be. www.flandersimage.com

ERIK MARTENS is editor of the DVD-releases at the Royal Belgian Film Archive and a freelance film critic for different media.

Bolivia José Sánchez-H.

The trend toward digital productions continues, many by first-time directors, as well as co-productions with other countries. Foreign productions are attracted to many of the spectacular locations Bolivia has to offer, such as the Uyuni Salt Flat, as well as being a significant boon for productions seeking to reduce costs.

Two films by first-time directors dealt with the issue of Bolivian emigration, a timely topic for a country suffering from a loss of its population abroad. Okie's **Sunday... Distant Lives** (*El domingo... vidas lejanas*) tells the story of two women from different social classes who embark on a journey in search of a better life. The film was shot in Cochabamba and Barcelona. Paz Padilla and Miguel Chavez's debut, **Looking for Paradise** (*En busca del paraiso*), tells the story of people attempting to achieve their dreams by emigrating to another country. Felicidad is an illegal immigrant living in Spain. Back in Bolivia her brother, Gerardo, awaits the money he needs from her to join her there. Adan Sarabia's **The Game of the Spider and the Butterfly** (*El juego de la araña y la mariposa*) tells a sombre story of incest and familial disintegration. The script was

Adan Sarabia's **The Game of the Spider and the Butterfly**

co-written by Sarabia and Bolivian actor Jorge Ortiz. When a mother leaves her family, the daughter is left behind to face a life of incest and sexual mistreatment at the hands of her father, played by Ortiz.

French director Denis Chapon made the impressive animated short, **Grandmother Cricket** (*Abuela grillo*), which was a Bolivian and Danish production. Based on a legend from the Ayoreo culture, the 12-minute film presents the struggle of a local people against the privatisation of water and exploitation by multinational corporations.

Two of the most notable foreign productions shot in Bolivia were Iciar Bollain's **Even the Rain** (*También la lluvia*), starring Mexico's

Okie's **Sunday... Distant Lives**

Iciar Bollain's **Even the Rain**

Gael Garcia Bernal, Spain's Luis Tosar, and the impressive Bolivian actor Carlos Aduviri. The film, with a script by Ken Loach's regular collaborator, Paul Laverty, tells the story of two filmmakers who arrive in Bolivia to make a film about Christopher Columbus' arrival on the American continent. In the middle of the production, the city of Cochabamba erupts in a 'water war' between the local inhabitants and a corporation intent on privatising the natural resource. Bollain sets up a parallel between the past and present exploitation of Latin America by foreign interests. Mateo Gil's **Blackthorn** has Bolivian producer Paolo Agazzi collaborating on a western based on the life of James Blackthorn, better known as Butch Cassidy. The film tells the story of the friendship between Blackthorn (Sam Shepard), who raises horses in Bolivia but contemplates returning to the US, and a young Spanish mining engineer (Eduardo Noriega). The film made great use of striking locations such as the Uyuni Salt Flat.

Mateo Gil's **Blackthorn**

Documentary films have offered a diverse look at various themes of interest. Fernando Martinez's **Fast Food Off the Shelf** (*¿Por qué quebró MacDonald's?*), a co-production between Bolivia, Argentina and Venezuela, explores cultural, sociological and economic factors that appear to have resulted in the global food chain's Bolivian franchises going broke in 2003, resulting in the nationwide closure of the restaurants.

The torture and murder of the Bolivian figurehead of human rights and social justice, Father Luis Espinal, by paramilitaries in 1980 is recreated in the docu-drama, **Lucho Saint of the People** (*Lucho San Pueblo*), directed by Jesuit priest Eduardo Pérez. It presents a lucid account of the life, death and legacy of this beloved figure, who was also known as an author, critic, and filmmaker.

Oliver Stone with Bolivian President Evo Morales, while filming **South of the Border**

South of the Border (*Al sur de la frontera*), the new documentary by Oliver Stone, was partially shot in Bolivia, where he spoke with President Evo Morales, one of the seven Latin American leaders interviewed in the film. It is a must-see for anyone wishing to understand contemporary Latin America.

Geraldine Ovando and Emiliano Longo's **Children of the End of the World** (*Los hijos del fin del mundo*) focuses on creating awareness about the destruction of the planet at the hands of a world seduced by consumerism. The filmmakers document their journey around the world, looking for

Geraldine Ovando and Emiliano Longo's **Children of the End of the World**

alternatives to save the planet by visiting eco-villas and eco-friendly neighbourhoods.

Kent Upshon's **Oruro's Carnaval** (*Carnaval de Oruro*) is a colourful documentary produced by the BBC for its strand **Grand Events**. Documenting the 2010 Oruro carnival, an event which dates back to 1780, the documentary is a wonderful showcase for Bolivia's music and folklore.

Forthcoming film production appears promising. This optimism owes much to digital technology and to the country's attraction as a low-budget option for foreign filmmakers

and international co-productions. However, domestic distribution remains a significant problem for local filmmakers.

The year's best films
Even the Rain (Iciar Bollaín)
Grandmother Cricket (Denis Chapon)
South of the Border (Oliver Stone)
Lucho Saint of the People (Eduardo Pérez)
Children of the End of the World (Geraldine Ovando, Emiliano Longo)

Quote of the year
'Our grandfathers fought in civil wars to gain national sovereignty. Our parents fought against military dictatorships seeking equality and freedom for all. What is the struggle that our generation will have to take on?' GERALDINE OVANDO *and* EMILIANO LONGO *asking themselves what change means in times of world crisis.*

Directory
All Tel/Fax numbers begin (+591)
Cinemateca Boliviana, Calle Oscar Soria, Prolongación Federico Zuazo s/n, Casilla 9933, La Paz. Tel: (2) 211 8759. informaciones@cinematecaboliviana.org, www.cinematecaboliviana.org.
Consejo Nacional de Cine (CONACINE), Calle Montevideo, Edificio Requimia, Piso 8, La Paz. Tel: (2) 244 4759. contacto@conacine.net. www.conacine.net.

JOSÉ SÁNCHEZ-H. is a filmmaker and author of *The Art and Politics of Bolivian Cinema*. He teaches in the department of Film and Electronic Art at California State University, Long Beach.

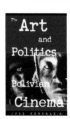

The Art and Politics of Bolivian Cinema
JOSÉ SÁNCHEZ-H

"Detailed information, not available elsewhere in English, fills the book, making it a major resource..." – *Film Quartely*

"...a very comprehensive history based not only on sound research, but also on interviews with Bolivia's most significant filmmakers..." – *British Bulletin of Publications on Latin America*

"...a valuable contribution to the still slim bibliography on Bolivian Cinema... a vivid and total mosaic of the history of Bolivian Cinema." – From the introduction by Jorge Ruiz, Bolivian Filmmaker

ISBN: 978-0810836259 • 328 pages • hardback

Denis Chapon's **Grandmother Cricket**

Bosnia & Herzegovina Rada Sesić

In spite of the country's huge governmental overhead, in which the budgets for culture have to be split among three separate administrative structures (the Federation of Bosnia and Herzegovina, the Republic of Srpska and the District of Brcko), and despite the economic crisis, several projects are currently in production, proving that the spirit of the country still stands tall. In face of such hardships, there are a number of exciting films, an expanding alternative film culture and even new film schools.

Ahmed Imamovic's **Belvedere**

Belvedere is the second feature film by Ahmed Imamovic, who first came to attention with his critically acclaimed short, *10 Minutes* and 2005 feature debut, *Go West*. He also scripted this painful drama about the survivors of the Srebrenica genocide. As Imamovic emphasises, it is a tale about those who are more dead inside than their appearance may let on. The story follows a family in camp Belvedere, which is still struggling to find the remains of their loved ones. Anticipating the complexity of the painful inner world of the survivors, the director shifts between sombre black-and-white images and more stylish colour sequences depicting bizarre reality shows.

The ever-resourceful Nedzad Begovic tackles the economic crisis by inventing an alternative way to make a film. Conceived as a post-modern story about relationships that exist via mobile phones, the film provides a funny and intriguing record of contemporary Bosnia. **Cell Phone Movie** is shot entirely by mobile phones and supplemented by footage from YouTube and other online sources.

Bosnian director Ines Tanovic, after directing part of the omnibus, *Some Other Stories*, which is still playing on the festival circuit, presented her second feature, **Our Everyday Life** (*Nasa svakodnevna prica*). An account of her own generation, this urban drama deals with people in their forties who remained in Bosnia, faced with the dilemmas of a post-war society and all the problems that entails. Sasha is still not able to own his own home and so lives with his parents. Through a series of turbulent changes in the family, we witness the tragic and comical aspects of family life in modern-day Sarajevo. The production was awarded an ARTE prize at CineLink, which is part of Sarajevo Film Festival.

One of the most exciting and much-anticipated films is **1395 Days Without Red** (*1395 Dana bez crvne*), by Sejla Kameric and Anri Sala. A co-production with the UK, it was also supported by several galleries and visual funds, as the Bosnian-Albanian directors' work is best known worldwide in terms of their visual art installations and exhibitions. Their intriguing and visually challenging film engages with the emotion of the siege of Sarajevo, which lasted one thousand three hundred and ninety five days. A woman today follows the route along the intersections on a stretch once known as Sniper Alley, where people had to run for their

Sejla Kameric and Anri Sala's **1395 Days Without Red**

lives, avoiding wearing red clothes as it was proven that snipers were attracted to bright colours like bulls to a red cape.

Documentary production has witnessed a marked decrease recently. Filmmakers rarely succeed in breaking out from conventional reportage to realise something more creative, with few local producers willing to undergo the time-consuming process and expense involved. One of the courageous few is Amra Camo Baksic, who produced two very different documentaries. **Don't Worry, It's Hidden** (*Ne brini, skriveno je*) is a new, investigative documentary by Alen Drljevic, exploring the background to an incident in which a boy finds his father's rifle and accidentally kills his baby sister. The film opens up the issue to cover a wider problem in society. The second documentary, **Cevljanovici**, by Namik Kabil, takes us to a village fair where dance, bull fights and people encounter each other once a year, at a location in the heart of the picturesque Bosnian countryside. The intensity of the film is established with almost no dialogue, but through close-ups and its stark imagery.

Feature films released late last year, such as Jasmila Zbanic's post-war drama, *On the Path*, still provoke discussions. The film has also won numerous awards at international festivals. The same goes for **Circus Columbia** by Oscar-winning Bosnian director Danis Tanovic. His latest drama, set prior to the outbreak of war, deals with the dilemma faced by people unsure whether to stay or leave the country. It is presented with humour and charm.

The students of Sarajevo have joined forces with experienced students from Amsterdam, who run the Kriterion cinema by themselves. Struggling for five years already, the students of Sarajevo's Kriterion recently opened its doors to film lovers.

Those who want to study cinema can now enrol at the new private university, which has opened a film faculty. At the same time, the state-run Academy for Fine Arts, which has existed for 25 years, opened a department for production, a profession that is increasingly in demand in this vibrant and quite successful film industry.

The year's best films
On the Path (Jasmila Zbanic)
Circus Columbia (Danis Tanovic)
Cevljanovici (Namik Kabil)
1395 Days Without Red (Sejla Kameric and Anri Sala)

Quote of the year
'Forbidding Angelina Jolie to shoot in B&H is the utter primitivism and totalitarianism.'
Golden Bear winner **JASMILA ZBANIC** *comments on the minister's decision not to allow the famous actress to make her film in Bosnia because her character, a war victim, falls in love with the perpetrator.*

Directory
All Tel/Fax numbers begin (+387)
Academy for Performing Arts, Obala, Sarajevo. Tel/Fax: 665 304.
Association of Filmmakers, Strosmajerova 1, Sarajevo. Tel: 667 452.
Cinematheque of Bosnia & Herzegovina, Alipasina 19, Sarajevo. Tel/Fax: 668 678. kinoteka@bih.net.ba.

RADA SESIĆ is a film critic, curator and a festival programmer based in the Netherlands. She is programme advisor of IFFR and one of the selectors of IDFA, also heading the documentary competition at SFF and lecturing at the Dutch Institute for Film Education (NIF). She makes documentaries and shorts.

Bulgaria Pavlina Jeleva

2010 saw Bulgaria plagued by the economic crisis, which affected most sectors of social life. Along with the severely affected performing arts, national cinema became the victim of severe budgetary cuts, with a reduction of almost 60% of the €9.5 million public support. According to the Bulgarian Observatory of Cultural Economics, during the last five years the financial structuring outlined in the Film Law has not been adhered to, resulting in €15 million never reaching the National Film Centre. Regardless of the announcements that 14 new titles would be produced by the end of the year, the financial restrictions forced the National Film Centre to cancel the regular selection committees, which were scheduled for the second half of the year.

During the 29th Golden Rose Varna National Film Festival, which screened 22 features produced during the last two years, filmmakers staged a public protest against the cuts to film funding. At the festival's opening, the director of the tear's most successful film, **Mission London**, Dimitar Mitovski, read a declaration signed by 34 members of the film community. The declaration was supported by the Union of Bulgarian Filmmakers and the festival jury, which announced a declaration of its own, defending the need for adequate financing of Bulgarian cinema. Representatives of professional guilds unified themselves around a firm belief that 'during the last years the artistic qualities of the Bulgarian films were growing and therefore the positive process must be treated with special care'. For the first time in its history, Bulgaria's premier film festival had no closing ceremony. The awarded artists, among whom was director Kamen Kalev, whose intimate

Dimitar Mitovski's **Mission London**

story of two brothers living in post-communist Sofia, **Eastern Plays**, received the Golden Rose, refused to officially accept the awards on stage.

One positive public initiative was the establishment of a National Film Academy, whose 500 members represent a cross-section of the film industry and who, for the first time, voted on the winners of the national film awards. Topping the list of eleven 2009 feature films as Film of the Year was *Eastern Plays*. The same film became Bulgaria's official entry for the Academy Awards.

The major box-office event of the year was Dimitar Mitovski's eccentric comedy, *Mission London*. Based on Alek Popov's satirical novel in which a freshly appointed ambassador in London is obliged to fulfil the ambition of Bulgaria's First Lady in bringing the Queen of England to a splashy diplomatic party on the eve of Bulgaria's EU membership, the film took full advantage of an extensive marketing campaign and the involvement of the private BTV channel.

Director and actor Tzvetodar Markov's teenage romance, **Hunting Down Small Predators**, became the country's first film to be shot in

High Definition and was screened in DCDM-equipped theatres. The plot, in which four Sofia teenagers mix with the underground world of powerful criminals, managed to win the unconditional adoration of the young.

An emotional love story set prior to the fall of the Berlin Wall, Victor Chuchkov Jr's ambitious feature debut, **Tilt**, received a positive critical response. As did Dragomir Sholev's **Shelter**, which was based on a script by the Romanian/Dutch couple, Razvan Radulescu and Melissa de Raaf. It was an exuberant profile of a young man who is too dependent on his parents.

Dragomir Sholev's **Shelter**

Ivaylo Hristov, another director and actor, presented a touching story about immigration during the communist period, **Footsteps in the Sand**. The film starred the popular actor Ivan Barnev, whose collaboration with Hristov produced a sympathetic portrait of a young man deeply in love.

2011 sees a number of significant productions. Kamen Kalev's second feature, **The Island**, stars French actress Laetitia Casta and Danish actor Thure Lindhardt and is focused on the emotional world of a man born in Bulgaria, but who now lives abroad. There is also Ilian Djevelekov's provocative feature debut, **Love.net,** which takes a very modern look at relationships.

PAVLINA JELEVA is a film critic and journalist, regularly contributing to many Bulgarian newspapers and magazines. Having been national representative on the boards of Eurimages and FIPRESCI, she is now artistic and foreign-relations director of her own film company.

The year's best films

Footsteps in the Sand (Ivaylo Hristov)
Mission London (Dimitar Mitovski)
Shelter (Dragomir Sholev)
Tilt (Victor Chuchkov Jr)
Hunting Down Small Predators
(Tzvetodar Markov)

Quote of the year

'I believe there wasn't a penalty action against *Mission London* targeting my participation in the filmmakers' protest against the financial cuts.' DIMITAR MITOVSKI *during the Varna Film Festival.*

Directory

All Tel/Fax numbers begin (+359)
Ministry of Culture, 17 Stamboliiski St, 1000 Sofia. Tel: (2) 980 6191. Fax: (2) 981 8559. www.culture.government.bg.
National Film Centre, 2A Dondukov Blvd, 1000 Sofia. Tel: (2) 987 4096. Fax: (2) 987 3626. www.nfc.bg.
Bulgarian National Television, 29 San Stefano St, 1000 Sofia. Tel: (2) 985 591. Fax: (2) 987 1871. www.bnt.bg .
National Academy of Theatre & Film Arts, 108A Rakovski Street, 1000 Sofia. Tel: (2) 9231 231/233.
Bulgarian National Film Library, 36 Gurko St, 1000 Sofia. Tel: (2) 987 0296. Fax: (2) 987 6004. bnf.bg/en/film_library/ or www.ceebd.co.uk/ceeed/un/bg/bg023.htm
Bulgarian Film Producers Association, Tel: (2) 8860 5350. Fax: (2) 963 0661. geopoly@gmail.com.
Union of Bulgarian Film Makers, 67 Dondukov Blvd, 1504 Sofia. Tel: (2) 946 1068. Fax: (2) 946 1069. www.filmmakersbg.org.

Ivaylo Hristov's **Footsteps in the Sand**

ABU DHĀBI FILM COMMISSION

Canada Tom McSorley

As the first decade of the 21st century closes, Canadian cinema finds itself in very familiar territory. On the one hand, there is the ongoing and considerable creativity of filmmakers producing absorbing, compelling, relevant work; on the other, those same filmmakers confronting the same intractable problem of a near-total lack of access to Canadian cinemas, of which roughly 95% are occupied by Hollywood releases. One of the happy consequences of this unhappy situation, however, is that the Canadian cinema has evolved, from the early 20th century onward, in a decidedly non-industrial, non-generic fashion. The lack of commercial imperatives can make for more adventurous film art, of course, but, nevertheless, the Canadian cinema's search for the *fata morgana* of domestic commercial success goes on, especially in English-speaking Canada.

In 2010 that search leads to two films that employ established film genres and adapt them to a Canadian context. Both fail, critically and commercially. William Phillip's **Gunless** is a gormless take on the Western in which an American gunslinger (gamely performed by Paul Gross), fleeing the law in the US, arrives in a small western Canadian town and soon discovers that gun culture north of the border is radically different. The promising comedic premise of national-cultural difference founders on a mediocre script and pedestrian direction. Michael MacGowan's earnest and not entirely unlikeable **Score: A Hockey Musical** weaves Canada's hockey obsession into a banal coming-of-age love story involving a young man named Farley (Noah Reid) who's been home-schooled by hippie pacifists and must face the challenges of the hockey world. In a musical where allegory meets atonality

Michael MacGowan's **Score: A Hockey Musical**

(there are few memorable songs), cameo appearances by Olivia Newton-John, Nelly Furtado, and several prominent professional hockey stars can neither salvage the film nor realise its commercial ambitions.

More securely anchored in the formally freewheeling, non-commercial independent Canadian filmmaking tradition are several impressive feature films, including two from indie veteran, Bruce McDonald. **This Movie Is Broken** revolves around a young couple falling in love and attempting to access the backstage area at a concert by the acclaimed Toronto band, Broken Social Scene; part romantic comedy, part concert film, it is neither and both simultaneously, and a successful hybrid. McDonald's second feature, **Trigger**, is the tale of Kat and Vic (Molly Parker and the late Tracy Wright, a McDonald regular who, sadly, died in 2010 at the age of 50), two women who once fronted a punk band together and whose lives have gone in different directions. Reunited after a decade, their thorny relationship is rekindled, as are their confrontations with time's passing, mortality, and a gnarled, shared past.

The equally prolific and adventurous Vancouver-based filmmaker Carl Bessai delivers **Repeaters**, a fascinating existential thriller involving recovering addicts who are given day passes from their rehab centre in order to make amends with those they have mistreated. Montreal writer-director Jacob Tierney's **Good Neighbours**, set in 1995 and involving a very peculiar love triangle (played by Jay Baruchel, Emily Hampshire, and Scott Speedman) and a series of unsolved homicides, is a promising follow-up to his previous film, *The Trotsky*. Michael Dowse returns to familiar territory with an admirable sequel, **Fubar II**, involving his quintessential Canadian headbanger 'hosers', Dean and Terry (Paul Spence and Dave Lawrence), as they celebrate five years of Dean's being cancer-free and the possibility of high-paying jobs in Alberta's oil industry.

Carl Bessai's **Repeaters**

Ingrid Veninger's **MODRA**, a low-budget coming-of-age tale of a young Canadian woman who goes to her family's native Slovakia, is an understated and engaging portrait of the search for identity. Experimental filmmaker and video artist Daniel Cockburn makes his feature debut with the offbeat and appealing **You Are Here**, an interwoven set of puzzling narratives involving an archivist, a scientist, and a man who's misplaced his computer password.

The cinema of Quebec continues to yield generation after generation of auteurist filmmakers, from Michel Brault to Denys Arcand to Robert Lepage to new talents like Denis Villeneuve and

Xavier Dolan's **Heartbeats**

Xavier Dolan. Not yet 22 years old, Dolan has already had both of his feature films selected for, and winning awards at, Cannes: his debut in 2009, *I Killed My Mother*, as well as his second, **Heartbeats** (*Les Mours imaginaires*), which screened in the Un Certain Regard section in 2010. Revolving around two friends, Francis and Marie (Dolan and Monia Chokri), and their mutual attraction to Nico (Niels Schneider), a young man who comes into their lives, *Heartbeats* is accomplished but less emotionally complex than its predecessor, and its stylishness occasionally verges on empty posture and affectation. Nonetheless, Dolan is clearly a talent to be reckoned with in the future.

The ever-idiosyncratic and intelligent cinema of Denis Cote continues with his fifth feature, **Curling**. Set in a small town in the depths of winter, Cote's twisted, deadpan tale of an unusual father-daughter relationship is a strangely affecting admixture of violence, repression, entrapment, and amusement. Catherine Martin's poetic, intensely moving drama, **Mourning For Anna** (*Trois temps après*

Denis Cote's **Curling**

la mort d'Anna), concerns the grief-stricken Françoise (Guylaine Tremblay) who leaves Montreal for wintry rural Quebec in order to come to terms with the violent death of her only daughter. Martin's extraordinary imagery, pacing, and sensitive direction not only convey the emotional devastation of her protagonist, but also hint at the possibilities of hope and transcendence. Arguably the most important of the current crop of Quebecois auteurs, Denis Villeneuve confirms, with **Incendies**, his position as one of the pre-eminent film directors in contemporary Canadian cinema, the heir apparent, in Quebec at least, to the mantle of Denys Arcand. Based on Lebanese-born Canadian Wajdi Mouawad's acclaimed play, Villeneuve's powerful, emotionally intense film tells the story of twins, Jeanne (Mélissa Désormeaux-Poulin) and Simon (Maxim Gaudette), who travel to a dangerous, war-torn Middle East in search of their roots to fulfill the wishes of their late mother's will.

Denis Villeneuve's **Incendies**

Canada's traditionally strong documentary tradition was dominated by veteran directors in 2010. William D. MacGillivray's **The Man of a Thousand Songs** is an intimate, insightful look at fabled Newfoundland singer-songwriter, Ron Hynes. Part portrait of an artist, part existential drama, MacGillivray's mature, assured style reveals much of Hynes' art and life. Similarly, veteran documentarian Michael Ostroff delivers an elegant exploration of the groundbreaking Canadian artist, Emily Carr, in **Winds of Heaven: Carvers, Carr and Spirits of the Forest**. Sturla Gunnarsson's **Force of Nature: The David Suzuki Movie** is a lively, thoughtful examination of the internationally renowned Canadian scientist-environmentalist-

William D. MacGillivray's **The Man of a Thousand Songs**

activist, Dr. David Suzuki. Shelley Saywell's **In the Name of the Family** offers a penetrating and deeply troubling study of the disturbing examples of 'honour killing' in North America, where fathers murder their daughters for perceived wrongdoings and betrayals of cultural orthodoxy. On the outer edges of the documentary tradition, meanwhile, Theodor Ushev's dark, oneiric, animated, essayistic ode to the late Canadian experimental filmmaker, Arthur Lipsett, **Lipsett Diaries**, features an evocative script by Ottawa International Animation Festival artistic director, Chris Robinson, and a stirring, haunting voiceover by filmmaker Xavier Dolan.

Theodor Ushev's **Lipsett Diaries**

Perhaps fittingly, given Canadian cinema's internationalist tendencies of the last half-decade, 2010 concluded with the mid-December release of the Canadian-Italian co-production, **Barney's Version**, starring Hollywood luminaries Paul Giamatti and Dustin Hoffman. An adaptation of the 1997 Mordecai Richler novel about a Montreal television producer recalling his turbulent, occasionally dissolute life and times, the film premiered

Paul Giamatti and Dustin Hoffman in **Barney's Version**

at the Venice Film Festival. Like all screen adaptations of his work (*The Apprenticeship of Duddy Kravitz* in 1974, which starred Richard Dreyfuss; and *Joshua Then and Now* in 1985, featuring James Woods), this film is a cross-border production featuring American star power, a not unfamiliar 'Canadian' production paradigm which will no doubt re-ignite all-too-familiar debates about Canadian cultural sovereignty and further illuminate the peculiar and often daunting enterprise that is filmmaking in Canada.

The year's best films
Curling (Denis Cote)
Trigger (Bruce McDonald)
Incendies (Denis Villeneuve)
The Man of a Thousand Songs
(William D. MacGillivray)
Lipsett Diaries (Theodor Ushev)

Quotes of the year
'I didn't want to be that American guy who screwed it up.' *American actor* PAUL GIAMATTI, *referring to his cross-border anxiety at taking the role as Canadian television producer, Barney Panosky, the lead character in* **Barney's Version**.

'Everyone loves to say they support Canadian films, but when it comes to the box office, no one wants to pay money to see them.' NIGEL AGNEW, *Toronto Underground Cinema*.

Directory
All Tel/Fax numbers begin with (+1)
Academy of Canadian Cinema & Television, 172 King St E, Toronto, Ontario, M5A 1J3. Tel: (416) 366 2227. Fax: (416) 366 8454. www.academy.ca.

Canadian Motion Picture Distributors Association (CMPDA), 22 St Clair Ave E, Suite 1603, Toronto, Ontario, M4T 2S4. Tel: (416) 961 1888. Fax: (416) 968 1016.
Canadian Film & Television Production Association, 151 Slater Street, Suite 605, Ottawa, Ontario, K1P 5H3. Tel: (613) 233 1444. Fax: (613) 233 0073. ottawa@cftpa.ca.
La Cinémathèque Québécoise, 335 Blvd de Maisonneuve E, Montreal, Quebec, H2X 1K1. Tel: (514) 842 9763. Fax: (514) 842 1816. info@cinematheque.qc.ca. www.cinematheque.qc.ca.
Directors Guild of Canada, 1 Eglinton Ave E, Suite 604, Toronto, Ontario, M4P 3A1. Tel: (416) 482 6640. Fax: (416) 486 6639. www.dgc.ca.
Motion Picture Theatre Associations of Canada, 146 Bloor Street W, 2nd Floor, Toronto, Ontario, M5S 1P3. Tel: (416) 969 7057. Fax: (416) 969 9852. www.mptac.ca.
National Archives of Canada, Visual & Sound Archives, 344 Wellington St, Ottawa, Ontario, K1A 0N3. Tel: (613) 995 5138. Fax: (613) 995 6274. www.archive.ca.
National Film Board of Canada, PO Box 6100, Station Centre-Ville, Montreal, Quebec, H3C 3H5. Tel: (514) 283 9246. Fax: (514) 283 8971. www.nfb.ca.
Telefilm Canada, 360 St Jacques Street W, Suite 700, Montreal, Quebec, H2Y 4A9. Tel: (514) 283 6363. Fax: (514) 283 8212. www.telefilm.gc.ca.

TOM McSORLEY is Executive Director of the Canadian Film Institute, a Sessional Lecturer in Film Studies at Carleton University, film critic for CBC Radio One, and a Contributing Editor to *POV* magazine.

Molly Parker and Tracy Wright in Bruce McDonald's **Trigger**

Chile Hugo Diaz Gutiérrez

With the arrival of a new government in 2010, Minister of Culture Luciano Cruz Coke decided to display Chile's potential on the global stage. Head executives of American studios such as Fox and Warner were invited to invest significantly in Chile, a deal that would include help with location scouting and FX development.

A number of events had a major impact on the country. An immense earthquake delayed many productions. And, later in the year, 33 miners were trapped 700 metres underground, which captured the attention of the nation and the world. The latter ended with an epic rescue and a number of countries have since announced film projects based around the incident.

With around 50 projects in production, only a few were likely to be released theatrically, or would be of such technical merit to warrant their release. However, many low-budget digital films proved to be surprisingly impressive.

José Manuel 'Ché' Sandoval's **You Think You Are the Prettiest (But You Are the Sluttiest)**

José Manuel 'Ché' Sandoval's **You Think You Are the Prettiest (But You Are the Sluttiest)** (*Te creís la más linda [pero erís la más puta]*), a low-budget comedy full of local slang, became an indie-hit. In it, 19-year-old Javier roams the night wondering if his ex-girlfriend Valentina and his best friend Nicolás are having sex. It plays out like a Chilean *Catcher in the Rye* with added sex.

EstebanRojas and Juan Olivares' **Burning Down the House**

The Chile-Argentina co-production **Burning Down the House** (*La casa por la ventana*) was shot as a guerrilla-film by Esteban Rojas and Juan Olivares in the pre-earthquake city of Concepción. Julio Sáez Jr, an architecture graduate, organises a boring New Year Eve bash that transforms into a wild rock party. Premiering at the third edition of the Cine B Film Festival, this innovative, strange and naïve comedy clearly continues in the tradition of 'geek' films such as *Napoleon Dynamite*.

The World Cup classification tournament was depicted in **Red Eyes** (*Ojos rojos*), a documentary by Juan Ignacio Sabatini, Juan Pablo Sallato and Ismael Larraín. It details the struggle faced by the national football team following their failure at Germany 2006, to the success of qualifying for South Africa 2010. It was the highest-grossing film of the year and the top-grossing documentary in Chilean history.

Ernesto Díaz Espinoza previously directed Marko Zaror in *Mirageman*. They re-teamed for **Mandrill**, where the 'Latin Dragon' plays a bounty hunter with a Bond-like attitude, albeit shot through with the impact of childhood trauma. Unlike *Mirageman*, *Mandrill* failed to light up the domestic box office, probably due to a delay in the release, following the earthquake, which affected its marketing campaign. The film fared better internationally, where it received the Best Film and Best Actor awards at the Fantastic Fest in Austin, Texas.

A new trend could be seen with Nicolás López's **F*ck My Life** (*Que pena tu vida*), a romantic comedy about Javier, a young publicist who is abandoned by his girlfriend and has to struggle against the technical hitches associated with the break-up on various social networks. Twitter fans seemingly adored the film, but reviews were mostly negative. However, the premise seduced Panamax Films, an American company, to acquire the rights for a remake.

Matías Bize's **The Life of Fish**

Matías Bize's **The Life of Fish** (*La vida de los peces*) centres on Andrés, a journalist who has lived abroad for 10 years, and the bittersweet farewell he offers his friends at a birthday party prior to his permanent departure for Berlin. He is briefly re-united with Beatriz, a love of old. The film is the Chilean submission to the 2011 Academy Awards. The simple set-up allows for an intimate and well-performed drama that should strengthen the film's chances with the Academy.

Juan Ignacio Sabatini', Juan Pablo Sallato and Ismael Larrains **Red Eyes**

The year's best films
The Life of The Fish (Matías Bize)
You Think You Are the Prettiest (But You Are the Sluttiest) (José Manuel 'Ché' Sandoval)
Red Eyes (Juan Ignacio Sabatini, Juan Pablo Sallato and Ismael Larraín)
Burning Down the House (Esteban Rojas y Juan Olivares)
Mandrill (Ernesto Díaz Espinoza)

Quote of the year
'It seems fine to me that the dictatorship has been left aside as an only recurring theme, even if I don't think that talking about the dictatorship nowadays has to be wrong.' CHÉ SANDOVAL, *interviewed by the Argentinean magazine 'El Amante'.*

Directory
All Tel/Fax numbers begin (+56)
Consejo Nacional de la Cultura y las Artes, Fondo de Fomento Audiovisual, Plaza Sotomayor 233, Valparaíso. Tel: (32) 232 66 12. claudia.gutierrez@consejodelacultura.cl. www.consejodelacultura.cl.
Corporación de Fomento de la Producción (CORFO), Moneda 921, Santiago. Tel: (2) 631 85 97. Fax: (2) 671 77 35. lordonez@corfo.cl. www.corfo.cl.
Ministerio de Relaciones Exteriores, Dirección de Asuntos Culturales, Teatinos 180, Santiago. Tel: (2) 679 44 07. Fax: (2) 699 07 83. acillero@minrel.gov.cl. www.minrel.cl.

HUGO DIAZ GUTIÉRREZ is a journalist, screenwriter, film critic, and former editor of the Catalogue of the Valdivia International Film Festival.

China Luna Lin

Following the boom of 2009, China's film industry continued to grow at a high speed in 2010. China's box office up to the end of November swelled to US$1.27 billion, a 93% increase on November 2009. The number of cinemas continued to expand across the country. Capital also flooded into production. There are two local film companies currently listed on the stock market, while another dozen receive funds from private equity companies or banks. With the guarantee of funds, filmmakers began making more diverse films across a variety of genres and topics. As a result, 2010 can be seen as a successful year across the film industry as a whole.

Feng Xiaogang's **Aftershock**

Disaster films are one of the rarely produced genres in China, mainly due to the lack of technical talent to produce convincing scenarios. Feng Xiaogang's disaster drama **Aftershock** (*Tangshan Da Dizhen*) is likely to change this situation. Set against the backdrop of the devastating Tangshan earthquake in 1976, the film tells the story of a family separated by the disaster who eventually reunite 32 years later. Unbeknownst to her family, a young girl miraculously survived the quake. She grew up in a foster family, filled with hatred and feelings of abandonment,

until she volunteered for the rescue team that aided victims in the 2008 Sichuan earthquake. There, she met her brother and was eventually reconciled with her guilt-ridden mother.

Feng, who is better known for his comedies, successfully delivers a heart-wrenching drama with impressive effects courtesy of the UK-based Moving Pictures Company. The film's box-office takings were in the region of US$100m, making it one of the most successful domestic films ever made.

China's State Administration of Radio, Film and Television (SARFT) estimates that, by the end of 2010, production will reach 500 films, a 10% increase on 2009. The total box-office revenue for 2010 is likely to reach US$1.49bn. As for SARFT estimates that there will be 1000 new screens by the end of 2010, taking the total to 5700.

The diversity of filmmaking is also exemplified in film topics and the emergence of new filmmakers. Li Fangfang's feature debut, **Heaven Eternal, Earth Everlasting** (*Baling Hou*), a contemporary story exploring a young Chinese woman's emotional world from her teenage years through to her late 20s, displayed the potential of a clever storyteller and talented filmmaker, with its well-structured

Li Fangfang's **Heaven Eternal, Earth Everlasting**

narrative and impressive visual style. More significantly, the film is one of the first to present stories about China's young adult generation – the generation born in the 1980s, who have grown up in a mostly peaceful period in contemporary Chinese history.

Li Yu's **Buddha Mountain**

Li Yu's **Buddha Mountain** (*Guanyin Shan*), starring Fan Bingbing, Silvia Chang and Berlin Chen, is another contemporary story about a group of twentysomething Chinese. Three friends move in to the house of a grieving mother. Initially detesting each their landlady – and vicer-versa – the four lost souls gradually bond; the youngsters learning to grow up, while the mother starts to embrace life again. Li Yu (*Lost In Beijing*) collaborated once again with producer and co-writer Fang Li, delivering a sharp and tightly constructed narrative. Fan Bingbing's performance won her the Best Actress award at the Tokyo International Film Festival.

Two action films stood out in 2010. **Detective Dee and Mystery of the Phantom Flame** (*Di Renjie Zhi Tongtian Diguo*), directed by

Tsui Hark's **Detective Dee and the Mystery of the Phantom Flame**

Tsui Hark, starring Andy Lau, Carina Lau and Li Bingbing, tells a Tang Dynasty story about the famous Detective Dee, who solved the mysterious deaths of state ministers in the grand palace. Blending period drama, martial arts and a Holmes-style detective story, Hark's film is highly entertaining, offering impressive production design and visual effects to match the star-studded cast.

Taiwanese director Su Chao-pin's **Reign of Assassins** (*Jian Yu*), produced by John Woo, presents an oft-told story of swordsmen hunting and battling against each other for the remains of a Buddhist monk. Possession of the remains guarantees supernatural powers that could help conquer the world. In addition to the thrill of their execution, the fight scenes are employed to explore the innermost desires of the swordsmen and the rivalries between them. Action director Stephen Tung designed a series of exhilarating action scenes that are imaginative, but believable, relying less on wire-generated choreography. With fine performances by Michelle Yeoh, Korean star Jeong Woo-seong, Hong Kong's Shaun Yue and China's Wang Xue-qi, *Reign of Assassins* was one of the more memorable films of 2010.

Su Chao-pin and John Woo's **Reign of Assassins**

As *Avatar* cemented the worldwide popularity of 3D cinema, Chinese filmmakers have been quick to profit from the trend. The first mainland Chinese 3D film was Agan's **Don Quixote** (*Tang Ji Ke De*), which presents a Chinese version of the classic Spanish story, about a Tang Dynasty man, obsessed with the world of martial arts, who sets out in

Tsui Hark's **Flying Swords of Dragon Gate**

search of his enemies. Not long after, director Tsui Hark announced he was shooting the period action film **Flying Swords of Dragon Gate** (*Longmen Feijia*) in 3D, with *Avatar's* stereographic visual effects director, Chuck Comisky, as consultant. Another 3D action film project, **Monkey King** (*Danao Tiangong*), directed by Soi Cheng, was announced. This time, *Alice in Wonderland's* visual effects director, David Ebner, was on board as consultant. These 3D films, slated for a summer 2011 release, aim to revolutionise traditional martial-arts films.

Meanwhile, renowned filmmaker Zhang Yimou made a drastic change in genre and style with the simple love story, **Under the Hawthorn Tree** (*Shan Zha Shu Zhi Lian*). Set during the Cultural Revolution, the film tells the story of a young girl sent to the countryside to be 're-educated' because of her 'rightwing family background'. She falls in love with a man who encourages her not to be ashamed of her family. She has no choice but to continue her re-education, but the two promise to meet under the hawthorn tree again. However,

Zhang Yimou's **Under the Hawthorn Tree**

she hears that her love is suffering with leukaemia. The central performances by two new discoveries and Zhang's restrained, but beautiful, cinematography and well-paced narrative make for a compelling film.

Although film production has increased, both in volume and diversity, not all films were profitable. According to a recent study, of the 50 local films released between January and August, only 12 broke even. Most were quickly made slapstick or romantic comedies. In 2009, romantic comedies appeared to be a popular new genre in China. In 2010, dozens of filmmakers attempted to cash in on the trend. However, actor-director Xu Jinglei's **Go Lala Go** (*Du Lala Shengzhi Ji*) was the only significant success. The film, about a woman climbing her way up in an international corporation, earned US$19.58 million at the box office.

Xu Jinglei's **Go Lala Go**

So, despite the high revenues generated, China's box office remains dominated by a handful of mega-blockbusters. At the same time, actors' salaries and production costs are rising. Chinese film scholars such as Yin Hong, from Ching Hua University, warned that the situation is not just unhealthy, it runs the risk of generating a bubble economy.

Under the façade of a thriving film industry, another undercurrent is the Chinese authorities' policy u-turn on the film-rating system. In late summer 2010, Chinese officials announced that the country would not introduce the rating system in the foreseeable future, which contradicted SARFT's policy direction six years ago. In 2004, the system appeared in the draft of a film-related law. However, in the latest Film Industry Promotion Law draft, the film-rating system is not, and will not, be included.

Chinese officials stated that the Chinese government had conducted research on the issue and the results showed that the system did not prove successful in curbing young people's access to 'inappropriate' films. And they believe that the current censorship process can successfully stop content such as violence and pornography from being made, hence there is no need for any amendment.

Lacking a film-rating system, all films entering Chinese cinemas are required to be appropriate for audiences of all ages. Films containing violence, sex, homosexuality and supernatural elements are considered inappropriate for young audiences, therefore likely to be barred by Chinese film censors.

LUNA LIN is a Beijing-based journalist who contributes to Beijing-based *City Weekend* magazine and Shanghai-based *Modern Weekly* magazine.

Zhang Yimou's **Under the Hawthorn Tree**

The year's best films
Reign of Assassins (Su Chao-pin, co-directed by John Woo)
Under the Hawthorn Tree (Zhang Yimou)
Buddha Mountain (Li Yu)
Aftershock (Feng Xiaogang)
Heaven Eternal, Earth Everlasting
(Li Fangfang)

Quote of the year
'Chinese movies are similar to Chinese football! Like the Chinese football [league], the Chinese movie industry is not short of money now. But speaking of skills, we are still a long way behind [Hollywood].' **FENG XIAOGANG** *speaking at a forum at Shanghai International Film Festival in June 2010.*

Directory
All Tel/Fax numbers begin (+86)
Beijing Film Academy, 4 Xitucheng Rd, Haidian District, Beijing 100088. Tel: (10) 8204 8899. http:www.bfa.edu.cn.
Beijing Film Studio, 77 Beisanhuan Central Rd, Haidan District, Beijing 100088. Tel: (10) 6200 3191. Fax: (10) 6201 2059.
China Film Archive, 3 Wenhuiyuan Rd., Xiao Xiao Xitian, Haidian District, Beijing 100088. Tel: (10) 6225 4422. chinafilm@cbn.com.cn.
China National Film Museum, 9, Nanying Rd, Beijing 100015. Tel: (10) 64319548. cnfm2007@ yahoo.com.cn

Colombia Jaime E. Manrique & Pedro Adrián Zuluaga

Six years have passed since the Ley del Cine (Filmmaking Law) was created and it is still too early to assess its impact on the industry. The last three years have seen an average of 10 releases, but audience attendance for local productions remains low and international recognition remains elusive. The Colombian Academy of Film Arts and Sciences was created in 2009 and its first public act was to award the Macondo Prizes in October 2010. The main winner was Carlos Gaviria's **Portraits in a Sea of Lies** (*Retratos en un mar de mentiras*), a road movie that premiered at the Berlin Film Festival. A light comedy riddled with clichés, it tells the story of a woman suffering from post-traumatic stress, the cause of which is revealed as she travels with her cousin to claim land that belonged to her family, which was lost to them because of internal conflict.

The co-production model continues to be an efficient formula in gaining access to international audiences, but still mostly fails to engage with local audiences. A Colombia-Germany-France-Peruvian production, Peruvian director Juan Fuentes León's **Undertow** (*Contracorriente*), is a melodrama about the relationship between a man, his wife and dead gay lover. **Of Love and Other Demons** (*Del amor y otros demonios*), a Colombia-Costa Rica production directed by Costa Rican Hilda Hidalgo, is an unsuccessful adaptation of García Marquez's novel about the love between an adolescent and a clergyman, set in Cartagena during the Inquisition. A Colombia-Spain-Ecuador production, **Rage** (*Rabia*), is an unusual and suspenseful love story between two South American immigrants in Spain. It was directed by Ecuadorian Sebastián Cordero. A thriller about a doorman who is betrayed by his wife, **García** was directed by José Luis Rugeles and co-produced by Brazil and Colombia. Although all these films featured a Colombian cast and crew, they all showed an interest in reaching out to a large global audience.

Ruben Mendoza's **The Spotlight Society**

Ruben Mendoza waved the flag of creative independence with **The Spotlight Society** (*La sociedad del semáforo*). The film continues the Colombian tradition of portraying the lives of marginal characters, in this case as they attempt to improve their living conditions as they work around a street light.

Three films were screened at international film festivals, but have yet to open domestically.

Sebastián Cordero's **Rage**

Jairo Carrillo and Óscar Andrade's **Little Voices**

Jairo Carrillo y Óscar Andrade's **Little Voices** (*Pequeñas voces*), an animated documentary about children caught up in the country's armed conflict, screened at Venice. Carlos Santa's **The Strange Presages of Leon Prozak** (*Los extraños presagios de León Prozak*), another animated film, which updates the Faust myth with a character who sells his soul in exchange for success, premiered at Annecy. Finally, Carlos César Arbeláez's **The Colours of the Mountain** (*Los colores de la montaña*), a realistic portrait of rural life told from the point of view of children, competed in the San Sebastián Film Festival, where it received the Kutxa Prize for New Directors.

Short films and documentaries remain a dynamic element in an industry uncertain about its future. Although there appears no immediate hope of significant domestic distribution or revenue generation, they are supported by a growing number of festivals and events that vary in size and scope. This vitality shows that there is an audience interested in other formats and modes of exhibition.

The year's best films
Little Voices (Jairo Carrillo and Óscar Andrade)
Rage (Sebastián Cordero)
This is Not a Gun (Pablo González)
The Colours of the Mountain (Carlos César Arbeláez)

JAIME E. MANRIQUE is a journalist and director of the showcases In Vitro Visual and Imaginaton. **PEDRO ADRIÁN ZULUAGA** is a journalist, film critic and curator of exhibitions.

Quote of the year
'Nowadays films are being made as bread but there is no oven. And there is no bed big enough for such number of people, because the film industry has always been dodging Colombian cinema. The national market is saturated with over 15 Colombian films. Production budgets increase as the audience decreases.' LUIS OSPINA's *acceptance speech at the ceremony that saw him receive the 2010 award for a lifetime dedicated to cinema from the Ministry of Culture.*

Directory
All Tel/Fax numbers begin (+57)
Colombian Association of Documentary Film Directors, Calle 34, No 6-59, Bogotá.
Tel: (1) 2459961. alados@aladoscolombia.com / www.aladoscolombia.com
Colombian Film Archives, Carrera 13, No 13-24, Piso 9, Bogotá. Tel: (1) 2815241.
Fax: (1) 3421485. info@patrimoniofilmico.org.co / www.patrimoniofilmico.org.co
Colombian Film Commission, Calle 35, No 4-89, Bogotá. Tel: (1) 2870103. Fax: (1) 2884828. info@filmingcolombia.com / www.filmingcolombia.com
Film Promotion Fund, Calle 35, No 4-89, Bogotá.
Tel: (1) 2870103. Fax: (1) 2884828.
claudiatriana@proimagenescolombia.com / www.proimagenescolombia.com
Ministry of Culture, Film Division, Calle 35, No 4-89, Bogotá. Tel: (1) 2882995. Fax: (1) 2855690.
cine@mincultura.gov.co / www.mincultura.gov.co
Kinetoscopio Magazine, Carrera 45, No 53-24, Medellín. Tel: (4) 5134444.
Fax: (4) 5132666. kinetoscopio@kinetoscopio.com / www.kinetoscopio.com
Cinemateca Distrital, Carrera 7, No 22-79, Bogotá. Tel: (1) 2837798. Fax: (1) 3343451.
direccioncinemateca@fgaa.gov.co / www.cinematecadistrital.gov.co

Croatia Tomislav Kurelec

The seven films produced in 2010 were more a product of quantity than quality. The most acclaimed of the releases was veteran director Rajko Grlić's **Just Between Us** (*Neka ostane među nama*). It received the Best Film and Best Director awards at the Pula Film Festival, alongside six prizes in other categories. It also received numerous international awards, including Best Screenplay at Karlovy Vary, as well as Best Feature and Best Actor at the 4th Gotham Screen Film Festival & Screenplay Contest in New York. It is something of a paradox that one of Croatia's best filmmakers should receive so many laurels for what is possibly his weakest film.

Rajko Grlić's **Just Between Us**

The main problem lies with his choice of the leading actor, Miki Manojlović, whose philanderer recalls the character he played in Grlić's best film to date, 1981's *You Only Live Once*. However, 30 years have passed since that film and some of the moments in *Just Between Us* fail to acknowledge that times have changed. The portrayal of a middle class that has radically changed under the new Croatian establishment is also unconvincing, resulting in a film that resembles a TV soap opera.

Even less convincing were two films by younger, but no less renowned, directors. Ognjen Sviličić's **2 Sunny Days** (*2 sunčana dana*) attempts to couple the romantic drama

Ognjen Sviličić's **2 Sunny Days**

of two foreign tourists lost on a treacherous mountain with the forces of nature. The film also attempts to portray Croat attitudes to foreigners. But poor characterisation gives the film little depth. Even worse is Dalibor Matanić's **Mother Of Asphalt** (*Majka asfalta*), whose tale of a young woman fleeing with her young son from an abusive husband fails because of its unconvincing portrait of daily life.

New directors fared much better. The most fascinating film was Nevio Marasović's **The Show Must Go On** (*The Show Must Go On*). Belying its minuscule budget, the film is a sci-fi drama which culminates in an nuclear attack on Zagreb, the reprisal for NATO's assault on Muslim countries. The special effects, which were produced at low cost by friends and business associates, were convincing, bolstering an interesting narrative of how the media responds to dramatic events, presented through the lives of a couple who work for competing networks. Ivan-Goran Vitez's

Nevio Marasović's **The Show Must Go On**

Forest Creatures (*Šuma summarum*), about a team-building trip undertaken by members of a marketing agency, which turns into a struggle for survival, also impressed. A novel exploration of Croatia's burgeoning capitalist culture, the film features its fair share of suspense and grotesque violence. In **72 Days** (*Sedamdeset i dva dana*), Danilo Šerbedžija (the son of the internationally acclaimed actor Rade Šerbedžija, who stars) presents an entertaining black comedy about village life, in which a family live off their grandmother's American pension and, following her death, look for a doppelganger, enabling them to continue receiving the payment. Dan Oki was in New York on September 11, 2001 and produced a unique documentary about what he saw. In **The Performance** (*Predstava*) he has conjoined footage from that day with the fictional story of a visit by an alternative theatre group from Croatia, documenting their reactions to a tragic event that changed their lives as individuals. Sadly, the film fails to gel the two strands in a coherent or convincing way.

The appearance of new directors might lead us to conclude that the Croatian film industry faces a bright future. However, there are numerous problems with funding and, on a qualitative level, this year has left much to be desired, particularly from more established directors. Such a situation can only dampen more optimistic opinions of the future of Croatian cinema.

The year's best films
The Show Must Go On (Nevio Marasović)
Forest Creatures (Ivan-Goran Vitez)
72 Days (Danilo Šerbedžija)
Just Between Us (Rajko Grlić)
The Performance (Dan Oki)

Quote of the year
'The situations that I react to with laughter in others would cause desperation, self-analysis, anger or sadness, so in a potential work of art they would apply their opposite approach.'
IVAN-GORAN VITEZ *talking about* **Forest Creatures.**

Directory
All Tel/Fax numbers begin with (+385)
Hrvatski filmski savez (Croatian Film Clubs' Association), Tuškanac 1, 10000 Zagreb. Tel / Fax: (1) 484 8764. vera@hfs.hr.
HAVC – Hrvatski audiovizualni centar (Croatian Audiovisual Centre), Zvonimirova 20, 10000 Zagreb. Tel: (1) 465 5439. Fax: (1) 465 5442. info@havc.hr.

Ivan-Goran Vitez's **Forest Creatures**

TOMISLAV KURELEC has been a film critic since 1965, mostly on radio and television. He has directed five short films and many television items. Since 2007, he has been the artistic director of the festival Days of the Croatian Cinema in Zagreb.

Cinematographic reflexology

english français italiano español

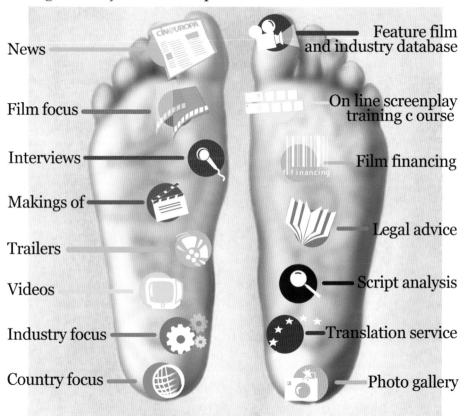

News

Film focus

Interviews

Makings of

Trailers

Videos

Industry focus

Country focus

Feature film
and industry database

On line screenplay
training c ourse

Film financing

Legal advice

Script analysis

Translation service

Photo gallery

● **THE SITE FOR** EUROPEAN CINEMA

cineUROPA.org

film's most relevant reflex points

MEDIA
A programme of the European Union

CINEUROPA.ORG IS THE ONLY PORTAL DEDICATED TO
THE EUROPEAN FILM INDUSTRY IN FOUR LANGUAGES

Cineuropa.org is an initiative co-financed by the MEDIA Programme of the
European Commission, the Italian Ministry of Culture, Cinema Centre of the Ministry
of French Community of Belgium, Swiss Films, Federal Cinema Office of Switzerland,
Centre National de la Cinématographie, ICAA - Institute of Cinematography and
Audiovisual Arts, German Films, Luxembourg Film Fund, Filmunio, Czech Film
Centre, Slovenian Film Fund, Malta Film Commission, the Irish Film Board

Cuba Jorge Yglesias

In contrast to the political and formal correctness of the Cuban cinema industry, the emergence of fresh talent working independently or supported by institutions such as the Higher Institute of Arts (ISA) or the International School of Cinema and TV (EICTV) continues to offer strong signs of revitalisation. In terms of film language, ISA productions veer towards the style of music videos, while those at the EICTV are more grounded in art house or experimental cinema.

Mayckell Pedrero's **Revolution**

Mayckell Pedrero´s **Revolution**, a portrait of the quasi-underground rap group, Los Aldeanos (The Villagers), received the top prize at an annual contest for young talent. Banned from exhibition, the film has been widely distributed via illegal DVD copies. Although the work suffers from a faster-than-life approach to editing that some see as quintessential cinema, the anti-establishment attitude and opinions of Los Aldeanos do find a curious correlative in such a style.

The childhood and adolescence of the Cuban national hero, José Martí, was recreated by Fernando Pérez in **José Martí, the Eye of the Canary** (*José Martí, el ojo del canario*). Covering his formative years, the film was

a blend of conventional hagiography and inventive *mise-en-scène*. Raúl Pérez Ureta's stunning cinematography, a winner of the National Prize for Cinema, makes the most of the country's stunning light.

Memories of Overdevelopment (*Memorias del desarrollo*), a US$50,000 film made over five years in the US and Cuba by guerrilla filmmmaker Miguel Coyula, is a unique companion to Tomás Gutiérrez Alea´s *Memories of Underdevelopment*, a classic of Cuban cinema. Sergio, an ideological relative of Alea's main character 40 years later, is now an exile in the United States, weighed down by memories and remorse for past actions. A product of the digital generation, the film ranks as one of the best this country has produced.

Miguel Coyula's **Memories of Overdevelopment**

Lisanka, a new comedy by Daniel Díaz Torres, tells the story of a young peasant woman, employed as a tractor driver near a military base during the middle of the Missile Crisis of October, 1962, who is courted by three possessive men. Some interpreted the main character as a representation of Cuba, as she refuses to be objectified by her suitors, one of whom is a Russian soldier.

Bárbaro Joel Ortiz's **20 Years**

Bárbaro Joel Ortiz's **20 Years** (*20 años*) is a landmark of Cuban animation. Based on a popular song, this short feature uses stop-motion technique to chart the rise and fall of a relationship. Influenced by the great Czech animator Jan Svankmajer, Ortiz worked for three years to achieve a work whose tender memories emerge painfully amidst a couple's daily routine.

Bárbaro Joel Ortiz's **20 Years**

Orisel Castro's **The Belly of the Whale** and **Music Box** are two good examples of how documentary filmmakers trained at the EICTV have an eye for depicting reality with subtlety. *The Belly of the Whale*, filmed in reverse, sees gestation as a heroic process made of efforts, fears, uncertainties, hopes and expectations; *Music Box* highlights the unintentional humour of registry-office weddings. In both cases, Orisel Castro employs a fragmented narrative, fake amateur cinematography and other devices to present his worlds. Another interesting documentary, albeit less ambitious, was Jessica Rodríguez and Zoe Miranda's **The World of Raúl** (*El mundo de Raúl*), which deals with an eccentric optometrist who talks about his tastes, daily life and how he became a peeping Tom.

If the young filmmakers remain immune to the Buena Vista Social Club syndrome and try to remain faithful to their visions instead of becoming prisoners of banality, Cuban cinema will remain lively, producing films that will be worth seeing.

The year's best films
Memories of Overdevelopment
(Miguel Coyula)
José Martí, the Eye of the Canary
(Fernando Pérez)
Revolution (Mayckell Pedrero)
The Belly of the Whale (Orisel Castro)
20 Years (Bárbaro Joel Ortiz)

Quote of the year
'I speak about Cuba's reality, because I live here. I don't know any other land, other lives than these. If I were living in France, I would speak about France. If I were living in New York, I would speak about New York.' *A member of Los Aldeanos.*

Directory
All Tel/Fax numbers begin (+53)
Cuban Institute of Art and Cinema Industry (ICAIC), Calle 23, No 1155, Entre 8 & 10, Vedado, Havana. Tel: (7) 8383650. Fax: 8333281. internacional@icaic.cu. www.cubacine.cu.
Escuela Internacional de Cine y TV, Carretera Vereda Nueva, Km 4½, San Antonio de Los Baños. Tel: (47) 383152. Fax: 382366. eictv@eictv.org.cu. www.eictv.org.
Festival Internacional del Nuevo Cine Latinoamericano, Calle 2, No. 411, Entre 17 & 19, Vedado, Havana, Cuba CP 10400. festival@festival.icaic.cu, habanafest@festival.icaic.cu (World Registration). www.habanafilmfestival.com.

JORGE YGLESIAS is a poet and film critic, and Professor of Film History and Chair of Humanites at the International School of Film and Television of San Antonio de los Baños, Cuba.

Cyprus Ninos-Fenek Mikelidis

The Film Funding Committee has continued its policy of funding feature, shorts and documentary films. For 2010, the Committee has funded the development of three feature films and the development of five screenplays. It has also funded one animated film, three shorts, two documentaries (one for script development) and five scripts for short films. Eight feature films, including two directorial debuts, seven documentaries and seven short films are nearing the final stages of development.

Already completed and released this year is **Knifer** (*Maherovgaltis*), a Greek-Cypriot co-production by Greek-Cypriot director Yiannis Economidis. It is a very dark, free adaptation of James M. Cain's *The Postman Always Rings Twice*, a love triangle among petit bourgeois/working-class characters, which leads to murder, set on the outskirts of Athens and shot in crisp black-and-white. Another new film, Marinos Kartikkis' psychological drama **By Miracle** (*Apo thavma*), which screened at the Thessaloniki Film Festival, is an intimate and affectionate look at the lives and problems of various characters, told through parallel storylines: a young homosexual living with his mother who seeks casual sex in a park; and a young couple trying to have a baby a year after their daughter's death.

Still in post-production is **Dinner With My Sisters** (*Dipno me tis adelfes mou*) by Michael Hapeshis, co-produced with the UK, about the secret a Greek doctor discovers when he returns to Cyprus in order to investigate his father's death. Other films in post-production include Aliki Danezi-Knutsen's **China Town – The Three Nails** (*China Town – Ta tria karfia*), Elias Dimitriou's **Oil in the fire** (*Ladi sti fotia*) and Christina Hadjizahariou's **Loveless Zorica**.

The recent global financial meltdown also struck the Cyprus economy, although not as deep as in other countries. Thankfully, film production so far seems to continue untouched by the problems, with producers and directors from Greece (including Theo Angelopoulos) seeking co-production deals. American films still dominate cinemas – around 90% – whilst films from Europe and other continents are usually screened at film events (some of them in the recently renovated 'Pallas' theatre), or by the Nicosia Film Society. However, the mooted Cultural Institution, which would offer a platform for all art forms and would help with the financing, production and distribution of films, was promised almost two years ago by the new Minister of Education and Culture. It is still being looked into, the major obstacle being the scale of funding involved for such a huge project.

The year's best films
Knifer (Yiannis Economidis)
By Miracle (Marinos Kartikkis)

Quote of the year
'The majority of contemporary Greek art – poetry, music, films – does not deal with the essence of life. This should have been the alpha and the omega, i.e. to speak with truth about the time you live in.' YIANNIS ECONOMIDIS, *the director of* **Knifer**.

NINOS-FENEK MIKELIDIS is an historian of Greek Cinema and film critic for *Eleftherotypia* daily newspaper. He is also the founder and director of the Panorama of European Cinema film festival in Athens.

FILMING in CYPRUS

Locations, Incentives, Resources

There's always a new world to discover.

Cyprus lies at the crossroads of three continents, where East meets West, where deep blue seas, sandy beaches, captivating forests, breathtaking mountains, unique archaeological sites, monasteries, churches and enchanting locations await for you to discover them.

Probably your next filming destination.

The "all in one" Filming Destination
One Island. One natural Studio with almost 360 days of Sunshine...

Ministry of Education and Culture of Cyprus
Cultural Department (Cinema Advisory Committee)
Kimonos and Thoukididou, 1434 Nicosia, Cyprus
Tel.: 0035722800982 Fax.: 0035722809506
Email: echristo@cytanet.com.cy   http:www.moec.gov.cy

Czech Republic Rudolf Schimera and Michal Kriz

One of the most important events in Czech cinematography in 2010 was the launch of the classical films digitalisation project. This project should include 200 films from the period 1898–1991, including the silent cinema (11 films), with the largest proportion of features coming from the Czech New Wave (80 films).

Another important change, promising a better future for Czech film, was the attempt to update the legislation concerning the financing of the industry through the 'Concept of Support and Development of Czech Cinematography and Film Industry in 2010–2016' which was passed in December.

The annual production has been relatively stable for several years, with approximately 30 releases a year. In 2010, 26 features and nine documentaries were produced. Once again, events from history played an important role, with many set in Communist-controlled Czechoslovakia. However, the national cinema still lacks an abundance of original voices, with surrealists Jan Švankmajer and David Jařab being rare exceptions.

One area that has seen the rise of strong, visionary filmmakers is documentary. Even audiences have been attracted to cinemas to see some of the more striking examples of non-fiction film on release. In particular, there is a strong tradition of female filmmakers. In addition to the older generation, (Helena Třeštíková, Olga Sommerová), younger filmmakers are gradually establishing themselves. Erika Hníková's **Matchmaking Mayor** (*Nesvatbov*) traces the extraordinary efforts of the mayor of a small village to attract new residents to the local community.

Erika Hníková's **Matchmaking Mayor**

Olga Špátová's **Eye over Prague** (*Oko nad Prahou*) maps the distressing and, from a Czech perspective, embarrassing tug of war over architect Jan Kaplický's designs for the National Library. Tereza Reichová highlights the absurdities of the global 'War on Terror' in **A Terrorist Manual** (*Manuál na výrobu teroristy*). Acclaimed filmmakers Vít Klusák and Filip Remunda presented another probe into the Czech psyche with **Czech Peace** (*Český mír*), which looked at the issues surrounding an American anti-missile radar project. Meanwhile, Ivan Vojnár's **Cinematherapy** (*Cinematerapie*) is a remarkable project that takes the testimonies of numerous people to blur the lines between a reality show and

Ivan Vojnár's **Cinematherapy**

documentary. David Čálek's **Heaven, Hell** (*Nebe, peklo*) follows three people with a penchant for unusual sexual and erotic practices, while Robert Sedláček's **The Greatest Czechs** (*Největší z Čechů*) was everything its title suggested.

David Čálek's **Heaven, Hell**

Genre film remains popular. Ondřej Trojan's bitter comedy, **Identity Card** (*Občanský průkaz*), is a solid adaptation of Petr Šabach's novel. Fairytales were represented by Milan Cieslar's **The Rain Fairy** (*Dešťová víla*), although the film lacked the spark such tales need to make them truly magical. More impressive was Juraj Herz's tackling of the expulsion of the Germans from Czechoslovakia after the Second World War in **Habermann´s Mill** (*Habermannův mlýn*), while the totalitarian regime of the 1980s was the backdrop for Radim Špaček's **Walking Too Fast** (*Pouta*). Alice Nellis' **Mamas & Papas**, like all her work, focuses on human relationships. This time she presented a mosaic of parental-themed narratives.

Alice Nellis' **Mamas & Papas**

Jan Hřebejk's **Kawasaki's Rose**

A number of films have been acclaimed at various international festivals. The most notable of these is David Jařab's **Head-Hands-Hearth** (*Hlava-ruce-srdce*), a mysterious story which unfolds during the First World War. Jan Hřebejk's **Kawasaki's Rose** (*Kawasakiho růže*) screened in the Panorama section of the Berlin Film Festival, while Jan Svěrák's variation on the fairytale, **Kooky** (*Kuky se vrací*), screened in the main competition of the Karlovy Vary Film Festival. One of the year's most eagerly anticipated films was Jan Švankmajer's **Surviving Life (Theory and Practice)** (*Přežít svůj život [teorie a praxe]*). Screening at the Venice Film Festival, the surrealist filmmaker's latest was another exploration of desire, through one man's dreams of a woman whose name changes every time he meets her, but which always begins with an 'E'.

Jan Svěrák's **Kooky**

New directors include Jitka Rudolfová with **Losers** (*Zoufalci*), which screened to acclaim at Karlovy Vary and Cottbus, Jaroslav Fuit with **Twosome** (*Dvojka*) and Tomáš Řehořek, whose sophomore feature, **PIKO**, presents a brutal and uncompromising account of drug addiction.

The commercially most successful films of the year included Petr Jákl Jr's **Kajínek**, which broke box-office records. The film's taut narrative, about the infamous criminal and multiple prison escapee, also performed well outside the Czech Republic. Jiří Vejdělek's comedy **Women in Temptation** (*Ženy v pokušení*), about a wayward woman in her forties' also attracted audiences, coming in second at the year's box office. Close behind was Tomáš Bařina's adaptation, **A Novel for Men** (*Román pro muže*).

Jiří Vejdělek's Women in Temptation

Next year will see the release of Petr Nikolaev's **Lidice** and the planned adaptation of the *Alois Nebel* comics.

The year's best films
Kawasaki's Rose (Jan Hřebejk)
Losers (Jitka Rudolfová)
Kooky (Jan Svěrák)
Head-Hands-Hearth (David Jařab)
Surviving Life (Theory and Practice) (Jan Švankmajer)

Quote of the year
'All my films oscillate on the border of horror and comedy or dark humour.' *Czech director and animator* JAN ŠVANKMAJER, *discussing his approach to filmmaking.*

RUDOLF SCHIMERA and **MICHAL KRIZ** are Czech freelance film critics. They write for the online journal *Fantom* and are also consultants at a number of film festivals.

Jitka Rudolfová's Losers

Directory
All Tel/Fax numbers begin (+420)
Association of Czech Filmmakers (FITES), Pod Nuselskymi Schody 3, 120 00 Prague 2. Tel: (2) 691 0310. Fax: (2) 691 1375.
Association of Producers, Národní 28, 110 00 Prague 1. Tel: (2) 2110 5321. Fax: (2) 2110 5303. www.apa.iol.cz.
Czech Film & Television Academy, Na Îertvách 40, 180 00 Prague 8. Tel: (2) 8482 1356. Fax: (2) 8482 1341.
Czech Film Centre, Národní 28, 110 00 Prague 1. Tel: (2) 2110 5302. Fax: (2) 2110 5303. www.filmcenter.cz.
FAMU, Film & Television Faculty, Academy of Performing Arts, Smetanovo 2, 116 65 Prague 1. Tel: (2) 2422 9176. Fax: (2) 2423 0285. kamera@f.amu.cz. Dean: Karel Kochman.
Ministry of Culture, Audiovisual Dept, Milady Horákové 139, 160 00 Prague 6. Tel: (2) 5708 5310. Fax: (2) 2431 8155.
National Film Archive, Malesická 12, 130 00 Prague 3. Tel: (2) 7177 0509. Fax: (2) 7177 0501. nfa@nfa.cz. www.nfa.cz.

Jan Švankmajer's Surviving Life (Theory and Practice)

Denmark Christian Monggaard

2009 was a catastrophic year for the Danish film industry in terms of box office sales. Several film companies were also struggling – some being forced to close – and everyone was hoping 2010 would be better. New films by a couple of the most popular Danish directors promised a brighter future and a better market share for Danish films. But, at the time of writing, the situation remains almost as bad.

The number of tickets sold for the 19 features that opened prior to November 2010 was two million, more or less on par with 2009 and less than half of the 2008 figure. With only two more Danish films scheduled for release before Christmas, things don't look good.

'The Danes are victims of their own success,' a Norwegian film journalist recently told the author of this article. Perhaps he is right. One could argue that, with the immense success that Danish films have enjoyed both at home and abroad over the last 10–15 years, we have perhaps foolishly believed this is how things would always be.

2010 got off to a bad start when Per Fly's new film, **The Woman Who Dreamt of a Man** (*Kvinden der drømte om en mand*), opened.

Per Fly's **The Woman Who Dreamt of a Man**

Wanting to try something completely new, he made an erotic psychological thriller with Sonja Richter in the lead. Unfortunately, Fly was out of his element. The film, which was shot in Paris and Warsaw, flopped spectacularly at the box office, selling only 28,000 tickets, a far cry from the 400,000 admissions for Fly's previous film, *Manslaughter*.

Christoffer Boe's **Everything Will Be Fine**

Christoffer Boe's **Everything Will Be Fine** (*Alting bliver godt igen*) also fared badly, with sales barely exceeding 11,000. However, the film was later chosen for the Director's Fortnight at the Cannes Film Festival. It is a beautifully shot thriller about a troubled filmmaker (Jens Albinus) who acquires photos showing the torture of prisoners in Iraq. A cleverly constructed film, which deserves to be seen again just to appreciate the complexity of the narrative.

The international interest in Danish films certainly seems as strong as ever. Two films were chosen for the main competition at the Berlin Film Festival: Thomas Vinterberg's **Submarino** and Pernille Fischer Christensen's **A Family** (*En familie*). A third film, Michael Noer and Tobias Lindholm's prison-drama, **R**, won the main prize at the Gothenburg Film Festival.

Thomas Vinterberg's **Submarino**

Both *Submarino*, a harsh look at alcoholism, drug abuse and the difficult relationship between two estranged brothers (Jacob Cedergren and newcomer Peter Plaugborg), and *R*, an even bleaker film about a prison system that doesn't work and a young man (Pilou Asbæk) trapped inside, received great reviews when they opened in the Danish cinemas. (*A Family* doesn't open until 2011.)

Both films were co-written by Tobias Lindholm, but failed to attract large audiences. *Submarino*'s admissions levelled out at 45,000, while *R* ended its run with 33,000. But both films displayed the artistic integrity and fearlessness that has been lacking in recent Danish films.

Michael Noer and Tobias Lindholm's **R**

Fearlessness was also on display in Nicolas Winding Refn's latest, English-language film. **Valhalla Rising** finds Mads Mikkelsen playing a mute, one-eyed warrior who joins a band of Christian Vikings searching for the Promised Land. The stylish and meditative film demands a lot of its audience, which may explain why only 8,000 people went to see it.

The big hits of the year were two so-called family films, Jørgen Lerdam's forgettable **Olsen Gang Gets Polished** (*Olsen Banden – på de bonede gulve*) and yet another entry in Claus Bjerre's terrible Father of Four franchise, **Father of Four – in Japanese Mode** (*Far til fire – på japansk*). There was also Susanne Bier's **In a Better World** (*Hævnen*), which picked up two major prizes at the Rome International Film Festival. Together, the three films sold more than 1.1 million tickets, which equals the attendance figure of the remaining 17 released Danish titles combined.

In a Better World tells the story of two bickering families and how small conflicts can lead to bigger ones, even wars, if they are not resolved. It received mixed reviews and, although it is a solid, impressively made and well-acted melodrama, it's all a little too obvious.

Susanne Bier's **In a Better World**

Kenneth Kainz' **Therapy** (*Parterapi*) is an amusing, well-made comedy about a couple in trouble, while Charlotte Sachs Bostrup's **Karla and Jonas** (*Karla og Jonas*) was a children's film that took its audience seriously. Both films attracted sizeable audiences, selling around 145,000 tickets.

The prolific director and screenwriter Nikolaj Arcel, who previously made the intelligent and popular political thriller *Kings Game* (and, with his writing partner Rasmus Heisterberg, he wrote the script for *The Girl With the Dragon Tattoo*), returned with the original, funny

Nikolaj Arcel's **Truth About Men**

and personal **Truth About Men** (*Sandheden om mænd*). Thure Lindhardt plays Mads, a screenwriter in his thirties who is feeling stuck, both personally and professionally, and decides to break free to pursue his dreams. The result is both hilarious and moving, as Arcel breaks free from various narrative conventions. Sadly, the film didn't quite live up to its potential, failing to attract more that 88,000.

Apart from *R*, a number of the new Danish films were feature debuts, but none performed especially well at the box office, even with positive reviews. Nicolo Donato's **Brotherhood** (*Broderskab*) told a dramatic story about homosexuality among a group of Neo-Nazis. Louise N.D. Friedberg's **The Experiment** (*Eksperimentet*) was a well-meaning, but clumsily told film about a dark part of Denmark's recent history when, in the 1950s, children in the Danish colony of Greenland were taken from their homes and moved to Denmark in order to raise them as Danes. Mikkel Munch-Fals' **Nothing's All Bad** (*Smukke mennesker*) was a darkly

Mikkel Munch-Fals' **Nothing's All Bad**

comic and slightly unsatisfying look at human interaction and loneliness in the style of Todd Solondz. Finally, Kaspar Munk made one of the year's best films with the youth-oriented **Hold Me Tight** (*Hold om mig*), which tells a beautifully observed and tragic story about a young girl, Sara (Julie Brochorst Andersen), who is harassed by her schoolmates. Like *Brotherhood* in 2009, Munk's film picked up a prize at the 2010 Rome Film Festival.

A number of exciting documentaries have been made in Denmark over the last few years, none more successful than Janus Metz's **Armadillo**, which sold 118,000 tickets domestically following its premiere at the Cannes Film Festival.

Janus Metz's **Armadillo**

With the invaluable help of cinematographer Lars Skree's haunting and cinematic images, often reminiscent of *Apocalypse Now* and *The Deer Hunter*, Metz portrays a unit of Danish soldiers in Afghanistan. Dispelling the notion that the conflict in Afghanistan is merely a peacekeeping mission, it presents the action in brutal and horrifying detail. The film immediately started a debate about the war and Denmark's involvement there and in Iraq. Metz has come to represent a new generation of Danish documentary filmmakers who tell important stories in a cinematic way.

As the year drew to a close and politicians had to negotiate a new four-year film plan, aimed at defining the economic and administrative framework of the government's support for

Danish film, a moment of introspection seized the film industry. The current plan proved unpopular from the very beginning, not least because it moved money and power from the Danish Film Institute (DFI) to the two public service TV-stations, DR and TV2. The CEO of DFI, Henrik Bo Nielsen, fought long and hard to ensure the whole film industry – producers, directors, distributors, exhibitors, etc. – backed the DFI's proposal for a new settlement.

For once, the politicians, both in government and the opposition, listened and, in October, a new plan was agreed, moving power back to DFI and giving the institute the ability to revise and simplify the current, somewhat complicated film-subsidy system. This would allow more freedom in a market that evolves constantly. Over four years, the politicians agreed on a budget of €280 million for Danish films, with a focus on making documentaries more visible in Denmark, and supporting smaller cinemas and art-house venues, who need to make that all-important transition to digital.

Although there remain many hurdles for the Danish film industry in the coming years, a certain degree of optimism can be detected following the agreement on the new plan.

2011 will see the return of Denmark's most famous filmmaker, Lars von Trier. He has described *Melancholia* as a psychological disaster film.

The year's best films
Truth About Men (Nikolaj Arcel)
R (Michael Noer and Tobias Lindholm)
Hold Me Tight (Kaspar Munk)
Submarino (Thomas Vinterberg)
Everything Will Be Fine (Christoffer Boe)

Quote of the year
'It's not a comeback, because I haven't been gone. Maybe you have been away, but I've been here all the time.' THOMAS VINTERBERG *at the press conference for* **Submarino** *in Berlin, where journalists suggested that the director had been struggling since his big breakthrough with* **Festen** *in 1998.*

Directory
All Tel/Fax numbers begin (+45)
Danish Film Institute/Archive & Cinematheque (DFI), Gothersgade 55, DK-1123 Copenhagen K. Tel: 3374 3400. Fax: 3374 3401. dfi@dfi.dk. www. dfi.dk. Also publishes the film magazine, *Film*.
Danish Actors' Association (DSF), Sankt Knuds Vej 26, DK-1903 Frederiksberg C. Tel: 3324 2200. Fax: 3324 8159. dsf@skuespillerforbundet.dk. www.skuespillerforbundet.dk.
Danish Film Directors (DF), Vermundsgade 19, 2nd Floor, DK-2100 Copenhagen Ø. Tel: 3583 8005. Fax: 3583 8006. mail@filmdir.dk. www.filmdir.dk.
Danish Film Distributors' Association (FAFID), Sundkrogsgade 9, DK-2100 Copenhagen Ø. Tel: 3363 9684. Fax: 3363 9660. www.fafid.dk.
Danish Film Studios, Blomstervaenget 52, DK-2800 Lyngby. Tel: 4587 2700. Fax: 4587 2705. ddf@filmstudie.dk. www.filmstudie.dk.
Danish Producers' Association, Bernhard Bangs Allé 25, DK-2000 Frederiksberg. Tel: 3386 2880. Fax: 3386 2888. info@pro-f.dk. www.producent-foreningen.dk.
National Film School of Denmark, Theodor Christensen's Plads 1, DK-1437 Copenhagen K. Tel: 3268 6400. Fax: 3268 6410. info@filmskolen.dk. www.filmskolen.dk.

Kaspar Munk's **Hold Me Tight**

CHRISTIAN MONGGAARD is the film editor and film critic at the daily Danish newspaper *Information*. He has written/contributed to books on films, he freelances for different magazines, and he regularly serves on FIPRESCI-juries at film festivals around the world.

Ecuador Gabriela Alemán

2010 closed with record-breaking box-office sales for three films: Fernando Mieles' **Deported Prometheus** (*Prometeo Deportado*), Carl West's **Zuquillo Express** and Sebastián Cordero's **Rage** (*Rabia*). Each film deals with issues surrounding the subject of migration.

Fernando Mieles' **Deported Prometeus**

Deported Prometheus is a chamber piece, set in an unspecified European airport. A plane filled with Ecuadorians lands, the passengers descend and, upon reaching customs, all of them are sent to a waiting lounge without being told why, or when they will be allowed to leave. The film, which was ten years in the making, won the Special Jury Prize for Best Director at the Festival Cero Latitud 2010 in Quito. *Zuquillo Express* is the first Ecuadorian feature film to be based on a local TV series. The comedy tells the story of four women who want to enter the US illegally, with the aid of a coyote. In its first seven weeks it attracted 10,000 spectators, an extraordinary success by Ecuadorian standards. *Rage* is a Mexican-Colombian-Spanish co-produced thriller set in Spain. It centres on the romance between two migrant workers and has picked up awards from festivals in Japan, Spain, Mexico and Chile.

Juan Diego Pérez's **Alfaro's Revolution: The Movie**

Although support for Ecuadorian films has increased, there were no other commercial features released in 2010. Juan Diego Pérez's historical drama, **Alfaro's Revolution: The Movie** (*La revolución de Alfaro, la película*), was a state-financed production about the Liberal Revolution.

The EDOC Documentary Film Festival has, for another year, helped maintain an exhibition circuit for the growing number of documentaries from Ecuador. Amongst the most interesting this year was Santiago Carcelén's **Camilo Egas, A Secretive Man** (*Camilo Egas, un hombre secreto*), about one

Sebastián Cordero's **Rage**

Gabriela Calvache's **The Silent Walls**

of the most acclaimed but not so well known figures of the Ecuadorian art scene during the 20th century. Carla Valencia's **Grandfathers** (*Abuelos*) deals with the different destinies of the director's grandfathers. One of them was murdered in Chile under Pinochet, while the other, a doctor and inventor, lived peacefully in Ecuador. The last documentary premiere of the year was Gabriela Calvache's **The Silent Walls** (*Labranza Oculta*), which documents the reconstruction of a deteriorated house (*La Casa del Alabado*, which was constructed in 1671) in historical downtown Quito, the first city considered by UNESCO as Cultural Patrimony of Humanity.

Of the shorts, Victor Carrera's **Streets** (*En mi tribuna*) follows various homeless children in the northern part of Quito, while Julián Larrea Arias's **Numtaketji, We Are the Same** (*Numtaketji, somos los mismos*) documents the first encounter, following the Cenepa War that affected Ecuador and Peru, between different shuar groups, who live on either side of the border.

If all goes well, 2011 will be a record year for feature releases in Ecuador. Four years after the creation of the National Film Council (*Consejo Nacional de Cine*), film production has finally reached some kind of equilibrium. Ten productions and co-productions were shot in 2010. Amongst them, there is the much-awaited new Sebastián Cordero release, **The Fisherman** (*El pescador*), Iván Mora's

Without Fall, Without Spring (*Sin otoño, sin primavera*), Alfredo Leon's **Monkeys with Chickens** (*Monos con Gallinas*) and Tito Jara's **Behind You** (*A tus espaldas*).

The year's best films
Deported Prometheus (Fernando Mieles)
Camilo Egas, A Secretive Man (Santiago Carcelén)
Grandfathers (Carla Valencia)
Streets (Victor Carrera)
Numtaketji, We Are the Same (Julián Larrea Arias)

Deported Prometheus *director Fernando Mieles*

Quote of the year
'There are different characters... that can be seen as fragments of a country that rebuilds itself thousands of miles away. After all, Ecuadorians literally carry all of Ecuador in their luggage.' XAVIER DONOSO, *talking about* **Deported Prometheus**.

Directory
All Tel/Fax numbers begin (+593)
INCINE, Vizcaya E13-39 & Valladolid, Tel. 290 4724, info@incine.edu.ec, www.incine.edu.ec
Cine Memoria Corporation, Veintimilla E8-125, Quito, Tel. 290 2250, info@cinememoria.org, www.cinememoria.org
Consejo Nacional de Cine (CNC), www.cncinecuador.blogspot.com

GABRIELA ALEMÁN is a freelance reporter and writer. She teaches film in various institutions.

Egypt Sherif Awad

I n 2010, approximately 30 Egyptian films – mostly comedies and dramas – were released domestically. The sole action film was a co-production, from Oscar/El-Massa/El-Nasr, featuring action star Ahmed El-Sakka. He appeared together with character actor Khaled Nabawy for the first time in Ahmad Saleh's **The Dealer**, which kick-started the summer season. Written by Medhat El-Adl who penned *Mafia* (2002) for El-Sakka, the predictable plot revolves around two rival drug dealers who are also competing for the affections of one woman. Partially shot in Europe, *The Dealer*'s much-publicised production troubles delayed its release for a couple of years and was reflected in the mostly incoherent narrative. Towards the end of the year, El-Sakka returned with the comedy **Council's Son**, while Nabawy fared better in a small role alongside Sean Penn and Naomi Watts in Doug Liman's **Fair Game**.

The highest-grossing film of the year, **Bloody Fist** (*El-Kabda El-Dameya*), was produced by Al-Arabia and was a parody of American action and Asian martial-arts films. It featured Ahmed Mekky as Adham, whose resemblance to a gangster finds him recruited by the police in order to infiltrate a drug ring. The second most popular film was **Light of My Eyes** (*Nour Einy*), starring singer Tamer Hosny. A romantic drama, it was a favourite with his many teen fans. He plays a young man who falls in love with a blind woman, played by Menna Shallay.

Mohamed Amin's **Egyptian Maidens**

Al-Arabia Company also produced a number of powerful dramas that found their way into local cinemas. Dawood Abdel-Sayed's **Messages from the Sea** (*Rassayel El Bahr*) featured Asser Yassin as a shy young man who falls desperately in love with a call girl. Mohamed Amin's more impressive **Egyptian Maidens** (*Bentein Min Misr*) tackled the problem of women whose age prevented them from finding an eligible suitor. It was helped by an outstanding performance from Jordanian-born TV star, Saba Mubarak, making her Egyptian film debut.

The Cairo Film Festival premiered Khalid Al-Haggar's new drama, **Lust** (*El-Shoq*). Starring

Menna Shallay and Tamer Hosny in **Light of My Eyes**

EGYPTIAN MEDIA CITY IN 2011

Established in the year 1997, **The Egyptian Media Production City** (EMPC) is set 30 km away from Downtown Cairo and 10 km away from the Giza Pyramids, thus representing a central location for not only indoor shooting, but outdoor shooting as well where the sky is clear all year long. Logistically, EMPC is provided with the latest state-of-the-art equipment, as well as experienced technicians and crews who work in local and international TV, Cinema and ads productions. EMPC comprises 67 video and cinema studios and 16 outdoor shooting locations with a variety of architectural and historical designs including Pharaonic, Islamic, Bedouin, rural, jungle and military areas, just to name a few.

There is also a five-star hotel to accommodate visiting crews, pre and post-production facilities and the Nile Sat uplinks with transcontinental footprints.

EMPC also operates under the umbrella of the Media Free Zone, which gives its clients tax-free unconstrained imports on their shooting equipment. Cinema City is also a major EMPC division that comprises soundstages, printing facilities, sound unit and camera.

With a major success and established reputation throughout the whole world, EMPC is continuing its leadership in film and TV production with major international companies coming to use its facilities. In 2010, **Ramses II, The Great Voyage**, a docu-drama that spans over the ages starting from ancient Egypt till the 21st century. Directed by Guillaume Hecht and Valerie Girie, the ninety minute is a co-production between the French company **Les films du Scribe** and **EMPC** that was entirely shot on location at EMPC facilities in January 2010.

In 2011, British filmmaker Christopher Miles will be helming **The Last Pharaoh**, an EMPC co-production of a WWII epic drama revolving around the last Egyptian king, Farouk the First. That is in addition to "Ali Baba and the Forty Thieves" which will be shot in the same year and directed by the Canadian director, Izidore Musallam.

Ahmed Abdalla's **Microphone**

Ruby and her real-life sister, Mayan, as two marginal girls traumatised by poverty and deprivation, its risqué scenes caused a great deal of outrage in the media.

The new wave of Egyptian 'indies' continued to challenge the mainstream, whilst garnering much local and international acclaim. Following Ibrahim El-Batout's *Ein Shams*, which was awarded the Golden Tauro at Taormina Film Festival 2008, and Ahmed Abdalla's *Heliopolis*, which received a special mention at the Cairo Film Festival in 2009, Abdalla's second feature, **Microphone**, picked up the main prize at the Carthage Film Festival, while El-Batout's **Hawi** was awarded the Best Arab Film prize at Doha Tribeca. Digitally shot and funded by minuscule budgets, both films take place in the Mediterranean city of Alexandria, where the filmmakers reflect, in docu-drama style, on the everyday lives of its cosmopolitan inhabitants. Through the eyes of Khaled (Khaled Abol-Naga, who also served as co-producer), *Microphone* employs vibrant hip-hop and metal music by new bands to tell its tales, which are set amongst the city's underground art and music scenes. The script is mostly improvised,

Ibrahim El-Batout's **Hawi**

following extensive workshops overseen by Abdalla, with a cast of non-professionals. The film captures glimpses of Alexandria's street life, where struggling teens are desperate for a breakthrough. *Hawi* employs a similar approach, presenting a series of interweaving stories about the daily struggle to find a place in life.

This new wave presents audiences with an exciting generation of Egyptian filmmakers who rely on strong, realistic stories and captivating characters, recalling the 'New Realism' era of the 1970s and 1980s, which gave us filmmakers like Mohamed Khan, Dawood Abdel-Sayed and Atef El-Tayeb. The trend looks set to continue in 2011, with a number of filmmakers working on ambitious projects.

Sherif Mandour's **Cairo Exit**

As the year drew to a close, Sherif Mandour, who produced *Ein Shams* and *Heliopolis*, premiered his new film, **Cairo Exit**, at the Dubai Film Festival. It marked the first Egyptian production for writer-director Hesham Essawi, an Egyptian-born filmmaker who studied in the United States, making a name for himself with the short *T for Terrorist* and his feature debut, *AmericanEast*, which starred Sayed Badreya. *Cairo Exit* stars Mohamed Ramadan and Maryan as two young Egyptian lovers, a Coptic girl and Muslim young man, who are desperate to leave their lives behind.

Ahmed Rashwan, whose feature debut, *Basra*, won the Best Screenplay award at the Cairo Film Festival in 2008, will begin shooting **Sahara** in 2011. Tamer El-Said is likely to finish his feature debut **In the Last Days of the City**, in which Khalid Abdalla makes his Egyptian

Al Arabia Cinema Production & Distribution
21 Ahmed Orabi Str. Mohandessine Cairo 12411 - Egypt
Tel: +202 33452461-62 / +202 33444688 Fax: +202 33444030 / +202 33445040
www.alarabiacinema.com   email: sales@arabiacinema.com

Founded in the year 2000, **Al Arabia Cinema Production & Distribution Co.** is a Cairo-based Egyptian entity that was the driving force behind the production and distribution of more than 100 feature films varying between Big-budget Blockbusters that scored smashing successes in Egypt and the Pan-Arab region and also acclaimed Arthouse and Films D'auteur coming from the creative minds of a new generation of Egyptian filmmakers. Al Arabia has in contract Egyptian big stars like Adel Imam and many young talents who are all top-billed in its annual line-up of colorful action, drama and comedy films. Moreover, Al Arabia has been the main studio supporting the Egyptian generation of 1980s neo-realism who are still contributing with their ongoing literate work as its first ever films included **A Citizen, A Detective and A Thief** by Daoud Abdel-Sayed and **Girl's Secrets** by Magdy Ahmed Aly. This collaboration continued in 2010 with Abdel-Sayed's **Messages from the Sea** and Aly's **Birds of the Nile** that were screened to great acclaim in Abu Dhabi and Cairo Festivals. Al Arabia also financed the entire work of writer-director Mohamed Amin including his latest acclaimed drama **Egyptian Maidens** starring Zeina and Jordanian-born Saba Mubarak. Moreover, Al Arabia also produced film debuts for rising filmmakers like **A Boy and a Girl** by Karim El-Adl and **Those Days** by Ahmed Fathy Ghanem. In acquiring the distribution rights of the independently produced, digitally shot **Heliopolis** by Ahmad Abdalla and Taormina's Golden Taura winner **Ein Shams** by Ibrahim El-Batout, Al Arabia became the first supporter of the New Wave of young filmmakers who are creating a new realm of Egyptian arthouse film experience with the narrowest financial resources. Now, Al Arabia tends to export its landmark catalogue to new territories in the entire world through its frequent participation of renowned film events including the American Film Market (AFM), the European Film Market (EFM) and le marché du film. Films produced by Arabia are frequently selected in major world festivals. In 2010, *Birds of the Nile* won Best Actor Award in Cairo Festival and *Messages from the Sea* competed in Taormina, Carthage and Abu-Dhabi Festivals.

cinema debut. Another Egyptian actor, Amr Waked, will appear in Lasse Hallström's *Salmon Fishing in the Yemen* and Steven Soderbergh's *Contagion* in 2011.

The year's best films
Microphone (Ahmad Abdalla)
Egyptian Maidens (Mohamed Amin)
Messages from the Sea (Dawood Abdel-Sayed)
Hawi (Ibrahim El-Batout)

Quote of the year
'All we need is the vision and the know-how, nothing else because recognition and appreciation have become possible on both the regional and international levels. The achievement does not undermine commercial filmmaking by any means. But it widens the variety for audiences. New cinema creates a richer environment, as it offers new perspectives and often tackles what's happening around us.' IBRAHIM EL-BATOUT, *after his success at Doha Tribeca Festival.*

Directory
All Tel/Fax numbers begin (+20)
Chamber of Film Industry, 1195 Kornish El Nil, Industries Union Bldg, Cairo. Tel: 578 5111. Fax: 575 1583.
Egyptian Radio & TV Union, Kornish El Nil, Maspero St, Cairo. Tel: 576 0014. Fax: 579 9316.
National Egyptian Film Archive, c/o Egyptian Film Centre, City of Arts, Al Ahram Rd, Guiza. Tel: 585 4801. Fax: 585 4701. President: Dr Mohamed Kamel El Kalyobi.
National Film Centre, Al-Ahram Ave, Giza. Tel: 585 4801. Fax: 585 4701.

SHERIF AWAD is an Egypt-based film/art critic who also curates cinema and art focuses across Europe. Besides his contribution to Arab and European publications, he produces TV shows in the pan-Arab area.

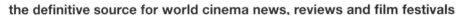

Estonia Jaan Ruus

Following a peak year in 2007, when no less than ten feature films were made, 2010 saw the completion of just two features. However, documentary and animation continue to excel.

There was much discussion in the media over the future of Estonian film. The coffers of the Estonian Film Foundation, the state agency that provides two thirds of funding, fell by 16% over the past two years, totalling €3.4 million in 2010, the level it was at in 2007. However, the ruling right-of-centre coalition has made an election-campaign promise to double the money available.

The grants handed out by the other state-run financier, the Cultural Endowment of Estonia, which receives its money from excises on gambling, alcohol and tobacco, and covers approximately one fifth of the nation's film funds, is in an even worse situation. People visit casinos less frequently, while the tax on alcohol and tobacco has made the products prohibitively expensive, thus limiting con-sumption. And even though the government's support of the domestic film industry is four times that of Lithuania and three times that of Latvia, with €5.5 million in 2010, it remains

insufficient. On the positive side, Estonian film financing for the near future remains relatively stable. For 2011, three major public sources of funding, the Estonian Film Foundation, the Estonian Cultural Endowment and the Ministry of Culture, have budgeted a total of €5 million, a minor cut considering the economic climate.

Karlo Funk, Head of Production and Development at the Estonian Film Foundation, declared that in order for domestic films to achieve respectable box-office results, at least a dozen new productions must be released in cinemas each year. He somberly added that the slogan 'More films!' will not increase state resources and 12 new films a year will remain utopian for such a small nation. Moreover, the country's simplistic tax system does not favour schemes based on tax exemptions that support film industries in other European countries.

In 2009, only 2% of viewers watched Estonian films in cinemas and the attendance figure for any single film never exceeded 7,000. Homegrown product on TV is a different matter. Even Soviet-era films, which are being shown to celebrate the 100th anniversary of the first Estonian feature film in 2012, are surprisingly popular.

15th Tallinn
Black Nights
Film Festival **PÖFF**

18 November –
4 December
2011

The general cinema attendance has remained stable over the past four years, reaching 1,783,780 viewers in 2009. Competition between multiplex cinemas during the economic recession has, for the first time, led to falling ticket prices. The average cinema ticket cost €4.2 in 2009, 7% less than the year before.

Director Andres Puustusmaa, who has directed a number of films in Russia, returned home with a dark criminal drama, **Red Mercury** (*Punane elavhõbe*). The film depicts Estonia in the 1990s, a shell-shocked society in transition, where the underground rules, police officers are drunks, slobs and thugs, and the state excels in metal exports. However, the film remains too superficial to truly convey the spirit of the era.

Andreas Puustusmaa's **Red Mercury**

Marko Raat's **The Snow Queen**

In Marko Raat's **The Snow Queen** (*Lumekuninganna*), Hans Christian Andersen's queen has become a wealthy middle-aged woman with fatal cancer, to whom a Lappish witch suggests the ice cold and a young boy's warm blood for remedy. A young boy leaves home to move in with the woman in her house of ice. The unearthly world of ice and snow, created by cinematographer Matzow Gulbrandsen and designers Jack van Domburg and Eva Maria Gramakovski, makes for a compelling atmosphere, but flat dialogue and dull performances result in an inert, one-dimensional fantasy drama.

Tanel Toom who began his studies at the Baltic Film and Media School in Tallinn and is now a student at the National Film and Television School in Beaconsfield, in the UK, won the 2010 Honorary Foreign Film award of the Student Academy Awards competition (given annually by the Academy of Motion Picture Arts and Sciences in California), for his short film **The Confession** (*Pihtimus*). Revolving around a schoolboy's first confession, the film explores ideas of conscience and truth. Toom's previous film, *The Second Coming* (*Teine tulemine*), had been included in the short film programme at the Venice Film Festival.

Public television produced a seven-part sequel to Ilmar Raag's 2007 drama, *The Class*, a story about school violence that has become the country's most popular film at festivals.

International cooperation has become a natural state of affairs. *The Snow Queen* is an Estonian-Norwegian joint project. Estonian producer Marianna Kaat is financing Belorusian director Yuri Khashchavatski's **Lobotomy**, which looks at the Russian media's role in the Georgian-Russian military conflict. She is also the director of the bleak Estonian-Ukrainian documentary, **Pit No 8**, about child miners.

Director Sergei Loznitsa picked Estonian performers for his film **My Joy** (Germany-Ukraine-Netherlands), which won the Grand Prix at Tallinn Black Nights Film Festival in December 2010. German-Austrian **The Poll Diaries** (*Poll*), by Chris Kraus, was awarded Best Screenplay at the same festival. It depicts the life of Baltic Germans and was shot mostly in Estonia, with the co-operation of a local producer (Estonia also contributed 2% of the film's budget).

In animation, Priit and Olga Pärn, as well as Mati Kütt and Kaspar Jancis, stand out. Mati Kütt's forceful, 45-minute surreal puppet film **Sky Song** (*Taevalaul*) employs pixilation, in a film that features Sigmund Freud, Salvador Dali and Alfred Hitchcock and explores the logic of dreams on a grand scale.

Mati Kütt's **Sky Song**

The grotesque and melancholic drawn animation about the joys of small people, **Crocodile** (*Krokodill*), by Kaspar Jancis,won the Cartoon d'Or, the traditional award of European animation, whose recipient is selected from the prize winners of 15 European animation festivals.

The year's best films
Sky Song (Mati Kütt)
The Confession (Tanel Toom)
Crocodile (Kaspar Jancis)
Pit No 8 (Marianna Kaat)

Quote of the year
'If six people praise you, one after the other, you may very well earn the title of genius.'
Director **PEETER SIMM** *on the influence of friendly circles.*

Kaspar Jancis' **Crocodile**

Directory

All Tel/Fax numbers begin (+372)
Estonian Film Foundation, Uus 3, 10111 Tallinn. Tel: (6) 276 060. Fax: (6) 276 061. film@efsa.ee. www.efsa.ee.
Estonian Association of Film Journalists, Narva mnt 11 E, 10151 Tallinn. Tel: 5533 894. Fax: (6) 698 154. margit.tonson@ekspress.ee.
Estonian Filmmakers Union, Uus 3, 10111 Tallinn. Tel: (6) 464 164. Fax: (6) 464 068. kinoliit@kinoliit.ee. www.kinoliit.ee.
Association of Estonian Film Producers, Lootuse pst 62, 11616 Tallinn. Tel: 5646 7769. produtsendid@produtsendid.ee.
Union of Estonian Cameramen, Faehlmanni 12, 15029 Tallinn. Tel: 5662 3069. Fax: (6) 568 401. bogavideo@hot.ee.
Association of Professional Actors of Estonia, Uus 5, 10111 Tallinn. Tel: (6) 464 512. Fax: (6) 464 516 enliit@enliit.ee. www.enliit.ee.
Estonian National Archive's Film Archive, Ristiku 84, 10318 Tallinn. Tel: (6) 938 613. Fax: (6) 938 611. filmiarhiiv@ra.ee. www.filmi.arhiiv.ee.
Media Desk Estonia c/o Estonian Film Foundation, Uus 3, 10111 Tallinn. Tel: (6) 276 065. Fax: (6) 276 061. mediadesk@efsa.ee. www.mediadesk.efsa.ee.
Tallinn University's Baltic Film and Media School, Sütiste tee 21, 13419 Tallinn. Tel: (6) 268 124. Fax: (6) 268 108. info.bf@tlu.ee.

JAAN RUUS works as a film critic for the leading Estonian weekly, *Eesti Ekspress*. He is the founder of Estonian FIPRESCI and the Artistic Director of Tallinn Black Nights Film Festival's competition programme.

Finland Antti Selkokari

There were 22 domestic releases in 2010, the result of several production subsidies from previous years taking effect over the last year. Of these films, eight dealt with the ever more vulnerable psyche of the Finnish male.

Joonas Berghäll and Mika Hotakainen's **Steam of Life** (*Miesten vuoro*) proved to be exceptionally popular. The film attracted more than 43,000 admissions, an outstanding figure for a documentary feature. Superficially, the film looks at the perennial Finnish penchant for the sauna. Several men were filmed sweating, bathing and discussing their lives, the heat and steam opening them up emotionally, offering an insight into the life of the everyday male. The film has been making the festival rounds, from Leipzig to Calgary, and is the Finnish entry for the Academy Awards. A similar documentary, exploring the contemporary male's propensity for emotional expression and physical endurance, is Mika Ronkainen's **Freetime Machos**. By looking at a hapless Finnish rugby team, Ronkainen identifies the sport as a way for the men to reclaim their machismo, whilst successfully capturing their fragility.

Aleksi Salmenperä's **Bad Family**

Somewhat similar territory is charted in Aleksi Salmenperä's third feature, **Bad Family** (*Paha perhe*). An overprotective father suspects his son is having an incestuous relationship with his sister. Salmenperä builds dramatic tension around the taut performance of Ville Virtanen, who plays the father, deteriorating from paranoia into madness. Cinematographer Tuomo Hutri excels in embellishing the film's emotions through a carefully selected palette of light and colour, with the camera's distance from the characters underpinning the emotional state of the family. Despite mostly positive reviews, the Aki Kaurismäki-produced film played to a slight audience of 16,000.

Short films also play a major role in Finland's film culture. One of the most significant voices when it comes to documentary shorts is Pia Andell, whose topics have ranged from life as a twin and religious sects to war-time memories from conquered towns. Once again using archive footage, Andell's **Göring's Baton** (*Göringin sauva*) tells how Finnish Field Marshal C.G. Mannerheim made a secret trip to Germany to greet Adolf Hitler in 1942, in response to Hitler's visit to greet Mannerheim on his birthday. Andell was fortunate enough to

Joonas Berghäll and Mika Hotakainen's **Steam of Life**

meet Finnish cameraman Felix Forsman, who documented both visits. She creates a vivid image of wartime Finnish history, combining pristine footage shot in Berchtesgaden with a commentary by Felix Forsman and the dramatisation of certain events.

Dome Karukoski's **Lapland Odyssey** (*Napapiirin sankarit*) is a comedy about an unemployed slacker, Janne, who is about to lose his girlfriend if he cannot return home with a converter that allows her to access cable TV. Janne takes his two best friends to assist in his quest, leading to various comic scenarios, mostly resulting from the boys spending all the money on beer. Karukoski and scriptwriter Pekko Pesonen maintain a cheerful mood, along with a smattering of morbid humour, playing up to one of the oldest tricks of Finnish comedies, of men going astray before settling down with their spouses.

Jalmari Helander's **Rare Exports: A Christmas Tale**

The most anticipated Finnish film of the year originated when Jalmari Helander was working for an advertisement agency. A simple idea stemming from the desire to see a different kind of Christmas film resulted in **Rare Exports: A Christmas Tale**. It has since become the best export of Finnish cinema in 2010. The film treats, with mischievous glee, the idea of the original Santa Claus being anything but a jovial old man.

The most popular Finnish film of the year was Mari Rantasila's follow-up to 2008's *Ricky Rapper*, **Ricky Rapper and the Bicycle Thief** (*Risto räppääjä ja polkupyörävaras*). A musical comedy, it found its audience in children and families, who went to see the film in droves.

Mari Rantasila's **Ricky Rapper and the Bicycle Thief**

It is based on the popular children's books, by sisters Tiina and Sinikka Nopola, who have so far published 14 volumes, and deals with the everyday adventures of a red-haired, sprightly young boy. In this instalment, he loses his brand-new bike and sets out to look for it with his best friend, Nelli. The quest for the bike leads them to meet ever more eccentric adults, who are portrayed in both book and film as caricatures. This, along with the candy colour scheme and slapstick-style acting, explains the success of the film, which has so far sold 328,000 tickets. It also has universal appeal, touring festivals as far afield as Cairo and Lübeck. A third film is on its way in 2012.

At the end of the year, it appeared that 2010 looked set to break records. Finnish cinema saw admissions approaching the two-million mark, which has not happened in decades.

Christmas saw the premiere of Lauri Nurkse's **The Night Is Still Young** (*Veijarit*), a tale of two best friends who want nothing more than to live life to the maximum. Nurkse, who is better known as an actor, elicits vivid performances from his young cast. However, the film fails to rise above routine fare, the director lacking the distance to portray these superficial lives.

Olli Saarela's **Priest of Evil** (*Harjunpää ja pahan pappi*) almost discards the source novel, by Matti Yrjänä Joensuu. Peter Franzén plays Detective Sergeant Harjunpää, whose investigation into a series of strange deaths at a number of metro stations in Helsinki puts him on the trail of the killer who murdered his

Olli Saarela's **Priest of Evil**

daughter. Saarela opts for action and style, reducing the existential anguish of Matti Yrjänä Joensuu's literary hero.

The year's best films
Lapland Odyssey (Dome Karukoski)
Steam Of Life (Joonas Berghäll & Mika Hotakainen)
Bad Family (Aleksi Salmenperä)
Göring's Baton (Pia Andell)
Rare Exports (Jalmari Helander)

Quote of the year
'The status of Finnish cinema must be legally confirmed.' IRINA KROHN, *CEO of the Finnish Film Foundation, about the reorganisation of administration and financing at the Finish Broadcasting Corporation, Yle.*

Directory
All Tel/Fax numbers begin (+358)
Finnish Film Foundation, Kanavakatu 12, FIN-00160. Tel: (9) 622 0300. Fax: (9) 622 0305. ses@ses.fi. www.ses.fi

ANTTI SELKOKARI is a freelance film critic and journalist, who lives in Helsinki.

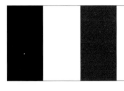

France Michel Ciment

At the beginning of 2010, the French cinema business was looking remarkably healthy. Once again, the economic crisis drew audiences back to watch more films. For the first time in 27 years, cinema attendance reached more than 200 million, an increase of 5.7%. French films fared less well, with a market share of 36.8% and just shy of 74 million tickets sold (down 14.7% on the previous year, which was buoyed by the astonishing success of *Welcome to the Sticks*, with more than 20 million tickets sold). Overall, 21 films sold more than two million tickets (14 in 2008) and seven films exceeded four million. The box office was up by 8%, partly due to an increase in ticket prices (by two or three Euros) due to 3D screenings.

American films reached their highest level since 2000, with a market share of 49.7% and 99.91 million seats (+21.6%). European films gave the wrong impression of being more popular (+10.8%), but those which allowed such a spectacular progression were similar, in form and content, to popular Hollywood blockbusters, such as the sixth instalment of the *Harry Potter* franchise (6 million) and *Slumdog Millionaire* (2.7 million), or the Swedish film, *The Girl with the Dragon Tattoo* (1.22 million seats).

The record cinema attendance was also probably linked to the increasing number of releases, 588 (as against 555 in 2008), which offered an even greater variety of titles. If a limited number of films garnered a maximum amount of money, the concentration was less prevalent than in the preceding years. One hundred films sold more than 500,000 tickets (5% more than in 2008 and an increase of 31.6% over 2007) and 50 films more than

one million (among them, 18 French and 28 American films). The most impressive box-office figures were achieved by animated films, which represented 6% of all new releases but owned 15.4% of total ticket sales. At the other end of the spectrum, documentaries (71 releases, compared to 50 in 2008), which represented 12.1% of all new releases, failed to attract more than 1.6% of the audience share, the only real success being *Michael Jackson's This Is It*, which sold over half a million seats.

The most popular genre remained comedy. Almost all the successes were American and French, with 15 of the 127 released selling more than one million seats. The national comedies fared particularly well, taking half of the tickets sold for this genre.

If auteur cinema cannot boast a home in France (more and more films playing at festivals fail to open on general release), it does remain relatively popular with French audiences compared to other countries (for instance, the Korean film *Poetry* still sold more than 200,000 tickets). Art-house films have also made significantly more progress commercially than many other films, retaining 37.4% of the market share, compared to 27.6% in 2008.

For the first time since 2001, no month registered audience figures of less than ten million. If, as expected, the majority audience share was concentrated over the weekend (54.9%), there is also a growing tendency for a spike in figures over the summer months.

Paris and its outskirts, as well as other big cities, garnered the maximum box office. Interestingly, more women (54.5%) than men (45.5%) went to the cinema. Half of the film population is over 35-years-old, but the age bracket 25–34 increased its appetite for films, as did university and high-school students. Retired people went less to cinemas and tended to prefer French films, while youngsters favoured American product.

Germany was the country where French films were most enjoyed, followed by the USA, Canada, Russia, Belgium, the United Kingdom, Ireland and Italy. The number of films produced domestically showed a slight decline, with 182 titles (as against 196 in 2008), 137 being entirely financed by French money and 45 co-produced with foreign investment.

The average budget for a film was €5.10 million (as against €6.42 million in 2008). This might be explained by another increase in first features (produced at a lower cost), with 77 films, the highest number from the last ten years. Second features achieved just half that number (37). Public channels partly financed 87 films with investment of €110 million (–23%), while cable channels Canal+ and TPS also decreased their contribution, but played a

Xavier Beauvois's **Of Gods and Men**

vital part in national production. The Avance sur recettes, as usual, helped the production of quality films (23.1% of the total number).

588 films were distributed, an increase of 33 titles, with 268 French films (+28) and 165 American films (–9). A total of 96 European films were screened, with a decline in German (–7), Italian (– 6), and Spanish (–3) releases.

The most spectacular development was, of course, the distribution of digital films (83 as against 57 in 2008, 30 in 2007 and 14 in 2006). Forty-nine came from American distributors and twenty-six from French. By the end of January 2010, 298 theatres boasted digital projection facilities and the CNC (National Centre of Cinema) is helping small venues with little money to acquire digital facilities. On the whole, the number of screens increased by 46, to a total of 5,470 across 2,006 venues.

Ten new multiplexes opened in 2009. In the provinces, multiplexes have been developed at the expense of local cinemas in the centre of cities, which often had more daring programming. In a town like Chartres, for instance, two cinemas (one had four screens, the other, one) have closed, while a multiplex with ten screens opened.

Sixteen films in 3D were released during the year, mostly distributed by American companies, which ranked top of the year's most successful distributors: 1. 20th Century Fox; 2. Warner Bros; 3. Pathé; 4. Sony Pictures; 5. Buena Vista; 6. SND; 7. TFI; 8. Mars; 9. Studio Canal; 10. Metropolitan.

From an artistic point of view, French cinema – as proven by the number of films selected for festivals, prizes won at Cannes and the attention of international film critics – has no rival in the European field for the sheer volume of quality films. Xavier Beauvois's **Of Gods and Men** (*Des hommes et des dieux*), which won the Grand Prix in Cannes, has been a huge success, with an audience of over three million. The true story of seven monks in an Algerian monastery, who died in mysterious circumstances, likely at the hands of Islamic fundamentalists, has resulted in an austere, yet moving, story of solidarity, courage and spiritual meditation in the face of adversity. For various reasons – a positive view of French people in a former colony, a return to moral values in a cynical and materialistic age, and the religious dimension – the film appealed to a wide spectrum of the population.

Mathieu Amalric's **On Tour**

Mathieu Amalric was awarded the Best Director prize at Cannes for **On Tour** (*Tournée*), his third and best film so far. It depicts, with energy and humour, a group of American burlesque artistes on a tour of French towns and their relationship with their manager, played by the director. The gusto and melancholy that permeates the film are enhanced by the charm of the women whose curvaceous physiques do not correspond to the canons of contemporary beauty.

The Princess of Montpensier (*La Princesse de Montpensier*), a period film by Bertrand Tavernier, adapted from a short story by Madame de La Fayette, shows the director at the peak of his powers, displaying his talent for recreating the past (the religious wars between Catholics and Protestants in the late 16th century) with energy. Mostly played by a host of new talents (except Lambert Wilson, following on from *Of Gods and Men* with another excellent performance), it is primarily a love story between a young princess, her

Bertrand Tavernier's **The Princess of Montpensier**

husband, whom she did not choose, her true beloved and the future king of France. The epic battles and more intimate scenes confirm once again the eclectic and wayward talent of Tavernier.

One of the highlights of Cannes was the screening of **Carlos** which, in its complete TV version of 5 hours and 20 minutes (the film version reduced to 2.30 bombed at the box office), is arguably Olivier Assayas' best film. Always maintaining the right distance, neither demonising nor extolling the complex personality of the famous terrorist, Assayas shows impressive assurance in his control of this epic, while analysing the intricacies of world politics and the suicidal behaviour of exalted ideologues.

Olivier Assayas' **Carlos**

Former Maoist and currently pro-Palestinian spokesman, Jean-Luc Godard, offered a disenchanted view of the world in **Film Socialisme**, his new and mostly esoteric meditation interspersed, as usual, with moments of visual beauty. The contrast with *Carlos* could not be more evident in its approach to political cinema.

Another period piece, **Au fond des bois**, by Benoît Jacquot, confirmed his talent for stylising the past. In 19th century France, a dim-witted man (close to Herzog's Gaspar Hauser or Truffaut's wild child) seduces a young girl from a bourgeois family and elopes with her to the mountainous forests of Ardèche. The film has a raw quality, which matches the unsettling story.

Abdellatif Kechiche's **Black Venus**

Abdellatif Kechiche in **Black Venus** (*Vénus noire*) was also inspired by a real historical event: the exhibition and degradation of an African woman, Saartjes Baartman, who was known as the 'Venus Hottentot', in early 19th century London and Paris, where she was ill-treated in salons and music halls by debauched aristocrats and leering crowds. This powerful subject, featuring some impressive sequences, was diluted by a repetitious narrative and an obviousness that failed to match Kechiche's earlier work.

Rachid Bouchareb's **Outside the Law** (*Hors la loi*) portrays, from the Algerian side and through the portrait of three brothers, the war of independence against France. Far from self-righteous, the film refuses to avoid some negative aspects of the quest for freedom and pursues the historical perspective begun with *Days of Glory*. In a lighter vein, Luc Besson's **The Extraordinary Adventures of Adèle Blanc Sec** (*Les Aventures extraordinaires d'Adèle Blanc Sec*), inspired by the famous

Tony Gatlif's **Liberté**

Period pieces were decidedly in vogue this season, with mostly impressive results. **Liberté** was one of the best efforts by gypsy filmmaker Tony Gatlif, who evokes the fate of the Romas during the German occupation of France and the complicity of the French police in their deportation to the camps. The film became all the more powerful when, a few months later, the government took drastic measures against the gypsy community.

Luc Besson's **The Extraordinary Adventures of Adèle Blanc Sec**

comic strip by Tardi, captures the spirit of the popular serials of the time and the films of Feuillade, set in *fin de siècle* Paris.

Claire Denis's **White Material** is more a travel in space than a travel in time. Isabelle Huppert gives another thrilling performance as a French settler in Africa, who tries to save her plantation while a civil war is raging. Denis's atmospheric sense of place and her powerful physical evocation of landscape and violence give the film a peculiar strength. Bertrand Blier's **The Sound of Ice Cubes** (*Le Bruit des glaçons*) signals a return to form for its director with his provocative and iconoclastic style. The protagonist's dialogue with the cancer that inhabits his body is informed by Blier's usual dark humour and pithy language.

Bertrand Blier's **The Sound of Ice Cubes**

The contribution of foreign directors currently living and working in France has always added an extra dimension to the national production. Iosseliani's **Chantrapas** is, notwithstanding the director's statement, a partly autobiographical film about a young Georgian director who has to find his way in his own country during the soviet era and bypasses the threats of censorship, until he goes to work in France and faces different kinds of problems. With his usual lightweight humour and elliptical narrative, Iosseliani perfectly illustrates Milos Forman's famous comment that filming in a communist country was like being behind the bars of a zoo but being fed every day while, in a liberal economy, you live in a jungle where only the strongest survive.

Is Raoul Ruiz's masterpiece, **Mysteries of Lisbon**, a French film? The jury of the Delluc Prize answered positively by awarding it the main prize. Partly spoken in French and set in Portugal and France, it is a multi-layered narrative with flashbacks and fascinating diversions, a baroque maze where one loses oneself with delight, captivated by the surrealist atmosphere and the gorgeous colours.

Benoît Delépine and Gustave Kervern's **Mammuth**

If Benoît Delépine and Gustave Kervern are French, their films belong to another world. **Mammuth** is a road movie with Gérard Depardieu at its centre, who rides a motorcycle searching for a way to have his pension paid. Outrageously funny, with absurd situations and larger-than-life characters (including Yolande Moreau as the wife of the protagonist), it is a work of mavericks all too rare in today's cinema.

Among the more classical and successful comedies of the year, **Potiche** stands out because of its huge success in France and on

François Ozon's **Potiche**

Marc Fitoussi's **Copacabana**

the festival circuit. Adapted from a boulevard play by Barillet and Gredy, it confirms François Ozon's sense of timing, his direction of actors (Catherine Deneuve and Gérard Depardieu at their peak), and his social satire. French provincial political life is observed with irony as Deneuve, a passive and ornamental woman married to a reactionary husband (Fabrice Luchini) facing a strike, takes command of her marriage and of the factory.

Michel Leclerc's **Le Nom des gens** holds up a mirror to French society with the double portrait of a woman of north-African origin and her boyfriend, a socialist, who are confronted with the social and political issues facing the country. Pierre Salvadori's **Full Treatment** (*De vrais mensonges*) echoes Ernst Lubitsch in a story of false letters, betrayals and romance. Jean-Pierre Améris's **Les Émotifs anonymes** is the most touching and charming of them all, with its portrayal of two shy characters, an employee of a chocolate factory (Isabelle Carré) and her boss (Benoît Poelvoords), who overcome their timidity and fall in

Pierre Salvadori's **Full Treatment**

love. In **Copacabana**, Marc Fitoussi allows Isabelle Huppert to show her comic talent as a superficial mother who wants to make amends in order to win the respect of her very conservative daughter. Once more, the performances of the actors contribute greatly to the success of these films.

Marc Dugain's **An Ordinary Execution**

Few achievements justify the sheer number of first films. Among them, the writer Marc Dugain's adaptation of his own novel, **An Ordinary Execution** (*Une exécution ordinaire*), stands out with its depiction of the last months in the life of Joseph Stalin (with an exceptional interpretation by André Dussolier as the cunning and perverse tyrant) and his relationship with a doctor (Marina Hands) who helps soothe his back ache. The comic-strip writer Joann Sfar was partly successful with his biopic **Gainsbourg (Vie héroïque)**. Some original visual ideas and another great performance by Eric Elmosnino are mixed with more conventional narrative devices. Another comic-strip artist, Pascal Rabaté, succeeds with **Les Petits Ruisseaux** in the portrayal of an elderly man who discovers a new life after the death of his wife.

Two prison films (very different from *A Prophet*) were directed by two new female filmmakers: Lea Fehner's **Silent Voice** (*Qu'un seul tienne et les autres suivront*) and Brigitte Sy's **Les Mains libres**. Both films avoid the conventions of the genre, the first taking place in the visiting room of a prison, while the other has a documentary director falling in love with an inmate.

Sylvain Chomet's **The Illusionist**

Two films stood out in the fields of documentary and animation. Nicolas Philibert's **Nénette** is a portrait of the orang-utan in the zoo at the jardin des Plantes in Paris. The animal is silent and the soundtrack is made up of comments by visitors. Sylvain Chomet's **The Illusionist** (*L'illusionniste*) is an adaptation of an original script by Jacques Tati, featuring a protagonist who looks like Hulot himself, who travels through England and Scotland in an attempt to find an audience for his magic tricks. Chomet's wonderful drawings recreate the landscape and the music hall with a poetic atmosphere and melancholy tone.

Joann Sfar's **Gainsbourg (Vie héroïque)**

MICHEL CIMENT is president of FIPRESCI, a member of the editorial board of *Positif*, a radio producer and author of more than a dozen books on cinema.

The year's best films
Au fond des bois (Benoît Jacquot)
Carlos (TV version) (Olivier Assayas)
Des hommes et des dieux (Xavier Beauvois)
Potiche (François Ozon)
La Princesse de Montpensier (Bertrand Tavernier)

Directory
All Tel/Fax numbers begin (+33)
Archives du Film, 7 bis rue Alexandre Turpault, 78395 Bois d'Arcy. Tel: (1) 3014 8000. Fax: (1) 3460 5225.
Cahiers du Cinema, 9 passage de la Boule Blanche, 75012 Paris. Tel: (1) 5344 7575. Fax: (1) 4343 9504. cducinema@lemonde.fr.
Centre National de la Cinématographie, 12 rue de Lubeck, 75016 Paris. Tel: (1) 4434 3440. Fax: (1) 4755 0491. webmaster@cnc.fr. www.cnc.fr.
Cinémathèque de Toulouse, BP 824, 31080 Toulouse Cedex 6. Tel: (5) 6230 3010. Fax: (5) 6230 3012. contact@lacinemathequedetoulouse.com. www.lacinemathequedetoulouse.com.
Cinémathèque Française, 4 rue de Longchamp, 75116 Paris. Tel: (1) 5365 7474. Fax: (1) 5365 7465. contact@cinemathequefrancaise.com. www.cinematequefrancaise.com.
Ile de France Film Commision, 11 rue du Colisée, 75008 Paris. Tel: (1) 5688 1280. Fax: (1) 5688 1219. idf-film@idf-film.com. www.iledefrance-film.com.
Institut Lumière, 25 rue du Premier-Film, BP 8051, 69352 Lyon Cedex 8. Tel: (4) 7878 1895. Fax: (4) 7878 3656. contact@institut-lumiere.org. www.institut-lumiere.org.
Positif, 3 rue Lhomond, 75005 Paris. Tel: (1) 4432 0590. Fax: (1) 4432 0591. www.johnmichelleplace.com.
Unifrance, 4 Villa Bosquet, 75007 Paris. Tel: (1) 4753 9580. Fax: (1) 4705 9655. info@unifrance.org. www.unifrance.org.

Benoît Jacquot's **Au fond des bois**

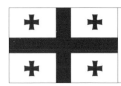

Georgia Nino Ekvtimishvili

The most remarkable event of Georgian cinema in 2010 was Levan Koguashvili's feature debut, **Street Days** (*Kuchis dgeebi*). Described in the press as starting 'a New Wave of Georgian cinema' and 'reviving the best tradition of Georgian neo-realistic film', it was nominated in the Best Feature Film competition at both the Rotterdam and Edinburgh International Film Festivals, going on to win the Golden Lily in Wiesbaden and the Tolerance Award and Special Mention of the Critics Jury, in Subotica, Serbia.

Guga Kotetishvili in Levan Koguashvili's **Street Days**

The action unfolds in present-day Tbilisi. A tragedy of a lost generation, which left behind its youthful days in the 1990s, the film's moral core is embodied by the main character, Checkie, an unemployed junkie. An all-too-human, honest and realistic drama, it stood in stark contrast to other Georgian films and successfully broke out of the festival circuit, its rights sold to both Canada and the United States. It also marks the first time in 20 years that a Georgian production has been screened in Russian cinemas.

Tornike Bziava's short, **The April Chill** (*Aprilis suskhi*), unfolds during the tragic events of the

Tbilisi Massacre, which took place on 9 April, 1989. A meeting between a Georgian dancer and a Soviet soldier draws out the latter's human side. It was awarded the best film prize at the Capalbio Short Film Festival and received a Special Jury Mention at Clermont-Ferrand.

Aleko Tsabadze's surreal **Rene Leaves for Hollywood** (*Rene midis holivudshi*) tells the story of a teacher at a film academy who moonlights as a delivery driver for a gas company. Existing mostly in an imaginary world, fantasy and reality soon blur, leading to his being pursued by imaginary enemies.

Levan Tutberidze's criminal drama, **I Will Die Without You** (*Ushenod mgoni movkvdebi*), describes a day in the life of two young men living in Tbilisi. They do not know each other, but love, friendship and revenge draw them towards a fatal encounter.

Salome Jashi's short documentary, **The Leader Is Always Right** (*Lideri yoveltvis martalia*), follows teenagers on a two-week break at one of the Presidential-funded Summer Camps for Patriots. The film's central thesis, how patriotism is perceived by contemporary Georgian society, attracted much outrage amongst audiences.

Rusudan Pirveli's **Susa** (*Susa*) tells the story of a 12-year-old who lives with his mother in a gloomy suburb, awaiting the return of his father and the hope of a happier life. His father's arrival disappoints the little dreamer, but he remains unwilling to accept his fate.

Two dramas, Keti Machavariani's **Salt White** (*Marilivit tetri*) and Giorgi Maskharashvili's

Avtandil Tetradze in Rusudan Pirveli's **Susa**

The Watchmaker (*Mesaate*), will be released in 2011. Machavariani's film is about a single woman working during the summer season at a resort on the Black Sea. *The Watchmaker* details the process of making a documentary film about a series of sensational murders.

The Georgian Film Commission will launch its website in early 2011. It is heralded as an opportunity to attract local and foreign filmmakers to the benefits of working in Georgia. (www.filmcommission.ge)

The year's best films
Street Days (Levan Koguashvili)
Susa (Rusudan Pirveli)
The April Chill (Tornike Bziava)
I Will Die Without You (Levan Tutberidze)
The Leader Is Always Right (Salome Jashi)

Quote of the year
'The time of realism has come, the time of poetry found in reality. Georgia's time is demanding it, as it is so dramatic and interesting. The time for fables and theatres, transposed into a cinema, has finished. It's time to go out to the streets and see what is happening there, to see real people, real situations, and real dialogue' LEVAN KOGUASHVILI *talking about* **Street Days**.

NINO EKVTIMISHVILI is a freelance journalist who specialises in cinema and art in Georgia.

Directory
All Tel/Fax numbers begin (+995)
Batumi International Arthouse Film Festival, 6000 Batumi, Heidar Abashidze St. 14. Tel./fax: (22) 272 479. info@biaff.org. www.biaff.org.
Film Studio – Remka, 36 Kostava St., 0179 Tbilisi, Tel: (32) 990 542. Fax: (32) 933 871. remka@remkafilm.ge. www.remkafilm.ge.
Georgian National Film Center, 0105 Tbilisi, Georgia # 4 Z. Gamsakhurdia Sanapiro, 4th Floor. Tel/Fax: (32) 999 200; (32) 999 102. info@gnfc.ge.
Independent Filmmakers' Association – South Caucasus (IFA-SC), Head Office – Georgia, Niko Nikoladze Street 1, Apt. 12, 0108 Tbilisi. Tel: (32) 93 12 50. Fax: (32) 50 60 68. ifasc@ifasc.org.ge.
Ministry of Culture, Monuments Protection and Sport, 4, marjvena sanapiro, 0105 Tbilisi, Georgia, Tel: (32) 987 430. info@mc.gov.ge
Sakdoc Film – 2007, 121 Zemo Vedzisi St., 0160 Tbilisi. Tel: (93) 24 32 72/(93) 32 39 29. info@sakdoc.ge. www.sakdoc.ge.
Sanguko Films, 7 Tamarashvili St., 0162 Tbilisi. Tel: (32) 22 40 61. info@sanguko.ge. www.sanguko.ge.
Shota Rustaveli Theater and Film Georgian State University, 0108 Tbilisi, 19 Rustaveli, Tel: (32) 99 94 11. Fax: (32) 98 30 79. www.tafu.edu.ge.
Studio 99, 10 Sharashidze St., 0162 Tbilisi. Tel: (32) 220 79064. Fax: (32) 230 412. Berlin office: Greifenhagener Str. 26, D-10437 Berlin, Germany, Tel: (+49 30) 44031861. Fax: (+49 30) 44031860.
Taia Group ltd., 74, Chavchavadze Ave., 0162 Tbilisi. Tel: (32) 912 945. Fax: (32) 253 072.
Tbilisi International Film Festival, 0112 Tbilisi, Agmashenebeli Ave. 164. Tel: 47 51 82. Fax: 35 67 60. office@tbilisifilmfestival.ge. www.tbilisifilmfestival.ge.

Levan Koguashvili's **Street Days**

Germany Andrea Dittgen

The ongoing financial crisis appears to have unleashed mysterious new forces in Germany, leading to the release of an extraordinarily wide range of genre films in 2010. Fantasy, thrillers, horror and sci-fi – once a no-go for the country's auteurs – have populated German cinemas, often with astonishing results.

Dennis Gansel's **We Are the Night** (*Wir sind die Nacht*) turns out to be a subtle and stylish film about female vampires who turn a comic-book Berlin upside down. Meanwhile, Marvin Kren's zombie love-story **Rammbock** – another welcome surprise – brings the end of civilisation to Germany's capital. The third and most ambitious work of the trio is **The Days to Come** (*Die kommenden Tage*), which finds Lars Kraume's political sci-fi drama unfolding in a dystopian Germany circa 2020. While the country is at war with Saudi Arabia over its remaining oil reserves, some young and errant members of a fractured family join a terrorist movement, while others – particularly the women – struggle between their middle-class life, unhappy love affairs and likely defeat.

Lars Kraume's **The Days to Come**

A young woman of Turkish descent fights for a self-determined life in Germany, despite her family's threats, in **When We Leave** (*Die Fremde*). The remarkable debut of writer/director Feo Aladag combines strong melodramatic and thriller elements. Once again, Sibel Kekilli, who played the lead in Fatih Akin's acclaimed *Head On* in 2002, gives an outstanding performance.

Despite the presence of narrative depth and strong visual style, none of these titles scored a large success at the box office. Only four films attracted an audience of over one million in 2010, all of which were comedies. **Zweiohrküken**, actor/producer/director Til Schweiger's follow-up to his *Rabbit Without Ears*, was released in December 2009 but racked up 4.2 million admissions during 2010. Markus Goller's **Friendship!** (1.5 million viewers) is an intermittently funny comedy, in which two East Germans travel from New York to San Francisco without the benefit of English-language skills or any real knowledge of the US. Fatih Akin's **Soul Kitchen**, in which a loser brings slow food and happiness to the unwashed masses of Hamburg, was released at Christmas-time in 2009 and managed to sell an additional 1.2 million tickets in the new year.

Dennis Gansel's **We Are the Night**

The fourth hit reflects the audiences' growing interest in 3D. **Animals United** (*Konferenz der Tiere*), animated by Werner Kloos and Ulrich Tappe and loosely based on a famous children's book, was Germany's first feature-length film shot in 3D. Its hero, the brave little meerkat, Billy, is a cute creature that appeals to children and adults. However, it's hardly an original character, bearing as it does a strong resemblance to Scrat from the *Ice Age* franchise. Together with a ragtag band of other animals, Billy fights a greedy hotel manager in order to bring water back to the African savannah. In terms of technology, the film stands well against Hollywood standards and it has so far attracted 1.1 admissions.

Werner Kloos and Ulrich Tappe's **Animals United**

No other children's films achieved more than one million in admissions, not only because other international 3D-movies stole their thunder in the first half of the year, but because nothing new or original was on offer. German producers reacted to the financial crisis by cutting back on budgets and ideas, favouring literary adaptations and variations of well-known themes, such as **Goethe!** The mixture of biopic and romantic comedy by Philipp Stölzl focuses on the writer's early years, where he fails at his studies but discovers that poems sometimes make for the best pick-up lines. **Single by Contract** (*Groupies bleiben nicht zum Frühstück*) uses the same territory for a different approach: its heroine unknowingly falls in love with a musician whose contract does not permit him to be seen with a girlfriend. Director Marc Rothemund delivers a breathtakingly fast comedy with just the right amount of love, music and burlesque.

Marc Rothemund's **Single by Contract**

The number of feature films produced didn't drop noticeably from the previous year and the German Federal Film Fund (DFFF) of €60 million was not reduced, but outside the field of low-budget productions, few risks were taken. Even Tom Tykwer went back to his roots with **Three** (*Drei*), an intimate love-triangle and his first German-language feature in a decade. The result was disappointing, the film's emotional core weighed down by the director's overly intellectual approach. Other well-known directors failed their audiences for the same reason, notably Joseph Vilsmaier with **Nanga Parbat**, about the fateful expedition during which Reinhold Messner lost his brother; Detlev Buck with **Same Same but Different**, an impossible German-Asian love story between a journalist and a prostitute; while Oskar Roehler's **Jew Suss: Rise and Fall** (*Jud Süß – Film ohne Gewissen*), about the production of the famous Nazi-propaganda film, turned out to be a real bore compared to the ill-intended, but well-made original.

Thomas Arslan surprised with his stylish thriller, **In the Shadows** (*Im Schatten*), focusing on

Thomas Arslan's **In the Shadows**

the details of a crime. But only Ralf Huettner, another acclaimed director, succeeded in attracting audiences (800,000 viewers). **Vincent Wants to Sea** (*Vincent will meer*) unites three young escapees from a psychiatric hospital, one with Tourettes syndrome, another with Obsessive Compulsive Disorder and a third who suffers from anorexia, on a voyage to Italy, with a helpless doctor and an anxious parent in pursuit.

Ralf Huettner's **Vincent Wants to Sea**

With only four bona-fide hits, even taking in the normally popular comedy and kids' sector, it is no surprise that the share of domestic ticket sales fell from 27.4 per cent in 2009 to 20 per cent during the first six months of the year. However, thanks to some directors' willingness to gamble, the overall quality and diversity of domestic releases made 2010 an unexpectedly rich one for German cinema.

The year's best films
When We Leave (Feo Aladag)
In the Shadows (Thomas Arslan)
We Are the Night (Dennis Gansel)
Vincent Wants to Sea (Ralf Huettner)
The Days to Come (Lars Kraume)

ANDREA DITTGEN is a film critic and editor of the daily newspaper *Die Rheinpfalz* and contributor to the magazine *Filmdienst*. She is also a member of the board of the German Film Critics Association and web editor for the International Federation of Film Critics (FIPRESCI)

Quote of the year
'We were never this close to the version that premiered in 1927.' *Film historian* **ANKE WILKENING** *at the presentation of the newest restoration of* **Metropolis** *with 30 additional minutes of footage.*

Directory
All Tel/Fax numbers begin (+49)
Deutsches Filminstitut-DIF, Schaumainkai 41, 60596 Frankfurt am Main. Tel: (69) 961 2200. Fax: (69) 620 060. info@deutsches-filminstitut.de. www. deutsches-filminstitut.de.
Deutsches Filmmuseum Frankfurt am Main, Schaumainkai 41, 60596 Frankfurt am Main. Tel: (69) 2123 8830. Fax: (69) 2123 7881. info@deutsches-filmmuseum.de. www.deutsches-filmmuseum.de.
Federal Film Board (FFA), Grosse Praesidentenstr 9, 10178 Berlin. Tel: (30) 275 770. Fax: (30) 2757 7111. www.ffa.de.
Filmmuseum Berlin-Deutsche Kinemathek, Potsdamer Str 2, 10785 Berlin. Tel: (49 30) 300 9030. Fax: 3009 0313. info@filmmuseum-berlin.de. www.filmmuseum-berlin.de.
German Films Service & Marketing GmbH, Herzog-Wilhelm-Strasse 16, 80331 Munich, Tel: (89) 599 787-0. Fax: (89) 599 78730. info@german-films.de. www.german-films.de.
Münchner Stadtmuseum/Filmmuseum, St Jakobsplatz 1, 80331 Munich. Tel: (89) 2332 2348. Fax: (89) 2332 3931. filmmuseum@muenchen.de. www.stadtmuseum-online.de/filmmu.htm.
New German Film Producers Association, Agnesstr 14, 80798 Munich. Tel: (89) 271 7430. Fax: (89) 271 9728. ag-spielfilm@t-online.de.
Umbrella Organisation of the Film Industry, Kreuzberger Ring 56, 65205 Wiesbaden. Tel: (611) 778 9114. Fax: (611) 778 9169. statistik@spio-fsk.de.

Feo Aldag's **When We Leave**

Greece Ninos-Fenek Mikelidis

The recent economic crisis has, unsurprisingly, had a negative impact on the country's cinema. Compared with last year, this year's production was more than halved (a number of films distributed this year were produced last year), resulting in the production of less than 20 new features. Another reason was the Greek Film Centre's (GFC) debt, which rose to almost €17 million (due to an excessive number of scripts being approved without any concrete financial support for them). Following the accounts report by the GFC's President at the annual General Assembly, a disapproval vote was recorded from the majority of its members.

The films that managed to make a reasonable profit at the box office were, once again, farcical comedies and melodramas, made for home consumption. Topping the year's box office was **I Love Karditsa**, which was seen by 355,000 people. Conversely, all the more artistically-inclined films, with the exception of two that attracted 30–60,000 entries, failed to attract sizable audiences. Some recorded less than one thousand box-office receipts.

Among the most important films of the year was Yiannis Economidis' **Knifer** (*Maherovgaltis*), a neo-noir in which envy and

Yiannis Economidis' **Knifer**

lust lead to extreme, unexpected results for alienated, lower-middle-class members of society. An interesting variation on James M. Cain's oft-filmed *The Postman Always Rings Twice*, Economidis has a young man, who works for his uncle, embark on a relationship with his aunt. The film provides a comment on social and economic repression in contemporary Greek society.

Nicos Panayiotopoulos' **The Fruit Trees of Athens**

Another important film was Nicos Panayiotopoulos' beautifully photographed **The Fruit Trees of Athens** (*Ta oporofora tis Athinas*), in which a tramp travels around the capital, searching out its wild fruit trees. Based on a novel by Sotiris Dimitriou, Panayiotopoulos successfully translates a difficult, seemingly unfilmable novel into a passionate, poetic hymn to Athens, embellishing it with humour – visual and verbal – and eroticism.

Athina Rachel Tsangari's **Attenberg**, screened in competition at the Venice Film Festival, is an interesting, visually beautiful, but uneven film. It tells the story of a young virgin girl, influenced by David Attenborough's TV documentaries, who, on the cusp of teenage romance, has to attend to her dying father.

Athina Rachel Tsangari's **Attenberg**

With her second feature Tsangari attempts – not always successfully – to combine the formal style of last year's critical success, *Dogtooth*, with a more realistic approach, particularly in the scenes with her father.

The other Venice entry, Syllas Tzoumerkas' **Homeland** (*Hora proelevsis*), deals with a family's problems in Greece's social and economic reality. Tzoumerkas employs an unnecessarily complicated approach, with an overuse of music and too many scenes that veer towards the didactic and overtly symbolic, to present the dramas that unfold within a middle-class family.

In **Voyage to Mytilene** (*Taksidi sti Mitilini*), Lakis Papastathis turns to the memories of a local who left the island 20 years earlier, to study cinema in Paris. He returns to the island to claim his inheritance. The director/protagonist records his experiences on video, the subjective point of view reminiscent of Robert Montgomery's character in *Lady in the Lake*. However, this detachment robs the film of any emotional engagement with the characters, resulting in a cold, often prosaic, atmosphere.

Renos Haralambidis' **Four Black Costumes** is a funny black comedy/road movie about four insolvent gravediggers who steal a coffin with a man in it, making their escape out of Athens and towards a distant village. They do so in the belief that the coffin contains a large sum of money. The naïve dialogue and directorial style often work against a plot that promised a madcap comedy in the style of Monty Python. Vardis Marinakis' **The Black Meadow** (*To

mavro livadi) unfolds in Ottoman-occupied Greece in 1654. It tells the story of an unrequited love affair between a Janissary and a young boy who is disguised as a nun. Although the film is flawed, it features beautiful images reminiscent of Andrei Tarkovsky's work.

Angelos Frantzis's **Into the Woods** (*Mesa sto dasos*) employs a similar approach to his previous film, *The Dog's Dream*, in telling the story of two boys and a girl who, lost in a forest, embark on a doomed love affair. In Margarita Manda's low-key **Gold Dust**, (*Chrysoskoni*), the sibling rivalry over the sale of a family house allows the director to explore the changing face of Athens and the loss of youth.

Documentary had a good year with a number

Angelos Frantzis' **Into the Woods**

of interesting films. Nicos Perakis' pseudo-documentary, **Art Therapy**, profiles three young, non-conformist artists – a street artist, an actor and a female singer – and their attempts to find a place for themselves on the fringes of society. In Dimitris Panayiotatos' **Strangers in a Strange Land** (*Ksenes se kseni hora*), the history of Greece's genre cinema (thriller, film noir, sci-fi and horror) is explored through interviews and clips. Meanwhile, Greek porn cinema from the 1960s to the 1980s is explored by Vassos Yiorgas in **Naked Cinema** (*To sinema yimno*), once again employing clips and interviews to present a rarely discussed history.

Angeliki Aristomenopoulou's **A Voyage-Prone Soul** (*Taxidiara psychi*) offers a fascinating portrait of the famous Greek singer, Yiannis Angelakas. In the solid **Dreams in Another

Language (*Onira se alli glossa*), Loukia Rikaki examines the problems encountered by school children of various nationalities (children of Greek Cypriot and immigrant origin) at a school in the centre of the old town of Nicosia, near the green line that divides the island between the Republic of Cyprus and the region occupied by the Turkish army.

The problems that arose due to the delay in the passing of a new bill regarding Greek cinema have now been resolved and Greek directors agreed to submit their films for this year's Thessaloniki Film Festival. A total of 27 films were entered, half of which were produced last year. However, the presentation of the ministry's new bill via the internet divided the film community, with most of the so-called 'Directors in the Mist' in agreement with it and the Union of Film Directors against it. Although the new bill rightly calls for an end to co-operativism, which had created serious problems in the past, and proposes various ways of financing (among these, measures to make TV channels plough 0.75 per cent of their revenue into film production), the bill has no specific policy on cinema, nor does it take any concrete measures regarding a broader education (a national archive, film societies, parallel circuit, etc.), that will help encourage a richer film environment. The bill also gives absolute power to the directors of various institutions, such as the GFC and Thessaloniki Film Festival, with little room for public accountability.

The year's best films
Knifer (Yiannis Economidis)
The Fruit Trees of Athens
(Nicos Panayiotopoulos)
Art Therapy (Nicos Perakis)
A Voyage-Prone Soul (Angeliki Aristomenopoulou)
Strangers in a Strange Land
(Dimitris Panayiotatos)
Attenberg (Athina Rachel Tsangari)

Quote of the year
'The worst enemy of the artist is the public... Because the public hasn't the generosity, the magnanimity, to get into another person's position, to look at one who is looking. Nobody today gets into the other person's position.' NICOS PANAYIOTOPOULOS, *director of* **The Fruit Trees of Athens**.

Directory
All Tel/Fax numbers begin (+30)
Association of Independent Producers of Audiovisual Works (SAPOE), 30 Aegialias, 151 25 Maroussi. Tel: (210) 683 3212. Fax: (210) 683 3606. sapoe-gr@otenet.gr.
Greek Film Centre, President: George Papalios, 7, Dionysiou Aeropagitou, 117 42 Athens. Tel: (210) 367 8500. Fax: (210) 364 8269. info@gfc.gr. www.gfc.gr.
Greek Film, Theatre & Television Directors Guild, 11 Tossitsa, 106 83 Athens. Tel: (210) 822 8936. Fax: (210) 821 1390. ees@ath.forthnet.gr.
Hellenic Ministry of Culture, 20 Bouboulinas, 106 82 Athens. Tel: (210) 820 1100. w3admin@culture. gr. http://culture.gr.
Hellenic Film Academy, 12 Athinas Street, 182 33, Athens. press@fogfilms.org.
Union of Greek Film Directors and Producers, 33 Methonis, 106 83 Athens. Tel: (210) 825 3065. Fax: (210) 825 3065.
Union of Greek Film, TV & Audiovisual Sector Technicians (ETEKT-OT), 25 Valtetsiou, 106 80 Athens. Tel: (210) 360 2379/361 5675. Fax: (210) 361 6442. etekt-ot@ath.forthnet.gr.

NINOS-FENEK MIKELIDIS is an historian of Greek Cinema and film critic for *Eleftherotypia* daily newspaper. He is also the founder and director of the Panorama of European Cinema film festival in Athens.

Nicos Perakis' **Art Therapy**

ABU DHABI FILM COMMISSION

Hong Kong Tim Youngs

Over the last year, Hong Kong filmmakers continued to juggle big hitters suitable for the huge mainland China market, while trying to keep audiences interested at home. The year before had seen the film industry make gains across the border, with summertime box-office successes ranging from comedy and animation to thrillers, but effort was still needed on the home turf, amid concerns about Hong Kong cinema losing its local character.

So it was encouraging to see a revival in mid-budget, locally focused cinema early in 2010, not least when the Hong Kong International Film Festival announced a roster of premieres and played up the films' Hong Kong character. The festival opened and closed with four local titles, a major push that kicked off with Ivy Ho's **Crossing Hennessy** (*Yuet muhn Hin Lei Si*), a gentle romantic comedy and grass-roots community snapshot. The smaller Hong Kong Asian Film Festival made a similar effort later in the year, opening with local films only and running others as premieres.

Among the best of these smaller films was **Gallants** (*Da lui toi*). Co-directors Derek Kwok

Derek Kwok and Clement Cheng's **Gallants**

and Clement Cheng whipped up a kung-fu concoction about ageing fighters protecting their master's martial-arts school from pushy landowners. Keen plotting, mixed-media flair and fight-film standards made festival tours a given, while local themes (community and heritage, modernity and tradition) gave it a firm Hong Kong identity. *Gallants'* property-market aspect later ran riot in Pang Ho-cheung's ultra-violent **Dream Home** (*Wai do lei ah yat ho*), a grisly slasher about an everyday office lady who would do anything to bring down real-estate prices.

Alex Law's **Echoes of the Rainbow** (*Shui yuet sun tau*) made an unexpected box-office splash. That the screenplay, a nostalgia piece about a boy growing up in late-1960s Hong Kong, was watered down (political detail was notably absent) didn't seem to bother a largely middle-age audience that linked the picture to rising concern over its cultural heritage. Classier historic detail arrived in **The Drunkard** (*Jau touh*), an involving literary adaptation by first-time director Freddie Wong. Taking a 1951 local novel as its base, the atmospheric, low-budget work followed a struggling writer's decline amid booze, women and sleazy commissions. Further glances to the past came in the form of Yan Yan Mak and Clement Cheng's **Merry-Go-Round** (*Tung boh fung*), which sees a girl head from San Francisco to Hong Kong, as personal histories are told around her and a mortuary worker.

Romance was also present. **Lover's Discourse** (*Luen yahn seui yu*) was the feature debut of Derek Tsang and Jimmy Wan, weaving stories of cheating, hidden crushes and the first hints of love in a neat package. Wan and Tsang are regulars behind the scenes with Pang Ho-

Derek Tsang and Jimmy Wan's **Lover's Discourse**

cheung, who shot and released **Love in a Puff** (*Ji ming yu chun giu*) on the quick, while his *Dream Home* awaited release. A casual, off-the-cuff work with ultra-colloquial dialogue, it traced wisps of affection between office workers exiled to alleyways after a workplace smoking ban.

In **La Comédie Humaine** (*Yahn gaan hei ket*), writer-directors Chan Hing-ka and Janet Chun continued the line of smart romantic comedies, this time basing relationships around a screenwriter's run-in with a film-obsessed hit man. And Barbara Wong's **Break-Up Club** (*Fun sau suet ngoi nei*), a rocky, youth-oriented romance shot in a clumsy faux-documentary style, won over teens who identified with its on-off romance and fresh-faced leads.

More on-the-streets Hong Kong themes cropped up in Kenneth Bi's **Girl$** (*Lui lui*), a ripped-from-the-headlines tale of young women and schoolgirls in the 'compensated dating' (youth prostitution) scene. Much more light-hearted was **72 Tenants of Prosperity** (*72*

ga jouh ha), a district-focused comedy about competitive shop owners, directed by Eric Tsang, Patrick Kong and Chung Shu-kai. And Felix Chong's **Once a Gangster** (*Fei sa fung jung jyun*), about two hoodlums hoping to go straight, subverted and refreshed the triad genre, once a staple of 1990s cinema.

These key, smaller-budget pictures take a pass on the mainland China market, or at least have no hope of a wide release there. The move frees up creative freedom for distinctly local themes. It also avoids censorship that, in the all-ages-only mainland system, covers not just political or sexual content, but can also rule out basic genre fodder like ghosts. Digital-filmmaking technologies also ensure films screen more efficiently and government financial support is becoming more prominent. Through the Film Development Fund, the government can back a portion of a medium-scale production's budget. Financing is generally capped at 35%, enough to get a project moving or allow the producers to forgo China.

Also of note are changes to Hong Kong–China co-production rules, such as the move to allow Hong Kong films to play in Guangdong province in Cantonese, thus preserving their wordplay and character. Meanwhile, some filmmakers are becoming far more active in promoting mid-budget pictures at home, such as getting stars to turn up at regular screenings to meet and greet audiences. It is also encouraging that quality films are increasingly being rewarded with a decent buzz around release time.

Any upswing in positive word of mouth is a good thing for the film industry, which has been dogged since the mid-1990s by local audiences shunning small-scale domestic fare. The situation is still precarious, with weak scripting still a major issue. Take **The Storm Warriors** (*Fung wan II*), from Oxide and Danny Pang. Despite being a bombastic saga of good battling evil in a green-screen fantasyland, audiences tired of the unimaginative storytelling. The Pangs' subsequent **The**

Oxide and Danny Pang's **The Child's Eye 3D**

Child's Eye 3D (*Tung ngan*), a horror show about kids in a haunted Bangkok hotel, was also undermined by weak writing.

The mainland market remains mixed for Hong Kong filmmakers. High-budget screen thrills keep coming, thanks to cross-border funding and the potential to reach large Chinese audiences. Yet problems in co-productions remain in wide-ranging censorship and awkward attempts at meeting mainland tastes. Just look at Wilson Yip's **Ip Man 2** (*Yip Man 2*), a biopic about Bruce Lee's '50s martial-arts mentor, which stands on historically shaky ground, or Andrew Lau's Shanghai-set, pre–World War II superhero action film, **Legend of the Fist: Return of Chen Zhen** (*Jing mo fung wan Chen Zhen*). Top-class martial-arts choreography brought in large crowds for both releases in Hong Kong and China, but their jingoistic climaxes (pitting heroes against the British and Japanese, respectively) seemed geared mainly toward mainland viewers more used to an overtly patriotic message.

Rifts in audience taste also turned up in the lower-budget arena. Lee Lik-chee's **Flirting Scholar 2** (*Tong Ba-fu dim Chau Heung 2*) and Chung Shu-kai's **Adventure of the King** (*Lung fung dim*), two nonsensical and loosely connected period screwball comedies, may have been conceived to go down a treat in China, but in Hong Kong they were met with audience silence and poor attendance. And Derek Yee, who could normally be relied on for detailed thrillers and working-class romances,

let down local audiences with the bland gun-buff-themed policier, **Triple Tap** (*Cheung wong ji wong*). Poor word-of-mouth hurt the picture in Hong Kong, yet mainland audiences propelled it to strong returns.

Other pictures hit their mark in both markets, however, preserving Hong Kong style without stumbling under ham-fisted screenplay twists aimed at pleasing large audiences and Chinese authorities. Dante Lam directed **Fire of Conscience** (*Fo lung*) and **Stool Pigeon** (*Sin yan*). *Fire of Conscience* saw a down-and-out Hong Kong policeman tangle with corrupt officers and visiting bomb-makers, while *Stool Pigeon* pitted a cop and his informer against jewel thieves. Both films' action set-pieces were big-screen sensations and mainland-friendly elements were cleverly integrated into moral grey areas and complex characterisation.

Teddy Chen's **Bodyguards and Assassins**

Teddy Chen took historical epics to new heights with **Bodyguards and Assassins** (*Sup yuet wai sing*), a taut thriller set in Hong Kong at the start of the 1900s, as hit men plan to kill visiting revolutionary Sun Yat-sen. Chen spent a decade developing the script and getting the elaborate production off the ground — an enormous set was built to re-create old city blocks — and the attention to detail shone through. Other Hong Kong filmmakers are also finding critical success with mainland Chinese period works. Director Tsui Hark returned to top form with **Detective Dee and the Mystery of the Phantom Flame** (*Dik Yan-kit ji tung tin dai gwok*), a taut whodunit about an assassination

Tsui Hark's **Detective Dee and the Mystery of the Phantom Flame**

plot, and John Woo produced and had a hand in directing (with Taiwan's Su Chao-pin) **Reign of Assassins** (*Gim yu*), about warriors tracking down an ancient relic, which became a throwback to older swordplay cinema.

Zipping forward to more contemporary stories, Wing Shya and Tony Chan's **Hot Summer Days** (*Chuen sing yit luen yit lat lat*) combined multiple romances in Hong Kong and mainland locales, straddling age groups and film techniques (from effects-laden fantasy to animated whimsy) with ease. The pop sensibility worked, earning 20th Century Fox a strong reception for its first Chinese-language production.

2010 drew to a close with Hong Kong filmgoers awaiting pictures as diverse as Wong Kar-wai's **The Grandmasters** (*Yat doi jung si*), based on the same martial-arts mentor covered in the Ip Man series, and Christopher Sun's classical softcore flick **3D Sex and Zen** (*3D yuk po tyun ji gik lok bo gaam*). And while period action spectacles were assured in the likes of Peter Chan's martial-arts saga **Wu Xia** (*Mou hap*), new works from Johnnie To and Soi Cheang were set to do their bit in keeping modern-day Hong Kong stories covered.

TIM YOUNGS is a Hong Kong-based writer and programme consultant for Italy's Udine Far East Film Festival.

The year's best films
Gallants (Clement Cheng and Derek Kwok)
Bodyguards and Assassins (Teddy Chen)
Lover's Discourse (Derek Tsang and Jimmy Wan)
Dream Home (Pang Ho-cheung)
The Drunkard (Freddie Wong)

Quote of the year
'Many of the medium-budgeted local productions released in early 2010 succeeded through good word of mouth, a sign of quality. It's significant for Hong Kong cinema's creative revival since it means films that target local audiences do not equate to poor quality or lacklustre box office.' GARY MAK, *Broadway Cinematheque director and HKAFF organiser*

Directory
All Tel/Fax numbers begin (+852)
Hong Kong Film Archive, 50 Lei King Rd, Sai Wan Ho. Tel: 2739 2139. Fax: 2311 5229. www.filmarchive.gov.hk.
Film Services Office, 40/F, Revenue Tower, 5 Gloucester Road, Wan Chai. Tel: 2594 5745. Fax: 2824 0595. www.fso-tela.gov.hk.
Federation of Hong Kong Filmmakers, 2/F, 35 Ho Man Tin St, Ho Man Tin, Kowloon. Tel: 2194 6955. Fax: 2194 6255. www.hkfilmmakers.com.
Hong Kong Film Directors' Guild, 2/F, 35 Ho Man Tin St, Ho Man Tin, Kowloon. Tel: 2760 0331. Fax: 2713 2373. www.hkfdg.com.
Hong Kong International Film Festival Society, 21/F, Millennium City 3, 370 Kwun Tong Rd, Kwun Tong. Tel: 2970 3300. Fax 2970 3011. www.hkiff.org.hk
Hong Kong, Kowloon and New Territories Motion Picture Industry Association (MPIA), Unit 1201, New Kowloon Plaza, 38 Tai Kok Tsui Rd, Kowloon. Tel: 2311 2692. Fax: 2311 1178. www.mpia.org.hk
Hong Kong Film Awards Association, Room 1601–1602, Austin Tower, 22–26 Austin Ave, Tsim Sha Tsui, Kowloon. Tel: 2367 7892. Fax: 2723 9597. www.hkfaa.com.

Hungary John Cunningham

It has been an uneven and difficult year for the Hungarian film industry, although it did appear to be riding the recession relatively well. However, the domestic box office is dominated by US imports to an extent unprecedented in recent years, while foreign production companies are queuing up to use Hungarian facilities and expertise, bringing with them much-needed capital.

State support for Hungarian films continues to shrink. There has been a distinct reduction in production and also talk of a proposed two-tier structure of filmmaking, with home filmmakers definitely on the bottom level. The economic health of the industry thus can be said to be thriving or sickly, depending on your stance. But, whatever problems there may be, new talent emerges all the time and 2010 has seen some interesting developments.

Szabolcs Hajdu's **Bibliotheque Pascal**

A good place to start, as always, is with the films shown at the Hungarian Film Week, held annually in February. A total of 16 features, 10 films for TV and 30 documentaries were in competition. Although no single film stood out, the coveted Golden Reel Award went to **Bibliotheque Pascal** (*Biblioteheque Pascal*) by Szabolcs Hajdu, an already established

Zsombor Dyga's **Question in Details**

and accomplished director whose career is currently experiencing an upward surge. The film's title is misleading – the Bibliotheque is not a library but a brothel, located in Liverpool, where the prostitutes, mainly Eastern Europeans, pose as literary characters. The Best Director award went to Zsombor Dyga for **Question in Details** (*Köntörfalak*), in which a blind date goes wrong and we follow the consequences. Dyga shared the prize with Robért Pejó, who directed **The Camera Murderer** (*Látogatás*). Although it was later to prove one of the most popular of this year's crop, Dénes Orosz's **Polygamy** (*Poligamy*), a strange tale of a man who discovers he can, more or less, sleep with any woman he wants,

Robért Pejó's **The Camera Murderer**

failed to win any prizes. Diana Groó has been consistently turning out interesting films for some years now and she did not disappoint with **Vespa**, about a young Gypsy boy who wins a national draw for a Vespa scooter. He travels to Budapest to claim his prize, which is where his troubles begin. Screening out of competition was veteran director Károly Makk's **The Way You Are** (*Igy ahogy vagytok*). Starring popular actors György Cserhalmi and Sándor Csányi, his film concerns a new town mayor who attempts to fight local corruption. The Best Documentary award, the Judit Ember Prize, went to Tamás Almási's very popular **Puskás Hungary**, an engaging biography of the brilliant footballer Ferenc Puskás, captain of the 'Arany Csapot' (the Golden Team of the 1950s), and arguably the most famous Hungarian in the world. The prize was shared with László Csáki's **Tin City** (*Bádogváros*), which looks at a particular district in the city of Miskolc.

Diana Groó's **Vespa**

Away from the Film Week limelight, Béla Tarr's long-awaited **The Turin Horse** did not make its hoped-for debut at Cannes, but is slated for release in the very near future. And Hungary's best-known director, István Szabó, continues to work on his latest film, **The Door** (*Az ajtó*), an adaptation of the novel of the same name by Magda Szabó (no relation), starring Helen Mirren. It is also set for a release very soon. The film is Szabó's latest re-working of a Hungarian novel, following his failure to secure sufficient funding for the proposed adaptation of Antal Szerb's *Journey by Moonlight* (*Utas es holdvilág*).

Agnes Kocsis' **Adrienn Pál**

Kornél Mundruczó, whose star continues to rise inexorably, premiered his latest film, **Tender Son – The Frankenstein Project** (*Szelíd teremetés – A Frankenstein-Terv*), at Cannes earlier in the year. Although the film impressed critics it failed to attract the acclaim of his previous offering, *Delta*. Also premiering at Cannes was **Adrienn Pál** (*Pál Adrienn*) by Agnes Kocsis, whose first feature length film, *Fresh Air*, made a major impact in 2006.

The Korda Studios at Etyek, on the outskirts of Budapest, continue to attract foreign film productions, although it now has a rival. Despite the recession, the $76m Raleigh Studios, boasting nine sound stages, is Hungary's latest filmmaking centre to open and is already doing brisk business. A partnership between the US Raleigh Studios and Hungary's Origo group, this huge facility looks set to become a major rival to Korda, with production on 20th Century Fox's romantic comedy, **Monte Carlo**, directed by Tom Bezucha and starring Selena Gomez and Katie Cassidy, beginning on 5 May. Not to be outdone, Korda are currently working on the new Showtime TV series, *The Borgias*, directed by Michael Hirst and starring Jeremy Irons. Whether or not two large studio complexes will be able to survive in the current economic climate in such a relatively small country remains to be seen. However, studio heads are enthusiastic about future prospects, aided by the generous provisions of Hungary's Film Law and recent devaluations of the Hungarian currency, which are a great financial boost to foreign companies. Other films being shot in and around Budapest include the New Line/Warner Brothers exorcism-horror production, **The Rite**, starring Anthony Hopkins. Hungary has now outstripped its main competitor, the Czech Republic, in attracting foreign film production. But a new rival, Romania, is emerging to the east.

All of which suggests that the overall picture for Hungary look quite rosy, although the Hungarian box-office figures for the last 12 months makes for rather grim reading. From 1st August 2009 to 31st August 2010, the best-selling Hungarian film was *Polygamy*, but that only managed number 31 in the charts. All other slots are held by American films with, inevitably, *Avatar* occupying first place. So far, *Polygamy* has been seen by 154,074 people, a paltry figure compared with *Avatar's* 1,182,669. This scenario is bad enough, bbut the recent news that the government has withdrawn a substantial amount of funding for domestic film production could be disastrous. And the HHungarian Film Week for 2011 has been postponed. Given such developments, it seems highly questionable as to whether the Hungarian film industry can maintain its present output; Hungarian films, many of which are now international co-productions of one kind or another, tend not to travel very well (although the bulk of the blame for this must lie with foreign distribution companies), despite their evident quality and popularity on the international film festival circuit.

Szabolcs Hajdu's **Bibliotheque Pascal**

The year's best films
Bibliotheque Pascal (Szabolcs Hajdu)
Tender Son – The Frankenstein Project
(Kornél Mundruzcó)
Vespa (Diana Groó)
The Way You Are (Károly Makk)
Puskás Hungary (Tamás Almási)

Quote of the year
'The next step for Budapest is to truly become one of Europe's main filmmaking centres.'
TAMÁS CSAPÓ, *President of Korda Studios.*

Directory
All Tel/Fax numbers begin (+36)
Association of Hungarian Filmmakers, Városligeti fasor 38. Budapest, Hungary-1068, filmszov@t-online.hu
Association of Hungarian Producers, Eszter utca 7/B. Budapest, Hungary-1022, mail@mpsz.org.hu, www.mpsz.org.hu
Hungarian Directors Guild, Ráday utca 31/K., Budapest, Hungary-1092, mrc@filmjus.hu, www.mmrc.hu
Hungarian Film Alliance (Magyar Filmunió), 38 Városligeti fasor, Budapest, Hungary - 1068. Tel: (1) 351 7760, 351 7761 Fax: (1) 352 6734. filmunio@filunion.hu
Hungarian Independent Producers Associations, Róna utca 174. Budapest, Hungary-1145, eurofilm@t-online.hu
Hungarian National Film Archive, Budakeszi út 51/E. Budapest, Hungary-1021, www.filmintezet.hu
Motion Picture Public Foundation of Hungary, Városligeti fasor 38. Budapest, Hungary-1068, mmka@mmka.hu, www.mmka.hu
National Film Office, Wesselényi utca 16. Budapest, Hungary-1075, info@filmoffice.hu, www.nationalfilmoffice.hu

JOHN CUNNINGHAM is Senior Lecturer in the Department of Stage and Screen at Sheffield Hallam University, UK. He is the Principal Editor of the journal *Studies in Eastern European Cinema* and his book on István Szabó will be published in 2011 by Wallflower Press.

Iceland Eddie Cockrell

'There is confidence that Icelandic cinema will survive, and thrive,' concluded last year's overview. While the latter is true, at least aesthetically, the former is a troubling question still very much up in the air and, agonisingly, just out of the industry's own control.

Ragnar Bragason's **Bjarnfreðarson**

The year began with a bang: the keenly anticipated spin-off feature of a remarkably successful TV trilogy. Director Ragnar Bragason's **Bjarnfreðarson** surfed the local zeitgeist with its deadpan saga of three very different misfits, led by the oblivious blowhard and self-proclaimed 'trained pedagogue' of the title (played by local comedian Jón Gnarr, nearly unrecognisable in the role). The film is a near-perfect storm of exaggerated grotesquery and social unease, tapping as it does into the modern, volatile Icelandic mix of economic fear and can-do spirit. Though perhaps too local in its focus to travel much overseas, it is nevertheless set to be remade for American television.

So popular was comedian Gnarr – the film defeated *Avatar* during its holiday weekend bow – that in June his satirical political machine, Best Party, promising 'sustainable transparency', won Reykjavik's municipal elections and he was installed as mayor; locals now call the town 'Gnarrenburg'. Can-do spirit indeed.

On a more serious, bittersweet note, New Year's Day saw Friðrik Þór Friðriksson unveil his latest drama, **Mamma Gógó**. The film is a quiet triumph of autobiographical storytelling, as the mother (Kristbjörg Kjeld) of a successful film director (Hilmir Snaer Gudnason) struggling with cash flow finds herself receding into Alzheimer's disease. Infused with a love of cinema and life, the film speaks eloquently to Friðriksson's commitment to his art and ranks alongside *Children of Nature* as one of his finest achievements. Like the earlier

film, it screened at numerous international festivals and was selected to represent Iceland in the Best Foreign Film category at the next Academy Awards.

Speaking of prizes, the delayed Eddas were finally held in late February and, to no one's surprise, *Bjarnfreðarson* swept the night, winning best film, director, screenplay, cinematography, lead actor and costume design. *Mamma Gógó* won for best actress, musical score and set design. By the time of the ceremony, it is estimated 25% of Iceland's 300,000 inhabitants had seen Bragason's film.

Then, disaster: as they had vowed to do in late 2009, the embattled Icelandic government slashed domestic film funding by just over a third. The offshore producer tax credit remains at an industry-leading 20%, but the blow is nevertheless a crippling one. 'The year we reached the goal of being a small industry it all came crashing down,' a clearly frustrated Bragason told icelandonscreen.com's Ben Hopkins. 'I'm hoping the government sees the errors of their actions. They still have a chance of correcting their mistake.'

Baltasar Kormákur's **Inhale**

Coincidentally, the bulk of the year's domestic releases occurred in September and October 2010. Such was the domestic logjam that, in late October, four of the top 10 films at the local box office were Icelandic. Amongst those were **Jitters**, debuting director Baldvin Z's confident ensemble drama about a teenaged boy's sexual indecision; *Jar City* director

Baltasar Kormákur's gritty, English-language thriller **Inhale**; Árni Ólafur Ásgeirsson's thoughtful fishing-boat drama **Brim**; and director Bragi Thór Hinriksson's **The Secret Spell**, the second outing in the immensely successful, kiddie-oriented Sveppi series.

Perhaps the year's most well-rounded and satisfying feature doubles as a cautionary reminder of why the funding of short films and documentaries is so critical to any successful industry. In 2007, young director Grímur Hákonarson won the Edda award for his short film **Wrestling**, which subsequently travelled to over 20 international film festivals. Hákonarson's first feature, **Summerland**, fulfils the promise on display in his short. To save the haunted house he's made of his home in order to attract the tourist trade, husband and father Oskar (Kjartan Gudjónsson) sells the elf stone in his back yard to a German art collector. Traumatised by this, his medium wife, Lara (Ólafía Hrönn Jónsdóttir), lapses into a coma that sends the hapless Oskar into inept damage control. The mellow comedy and warm humanism on display is reminiscent of Bill Forsyth at his finest, as these local heroes try to get along in a mysterious world.

Also screening, with various degrees of success, were: *Country Wedding* director Valdis Óskarsdóttir's sophomore feature, the quirky but ill-conceived trailer-park comedy **King's Road**; the agreeably low-rent concert documentary **Backyard**; the independently produced supernatural thriller **The Messenger**; and Gunnar B. Gudmundsson's coming-of-age drama, **Hullaballoo**.

Valdis Óskarsdóttir's **King's Road**

In all, business was brisk. The nine full-length domestic dramatic features released in 2010 nearly doubled the previous year's five. The domestic box office for all releases between January and October was approximately US$11.3 million, up significantly from the 2009 total of US$10.2 million and well within shouting distance of 2008's US$13 million take. Not bad for an industry struggling with so much adversity and unease.

The government's evisceration isn't immediately fatal, as almost a dozen films are nearing completion. Kormákur is finishing the Icelandic survival drama, **The Deep**, while *The Amazing Truth About Queen Raquela* director Olaf de Fleur has three films in post-production (the action-drama **City State**, the dramatic comedy **Polite People** and, as producer, the documentary **Adequate Beings**). The long-in-production animated epic, **Legends of Valhalla: Thor** – now in 3D! – is slated for late 2011.

Mindful of its precarious position, yet sincere in its commitment to cinema, the industry awarded a special honorary Edda to 'the Icelandic nation, for its strong support of Icelandic films through the years'. Now, more than ever, that support is vital. It is hoped the government will recognise this need and reverse its decision, allowing the Icelandic film industry to get back to the serious – and seriously successful – business of entertaining both its own loyal citizenry and audiences the world over.

The year's best films
Summerland (Grímur Hákonarson)
Mamma Gógó (Friðrik Þór Friðriksson)
Bjarnfreðarson (Ragnar Bragason)

Quote of the year
'I don't know if we can teach the world anything new but we can try to keep up a conversation with it... I think we are pretty good at making films look more expensive than they are. I am sure someone could learn something from that. It is a very small industry which can be both a strength and a weakness

at the same time.' BALTASAR KORMÁKUR, *speaking with icelandonscreen's Ben Hopkins.*

Directory
All Tel/Fax numbers begin (+354)
Association of Film-Rights Holder in Iceland, Laugavegur 182, 105 Reykjavík. Fax: 588 3800. smais@smais.is. www.smais.is.
Film Directors Guild of Iceland, Hverfisgata 54, 101 Reykjavík. Fax: 562 7171. ragnarb@hive.is. http://skl-filmdirectors.net.
Film in Iceland Agency, Borgartún 35, 105 Reykjavík. Tel: 561 5200. Fax: 511 4040. info@filminiceland.com. www.filminiceland.com.
Icelandic Film Centre, Hverfisgata 54, 101 Reykjavík. Tel: 562 3580. Fax: 562 7171. info@icelandicfilmcentre.is. www.icelandicfilmcentre.is.
Icelandic Film Makers Association, Hverfisgata 54, PO Box 1652, 121 Reykjavík. formadur@filmmakers.is. www.filmmakers.is.
Icelandic Film & Television Academy/EDDA Awards, Hverfisgata 54, 101 Reykjavík. Tel: 562 3580. Fax: 562 7171. hilmar@eddan.is. http://eddan.is.
National Film Archive of Iceland, Hvaleyrarbraut 13, 220 Hafnarfjordur. Tel: 565 5993. Fax: 565 5994. kvikmyndasafn@kvikmyndasafn.is.
SÍK - Association of Icelandic Film Producers, Hverfisgata 54, PO Box 5367, 125 Reykjavík. sik@producers.is. www.producers.is.
Statistics Iceland, Borgartún 21a, 150 Reykjavík. Tel: 528 1000. Fax: 528 1099. information@statice.is. www.statice.is/statistics/culture/cinemas.

EDDIE COCKRELL is a film critic and consulting programmer whose reviews and movie writing have appeared in *Variety*, *the Washington Post*, *the Sydney Morning Herald* and *the Australian*.

Friðrik Þór Friðriksson's **Mamma Gógó**

ABU DHABI FILM COMMISSION

India Uma Da Cunha

Two things are currently happening within the Indian film industry. As the country grows in economic stature (an estimated GDP growth rate of over 8% in 2010/2011), it catches the eye of foreign investment. Equally, Indian industry eyes mainstream cinema in the United States and elsewhere. It is looking to move beyond loyal Diaspora audiences.

Danny Boyle's *Slumdog Millionaire* raised the buzz around India many decibel points a couple of years ago and the industry has since expanded in various directions. Filmmakers from around the world are scouting locations here, to explore universal themes and to examine the country's unique culture and history. An 'Indo-Anglian' genre may be emerging, with top directors and stars from both sides. The lure is an expanding box-office with huge domiciled Indian and Asian populations.

In recent times, India has welcomed a dizzying list of film celebrities. Julia Roberts shot in Rajasthan for *Eat Love and Pray*, with India as her source for spiritual healing. British director John Madden and Judi Dench, Tom Wilkinson, Dev Patel and Maggie Smith are in Jaipur shooting *Best Exotic Marigold Hotel*, based on the Deborah Moggach novel. Roland Joffe has started filming *Singularity*, which links an Indian past with a British present. The alluring Bipasha Basu has bagged the lead, alongside Chris Pine and Josh Hartnett.

The press declared that the much-hyped *Mission Impossible 4*, starring Tom Cruise and Anil Kapoor, would be shot in India. From Hong Kong, the celebrated Ang Lee made headlines when he introduced his Indian find, 17-year-old Suraj Sharma, for the main role in *Life of Pi*, based on Yann Martel's Man Booker prize-winning novel. In *The Driver*, by Bill Duke, Mexican Selma Hayek will be the Indian wife of veteran baddie Gulshan Griver. Al Pacino was scouting in the northern hills for *Love Me Forever*. Bruce Willis was said to be on his way, with a project in mind. Drew Barrymore is slated to star in a Hindi film, *The Lifestyle*. Pamela Anderson was mobbed when she arrived in Mumbai to appear on a Hindi reality TV show. And noted director, Vidhu Vinod Chopra, was rumoured to have signed Nicolas Cage for his film *Broken Horses*. This heady list continues…

My Name is Khan

India's impressive international footprint is backed by financial alliances. In mid-November, Rajiv Dalal, Managing Director of the Motion Picture Association of America, announced the formation of the Los Angeles-Indian Film Council. It would promote the making of Indian films in California. Los Angeles is a favoured destination, as was shown in **Kites** and **My Name is Khan**, as well as 2009's *Damn Love*.

The drive for global reach has its downside. It may cost India its unique cinematic identity, which has withstood the onslaught of Hollywood and Hong Kong for decades. Non-Indian films have had a minuscule share of the country's huge audience. But the gap is narrowing. From roughly 3% ten years ago, the audience for foreign films rose to 5% in 2008 and is close to 12% in 2010.

Indian audiences are more inclined than ever to watch foreign films, especially if they are dubbed. There are also at least five TV channels exclusively screening foreign films and international releases are becoming more frequent. A testament to this shift is the third Narnia film, **The Voyage of the Dawn Treader**, which will premiere in India on December 3, a week ahead of the US release. Vijay Singh, CEO of Fox Star Studios, India commented, 'We are delighted to offer our *Narnia* fans this opportunity in 3D and multiple Indian languages.'

Mid-November saw one of 2010's biggest releases, Sanjay Leela Bhansali's **Request** (Guzaarish), starring top-liners Hrithik Roshan and Aishwaria Rai. It tells the story of a young quadriplegic seeking an end to his life, who is caught between two women, his lawyer and his nurse. It was released on 1,000 prints on the same day as *Harry Potter and the Deathly Hallows Part I* (around 400 prints). Surprising for an Indian audience, the Potter film had more advanced bookings.

Hindi blockbusters are getting to be less and less Indian in content, dress code, music, language (often a rapid-fire mix of English and Hindi) and even locations. Most of them are now shot outside India. With the soft-pedaling

Sanjay Leela Bhansali's **Request**

of Indian themes of this kind, such influences on and off screen will likely weaken over time. Current marketing practices also cause some concern, with the film industry on a headlong spending binge.

Also in mid-November, two industry leaders, Yash Chopra and Ronnie Screwvala, gathered together key individuals to evaluate the industry's shortsightedness. But the Indian film industry is not known for discipline or networking. Vision and strategising rest with some eight or ten top stars who demand astronomic fees, no matter that some 80% of the films fail to light up the box-office.

Mani Ratnam's **Raavan**

In what is becoming a predictably depressing routine, the first nine months of 2010 were marked by a series of commercial failures. Mani Ratnam led the way with his starry bonanza, **Raavan**, a modern-day adaptation of the epic 'Ramayan', starring Aishwaria Rai and Abhishek Bachchan. Other surprise flops were Anurag Basu's highly publicised *Kites*, an embarrassingly poor story of a man (Hrithik Roshan) pursued by criminals into the Mexican desert because of his love for a local woman (Barbara Mori), and Abbas Tyrewala's **Lies Are Okay** (*Jhoota Hi Sahi*). Shot in London, with John Abraham in the lead, it follows an angst-ridden woman in love with a geeky bookstore employee who anonymously offers helpline advice.

By the middle of the year, only one film had seen some success at the box office. The

Tamil film **Enthiran** (the Hindi version was called *Robot*) starred the demi-god of southern screens, Rajnikanth, as an andro-humanoid robot with a prodigious memory processor.

High hopes rested on 2010's last quarter, with its festivals and box-office spikes. The huge line-up of big titles leads to a scramble for vantage dates, forcing two or three films to open on the same day. Both Dharma Productions' **We Are Family** (a remake of *Stepmom*) and Arbaaz Khan Productions' **Fearless** (*Dabanng*) were released over September's Muslim festival of Eid. The former sank into oblivion, whereas Abhinav Kashyap's directorial debut turned out to be a surprising hit. Macho-star Salmaan Khan plays a fearless police officer whose alienation from his family adversely affects his behavior.

In November, two acclaimed films hit the screens over Diwali, the Festival of Lights. Vipul Shah's **Action Replay**, a sci-fi comedy, flopped despite the presence of Aishwaria Rai and Akshay Kumar. The other, Rohit Shetty's **Gol Maal 3** (the title translates as *Hotchpotch*) did brisk business. Ajay Devgan starred in the story of the theft of a necklace and a woman who suspects her husband is having an affair.

Thanksgiving and Christmas, holidays that are anything but Indian, are now key release dates for potential commercial successes. Kunal Kohli's much-touted **After the Break** (*Break ke Baad*) stars Ranbir Kapoor and Dipika Padukone, and was timed for Thanksgiving, with its eyes trained on an overseas market. Three successive Christmas hits from Aamir Khan were followed by the success of **Three Idiots**, India's highest-grossing Bollywood film. This slick entertainer urges students to rely on their own instincts and not be constrained by staid elders.

However, it is the successful art-house film that heartens the most. There has been a happy sea change in content and creativity from the better-financed independent film in centres such as Mumbai, Kolkata and Kerala, as well as the struggling film cultures in other regional languages.

In Mumbai, younger directors with a strong, individual style have emerged. Their films are linked to a contemporary reality. **The Flight** (*Udaan*) surfaced at Cannes in *Un Certain Regard* selection, albeit seven years after its completion. This debut work by Vikramjit Motwane is a study of growing up, in which an adolescent attempts to free himself from an abusive parent.

Two films premiered at the Toronto International Film Festival: Aamir Bashir's *Harud*, set in Kashmir, in which a young man's existence is threatened from all angles, and Siddharth Srinivasan's **Soul of Sand** (*Pairon Talle*), which unfolds in the rural outskirts of Delhi and details the degradation meted out to a factory watchman by his superiors.

Deepankar Bannerjee's **Love, Sex aur Dhoka**

It was Anuraag Kashyap who, some 15 years ago, was the leading light in the new energy and spirit of Indian cinema. Now a familiar face on festival circuits, his films dissect current social norms and lifestyles, particularly those in which young people find themselves. His latest, *The Girl In Yellow Boots*, which screened in Venice and Toronto, follows a young girl in the murky under-city where she ekes out a living. Another influential director is Deepankar Bannerjee. His **Love, Sex aur Dhoka** bristles with energy as it satirises the news media and social voyeurism.

Kiran Rao's **Dhobi Ghat**

Powerful inspiration and support for the art-house film has come most unexpectedly from the heart of Bollywood itself. Superstar and powerful producer Aamir Khan backed two films by debuting female directors. Anusha Rizvi's **Peepli Live**, which premiered at Sundance, followed by Berlin, and has had a measured success since, features no musical numbers. It looks at village life and the media with a wickedly satirical eye. Aamir Khan's astute marketing earned the film a profit in a Bollywood-driven market. The other film, directed by Kiran Rao, Aamir Khan's wife, is **Dhobi Ghat**. It premiered at Toronto to positive reviews. It looks, gently and poignantly, at life on the backstreets of Mumbai. Aamir Khan plays a lead role in the film, but has shied away from publicity, ensuring his wife holds centre stage. The film is slated for release early in 2011.

The year's best films
Harud (Aamir Bashir)
Dhobi Ghat (Kiran Rao)
Udaan (Vikramjit Motwane)
Peepli Live (Anusha Rizvi)
Memories in March (Sanjoy Nag)

Quote of the year
'I will never endorse fairness creams or cigarettes. Promoting fairness creams is like promoting racism and casteism… Generally, top heroes like SRK [Shahrukh Khan] should be telling people that it does not matter if one is fair or dark and all that matters is the brain. But it is really alarming that these very heroes are promoting casteism (by endorsing such products).' *Actor* ABHAY DEOL.

Directory
All Tel/Fax numbers begin (+91)
Film & Television Institute of India, Law College Rd, Pune 411 004. Tel: (20) 543 1817/3016/0017. www.ftiindia.com.
Film Federation of India, B/3 Everest Bldg, Tardeo, Bombay 400 034. Tel/Fax: (22) 2351 5531. Fax: 2352 2062. supransen.filmfed@hotmail.com. www.filmfed.org.
Film Producers Guild of India, G-1, Morya House, Veera Industrial Estate, OShiwara Link Road, Andheri (W), Mumbai 400 053. Tel: (22) 6691 0662/2673 3065. Fax: (22) 6691 0661. guild@filmtvguildindia.org. www.filmtvguildindia.org.
National Film Archive of India, P.O. Box No. 810, Law College Rd, Pune 411 004. Tel: (20) 2565 2259. Fax: (20) 2567 0027. nfaipune@gmail.com. www.nfaipune.gov.in.
National Film Development Corporation Ltd, Discovery of India Bldg, Nehru Centre, 6th Floor, Dr Annie Besant Rd, Worli, Bombay 400 018. Tel: (22) 2496 5643/2435 5069/2494 9856. Fax: 2496 5646. nfdc@nfdcindia.com. www.nfdcindia.com.
Central Board of Film Certification, Bharat Bhavan, 91 E Walkeshwar Road, Mumbai 400 006. Tel: (22) 2362 5770 Fax: (22) 2369 0083. rocbfcmum@rediffmail.com

UMA DA CUNHA is based in Mumbai. She edits the quarterly *Film India Worldwide* and works as a researcher and freelance journalist on film and also as a programmer for international film festivals, specialising in new Indian cinema. She organises specialised film industry events.

Vikramjit Motwane's **The Flight**

Iran Amir Esfandiari & Kamyar Mohsenin

The main problem in Iran's fast-growing film industry remains the same: the increase in the annual rate of productions when there are not enough venues to screen the films. Unofficial statistics indicate that over 100 features are completed and ready for release in Iran each year, a country with a population of 70 million to watch them. But there are a mere 265 cinemas in operation throughout the country. Between January and October 2010, 43 national productions and six foreign films were released in Iran, and an additional five cineplexes were built.

Most of the theatrically released films are once again escapist, with popular comedies attracting audiences and critical opprobrium in equal measure. Among these comedies, Behrouz Afkhami's **Saint Petersburg** (*San Petersbourg*) stands out. The story of a duo searching for the lost treasure of the last tsar, what begins as a witty, crowd-pleasing comedy loses all humour by the end.

Interestingly, the year's biggest commercial success was not a comedy. One of the most expensive projects in the history of Iranian cinema, Shahriar Bahrani's **The Kingdom**

Shahriar Bahrani's **The Kingdom of Solomon**

of Solomon (*Molk-e Soleiman*) is an epic inspired by the holy stories, focusing on the struggle of the Prophet Solomon (PBUH) against haunting, unearthly creatures. It netted US$2 million at the box office. Although some critics highlighted the film's weak script, the film nevertheless presents a new dimension of Iranian cinema, particularly in the use of special effects and sound design.

Mojtaba Raie's **Iraq, The Evening of the 10th Day**

But the main attraction of Iranian cinema this year was the screening of previously banned films at the 28th Fajr International Film Festival and their subsequent theatrical release. The winner of the national competition, Ebrahim Hatamikia's **As the Color of Purple** (*Beh rang-e arghavan*), depicts a love/hate relationship between a secret agent and the daughter of a fugitive, set against the stunning backdrop of Northern Iran. Contemplating the conflict between human desires and patriotic duties, it is a moving tale about the relationship between those who watch and the ones they are watching. Religious concerns were evident in Mojtaba Raie's **Iraq, The Evening of the 10th Day** (*Aragh, asr-e rouz-e dahom*), a drama shot in a documentary style, which looks at Shiite traditions in contemporary Iraq.

Alireza Raisian's **Love at Forty**

Some of the other highlights of the festival were Alireza Raisian's **Love at Forty** (*Chehel Salegi*), an updated adaptation of the first tale of Rumi, reflecting the labours of love in Iran today; Homayoun Asa'adian's **Gold and Copper** (*Tala va Mes*), which featured some excellent performances and emphasised the importance of life and its greatest values, which usurp traditional rules, particularly when life is hard; and Mohsen Abdolvahab's **Please Do Not Disturb** (*Lotfan mozahem nashavid*), which links three episodes that reflect, with drama and wit, on a series of moral dilemmas experienced by different people (a TV host and his wife, a clergyman and a pickpocket, an old couple and a drug addicted TV repairman and his baby).

Mohsen Abdolvahab's **Please Do Not Disturb**

Gold and Copper and *Please Do Not Disturb* did the rounds on the international film festival circuit. Another banned film screened at Fajr 2010: Tahmineh Milani's **Payback** (*Tasvieh Hesab*) was an official competition entry at the Shanghai Film Festival. Dwelling on four girls released from prison, it shows their

determination to exact blind vengeance on their unfaithful men. It was criticised in Iran for its misandry.

There were two Iranian entries at the Montreal Film Festival. **Tehran, Tehran**, an episodic venture by veteran Dariush Mehrjui and the energetic Mehdi Karampour, details two completely different pictures of the contemporary Iranian metropolis. Mehrjui's opening section, a romantic approach to the city and its relics in the form of a modern fairytale, contrasted, narratively and visually, with a look at the obstacles faced by the independent, youth-music scene in Karampour's closing episode. Majid Barzegar's directorial debut, **Rainy Seasons** (*Fasl-e Baran-ha-ye Mousami*), deals with adolescent dilemmas in a style familiar from the most popular films of New Iranian Cinema.

Dariush Mehrjui and Mehdi Karampour's **Tehran, Tehran**

In Warsaw, Bijan Mirbagheri's **Third Floor** (*Tabagheh-ye Sevvom*), a stagy encounter between an isolated woman and an alienated girl, was screened in the competition section. Meanwhile, Rafi Pitts's **The Hunter** (*Shekarchi*) premiered in the main competition of the Berlinale. A revenge story, it is a film of two incoherent parts. Initially, it shows the failed attempts of an ex-convict to rebuild his life with his wife and daughter, which is clumsily connected, in post-production, to the events following the 2009 election. The shocking news of his wife's death in a shooting incident results in his random killing of a police officer. In the film's second half, Pitts employs a poor

Mehdi Naderi's **Farewell Baghdad**

adaptation of one of Iran's most beloved short stories, about the relationship between a prisoner and two soldiers.

A film by a first-time director, Mehdi Naderi's **Farewell Baghdad** (*Bedoroud Baghdad*), is Iran's submission to the Academy Awards in the Best Foreign Film category. It is an amateurish film depicting the lives of the US soldiers and the Iraqi people in Iraq today.

AMIR ESFANDIARI is Head of International Affairs at Farabi Cinema Foundation. He is a board member of the Asia-Pacific Film Festival and has written and presented various papers and articles on the promotion and marketing of quality films for more than two decades.

KAMYAR MOHSENIN has worked as a film critic and TV host for over 15 years. He is also in charge of Research in International Affairs at the Farabi Cinema Foundation.

The year's best films
Tehran, Tehran (Dariush Mehrjui, Mehdi Karampour)
Love at Forty (Alireza Raisian)
Gold and Copper (Homayoun Asa'adian)
As the Color of Purple (Ebrahim Hatamikia)
Saint Petersburg (Behrouz Afkhami)

Quote of the year
'If the subsidaries are omitted, the film production will be affected severely. A raise of 20 to 30 per cent is predictable in the production expenses, when people have already expressed their complaint from the expensive tickets.' *Film Producer and Critic* ALI MOALLEM.

Directory
All Tel/Fax numbers begin (+98)
Farabi Cinema Foundation – International Affairs, Tel: (21) 22741254. Fax: (21) 22734953. fcf1@dpi.net.ir.
IRIB Media Trade, Tel: (21) 22548032. Fax: (21) 22551914. info@iribmediatrade.com.
Documentary and Experimental Film Center, Tel: (21) 88511241. Fax: (21) 88511242. int@defc.ir.
Iranian Young Cinema Society, Tel: (21) 88773114. Fax: (21) 88779073. intl@iycs.ir.

Ebrahim Hatamikia's **As the Color of Purple**

ABU DHABI FILM COMMISSION

Ireland Donald Clarke

Once again, like their British counterparts across the Sea, Irish filmmakers found themselves worrying about the government's plans to cut investment in the industry. Since the Irish Film Board was reconstituted in 1993, barely a year has gone past without some sage predicting its imminent destruction. Yet, at time of writing, it seemed as if the Board might live to fight another year. The economic devastation has certainly affected the business, as it has every other area of Irish life. After all, one of the most notoriously dysfunctional financial bodies in Europe – Anglo-Irish Bank – was a partner with the Film Board in the Company Development Initiative scheme.

And yet, 2010 was far from a disastrous year for Irish film. Facilities in the Republic and Northern Ireland welcomed an impressive array of big-budget international film and TV productions, including HBO's *Game of Thrones*, the adaptation of George R. R. Martin's fantasy sequence, and Starz' Camelot, yet another TV variation on the Arthurian myth, which utilised both Irish locations and personnel. *Il Divo* director Paolo Sorrentino arrived in Dublin to shoot **This Must be the Place** with Sean Penn. And Rodrigo Garcia brought Glenn Close to Ireland for his period piece, **Albert Nobbs**.

Meanwhile, a low-budget Irish film registered a notable success at the domestic box office. **His & Hers**, Ken Wardrop's delightfully peculiar documentary, examining the lives of women from the Irish midlands, proved to be the most successful documentary in Irish cinemas since Michael Moore's *Fahrenheit 9/11*. Cleverly exploited by Access Cinema, a body devoted to promoting less mainstream films in the provinces, it was that rare commodity that

actually managed to increase its takings after the opening weekend. Later in the year, the DVD release topped the charts, ahead of titles such as *Alice in Wonderland*.

The Jameson Dublin International Film Festival, founded by Michael Dwyer, who sadly died at the start of the year, is the first major film festival of the year. *His & Hers* played there to much acclaim, but the Dublin Film Critics Circle, which hands out gongs every year, awarded the best Irish film prize to Ivan Kavanagh's **The Fading Light**. A stunningly grim piece – much in the mode of Ingmar Bergman – the film is an unrelenting portrait of a family facing up to a mother's imminent death. Patrick O'Donnell's performance as a son with learning difficulties was particularly noteworthy.

Also premiering at the event was Neil Jordan's **Ondine**. A whimsical piece, the picture detailed the adventures of a fisherman, played by a dishevelled Colin Farrell, as he discovers a girl who might be a mermaid in his net. The picture received respectful views, but failed to light up the box office.

Neil Jordan's **Ondine**

Lotte Verbeek's **Nothing Personal**

Mark O'Connor's scrappy **Between the Canals**, a drama set in working-class Dublin, marked the arrival of a rough, developing talent, while Lotte Verbeek's **Nothing Personal** and Mira Fornay's **Foxes** confirmed that young directors from mainland Europe could bring fresh light to Irish situations.

Alicia Duffy's **All Good Children**

Cannes was a quiet time for Irish cinema. The only nominally Irish production competing in any of the main events was Alicia Duffy's **All Good Children**, which turned up at the Directors' Fortnight. Co-produced by the Irish Film Board, featuring a largely Irish cast, it followed troubled children in a remote area of France. The film proved to be an impressive slice of post-Tarkovsky, high-brow melancholy. It received a limited commercial release at the close of 2010.

The big event for Irish features remains the Galway Film Fleadh in July. This year, once again, domestic directors defied the miserable mood and delivered a surprisingly diverse array of original pictures.

Tom Hall, an experienced TV professional, presented the insidiously creepy sex drama **Sensation**. Following a lonely man as he opens a brothel in the country, the picture is as weird as it is original. It starred Domhnall Gleeson.

P. J. Dillon's **Rewind** stars Amy Huberman as a middle-class woman whose awful past comes back to haunt her. The film (though short) has enough slick grace to secure some sort of commercial life.

Carmel Winters' **Snap**

Carmel Winters, a gifted playwright, directed a terrifying, impressively experimental film entitled **Snap**. Beautifully shot by Kate McCullough, one of the nation's most promising young cinematographers, the film follows a mother whose past features a bizarre tragedy, the details of which emerge slowly.

There was much applause for **My Brothers**, the directorial debut of Paul Fraser, a frequent collaborator of Shane Meadows, about siblings who seek to replace their dying father's watch.

Paul Fraser's **My Brothers**

The celebrations over *My Brothers* were modest compared with the whooping that greeted Risteard Ó Domhnaill's **The Pipe**, a documentary following Shell's efforts – vigorously resisted by locals – to lay a gas pipeline across a remote, hitherto untouched corner of County Mayo. The picture won the Fleadh's best documentary prize.

The best Irish Feature prize (an audience award) went to Ian Power's charming, sentimental **The Runway**, concerning a South American pilot who accidentally landed his plane in County Cork.

Few of these films have yet received any commercial release. However, there was space for Maya Derrington's charming documentary, **Pyjama Girls**. It profiled two children from inner-city Dublin and even offered hope of future audiences for Irish features. During the film, the girls compare their own experiences to two Irish productions: Peter Mullan's *The Magdalene Sisters* and Lenny Abrahamson's *Adam & Paul*. It seems we are watching our own films, after all!

Maya Derrington's **Pyjama Girls**

DONALD CLARKE is a film critic and feature writer for *the Irish Times*. He makes frequent appearances on RTÉ radio and is a regular panellist on the television arts show, *The View*. He has also written two successful short films – *My Dinner With Oswald* and *Pitch 'n' Putt with Beckett 'n' Joyce* – the latter of which he also directed.

Ivan Kavanagh's **The Fading Light**

The year's best films
The Fading Light (Ivan Kavanagh)
Pyjama Girls (Maya Derrington)
The Pipe (Risteard Ó Domhnaill)
Snap (Carmel Winters)
Rewind (P. J. Dillon)

Quote of the year
'The criticism that many of the films aren't good enough to perform in the marketplace is the elephant in the auditorium which many people in the trade will not address on the record. "It's too glib to say he films aren't good enough; it's a lot more complex than that," is how one experienced producer puts it.' *Journalist* **TED SHEEHY** *discusss the state of the country's films an article he wrote for the Irish Times on 3 June 2010.*

Directory
All Tel/Fax numbers begin (+353)
Film Censor's Office, 16 Harcourt Terrace, Dublin 2. Tel: (1) 799 6100. Fax: (1) 676 1898. info@ifco.gov.ie.
Film Institute of Ireland, 6 Eustace St, Dublin 2. Tel: (1) 679 5744. Fax: (1) 679 9657. www.fii.ie.
Irish Film Board, Rockfort House, St Augustine St, Galway, Co Galway. Tel: (91) 561 398. Fax: (91) 561 405. www.filmboard.ie.
Screen Directors Guild of Ireland, 18 Eustace St, Temple Bar, Dublin 2. Tel: (1) 633 7433. Fax: (1) 478 4807. info@sdgi.ie.
Screen Producers Ireland, The Studio Bldg, Meeting House Sq, Temple Bar, Dublin 2. Tel: (1) 671 3525. Fax: (1) 671 4292. www.screenproducers-ireland.com.

Israel Dan Fainaru

It is reckoning time for Israeli cinema. For the last ten years, riding high with critics and audiences alike, swept away on the wings of such films as *Late Marriage*, *Broken Wings*, *The Syrian Bride*, *My Father My Lord*, *Walk on Water*, *The Band's Visit*, *Waltz with Bashir* and *Ajami*, to mention but a few, they had managed to break the old pattern of well-meaning, virtuous pictures with much to say but very little interest in the way it was being said. Now it's time to move on.

The next question everyone asks is: 'Do they have to offer anything for an encore?' No clear answer yet but, judging by this year's crop, some tendencies are becoming clear. For instance, it seems that original scripts, usually written by or with the participation of the filmmaker, who was intimately familiar with the subject and the background of the story, are being replaced by adaptations, some of highly respectable literary sources, but more often than not removed from the personal or the physical experience of those behind the camera. No less evident is the age that interests most Israeli filmmakers: adolescence, often blossoming under dark and unspoken, but clearly present, shadows of the Holocaust. Also, an interest in the early days of Israel appears evident, given the number of historical reconstructions attempted this year.

After eight years of TV drama, Nir Bergman (*Broken Wings*) is back making theatrical films. **Inner Grammar** (*HaDikduk HaPinimi*) is his own version of a highly regarded novel by David Grossman, about a 12-year-old whose body refuses to grow, most likely because subconsciously he hates the idea of joining the adult world he observes around him. Bergman's film (recently awarded top prize in

Avi Nesher's **The Matchmaker**

Tokyo) unfolds in 1968. As does Avi Nesher's **The Matchmaker** (originally titled *Once I Was*, the exact translation of the Hebrew title, *Paam Hayiti*). But whereas Bergman's film takes place in Jerusalem, *The Matchmaker* is set in Haifa, with a 16-year-old hero. In both cases, the Holocaust weighs heavy on the older generation, which impacts the younger generation. Joshua Knaz's *Hitganvut Yehidim* was adapted by Dover Kozashvili (*Late Marriage*) as **Infiltration**. One of the best modern Israeli novels, it travels back to 1956 and a training camp for physically impaired recruits, for a glimpse at the raw material that formed Israeli society.

If there is a problem with these three films, it is their failure to recreate the past in a credible manner, quite possibly because none is the physical and psychological background they deal with, or are comfortable with non-contemporary material.

More adolescence in trouble, but in the present, was presented in Guy Nattiv's **Flood** (*Mabul*). His first outing as a solo director (he had co-directed *Strangers* and *A Matter of Size* with Erez Tadmor), the film is based on a Noah Berman-Herzberg short story, about Yoni (an astonishingly sensitive and intelligent performance by Yoav Rotman), a smart, quick-witted but physically underdeveloped adolescent and the conflicts that take place amongst his badly dysfunctional family, caused by the return of his older, autistic brother, Tomer (Michael Moshonov). The father is a grounded pilot, the mother has an affair with the neighbour, while Yoni is preparing for his Bar Mitzvah, which symbolises his entrance into the very inauspicious world of adulthood.

Eitan Tzur's **Noemi**

Noemi (*Hitpartzut X*), the feature debut of TV director Eitan Tzur, is playwright Edna Mazia's adaptation of her own novel. It could be described as a film about very late adolescence. The astrophysics professor who kills his young wife's lover may be close to 60, but he is entirely dependent on his mother (played by Orna Porath, one of the country's great stage actresses), who is determined not to let her son down, even at the cost of her own life.

Israel's only representative in Cannes, Avishai Sivan's **The Wanderer** (*Hameshotet*), has a deeply troubled, religious teenager mulling over his coming-of-age while wandering the streets late at night. On the verge of experimental, with almost no dialogue, the film appears to take place within the confines of an extreme orthodox society, whilst attempting to take on more meaningful and general issues, but the approach is so excessively schematic that it risks leaving most audiences indifferent.

Eran Riklis' **Human Resources Manager**

Production-wise, **Human Resources Manager** (*Mashabey Enosh*) is probably the most ambitious venture of the year. Eran Riklis adapts a story by A.B. Yehoshua, who is one of Israel's most internationally renowned authors, transported his cast and crew from modern-day Jerusalem to somewhere in Eastern Europe (the film was shot in Romania but the location is not mentioned in the film), to follow a Human Resources Manager who wants to return the body of a foreign worker killed in a terrorist attack. A strong performance by Mark Iwanir ensures the film's credibility, even during the shifts in style, which are mostly caused by a script that has trouble focusing on the issues it has chosen to grapple with.

In a completely different mode, one of the year's top box-office attractions, **This is Sodom** has no ambition to take on serious matters. The cast of the most popular Israeli TV show, the wildly irreverent political satire *A Wonderful Country* (*Eretz Nehedereth*), threw politics out of the window in an unbridled,

Avishai Sivan's **The Wanderer**

lowbrow, belly-laughs comedy, targeting local audiences exclusively and bringing forth their own version of the Sodom and Gomorrah biblical story. Needless to say, it has very little to do with the Bible.

Soon to be released, the mockumentary **Guide for a Revolution** (*Madrikh LaMahapeckha*) promises to create quite a splash. Employing hidden camera footage from the Israeli Broadcasting Authority corridors and combining it with some fictional material, it is a biting satire of public broadcasting in Israel, recounting the long-term struggle of its two authors, filmmakers Doron Tzabari and Ori Inbar, to beat a fiendishly dubious and bureaucractic system.

Shlomi Eldar's **A Precious Life**

No report would be complete without the two documentaries already travelling extensively around the world. Yael Hersonski's **A Film Unfinished** (*Shtikat HaArkhion*) confronts a previously unreleased film shot by the Nazis in the Warsaw Ghetto with the actual survivors of the Ghetto, proposing a different manner of looking at Holocaust footage. In **A Precious Life** (*Khayim Yekarim*), TV reporter Shlomi Eldar tells the story of a Gaza infant he took for treatment at the largest medical centre in Israel, after being given up for dead at home. It is a moving human-interest story that emerges from the heart of darkness. Politically, it will probably be attacked from different quarters, right and left alike, but, on an emotional level, it is difficult to deny its impact.

Yael Hersonski's **A Film Unfinished**

The year's best films
A Film Unfinished (Yael Hersonski)
Flood (Guy Nattiv)
The Wanderer (Avishai Sivan)
A Precious Life (Shlomi Eldar)
Human Resources Manager (Eran Riklis)

Quote of the year
'They don't always like us but they can't deny our films are reaching large audiences around the world.' KATRIEL SCHORY, *the head of the Israeli Film Fund.*

Directory
All Tel/Fax numbers begin (+972)
Israel Film Archive, Jerusalem Film Centre, Derech Hebron, PO Box 8561, Jerusalem 91083. Tel: (2) 565 4333. Fax: (2) 565 4335. jer-cin@jer-cin.org.il. www.jer-cin.org.il.
Israel Film Fund, 12 Yehudith Blvd, Tel Aviv 67016. Tel: (2) 562 8180. Fax: (2) 562 5992. info@filmfund.org.il. www.filmfund.org.il.
Israeli Film Council, 14 Hamasger St, PO Box 57577, Tel Aviv 61575. Tel: (3) 636 7288. Fax: (3) 639 0098. etic@most.gov.il.
Tel Aviv Cinema Project, 29, Idelson St, Tel Aviv 65241. Tel. (2) 525 5020. info@cinemaproject.co.il. www.cinemaproject.org.il.
The New Fund for Cinema and Television, 112, Hayarkon St, Tel Aviv. Tel. (3) 522 0909. info@nfct.org.il. www.nfct.org.il.

DAN FAINARU is co-editor of Israel's only film magazine, *Cinematheque*, and a former director of the Israeli Film Institute. He reviews regularly for *Screen International*.

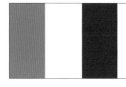
Italy Lorenzo Codelli

2010 was another calamitous year of clashes between the film industry as a whole – 250,000 professionals at the last count – and Silvio Berlusconi's ministers, who were abolishing most public subsidies as well as a vital tax-shelter system. Since the majority of filmmakers, including those on the political right, are exposing in their works the unflattering sides of a decaying country, why should the ruling media and propaganda baron grant them any support?

Despite hard times, rampant piracy and an increase in the number of satellite channels, Italian films accounted for 26% of the annual gross, thanks, of course, to a handful of comedy hits. Christmas and other holiday-period farces from Aurelio De Laurentiis' studio performed less well than usual, perhaps because his staff of jesters, headed by evergreen Christian De Sica in **Christmas in South Africa** (*Natale in Sudafrica*), are not quite as in touch with audience tastes as they should be. Giovanni Veronesi's **Parents and Children: Shake Well Before Use** (*Genitori e figli: agitare bene prima dell'uso*) attempted to refurbish De Laurentiis' familiar portmanteau formula, adding such spry faces as Silvio Orlando, Luciana Litizzetto and Margherita Buy.

The sleeper hit of the year was Luca Miniero's **Welcome to the South** (*Benvenuti al Sud*), a remake of the 2008 French hit, *Welcome to the Sticks*. Its wide appeal lies in playing to clichés about hyperactive Northerner versus lazy Southerners. A Milanese manager (Claudio Bisio) and Neapolitan bon vivant (Alessandro Siani) do their best to imitate, scene by scene, the ingenious clash between French stars Dany Boon and Kad Merad. Miniero just keeps the camera rolling and avoids any links with

Luca Miniero's **Welcome to the South**

real, tragic disparities between the Peninsula's richest and poorest ends, which could be seen to mirror the policy of the film's producer-distributor, Medusa, which is owned by Silvio Berlusconi.

Playing a soulful priest surviving in a godless society, Carlo Verdone starred in and directed his most popular vehicle in years, **Me, Them and Lara** (*Io, loro e Lara*). It is a pleasant variation on Alberto Sordi's style of comedy. Gabriele Muccino's **Kiss Me Again** (*Baciami ancora*) attempted to re-visit the group of flirtatious pals who appeared in his 2001 gem, *The Last Kiss* (*L'ultimo bacio*). Sadly, the thirtysomethings have lost all their ideals and romanticism, and their Hollywood-based director no longer appears to care about their misfortune. Armies of their fans did care, however, and were charmed by Jovanotti's catchy title song. Gay and straight audiences applauded Ferzan Ozpetek's family farce, **Loose Cannons** (*Mine vaganti*), which starred the cobalt-eyed Riccardo Scamarcio.

Within the same trend of easy-to-digest family dramas, but noticeably more upmarket and sophisticated, was Sergio Castellitto's **The Donkey's Beauty** (*La bellezza del somaro*). The multitalented actor-director pokes fun at snobbish parents who don't seem to want to grow old.

Mario Martone, a prominent stage and opera director, had to wait eight years in order to get financing for **We Believed** (*Noi credevamo*), an ambitious fresco about the Risorgimento wars for independence, which follows in the path of Roberto Rossellini and Luchino Visconti. Like a four-act opera, imbued with Verdi, Bellini and Rossini's music, it covers the ill-fated lives of three young conspirators from Campania, who are fighting for Italy's unity. Inspired by political dogmas of the radical leader Giuseppe Mazzini, hypnotically played by a devilish Toni Servillo, they eventually become terrorists and assassins. Martone avoids the conventions of a leaden costume drama, setting his sweeping epic in a very contemporary-looking 1800, and convincingly compares past and present sacrifices for democracy and the dream of a social utopia. His polemical thesis provoked widespread discussions in the lead-up to the celebration of Italy's 150th anniversary, in 2011.

Mario Martone's **We Believed**

Toni Servillo also graced **Gorbaciof**, a dark Neapolitan comedy by Stefano Incerti, and Claudio Cupellini's **A Quiet Life** (*Una vita tranquilla*), a mafia thriller set in Germany.

In the summer classes he holds at his villa on Bobbio's green hill (where he shot *Fists in the Pocket*), Marco Bellocchio showed how he has maintained his extraordinary visual and ethical standards. Edited together for **Sisters Never** (*Sorelle Mai*) are six shorts shot with his pupils since 1997, starring his own sisters, sons and

Marco Bellocchio's **Sisters Never**

friends, side-by-side with professionals. The result is a 'fantasy autobiography', rich in mood and echoes of the past. Every 'ballade', with its light humour and tender poetry, allows us further access to Bellocchio's rich imagination. It is a gem, albeit one never destined for commercial release.

Carlo Mazzacurati's **The Passion** (*La passione*) offers an updated variation on Fellini's *8 ½*, presenting the parable of a jobless film director forced to stage a Passion Play in a Tuscan village. This hilarious satire gently mocks greedy producers, arrogant starlets, TV icons, superficial audiences and miracle-maker politicians. The large and sparkling cast includes the irresistible clowns Silvio Orlando, Paolo Guzzanti, and Giuseppe Battiston. Meanwhile, in his bittersweet real-life miniature, **Six Venice** (*Sei Venezia*), Mazzacurati presented a portrait of six bizarre inhabitants of the lagoon city.

The Best Actor award at the Cannes Film Festival went to Elio Germano – ex aequo with Javier Bardem – for his energetic performance in **Our Life** (*La nostra vita*), as a petty construction boss losing his dignity in a harsh rat race. Daniele Luchetti's comedy drama, featuring a subtle script by Sandro Petraglia and Stefano Rulli, is shot in the vein of Ken Loach's films, highlighting the illegal activities nowadays considered normal in 'our life'.

Petraglia and Rulli struck again with a 'sequel' to their 2003 masterpiece, *Best of Youth*. Another four-part mini-series for Rai,

Longlasting Youth (*Le cose che restano*) was entrusted to experienced director, Gianluca Maria Tavarelli. An astonishing mural of a contemporary Roman bourgeois family, shattered by betrayals and compromises, it details how modern values, from changing attitudes to politics, immigration and sexuality, help each character's life. One can only hope it is as universally successful as the earlier film.

Veteran Pupi Avati successfully pulled out two aces. In **The Youngest Son** (*Il figlio più piccolo*), he upgraded Christian De Sica's trashy routines and transformed him into a greedy stock-market tycoon who is about to lose his empire and his beloved son. De Sica's fans rejected this mini-*Wall Street*, which was perhaps too uncomfortable for their tastes, and too 'anti-Berlusconian', even if it was produced by Medusa. **A Second Childhood** (*Una sconfinata giovinezza*), about a sports reporter struck by Alzheimer's and regressing to his childhood, underlined Avati's peculiar skill for exploring a character's roots. The idyllic flashback sequences, set in Avati's Emilian countryside, count among his finest achievements. Paolo Virzì also tried to catch moments from his youth in **The First Beautiful Thing** (*La prima cosa bella*), which was set in an enchanted home in Livorno. However, annoying mannerisms and a creeping sense of déjà vu plagued his nostalgic memoir.

20th Century Fox is investing heavily in the Italian film industry, although it favours commercially exportable products like **Vallanzasca – The Flower of Evil** (*Vallanzasca: gli angeli del male*), which was directed by

Elio Germani in Daniele Luchetti's **Our Life**

Michele Placido. A gangster saga about a real-life bandit in the 1970s, it guarantees as many robberies, gunfights and blood as anyone could wish for, and more. Placido's handling is indeed weaker and much less personal than it was in *Romanzo criminale.*

Sabina Guzzanti's **Draquila**

With her successful documentary, **Draquila**, Sabina Guzzanti dared to investigate behind the scenes of Berlusconi's exploitation of the catastrophic earthquake at L'Aquila in 2008. A whole ancient town was erased from the map, along with much of its population, but the ineffectual efforts of the government were ignored by the media. There are no easy solutions to such a corrupted regime, suggests Guzzanti, in her vengeful and powerful film.

Escaping out of Italy's boundaries seems to be a necessity for some filmmakers. Italo Spinelli's **Gangor**, an India-set, Bengali-speaking, feminist exposé was so convincingly authentic, it could have easily been mistaken for the work of a local director. Inspired by Mahasweta Devi's novel, it tells the story of a proletarian girl who is photographed breast feeding and, as a result of the media furore, becomes a social outcast. A genuine and moving tale, it is the second partnership between Italy and India, following Francesca Archibugi's 2007 film, *Flying Lessons.* Guido Chiesa shot **I Am with You** (*Io sono con te*) in Tunisia, which presents the story of Jesus' mother, Mary, and employed actors who spoke in ancient Greek and Aramaic. In style, it failed to capture the atmosphere and tone of Pier Paolo Pasolini's *Gospel According to St Matthew.*

Some low-budget digital films received limited distribution. The enterprising Indigo Film supported two promising youngsters. Pietro Marcello's **The Wolf's Mouth** (*La bocca del lupo*) was a lyrical documentary, while Massimo Coppola's **Afraid of the Dark** (*Hai paura del buio*) presented the gloomy odyssey of a Romanian immigrant.

Michelangelo Frammartino's second opus, **Le quattro volte**, a philosophical, speechless dissertation about how natural things mutate, was presented at Cannes' Directors' Fortnight and was heralded by some as a stunning experience, while snubbed by others as an empty bore. Likewise, Ascanio Celestini's debut, **The Black Sheep** (*La pecora nera*), received a mixed response at the Venice Festival. The film is a repetitive monologue by Celestini himself, as an asylum inmate who appears smarter than his guardians.

The 50th anniversary of *La dolce vita* and Federico Fellini's 90th birthday were celebrated across the country, with screenings of a new digital restoration of the filmmaker's masterpiece, which was carried out by Cineteca di Bologna and sponsored by Martin Scorsese's Film Foundation. Unfortunately, Rimini's Fellini Foundation is crumbling under immense debts, while several other archives, schools, studios, and museums are threatened by the bureaucrats' axe.

2011 should bring us Nanni Moretti's much-anticipated **Habemus Papam**, Paolo Sorrentino's big-budget **This Must Be the Place**, Gianni Amelio's Algiers-set **The First Man** (*Il primo uomo*), Gianni di Gregorio's **The Salt of Life** (*Il sale della vita*), Ermanno Olmi's comeback, **The Cardboard Village** (*Il villaggio di cartone*), and Marco Tullio Giordana's epic **Piazza Fontana**.

LORENZO CODELLI is on the board of Cineteca del Friuli, a Cannes Film Festival adviser and a regular contributor to *Positif* and other cinema-related publications.

Carlo Mazzacurati's **The Passion**

The year's best films
We Believed (Mario Martone)
Sisters Never (Marco Bellocchio)
The Passion (Carlo Mazzacurati)
Draquila (Sabina Guzzanti)
Our Life (Daniele Luchetti)

Quote of the year
'All of you go home!' *Italian producers' and filmmakers' shared plea to the government.*

Directory
All Tel/Fax numbers begin (+39)
Filmitalia-Cinecittà, Via Tuscolana 1055, 00173 Rome. Tel. (06) 722 861. Fax: (06) 7228 6324. www.filmitalia.org/mission.asp?lang=ing.
Cineteca del Comune, Via Riva di Reno, 40122 Bologna. Tel: (051) 204 820. www.cinetecadibologna.it.
Cineteca del Friuli, Via Bini 50, Palazzo Gurisatti, 33013 Gemona del Friuli, Udine. Tel: (04) 3298 0458. Fax: (04) 3297 0542. cdf@cinetecadelfriuli. org. http://cinetecadelfriuli.org.
Cineteca Nazionale, Via Tuscolana 1524, 00173 Rome. Tel: (06) 722 941. www.snc.it.
Fondazione Cineteca Italiana, Villa Reale, Via Palestro 16, 20121 Milan. Tel: (02) 799 224. Fax: (02) 798 289. info@cinetecamilano.it. www.cinetecamilano.it.
Fondazione Federico Fellini, Via Oberdan 1, 47900 Rimini. Tel (0541) 50085. Fax: (0541) 57378. fondazione@federicofellini.it. www.federicofellini.it/.
Museo Nazionale del Cinema, Via Montebello 15, 10124 Turin. Tel: (011) 812 2814. www.museonazionaledelcinema.org.

Japan Katsuta Tomomi

For the first time in four years, the top three positions in Japan's annual box-office figures failed to show a domestic release. Hollywood's 3D explosion, dominated by *Avatar*, *Alice in Wonderland* and *Toy Story 3*, each of which exceeded 10 billion yen, saw to this. But signs of hope prevailed. Japan's own 3D release, **Umizaru: The Last Message**, the second sequel of the action drama about coast guard rescue divers, came in fifth, with eight billion yen. It was a flashy extravaganza converted to 3D in post-production.

Although the local majors, Toho, Toei and Shochiku, were seemingly unwilling to make 3D films on their own due to the high cost and the uncertainty of the trend's long-term popularity, they finally accepted the need to catch this commercially profitable wave. *Umizaru* is Toho's first 3D production. Toei is set to follow.

While 3D cinema increased box-office coffers, middle-to-low budget films became increasingly difficult to finance. The production committee has become a common way of financing films in Japan. It is dominated by television stations, but also features advertising agencies, publishers, talent agencies and any companies that might help in marketing or would benefit from a film's success. However, the number of box-office duds and the economic recession proved sobering for many investors who had previously swarmed over the industry, expecting high returns and the honour of being associated with a hit film. Projects with no history, either in fiction or TV franchises, became increasingly difficult to green-light. And any ambitious projects found funding almost impossible amongst the committees.

As a result, the total number of domestic releases for 2010 was 250, a reduction of 150 on the previous year.

Not all filmmakers were satisfied with playing safe. A number of producers at major studios have started to tackle tougher material. Toho released two controversial films: **Villain** (*Akunin*) by Lee San-il and Nakashima Tetsuya's **Confession** (*Kokuhaku*). Produced outside the production-committee structure and denying audiences a happy ending, each film grossed two billion yen, double the amount that signifies a commercial success for a film in Japan.

Lee San-il's **Villain**

Villain details the love affair that unfolds between an unwitting murderer and a single woman in her thirties, who meet via an online-dating site. Lee, who previously directed *Hula Girl*, attracted critical acclaim for his study of isolation and solitude in modern society. *Confession* is a tale of the vengeance carried out by a schoolteacher following the death of her son at the hands of her students. Socially relevant issues such as school bullying were presented through dazzling imagery and a narrative style that appealed to a young audience.

Indie filmmakers also proved aggressive in their vision. Wakamatsu Koji's grotesque satire, **Caterpillar** (*Kyatapira*), is set during World War II, and delivers a strong anti-war message through the bizarre relationship between a multiple-amputee veteran and his wife, who is weighed down by societal conventions. Terajima Shinobu's outstanding performance won her the Best Actress award in Berlin.

Kobayashi Mashiro's **A Journey With Haru**

Kobayashi Mashiro's **A Journey With Haru** (*Haru tono Tabi*) starts out bitterly, but eventually becomes a heart-warming road movie about an old man and his young granddaughter. An homage to Ozu Yasujiro's *Tokyo Story*, Kobayashi's sensitivity to his material elevated the film above the conventional family drama, with word-of-mouth recommendations making it a success.

Two established directors offered up graphically violent films. Izutsu Kazuyuki's **The Hero Show** has a skirmish about a girl between some teenagers escalate into a brutal crime, while Takeshi Kitano's **Outrage**

Izutsu Kazuyuki's **The Hero Show**

Takeshi Kitano's **Outrage**

(*Autoreiji*) details a deadly turf battle between Yakuza clans. While Izutsu's attempt to push the boundary of violence on the screen garnered favourable critical responses but disappointing box-office returns, Kitano's rehash of his early works attracted a sizeable audience but mixed reviews.

Younger filmmakers were also uncompromising in the diverse material they tackled. Omori Tatsushi's second feature, **A Crowd of Three** (*Kenta to Jun to Kayo-chan no Kuni*), is an account of a trip made by three youths, underpinning the air of disaffection and hopelessness experienced by their generation. Ishii Yuya showed some promise in **Sawako Decides** (*Kawa no soko kara Konnichiwa*), a comedy-drama about a lower-middle-class girl.

Ogigami Naoko's **Toilet**

Female directors also presented a number of interesting films. While Ogigami Naoko attracted audiences with her off-beat domestic drama, **Toilet** (*Toiretto*), O Mipo's **Here Comes the Bride, My Mom** (*Okan no Yomeiri*)

witnessed the fallout of a mother announcing she was marrying a man 20 years her junior. Both films offered unique takes on family life, mixed with a sharp sense of humour.

Of all the independent films released in 2010, the highlight was Zeze Takahisa's self-financed **Heaven's Story** (*Hebunzu Sutori*). Over four hours long, it presented a portrait of over a dozen characters and the changes that take place in their lives across a decade. They include a man whose wife and son have been killed and who is intent on avenging them, a girl who has survived the massacre of her family, and a policeman who moonlights as a contract killer. Zeze weaves a harsh, but visually stunning, tapestry of death and birth, hatred and forgiveness, and guilt and punishment. Like a Buddhist Mandala, it is an epic vision of the world.

Zeze Takahisa's **Heaven's Story**

Epic samurai films, an old-fashioned genre, saw a resurgence in their popularity over the last year. An increase in the national average age has seen older people, who have time and money to spare, and who witnessed the heyday of the samurai epic in the 50s and 60s, attend the cinema. At the same time, the samurais' stoicism and nobility have become an attraction to a society perceived as overrun by indiscipline and disorder.

Miike Takashi's **13 Assassins** (*Jusan-nin no Shikaku*), a remake of a 1963 film, features a group of samurais assigned to kill a cruel Lord. Miike, a prolific cult director, plays up staple elements of the genre, whilst adding

Miike Takashi's **13 Assassins**

his own distinctive touches, such as 50-minute sword fight between 13 samurais and 200 of the cruel Lord's guards. Hirayama Hideyuki's **Sword of Desperation** (*Hisshiken Torisashi*) is more traditional genre fare, in which a highly loyal samurai betrayed by the feudal clan he belonged to decides to fight back. **Sakurada Gate Incident** (*Sakuradamongai no Hen*) by veteran director Sato Junya, is based on an historical event that took place in the Edo era, when a group of terrorists kill a high-ranking vassal of the Shogunate in order to change foreign policy. Morita Yoshimitsu's **Abacus and Sword** (*Bushi no Kakeibo*) added a twist to the genre, featuring a samurai more as a bureaucrat who loves peace and his family.

Sato Junya's **Sakurada Gate Incident**

A new generation of animators have also appeared, and look set to rank alongside Hayao Miyazaki and Mamoru Oshii. Studio Ghibli released **Arrietty** (*Karigurashi no Arietti*), an adaptation of Mary Norton's children's fantasy novel, about a community of tiny people who live under the floorboards of a country house.

First-time director Yonebayashi Hiromasa, one of Ghibli's animators, presents a beautifully detailed account of the community's life. Hara Keiichi, who had previously attracted acclaim for *Summer Days with Coo* in 2007, directed **Colorful** (*Colorful*). It daringly follows the soul of a teen suicide victim, who is given a second chance on the earth. Koike Takashi's feature debut, **Red Line** (*Red Line*), is an action-packed sci-fi tale about an illegal road race that takes place on another planet. Koike and his team drew over 100,000,000 drawings without CGI to create the original and often hilarious race.

Koike Takashi's **Red Line**

The death of Kon Satoshi in October struck a note with the industry. One of Japan's most prominent filmmakers, who had directed *Tokyo Godfathers* and *Paprika*, his absence is a great loss for Japanese animation.

2011 shows no weakening of the dominance of either the TV networks or Toho, the largest of the three majors. The scramble to acquire popular comic books or bestselling novels for adaptation will continue. However, independent filmmakers are unlikely to stop persevering to find new ways of realising their project. But the tougher the competition becomes, the more inventive filmmakers will have to be.

A possible future trend is the live-action adaptation of manga. As this book goes to press, Yamazaki Takashi's **The Space Battleship Yamato**, originally a 1970s space-opera made for TV, is set to open. It will be followed by **Tomorrow's Joe** (*Ashita no Jo*), about an orphan boxer and based on a popular comic book from the 1960s and 1970s.

Omori Tatsushi's **A Crowd of Three**

The year's best films
Heaven's Story (Zeze Takahisa)
A Crowd of Three (Omori Tatsushi)
A Journey With Haru (Kobayashi Masahiro)
Sword of Desperation (Hirayama Hideyuki)
Here Comes the bride, My Mom (O Mipo)

Quote of the year
'No war can be cool, it's just the brutal killing of each other. I'd like to show how a war sacrifices and ordinary people [suffer]... I'll be happy if young people see this film, who don't even know there was a war between Japan and USA.' WAKAMATSU KOJI, *explaining his intention of making* **Caterpillar**.

Directory
All Tel/Fax numbers begin (+81)
Motion Picture Producers Association of Japan, Tokyu Ginza Bldg 3F, 2-15-2 Ginza, Chuo-ku, Tokyo 104-0061. Tel: 3547 1800. Fax: 3547 0909. eiren@mc.neweb.ne.jp.
National Film Center, 3-7-6 Kyobashi, Chuo-ku, Tokyo 104-0031. Tel: 5777 8600. www.momat.go.jp.

KATSUTA TOMOMI is a journalist for the Mainichi newspapers in charge of films and has published a book about the actress Kagawa Kyoko who performed in the films of Kurosawa, Mizoguchi, Naruse and Ozu.

Kazakhstan Gulnara Abikeyeva

Despite the growth of film production in Kazakhstan – there were over 30 films at various stages of production throughout 2010 – the market share of Kazakhstani films remains extremely low, at only three per cent. Of the 260 films screened in local cinemas throughout the year, only eight were Kazakh.

There are currently three tendencies in Kazakh cinema: commercial films aimed at local and Russian markets; films aimed at luring younger audiences; and a determined drive to produce serious or art-house cinema, mainly through co-productions.

Erzan Rustembeekov and Alexander Chernyaev's **Irony of Love**

As a result of Kazakhfilm Studios' efforts in promoting Kazakh films on the Russian market, Erzhan Rustembekov and Alexander Chernyaev's **Irony of Love** was released in March 2010. With the support of Russian co-producer Renat Davlet'yarov, the film went on to earn US$700,000 at the Russian box office. This should have made the film an unqualified success. However, back in Kazakhstan, the film attracted criticism from the Parliament and in the media because of its story. The film is about a glamorous young Kazakh woman, Asel, who lives in Moscow. Just prior to her wedding to her rich Kazakh boyfriend, she runs away with a Russian man. The question of priorities was raised. Should the film be seen as a commercial success or does it mark a 'return to the elder Russian brother'?

Kanagat Mustafin's **The Dash**

A number of youth-oriented films were released in the last year. Kanagat Mustafin's **The Dash** is a sports drama about a basketball player who suffers a knee trauma, but is eventually able to return to the game. Farkhat Sharipov's **Tale of a Pink Hare**, a success amongst younger audiences, presented a very modern account of youths living in the city. A young man makes money by distributing leaflets dressed as a big pink hare. Whilst working, he witnesses a fatal car accident, recognising the driver of the car that leaves the

Farkhat Sharipov's **Tale of a Pink Hare**

scene before the authorities arrive. Adopting a detective narrative, the film presents a powerful portrait of contemporary society.

The most interesting film shot by the so-called 'Children of Independence' – the generation of cinematographers aged from 22 to 25 – is Talgat Bektursunov's **The Wanderer**. Young Marat comes to Almaty in order to continue his studies. But he faces many problems: the death of the mother, expulsion from the institute, problems with lodgings, conflicts in his hostel and the break-up of his relationship. The film was shot on a minuscule budget, but the quality of its cinematography and its detailed examination of human relationships set Bektursunov apart as a filmmaker to watch.

While commercial films focus on Kazakhstani audiences, art-house projects tend to be the result of co-productions and thus look at potential audiences further afield. Kyrgyz director Aktan Arym Kubat's **Mother's Paradise** is a good example of such a production. A young widow is left to look after her two sons and parent-in-law. In a small provincial town with little prospects, she has no choice other than to turn to prostitution.

Tajik filmmaker Bakhtiyar Khudoinazarov's Kazakhstan-Russia-France-produced **Waiting the Sea** will be completed in 2011. It tells the story of a ship captain who ends up without a ship and a crew. The tragedy of one man is presented as the tragedy of many people who continue to live a precarious life on the coast of the disappearing Aral Sea.

Another much-anticipated film is Amir Karakulov's youth drama, **Unreal Love**, which looks at online dating. Having used nicknames online, a young couple who meet via the site have no idea that they work at the same advertising agency. Young director Akhat Ibrayev is currently finishing one of next year's more technologically challenging releases. **Fairytale Forest** is based on a series of Tengri fairytales and features a cast of real and animated characters.

Sabit Kurmanbekov's **Unexpected Love**

Ammong the commercial co-productions scheduled for release in 2011 is Sabit Kurmanbekov's comedy, **Unexpected Love**, about three old men looking for new wives, one of whom is played by French actor Gérard Depardieu. And British footballer-turned-film actor, Vinnie Jones, will play a killer in **Liquidator**, a tale of revenge directed by Akhan Sataev.

The year's best films
The Wanderer (Talgat Bektursunov)
Tale of a Pink Hare (Farkhat Sharipov)
Mother's Paradise (Aktan Arym Kubat)
The Dash (Kanagat Mustafin)
Who Are You, Mister Ka? (Khuat Akhmetov)

Quote of the year
'The main challenge of this cinematic year is the entrance of the so-called generation of 'Children of Independence' – Adilkhan Erzhan, Akhat Ibrayev, Serik Abishev, Talgat Bektursynov and others. They will determine the future of Kazakh cinema.' *Film critic* INNA SMAILOVA.

GULNARA ABIKEYEVA is a famous Kazakh film critic and an author of five books about the cinema of Central Asia. She is artistic director of 'Eurasia' Film Festival which is held annually in Almaty, Kazakhstan.

Latvia Toms Treibergs

Key issues for the Latvian film industry over the last year were the establishment of the film law and the participation of a number of films in several prestigious film festivals. There was also an increased presence of foreign production companies filming in Latvia, thanks to the newly established Riga Film Fund, run by the Riga city municipality. It provides foreign production companies with a 15% cash rebate.

The year opened with Jānis Streičs' big-budget period-comedy, **Rudolph's Heritage**. A central figure in Latvian cinema, who has been making films since the 1960s, Streičs' latest is set in the 19th century and presents a comical account of the relationship between Latvian peasants and German nobility. The light mood of the film is a rare one for domestic films.

As the year drew to a close, the first Latvian-Hong Kong co-production was premiered. Māris Martinsons' **Hong-Kong Confidential** finds an eclectic group of people living out their lives in the alienated urban surroundings of Hong Kong's Central district. Poetically shot by acclaimed Latvian cinematographer Gints Berzins, the film lacks coherence and is ultimately undermined by unconvincing performances.

The much-anticipated feature debut of director Gatis Šmits, **The Return of Sergeant Lapins**, which looks at the impact of the Iraq war on soldiers returning home, was worth the wait. Premiering at the Pusan Film Festival, the portrayal of the contrast between the petty problems of everyday people and the war still raging inside the returning sergeant's mind made for an impressive film.

Laila Pakalniņa's **On Rubik's Road**

Of the year's documentaries, Laila Pakalnina's short, **On Rubik's Road**, was chosen to screen in the Orizzonti strand of the Venice Film Festival. Pakalnina recorded daily life on a bicycle path built under the aegis of the last Communist leader of Soviet Latvia. A tender film, it captures quiet movements in the daily lives of Riga's suburbanites, with testimonies recalling days gone by. Andris Gauja began his career as a TV reporter. One of his experiences has now been made into **The Family Instinct**, which screened at the International Documentary Festival Amsterdam.

Latvian animation has long garnered respect at festivals around the world. Nils Skapāns' plasticine stop-motion film, **Wonderful Day**, was selected for the Generation programme

Nils Skapāns' **Wonderful Day**

at the Berlin Film Festival, introducing young viewers to an extraordinary lady who lives with her cat and owns a magic button that can create many wonderful things.

Jurģis Krāsons' short, **To Swallow a Toad**, is a portrait of a character from Latvian folklore. It was screened at Cannes and received the *Grand Prix* at the ZINEBI Film Festival, in Spain. Another animated film, Kārlis Vītols' meditative and symbolic **Eclipse**, was shown out of competition at the Annecy Film Festival.

The year's best film
The Return of Sergeant Lapins (Gatis Šmits)

Quote of the year
'I think cinema is not an art. It is a mover, pusher, something quite simple, unlike the High Art of Whatever. Cinema is entertainment.' D*irector* GATIS ŠMITS.

Gatis Šmits' The Return of Sergeant Lapins

TOMS TREIBERGS is a freelance film and theatre critic who, for the last three years has contributed the film section in Latvia's exclusive culture weekly *Culture Forum*.

Directory
All Tel/Fax numbers begin (+371)
National Film Centre of Latvia (NFC), Peitavas 10/12, Rīga LV1050. Tel: 6735 8878. Fax: 6735 8877. nfc@nfc.gov.lv. www.nfc.lv.
State Culture Capital Foundation, Vīlandes 3, Rīga LV1010. Tel: 6750 3177. Fax: 6750 3897. kkf@kkf.lv. www.vkkf.lv.
Riga Film Museum, Peitavas 10/12, Rīga LV1050. Tel: 6735 8873. Fax: 6754 5099. kinomuzejs@kinomuzejs.lv. www.kinomuzejs.lv.
MEDIA Desk Latvia, Peitavas 10/12, Rīga LV1050. Tel: 6735 8857. Fax: 6735 8877. mediadesk@nfc.gov.lv. www.mediadesklatvia.eu.
EURIMAGES National Representative, Peitavas 10/12, Rīga LV1050. Tel: 6735 8862. Fax: 6735 8877. eurimages@nfc.gov.lv.
Film Producers Association of Latvia, Elizabetes 49, Rīga LV1010. info@filmlatvia.lv. www.filmlatvia.lv.
Filmmakers Union of Latvia, Elizabetes 49, Rīga LV1010. Tel: 6728 8536. Fax: 6724 0543. lks@delfi.lv.
Latvia State Archive of Audiovisual Documents, Šmerļa 5, Rīga LV1006. Tel: 6752 9822. Fax: 6752 9954. fonds@delfi.lv. www.arhivi.lv.
Department of Screen and Stage Art, Academy of Culture, Dzirnavu 46, Rīga LV1010. Tel: 6724 3393. Fax: 6714 1012. zirgupasts@lka.edu.lv. www.lka.edu.lv.

Lithuania Ilona Jurkonytė

Šarūnas Bartas' **Eastern Drift** (*Eurazijos aborigenas*) premiered in the Forum programme of the Berlin International Film Festival in February, going on to play at several festivals throughout 2010. Though recognised as the best Lithuanian film of the year, local audiences had to wait for the domestic release until early October and its premiere at the Kaunas Film Festival. The film takes place following the collapse of the Soviet Union. Gena has connections with the Russian crime world and finds himself torn between two women and two worlds. The film has great potential among local audiences who lived during that time and in a place that was caught between East and West.

Šarūnas Bartas' **Eastern Drift**

The biggest commercial release this year was Emilis Vėlyvis' comedy thriller, **Zero 2**. Described by the director as a 'detective soap', the plot revolves around a group of gangsters charged with finding a kidnapped dealer. Aimed squarely at the local market, the film has little of interest for international audiences.

It took 15 years for Tomas Donela's **Farewell** (*Atsisveikinimas*) to reach the screen. A man

diagnosed with a terminal disease makes his last journey to visit those close to him, confronting the life he has lived for a final time. Uneven as a whole, there are moments of great beauty in the film. It may have taken an inordinately long time to make the film, but *Farewell* is worth watching.

Another much anticipated fim, Kristijonas Vildžiūnas's **In Your Arms** (*Kai apkabinsiu tave*), failed to live up to many audience's expectations. Based on the true story of a Lithuanian family torn apart by the erection of the Berlin Wall in 1961, a father and daughter separated by the Second World War try to meet in Berlin. The father comes from Soviet-occupied Lithuania, while the daughter flies in from the USA. The film ultimately fails in its attempt to detail the failure of this family reunion.

Lithuanian documentary has proven to be a bedrock of strong talent over the last few years. The last year is no different. Julija Gruodienė and Rimantas Gruodis attracted a great deal of acclaim on the international festival circuit for their short, **The River** (*Upė*). It profiles the village of Saleninkai, known as the Lithuanian Venice, which is surrounded by the Šventoji and Neris Rivers. In the 1990s, a chemical plant had an accident and the local population was evacuated, except for the villagers, who were cut off by the water.

Young filmmaker Aušra Linkevičiūtė presented the witty and insightful **Anything But Black** (*Tik ne su juoda*), about the traditions of old Lithuanian villages. The elderly women have a tradition of showing the dresses they have prepared for wearing at their own funerals. There is no fear, just smiling faces and a serenity at the inevitability of their demise. Jeremiah Cullinane's **The Book Smugglers** (*Knygnešiai*) is about an Irish songwriter and poet who travels to Lithuania to tell the story of the 19th century *knygnešiai*, or book smugglers. These people risked their lives to protect the Lithuanian language against Russification. Books, newspapers and magazines were smuggled into the country from Prussia and distributed through clandestine networks. The film is an articulate examination of the relationship between language and nationality, as well as personal identity.

Among the short films this year, Dovilė Šarutytė's engaging **I Know You** (*Aš tave žinau*) was a highlight. It told the story of a 15-year-old girl's inner world, in which her room, her district, her school and everything around her feels too small.

The ICO and Lux commissioned **Ausgetraümt**, the latest work by Deimantas Narkevičius, which premiered at London's Tate Modern in Spring 2010. The word *ausgetraümt* has no direct translation. It suggests a state between a dream and reality, in the moments before we wake up. An examination of naïveté and idealism, the musical short also features impressive cinematography.

A number of government initiatives have been put into place, which aim to enhance the development of the local film industry, in terms of production and infrastructure. The national film centre has yet to start functioning and there is little information as to when this situation will change. In the meantime, Lithuania awaits a much-needed boost, both in terms of support and a greater flourishing of creative talent.

ILONA JURKONYTĖ is a director of Kaunas International Film Festival, a journalist writing about film and art for *IQ The Economist* and co-author of the Internet portal about Lithuanian film, www.lfc.lt.

Julija Gruodienė and Rimantas Gruodis' **The River**

The year's best films

Eastern Drift (Šarūnas Bartas)
The River (Julija Gruodienė and Rimantas Gruodžiai)
Ausgetraümt (Deimantas Narkevičius)
I Know You (Dovilė Šarutytė)
Anything But Black (Aušra Linkevičiūtė)

Quote of the year

'If anyone asks me at the end of the year to name major events of 2010 in Lithuania, I will certainly mention the bronze medals won by our national basketball team in the FIBA World Championship in Istanbul, and the retrospective of Béla Tarr's films at the Kaunas International Film Festival with the participation of the director in person.' *Documentary filmmaker* **AUDRIUS STONYS**.

Directory

All Tel/Fax numbers begin (+370)
The Ministry of Culture of Republic of Lithuania, J. Basanavičiaus g. 5, LT-01118 Vilnius. Tel: (5) 219 3400. Fax: (5) 262 3120. culture@lrkm.lt www.lrkm.lt.
Lithuanian Filmmakers Union, Vasario 16-osios g. 13 / Šermukšnių g. 1, LT-01002 Vilnius. Tel/Fax: (5) 212 0759. info@kinosajunga.lt www.kinosajunga.lt.
Lithuanian Theatre, Music and Cinema Museum, Vilniaus g. 41, LT-01119 Vilnius. Tel/Fax: (5) 262 2406. ltmkm@takas.lt http://teatras.mch.mii.lt.
Lithuanian Central State Archives, O. Milašiaus g. 21, LT-10102 Vilnius. Tel: (5) 247 7811 Fax: (5) 276 5318. lcva@archyvai.lt www.archyvai.lt.
www.lfc.lt (Information about Lithuanian film online) info@lfc.lt.

Luxembourg Boyd van Hoeij

As the country with the world's highest Gross Domestic Product per capita, there is hardly any poverty in Luxembourg. This affluence allows the government, via the Luxembourg Film Fund, to channel millions into a small but flourishing audiovisual sector that predominantly thrives on international co-productions. Some 15 features from 2010, including Ireland's **The Runway**, Belgium's **Illegal**, Switzerland's **The Little Room**, Canada's **The Last Escape** and France's **Special Treatment** and **Top Floor, Left Wing** are Luxembourg co-productions.

In many countries, financial poverty is one of the main incentives behind a flourishing counter-culture, which in turn feeds into the creative mainstream. Though Luxembourg is a rich nation, this year's small crop of purely local films proves, somewhat surprisingly, that there exists a vibrant counter-culture with its own virtues and limits.

Luxembourg's most prolific director, Andy Bausch, released two films, including 2010's only fiction feature, **Trouble No More**. The closing part of the largely Luxembourgish-language *Troublemaker* trilogy again looks at a group of working-class dead beats involved in petty crime, although it had to do without the charismatic presence of actor (and series frontman) Thierry Van Werveke, who died in 2009.

Bausch is again influenced by U.S. cinema of yesteryear and blends this with a distinctly local feel. Some of the humour and action sequences are awkwardly handled, and the film celebrates a class that has all but disappeared, giving the film an old-school feel. Bausch has always been more successful in shaping narratives than imagining them from scratch, which is why his documentaries are often stronger. His latest, **Chocolate, Chewing Gum and Brown Babies** (*Schockela, Knätschgummi a Brong Puppelcher*), ranks alongside his best. The talking-heads documentary looks at the presence and influence of American soldiers in Luxembourg during and after the Second World War and presents a surprisingly nuanced picture that doesn't portray every G.I. as a hero.

Despite the existence of countless war-related films, the subject continues to inspire filmmakers, including screenwriter Pol Tousch and director Marc Thoma, whose **Emil** is a docu-fiction hybrid about the titular Luxembourger who went into hiding when he was drafted by the Nazis (which also inspired Nicolas Steil's feature, *Draft Dodgers*, last year). However, like *Chocolate*, the film's period re-enactments prove an unnecessary weak link.

A lesser-known chapter in Luxembourg military history is explored in Frank Grötz's dutiful **Tour of Duty**, which looks at a Luxembourg veteran who fought in the Korean War and who travels to North America to meet some old acquaintances.

Andy Bausch's **Trouble No More**

Two non-fiction films with more contemporary subjects offered more interest. Alain Tschinza's **Hamilius: Hip Hop Culture in Luxembourg** is a fascinating look at the local scene of street artists, rappers, DJs and break-dancers. Tschinza explores the foreign influences on them, as well as their evolution over time. This classically constructed, fascinating film offers many insights into an unknown side of Luxembourg culture and features conversations with artists intercut with vintage recordings and well-edited musical interludes.

Govinda Van Maele's **We Might As Well Fail**

Equally interested in marginalised characters and music is Govinda Van Maele's **We Might As Well Fail** (*Rocdoc*). Divided between an atmospherically shot concert film and a look at the inherent contradiction in being a musician in a rich country that is nonetheless too small to support emerging professional musicians, Van Maele is not afraid to tackle complex issues in his first feature-length project. He's definitely a name to watch and his film perfectly complements Tschinza's.

Self-taught filmmaker Adolf El Assal, who emerged from the underground scene depicted in *Hamilius*, made two shorts: the guerrilla effort **Mano De Dios**, about an illegal Argentinean in Luxembourg, and the Film Fund-supported **The Notorious Road** (*La fameuse route*), a stoner road-trip comedy. Interestingly, the self-produced film (made by the same crew) is the strongest. Its strength lies in more nuanced emotions than the cartoonish silliness of *Road*, suggesting, like *Hamilius* and *We Might...*, that the Luxembourg underground is a viable cultural outlet that deserves more attention and respect.

2011 is shaping up to be a strong year for Luxembourg cinema, with several young filmmakers moving from shorts to feature-length projects, including Beryl Koltz, whose sauna dramedy **Hot Hot Hot** is, well, hotly anticipated.

The year's best films
Hamilius: Hip Hop Culture in Luxembourg (Alain Tschinza)
We Might As Well Fail (Govinda van Maele)
Mano De Dios (Adolf El Assal)
Chocolate, Chewing Gum and Brown Babies (Andy Bausch)

Quote of the year
'I wanted to show that, even if you're fully integrated, a small mistake could change your life forever because you don't own the right passport.' *Director* ADOLF EL ASSAL *on* **Mano De Dios**.

Directory
All Tel/Fax numbers begin (+352)
Film Fund Luxembourg, Maison de Cassal, 5 rue Large, L-1917 Luxembourg. Tel: 2478 2065. Fax: 22 09 63. info@filmfund.etat.lu http://en.filmfund.lu

---

BOYD VAN HOEIJ is a freelance film writer for *Variety*, cineuropa.org and *Winq* magazine, amongst others. His book *10/10: 10 Directors, 10 Years of French-Language Belgian Cinema, The 2000s* was published in September 2010.

Adolf El Assal's **The Notorious Road**

Malta Daniel Rosenthal

Although the wait continues for locally produced feature films telling Maltese stories to an international audience, Malta's film, TV and commercials servicing industry experienced record levels of visiting productions in 2010, with more than 300 shooting days. The presence of crews filming Lee Tamahori's fact-based drama, *The Devil's Double*, and, in particular, the HBO medieval fantasy series *Game of Thrones*, led Tonio Fenech, Minister of Finance, the Economy and Investment, to comment: 'As the local film-servicing sector continues to grow, this steady influx of productions will contribute considerable added value to the economy, and in addition the presence of a company such as HBO will consolidate our reputation as a viable, efficient film destination in face of the stiff competition from other countries.'

Film Commissioner Luisa Bonello indicated that, apart from a downturn in early 2009, immediately after the credit crunch hit film finance worldwide, the islands had been enjoying an encouragingly consistent flow of incoming projects since early 2007, moving away from a stop-start cycle. The Commission's statistics for 2007–10 show estimated total spending by visiting

Dominic Cooper as Uday Hussein in Lee Tamahori's **The Devil's Double**

productions of more than €72m, which led to rebates of more than €11m.

Bonello added: 'The efficacy and practicality of Malta's film-incentives scheme continues to be crucial to most decisions to film on the island.' There had been firm state backing for the audio-visual sector, and a stream of fairly regular work for Maltese technicians and support staff, many from an emerging, younger generation, was developing an increasingly broad and experienced skills base – an important factor for visiting producers in choosing where to shoot.

For Tamahori's €15m *The Devil's Double*, a Belgian production that spent 50 shooting days on Malta, which stood in for Iraq. It is the story of Latif Yahia, who was a double for Saddam Hussein's son, Uday, and was forced against his will to stand in for Uday in potentially dangerous situations. Dominic Cooper plays both men, alongside Philip Quast as Saddam, and French star Ludivine Saignier.

From September to November, Malta was the secondary location for HBO's $55m *Game of Thrones*, a ten-part series (shot mainly in Belfast), and adapted from George R. R. Martin's best-selling *A Song of Ice and Fire* series of novels. It is set in a medieval fantasy world 'where summers span decades and winters can last a lifetime. Kings and queens, knights and renegades, liars and noblemen vie for power in the bloody struggle for the Iron Throne.' A €22m Russian TV movie, *Last Romans*, was on Malta for seven weeks, overlapping with the Italian TV movie *Kammerspiel* in the spring of 2010.

Other productions in 2010 included a French feature, *The Fisherman*, with Malta doubling for Gaza, and a sequel to German children's blockbuster *Vicky the Viking*, which shot in 3D for a month at the water tanks of Mediterranean Film Studios (the original *Vicky* was partially filmed in Malta in 2008). July saw the filming of a Russian docu-drama, *Lent, Easter, Christmas*, a UK docu-drama, *Adrift*, and another Italian TV movie, *Tailor-Made Murder*.

At press time, projects scheduled for 2011 included a US/Italy mini-series, *Robinson Crusoe* (an estimated 20 days' shooting on Malta), and UK satellite broadcaster Sky 1's 13 x 60-minute *Sinbad* series (an estimated 70 days' local shooting), from Impossible Pictures (*Primeval*), whose publicity material promised a reinvigorating 21st century take on the much-filmed adventures of the eigth century action hero.

2010 also saw the broadcast of *Moby Dick*, a three-hour, two-part TV adaptation of Herman Melville's classic novel, directed by

William Hurt in the TV production of Herman Melville's **Moby Dick**

Mike Barker. It was filmed on the island in September 2009. One local production, the docu-drama **Valletta: Living History**, shot for seven days in June 2010.

It was announced in December that Malta will host the 2012 European Film Academy Awards ceremony, following a bid originally submitted by the film commission in 2009.

Directory
All Tel/Fax numbers begin (+356)
Malta Film Commission, Caraffa Stores, Cottonera Waterfront, Vittoriosa BRG 1721. Tel: 2180 9135 Fax: 2780 9136. info@mfc.com.mt www.mfc.com.mt.
Mediterranean Film Studios, St. Rocco Street, Kalkara KKR3000. Tel: 2166 8194 (production) / 2137 8852 (admin.) Fax: 2138 3357. www.mfsstudios.com.
Ministry of Finance, the Economy and Investment, 'Maison Demandols', 30 South Street, Valletta VLT 1102. Tel: 2599 8244 / 2599 8202. Fax: 2123 3605. www.finance.gov.mt

DANIEL ROSENTHAL was dditor of the *IFG* from 2002 to 2006. He is the author of *100 Shakespeare Films* (BFI, 2007) and teaches 'Shakespeare on Film' and 'Arts Journalism' classes for the International Programmes department of Pembroke College, Cambridge. He is completing a major new history of Britain's National Theatre for Oberon Books.

Mexico Carlos Bonfil

As six multinational enterprises control film distribution in Mexico, they are also able to adjust the release of local screenings to serve their own interests, with American blockbusters allowed the most advantageous marketing conditions. Needless to say, this situation, aggravated by the legal framework created by the NAFTA (North American Free Trade Agreement), which favours the US economy with preferential trade tariffs and taxes, has reduced the possibility for a true consolidation of a local film industry. In 2010, some 70 films were produced in Mexico, but only 45 have so far been screened and most of them are big-budget films with predictably conventional narratives. Mexican independent films are still celebrated abroad while they remain ignored at home. This is a situation that has been repeatedly reported during the past few years, but it now seriously threatens the viability of upcoming independent productions.

A sign of this is the government's decision this year to reduce the budget ascribed to the National Film Institute (IMCINE) as part of a financial move that favours a substantial increase of federal funds to support the hitherto unsuccessful fight against drug trafficking, to the detriment of both education and culture.

The majority of films produced or co-produced in Mexico have some state financing, normally through cultural institutions. Private investors, particularly the two big television network monopolies (Televisa and TV Azteca), have shown scarce interest in financing films, in part due to the fact that producers receive a very small return, with most of the profits going to distribution and exhibition. With such meagre

Carlos Carrera's **From Childhood**

rewards, it is hardly surprising that private enterprise is reluctant to risk its capital on film production. They are more eager to invest in satellite communications and a state-of-the-art audiovisual development. Cinema production is thus regarded by private investors and federal government alike as an anachronistic business with little if any financial appeal, or even cultural relevance.

In spite of this discouraging situation, independent filmmakers continue to demand the support of local cultural institutions and international funding, knowing very well that once a film is completed its chances of competing in the domestic commercial arena are limited and invariably frustrating. Film festivals are the best and often the only opportunity to promote their films. A success at Cannes, Venice or Berlin may allow a film director enough publicity and support to attract funding for a new project, without ever hitting the local market or attracting the audiences that have been lured by Hollywood's recycling of formulaic entertainment.

There is little chance that Mexican audiences will have the opportunity to appreciate the work of young filmmakers such as Nicolas Pereda, who, at the age of 28, has produced an impressive and challenging body of work. His two latest films, **Perpetuum mobile** and **Summer of Goliath** (*Verano de Goliat*), employ elaborate metaphors in their exploration of the aimlessness and violent behaviour of young people caught in the grip of chronic unemployment and the loss of faith in both their own future and in social and political progress.

Australian-born Michael Rowe's **Leap Year** (*Año bisiesto*) focuses on the desolate erotic experience of an indigenous woman betrayed by a man, but also undermined by her own expectations regarding love and companionship. It is a fascinating study of urban solitude and the exploration of limits in a relationship that unexpectedly combines violence and sexual gratification.

Luis Estrada's **Hell**

Two other filmmakers, Carlos Carrera and Jorge Michel Grau, deal with domestic violence in **From Childhood** (*De la infancia*) and **We Are What We Are** (*Somos lo que hay*). Carrera describes the experience of a young boy freeing himself through fantasy from the moral misery of his family life, while Grau offers an horrific tale of cannibalism to portray the unrelenting decay of a dysfunctional family. Social violence reaches its peak in Luis Estrada's **Hell** (*El infierno*). As in his previous film, *Herod's Law*, the director employs political satire and farcical humour to describe the current situation of over-arching corruption in Mexico. Politicians, members of the army and the police,

clergymen and businessmen alike participate in a masquerade in which drug trafficking is supposedly battled against, while everybody profits from its financial success. It is a cynical look at the flaws of the Mexican political system, rendered in a tone of self-indulgent Grand Guignol that is not always rewarding.

Jorge Michel Grau's **We Are What We Are**

Other films worked on a more personal level, as they dealt with the subjects of physical illness, existential uneasiness and the solitude of Mexican immigrants in America. Maria Novaro's **The Good Herbs** (*Las buenas hierbas*) explores euthanasia as the moral choice of a young woman witnessing the total decay of her mother through the ravages of Alzheimers. Rubén Imaz' **Cephalopod** (*Cefalópodo*) focuses on the long process of mourning experienced by a young painter following the death of his girlfriend and his search for a giant squid in the waters of Northern Mexico. Another interesting film, **Nomads** (*Nómadas*), shot in New York,

Rubén Imaz' **Cephalopod**

Maria Novaro's **The Good Herbs**

describes the experience of a group of illegal Mexican workers as they try to overcome cultural alienation and moral distress through friendship and mutual understanding. Of these films only *Hell* has enjoyed some commercial success, while others still await a release that will offer them some chance of success.

A similar situation affects documentary film, which has a thriving culture, but few films are ever screened on a commercial basis. The result is generally a few small screenings to art-house audiences, where they enjoy a brief, but welcome, life.

The year's best films
Leap Year (Michael Rowe)
Summer of Goliath/Perpetuum mobile
(Nicolas Pereda)
Hell (Luis Estrada)

Quote of the year
'When we hear people talk about Mexican cinema today, we have the illusion of seeming prosperity, when in fact we are currently living quite the contrary.' VÍCTOR UGLADE, *Head of the Mexican Association of Filmmakers, and a filmmaker himself.*

CARLOS BONFIL is a film critic, contributing a weekly article on cinema to *La Jornada*, a leading Mexican newspaper. He is the author of *Through the Mirror: Mexican Cinema and Its Audiences* (1994).

Directory
All Tel/Fax numbers begin (+52)
Cineteca Nacional, Avenida México-Coyoacán 389, Col Xoco, México DF. Tel: 1253 9314. www.cinetecanacional.net.
Association of Mexican Film Producers & Distributors, Avenida División del Norte 2462, Piso 8, Colonia Portales, México DF. Tel: 5688 0705. Fax: 5688 7251.
Cinema Production Workers Syndicate (STPC), Plateros 109 Col San José Insurgentes, México DF. Tel: 5680 6292. cctpc@terra.com.mx.
Dirección General de Radio, Televisión y Cinematografía (RTC), Roma 41, Col Juárez, México DF. Tel: 5140 8010. ecardenas@segob.gob.mx.
Instituto Mexicano de Cinematografía (IMCINE), Insurgentes Sur 674 Col del Valle, CP 03100, México DF. Tel: 5448 5300. mercaint@institutomexicanodecinematografía.gob.mx.

Michael Rowe's **Leap Year**

Morocco Maryam Touzani

With around 15 produced each year, Morocco is now ranked third in Africa in terms of production of full-length features. However, the largest film producer is the state, which rarely sees a return on its investment. Even the country's most popular films have had little impact at the box office. So the industry is kept afloat by state grants.

Almost all feature films produced in Morocco benefit from the assistance fund of the Moroccan Cinematographic Centre (CCM), which is involved in the production of over 75 per cent of projects and whose resources are constantly increasing. Other support agencies include national television and Fonds Sud, which is affiliated to the French Cinema Centre. The number of production companies has increased dramatically in recent years, but most are involved in the more profitable television sector. Nonetheless, a relatively large number of films exploring diverse themes still manage to be produced.

Mohamed Ismail returned with **Townfolks**, (*Awlad Lablad*), the story of three graduates desperate to find work. One becomes a Muslim fundamentalist, another starts a public

Swel and Imad Noury's **The Man Who Sold the World**

transport business while the third descends into crime and drug dealing. Swel and Imad Noury's **The Man Who Sold the World**, which featured in the Panorama section of the Berlin Film Festival, is an adaptation of Dostoevsky's *A Weak Heart*. Though visually enthralling, its narrative fails to engage, as it shifts between fantasy and reality. Hicham Ayouch's controversial second feature, **Cracks** (*Fissures*), was shot with no script and no real crew. It unfolds in Tangiers, where three characters in search of love and deliverance meet. Mohamed Lyounssi's **Allo 15** is a touching film about adolescence and the bonds of friendship and family, while Driss Chouika's **Crossed Destinies** (*Destins Croisés*) finds three couples in their forties, having lost touch since their wild university years, reunited through another friend. They relive their past, which was marked by the extreme politics of the 1970s. In Hassan Benjelloun's **Forgotten** (*Les Oubliés de l'Histoire*), two lovers decide to emigrate to Belgium, only to encounter a human trafficking network.

Angels' Terminal (*Terminus des Anges*) is a portmanteau of three short films by Narjiss Nejjar, Hicham Lasri and Mohamed Mouftakir. The stories intertwine around the suicide of a man with AIDS and is told through the eyes of his two wives and neighbour, detailing the ignorance, stigma and isolation surrounding the disease. A plea for tolerance could also be found in veteran film director Latif Lahlou's **The Big Villa** (*La Grande Villa*), about a family who decide to leave Paris and settle in Morocco. Ismaël Saidi's **Ahmed Gassiaux** tells the story of Ahmed Guessous, whose family was killed by the French army during the war of Taza in 1924.

Latif Lahlou's **The Big Villa**

Mohamed Mouftakir's first feature, **Pegasus** (*Pégase*), received the top honours at the Tangiers National Film Festival. He tells the story of Zineb, a psychiatrist in a mental asylum who attempts to unravel the mystery of Rihana, a terrified country girl who believes she's pregnant by Zayd, a boy from her village, and that her pregnancy is blessed by a spirit her father venerates.

Though a large number of short films are produced, they are rarely screened (production companies are required by law to make three short films or one feature film in order to operate). Among this year's better projects is Adil El Fadili's **Short Life** (*Courte Vie*), a film about the curse of bad luck, which won the

Grand Prix at the Tangiers Mediterranean Short Film Festival. In Samia Charkioui's **Fatma**, a crippled old woman works as a maid in a luxurious property in Marrakech, preparing it for the arrival of her boss, 'Mister Jacques'. Jihane El Bahhar's **Lost Soul** (*L'Ame Perdue*) relates the story of Murad, a young street artist who lives in a miserable room and whose universe exists in the portraits he paints.

The expected boom in the audiovisual sector and the creation of many production companies that preceded it have led to film schools opening across the country. Moreover, a strategy is planned, with the objective of increasing cinema attendance for domestic features. There is also a plan to double the number of films produced, as well as the increased promotion and participation of these films at international festivals. There is also talk of supporting the overseas sales of Moroccan films and to continue to attract foreign productions to the country. There is still a long way to go.

The year's best film
Pegasus (Mohamed Mouftakir)

Quote of the year
'For me a good film is a film that is thought of and conceived in a cinematographic approach from the very beginning. The pure language of cinema has to be at its essence.' MOHAMED MOUFTAKIR, *director of* **Pegasus**.

MARYAM TOUZANI is a freelance journalist based in Morocco and working internationally, specialising in Art and Culture.

Mohamed Mouftakir's **Pegasus**

Mozambique Guido Convents

2010 can be seen as a special year for Mozambican cinema. Despite the absence of financial help from the government, over 20 features, short films and documentaries were produced and an international documentary festival was organised.

The Dockanema Film Festival celebrated its 5th edition. It has proved to be a driving force for local cinema culture, a showcase for the national and international documentaries and a space for reflection on cinema policy and culture. It has re-evaluated the audiovisual heritage, developed substantially the cinematographic culture and promoted filmmaking in general and young filmmakers in particular.

The festival is an initiative of Pedro Pimenta. He has been involved in Mozambican cinema since 1977 and is one of the co-founders with Luís Carlos Cabaço and the filmmakers Camilo de Sousa, Isabel Noronha, Licínio de Azevedo, of Ebano Multimedia Ltd, which produces the festival in association with AMOCINE (Association of Mozambican Filmmakers). For the 5th edition, Pimenta organised the first international symposium on the history of film in Mozambique with participants from Brazil, Belgium, the UK, Portugal, and the US. At this occasion a restored version of *Behind the Lines* (1970) was presented, with its British director, Margaret Dickinson, present for the screening. It was the first western film made about the social, political and military organisation of the liberation movement FRELIMO, in the liberated Niassa province of Mozambique. The film was used internationally in the protest campaigns against the Portuguese colonial wars.

Since the liberalisation of the media in 1991, about a dozen private production houses have been founded. Ebano Multimedia Ltd, Promarte and Íris Imaginações are still very active and are often partners in international co-productions. Zoom: Produção, Gráfica e Vídeo and Nova Mahla Filmes were formed more recently. Zoom is responsible for Diana Manhiça's documentary, **The Bridge: A History of the Ferryboat Bagamoyo** (*Ponte-História do Ferryboat Bagamoyo*), which not only presents a day in the life of the ferryboat, but locates it in terms of the historical link it provided between Catembe and Maputo. It is a world that will likely disappear with the building of a new bridge connecting the island to Mozambique's capital.

Diana Manhiça's **The Bridge: A History of the Ferryboat Bagamoyo**

Nova Mahla Filmes produced Pipas Forjaz and Mikey Fonseca's tragic-comic short, **Mahla**. It tells the story of an alcoholic businessman who beats his wife. But for all the abuse meted out to her, the wife finds it difficult to leave him. A pioneer of films about children, Isabel Noronha re-teamed with French director Vivian Altman for **Salani**, which interweaves animation and documentary in its account of the trafficking of Mozambican children to South Africa by their families.

Three feature films were produced in 2010. João Ribeiro presented **The Last Flight of the Flamingo** (*O Último Voo do Flamingo*) at the Cinemas of the World section of the Cannes Film festival. It is based on a book by local magical realist author Mia Couto and unfolds in the early 1990s, in Mozambique's interior, where UN troops keep the peace. Five soldiers are killed in an explosion, with only their genitals found. During the official enquiry into this event the complex history of the Mozambican people is depicted.

Between April and June, Ebano Multimedia co-produced two feature films: Licínio de Azevedo's **Margarida** and Guinea-Bissau director Flora Gomes' **The Children's Republic** (*A república di mininus*). *Margarida* goes back to the early days of Mozambican independence, in Mozambique in 1975. It was a moment of optimism, with hope that the future would be better for Mozambicans, following 500 years of colonialism. By contrast, Gomes' film is far from plausible. It is a story about child soldiers and the formation of a new society without adults.

This year, the video art Associação de Vídeo Arte de Moçambique (AVIDEOARTE) celebrated its fifth anniversary. It is an exceptional organisation in Africa, but understandable given Mozambique's audiovisual history. In 1978, Jean-Luc Godard visited and introduced video and his ideas about experimental filmmaking. In the 1990s, filmmakers and video artists such as Chico Carneiro and Pompílio Hilário (Gemuce) were already experimenting with video art. In 2009, AVIDEOARTE organised an international festival promoting national and international video art in Maputo and Beira. And for the last two years, the works of Mozambican video artists have been presented at Dockanema. Not only those of pioneers like Aladino Jasse, but also a new generation, such as Maimuna Adam with her film **O Lar** (*4',20'*). The film shows a room with

João Ribeiro's **The Last Flight of the Flamingo**

a window and a door, which represents home and the nostalgia of having a place from which to look out to the world, and the idea that in the world one has a place.

The year's best films
The Bridge: A History of the Ferryboat Bagamoyo (Diana Manhiça)
Salani (Isabel Noronha and Vivian Altman)
The Last Flight of the Flamingo (João Ribeiro)
O Lar (Maimuna Adam)

Quote of the year
'I have no regrets of the documentaries we filmmakers made during the regime of Samora Machel. [At that] moment we had to contribute to the construction of national unity and Mozambican cultural identity. We Mozambicans didn't know each other, so our role was to bring the people together... Today, it is not easy to make films in a wild capitalistic system and the Government doesn't show any interest in promoting Mozambican cinema. But this doesn't hinder us in producing films we want to make and in the [style] we prefer, and to play a role in [questioning] our country.' CAMILO DE SOUSA *in an interview recorded in Maputo, September 2010.*

GUIDO CONVENTS is a Belgian film historian specialising in colonial and non-western cinema. He has published seven books on African Cinema. He works as a journalist for the World Catholic Association for Communication (SIGNIS) in Brussels. Since 1996 he has been president of the Afrika Filmfestival in Leuven (Belgium).

Netherlands Leo Bankersen

2010 started off with the birth of a new organisation: EYE Film Institute Netherlands. Maybe not as brand new as it might seem at first glance, but still an ambitious merger of four existing organisations, each with their own specialisation. The Filmmuseum (collection, presentation, distribution), Holland Film (international promotion), the Netherlands Institute for Film Education and the Filmbank (experimental film) pooled their resources to form a nationwide umbrella institute, promising a more coherent support of national film culture.

EYE's first job is the presentation of a plan for the nationwide digitalisation of cinemas, making it possible even for small arthouse venues to make the digital transition. Implementation will hopefully start in 2011.

Despite economic crisis, the total box office is still on the rise. At the time of writing, admissions for 2010 were expected to surpass last year's figure of 27 million. Dutch market share is fairly well maintained, at 11 per cent for the first ten months, similar to 2009.

The kind of Dutch film that does well with the home audience is exemplified by Antoinette Beumer's **The Happy Housewife** (*De gelukkige huisvrouw*), a drama with a touch of irony and sex, about post-natal psychosis, based on a semi-autobiographical bestseller. Films aimed at children and families also performed well and were often quite enjoyable, such as Joram Lürsen's festive comedy **The Magician** (*Het geheim*).

Potential Yuletide hits may give the market share an additional boost, although it will probably be difficult to equal the 17 per cent bump witnessed last year. Much will depend on how well Dick Maas' horror film **Saint** (*Sint*) performs against the latest Harry Potter film. *Saint* is an entertaining piece of cultural blasphemy in which Sint Nicolaas, the Dutch equivalent of Santa Claus, turns out to be a serial killer. If first weekends are anything to go by, the film is a hit.

A dark cloud appeared on the horizon when the new centre-right government took office on October 14th and announced severe cuts across culture and the arts. A reduction of 22 per cent was mooted, reason for immediate alarm. Doreen Boonekamp, CEO of the Netherlands Film Fund, warned that 'this could effect the total Dutch film industry. The production volume of films both for a wide audience as well as art films would drop,' adding that 'even without cuts, the Netherlands should establish a soft money scheme to strengthen economic revenues for film production.'

An older and by now well-known problem that won't go away is that the more artistic Dutch film continues to under perform at the box office. A good example is **Joy** by

Antoinette Beumer's **The Happy Housewife**

Mijke de Jong, a study of a strong, but anguished, teenager who wrestles with the mixed emotions she feels for her mother, who abandoned her as a baby. When the Netherlands Film Festival jury awarded *Joy* the Best Film prize it provoked two reactions. Some praised the decision as a boost for the arthouse film, while others protested it wasn't right to give such an important prize to a film with a cinema attendance of only 2300.

The number of Dutch features that received a cinema release (36 including 12 documentaries) was satisfying compared to the 31 released in 2009, but the majority of them only attracted a small audience. This also proved the case with acclaimed titles such as David Verbeek's subtle contemporary tale about a virtual relationship, **R U There**, which was selected for Un Certain Regard in Cannes. More daring, yet no more successful, was Ineke Smits' Second World War drama, **The Aviatrix of Kazbek** (*De vliegenierster van Kazbek*). It recounted the bloody uprising of a battalion of Georgian POWs, presented in a magical-realist style.

Ineke Smits' **The Aviatrix of Kazbek**

The Netherlands Film Festival celebrated its 30th edition with the *Mirror of Holland* programme – a selection of films from the past 30 years that reflect the changing zeitgeist. Obvious as this theme may appear, Dutch filmmakers have never previously been know to have their fingers on the pulse of current affairs, although this seems to be changing. More young filmmakers find themselves inspired by stories in modern settings.

Hanro Smitsman's **Dusk**

Mark de Cloe's **Shocking Blue** uses the Dutch bulb-growing region as a realistic backdrop for a grim yet poetic teen drama. In a similar vein, Sander Burger's **Hunting & Sons** (*Hunting & Zn*) peers behind the neat facade of a small village, where the pregnancy of a young married woman turns into a nightmare. Arguably the most impressive example of a more contemporary style of filmmaking is Hanro Smitsman's **Dusk** (*Schemer*). Loosely based on a real murder case, it shows the destructive aspects of group behaviour within a band of youngsters. It was lauded by Dutch film critics, but was refused distribution through Pathé cinemas, the largest cinema chain in the Netherlands.

One of the few films that managed to combine artistic achievement with healthy box-office returns was **Tirza**, by Rudolf van den Berg and based on a much-praised novel by Arnon Grunberg. This dark and confrontational exploration of the loneliness and despair of a modern man was chosen as Dutch entry for the Academy Awards.

Rudolf van den Berg's **Tirza**

Another film that managed to charm audience and critics alike was the children's film **Eep!** (*Iep!*), which was selected for the Berlin Film Festival. A philosophical fairy tale about a small girl with wings, it was marred by the unresolved conflict between director Rita Horst and her producer regarding the final cut. Horst had her name removed from the credits.

Rita Horst's **Eep!**

A rare example of Dutch political drama, Peter de Baan's **Majesty** (*Majesteit*) subtly crosses the boundary between fact and fiction by imagining what might have happened if Queen Beatrix had chosen to contradict the government.

The most impressive documentary amongst the year's strong line-up was **Farewell**, by Ditteke Mensink and film researcher Gerard Nijssen. For this slightly fictionalised adventure of a female journalist flying around the world in the Graf Zeppelin, only archive footage was used. Robert Oey's **The Lie** (*De leugen*) dealt

Ditteke Mensink and Gerard Nijssen's **Farewell**

with the controversy surrounding Ayaan Hirsi Ali, a former Dutch MP of Somalian descent. The film's pièce de résistance is a series of musical scenes, in which Oey convinced MPs and the former PM to partake.

This year's International Film Festival Rotterdam appeared in a slightly trimmed state. With two major sponsors lost, the crisis didn't go unnoticed. Still, there was the familiar wealth of adventurous world cinema, with a focus on new talent and experimentation. The most interesting sidebar this year was the section devoted to African cinema. The programme not only featured the usual overview and tributes; there were also a number of specially commissioned films, the result of co-operation between non-African directors and local filmmakers. Such a programme highlighted once again the importance of Rotterdam, not only as a platform for exhibition, but as an essential outlet for creative talent.

The International Documentary Festival Amsterdam, the other important international film event, opened with the new Dutch documentary **Position Among the Stars** (*Stand van de sterren*), the concluding part of Leonard Retel Helmrich's trilogy on the life of a poor Indonesian family. In a fluid and dynamic style and with surprising humor Retel Helmrich captures the heartbeat of the country. Also at IDFA was veteran director George Sluizer's **Homeland**, the follow-up to his earlier films on the Palestinian cause. It went on to win the Best Documentary award at Abu Dhabi Film Festival.

Nanouk Leopold's daring analysis of a relationship, **Brownian Movement**, premiered at Toronto but will not open in the Netherlands until March 2011. After debuting with her arthouse hit *Nothing Personal*, Urszula Antoniak saw her second project, **Code Blue**, selected by the Cinefondation Atelier in Cannes. Filming began in September 2010. 2011 also sees new films by Paul Verhoeven and Martin Koolhoven, both working on stories situated in the former Netherlands East Indies, now Indonesia.

Mijke de Jong's **Joy**

The year's best films

Dusk (Hanro Smitsman)
Tirza (Rudolf van den Berg)
The Aviatrix of Kazbek (Ineke Smits)
Farewell (Ditteke Mensink and Gerard Nijssen)
Joy (Mijke de Jong)

Quotes of the year

'If there is no engagement in it I find it
nothing. Something should be at stake.'
HANRO SMITSMAN, *director of* **Dusk**, *about the
kind of cinema he prefers.*

'Go with the flow.' PAUL VERHOEVEN, *when
asked what advice he would give to young filmmakers
aspiring to a career in the U.S.A.*

Directory

All Tel/Fax numbers begin (+31)
Association of Dutch Film Critics (KNF), PO Box
10650, 1001 ER Amsterdam. Tel: (6) 2153 4555.
info@filmjournalisten.nl. www.filmjournalisten.nl.
Cobo Fund, PO Box 26444, Postvak M54, 1202 JJ
Hilversum. Tel: (35) 677 5348. Fax: (35) 677 1955.
cobo@cobofonds.nl. portal.omroep.nl/cobofonds/.
Contact: Jeanine Hage.
Dutch Federation for Cinematography (NFC),
PO Box 143, 1180 AC Amstelveen. Tel: (20) 426
6100. Fax: (20) 426 6110. info@nvbbureau.nl. www.
nfcstatistiek.nl/index2.html. Contact: Wilco Wolfers.
EYE Film Institute Netherlands, Sandra den
Hamer, Vondelpark 3, PO Box 74782, 1070 BT
Amsterdam. Tel: (20) 589 1400. Fax: (20) 683 3401.
info@eyefilm.nl. www.eyefilm.nl.
Filmmuseum, Sandra den Hamer, Vondelpark 3,
PO Box 74782, 1070 BT Amsterdam. Tel: (20) 589
1400. Fax: (20) 683 3401. info@filmmuseum.nl.
www.filmmuseum.nl.
Holland Film, Claudia Landsberger, Jan
Luykenstraat 2, 1071 CM Amsterdam. Tel: (20) 570

7575. Fax: (20) 570 7570. hf@hollandfilm.nl.
www.hollandfilm.nl.
**International Documentary Film Festival
Amsterdam**, Frederiksplein 52, 1017 XN
Amsterdam. Tel: (020) 627 3329. Fax: (020) 638
5388. info@idfa.nl. www.idfa.nl.
International Film Festival Rotterdam, PO Box
21696, 3001 AR Rotterdam. Tel: (10) 890 9090. Fax:
(10) 890 9091. tiger@filmfestivalrotterdam.com.
www.filmfestivalrotterdam.com.
Ministry of Education, Culture and Science, Arts
Dept, PO Box 16375, 2500 BJ Den Haag. Tel: (70)
412 3456. Fax: (70) 412 3450. www.rijksoverheid.
nl/ministeries/ocw.
**Netherlands Film and Television Academy
(NFTA)**, Markenplein 1, 1011 MV Amsterdam.
Tel: (20) 527 7333. Fax: (20) 527 7344.
info@filmacademie.nl. www.filmacademie.nl.
Contact: Sytze van der Laan.
Netherlands Film Festival, Willemien van Aalst,
PO Box 1581, 3500 BN Utrecht. Tel: (30) 230 3800.
Fax: (30) 230 3801. info@filmfestival.nl.
www.filmfestival.nl.
Netherlands Film Fund, Jan Luykenstraat 2,
1071 CM Amsterdam. Tel: (20) 570 7676.
Fax: (20) 570 7689. info@filmfonds.nl. www.
filmfund.nl. Contact: Doreen Boonekamp.
Netherlands Institute for Animation Film (NIAf),
PO Box 9358, 5000 HJ Tilburg. Tel: (13) 532 4070.
Fax: (13) 580 0057. niaf@niaf.nl. www.niaf.nl.
Contact: Ton Crone.
Netherlands Institute for Sound and Vision,
Sumatralaan 45, 1217 GP Hilversum. Tel: (35) 677
5555. Fax: (35) 677 3307.
Rotterdam Media Fund, Lloydstraat 9F, 3025 EA
Rotterdam. Tel: (10) 436 0747. Fax: (10) 436 0553.
info@rmf.rotterdam.nl. www.rff.rotterdam.nl.
Contact: Jacques van Heijningen.

LEO BANKERSEN is a freelance film critic,
contributing regularly to *de Filmkrant*, the
largest independent film magazine in the
Netherlands.

New Zealand Peter Calder

His adaptation of the *Lord of the Rings* prequel, **The Hobbit**, may have spent much of the year mired in production delays, but the emperor of Wellywood (as his hometown Wellington is dubbed), Peter Jackson, was still centre-stage in the local cinema business in 2010.

The latter part of the year was dominated by a poorly handled dispute between Warner Bros, the studio behind the two-film project, and local actors. The scrap arose out of a boycott call from the Equity chapter's Australian parent union, which in turn was having its strings pulled by SAG in the US, and purported to be about working conditions for actors on local productions. But the plan backfired spectacularly: the public perception was of an Australian bully-boy holding the revered Jackson to ransom, and tech guilds, whose members initially maintained a telling silence, finally came out vociferously and vituperatively against the actors.

The situation was only saved when the government controversially changed the law to guarantee Warners industrial peace and sweetened the deal with increased tax breaks, but the damage done to New Zealand's reputation as a good place for studios to shoot was incalculable.

Jackson also figured in the August release of a report into the New Zealand Film Commission, a state-funded project-development agency which he has been sharply critical of in the past. He and Australian film academic David Court spent nearly a year interviewing stakeholders and industry experts, revealing a deep unease within an organisation that communicated poorly with the production

Gaylene Preston's **Home By Christmas**

sector and created an 'adversarial culture'. Many of the report's findings were overtaken by events, since the regime of the little-liked previous chief executive, Ruth Harley, had ended in the interim, when she took up a similar job in Australia. However, the review made a number of recommendations, including a move towards focusing on quality, not quantity, in the development of projects.

If off-screen life was fraught, there was much to be pleased about on-screen. **Boy**, a bitter-sweet coming-of-age comedy set in a remote rural community, became the biggest-grossing local film at the domestic box office, surpassing Roger Donaldson's runaway 2005 hit, *The World's Fastest Indian*. It was the second feature for the preternaturally gifted Taika Waititi, following 2007's oddball rom-com *Eagle vs Shark*. He also proved himself a gifted comic talent in a lead role as the title character's father, a shiftless but good-hearted dreamer. Unsurprisingly, the critically acclaimed film swept up at the local film awards.

The second notable success, albeit more artistic than financial, was a heartfelt work by industry veteran, Gaylene Preston (*War Stories*

Our Mothers Never Told Us; Bread and Roses). **Home By Christmas** is her father's story, and is a shining example of that special genre, an enacted documentary, in which actor Tony Barry riffed on audio interviews Preston had conducted with her father before his death, in the early 90s. The result, which interleaved archive footage, dramatised sequences and re-enacted interviews, was that rarest of things – a newly minted work that instantly became a precious cultural artefact.

Other films struggled at the local box office, but in the case of two, it was not for want of quality. **Matariki** is the first feature by Michael Bennett, a seasoned television director. His small but compelling drama is set at the time of year when the star cluster Pleiades, called Matariki by Maori, first appears. The film adopted a multi-strand narrative approach and, if directorial control was unsure at times, the ensemble work is terrific and the film perfectly captures its setting – Polynesian-dominated South Auckland, which was so grimly portrayed in 1994's *Once Were Warriors*.

Michael Bennett's **Matariki**

A sure sense of place distinguished the most improbable success of the year, the ultra-low-budget charmer, **The Insatiable Moon**. Mike Riddell adapted his semi-autobiographical novel about a Baptist minister in a once-raffish, now-genteel part of the inner-city, who befriends a genial schizophrenic called Arthur. The latter thinks he is the second Son of God and is looking for his Queen of Heaven to replay the Immaculate Conception. On paper, it sounds dire and it was perhaps unsurprising

Rosemary Riddell's **The Insatiable Moon**

that the Film Commission got cold feet after it was almost agreed as a UK/New Zealand co-production, with Timothy Spall and James Nesbitt attached, and Gillies Mackinnon directing. But the project went ahead anyway, directed by Mike's wife, Rosemary, a magistrate with theatre experience. On a budget of US$250,000, they captured a humane and utterly winning comedy drama thanks largely to some splendid performances from the likes of Rawiri Paratene (*Whale Rider*) and lustrous leading lady, Sara Wiseman, who also impressed in *Matariki*. The film profited from warm reviews and great word of mouth. As this book was going to press, the film finally secured a UK distribution deal.

Less impressive was **Predicament**, Jason Stutter's wooden adaptation of a novel by local writer Ronald Hugh Morrieson, a mid-century practitioner of small-town Gothic. Morrieson's other three novels have previously been filmed and this film, a tepid mystery about various scoundrels involved in blackmail and murder, showed why *Predicament* had not. Likewise,

Jason Stutter's **Predicament**

The Hopes and Dreams of Gazza Snell, in which Australian import William Macinnes played a suburban father obsessed with kart racing, was a heavy-handed domestic melodrama with a wearyingly predictable outcome.

A notable documentary early in the year was Florian Habicht's **Land of the Long White Cloud** (the title is the English translation of a Maori name for these islands), which charted a summer fishing competition on a famous Northland beach and provided a slice of pure Kiwiana almost as good as the director's earlier *Kaikohe Demolition*.

Florian Habicht's **Land of the Long White Cloud**

The year ahead does not promise a frenzy of activity, although *The Hobbit*, due to start shooting in February, will soak up much of the talent pool on both sides of the camera. Comedian Bret McKenzie (the smaller member of the *Flight of the Concords* cast) and Australian comic Hamish Blake will star in the comedy **Two Little Boys**, which begins filming in Southland, in January 2011. The third outing for Robert Sarkies (*Out of the Blue*, *Scarfies*), it is based on the novel of the same name by his brother, Duncan, and concerns the estrangement of two best friends.

Otherwise, as the Film Commission digests its new remit and the economy digests a national debt that costs US$190 million a week to finance, things look very quiet indeed.

PETER CALDER is the chief film critic for the *New Zealand Herald*, the country's major newspaper

The year's best films
Boy (Taika Waititi)
Home By Christmas (Gaylene Preston)
The Insatiable Moon (Rosemary Riddell)
Matariki (Michael Bennett)
Land of the Long White Cloud (Florian Habicht)

Quote of the year
'We're not rich. We make a lot of money, but we're not rich.' TAIKA WAITITI, *picking up a People's Choice Award for film of the year for* **Boy**.

Directory
All Tel/Fax numbers begin (+64)
Film New Zealand, PO Box 24142, Wellington. Tel: (4) 385 0766. Fax: (4) 384 5840. info@filmnz.org.nz. www.filmnz.com.
New Zealand Film Archive, PO Box 11449, Wellington. Tel: (4) 384 7647. Fax: (4) 382 9595. nzfa@actrix.gen.nz. www.filmarchive.org.nz.
New Zealand Film Commission, PO Box 11546, Wellington. Tel: (4) 382 7680. Fax: (4) 384 9719. marketing@nzfilm.co.nz.
Ministry of Economic Development, 33 Bowen St, PO Box 1473, Wellington. Tel: (4) 472 0030. Fax: (4) 473 4638. www.med.govt.nz.
Office of Film & Literature Classification, PO Box 1999, Wellington. Tel: (64) 471 6770. Fax: (4) 471 6781. information@censorship.govt.nz.
Screen Production & Development Association (SPADA), PO Box 9567, Wellington. Tel: (4) 939 6934. Fax: (4) 939 6935. info@spada.co.nz.

Taika Waititi's **Boy**

ABU DHABI FILM COMMISSION

Nigeria Steve Ayorinde

The Nigerian film industry has found a new passion that ran throughout 2010. Nearly every filmmaker of note was subject to a glamorous premiere, often across a number of cities, to launch their films.

All the year's top films had their moment on the red carpet, signifying that cinemagoing is back. No longer is Nollywood, as popular Nigerian cinema is known, the remit of home entertainment. It has returned to the big screen, all over the country. It prompted a celebration of sorts, with both the Nigerian Film Corporation and the National Film and Video Censors Board consciously campaigning for the revitalisation of cinemas. And all this in the same year as the 50th anniversary of the country's independence.

Chinese Anyaene's **The Journey**

One of the cinematic highlights was a Nollywood-Hollywood collaboration, **The Journey** (*Ije*), a beautiful drama directed by Chinese Anyaene, who originally used the film as her graduation film. Few films have had such a rapturous reception as *The Journey* had, with audiences riveted by the stylish

depiction of a Nigerian starlet, desperate for stardom in the US, and how her younger sister comes to her aid.

In an industry where 35mm films are rare, *The Journey* was a welcome presence. As were local films such as Desmond Elliot and Emem Isong's **Bursting Out**, a romantic thriller set in Lagos, and Lancelot Imasuen's satirical drama, **Bent Arrow**, which featured Nollywood stars Joke Sylva and her husband, Olu Jacobs.

Jeta Amata's **Inale**

Four years after *Amazing Grace* was screened in the Cannes film market, Jeta Amata returned with **Inale**, a fairytale romantic drama set in a 19th century Nigerian village. Bongos Ikwe, one of Nigeria's best-known composers and singers wrote and performed the film's score and was also its Executive Director.

Not everything has been so rosy. Niyi Akinmolayan's **Commonwealth** (*Kajola*), Nigeria's first attempt at sci-fi, was a spectacular failure, with audiences unhappy at the film's portrayal of the country as a totalitarian state in 2059. The outrage, which led to some cinemas refunding audiences, led to the film being pulled from exhibition at many venues. Nollywood just didn't seem ready for it, despite the occasional flash of brilliance.

Indigenous films continued to hold their own against English-language productions. For its arty candour and inspiring use of cultural insignias, Tunde Olaoye's **Malaika**, produced by the award-winning Kafidipe sisters, stood out among the late offerings of 2010. Whereas Daniel Ademinokan's **Third Eye** (*Eti Keta*) struggled to earn favour with its taut – and tautly edited – tale of love and betrayal in the city.

The Association of Core Nollywood Producers was formed, a clear indication that internal strife in the industry is far from over, with debates over who has the right to institute a film fund after the government's failed attempt to set one up. Nevertheless, the year was defined largely by the creative enterprise of filmmakers like Obi Edozien whose *Save Our Soul*, an urban drama set in Lagos and London, focused on the ravages brought about by cancer.

A number of impressive films are currently in various stages of post-production. Niji Akanni's epic, **Aramoto**, an historical foray into the legends of traditional masquerades, and Jeta Amata's **Black Gold**, an action thriller and a bold examination of the corruption within the oil business in the volatile Niger Delta region, will be released in 2011. The doyen of Nigerian filmmakers, Tunde Kelani, is on location shooting his much-anticipated **Maami**, while director Charles Novia is preparing to shoot **Majek**, a biopic of Nigerian reggae star, Majek Fashek.

Promotional image for Chinese Anyaene's **The Journey**

The year's best films
The Journey (Chinese Anyaene)
Inale (Jeta Amata)
Malaika (Tunde Olaoye)
Commonwealth (Niyi Akinmolayan)
Bursting Out (Desmond Elliot and Emem Isong)

Quote of the year
'Piracy, to me, is an economic crime and a solution is not reached by closing them down. I do not wish to make excuses for the crime, but I think it is better to work towards making them (pirates) your officials in order to have a win-win situation.' BABATUNDE FASHOLA, *the governor of Lagos State of Nigeria, responding to an enquiry by filmmakers and musicians on how best to tackle the growing menace of piracy in Nigeria.*

STEVE AYORINDE is a film critic and editor of *National Mirror* newspaper. He is a member of FIPRESCI and sits on the Jury of the African Movie Academy Awards (AMAA). He is the author of *Masterpieces: A Critic's Timeless Report*.

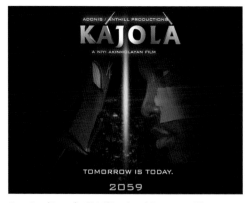

Promotional image for Niyi Akinmolayan's **Commonwealth**

Norway Trond Olav Svendsen

The Norwegian film industry is healthy. For a decade now, domestic product has generated significantly more excitement than it used to. Over 20 Norwegian films are released each year, attracting a significant percentage of the market share. This new level of energy has attracted the interest of foreign distributors and the increased quality of films has seen them play at an increasing number of international festivals.

There has been criticism that an 'artificially' high production rate displays a lack of thought over the presence of an audience sizeable enough to watch all the films, creating an unhealthy level of competition amongst the home-grown product. Others complain that too many genre films, such as the *Cold Prey* series, are being made. There certainly exist a number of young directors satisfied with copying a mainstream Hollywood model. But the results can be entertaining. Above all, the current system allows for young mavericks or established talent, whether they have more esoteric, art-house or commercial instincts, more opportunities to makes films.

Films by established figures were not so successful this year. Marius Holst, Bent

Marius Holst's **King of Devil's Island**

Hamer, Erik Skjoldbjærg and Petter Næss, who made **King of Devil's Island** (*Kongen av Bastøy*), **Home for Christmas** (*Hjem til jul*), **Nokas** and **Shameless** (*Maskeblomstfamilien*) respectively, all handled painful subjects with conviction, but their efforts were not rewarded commercially. Holst tells a story about the clash of strong wills at a correctional facility for boys in the early decades of the 20th century, with Stellan Skarsgård as the brutal warden. The film is effective in its portrayal of a degrading environment, but often appears more a series of interconnected images than a real drama. Hamer's film, which mixes together a number of stories and characters at Christmas time, is typical of his work and certainly very watchable. But it is ultimately too fragmented. Skjoldbjærg tells the story of a robbery that

Erik Skjoldbjærg's **Nokas**

took place in 2004, but the style is so close to a documentary it diminished the dramatic elements of the film, leaving the audience with little more knowledge of the crime than what they learned from the news. Finally, Peter Næss' portrayal of a troubled young man felt constrained by its literary source, with both dialogue and mood veering uneasily off-target.

Hans Petter Moland fared better with **A Somewhat Gentle Man** (*En ganske snill mann*), a festival hit and an example of a successful international co-production, featuring a script by a Dane, Kim Fupz Aakeson, and with Stellan Skarsgård (Sweden) in the lead role. Ulrik is released from prison, after having been convicted for killing a man. The film details his attempts to re-enter society, reconcile with his family and to escape the criminal links that saw him incarcerated in the first place. Although it veers close to familiar genre territory, Moland's film unfolds in its own lively way, hovering between tragedy and comedy, with Skarsgård building his performance with steady conviction. Social realist in tone, the film's tension is always threatening to erupt.

Hans Petter Moland's **A Somewhat Gentle Man**

Equally secure in its handling of edgy realism is Maria Sødahl's **Limbo**, a return to the fray for a filmmaker who had made an impression with her short films in the early 1990s. Her feature debut, which she also wrote, is set in an enclave for foreign engineers in Trinidad, in the 1970s. Sonia (the excellent Line Verndal) is the wife of an engineer (Henrik Rafaelsen), who is already stationed on the island. When she arrives with their two children, it soon

Maria Sødahl's **Limbo**

becomes clear that he has had an affair. She also clashes with her children's schoolteacher. And what is expected of a foreign engineer's wife in a developing country? The troubles of the Norwegians are effectively contrasted with that of a more seasoned couple played, by Bryan Brown and Lena Endre. Sødahl draws out a strong feminist subtext although the film's attempt to deal with too many issues and the unnecessary final scenes threaten to undermine it. The cinematography also fails to capture the heat and humidity of Trinidad, but the handling of the relationships between the female and male characters always ensures the film is never less than riveting.

Autumn saw lighter fare and something for fans of fantasy. **The Trollhunter** (*Trolljegeren*) is a mockumentary directed by newcomer André Øvredal. Its striking premise is that the legends about Norwegian trolls are actually true. They are contained in secret hydroelectric installations that exist in practically every

André Øvredal's **The Trollhunter**

Norwegian mountain. The film opens more in a horror vein, albeit filmed like a documentary, before settling into a lighter mood. With well-known stand-up comedians among the cast, Øvredal displays an impressive talent for blending horror and comedy.

Much of the criticism against the present Norwegian industry is unreasonable. Some critics want fewer films made. Some want a quota system to increase the number of female directors. This would, of course, immediately solve the problem, at least as seen by the politicians, but introducing this kind of regulating bureaucracy in a field of artists and artisans also has its dangers. The best policy for Norway is to maintain a steady rate of 25 releases per year and to focus on marketing them to domestic and international audiences. Maintaining such an industry offers more guarantee that the filmmakers will have more opportunities to present us with the very best of their work.

The year's best films
A Somewhat Gentle Man
(Hans Petter Moland)
Limbo (Maria Sødahl)
The Trollhunter (André Øvredal)
Home for Christmas (Bent Hamer)
King of Devil's Island (Marius Holst)

Quotes of the year
'We lack a Lars von Trier.' GEIR KAMSVÅG,
editor of the magazine Film & Kino on the state of the Norwegian industry.

'Abroad we are building the brand "Norwegian film" slowly but surely.' IVAR KØHN, *Film Institute department director, in an interview in the newspaper Aftenposten.*

Directory
All Tel/Fax numbers begin (+47)
Henie-Onstad Art Centre, Sonja Henie vei 31, 1311 Høvikodden. Tel: 6780 4880. post@hok.no.
Norwegian Film Institute, PO Box 482 Sentrum, 0105 Oslo. Tel: 2247 4500. Fax: 2247 4599. post@nfi.no. www.nfi.no. Contact: Lise Gustavson.

Bent Hamer's **Home for Christmas**

Norwegian Film Development, Dronningens gt. 16, 0152 Oslo. Tel: 2282 2400. Fax: 2282 2422. mail@nfu.no. Contact: Kirsten Bryhni.
Norwegian Film and TV Producers Association, Dronningens gt. 16, 0152 Oslo, Tel: 2311 9311. Fax: 2311 9316. leif@produsentforeningen.no. Contact: Leif Holst Jensen.
Norwegian Film Workers Association, Dronningens gt. 16, 0152 Oslo. Tel: 2247 4640. Fax: 2247 4689. post@filmforbundet.no. Contact: Sverre Pedersen.
Norwegian Media Authority, Nygata 4, 1607 Fredrikstad. Tel: 6930 1200. Fax: 6930 1201. post@medietilsynet.no. Contact: Tom Thoresen.

TROND OLAV SVENDSEN is a historian from the University of Oslo. He has worked as a newspaper film critic and an editor in the Oslo publishing house of Kunnskapsforlaget. Among his publications is a Theatre and Film encyclopedia.

Poland Barbara Hollender

The Polish Film Institute celebrated its fifth year of operation in 2010. The period since its inception has been marked by the rapid development of the Polish film industry. Annual production skyrocketed from 20 titles per year to around 60. Almost 100 new production companies appeared on the scene, along with 13 regional funds. Making a first film has never been easy for young filmmakers, but the programme *30 minutes* commissioned over 50 short films, with 60 features subsequently shot.

Agnieszka Odorowicz, who was reinstated as director of the Polish Film Institute for another five-year term in October 2010, commented, 'Now is the time to change quantity into quality. We focused on enlivening the Polish film industry, but we co-financed too many weak pictures with state funds. Presently, we are devoted to quality, and we will evaluate projects more rigorously.'

Jerzy Skolimowski's **Essential Killing**

Results of a revival are already visible. In 2010, Polish films competed at numerous prestigious film festivals. At the Venice Film Festival, Jerzy Skolimowski's **Essential Killing** (*Essential Killing*) won the Special Jury Prize and director award. Young documentary filmmaker Bartek Konopka was nominated for an Academy

Bartek Konopka's **Rabbit a'la Berlin**

Award for his short, **Rabbit a'la Berlin** (*Królik po berlińsku*), a story about socialism and transformation, which was viewed from the perspective of rabbits living between the walls that separated West and East Berlin.

Young filmmakers are actively engaged with issues in contemporary Poland, shining a light on its problems. Marcin Wrona's **The Christening** (*Chrzest*) is a faultlessly shot film about a man who tries to secure the wellbeing of his family after the mafia have passed sentence on him. It is a story about a past from which one cannot escape, about responsibility for one's own life and the importance of choices made as well as the difficulty of friendship between men. This monstrously brutal film surprises with the subtlety of the feelings expressed in it.

A study of aggression is also the subject of Przemysław Wojcieszek's **Made in Poland** (*Made in Poland*) and playwright Paweł Sala's **Mother Theresa of Cats** (*Matka Teresa od kotów*). Wojcieszek's film has a young boy who tattoos the words 'FUCK OFF' on his forehead, hates everybody and favours a metal rod over talking. 'Being pissed off is the AIDS of the 20th century,' he says. In Sala's film, based

on a true story, two brothers kill their mother. Violence is in the air and has no specific cause. It is just present, an easy remedy for frustration, lack of fulfilment and helplessness.

A counterbalance to these films, Marek Lechki's **Erratum** (*Erratum*) features a young man who accidentally finds himself in his home town and tries to reconcile with his father. It is an intimate journey to one's roots, with hope for a happy outcome. Dorota Kędzierzawska also joined the group of young filmmakers dealing with present-day issues. **Tomorrow Will be Better** (*Jutro będzie lepiej*) is the story of two small boys from Russia who search for a better life in Poland only to find their dreams clashing with reality.

Marek Lechki's **Erratum**

The older generation of filmmakers took a different approach, often looking at life from a distance; searching for universal subjects and drawing on the past. Most importantly, they avoided any schematic response to humanity's problems, detailing the complexity of human affairs. Jan Kidawa-Błoński's **Little Rose** (*Różyczka*) unfolds in 1968, presenting the tortured ménage à trois between a Security Service employee who bullies his girlfriend into taking a famous writer as her lover, so that she can provide the authorities with information about him. Kidawa-Błoński shows how the mechanisms of totalitarianism inveigled their way into the lives of ordinary people, detailing the gradual deterioration of his character's moral compass. Janusz Majewski, in the partially autobiographical **The Rite of**

Jan Kidawa-Błoński's **Little Rose**

Passage (*Mała matura 1947*), recounts a story of growing up during the post-war years. In **Joanna**, Feliks Falk uses extraordinary means to tell the story of a woman who hid a Jewish girl during the German occupation and was unjustly accused of having an affair with a German. Jan Jakub Kolski's **Venice** (*Wenecja*) is set in 1939 and takes a look at the tragic fate of Poland through the eyes of a child, who desperately tries to look past an impending war, solitude and death.

There was also a marked distinction between the styles used by the two generations. Whereas older directors prefer traditional cinema, employing elaborate set-ups and creating a specific atmosphere, younger directors make the most of the rapid speed of modern life, capturing its rhythms in the editing. Interestingly, the two styles complement each other.

Jerzy Skolimowski's *Essential Killing* stands out as one of 2010's most unique films. It is a story of a prisoner from Afghanistan, probably a terrorist, who escapes when he is transported to a prison in a central European country. In a completely foreign environment, alone against an American army equipped with helicopters, he fights for every moment of his life, killing in order to survive. It is a masterly, provocative film. Sadly, limited distribution prevented it from being seen by a wider audience. Unlike Filip Bajon's nineteenth century comedy, **Maiden Vows** (*Śluby panieńskie*), written by Aleksander Fredro. A slightly modernised version of a staple text attracted almost one million viewers, but was a disappointment artistically.

The box office was dominated by romantic comedies, such as Patryk Vega's **The Cake** (*Ciacho*), Wojciech Wójcik's **Blind Date** (*Randka w ciemno*) and Krzysztof Lange's **Breakfast in Bed** (*Śniadanie do łóżka*). The films received little praise from critics, who were more impressed with the modest, intelligent debut of actor Arkadiusz Jakubik, **A Simple Story About Love** (*Prosta historia o miłości*). Reality and fiction blur in a subtle story that unfolds on the set of a film.

What will the year 2011 bring? The master of Polish cinema, Andrzej Wajda, is making a film about Lech Wałęsa. There are also a number of other historical films. Jerzy Hoffman is completing work on **Battle of Warsaw 1920** (*Bitwa Warszawska 1920*), which deals with the 1920 conflict between Poland and Russia. Antoni Krauze is putting finishing touches to **Black Thursday** (*Czarny czwartek*), about tragic events that took place in Gdynia in 1970. Wojciech Smarzowski is shooting **Rose from Mazury** (*Róża z Mazur*), which unfolds in the Regained Territories (at the Polish and German border) in 1945, while Janusz Zaorski is working on **Syberiada**, which recounts the story of the Poles deported by the NKVD in 1940.

There are also two contemporary debuts: Bartek Konopka's **Fear of Heights** (*Lęk wysokości*) and Jan Komasa's **Suicide Room** (*Sala samobójców*). Małgorzata Szumowska's Polish, French and Danish co-production, **Sponsoring**, about student prostitutes and featuring Juliette Binoche, is also highly anticipated.

BARBARA HOLLENDER is a Warsaw-based journalist and film critic for a daily *Rzeczpospolita*. She covers many major film festivals, and has written, among other works, a study of *Studio Tor* (2000).

The year's best films
The Christening (Marcin Wrona)
Essential Killing (Jerzy Skolimowski)
Erratum (Marek Lechki)
Rabbit a'la Berlin (Bartek Konopka)
Little Rose (Jan Kidawa-Błoński)

Quote of the year
'I don't want only to play with the cinema. If the film is not important for me, it will not be important for other people.' MARCIN WRONA *talking about* The Christening.

Directory
All Tel/Fax numbers begin (+48)
Polish Film Institute, 00-071 Warsaw, ul., Krakowskie Przedmieście 21/23, Tel: (22) 421 0518, Fax: (22) 421 0241. pisf@pisf.pl www.pisf.pl
Polish Filmmakers Association, 00-068 Warsaw, Krakowskie Przedmieście 7. Tel: (22) 556 5440, (22) 845 5132 Fax: (22) 845 3908. biuro@sfp.org.pl www.sfp.org.pl
National Chamber of Audiovisual Producers, ul. Chełmska 21 bud.28 C, 00-724 Warszawa Tel: (22) 840 5901 Fax: (22) 840 5901. kipa@kipa.pl www.kipa.pl
National Film Archive, 00-975 Warsaw, ul., Puławska 61. Tel: (22) 845 5074 Fax: (22) 646 5373. filmoteka@fn.org.pl www.fn.org.pl
Media Desk Poland, 00-724 Warsaw, ul., Chełmska 19/21 p. 229. Tel/Fax: (22) 851 1074, Tel. (22) 559 33 10. biuro@mediadeskpoland.eu www.mediadeskpoland.eu

Marcin Wrona's The Christening

Portugal Martin Dale

Wracked by a major sovereign debt crisis, government cuts, slumping TV advertising revenues and a 'gloom and doom' atmosphere of economic and psychological depression, it hasn't been one of Portugal's better years.

The national film institute, ICA, was obliged to cut production support, given falling income from the levy on TV channels. The activities of the film and TV fund FICA, set up in 2007, were frozen due to lack of contributions from the State and TV companies.

In early 2010, the last straw was delivered when the Minister of Culture, Gabriela Canavilhas, attempted to retain 10% of film-funding grants already awarded, which resulted in a major demonstration from local film talent and unions. The Minister then back-pedalled on the 10% retention, appointed a new management firm for FICA and promised a new Film Law by the end of 2010, which dampened the voices of dissent.

In the meantime, the state-owned national film lab, Tobis, already suffering from the celluloid-to-digital switch and competition from foreign labs, entered into tailspin and was put up for sale in November 2010.

Portuguese films enjoyed very modest returns in 2010, once again seeing no more than 3% of the national box office and no film in the Top 40.

Acclaimed director João Botelho brilliantly captured the ongoing sense of unease in Portugal with his adaptation of the *Book of Disquiet*, by the country's best-known poet, Fernando Pessoa (1888-1935). **Film of Disquiet** (*Filme de Desassossego*) is one of the year's

most powerful films. Botelho is renowned for his powerful visuals, but he can leave the spectator cold. Here he provides an ode to an eternal and labyrinthine Lisbon, employing special effects to show impossible cityscapes, with buildings stretching up to the heavens. The film achieves the daunting feat of combining visceral images with the existential questioning that underlies Pessoa's work and also much of contemporary Portuguese culture. Vexed with God's existence, the main character, Bernardo Soares, one of Pessoa's heteronyms, reaches the conclusion, 'I am God.'

Claúdio da Silva plays Bernardo Soares in **Film of Disquiet**

Frustrated by the low turnout for his last film, *The Northern Land*, which clocked up just 5,000 admissions, unsurprising given the virtually non-existent domestic art-house circuit, Botelho decided on a DIY digital distribution approach, organising a series of director-hosted screenings in over 60 venues throughout the country, for the general public and schools and universities.

With 10,000 admissions in the first four weeks of this strategy, other Portuguese producers such as Paulo Branco are reportedly planning to emulate Botelho's self-distribution model. The Minister of Culture has even announced

Carlos Coelho da Silva's **Adventure in a Haunted House**

plans to build a digital cinema network favouring art-house films.

In the traditional exhibition circuit, the biggest local hit was Carlos Coelho da Silva's **Adventure in a Haunted House** (*Uma Aventura na Casa Assombrada*), an action-thriller based on the children's *Aventura* fiction series written by Isabel Alçada. With a 50-screen Christmas release, the film attracted 125,000 spectators, but in quality was closer to a TV-movie than a cinematic feature.

Veteran director António-Pedro Vasconcelos, responsible for some of Portugal's biggest box-office hits, shifted gear from his favourite genre, film noir, to direct the romantic comedy, **Beauty and the Paparazzo** (*A Bela e a Paparazzi*), which was shot in some of Lisbon's most emblematic locations. The film also marked a genre shift for lead actress, Soraia Chaves, who hitherto has been typecast in erotic roles, including Vasconcelos' previous local hit, *Call Girl*. Beauty did modest business, with 99,000

Soraia Chaves in **Beauty and the Paparazzo**

spectators, but suffered from being excessively lightweight and insufficiently comic.

US-based Fernando Fragata directed an English-language supernatural thriller, **Backlight** (*Contraluz*), starring Joaquim d'Almeida. Advertised as 'the first Hollywood film by a Portugese director', the film combined impressive visuals with a powerful soundtrack, but despite its strong premise – five unrelated characters suffering life crises – the plot is disjointed and the dialogue hackneyed.

Maria João Bastos and João Baptista play Ângela de Lima and D. Pedro da Silva in **Mysteries of Lisbon**

Portugal's most prolific producer, Paulo Branco, who is also director of the Estoril Film Festival, unveiled Raul Ruiz's 4-½ hour epic, **Mysteries of Lisbon**, based on the Portuguese novel by Camilo Castelo Branco and with script by Carlos Saboga. Brilliantly exploring the psychological intrigues of aristocratic nineteenth century Lisbon, with highly polished visuals, Chilean-born Ruiz has delivered one of Portugal's most accomplished films to date.

2010 saw the sophomore outings of two of Portugal's most promising young directors – Antonio Ferreira and Marco Martins – but, sadly, both fell short of their debut films. Ferreira's **Embargo** is based on the novel by the late José Saramago. The main character invents a foot digitaliser, which promises to revolutionise the shoe industry, but his dreams are dashed when he gets locked into his car. An amusing premise loses its way over the course of the film.

لجنة أبوظبي للأفلام
ABU DHABI FILM COMMISSION

Martins' **How to Draw a Perfect Circle** (*Como Desenhar um Círculo Perfeito*) once again employs the powerful imagery and strong performances that marked out his first feature, *Alice*, but this time round everything is less convincing. Dealing with incestuous teenage twins in a dysfunctional family who try to make sense of life and their own sexuality, the film fails to engage.

The main ray of hope for the crisis-ridden Portuguese film industry is the promise of a new film law, although the net result of legal changes in the past has been *plus ça change, plus c'est la même chose.*

A draft law was unveiled in September, promising to introduce tax credits of up to €2.5 million per film. The draft law also includes a phasing out of the $112 million film fund, FICA, and rediverting some of its statutory funds to the cash-strapped ICA. It proposes the introduction of investment obligations for free-TV operators and film distributors, thus decentralising some decision-making power from ICA.

The main stumbling block of the new proposal is an attempt to introduce an ambitious levy system on free- and pay-TV operators, cable TV distributors, exhibitors and telecommunications firms. This has been fiercely contested, including the threat of legal action.

A long road lies ahead before Portuguese cinema establishes a clear legal framework, wider critical success and, above all, a stronger bond with audiences.

MARTIN DALE has lived in Lisbon and the North of Portugal since 1994 and works as an independent media consultant and a contributor to *Variety*. He has written several books on the film industry, including *The Movie Game* (1997).

Lourdes Castro profiled in **Through Shadows**

The year's best films
Film of Disquiet (João Botelho)
Mysteries of Lisbon (Raul Ruiz)
Through Shadows (Catarina Mourão)
Lusitanian Illusion (João Canijo)
Beauty and the Paparazzo (António-Pedro Vasconcelos)

Quotes of the year
'On my films I'm the director but also the editor and I often take care of the photography and sound. This gives me a great liberty of action. The film is for nobody, but at the same time it presents the best of me.' JOÃO BOTELHO, *director of* **Film of Disquiet**.

'The state's intervention in Portuguese cinema is tragic and absolutely inadmissible in a democratic society.' ANTÓNIO-PEDRO VASCONCELOS, *director of* **Beauty and the Paparazzo**.

Directory
All Tel/Fax numbers begin (+351)
Cinemateca Portuguesa, Rua Barata Salgueiro 63, 1269-059 Lisbon. Tel: (21) 359 6200. Fax: (21) 352 3180. www.cinemateca.pt
Institute of Cinema, Audiovisual & Multimedia (ICAM), Rua de S Pedro de Alcântara 45, 1°, 1250 Lisbon. Tel: (21) 323 0800. Fax: (21) 343 1952. mail@icam.pt. www.icam.pt

Romania Cristina Corciovescu

Romanian cinema continues to enjoy its status as a leading light for contemporary film. 2010 boasted 17 features, with another ten in various stages of production. Many of the released films enjoyed festival success and received a wealth of awards. With each passing year, the Romanian film industry operates more efficiently, helped in no small part by its most significant financier, the National Centre of Cinematography.

Mihai Ionescu and Tiberiu Iordan's **Different Mothers**

An independent cinema is also emerging, comprising mostly young, new directors, who are keen for their work to be recognised, thus achieving wider distribution. Of these, the highlights include Dan Chisu's **WebSideStory**, about a girl who wants to avenge the death of her only friend, and **Different Mothers** (*Despre alte mame*), by Mihai Ionescu and Tiberiu Iordan, in which a film crew spend a night in Bucharest Central Station in order to find interviewees for a documentary they are making. Despite certain weaknesses in the way they are made, both films have a certain freshness, which drew the attention of festivals such as Mons, Valladolid and Moscow.

However, the image of Romanian cinema enjoying a perfect situation is not quite

accurate, as was pointed out by participants at the 3rd edition of the 'Romania on the Movie Map' International Conference, organised by the Film Critics Association during the Transylvania Film Festival (TIFF), in June 2010. They noted the meagre domestic box-office returns of Romanian films. 'International success is not enough, the value of a cinema must be validated by its domestic viewers, they claimed. The Romanian populace, whose passion for cinema has never been all consuming, rarely watch a Romanian film. This explains why no Romanian productions appear in the top 70 films at the 2009 box office, or the fact that Romanian films are withdrawn from exhibition after a maximum of 10 weeks, with disappointing results. The causes and the solutions could be extensively discussed, spanning from the total lack of cine-literacy to the insignificant budgets distributors have to advertise their films.

2010 began with a surprise, when Florin Serban's **If I Want to Whistle, I Whistle** (*Eu cand vreau sa fluier, fluier*) was awarded the Silver Bear at the Berlin Film Festival. It takes place in a rural prison for young male offenders. The central character is willing to

Florin Serban's **If I Want to Whistle, I Whistle**

Constantin Popescu's **Portrait of the Fighter as a Young Man**

risk further time behind bars when he finds out about a family problem that needs resolving. It's a simple and sincere film, with a cast comprising mostly non-professionals, many of whom are actual inmates. It is also a subtle shift away from the minimalism of other, recent Romanian productions. Also screening at Berlin, in the Forum section, and no less daring is Constantin Popescu's **Portrait of the Fighter as a Young Man** (*Potretul luptatorului la tinerete*), which recalls a dramatic episode from post-war Romanian history, when there was resistance to the new Soviet regime and the lengths authorities went to in order to hunt down those opposed to them. Popescu has said it is the first part of a trilogy of films that looks back to Romania's recent past.

Andrei Ujica's **The Autobiography of Nicolae Ceausescu**

History also played a major role in the films of directors who were too young to witness the times they present on screen. Titus Muntean's adaptation of a short story by Ioan Grosan, **Kino Caravan** (*Caravana cinematografica*), is set in a small village in the 1950s, a time when collectivisation was reinforced through the ideological manipulation of cinema. A comedy

drama, the film pits the stupidity and obstinacy of a party activist and a Securitat officer, who acts as driver and cinema projectionist, against a group of locals. The past comes to life in Andrei Ujica's **The Autobiography of Nicolae Ceausescu** (*Autobiografia lui Nicolae Ceausescu*) which presents an unsurprisingly unflattering portrait of the dead dictator, highlighting how the Romanian population were an abstraction to him, whose reality he chose to pay no attention to. The film was shown out of competition at Cannes.

Marian Crisan's **Morgen**

There were other fine films. Communication – or the lack of it – and illegal immigration takes centre stage in **Morgen**, the debut of writer-director Marian Crisan. It follows a Turkish man who attempts to emigrate, illegally, to German, but finds himself stuck with a Transylvanian peasant. It received the Special Jury Prize at the Locarno Film Festival. Marital conflict and adultery are the main themes of Radu Muntean's **Tuesday, after Christmas** (*Marti,*

Razvan Radulescu's **First of All, Felicia**

ABU DHABI FILM COMMISSION

dupa Craciun), while Razvan Radulescu's **First of All, Felicia** (*Felicia inainte de toate*) looks at the relationship between a caring mother and her daughter, who lives abroad.

Calin Peter Netzer's **Medal of Honor**

With his second feature, **Medal of Honor** (*Medalia de onoare*), Calin Peter Netzer details the story of a man who receives a medal that doesn't belong to him. His attempts to return it are milked for all they're worth as a satire on contemporary society.

Cristi Puiu's **Aurora**

Aurora, which was selected in the Un Certain Regard section of Cannes 2010, marks the long-awaited return of writer-director Cristi Puiu after a five-year break. It is an ambitious and challenging film. The director describes it as 'a crime story from a different perspective'. Coming in just shy of three hours, it is a long and slow-paced portrait of a middle-aged, disturbed sociopath who commits three crimes with no plausible motivation. With his impenetrable face, the main character – played by Puiu in his acting debut – wanders around

a grey Bucharest, meets some people who remain anonymous, spies a blonde woman (apparently his ex-wife) and concocts his revenge. It will premiere in Romania in 2011.

The year's best films
If I Want to Whistle, I Whistle (Florin Serban)
Tuesday, after Christmas (Radu Muntean)
Morgen (Marian Crisan)
The Autobiography of Nicolae Ceausescu (Andrei Ujica)
First of All, Felicia (Razvan Radulescu, Melissa de Raaf)

Quote of the year
'Kafka would be ten times greater if he lived under the rule of Nicolae Ceausescu.' RADU MIHAILEANU, *director of the French-Romanian co-production* The Concert.

Directory
All Tel/Fax numbers begin (+4)
Centrul National al Cinematografiei, Str. Dem I Dobrescu nr. 4-6, sector 1, 010026, Bucuresti. Tel: 021 310 43 01. Fax: 021 310 43 00. www.cncinema.ro.
Uniunea Cineastilor, Str. Mendeleev nr. 28-30, sector 1, Bucuresti. Tel: 021 316 80 83. Fax: 021 311 12 46. www.ucin.ro.
Arhiva Nationala de Filme, Soseaua Sabarului nr. 20, com Jilava. Tel/Fax: 021 450 12 67. anf@xnet.ro.

CRISTINA CORCIOVESCU is a film critic and historian, and the author of several specialised dictionaries.

Radu Muntean's **Tuesday, after Christmas**

Russia Kirill Razlogov

The main discussion point of the last year has been the creation of the Federal Fund for Social and Economic Support of National Cinematography, or *Cinema Fund*. With extensive public funding (almost US$100 million), it reduced the role of the Ministry of Culture in supporting film projects. The Fund selected eight 'major' beneficiaries, enabling the chosen studios the possibility of funding projects of their own choice for three years. Well, on paper at least. This decision was contested by the Federal Anti-Monopoly Service, but was eventually adopted following the intervention of Prime Minister Putin. The Fund also selected several 'socially important' projects, some historical and literary, as well as works by important filmmakers such as Andrey Zvyagintsev. A bio-pic of the late rock star, Viktor Tsoy, was also green lit.

Alexei Balabanov's **Stoker**

Conflict surrounding these decisions, as well as the legal and financial problems of implementing the new system, resulted in some difficulties, with the rescheduling of many current projects. The first releases mentioning the Fund support in their credits were not the patriotic blockbusters everybody had expected, but low budget art-house movies such as Alexei Balabanov's **Stoker**

(*Kochegar*), a dark tale of sex, greed and betrayal.

Another curiosity, which received the main award at the 'Window to Europe' national film festival, was Roman Karimov's first film, **Inadequate People** (*Neadekvatnye lyudi*), a tragi-comedy about an affair between a middle-aged man and a high-school girl, which owed a debt to the late Siberian cult actor-director, Vassily Shukshin. It shared also the 'Hambourg count' prize (given to the best film of all sections of the festival) with Stanislav Govorukhin's old-fashioned **In the Jazz Style** (*... v Stile Dzhaza*).

The controversy surrounding the Russian film industry began some time ago, with a discussion about the future of the Filmmakers' Union and the legitimacy of its leader, the charismatic actor-director, Nikita Mikhalkov. The Congress of Russian Filmmakers had attempted to oust Mikhalkov, but their vote was declared illegal and, in the following Autumn, the General Assembly confirmed Mikhalkov as the Union's President. As a result, a powerful anti-Mikhalkov campaign appeared, led mostly by critics and several

Nikita Mikhalkov's **Burned by the Sun 2: Exodus**

important directors, who considered themselves as worthy successors to him. An alternative Filmmakers' Union of Russia was formed, led by documentarian Vitaly Mansky, the editor-in-chief of *Iskusstvo Kino*, Daniil Dondurei, and the young director, Boris Khlebnikov, who was eventually elected president of the new organisation. The conflict intensified with the criticism attracted by Mikhalkov's expensive art-house sequel, **Burned by the Sun 2: Exodus** (*Utomlennye solntsem 2: Predstoyanie*), which continued at Cannes, where a direct attack by Russian critics was launched against the director.

Sergei Loznitsa's **My Joy**

Acclaimed documentary filmmaker Sergei Loznitsa's feature debut, **My Joy** (*Schastye moe*), also screened at Cannes and was seen as direct competition to Mikhalkov's film. Co-produced by Ukraine, Germany and the Netherlands, the film was considered anti-Russian (Russian authorities refused their support). It was shot in Russian with Russian actors in the Ukraine and presented a bleak portrait of contemporary life, where Russia is seen to corrupt innocents and transform ordinary people into murderers. Some foreign critics perceived the film as a genre work, but former Russian satellites took it seriously, with Loznitsa collecting numerous regional awards, the most controversial of which was the Best Director prize at the Knotavr Film Festival, in Sochi.

Alexey Fedorchenko's **Silent Souls** (*Ovsyanky*) played to great acclaim at the Venice Film Festival, where it received the Critics' Prize

Alexey Fedorchenko's **Silent Souls**

and cinematographer Mikhail Krichman was awarded the Ozella. Based on a screenplay by Denis Osokin, it details rural life on the Volga river as a widower's friends set out on a road trip to bury the man's wife. Having lost out to Venice with the premiere of this film, Moscow Film Festival instead presented two special discoveries: documentary filmmaker Yuri Shiller's feature, **The Sparrow** (*Vorobei*), and Yuri Feting's Tatar drama, **Bibinur**. Other festival successes during 2010 included Alexei Popogrebsky's psychological drama, **How I Ended This Summer** (*Kak ya provel etim letom*), which was shot by documentary filmmaker Pavel Kostomarov. Sergei Puskepalis and Gregory Dobrynin were awarded for their performances at the Berlin Film Festival. Svetlana Proskurina's **The Truce** (*Peremirie*) won the Kinotavr competition, while Alexey Uchitel's **The Edge** (*Kray*), a powerful drama set in a remote labour camp around the time of the Second World War, is Russia's entry for the Academy Awards. The film explores the relations between Russians and Germans, Russians and Lithuanians, Communist, Stalinists and anti-Communists, prisoners and their guards, and men and women. The high

Alexei Popogrebsky's **How I Ended This Summer**

production values and excellent performances could be undermined, for foreign audiences at least, by the complex plot.

If the festival results are satisfying, the performance of Russian films at the domestic box office is not. After attaining almost 30% of the annual receipts just two years ago, the last year will have seen a drop to below 20%, mainly due to the absence of home-grown blockbusters.

Avatar reigned supreme, with a gross of US$117 million (it was still screening at the end of October), more than double the amount earned by the most successful Russian film, *Irony of Fate 2*. The most successful Russian film of 2010 – the only one to feature in the top ten – was the eccentric comedy, **Our Russia: The Balls of Fate** (*Nasha Russia: Yaitsa Sud'by*), which came six places behind, with US$22 million. Next was **Black Lightning** (*Chernaya Molniya*), a fantasy blockbuster produced by Timur Bekmambetov, with almost US$20 million. That film's fortunes may have been better without the presence of James Cameron's film.

One of the reasons why post-Soviet cinema has failed to attract young audiences is the overwhelming pessimism of the better films, a trend that has dominated Russian film for much of the last three decades. On the official side, there were the super-productions from Mikhalkov (US$8 million), as well as *The Edge*

Alexandr Kott's **The Fortress of Brest**

(US$5 million) and the Russian-Belorussian co-production, **The Fortress of Brest** (*Brestskaya Krepost*) by Alexandr Kott. The performance of these films showed that spectators have tired of patriotic war epics.

Dmitry Mamulia's **Another Sky**

An interest in immigrants from former Soviet republics and their tragic fate can be found in Uzbek director Yusup Razykov's **Gastarbeiter**, Georgian Dmitry Mamulia's **Another Sky** (*Drugoe nebo*) and Andrey Stempkovsky's **Reverse Motion** (*Obratnoe Dvizhenie*), all of which were better received internationally than at home.

The curious mix of animation and live acting, the trademark of Irina Evteeva, could be found in her adaptation of Pushkin's **Little Tragedies** (*Malen'kie Tragedii*). But, again, the film failed to attract audiences.

New trends, particularly between film and the plastic arts, were witnessed by the success of the Media-Forum at the Moscow International

Alexey Uchitel's **The Edge**

Film Festival and the Horizons programme in Venice, where several Russian artists presented their work, including the group Provmyza.

By the end of the year, new measures were taken to support local film production. 1% of all sales of virgin discs and cassettes, as well as electronic equipment to register and duplicate films, will be given to a special rights owners organisation created by the Filmmakers' Union. Nikita Mikhalkov's 65th birthday was commemorated by extensive screenings of his film on the main TV channels.

The year's best films
The Stoker (Alexei Balabanov)
Silent Souls (Alexei Fedorchenko)
Burned by the Sun 2: Exodus
(Nikita Mikhalkov)
Bibinur (Yuri Feting)
How I Ended This Summer
(Alexei Popogrebski)

Quote of the year
'On the global level Russian cinema is still associated with the artistic top-model, created during the Soviet period. Its main characteristic is the exalted spirituality, and its leading cultural hero, who gives this model his image, is Andrei Tarkovsky. Western intellectuals perceive the codes Tarkovsky established in *The Return* of Andrei Zwyagintsev and *Silent Souls* by Alexei Fedorchenko. ... Alexei Balabanov, who refused to conform to this canon, has been cut off from the festival process. None of his films has ever been accepted into Cannes, Venice, or Berlin competitions – and that is a shame for these festivals.' ANDREI PLAKHOV, *quoted in the newspaper Kommersant.*

Yuri Feting's **Bibinur**

Directory
All Tel/Fax numbers begin (+7)
Alliance of Independent Distribution Companies, Tel: 243 4741. Fax: 243 5582. felix_rosental@yahoo.com.
Ministry of Culture (without Mass Communications) of the Russian Federation, 7, Maly Gnezdnikovsky Lane, Moscow 103877 Tel: 495-923-2420 and 629-7055.
National Academy of Cinema Arts & Sciences, 13 Vassilyevskaya St, Moscow 123825. Tel: 200 4284. fax: 251 5370. unikino@aha.ru.
Russian Guild of Film Directors, 13 Vassilyevskaya St, Moscow 123825. Tel: 251 5889. fax: 254 2100. stalkerfest@mtu-net.ru.
Russian Guild of Producers, 1 Mosfilmovskaya St, Moscow 119858. Tel: 745 5635/143 9028. plechev@mtu-net.ru.
Union of Filmmakers of Russia, 13 Vassilyevskaya St, Moscow 123825. Tel: 250 4114. fax: 250 5370. unikino@aha.ru.

KIRILL RAZLOGOV is Director of the Russian Institute for Cultural Research and Programme Director of the Moscow International Film Festival. He has written 17 books on cinema and culture and hosts Kultura's weekly TV show, *Movie Cult.*

Serbia Goran Gocić

Skinning (*Sisanje*) written by Dimitrije Vojnov and directed by Stevan Filipovic is a thriller about a right-wing gang who drag a young apprentice into a vortex of deadly violence. The film proved to be strangely prophetic: four days after its premiere in October 2010, Belgrade was vandalised by similar characters. It stars Bojana Novakovic, a promising young actress who has appeared in a number of American, British and Australian films, including the thriller *Edge of Darkness*.

Aleksandar Janković's **Flashback**

Newcomer Aleksandar Janković's **Flashback** (*Flesbek*), stylishly shot in black and white, is about an ex-convict who attempts to sort out his life again and reconnect with his estranged wife and daughter. Janko Baljak's **Blue Train** (*Plavi voz*) is a teenage comedy set in the week following President Tito's death in 1980. Miroslav Petkovic's **Oh, He's Not Like That** (*Ma nije on takav*) is about a Serbian fraudster who coerced money from his numerous spouses.

Stevan Filipovic's **Skinning**

The most talked about film this season was **The Woman with a Broken Nose** (*Žena sa slomljenim nosem*), which premiered in Karlovy Vary and has had a good festival run in Serbia. Written and directed by Srdjan Koljevic, it is an endearing melodrama about a Belgrade taxi driver who takes care of a baby left behind in his cab by a suicidal woman. **Motel Nana**, directed by Predrag Velinovic and written by Ranko Bozic (best known as the writer of Emir Kusturica's *Life is a Miracle*), is a co-production between Bosnia-Herzegovina and Serbia. The story of a teacher who is suspended from their post at a Belgrade grammar school then receives a chance to begin anew in a Bosnian backwater, it is a typical local melodrama.

Actor and director Rados Bajic adapted a local TV series for **Village is Burning... and So On** (*Selo gori... i tako*), hence the film's broad appeal to domestic audiences. The film is

Srdjan Koljevic's **The Woman with a Broken Nose**

Nikola Lezajic's **Tilva Rosh**

composed from a popular TV series set in rural Serbia with broad appeal. Rados Bajic starred and directed it – the latter for the first time in his 35-year-long career as an actor. An even bigger crowd pleaser was writer-director – and popular singer – Djordje Balasevic's **An Early Frost** (*Kao rani mraz*), a period melodrama set around the First World War.

Oleg Novkovic's **White, White World**

The biggest international success has been **Tilva Rosh**, the debut of writer-director Nikola Lezajic. A coming-of-age drama about a group of despondent youths who attempt to come to terms with their future, it was the first Serbian film to win the Sarajevo Film Festival's main prize, *Heart of Sarajevo*. It also picked up the Internationa Film Guide Inspiration Award at Film Festival Cottbus. Hopes were also high for the Serbian-German-Swedish musical **White, White World** (*Beli, beli svet*), which premiered at Locarno. Director Oleg Novkovic had to settle for the prizes for the Best Art Film and Best Actress, which went to Jasna Djuricic. It went on to win the Best Film Prize at Cottbus. An opera-of-sorts (each character has a song, with the entire acting ensemble singing the final composition) it looks at the

drudgery experienced by a number of families and their friends. Interestingly, both *Tilva Rosh* and *White, White World* are set in the polluted and hopeless mining town, Bor, probably best remembered by cinema fans as the setting of Dusan Makavejev's 1965 feature debut, *Man is Not a Bird*.

US-financed **The Choice**, written and directed by Chicago-based Serbian expatriate, Misha Toth, is an elegant drama about a strange man who visits a young Serbian widow claiming that he had lent money to her dead husband. It features an all-American cast – aside from Serbian actress Irena Micijevic – but its creative team is Serbian. An impressive film, it deserved a more aggressive marketing campaign to sell it to international markets. On the other hand, *A Serbian Movie* (see IFG 2010) is as aggressive as things get, both in content and distribution. It was shown at a dozen specialised festivals around the world, picking up a few awards at the Festival of Fantasy, in Montreal. It is still shocking its audience wherever it appears. After it secured a distributor in the UK, the British Board of Film Classification requested 49 cuts before it was given a certificate.

Co-productions between ex-Yugoslav republics are gaining momentum. **Some Other Stories** (*Neke druge price*) is an omnibus piece about five women struggling with motherhood in difficult times, directed by five women from the ex-Yugoslav region: Ivona Juka, Ana Maria Rossi, Ines Tanovic, Marija Dzidzeva and Hanna

Rajko Grlic's **Just Between Us**

Danilo Serbedzija's **Seventy Two Days**

Slak. There are other similar projects, such as the Croatian-Serbian-Slovenian drama **Just Between Us** (*Neka ostane među nama*), directed by veteran filmmaker, Rajko Grlic, and newcomer Danilo Serbedzija's Croatian-Serbian drama, **Seventy Two Days** (*72 dana*). Sasa Hajdukovic's *32nd December* is set in Bosnia, while Branko Smit's *Metastases* unfolds in Croatia and Damjan Kozole's *Slovenian Girl* takes place in Slovenia. These films were all produced in 2009 and received some Serbian funding.

Belgrade actor Nebojsa Glogovac starred in *The Woman with a Broken Nose*, *White, White World* and *72 days*. Predrag 'Miki' Manojlovic starred in *Just Between Us* as well as the Bosnian production *Circus Columbia* this year. He still appears in up to five films a year, from Bulgaria to France, at the healthy age of 60. Many other Serbian actors are involved in ex-Yugoslav productions, recalling the best times, when 'brotherhood and unity' reigned. Judging by the current cinema, ex-Yugoslavia has clearly restored some kind of common market.

GORAN GOCIĆ is a broadcast and print journalist whose works have been published by over 30 media outlets in eight languages. He has written chapters in 16 books on the mass media, edited several magazines, authored studies on Warhol, Kusturica, illness in cinema and pornography and directed two feature-length documentaries.

The year's best films
A Serbian Movie (Srdjan Spasojevic)
Skinning (Stevan Filipovic)
The Choice (Misha Toth)
The Woman with a Broken Nose (Srdjan Koljevic)
Voices (Aleksandar Nikolic)

Misha Toth's **The Choice**

Quote of the year
'I've been living abroad for 20 years. When I first read the script, I called Steva and told him that it was nonsense, that he created something which strives to be real but was not, that it was not happening [in Serbia]. Then he started sending me articles and links and I realised that events depicted in the film are not a metaphor, but reality. And then they happened in full force after the film.' *Actress* **BOJANA NOVAKOVIC** *talking about Stevan Filipovic's* **Skinning**.

Directory
All Tel/Fax numbers begin (+381 11)
Film Center Serbia, Zagrebacka 9/III, 11000 Belgrade. Tel: 262 51 31. Fax: 263 42 53. fcs.office@fcs.rs www.fcs.rs.
Yugoslav Film Archive, Knez Mihajlova 19, 11000 Belgrade. Tel/Fax: 262 25 55. kinoteka@org.rs. www.kinoteka.org.yu.
Faculty of Dramatic Arts, Bulevar Umetnosti 20, 11070 Belgrade. Tel: 213 56 84. Fax: 213 08 62. fduinfo@eunet.rs www.fdubg.com.
Film in Serbia, Dalmatinska 17, 11000 Belgrade. Tel/Fax: 329 20 24. info@filminserbia.com. www.filminserbia.com.

Singapore Yvonne Ng

2010 was a lacklustre year for Singapore's film production, both in quality and at the box office. Jack Neo, Singapore's popular director and star has taken a temporary hiatus from filmmaking due to his heavily publicised extra-marital affair. The scandal likely affected the ticket sales of his latest satirical comedy, **Being Human** (*Suo ren*), about an unscrupulous businessman, replete with Neo's usual dose of laughs, melodrama and moralising. Kelvin Tong, another popular director, released his blood-splattered suspense thriller, **Kidnapper**, about a taxi driver whose son is mistakenly abducted. **Roulette City** is Thomas Lim's Cantonese-language action drama set in Macau. First-time feature director Lim plays Tak, a Chinese mainlander who tries his luck at the city's underground gambling dens in hopes of helping his sick mother. **Gurushetram – 24 Hours of Anger** by T. T. Dhavamanni is a rare Singapore film made in Tamil, as most productions here are mainly in Mandarin or English. The thriller focuses on 17-year-old Prakarsh, who attempts to protect his mentally disabled brother as both are drawn into a world of gangsters and drugs.

Andrew Lau's **Haunted Changi**, a low-budget mockumentary, is a *Blair Witch*-style journey to Singapore's abandoned and notoriously haunted Old Changi Hospital, a former Japanese military hospital during the Second World War. An effective online publicity campaign helped this amateurish horror film top the local box office during its opening weekend in September.

One documentary that made waves internationally when its trailer went viral on YouTube was Singapore resident Amit Virmani's **Cowboys in Paradise**. Set in Bali, it is an eye-opener on the lives, loves and motivations of the 'Kuta cowboys', young men on the island's famous beach who offer female tourists romance and sex.

Sherman Ong's **Memories of a Burning Tree** (*Kumbukumbu Sa Mti Uunguao*) was commissioned by Rotterdam International Film Festival for their Forget Africa programme. Set in Dar es Salaam, the film was shot in Swahili with non-professional actors. The story centres on a man who enlists the help of locals in looking for his mother's grave. This noteworthy effort blurs the boundaries between reality and fiction, while bestowing the characters and landscape with quiet dignity.

Probably the most accomplished production in 2010 was Boo Junfeng's debut feature **Sandcastle**, selected for the Critics' Week at Cannes. The story revolves around 18-year-old En and his desire to know about his deceased father's student activist past, which the family is determined to keep buried. The film touches on family relationships, dementia, death, first love and identity. It is the first time a Singapore fiction feature has highlighted the tumultuous

Boo Junfeng's **Sandcastle**

political period of the late 1950s that, until recently, was rarely remarked upon officially.

The fact that nine shorts and two features from Singapore were shown at Rotterdam suggests that independent films are catching the attention of the international film circuit, if not the local box office. Both features are by Sherman Ong: the aforementioned *Memories* and his earlier *Flooding in the Time of Drought* (2009), an inventive blend of documentary and fiction, which looks at life in Singapore through the eyes of eight immigrant couples, as a water crisis looms. *Flooding* was made by 13 Little Pictures, a production company founded in 2009, comprising a group of young filmmakers. It has so far completed more than half a dozen features. Its productions include Liao Jiekai's debut, **Red Dragonflies**, a personal film that gently evokes memories of childhood and a wistful sense of loss, and Chris Yeo Siew Hua's magical identity swap tale, **In the House of Straw**.

Liao Jiekai's **Red Dragonflies**

Singapore's Media Development Authority, which has been promoting the local media industry, must have felt gratified when the important China-Singapore co-production agreement was signed in July. Covering theatrical features and tele-films, it is expected to pave the way for more co-operation between the two countries.

YVONNE NG is on the editorial board of *KINEMA*. She is co-author of *Latent Images: Film in Singapore* (2000), *Latent Images: Film in Singapore CD-ROM* (2003) and *Latent Images: Film in Singapore* Second Edition (2010).

The year's best films
Sandcastle (Boo Junfeng)
Memories of a Burning Tree (Sherman Ong)
Cowboys in Paradise (Amit Virmani)
Old Places (Royston Tan, Victric Thng, Eva Tang)
When Hainan Meets Teochew (JoHan Yew Kwang)

Quote of the year
'I feel that old places always have a lot of stories. Even a crack in the wall. I know it sounds very clichéd, but every time I see something like a rusty lamppost or anything, I think there's a story there.' ROYSTON TAN *on his interest in nostalgia.*

Directory
All Tel/Fax numbers begin (+65)
Cinematograph Film Exhibitors Association, 13th & 14th Storey, Shaw Centre, 1 Scotts Rd, Singapore 228208. Tel: 6235 2077. Fax: 6235 2860.
Singapore Film Commission, 140 Hill St, Mita Bldg #04-01, Singapore 179369. Tel: 6837 9943. Fax: 6336 1170. www.sfc.org.sg.
Singapore Film Society, 5A Raffles Ave, #03-01 Marina Leisureplex, Singapore 039801. Fax: 6250 6167. ktan@sfs.org.sg. www.sfs.org.sg.

لجنـــة أبـوظـبــي للأفـــلام
ABU DHABI FILM COMMISSION

Slovakia Miro Ulman

The last year failed to keep up the pace of 2009. Even though the Act on the Audiovisual Fund (AVF) came into effect on 1 January, 2009, this new public institution, created for the support and development of the audiovisual industry, replacing the old AudioVision grant programme of the Ministry of Culture, only began distributing funds in 2010.

The strong position of Slovak production was confirmed by the Slovak entries for the Best Foreign Film category of the American Academy Awards in 2009 (*Blind Loves*) and 2010 (*The Border*). Twenty-one cinemas (almost 10% of screens in the country) are now also able to screen 3D films.

As of September 30, the annual box office recorded 8% less filmgoers than in 2009, of which domestic production comprised just 2.5%. Only nine local films opened, of which four were mostly funded by Slovakia. Mariana Čengel Solčanská's **The Legend of Flying Cyprian** (*Legenda o Lietajúcom Cypriánovi*), about a monk from the 18th century who constructed a flying machine, was the only Slovak fiction feature. Dealing with the monk's search for peace and reconciliation within himself, it lacked structure but impressed with its period detail.

Peter Begányi's **Erotic Nation**

The Czech branch of HBO launched its own production arm. Its first film, Peter Begányi's **Erotic Nation**, was shown on wide release. It focuses on a family-run sex shop that has been in operation since 1991. On a larger scale, the film details how social and political life have changed since the fall of Communism in 1989. It is a daring film, but the parallels drawn between the political and erotic worlds appear artificially constructed.

In **Mongolia** (*Mongolsko – V tieni Džingischána*), Pavol Barabáš, who specialises in mountain films, applies elements from fiction films for the first time in his work. Scenes from the journey of five Slovaks across Mongolia are combined with re-enacted historical scenes. However, its tightly scripted narrative notwithstanding, it is less visually daring than Barabáš's previous films.

Pavol Barabáš's **Mongolia**

Martin Šulík's two-part documentary, **25 From the Sixties, or the Czechoslovak New Wave** (*25 ze šedesátých aneb Československá nová vlna*) looks at major films from that famous movement, featuring interviews with filmmakers and film historians, discussing the golden era of Czechoslovak cinema.

Martin Šulík's 25 From the Sixties, or the Czechoslovak New Wave

Adam Hanuljak's **Protected Territory** (*Chránené územie*) follows the US tour by the Theatre from the Passage, an ensemble of mentally handicapped actors. It highlights the almost non-existent discourse about the situation of the handicapped and their place in the world.

Adam Hanuljak's Protected Territory

Spring 2011 will see the premiere of Matej Mináč's latest documentary, **Nicky's Family** (*Nickyho rodina*). After his Emmy Award-winning *Nicholas Winton – The Power of Good*, the director returns to look at the life of the man who saved 669 Czech and Slovak children prior to the outbreak of the Second World War. The film reveals unpublished facts, testimonies and stories of newly discovered 'Winton children'.

Mariana Čengel Solčanská's The Legend of Flying Cyprian

The year's best films
The Legend of Flying Cyprian
(Mariana Čengel Solčanská)
25 From the Sixties, or the Czechoslovak New Wave (Martin Šulík)

Quote of the year
'I promise to do better next time and to make a documentary, so that the Academy will realise that I am both a screenwriter and a film director.' JURAJ JAKUBISKO, *screenwriter and director of the box-office hit* **Bathory**, *in reaction to the announcement that only documentaries had been nominated for Best Screenplay and Best Direction at the National Film Awards.*

MIRO ULMAN is a freelance journalist. He works for the Slovak Film Institute and is a programmer for the Art Film Festival Trenčianske Teplice – Trenčín.

Slovenia Ziva Emersic

Slovenian cinema showed surprising persistency and resistence in light of various shifts in the Slovenian film industry. A new structure of cinema production developed out of a new law legislating the Film Fund and Film Centre. Bureaucracy aside, the annual production schedule saw seven features released, as well as some 30 shorts, and, through co-operation with public television, over 20 documentaries. Slovenian cinema is as tough as it is small, a modest little brother to stronger and more important cultural branches of the arts, such as the prestigious literature and theatre scenes. But it is Slovenian cinema that has the widest reach outside the country's borders.

Janez Burger's **Circus Fantasticus**

Janez Burger, director of *Idle Running*, won over critics and festival juries with his dialogue-free drama, **Circus Fantasticus**. The 'futuristic war allegory' that features no soldiers was originally turned down by Slovenian Film Fund in 2003, but was later picked by the Sundance Institute. The film was co-produced by 17 countries and gathered an impressive body of internationally acclaimed actors and real circus performers. There's no doubt that Burger's

deeply personal and highly artistic film will bitterly divide audiences over the question of what films receive subsidies.

Slovenian wunderkind Goran Vojnovic's **Piran-Pirano** unfolds in Istria both during and after the Second World War. He attempts to deal with issues that have defined the area in modern times, from Communist rule to the exile of Italians – a matter still regarded as taboo. However, Vojnovic's ambitions are not matched by his skill, resulting in an unsatisfying film that failed to win an audience, a matter not helped by poor distribution.

The same topic and a very different approach worked better in the short **Trieste is Ours!** (*Trst je naš*), directed by film student Ziga Virc. A genuinely funny plot tells the story of a group of people who attempt to 'remake' history, repeating the Partisan's attack on Trieste. A normally serious topic is treated with irony and humour with successful results and no offence caused.

Vlado Skafar was the first Slovenian director to appear in Critics' Week at the Venice Film Festival. The second part of his 'family trilogy',

Ziga Virc's **Trieste is Ours!**

The Father (*Oca*) follows on from 2008's *The Children* and deals with the relationship between a man and his son. A powerful atmosphere prevails throughout, with glances and minimal dialogue, spoken in the dialect of the northern Slovenian region of Prekmurje, revealing the delicate balance of human relationships. The film has been picked for numerous international festivals.

This year also saw success for a comedy aimed at younger audiences, Miha Hocevar's **We Go Our Own Way** (*Gremo mi po svoje*). The winner of the audience award at the national film festival in Portoroz, it went on to attract an audience in excess of 90,000, more than the last *Harry Potter* film. Employing a major TV star, it is unlikely that the film's success will be repeated too often.

Srdjan Karanovic's **Solemn Oath**

There were a number of co-productions of varying quality. They included Serbian director Srdjan Karanovic's drama **Solemn Oath** (*Besa*), in which Slovenian actress Iva Kranjc plays opposite Miki Manojlovic. At the outbreak of the First World War, a Serbian teacher about to depart to the Front makes a traditional pact (a Besa, or sworn oath) with an Albanian (Manojlovic), who promises to protect the teacher's wife, Lea (Kranjc). Bored and restless, Lea's relationship with her devout Muslim guardian grows more intimate and their feelings for each other more complex.

Slovenian producers also supported the latest film by French-based, Oscar-winning Bosnian

director, Danis Tanovic, **Circus Colombia**. Another famous director from ex-Yugoslavia, Croat Rajko Grlic, received Slovenian support for **Just Between Us**.

Another interesting collaboration that evoked the heyday of a once strong Yugoslav cinema was the omnibus **Some Other Stories** (*Neke druge zgodbe*), composed of five stories from five former republics, all written and directed by women, with one central topic: the destiny of women in the post-war region. The Slovenian contribution was made by Hana A.W. Slak.

The year's best films
Trieste is ours! (Ziga Virc)
Solemn Oath (Srdjan Karanovic)

Quote of the year
'Each of my films is very "Burgerian", there's no other way. It is like having children; all are very much yours, but one might have been conceived by your neighbour.' JANEZ BURGER, *the director of* **Circus Fantasticus**.

Directory
All Tel/Fax numbers begin (+386)
Association of Slovenian Film Makers, Miklošičeva 26, Ljubljana. e-mail. dsfu@guest. arnes.si.
Association of Slovenian Film Producers, Brodišče 23, Trzin, 1234 Mengeš. dunja.klemenc@ guest.arnes.si.
Slovenian Cinematheque, Miklošičeva 38, Ljubljana. Tel: 434 2520. silvan.furlan@kinoteka.si.
Slovenian Film Fund, Miklošičeva 38, 1000 Ljubljana. Tel: 431 3175. info@film-sklad.si.

ZIVA EMERSIC is a film critic, a former program director of Slovenian National Film Festival in Portorož, and currently the head of documentary film production at TV Slovenia.

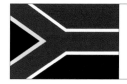

ABU DHABI FILM COMMISSION

South Africa Martin P. Botha

The past year has been characterised by award-winning features about people on the periphery of South African society, a revival in Afrikaans-language cinema, fascinating documentaries about environmental concerns and the launch of the largest film studio on the African continent. For the first time since 1991, more than 20 features were produced domestically. Several of them went on to garner international acclaim.

One of the major releases of last year, *Shirley Adams*, continued its remarkable run at international films festivals. Oliver Hermanus' powerful portrait of a woman coping with her disabled son, the victim of a gangland shooting, won the South African Film and Television Award for Best Feature Film, the Best Director Award and the Best Actress Award for Denise Newman, who also received the same accolade at the 3rd edition of the Cape Winelands Film Festival. Hermanus' international recognition was further enhanced by his induction into the Cinefondation residency programme at the Cannes Film Festival, where he developed his next feature.

Oliver Schmitz, currently living in Germany, returned to South Africa after almost a decade to direct **Life, Above All**. Based on Allan Stratton's novel, *Chanda's Secrets*, the film received a standing ovation at the 2010 Cannes Film Festival and has since been selected as South Africa's official entry for the 2011 Academy Awards. It is an emotional drama about a young girl (played by debutant Khomotso Manyaka) who fights the fear and shame that have poisoned her community. The film vividly captures the enduring strength of loyalty and a courage powered

Oliver Schmitz' **Life, Above All**

by the heart. Its characters are part of the cinema of marginality that has characterised post-apartheid cinema.

Stefanie Sycholt's **Themba – A Boy Called Hope** was awarded the Best Feature prize at the Zanzibar International Film Festival, in addition to awards at other international festivals. It also examines individuals on the edges of South African society. Visually stunning, it is a coming-of-age drama about a young South African boy's escape from poverty and the pursuit of his dream to be a football star. The film couldn't have come at a better time. It was released in the aftermath of the hugely successful 2010 FIFA World Cup in South Africa. Ultimately, the film is less

Stefanie Sycholt's **Themba – A Boy Called Hope**

about football and more about the triumph of the human spirit against social, economic and familial adversity.

Minky Schlesinger's **Gugu and Andile**, which was developed through the NFVF's (National Film & Video Foundation) Sediba Script Training Programme with the SABC (South African Broadcasting Corporation), won the Best South African Feature award at the 3rd edition of the Cape Winelands Film Festival. It also received three prizes at the African Movie Academy Awards in Nigeria, including Best Picture in an African Language. It was also selected for competition at FESPACO in Burkina Faso, and won first prize for Best Youth Film at the Lola Kenya Screen. The story is set during 1993, when democracy is at hand but the country's townships are burning. Gugu, a 16-year-old from a Zulu family, falls in love with Andile, an 18-year-old Xhosa youth. Their love is frowned upon by both communities. Based on Shakespeare's *Romeo and Juliet* it is a moving tale of love, death and reconciliation.

For the first time since the 1970s, Afrikaans-language cinema is blossoming, characterised by the emergence of new voices and a diversification of themes. Regardt van den Bergh's latest film, **The Incredible Adventures of Hanna Why** (*Die Ongelooflike Avonture van Hanna Hoekom*), is a departure from the thematic concerns of faith and personal healing that dominated his previous work. It tells the tale of Hanna (Anneke Weidemann), a teenager with a wild imagination, and her unconventional family. Actress Anna-Mart van

Regardt van den Bergh's **The Incredible Adventures of Hanna Why**

der Merwe brilliantly plays Hanna's artistic mother, while Gys de Villers is her would-be-actor stepfather. An adaptation of Marita van der Vyver's novel, the film offers a refreshing portrait of an extended Afrikaner family, which in many ways deconstructs the image of conservative Afrikaners that populated cinema in the 1970s. Hanna's biological father, for example, is flamboyantly gay (a fine performance by Tertius Meintjies), while the children embrace hip hop and are very much part of a post-apartheid South Africa.

Bakgat 2

Other Afrikaans films included the highly popular teen comedy **Bakgat 2**, Darrell Roodt's latest film, **Jakhalsdans**, about the efforts of a teacher to save a school in a remote Karoo town, as well as **Liefling: The Movie**, the first Afrikaans-language musical since 1980. The film, conceptualised by producer Paul Krüger, takes its name from the well-known Gé Korsten song, 'Liefling', and tells the story of Liefling Marais (Lika Berning), an adventure-loving young girl with a passion for life. She lives on a farm in Hartbeespoort with her father Simon (Alwyn Swart), mother Linda (Sonja Herholdt), grandfather Karel (Rouel Beukes), brother Kobus (Paul du Toit) and housekeeper Katy (Clementine Mosimane). Simon is a professor at the university and in his class are three friends, Jan (Bobby van Jaarsveld), Pieter (Gert Wolmarans), and Gert (Willem Botha), who also live on the outskirts of the city in Hartbeespoort. It's the December holidays and Jan, a civil engineering student raised by his grandmother, has his eye on Liefling, but spoilt little rich girl Melanie

(Marlee van der Merwe) has other ideas. Fate intervenes and brings lovers, friends and enemies together in a musical celebration.

Sara Blecher and Dimakhatso Raphoto's **Surfing Soweto**

Documentary filmmakers Damon and Craig Foster, who became internationally known for their masterful *The Great Dance: A Hunter's Story* and *Cosmic Africa*, have cemented their reputation as world-class filmmakers with an outstanding new film. **My Hunter's Heart**, shot over three and a half years, explores the world's most ancient shamanic culture and how it is perilously close to becoming extinct. It tracks the Khomani San of the Central Kalahari, the oldest living indigenous tribe in the world, who are genetically linked to every human being. In modern times, their traditional nomadic way of life has changed and westernisation has severed their link to land and animal. The children feel there is no future and the elders are faced with haunting reminders of their past. The film follows younger members of the clan as they embark on an epic journey to recapture some of the knowledge and skills of their ancestors. Produced by the Foster brothers, Anant Singh and Helena Spring, the evocative score was composed by Trevor Jones. The film was developed and produced with financial assistance from the NFVF. Other documentary titles funded by the NFVF include Sara Blecher and Dimakhatso Raphoto's Tri-continent festival winner, **Surfing Soweto**, and Rehad Desai's **Battle for Johannesburg**.

The Foster Brothers also directed **Iceman: The Lewis Gordon Pugh Story**, which serves as a visual experience of one man's attempts to draw attention to the oceans and raise awareness of climate change, by swimming in the freezing waters around both the North and South Pole. **The Nature of Life** also saw the brothers tackling climate change, highlighting ground-breaking examples of sustainable development across the world, inspired by examples from Africa and the natural world.

Damon and Craig Foster's **Iceman: The Lewis Gordon Pugh Story**

During August 2010 Nico Dekker, CEO of Cape Town Film Studios, South Africa's largest and newest film complex, announced that the studio has secured the first major 3D action film to be made in Africa, **Judge Dredd**. Cape Town Film Studios, which officially opened its doors at the end of 2010, is the first custom-built Hollywood-style film studio complex of its kind in Africa. It is owned and financed by Anant Singh's Videovision Entertainment and Marcel Golding's Sabido Investments (the owners of e.tv and e.sat).

MARTIN P. BOTHA has published five books on South African cinema, including an anthology on post-apartheid cinema entitled *Marginal Lives and Painful Pasts: South African Cinema After Apartheid*. He is a professor of film studies in the Centre for Film and Media Studies at the University of Cape Town. His latest book is a survey of South African cinema from 1896 till 2010.

International Film Guide.com

the definitive source for world cinema news, reviews and film festivals

Spotlight on...

As part of the IFG website's focus on various aspects of the constantly shifting film landscape, Spotlight is an opportunity to focus in on the work of an organisation or film festival, offering an overview or day-by-day update on their impact on the industry. Throughout 2011, the Spotlight will focus on:

- Festival Partnerships: a daily update of the events, screenings and activities of our Festival Partners.

- Company Spotlight: profiles of companies at the cutting edge of film technology and production.

For more information about the IFG Spotlight or becoming a Festival Partner, contact: Sara Tyler, International Business Manager
tel: +44 (0)1349 854931
email: saraifg@aol.com

www.internationalfilmguide.com

The year's best films
Life, Above All (Oliver Schmitz)
My Hunter's Heart (Damon and Craig Foster)
Gugu and Andile (Minky Schlesinger)
Die Ongelooflike Avonture van Hanna Hoekom (Regardt van den Bergh)
Themba – A Boy Called Hope (Stefanie Sycholt)

Quote of the year
'*Life, Above All* is a beautiful movie about strength, survival, friendship, love and all the good things about Africa. It's a beautifully made film by a beautiful director with absolutely extraordinary performances by actors who deserve to be seen by the world.' *Filmmaker* **THANDI BREWER**, *who was part of the South African Academy Awards Selection Committee, who has chosen* Life, Above All *for consideration as South Africa's official Entry into the Best Foreign Film Category for the 83rd Academy Awards.*

Directory
All Tel/Fax numbers begin (+27)
Cape Film Commission, 6th Floor, NBS Waldorf Bldg, 80 St George's Mall, Cape Town 8001. Tel: (21) 483 9070. Fax: (21) 483 9071. www.capefilmcommission.co.za.
Independent Producers Organisation, PO Box 2631, Saxonwold 2132. Tel: (11) 726 1189. Fax: (11) 482 4621. info@ipo.org.za. www.ipo.org.za.
National Film & Video Foundation, 87 Central St, Houghton, Private Bag x04, Northlands 2116. Tel: (11) 483 0880. Fax: (11) 483 0881. info@nfvf.co.za. www.nvfv.co.za.
South African Broadcasting Co (SABC), Private Bag 1, Auckland Park, Johannesburg 2006. Tel: (11) 714 9797. Fax: (11) 714 3106. www.sabc.co.za.

South Korea Nikki J. Y. Lee

'What kind of film do you want to be in next?' a young actress asks Kim Ok-bin, who has just finished shooting Park Chan-wook's vampire film *Thirst*. 'A film in which a number of female actresses appear, or a film in which female actresses love one another…', replies Ok-bin vehemently. This conversation is featured in E J-yong's heart-warming and experimental **Actresses** (*Yeobaeudeul*), in which six leading actresses are cast as themselves. The film's self-referential statement may be considered a subtle yet critical comment on one of the predominant trends of South Korean cinema in 2010. For this is a year when action thrillers and crime films have prevailed as popular genres. Moreover, the majority of such films have starred top male actors as main characters, caught up in conflicts that are both cruel and extremely violent.

E J-yong's **Actresses**

Another noticeable characteristic is the trend for media convergence or diversification of film production and distribution conditions. The two major internet portal sites, Daum and Naver, commenced legal downloading services early this year, helping to consolidate film-file downloading, or VOD (video on demand),

as one of South Korea's key distribution platforms. Such changes have helped induce the emergence of new popular genres, as well as a new spirit of adventure in low-budget independent production. For example, Kim Gyu-tae and Yang Yun-ho's **Iris the Film** (*Airiseu: Deu Mubi*) is a sequel to a glossy blockbuster spy television drama series, **Iris**, and was released through internet portal sites and PPV channels. The **Korea Meets Films** (*Hanguk, Yeonghwareul Mannada*) series, produced by Arirang TV (Korean English-language broadcasting channel), comprises five films promoting the five different cities in which the respective entries are set (Seoul, Incheon, Chuncheon, Jeju and Pusan). The films were broadcast on Arirang TV, while also being made available for legal internet downloading.

In contrast to previous years, no record-breaking Korean blockbusters ruled at the box office in 2010. Instead, the top ten domestic films all achieved relatively similar levels of commercial success. Lee Jeong-beom's **The Man from Nowhere** (*Ajeossi*) was the leading domestic hit. Described as the Korean *Leon*, it successfully re-presented Won Bin, one of

Lee Jeong-beom's **The Man from Nowhere**

Ryu Seung-wan's **The Unjust**

Korea's young flower-beauty male stars, as a cool lone action man with divine muscles and a dark personal history. Korean blockbuster director Kang Woo-suk's **Moss** (*Ikki*) ranked fourth among domestic films at the box office. At a time when an abundance of violent and cruel male-body genre films are being made, it stands out as a mesmerising piece due to its enthralling theme and plot based on the original manga by Yun Tae-ho (which appeared serially at a web portal site) and powerful acting by the male cast (Jeong Jae-young, Yu Hae-jin, Kim Sang-ho, Kim Jun-bae and Park Hae-il). Ryu Seung-wan's action noir, **The Unjust** (*Budanggeorae*), was the eighth most commercially successful domestic film of the year. Like *Moss*, it also touches on the dark currents of Korean society; here, a dog-eat-dog chain is explored linking a prosecutor, policeman and criminal involved in creating a fake suspect for a serial murder case. **I Saw the Devil** (*Angmareul Boatda*) is Kim Ji-woon's ambitious engagement with the hard gore genre. Although one minute and thirty seconds had to be cut for its theatrical release, the film still repelled many audiences, not only because of its extreme violence, but also the lack of entertainment value.

Choi Dong-hoon's **Jeon Woo Chi, The Taoist Wizard** (*Jeon U Chi*), the second-biggest domestic hit film, is a comically, action-packed, hybrid sci-fi period drama, which relies heavily upon wire action and CGI. It cleverly interweaves a number of key elements from current popular Korean cinema into a light, audience-pleasing entertainment. The ensemble of funny-talking and chatty male characters includes Baek Yun-sik, Yu Hae-jin, Kim Sang-ho, Song Young-chang and Joo Jin-mo, while Kang Dong-won's performance as the main hero, Woochi, consolidates his reputation, not just as eye-candy, but also a credible actor.

Jang Hoon's **Secret Reunion** (*Uihyeongje*), the third-biggest domestic hit film, also features Kang Dong-won, this time as a North Korean spy who spars with Song Gang-ho's South Korean ex-security agent. Adopting a light, humourous tone, it deals with the unlikely friendship between the two men, both isolated from their family and government

Kim Dae-woo's **The Servant**

Kim Dae-woo's **The Servant** (*Bangjajeon*) is another brilliant example of the fruitful trend for hybrid epic dramas. It does not deliver spectacular action but rather explicit sex scenes, beautiful scenery and revisionist storytelling in its take on *Chunghyang Jeon*, one of Korea's most famous folktales, which has been adapted for the big screen more than 15 times.

John H. Lee's **71-Into the Fire** (*Pohwa Sogeuro*) is a big-budget war film about a group of young South Korean volunteer soldiers during the Korean War. As a title commemorating the fiftieth anniversary of its outbreak, the film obviously aimed to recuperate the lineage of recent Korean War-related blockbusters, but fell short.

Kang Dae-gyu's **Harmony** (*Hamoni*) is a touching story of female prisoners who form a choir. The film's success evidences the fact that it is middle-aged women who comprise an increasingly large segment of the theatregoing audience in South Korea. Other recent films designed to appeal to middle-aged women include Kang Hyo-jin's **Robbery** (*Yukhyeolpogangdodan*), a comedy drama about three bank-robbing grannies, and You Seong-yub's **A Long Visit** (*Chinjeong Eomma*), a tear-jerking melodrama about a mother's dedicated love.

On the other hand, romantic comedy has remained a long-lasting and prolific genre that appeals to both young male and female audiences. Kim Hyun-seok's **Cyrano Agency** (*Sirano: Yeonae Jojakdan*) is a contemporary take on *Cyrano de Bergerac*. Exhibiting a self-reflective and mature approach to love, it revamps the genre while distinguishing itself from other more conventional titles that place an emphasis on clichéd comedy rather than bother to explore relationships.

Among a number of comic films that came out this year, Yook Sang-hyo's **Banga? Banga!** (*Bangga? Bangga!*) is a little gem. Its treatment of the cold and cruel reality of people living on the periphery of society (illegal immigrant workers and a young jobless man) is peppered with slapstick and verbal comedy, ultimately leading to some kind of catharsis.

This year's Korean competitors at the Cannes Film Festival were Lee Chang-dong's moral drama **Poetry** (*Si*), Im Sang-soo's **The Housemaid** (*Hanyeo*) and Hong Sang-soo's tenth feature, **Ha Ha Ha** (*Hahaha*). While *Poetry* won the Cannes award for Best Screenplay and *Ha Ha Ha* won the Un Certain Regard prize, Im's *The Housemaid* – a remake of Kim Ki-young's classic 1960 film – failed to win anything, but turned out to be the most talked-about film and went on to end the top ten domestic hits of the year. The sex scenes between top stars Jeon Do-yeon and Lee Jeong-jae provided the focal point

Park Chan-ok's **Paju**

for marketing the film. But critical attention was also drawn to Im's contemporary take on class issues in Korean society. This year's opening film at the International Film Festival Rotterdam, Park Chan-ok's **Paju** (*Paju*) is a stunning cinematic achievement which subtly delineates the complex emotions and memories of one young girl against the backdrop of a barren border town. **Bedevilled** (*Gimbongnam Sarinsageonui Jeonmal*) is the well-made debut feature of Jang Cheol-soo, who previously worked as assistant to Kim Ki-duk. While highly praised by many Korean film critics, the film unfailingly exhibits the kind of 'extreme' elements with which many contemporary Korean films are internationally associated.

The new environment of digital filmmaking and internet distribution facilitated various ventures in low-budget independent filmmaking. There were a number of single-themed omnibus titles, such as **One Night Stand** (*Won Nait*

Im Sang-soo's **The Housemaid**

Seutaendeu), **Nice Shorts** (Sasakkeonkkeon) and **The Neighbour Zombie** (Iutjib Jombi). Fresh new takes on staple genres were also noteworthy. Lee Eung-il's **The Uninvited** (Bulcheonggaek) turns a small, dark basement flat – the common habitat of young people preparing to sit exams to enter the professions – into a creepy set for a super, low-budget sci-fi fantasy.

Independent film director Yoon Seong-ho's indie comedy **Read My Lips** (Halsuitneunjaga Guhara) stirred up much public interest. Filled with black humour and sexual jokes, it comprises ten five-minute episodes, with each episode uploaded on to the internet so that viewers could watch them for free. The Director's Version was also released on the internet in early December.

The Korean independent music scene is a small but creative haven for young Korean people. Independent musicians appear in such documentaries as Baek Seung-hwa's **Turn it Up to 11** (Bandeusi Keuge Deuleulgeot) and Min Hwan-gi's **Sogyumo Acacia Band's Story** (Sogyumo Akasia Baendeu Iyagi), as well as in feature films like Yu Sang-heon's **Acoustic** (Eokustik) and Kim Hyo-jeong and Park Seong-yong's **Dancing Zoo** (Chumchuneun Dongmulwon).

Major films due for release at the end of 2010 include Lee Seung-mu's western co-production, **The Warrior's Way** (Weorieojeu Wei) and Na Hong-jin's thriller **Hwanghae** (Hwanghae), which again casts Ha Jeong-woo and Kim Yun-suk, the two top male actors from Na's debut feature, The Chaser. 2011 may witness the return of big-budget Korean blockbusters. Kim Ji-hoon's **The 7th Sea Mining Area** (Chil Gwangu), a large-scale 3D monster film, is in post-production. **My Way** (Mai Wei), Kang Je-gyu's World War Two blockbuster, with an international cast, and Jang Hun's Korean War film **Gojijeon** (Gojijeon) are both in production.

Lee Eung-il's The Uninvited

The year's best films
Actresses (E J-yong)
Banga? Banga! (Yook Sang-hyo)
Paju (Park Chan-ok)
The Servant (Kim Dae-woo)
The Uninvited (Lee Eung-il)

Quotes of the year
'If I see another South Korean gangster or serial-killer film with a cocky young thug in a tailored black suit, I think I may burn the cinema down.' DEREK ELLEY, *chief film reviewer of* Film Business Asia, *on the current trend for South Korean action thriller films.*

'I was worried that what is supposed to be extreme revenge may turn into extremely boring revenge after the cuts.' KIM JI-WOON *on the cuts that had to be made in order for* **I Saw the Devil** *to get a theatrical release.*

Directory
All Tel/Fax numbers begin (+82)
Korean Film Archive, 1602 DMC, Sangam-dong, Mapo-gu, Seoul 120-270. Tel: (2) 3153 2001. Fax: (2) 3153 2080. www.koreafilm.or.kr.
Korean Film Council (KOFIC), 206-46 Cheongnyangni-dong, Tongdaemun-gu, Seoul 130-010. Tel: (2) 9587 581~6. Fax: (2) 9587 590. www.kofic.or.kr.

Dr NIKKI J.Y. LEE is a film researcher based in the UK. She mainly writes on the Korean film industry, directors and films, and is co-editor of *The Korean Cinema Book*

لجنـة أبوظبي للأفلام
ABU DHABI FILM COMMISSION

Spain Jonathan Holland

There is a sea change in the Spanish film industry, where, to the relief of some and the horror of others, films are increasingly being seen more as consumer, rather than cultural, products. 2009 ended with the Spanish box office looking set for a breakout, largely driven by a single project – Daniel Monzon's prison drama **Cell 211**, which, unusually for a domestic film, kept both critics and audiences happy. The year brought a small increase in ticket sales – a figure that had plunged, under a cloud of apathy, piracy and alternative sources of entertainment – from 146 million in 2001 to less than 110 million in 2008.

But at 2010's halfway point, *Cell 211*, which was released in November 2009, still represented Spanish cinema's second-highest-grossing film of the year, suggesting that it may have been a one-off, rather than a new dawn. The box office for 2010 is unlikely to reach 2009 levels.

The year saw an overhaul of Spanish subsidy regulations, with controversy surrounding a number of incentives being reserved for films budgeted at US$2.8 million and above. Spain's austerity plans, announced in summer 2010, bit deeply, with the maximum subsidy

Félix Fernández de Castro's **Maria and I**

a film can receive falling from US$2.6 million to US$1.9 million. Until recently, subsidies and TV have represented 80% of an average film's financing. Producers are now being encouraged to take the 18% tax break available for foreign investors in film.

Many commentators believe that the survival of Spanish film depends on whether the industry is able to work out a new financing model, built around these new attitudes and regulations.

On the artistic side, the year brought a series of fine documentaries notable for their insistence on revealing often uncomfortable truths. Félix Fernández de Castro's **María and I** (*Maria y yo*) looked at life through the eyes of an autistic girl, her artist father and

Jo Sol's **Fake Orgasm**

their wonderful relationship, finding joys in unexpected places, while Jo Sol's challenging **Fake Orgasm** unpicked issues of sexuality and gender through an in-depth study of the life and opinions of performance artist Lazlo Perlman.

José Luis Guerín continued his exploration of the frontiers between life and art in **Guest**, in which he looks at the reality of life in the festival cities he has been invited to. Though typically provocative, full of energy and epic in scale, the film's almost exclusive focus on poverty felt like a missed opportunity for a truly global view. The year's standout documentary was Edmon Roch's debut, **Garbo**, which fused interviews, film clips and recreations into a compelling, stranger-than-fiction study of a Catalan spy who changed the course of World War Two.

Edmon Roch's **Garbo**

As usual, women's issues were very much a secondary issue, with only a handful of female directors able to see their projects through to release. Laura Maña's comedy **Life Begins Today** (*La vida empieza hoy*) represented a worthy addition to the burgeoning number of films about third-age sexuality and confirmed its director as one of Spain's more accomplished genre hoppers.

Julio Medem also focused on women. At one time considered second only to Almodóvar in the Spanish auteur stakes, he delivered **Room in Rome**, in which two actresses shed their inhibitions and their clothes over a single intense night in the city. Typically for Medem, critics were split between those who admired the artistry and those who saw only soft porn.

Julio Medem's **Room in Rome**

The idea of a 'sophisticated comedy' still appears to be an alien concept to most Spanish film producers. The last twelve months have seen **Death to Ugly People** (*Que se mueren los feos*), a crowd-pleasing rural comedy about the frustrated love affair between an aesthetically challenged farmer and his sister-in-law, which did find room for moments of human tenderness, and **Spanish Film**, a parody, à la *Scary Movie*, of the likes of Almodóvar, Amenábar and del Toro, which seems to have been conceived on the principle that humour is defined by the blatantly obvious and copious amounts of farting, which for many seems to be the case. Both performed well at the box office. Altogether better was Paco Cabezas' feature debut, the as-yet-unreleased **Neon Flesh** (*Carne de Neón*). This blood-

Death to Ugly People

Oskar Santos' **For the Good of Others**

spattered, high-testosterone fantasy about a Barcelona street kid trying to come good for Mom, is less a comedy than a Guy Ritchie-style thriller, but actually delivered more laughs than the other two films combined.

The big-budget end of Spanish production recently seems to have taken on board the principles of M. Night Shayamalan and several high-profile US TV shows in determining that there's good entertainment to be had in marrying medical problems to a thriller plot. **Agnosia**, a tale of industrial espionage set in Barcelona at the turn of the twentieth century, and featuring a young woman with problems of perception, was a grand folly – delicious looking, but empty and confused, despite being penned by *The Devil's Backbone* scribe, Antonio Trashorras. Alejandro Amenábar's first production not directed by him, Oskar Santos' morality tale, **For the Good of Others** (*El mal ajeno*), features Eduardo Noriega as a doctor both blessed and cursed with the miraculous ability to save the lives of people he doesn't know. It's a wonderful idea that the script fails to fully exploit. The best of the bunch and a big-box office hit at the end of the year was **Julia's Eyes** (*Los ojos de Julia*), directed by Guillem Morales and starring Belén Rueda as a woman slowly going blind as she pursues the truth about her sister's death. Again, striking visuals tied beautifully into the theme, but failed to compensate for an overly complex narrative. As 2010 ended, the film had overtaken *Death to Ugly People* as the year's biggest commercial success.

All the above films have their eyes firmly set on the overseas market. But the one major international success story of the last twelve months has been Rodrigo Cortés' **Buried**, starring Ryan Reynolds as a kidnapped truck driver in Iraq, who spends the duration of the film in a coffin. Shot in English, with a strong American-orientated theme and with an American actor, it was nonetheless a Spanish project at production and crew levels. Filmmakers on both sides of the Atlantic will have noted with interest the project's development.

Rodrigo Cortés' **Buried**

Film directors continue to plunder Spain's past. Andrucha Waddington's **Lope**, set in the 16th century, was the year's biggest costume drama, offering a take on the life, loves and literature of Spain's greatest playwright, Lope de Vega. The film nicely combines epic sweep with a sense of intimacy. **Paper Birds** (*Pajaros de papel*), the debut from seasoned actor turned media mogul Emilio Aragón, fashioned polished entertainment from the trials of a vaudeville troupe in post-Civil War Spain, but

Guillem Morales's **Julia's Eyes**

Agusti Villaronga's **Black Bread**

Agusti Villaronga's **Black Bread** (*Pa negre*), also about a young man's awakening to the harsh realities of life in the 1940s, exists on a different plane altogether. Dark to its heart and breathlessly watchable, it is Villaronga's most mainstream film but nonetheless retains the director's trademark subversive edge. It is the finest Spanish film of the last 12 months.

Alex de la Iglesias' **Sad Trumpet Ballad**

Meanwhile, Alex de la Iglesias' **Sad Trumpet Ballad** (*Balada triste de trompeta*) took the Golden Lion and split opinions at Venice. Depending on how you looked at it, the film is either self-indulgent and overcooked, or a powerful cinematic howl of rage. The tale of two disfigured clowns, fighting for the love of an acrobat, represented perhaps the year's most disturbing cinematic experience, and showed that de la Iglesias retains his wild edge despite most often being seen in a suit as president of the Spanish Film Academy. Space should be reserved for a handful of films that barely registered at the box office, but which deserve a mention. Pau Freixas' tender-

hearted **Forever Young** (*Heroes*) is, on paper, a dewy-eyed nostalgia trip back to a summer vacation in the 1980s, but it possesses an air of sincerity that generates more emotion than sentimentality. Luis Aviles Baquero's sombre **Returns**, the tale of a man unwittingly attracting intrigue when he returns to his rainy Galician village following his father's death, was perhaps the year's strongest debut and is suffused with an air of authentic tragedy. Also debuting strongly in yet another year that featured a paucity of female directors, was Juana Macias' **Plans for Tomorrow** (*Planes para mañana*), a small-scale production featuring three stories about women making big, life-changing decisions. It was marked by a clutch of excellent performances.

Juana Macias' **Plans for Tomorrow**

The next twelve months are likely to see fewer Spanish films, the result of the new ministerial order restricting the subsidies on which all areas of the industry have depended for so long. It is likely that a significant number will be smaller in scale and budget. It is no surprise that the future seems to be in co-production and it appears to be a pivotal moment for Spanish genre fare internationally, if the buzz at 2010's Sitges Film Festival is anything to go by.

Artistically, one high point of the coming year will be a new Pedro Almodóvar film, **The Skin I Live In** (*La piel que habito*), in which Antonio Banderas plays a plastic surgeon bent on revenge. Almodóvar promises us a film unlike any he's made before.

Pau Freixas' **Forever Young**

The year's best films

Anything You Want (Achero Mañas)
Garbo, the Man Who Changed the World
(Edmon Roch)
Neon Flesh (Paco Cabezas)
Black Bread (Agustí Villaronga)
Returns (Luis Aviles Baquero)

Quotes of the year

'I have a daughter who, every time she sees a film in black and white, thinks the television's broken.' ALEX DE LA IGLESIAS, *film director.*

'My name is Sara Montiel and I don't go to the supermarket. I've never set foot in one. They're not the place for me.' SARA MONTIEL, *veteran actress.*

Directory

All Tel/Fax numbers begin (+34)

Escuela de Cinematografia y de la Audiovisual de la Comunidad de Madrdid (ECAM), Centra de Madrid a Boadilla, Km 2200, 28223 Madrid. Tel: (91) 411 0497. www.ecam.es.

Federation of Associations of Spanish Audiovisual Producers (FAPAE), Calle Luis Bunuel 2-2° Izquierda, Ciudad de la Imagen, Pozuelo de Alarcón, 28223 Madrid. Tel: (91) 512 1660. Fax: (91) 512 0148. web@fapae.es. www.fapae.es.

Federation of Cinema Distributors (FEDICINE), Orense 33, 3°B, 28020 Madrid. Tel: (91) 556 9755. Fax: (91) 555 6697. www.fedicine.com.

Filmoteca de la Generalitat de Catalunya, Carrer del Portal de Santa Madrona 6-8, Barcelona 08001. Tel: (93) 316 2780. Fax: (93) 316 2783. filmoteca.cultura@gencat.net.

Filmoteca Espanola, Calle Magdalena 10, 28012 Madrid. Tel: (91) 467 2600. Fax: (91) 467 2611. www.cultura.mecd.es/cine/film/filmoteca.isp.

Filmoteca Vasca, Avenida Sancho el Sabio, 17 Trasera, Donostia, 20010 San Sebastián. Tel: (943) 468 484. Fax: (943) 469 998. www.filmotecavasca.com. andaluciafilmcom@fundacionava.org.

Paco Cabezas' **Neon Flesh**

JONATHAN HOLLAND is a university teacher and journalist based in Madrid. He reviews Spanish films for *Variety*.

Sweden Gunnar Rehlin

2010 was a banner year for Swedish cinema, with films, actors and directors making an impression around the world. The *Millennium* trilogy earned more than US$200 million at the international box office. They also landed their stars international careers – Noomi Rapace plays one of the leads in **Sherlock Holmes 2** and Michael Nyqvist is the main bad guy in **Mission Impossible 4**. And in the fall David Fincher travelled to Sweden to shoot the US version of the first *Millennium* novel, **The Girl with the Dragon Tattoo**.

Let the Right One In director Tomas Alfredson started shooting **Tinker, Tailor, Soldier, Spy** in the UK, with Gary Oldman and Colin Firth. **Easy Money** (*Snabba cash*) star Joel Kinnaman went to Moscow to shoot the US sci-fi thriller **The Darkest Hour**, while its director Daniel Espinosa signed on to shoot the thriller **Safe House**, with Ryan Reynolds and Denzel Washington. Meanwhile, back in Sweden…

Pernilla August's **Beyond**

Things continued to look very bright indeed. 2010 witnessed a string of well-made, frequently provocative films, with most winning over critics and audiences alike. And it finally seemed that female directors were at the forefront, producing many of the year's best films. They included actress Pernilla August, who won several awards, including the audience award at the Venice Film Festival, for her tough and tragic family story, **Beyond** (*Svinalängorna*), which stars Noomi Rapace.

To go back to the end of 2009, when *Easy Money* hit cinemas. Based on a best-selling novel, it is a tough and often violent depiction of the Stockholm underworld, with Joel Kinnaman as a taxi driver by day and drug dealer by night. The film was sold to the US, where it is to be remade with Zac Efron in the lead role. If Espinosa and Kinnaman have time and feel the scripts are right, there will be two sequels.

Hakon Liu directed **Miss Kicki**, with Pernilla August playing a mother searching for her son in Asia. The film had its international premiere at the Pusan Film Festival, where it received rave reviews. Also championed by critics was the tragic youth drama, **Sebbe**, directed by Babak Najafi. The story of the strained relations between a mother and her teenage son won the Best First Feature award at the Berlin Film Festival and went on to pick up awards at a string of festivals, among them Athens and Seoul.

There were two commercial disappointments in the spring: Josef Fares' light comedy, **Dad** (*Farsan*), with his own father, Jan, as a single man looking for a new woman; and Johan Brisinger's **Among Us** (*Änglavakt*), about a dying child and how belief in a guardian angel saves his life. *Dad* received modest reviews, but less box-office takings than Fares is normally used to. Brisinger's moody film was inexplicably savaged by most critics and as a result failed to attract viewers. A US remake has been mooted.

Johan Brisinger's **Among Us**

Summer saw the premiere of the police parody **Kommissarie Spack**, of which the less said, the better. The same goes for Kjell Sundvall's comedy about twins, **The Brothers Karlsson** (*Bröderna Karlsson*), which left no cliché unused. The best film of the summer was Othman Karim's **Dear Alice** (*För kärleken*), an Altman-esque drama featuring Danny Glover. The film won the critics' award at the Kaliningrad Film Festival.

Alexander Skarsgård in Johan Kling's **Trust Me**

Autumn's releases were among the best Swedish cinema has seen in years. Among the highlights – and there were many – were Johan Kling's theatre-set comedy, **Trust Me** (*Puss*), starring Skarsgård brothers Alexander and Gustaf, Hannes Holm's excellent 1970s set thriller, **Behind Blue Skies** (*Himlen är oskyldigt blå*), and Andreas Ohman's dark comedy, **Simple Simon** (*I rymden finns inga känslor*), which is Sweden's entry for the Oscars. The latter two films starred Bill Skarsgård. With Stellan Skarsgård appearing in the US films **Thor** and **The Girl with the Dragon Tattoo**, as well as the Norwegian

production **King of Devil's Island**, Gustaf in Peter Weir's **The Way Back** and Alexander in the hit TV show, *True Blood*, as well as the features **Straw Dogs** and **Battleship**, we can conclude that the Skarsgård family is taking over the world in 2011.

Hannes Holm's **Behind Blue Skies**

Other excellent films were Peter Schildt's **A Thousand Times Stronger** (*Tusen gånger starkare*), a drama that could best be described as *One Flew Over the Cuckoo's Nest* set in a high school, and Lisa Langseth's spare and haunting **Beloved** (*Till det som är vackert*), in which a 22-year-old girl embarks on an affair with a 50-year-old concert conductor, leading to disastrous consequences. Langseth's film won one of the major awards at the Pusan Film Festival and should have a strong international run, with young actress Alicia Vikander someone to watch out for.

Controversial Dutch singer/composer Cornelis Vreeswijk was portrayed in Amir Chamdin's well made bio-pic **Cornelis**, starring the

Ola Simonsson and Johannes Stjäme Nilsson's **Sound of Noise**

scaringly lookalike Hans-Erik Dyvik Husby. The
Cannes entry **Sound of Noise**, directed with
musical flair by Ola Simonsson and Johannes
Stjärne Nilsson, finally had its domestic
premiere, while Colin Nutley unspooled **House
of Angels 3** (*Änglagård – tredje gången gillt*),
some 14 years after the previous sequel, about
a small town in rural Sweden.

However, the year's biggest breakthrough was
Pernilla August's feature debut. The eminent
actress proved herself equally excellent behind
the camera. A very dark story about domestic
abuse, alcoholism and children trying to
survive in that world, *Beyond* opened in time
for Christmas, resulting in ironic comments
about 'a typical Swedish Christmas movie'. The
film won the Critics' Week at the Venice Film
Festival and will be a very strong contender for
the 2011 Swedish Oscar entry.

And 2011? Danish director Susanne Bier will
hopefully start shooting her Ingmar Bergman
biopic, scripted by Henning Mankell. Kjell
Sundvall will present **The Hunters 2**. Björn
Runge's **Happy End**, starring Gustaf Skarsgård
(yes, again) is one of the films to look forward
to. And at the end of the year we will see
David Fincher's interpretation of *The Girl with
the Dragon Tattoo*. It is an American film, but
based on a Swedish novel, shot in Sweden
and co-starring several Swedish actors. The
Swedish film was efficiently made in an
American way. 'I want to capture Sweden. I
hope for a Chinatown-esque feeling,' Fincher
commented. It sounds promising. Perhaps we
Swedes will finally get a realistic portrait of
who we are.

GUNNAR REHLIN is a Swedish journalist/
critic, working for several international media,
among them Swedish news agency TT Spektra,
Norwegian magazine *Film & Kino* and *Variety*.
His four years as a TV host was the subject of
a one-hour mockumentary, directed by *Let the
Right One In* director Tomas Alfredson.

Lisa Langseth's **Beloved**

The year's best films
Among Us (Johan Brisinger)
Behind Blue Skies (Hannes Holm)
Beloved (Lisa Langseth)
Beyond (Pernilla August)
Trust Me (Johan Kling)

Quote of the year
'My mother has always said that a father can
support his children, but the children can not
support their father. I'm going to prove her
wrong.' *Actor* STELLAN SKARSGÅRD

Directory
All Tel/Fax numbers begin (+46)
Cinemateket, Swedish Film Institute, Box 27126,
SE-102 52 Stockholm. Tel: (8) 665 1100. Fax: (8) 666
3698. info@sfi.se. www.sfi.se. .
Swedish Film Institute, Box 27126, SE-10252
Stockholm. Tel: (8) 665 1100. Fax: (8) 666 3698.
info@sfi.se.
Swedish Film Producers Association, Box 27298,
SE-102 53 Stockholm. Tel: (8) 665 1255. Fax: (8) 666
3748. info@frf.net.
**Swedish National Archive for Recorded
Sound & Moving Images**, Box 24124, SE-10451
Stockholm. Tel: (8) 783 3700. Fax: (8) 663 1811.
info@ljudochbildarkivet.se.

Switzerland Marcy Goldberg

The first half of 2010 was dominated by a series of outstanding documentary films, while the second half of the year saw the domestic release of an unprecedented number of fiction features. Market share, however, remained disappointingly stable, continuing to hover around 5%. Critics pointed out the short-term drawbacks of increased competition for the same number of spectators and theatrical slots. But most of the industry seems to agree that, in the longer term, the boom in production will raise the overall quality and enhance the visibility of Swiss cinema, both at home and abroad.

The most talked-about film of 2010 was unquestionably **Sennentuntschi**, Michael Steiner's reworking of an Alpine folktale about a lonely herdsman who fashions a sex doll out of straw (the 'Sennentuntschi' of the title), only to see her come alive and take revenge on her tormentors. The production's financial difficulties and supposedly risqué scenes had already generated malicious headlines for over a year, but *Sennentuntschi* turned out to be one of the best and most original films made in Switzerland in a long time. Steiner's update of the traditional tale includes some provocative contemporary plot twists, and

Michael Steiner's **Sennentuntschi**

deftly combines Alpine folklore and topography with the vocabulary of the horror and thriller genres, balancing effectively between the realistic and the supernatural.

Equally controversial, but for different reasons, was Jean-Luc Godard's **Film Socialisme**, a fragmented collage essay that takes on nothing less than the history of the cinema, the political tragedies of the twentieth century and Western thought altogether. Although Godard continues to be perceived as a French filmmaker, he is a Swiss citizen and has been living and working here for many years. *Film Socialisme* was produced by Zurich-based Vega Film and supported by several key Swiss film funds. It premiered in the Un Certain Regard

section at Cannes, where Godard made a point of maintaining a conspicuous absence (as he did again in November by ignoring an Academy Award ceremony for his Lifetime Achievement award). Predictably, the film polarised critics and audiences, who either found it brilliant and trenchant or infuriatingly inaccessible and politically confused. At 79, Godard has clearly not lost his ability to provoke.

Stéphanie Chuat and Véronique Reymond's **The Little Room**

Vega Film also produced the year's most noteworthy debut: **The Little Room** (*La petite chambre*), the first fiction feature by Stéphanie Chuat and Véronique Reymond. The film traces the unlikely friendship that develops between an elderly man confronting his own mortality (octogenarian French actor Michel Bouquet) and his young nurse (Florence Loiret Caille), still grieving over a miscarriage. The story unfolds with sensitivity, intelligence and some unexpected humour, and showcases the cold beauty of the Lake Geneva region and the surrounding mountains.

Switzerland distinguished itself once again this year with a slew of first-rate documentaries, demonstrating that the country has not lost its penchant for non-fiction. **Daniel Schmid – The Thinking Cat** (*Daniel Schmid – Le chat qui pense*) is a fascinating portrait of the Swiss auteur, who died of cancer in 2006. Remarkably, this homage to Schmid and his work (*La Paloma*, *Hécate*, *Il Bacio di Tosca*), which premiered at the Berlinale, was conceived as a graduation project by

Zurich film students Benny Jaberg and Pascal Hofmann. The film has since toured festivals on several continents and will hopefully continue to make Schmid's work known to a new generation of cinephiles.

Aisheen (Still Alive in Gaza) also premiered at the Berlinale, where it won the Ecumenical Jury Prize. Geneva-based Nicolas Wadimoff and Béatrice Guelpa arrived in Gaza in January 2009, just weeks after the Israeli offensive, but chose – refreshingly – to avoid the officials' rhetoric and focus on a small number of telling personal stories. Vignettes from everyday life include the obligatory visits to a UN food centre and a children's shelter, but also some more unusual locations, like the Gaza zoo, a ruined amusement park and – in one of the film's most interesting scenes – a radio station, where they filmed a tense interview between a head-scarved radio host and a pair of rebellious rappers from the Gaza hip hop group DARG Team.

The Cannes Directors' Fortnight saw the premiere of **Cleveland vs. Wall Street**, Jean-Stéphane Bron's instructive take on the flawed banking system. In an innovative twist on the courtroom re-enactment genre, Bron chose to depict a trial that was never able to take place: the city of Cleveland's thwarted attempt to bring a lawsuit against the 21 US banks they blamed for bankrupting their city. Although the trial was staged for the film, all the participants play themselves, and their testimony is real. Their insights into the causes and effects of the financial crisis make for essential viewing.

Jean-Stéphane Bron's **Cleveland vs. Wall Street**

Finally, Vadim Jendreyko's **The Woman with the 5 Elephants** (*Die Frau mit den 5 Elefanten*) is an amusing and inspiring portrait of acclaimed translator Swetlana Geier, best known for her benchmark translations of Dostoyevsky's five classic novels (the five elephants of the title) into German. The film premiered in 2009 at Visions du réel in Nyon, where it won several awards. After winning the Best Swiss Documentary award in early 2010, it went on to worldwide festival success, picking up a dozen more awards. Jendreyko's rapport with the feisty literary scholar (who died at the age of 87 in November 2010) led to in-depth conversations about her work as a translator, her home life as wife, mother and grandmother, and – the dark spot in Geier's biography – her stint as a translator for the Nazis in wartime Ukraine, which allowed her and her mother to survive.

2010 also saw the changing of the guards at two major Swiss festivals. In Locarno, Olivier Père (of the Cannes Directors' Fortnight) succeeded Frédéric Maire, who was appointed director of the Swiss Cinémathèque. And longtime director Jean Perret stepped down from Visions du réel in Nyon, to be succeeded by Luciano Barisone of the Festival dei Popoli in Florence. In addition, the controversial Federal Film Office chief, Nicolas Bideau, has left his post, leaving the door open for new film policies in 2011.

MARCY GOLDBERG is a film historian and independent media consultant based in Zurich.

Benny Jaberg and Pascal Hofmann's **Daniel Schmid – The Thinking Cat**

The year's best films
Sennentuntschi (Michael Steiner)
The Little Room (Stéphanie Chuat and Véronique Reymond)
Cleveland vs. Wall Street (Jean-Stéphane Bron)
Daniel Schmid – The Thinking Cat (Pascal Hofmann and Benny Jaberg)
The Woman With the 5 Elephants (Vadim Jendreyko)

Quote of the year
'There's no such thing as intellectual property, there's only intellectual responsibility.' JEAN-LUC GODARD *quoted in* Variety, *May 17, 2010.*

Directory
All Tel/Fax numbers begin (+41)
Swiss Films, Neugasse 6, P.O. Box, CH-8031 Zurich. Tel: (43) 211 40 50. Fax: (43) 211 40 60. info@swissfilms.ch www.swissfilms.ch.
Swiss Films Genève, Maison des Arts du Grütli, 16, rue Général Dufour, CH-1204 Genève. Tel: (22) 308 12 40. Fax: (22) 308 12 41. geneva@ swissfilms.ch www.swissfilms.ch.

Taiwan David Frazier

At the Tokyo International Film Festival in late October, Taiwanese government agencies promoting film were confident enough to usher in stars from six recent releases under the banner 'Taiwan Cinema Renaissance 2010'. They had something to celebrate. For the second time in three years, a Taiwanese film had been among the domestic box-office leaders.

In 2010, Doze Niu's **Monga**, a period gangster piece, raked in NT$231 million, led Taipei box offices for three weekends, and, in terms of total receipts, finished third for the year behind **Inception** and **Iron Man 2**. The tale of brotherhood and betrayal is Taiwan's first

Doze Niu's **Monga**

underworld shoot-em-up to rival similar Hong Kong fare – think Johnnie To's *Election* or Alan Mak's *Infernal Affairs* – in scope, budget and intensity, though the story is more a teary melodrama than a hardboiled action thriller. It was made with significant assistance from Taiwan's government; a cooperation with Taipei City involved restoring old-town street corners to a vintage 1970s look, then leaving them that way as tourist attractions. According to Taiwanese media reports, *Monga* will be the first Taiwanese film to have a major release in Japan in 18 years. The lush cinematography was by Jake Pollock, a Taiwan-based American ex-pat who looks set to be the next Christopher Doyle.

Unfortunately, *Monga*'s stars were prevented from enjoying the Tokyo festival's entrance parade by the unexpected eruption of an East Asian political spat. Literally minutes before the festival's awards ceremony, Chinese bureaucrat Jiang Ping, deputy director-general of China's State Administration of Radio, Film and Television, raised a furore with Japanese organisers, demanding Taiwan's delegation not be allowed to enter the awards hall under the banner 'Taiwan'. For decades, China has moved to exclude Taiwan from international bodies and conventions, and now this apparently includes film festivals. China claims Taiwan as part of its territory, and Jiang, throwing what was likely a premeditated temper tantrum, insisted 'Taiwan' call itself 'Chinese Taipei' or 'Taiwan, China'. Furthermore, he threatened to pull all Chinese films out of the festival if the organisers did not comply. Jiang reportedly told a Taiwanese group, 'Don't you want to sell your films in the mainland. Aren't you all Chinese?' To which the top Taiwanese official there replied, 'You are Chinese, I am

Taiwanese.' In the end, Jiang's antics resulted in stars from both China and Taiwan missing the event, simply because his bullying created a huge delay. No films were pulled from the festival and Tokyo organisers later apologised to Taiwan, confirming that they would continue to use the designation 'Taiwan' in the future.

At both national and local levels, Taiwan's government has devoted more energy and funds to its film industry in recent years. The central government has marked a budget of NT$26.2 billion (US$850 million) to be spent on the arts between 2009 and 2013, with film as one of six targeted areas. Taiwan's two largest cities, Taipei and Kaohsiung, both operate film commissions to assist foreign productions, and Taipei reported that it cooperated with 15 countries in the production of 25 projects last year. Taiwan's national government reaffirmed in late 2010 that it will continue to bar all investment from mainland China in film and publishing industries.

Taiwan's reigning auteur-in-residence, Tsai Ming-liang, was awarded Asian Filmmaker of the Year at the 2010 Pusan Film Festival. His next project, **The Diary of a Young Boy**, should begin filming in 2011.

Arvin Chen's **Au Revoir Taipei**

Tsai's award and *Monga's* success are good news for Taiwan, but of the 37 films produced in the first 11 months of 2010, many were by debut or sophomore directors, an indication that the industry is still trying to find itself. Internationally, the country's most talked-about

film was 31-year-old director Arvin Chen's debut, **Au Revoir Taipei**, a zippy and brightly coloured romantic comedy. Produced by Wim Wenders, who discovered Chen after seeing his graduation short at the Berlin Film Festival in 2007, the film won the Best Asian Film Award from the Network for the Promotion of Asian Cinema (NETPAC) in Berlin.

Chung Mong-hong's **The Fourth Portrait**

The Fourth Portrait, the second feature by Chung Mong-hong, presents the sensitive story of a young boy's disturbed childhood, eventually taking on a surreal dimension. It was awarded the Best Feature Film prize at the Taipei Film Festival and garnered nominations in seven categories at the 'Chinese Oscars', the Golden Horse Awards.

Other young directors' efforts were less successful. Cho Li's feature debut, **Zoom Hunting**, was an attempt at the erotic thriller, with a narrative that recalled Antonioni's *Blow Up*. The critic's response was 'nice

Cho Li's **Zoom Hunting**

Hsiao Ya-chuan's **Taipei Exchanges**

try.' **Taipei Exchanges** by Hsiao Ya-chuan, whose background is in advertising, delivered a thinly scripted story about a woman who opens a Taipei coffee shop, but struggles to make it work. Commissioned by Taipei City Government's Department of Information & Tourism, its main attraction was the actress Guey Lun-mei.

Three young directors combined their talents for the portmanteau film, **Juliets**, which offered three short reinterpretations of Shakespeare's tragic heroine: *Juliet's Choice* by Hou Chi-jan, *Two Juliets* by Shen Ko-shang and Chen Yu-hsun's *One More Juliet*.

Ho Wi-ding was the newcomer with the best credentials. He had previously won the Kodak prize at Cannes for his 2005 short, *Respire*. His social comedy, **Pinoy Sunday**, was Taiwan's first feature to focus on its population of 300,000 migrant workers, telling the story of Filipino workers who, on their one day off, discover a sofa and try to carry it back to their dormitory. The leads are all top Filipino stars – Meryll Soriano, Alessandra De Rossi, Bayam Agbayani and Jeffrey 'Epy' Quizon – and almost all the dialogue is in Tagalog. A big release in the Philippines is planned for 2011.

Given the mixed response to the younger directors' films, it was no surprise that an experienced filmmaker should steal the limelight at the Golden Horse Awards. At 49, Chang Tso-chi, former assistant to Hou Hsiao-hsien, is one of Taiwan's finest filmmakers, who possesses his own distinctive style.

His latest, **When Love Comes**, received 14 nominations and picked up the festival's Best Film award. It offers a roving, naturalistic portrait of a teenage girl living in a dysfunctional lower-middle-class family, and, as with Chang's earlier work, his interest lies in those on the margins of society.

In the arena of pop cinema, the high-octane martial-arts epic **Reign of Assassins** was a collaboration between the legendary Hong Kong director of shoot-em-ups, John Woo, and Taiwan's Su Chao-pin, co-directing what was mainly a Taiwan production. The pan-Asian cast of A-list stars included Hong Kong's Michelle Yeoh, Barbie Hsu and Leon Dai from Taiwan, as well as South Korean Jung Woo-song. According to reports, it will see major distribution in North America and other big markets.

Documentaries of note include Jiang Xiuquiong and Pung-Leung Kwan's **Let the Wind Carry Me**, a profile of cinematographer

Ho Wi-ding's **Pinoy Sunday**

Mark Lee, who shot virtually every Hou Hsiao-hsien film, as well as Wang Kar-wai's *In the Mood for Love,* amongst many others. Another, Su Che-hsien's **Hip Hop Storm**, tells the story of two generations of Taiwanese break-dancers.

Su Che-hsien's **Hip Hop Storm**

In 2011, Ang Lee will start shooting a 3-D adaptation of Yann Martel's best-selling novel **Life of Pi**, with location shooting in Taiwan and India. Anticipation is also very high for the US$18.9 million **Seediq Bale**, the sophomore effort of Wei Te-sheng, who shattered Taiwan's box-office records with his 2008 debut, *Cape No. 7.* This historical epic chronicles a Formosan aboriginal tribe's uprising against the Japanese in the 1930s and will be released in two parts.

DAVID FRAZIER is founder and programmer of the Urban Nomad Film Fest (www. urbannomad.tw), a major platform in Taiwan for indie and underground film. As a writer, he has contributed to numerous publications, including *The International Herald Tribune, Wallpaper, Art in America, Art AsiaPacific, Taipei Times, Japan Times* and *South China Morning Post.*

The year's best films
Monga (Doze Niu)
When Love Comes (Chang Tso-chi)
Reign of Assassins (Su Chao-pin and John Woo)
Au Revoir Taipei (Arvin Chen)

Quote of the year
'You are Chinese, I am Taiwanese.' CHEN CHIH-KUAN, *Head of the Department of Motion Pictures at Taiwan's Government Information Office, upon being told by a Chinese bureaucrat that the Taiwanese delegation should change it's name to 'Chinese Taipei'.*

Directory
All Tel/Fax numbers begin (+886)
Chinese Taipei Film Archive, 4F, 7 Chingtao East Rd, Taipei. Tel: (2) 2392 4243. Fax: (2) 2392 6359. www.ctfa.org.tw.
Government Information Office, Department of Motion Picture Affairs, 2 Tientsin St, Taipei 100. Tel: (2) 3356 7870. Fax: (2) 2341 0360. www.gio.gov.tw.
Motion Picture Association of Taipei, 5F, 196 Chunghwa Rd, Sec 1, Taipei. Tel: (2) 2331 4672. Fax: (2) 2381 4341.
Taipei Film Commission, 4F, #99, Section 5, Civic Blvd., Taipei. Tel: (2) 2528-9580. Fax: (2) 2528-9580. www.taipeifilmcommission.org.

Su Chao-pin and John Woo's **Reign of Assassins**

Thailand Anchalee Chaiworaporn

Thailand experienced a turbulent year, including the country's month-long political upheavals. Surprises also rocked the film industry. The local box office nosedived, but the number of productions increased. And then, amidst the political crisis, Apichatpong Weerasethakul became the first Thai director to win the Palme d'Or, for **Uncle Boonmee Who Can Recall His Past Lives**. Another surprise was the government's investment of US$6.7 million to support local filmmaking. These events caused shockwaves that are likely to impact the industry for the next few years.

Over the first half of the year, film business soared, particularly during March and May, as the political situation intensified. But then summer arrived and admissions dropped off considerably. Several films were rescheduled and takings shrank, even for the surefire sequels, **My Trip with Che** (*Saranae Sib Lor*) and **Ong Bak 3: The Final Battle**.

My Trip with Che, the follow-up to the 2009 hit **God Bless Trainees**, only earned US$2.2 million, a third less than the earlier film. Rather than the Candid Camera style of the earlier film, *My Trip with Che* was a scripted tale of a young man's journey to adulthood. Tony Jaa and Panna Rittikari's final entry in the martial-arts trilogy attracted just US$1.40 million. However, the figures were enough to place both films in the list of the year's five top box-office successes.

As the country descended into violence in May, everyone appeared to forget that a Thai film was competing at Cannes. And then, on the first Monday morning following the crisis, news came in of *Uncle Boonmee*'s success.

Apichatpong Weerasethakul's **Uncle Boonmee Who Can Recall His Past Lives**

Apichatpong came back home with the best present for the country. For the first time, the film was immediately released domestically at just one theatre at a time, playing once each day. After three months of screenings in Bangkok, the northeast, central, and southern parts of the country, it had earned US$350,000.

The triumph of *Uncle Boonmee* saw a friendlier approach to independent films in Thailand. Instead of garnering recognition abroad and then securing a domestic release, it is hoped that they could be given an earlier release at home. Seven local independent films were given limited releases over the last year, a significant improvement on the one or two films of previous years. They included Uruphong Raksasad's *Agrarian Utopia* and Anocha Suwichakornpong's *Mundane History*.

Other interesting independent works included Tanwarin Sukkhapisit's **Insects in the Backyard**, about a family's response to homosexuality, and Sivaroj Kongsakul's **Eternity**, which detailed the romance of the director's own parents.

Sivaroj Kongsakul's **Eternity**

If independent films flourished, the plight of mainstream cinema remained uncertain. Production rose from 50 to 61 features, but poor box-office results, even in the aftermath of civil disorder, was alarming. It took almost three months for the business to settle. Audiences returned to see two romantic comedies: Banjong Pisanthanakun's **Hello Stranger** and debut directors Wasin Pokplong and Phuttipong Phromsaka Na Sakonnakorn's **First Love**. Pisanthanakun's film detailed the growing romance between two strangers in Korea. An old hand at this style of film, with *Shutter* and *Alone*, Pisanthanakun walked away with the year's box-office honours after his film attracted US$4.40 million. *First Love* also performed well. The secret love between a younger girl and an older man earned US$2.60 million.

Banjong Pisanthanakun's **Hello Stranger**

Other productions failed to attract audiences, with one film earning just US$2,100. One third of all the year's releases failed to break US$300,000. Even the year's most eagerly awaited film, Wisit Sasanatieng's **The Red**

Eagle, collected just US$400,000. A remake of *The Golden Eagle*, whose status stems from the death of Thai star Mitr Chaibancha in a helicopter accident during production, Sasanatieng's film was updated, with the anti-hero disposing of corrupt politicians.

Wisit Sasanatieng's **The Red Eagle**

The Thai government's new film fund will allot US$6.7 million to 69 feature and 21 television projects, as well as other platforms and support initiatives. However, not every project will receive full support and, even then, only a number of the funded projects will reach completion. Apichatpong's Cannes winner was a recipient, as is Pen-Ek Ratanaruang's **Headshot**, a film noir about a hitman and his experiences after he is shot in the head. Other films that will benefit from the fund include Aditya Assarat's semi-autobiographical feature, **Hi-So**, about a man living in two cultures; Kong Rithdee and Panu Aree's **Baby Arabia**, a documentary on the lives and music of a Muslim band; and Ekachai Eukrongtham's **Enemies**, which focuses on the relationships between a group of friends.

Aditya Assarat's **Hi-So**

The next few years are likely to see a thriving independent sector, while the mainstream will need to reassess its situation.

The year's best films
First Love (Wasin Pokplong and Phuttipong Phromsaka Na Sakonnakorn)
Uncle Boonmee Who Can Recall His Past Lives (Apichatpong Weerasethakul)
The Red Eagle (Wisit Sasanatieng)
Hi-So (Aditya Assarat)
Insects in the Backyard (Tanwarin Sukkhapisit)
Eternity (Sivaroj Kongsakul)

Quote of the year
'I would like to thank for all the spirits and ghosts in Thailand who made it possible for me to be here.' APICHATPONG WEERASETHAKUL *on receiving the Palme d'Or.*

Tanwarin Sukkhapisit's **Insects in the Backyard**

Directory
All Tel/Fax numbers begin (+66)
Federation of National Film Association of Thailand, 31/9 UMG Theatre 2 Fl., Royal City Avenue, New Petchburi Road, Bangkapi, Bangkok 10310. Tel: (2) 6415917-8. www.thainationalfilm.com.
National Film Archive, 93 Moo 3, Phutthamonthon Soi 5 Phutthamonthon, Nakorn Prathom 73120. Tel: (2) 4822013-5. www.nfat.org.
Office of Contemporary Arts and Culture, Ministry of Culture, 666 Baromrajchonnanee Road, Bangplad, Bangkok 10700. Tel: (2) 4228819-20. http://www.ocac.go.th.

ANCHALEE CHAIWORAPORN is a film critic based in Thailand. She won Thailand's 2000 Best ML Bunlua Thepphayasuwan Film Critic and 2002's Best MR Ayumongkol Article Writer. She runs a bilingual website on Thai cinema, www.thaicinema.org.

Tunisia Maryam Touzani

t was announced that 2010 would be the year of cinema in Tunisia, following President Ben Ali's decision to devote one year to the celebration of every art. The bi-annual Carthage Film Festival – the oldest in Africa and the Arab world – celebrated its 45th year and 23rd edition this year. But it unfolded against the backdrop of a national cinema in disarray.

Remaining true to its original purpose of being a platform for African and Arab cinema, the festival faced the usual struggle with domestic productions. Tunisia produces on average a meagre four features each year. Among the films present was veteran film director Abdelatif ben Ammar's Tunisian-Algerian co-production, **The Wounded Palm Trees** (*Les Palmiers Blessés*), which recounts the story of Chama, a young Tunisian woman who has graduated in sociology and, while looking for a job, accepts temporary employment typing up a novelist's manuscript. As she types the document, a historical quest for truth develops within her.

Also competing for Carthage's top prize, the Gold Tanit, was Ayda Ben Aleya's **Chronicles of an Agony** (*Chronique d'une agonie*), the story of Donia, a lonely young girl who tries by all means to survive her difficult life. Ben Aleya, prior to directing her latest feature, also directed **Dar Joued**, the story of four women locked up for disobedience. Some recant their behaviour, while the others refuse.

In Moez Kamoun's sophomore feature, **Late December** (*Fin Décembre*), the paths of three characters cross in a peaceful village. Aicha, a 20-year-old worker, betrayed by her love, takes refuge in solitude, while Adam, a disillusioned doctor, accepts a position in this same village,

Moez Kamoun's **Late December**

and Sofiéne, who has emigrated, returns to his village to find a wife.

Doc à Tunis is instrumental in promoting documentary production in Tunisia and is responsible for playing a part in many of the year's non-fiction releases.

Hichem Ben Ammar returned with **Once Upon Our Time** (*Un Conte de Faits*), which follows Anès, whose father believes he will be a great musician and who is accepted at at the Yehudi Menuhin School. Fathi Saidi's **Separations** focuses on the experiences of Mohamed, a

Hichem Ben Ammar's **Once Upon Our Time**

Tunisian emigrant, who boarded a boat from Libya to Italy, hoping for a new life in Europe.

Tunisia produces around 20 short films per year. Youssef Chebbi's short **Towards the North** (*Vers le Nord*) is a story that takes place on a dark night, on a beach in the middle of nowhere, where Mehdi and Nito try to make a human traffic deal with the Albanese mafia; things change when Mehdi learns that his younger brother, Mouja, has been chosen for the voyage. **Dirty Linen** (*Linge Sale*), directed by Malik Amara, is the story of submissive Radhi, 50, who is married to a terrible, mistreating shrew and has resigned himself to this life until she accidently falls from the second story of the building but only sprains her wrist.

A number of ex-pat filmmakers were at work around the world. Karim Dridi's **The Last Flight** (*Le Dernier Vol*) stars Marion Cotillard as aviator Marie Vallières de Beaumont, while *Couscous* director Abdellatif Kechiche's **Black Venus** (*Venus Noire*) was a bio-pic of Sarah Baartman, the 'Hottentot Venus'. It screened in competition at the Venice Film Festival.

Veteran filmmaker Ferid Boughedir was appointed chair of an advisory committee whose mission is to foster growth and development in the audiovisual industry. The Ministry of Culture will offer support to nine feature projects, a significant increase on previous years.

It is hoped that digital cinema will allow filmmakers more ease and access, enabling them to produce more films at home. The President also authorised the construction of multiplex cinemas, a welcome project for a country that boasts just 15 dedicated cinemas.

The year's best films
Late December (Moez Kamoun)
The Wounded Palm Trees (Abdelatif ben Ammar)

Moez Kamoun's **Late December**

Quote of the year
'This film originated with an idea of a young modern Tunisian woman growing up in a crumbling mountain-top village. As there is so much more time to talk in a village than in a town there are more stories to tell... I also wanted to show the beauty of rural Tunisia and the wonderful character of some of my country's poorest people.' *Director* MOEZ KAMOUN *on* **Late December**.

MARYAM TOUZANI is a freelance journalist based in Morocco and working internationally, specialising in Art and Culture.

Turkey Atilla Dorsay

Turkish cinema, considerably helped by the relative health of the economic situation (one of the few countries that expects to report significant growth – around 5% – for 2010), continued to do well. Local production increased again, reaching over 60 films. The total admissions climbed as well reaching 42 million, an increase of over four million on last year.

The new wonder boy of Turkish cinema, musical icon-turned-director, Mahsun Kirmizigül, realised his dream project, **New York'da Bes Minare** (*Five Minarets in New York*). Having been responsible for two major successes in as many years (*The White Angel* and *I Saw the Sun*), Kirmizigül's latest is his most ambitious yet, costing no less than an unprecedented US$12 million. A Turkish-American co-production, with the participation of Hollywood stars Danny Glover, Gina Gershon and Robert Patrick, it opens in Bitlis, a remote Turkish town and continues in Istanbul and New York, before finally returning to Bitlis. Cultural and religious conflicts, blood feuds and American imperialism are just some of the elements in an impressively presented and wisely balanced drama, which sold two millions tickets in the first two weeks of its domestic release.

Mahsun Kirmizigül's **Five Minarets in New York**

International distribution has been secured for the film. However, the sincerity of Kirmizigül's two previous features is missing here.

Another box-office hit, **Recep Ivedik 3**, saw director Togan Gökbakan reunite with his immensely popular comedian brother, Sahan Gökbakan. The continuing story of the vulgar, uneducated, misogynist anti-hero, Recep, it went further than the previous films in its grotesque humour. However, this Turkish Mr Bean broke all records – both in box office and bad taste!

Ata Demirer in Hakan Algül's **Oh My God**

Other comedies also fared well. Murat Aykul's **Kanal-I-Zasyon** and Kemal Uzun's **Oh Dude** (*Vay Arkadas*) are pretty hard to defend. Some were better. The talented comedian, writer and director Yilmaz Erdogan's **Happy Days** (*Neseli Günler*) was a charming little comedy, maybe the first Christmas movie from a Muslim society. A man searching for a job is only able to find one that requires him to dress up as Santa Claus in a big city mall. It is unusual, sentimental and very funny. Omer Faruk Sorak's **The Beautiful West** (*Yahşi Bati*) relied on the immense talent of comedian Cem Yilmaz, while Hakan Algül employed another funny man, Ata Demirer, for **Oh My God** (*Eyvah Eyvah*).

Honey (*Bal*) completes Semih Kaplanoğlu's 'trilogy of Yusuf', after *Milk and Egg*, this time dealing with his hero's childhood and paternal relations, set against a gorgeous and vividly filmed rural backdrop. It was the winner of the Golden Bear at the Berlin Film Festival. Reha Erdem, another master, gave us **Kosmos**, a complex and poetic film about the arrival in Kars of a mysterious man, a kind of prophet who can cure sick people with his touch, and his relations with the local people, in particular a half-witted girl. Mixing Muslim, Christian and heathen traditions, he uses Kars (an old city in east Turkey, on the Russian border, which is usually under snow and is the setting of novelist Orhan Pamuk's *Snow*) as an element in his drama. This unique film cast a spell over audiences.

Semih Kaplanoğlu's **Honey**

Tayfun Pirselimoglu's fourth film, **Haze** (*Pus*), is a masterpiece of minimalism, dealing with the lives of four people in the suburbs of a town and creating a rare sense of realism.

Of the newcomers, Inan Temelkuran's **Bornova Bornova** looked at dissolute youth in a small, rural Anatolian town. Selim Demircan's **Junction** (*Kavsak*) presents a series of convincing, interwoven stories about a group of people, while Seren Yüce's Grand Prix winner at Anatalya, **Cogunluk**, depicts the life of a nouveau riche family and their estranged, overweight son, who seeks an impossible relationship with a Kurdish girl. Ilksen Basarir's **Love in Another Language** (*Baska Dilde Ask*) is a touching film about a deaf-and-mute young man and the girl he loves. Even an American residing

Seren Yüce's **Cogunluk**

in Turkey, university professor Theron Patterson, caught the current trend towards some kind of realism with **The Unlucky One** (*Bahti Kara*), an astute account of life in the suburbs.

Politically themed films were still an important element of Turkish cinema. Popular musician-writer-director Zülfü Livaneli contributed to a number of films about the great Atatürk with his dramatic feature, **Farewell** (*Veda*). The film re-opened the endless polemic about the founder of the Turkish Republic and its first President, but was well liked by audiences and a number of critics, including myself. Atıl Inac's **The Big Game** (*Büyük Oyun*) offered an impressive portrait of present-day Iraq through the sad story of a Kurdish girl whose family is killed by American soldiers and leaves for Turkey in search of her elder brother. Alper Caglar's **Büsra**, a so-called Islamist film, impresses with its tact and objectivity in dealing with the daily life of a girl who wears a hijab and her efforts to exist in a modern society. Turkish-Kurdish director Miraz Bezar's **I Saw It Too** (*Min Dit*) is a courageous film with strong messages, while Yusuf Kurcenli's **Ask Your Heart** (*Yuregine Sor*) portrays the difficult relations between Muslim Turks and Orthodox Greeks in the Black Sea coastal region circa 1870. With a central narrative that recalls Shakespeare's *Romeo and Juliet*, it is a beautifully shot and well-acted film, with a rich seam of folklore running through it. German director Ben Verbong explores different cultural encounters in **Takiye**. The film shines a light on Islamic links between Germany and Turkey, where large sums of money are collected from believers for apparently noble purposes, with a lack of any serious control on the part of either government. It is a brave, but ultimately unconvincing drama.

A number of good genre films were released over the last year. Actor-director Ugur Yücel's **The Dragon Trap** (*Ejder Kapani*) b, the, was a good and atmospheric 'police story' with a twist. **The Voice** (*Ses*), by the interesting Ümit Ünal, was a rare example of a fantastic film in our cinema, and also quite successful. Ünal was also responsible for **Captain Sky** (*Kaptan Feza*), a thriller with fantastic touches, albeit not very convincing. Instead, a film that came towards the end of the year, **The Sleeping Princess** (*Prensesin Uykusu*) by the prolific Cagan Irmak, was a real revelation. Combining a few 'genres', adding up classic tales, animation sequences and quite a number of special effects, it was fun to watch.

And there were documentaries, both in specialised festivals and competitions. But some were also released. Highlights amongst these were Kurdish director Kazim Öz's **Savaks – The Last Season** (*Son Mevsim - Savaklar*), about the nomadic Kurds of the Dersim area, and Nezih Önen's masterly overview of the mostly forgotten songs and dances of Anatolia's minorities, **The Lost Songs of Anatolia** (*Anadolu'nun Kayip Sarkilari*).

The Anatalya Film Festival once again highlighted the fine health of contemporary Turkish cinema. There were many solid films, with almost all the awards going to the new generation of filmmakers. Many of these will be released over the course of the next year, along with the anticipated releases of Ceylan, Demirkubuz, Tugrul and Zaim. So the future seems assured.

ATILLA DORSAY has been a film critic since 1966 and has published over 40 books. He is the founder and honorary president of SIYAD-Association of the Turkish Critics and one of the founders of the Istanbul Film Festival.

Reha Erdem's **Kosmos**

The year's best films
Kosmos (Reha Erdem)
Honey (Semih Kaplanoğlu)
The Sleeping Princess (Cagan Irmak)
Ask Your Heart (Yusuf Kurcenli)
Majority (Seren Yüce)

Quote of the year
'We certainly have a child-like side. Who can say that cinema is not a child's game? Making a film is also a very amusing effort. But I don't want to give an impression of self-importance. We are, after all, the humble followers of 100 years of movie making.' CAGAN IRMAK *speaking about* The Sleeping Princess.

Directory
All Tel/Fax numbers begin (+90)
CASOD (The Association of Actors), Istiklal Caddesi, Atlas Sinemasi Pasaj- C Blok 53/3 - Beyoglu/ Istanbul. Tel: 212 251 97 75 Fax : 212 251 97 79. casod@casod.org.
FILM-YÖN (The Association of Directors), Ayhan Isik Sokak, 28/1- Beyoglu/ Istanbul. Tel: 212 293 90 01.
IKSV- Istanbul Kültür ve Sanat Vakfi (The Istanbul Culture and Arts Foundation), Sadi Konuralp Caddesi No 5/ Deniz Palas, Evliya Çelebi Mahallesi- 34433, Sishane/ Istanbul. Tel: 212 334 07 00. Fax: 212 334 07 02. film.fest@istfest.org.
SIYAD- Sinema Yazarları Dernegi (The Association of Film Critics), Erol Dernek Sokak No 7/1-A, Beyoglu 80600/ Istanbul. Tel: 212 251 56 47. Fax: 212 251 63 27. denizyavuz@superonline.com.
TÜRSAK (The Turkish Cinema and Audiovisual Culture Foundation), Gazeteci Erol Dernek Sokak, 11/ 2 Hanif Han- Beyoglu/ Istanbul. Tel: 212 244 52 51. Fax: 212 251 67 70. tursak@superonline.com.

Ukraine Volodymyr Voytenko

Despite the crisis in Ukraine in recent years and slow growth in the number of new cinemas (there are currently 300), the box office has grown steadily. By September 2010, it had grown by 48% on the previous year, from US$36 million to US$53.85 million.

With the change in leader (the new President, Viktor Yanukovych, has been an implacable opponent of Viktor Yushchenko since the Orange Revolution of 2004), there was a shift in public policy and ideology, with a return to stonger Russian influence and its corresponding values. In film distribution, the preference for Ukrainian as the main language in the dubbing and post-synching of foreign-language films lost out to Russian. However, a regulation was passed stipulating that film prints should be post-synched and dubbed exclusively by Ukrainian companies.

The state support for filmmaking was miserable. By the end of October, the film industry saw its budget drop from US$3 million to less than US$1 million, elevating the importance of independent projects, often seen as a challenge to the frail state film policy. Such was the funding behind the portmanteau of 14 short films, **F***ers.**

F***ers. *Arabesques*

Arabesques (*Mudaky. Arabesky*), a collection of social satires. All films were shot on a low-to-no-budget basis and have had a good run at festivals. Myroslav Slaboshpytskiy's **Deafness** (*Glukhota*) was produced in the same way, going on to compete at the Berlin Film Festival. The same group of enthusiasts, led by Volodymyr Tykhiy, have already begun work on a new collection, **Ukraine, Good Bye**, looking at the levels of emigration out of the country and the reasons behind it.

Sergei Loznitsa's **My Joy**

Another breakthrough was the Ukraine-German-Netherlands co-production, **My Joy** (*Schastie moyo*), the feature debut of documentary filmmaker Sergei Loznitsa. It was the first Ukrainian film to feature in competition at the Cannes Film Festival. It was a disturbing tale of the corrupting influence of power. The film's producer Oleg Kokhan also co-produced **Chantrapas**, directed by Otar Iosseliani, which reflects on the place of the artist in democratic and totalitarian societies.

Alexander Shapiro's **Dnipro** (*Dnepr*) is a slight film poem, a peaen to the great Ukrainian river, with the director's footage intercut with official newsreels from the past. Dmytro Tyazhlov's documentary **I am a Monument to Myself** (*Ya pamyatnyk sobi*) tells the story

Dmytro Tyazhlov's **I am a Monument to Myself**

of an amateur sculptor whose work aims to reconcile a politicised community, constructing a number of monuments to former enemies of the people.

Three new films were co-productions with Russia: Alexei Lukanev's **Stradivari Gun** (*Pistolet Stradivari*), Vilen Novak's **Shoot Immediately!** (*Strelyai nemedlenno!*), and Leonid Gorovets' **My Widow's Husband** (*Muzh moyei vdovy*), an adventurous crime story with humorous elements that failed to convince audience and critics.

The only project made with some State support was the animated series **Ukraine is My Country** (*Moya kraina – Ukraina*), a collection of three-minute episodes that present the history of a particular geographical area, which succeeded in pleasing audiences and was artful throughout.

In the meantime, a number of feature films under-funded by the State are waiting for completion in 2011. In particular, Russian filmmaker Ilya Khrzhanovsky's biographical drama, **Dau**. It is the fateful story of the prominent physicist, Lev Landau, who worked in Ukraine during the 1930s.

Meanwhile, from January 1, 2011 changes to the 'Law on Cinema' come into effect. Investment in all stages of domestic films, from production to exhibition, will be exempt from tax for a period of five years. However, there is much doubt over how well this will work.

The year's best films
My Joy (Sergei Loznitsa)
F***ers. Arabesques (Volodymyr Tykhiy, Myroslav Slaboshpytskiy et al)
Ukraine is My Country (Stepan Koval et al)
I am a Monument to Myself (Dmytro Tyazhlov)

Quote of the year
'The subject of f***ers (or assholes) can not be exhausted. We should shoot a sequel, like 'F***ers. Ukraine in Flames'. Being an asshole is the main way of life in the country. People don't give a damn for the past and future, they live only according to their whims.'
VOLODYMYR TYKHIY, *producer and director of* F***ers. Arabesques.

Directory
All Tel/Fax numbers begin (+380)
National Oleksandr Dovzhenko Center (State Film Archives), 1 Vasylkivska St, Kyiv 03040. Tel: 257 7698 Fax: 201 6547.
Central State Archives of Film, Photo & Sound Documents, 24 Solomyanska St, Kyiv 03601. Tel: 275 3777 Fax: 275 3655. tsdkffa@archives.gov.ua.
Institute of Screen Art, Kyiv National University of Theatre, Cinema and Television, 40 Yaroslaviv Val St, Kyiv 01034. Tel: 272 1032 Fax: 272 0220. info@knutkt.kiev.ua http://knutkt.kiev.ua.
Ukrainian Cinema Foundation, 6 Saksahansky St, Kyiv 01033. Tel/Fax: 287 6618. info@ucf.org.ua www.ucf.org.ua.
Ministry of Culture and Tourism of Ukraine, State Cinema Service, 19 Ivan Franko St, Kyiv 01601. Tel/Fax: 234 4094, 234 6951. ros@mincult.gov.ua http://dergkino.gov.ua/.
Kyiv International Film Festival Molodist, 6 Saksahansky St, Kyiv 01033. Tel/Fax: 461 9803. info@molodist.com www.molodist.com.
Krok International Animated Film Festival, Suite 208, 6, Saksagansky St, Kyiv 01033. Tel/Fax: 287 52 80. krokfestival@gmail.com www.krokfestival.com.

VOLODYMYR VOYTENKO is a film critic, editor-in-chief of internet portal www.kinokolo.ua and presenter of the weekly programme about art cinema at the national TV channel *1+1*.

United Kingdom Jason Wood

The United Kingdom was almost entirely dominated by the abrupt shock announcement by the Department for Culture Media and Sport on Monday 26 July that the UK Film Council – the Government's lead agency for film in the UK – was to be abolished. The response from Tim Bevan, the Chairman of the UK Film Council, was equally swift and unequivocal. 'Abolishing the most successful film support organisation the UK has ever had is a bad decision, imposed without any consultation or evaluation. People will rightly look back on today's announcement and say it was a big mistake, driven by short-term thinking and political expediency. British film, which is one of the UK's more successful growth industries, deserves better.' Chief Executive John Woodward tended his resignation.

The organisation's detractors were quick to point out that the UKFC made a number of questionable decisions and there was criticism too of a salary structure that handsomely rewarded executives in its upper echelons. However, since its creation in 2000 the UKFC has undoubtedly striven to be a force for good, investing over GB€160m of Lottery funding into more than 900 films which have entertained over 200 million people and helped generate over GB€700 million at the box office worldwide, generating GB€5 for every GB€1 of Lottery money it has invested. The UKFC has helped develop new filmmakers, funded a number of ambitious new British films and filmmakers (but equally, it can be countered, spurned many others) and striven to present a wider choice of films to audiences throughout the UK. A roll call of titles supported by the UKFC since its inception in 2000 includes: *Bend it like Beckham*, *The Sex Lives of the Potato Men* (the organisation's nadir and the

Streetdance 3D

stick so often used to beat it), *Bright Star*, *The Constant Gardener*, *Fish Tank*, *Gosford Park*, *Bullet Boy*, *In the Loop*, *The Last King of Scotland*, *Man on Wire*, *Nowhere Boy*, *Red Road*, *St Trinian's*, *This is England*, *Touching the Void*, *Vera Drake*, *The Wind That Shakes the Barley*, **Streetdance 3D**, **The King's Speech**, **NEDS**, and the upcoming **Attack the Block** (Joe Cornish), **We Need To Talk About Kevin** (Lynne Ramsay) and Andrea Arnold's **Wuthering Heights**.

Prominent amongst the UKFC's numerous successful funding initiatives is its contribution to the creation of the world's first Digital Screen Network, which has invested in 240 digital screens in cinemas across the UK (the highest anywhere in Europe), increasing film choice to audiences throughout the country. This initiative has altered the exhibition and distribution model, most notably in regards to the rise of alternative content on UK screens and the astonishing success UK exhibitors have enjoyed when presenting live opera (the Metropolitan is particularly noteworthy), theatre and other satellite events. When opposing the abolishment, Tim Bevan was also able to cite a number of persuasive statistics as to why

the organisation should have been preserved. The UK box office has grown by 62% since the UK Film Council was created (in 2009 it reached record levels of GB€944 million), with British films accounting for 23% of all UK cinema takings over the ten years to 2009. Recent figures also show that in 2009 cinema admissions rose to 174 million, the highest figure for seven years. This upward trend largely continued in 2010, due mainly to the increased ticket prices that accompany the huge amount of films now being released in the 3D format.

As high-profile figures including Clint Eastwood, Steven Spielberg, Ken Loach and Mike Leigh continued to question the decision, speculation regarding the coalition government's plans for the public funding of UK film consumed both the trade press and the broadsheets. On 29 November, Culture Minister Ed Vaizey revealed the resolution many predicted when he announced that the British Film Institute would become the lottery distributor for film in the UK. Reaffirming the government's commitment to the current Film Tax Relief, Vaizey also revealed that inward investment work would transfer to Film London (abolishing the regional screen agencies) in a public/private partnership with the Production Guild, UK Screen, Pinewood Shepperton Studios and others in the industry. Vaizey also confirmed that lottery funding for film would grow from GB€27m in 2010 to around GB€43m by 2014.

Tom Hooper's **The King's Speech**

BFI Chairman Greg Dyke welcomed the news. 'This decision is a great vote of confidence in the BFI. It is a bold move to create a single champion for film in the UK and we welcome it. We want to achieve greater coherence across the whole film sector and to strike a balance between cultural and commercial. We see an opportunity to reduce overhead costs which in turn will allow us to put more of the Lottery funds into frontline activities and provide greater public value. It is our aim to increase the Production budget for film from GB€15 million to GB€18 million in the coming year and this is only possible because of the cut in overhead costs.'

There is a certain irony in the decision given that at its inception the then incoming UKFC Chief Executive John Woodward was scathing of the kind of work associated with the BFI production unit and outlined his plans to finance films that people would actually want to see in cinemas. Experimentation was out, entertainment and accessibility was very much in. Of course the UKFC would go on to be involved in numerous projects that blurred the boundaries with films such as *My Summer of Love* and Peter Greenaway's (the bête-noire of former UKFC chairman Alan Parker) *Nightwatching* all being ushered into production.

The above dichotomy very much encapsulates the challenges faced by the BFI in its new role. An organisation facing its own significant funding cuts and already in need of a radical overhaul and transformation, it now has to carry the responsibility of administering lottery funding to invest in populist fare such as **The King's Speech** whilst also maintaining its heritage and policy of diversity in its support of projects such as Gillian Wearing's **Self Made** and Terence Davies's **The Deep Blue Sea**. Dyke has promised to 'develop a new, exciting and coherent vision for film in Britain going forward'. These could be exiting times. Let's wait and see.

Against the backdrop of these major structural changes, 2010 proved to be an interesting

David Yates' **Harry Potter and the Deathly Hallows Part One**

year for UK cinema, both aesthetically and commercially. **Harry Potter and the Deathly Hallows Part One** arrived to mediocre reviews but record-breaking business. A two-parter that brings the curtain down on one of the cinema's most lucrative franchises, the David Yates-directed film finds Harry, Ron and Hermione attempting to track down and destroy the secret to Voldemort's immortality. Alarm bells began to ring when Warner Bros announced that the film would not in fact be released in the 3D format but nerves were quickly soothed when the film opened in November. Amongst its numerous box-office achievements are: the biggest 3-day weekend ever and the biggest 7-day figure ever. At the time of writing the film's UK box office stands at an astonishing GB€33.7 million. Perhaps the most unexpected hit of the year was **Streetdance 3D**. The first British film to be shot using the 3D format, the tale of a London dance crew's unlikely collaboration with a troupe of ballet dancers went on to take over GB€11 million. It was lent added gravitas by the inclusion of Charlotte Rampling amongst the cast of real-life performers. A sequel is already in production. Also enjoying perhaps

Josh Appignanesi's **The Infidel**

unexpected success was Josh Appignanesi's identity-crisis comedy **The Infidel**. Well-scripted by David Baddiel, making light of racial, religious and political differences, the film was released on a modest 29 screens (expanding to a maximum of 57) and grossed a shade under GB€600,000. A strong return for a modestly budgeted British comedy.

Nigel Cole's **Made In Dagenham**

Expectations were rather higher for Nigel Cole's **Made In Dagenham**. Inspired by 1968 events at the Ford plant in Dagenham where a group of women went out on strike in protest at their working conditions and a pay structure that classified them as unskilled labourers, this entertaining look at British sexual politics featured an impressive ensemble cast including the characteristically brilliant Sally Hawkins (who will be seen next year in both **Never Let Me Go**, a solid but somewhat stilted adaptation of the Kazuo Ishiguro sci-fi about genetic engineering, and Richard Ayoade's hugely likeable **Submarine**), Miranda Richardson and the stalwart Bob Hoskins. Released at the beginning of October after a stagnant September relatively starved of awards titles (a period hot on the heels of a summer parched by a heat wave and the World Cup) the film was slow to get out of the traps (scraping to an opening 3-day of GB€674,059 from 354 screens) but went on to build through strong word of mouth to a respectable GB€3,631,485. Faring less well was Stephen Frears' **Tamara Drewe**. An adaptation of the Posy Simmonds *Guardian* cartoon strip, the film featured a simmering performance from

Stephen Frears' **Tamara Drewe**

Gemma Arterton (equally impressive in gritty kidnap drama **The Disappearance of Alice Creed**) as a London journalist returning home to country roots and the ghosts of her past. Lauded, a little perplexingly, at Cannes, the film is not amongst the director's finest work and failed to find critical or commercial favour.

Mike Leigh's **Another Year**

Of the veteran British filmmakers, Mike Leigh arguably had the best year with **Another Year**. Utilising an ensemble cast of Leigh veterans including Jim Broadbent, Ruth Sheen and Lesley Manville, this Rohmerian tale of happiness, companionship, death, loss and the ageing process drew almost unanimous rave reviews and was perceived by many to be amongst the finest films of the director's career. Audiences responded well to the film too, and, at the time of writing, six weeks after its initial release, *Another Year* is still a fixture at art-house cinemas. A less high-profile figure, but an important one none the less, Patrick Keiller returned with **Robinson In Ruins**, the continuing tale of our eponymous

narrator's wanderings and meditations on contemporary life. Deftly assembled, the film proved a valuable continuation of *London* and *Robinson In Space*. Another cinematic essay that impressed was Chris Petit's **Content**.

Patrick Keiller's **Robinson In Ruins**

Proving that experimental film in the UK is in rude health, **The Arbor** and *Self Made* both staked claims as being amongst the most vital viewing experiences of the year. The debut feature of Clio Barnard, *The Arbor* offers a fascinating fusion of narrative and documentary filmmaking as it unflinchingly relates the troubled personal and professional life of Bradford playwright Andrea Dunbar. A haunting, original and poetic work, it is beautifully complemented by artist and filmmaker Gillian Wearing's *Self Made*, a similarly striking and perfectly realised analysis of memory and fantasy that also offers a potent portrait of catharsis. Albeit more conventional, amongst the other debut features that stood out was Brian Welsh's **In Our Name**. Dealing with the subject of post-war trauma with integrity and insight, National Film and Television School

Clio Barnard's **The Arbor**

graduate Welsh is well served by newcomer Joanne Froggatt in the central role. The performance has already earned Froggatt a British Independent Film Award. The film is also notable for being the first in a new initiative by Curzon Artificial Eye, labelled Curzon On Demand. A service that aims to tackle digital piracy, it also hopes to allow people access to a greater diversity of films.

Facilitating a similar role, but located in the cinema context, Soda Pictures' New British Cinema Quarterly (NBCQ) fulfils a similar function and proves how far the UK has come in terms of utilising the potential of digital to its fullest. The successful restoration and re-issue of classic titles including *The Red Shoes*, *Peeping Tom* and *The Queen of Spades* further emphasises the impact of the digital revolution. The NBCQ takes films from fledgling filmmakers and tours them as one-off screening events with director Q&A's, and the scheme yielded particular dividends with Nick Whitfield's Edinburgh-prize-winning **Skeletons**. Michael Whyte's **No Greater Love**, an intimate documentary about the Most Holy Trinity monastery in London's Notting Hill also stood out. Other documentaries of note in 2010 were veteran Kim Longinotto's **Pink Saris**, a characteristically direct celebration of Sampat Pal, a campaigner for women's

Nick Whitfield's **Skeletons**

rights in Northern India, and Jez Lewis's **Shed Your Tears And Walk Away**. A passionate portrait of Lewis's Hebden Bridge hometown, an area of immense beauty and outward placidity that conceals a deep malaise and vortex of drink- and drug-related misery, it is compelling, personal and heartfelt fare. **Oil City Confidential**, Julien Temple's affectionate account of Canvey island rockers Dr Feelgood, also set the pulses racing.

Chris Morris' **Four Lions**

Other impressive debutants were satirist Chris Morris and special-effects maestro Gareth Edwards. Morris' **Four Lions** attracted, but never courted, controversy for its plot concerning a quartet of hapless British jihadists, who push their abstract dreams of glory to breaking point. As the wheels fly off and their competing motivations clash, Morris and co-writers Jesse Armstrong and Sam Bain reveal, with quote astonishing plausibility, that while terrorism is about ideology, it is also about idiots. This year's *Moon*, Edwards's **Monsters** is a formidable achievement. A space probe carrying samples of alien life crashes in Central America and soon half of Mexico is quarantined as an Infected Zone. Six years later, the Infected Zone remains a hostile territory filled with unearthly life. On assignment in Mexico, photojournalist Andrew Kaulder is charged with ensuring that the daughter of his mogul boss gets home safely. A low-budget miracle that merges *In Search of a Midnight Kiss* with *District 9*, *Monsters* is both a convincing creature film – with Edwards himself doing all the special effects – and an intimate and romantic tale of strangers connecting.

Mat Whitecross's **Sex and Drugs and Rock and Roll**

Two of the highest-profile bio-pics of the year were Mat Whitecross's **Sex and Drugs and Rock and Roll** and Bernard Rose's **Mr Nice**. Both take a 'print the legend' approach and feature strong central performances from Andy Serkis (as chief Blockhead Ian Dury) and Rhys Ifans (as happy-go-lucky drug smuggler-turned-writer-turned-raconteur Howard Marks) respectively. Flawed though watchable affairs, both met with mediocre commercial success. Although the award for misfire of the year goes to **44 Inch Chest**, a regrettable and tired Pinteresque gangster flick from the writers of *Sexy Beast*.

Peering tentatively into 2011, two early titles suggest themselves as standouts. First, there is Tom Hooper's multiple-awards contender **The King's Speech**. After the death of his father King George V and the scandalous abdication of Edward VII, Bertie (Oscar bait Colin Firth), who has suffered from a debilitating speech impediment all his life, is suddenly crowned King George VI. With his country on the brink of war and in desperate need of a leader, his wife, Elizabeth, arranges for her husband to see an eccentric speech therapist, Lionel Logue (Geoffrey Rush). After a rough start, the two delve into an unorthodox course of treatment and eventually form an unbreakable bond. Handsome, well performed and rich in period detail, *The King's Speech* is sure to be one of 2011's major successes.

Peter Mullan's third feature as director, **NEDS** (Non-Educated Delinquents), is a personal but non-autobiographical work that combines

realism with audacious flashes of fantasy. Glasgow, 1973. On the brink of adolescence, young John McGill is about to start secondary school. He's a bright and sensitive boy, but the cards are stacked against him. The McGill family's dirt poor, his hated father is a drunken bully and his teachers – punishing John for the sins of his older brother – are down on him from the start. And then there's the gangs with their culture of drugs, drink and violence… A distinctive work, Mullan wears his integrity and compassion firmly on his sleeve.

Peter Mullan's **NEDS**

The year's best films
The Arbor (Clio Barnard)
Self Made (Gillian Wearing)
Another Year (Mike Leigh)
Robinson In Ruins (Patrick Keiller)
Monsters (Gareth Edwards)

Gareth Edwards' homegrown sci-fi, **Monsters**

Quotes of the year

'Just imagine, if you went into the library and the bookshelves were stacked with 63% to 80% American fiction, 15% to 30% half-American, half-British fiction, and then all the other writers in the whole world just 3%. Imagine that in the art galleries, in terms of pictures; imagine it in the theatres. You can't, it is inconceivable – and yet this is what we do to the cinema, which we think is a most beautiful art.' KEN LOACH's *BFI London Film Festival Keynote speech.*

'I wanted to show that if you choose to kill someone by punching them, it's a long, slow, difficult process. Also, I want you to have the space to think about what's going on. Why is he doing this when he loves her? It's the pointlessness of it. That's the key thing: how pointless it is.' MICHAEL WINTERBOTTOM *defending the violence in* **The Killer Inside Me**, The Observer, *Sunday May 23rd.*

Directory

All Tel/Fax numbers begin (+44)
British Academy of Film & Television Arts (BAFTA), 195 Piccadilly, London, W1J 9LN. Tel: (20) 7734 0022. Fax: (20) 7734 1792. www.bafta.org.
British Actors Equity Association, Guild House, Upper St Martins Lane, London, WC2H 9EG. Tel: (20) 7379 6000. Fax: (20) 7379 7001. info@equity.org.uk. www.equity.org.uk.
British Board of Film Classification (BBFC), 3 Soho Square, London W1D 3HD. Tel: (20) 7440 1570. Fax: (20) 7287 0141. webmaster@bbfc.co.uk. www.bbfc.co.uk.
British Film Institute, 21 Stephen St, London, W1T 1LN. Tel: (20) 7255 1444. Fax: (20) 7436 7950. sales.films@bfi.org.uk. www.bfi.org.uk.
Creative Scotland, 12 Manor Place, Edinburgh EH3 7DD. Tel: (131) 226 6051. enquiries@creativescotland.com. www.creativescotland.com.
Directors Guild Trust & DGGB CIC Ltd, Studio 24, Royal Victoria Patriotic Building, John Archer Way, London, SW18 3SX. Tel: (20) 8871 1660. guild@dggb.org. www.dggb.org.

```
1996 Modem Festival
http://1996modfest.blogspot.com


to be continued
```

National Film & Television Archive, British Film Institute, 21 Stephen St, London W1P 1LN. Tel: (20) 7255 1444. Fax: (20) 7436 0439.
Scottish Screen Archive, 1 Bowmont Gardens, Glasgow G12 9LR. Tel: (141) 337 7400. Fax: (20) 337 7413. archive@scottishscreen.com. www.scottishscreen.com.

UK Film Council (until 31 March 2011), 10 Little Portland Street, London W1W 7JG. Tel: (20) 7861 7861. Fax: (20) 7861 784. info@ukfilmcouncil.org.uk. www.ukfilmcouncil.org.uk.
Office of the British Film Commissioner (from 1 April 2011), Film London, The Tea Building 56 Shoreditch High Street, London E1 6JJ. Tel: (20) 7613 7676. Fax: (20) 7613 7677. info@filmlondon.org.uk.
UK Film Council's Film Fund, Distribution and Exhibition Department (from 1 April 2011), MEDIA Desk UK, Certification Film Unit, UK Partnerships, British Film Institute, 21 Stephen Street, London W1T 1LN. Tel: (02) 7255 1444. Fax: (20) 7436 6950.

NB: During the transition of the UK Film Council's activities to the British Film Institute and Film London, information will be published on www.ukfilmcouncil.org.uk.

JASON WOOD is a Film Programmer and contributor to *Sight and Sound* and *the Guardian*. He has also published several books on cinema.

United States Tom Charity

A year that began with the blockbuster success of James Cameron's *Avatar* by and large failed to live up to commercial expectations.

According to projections, total box-office revenue should reach approximately US$10.5 billion. But that extra revenue can be attributed to a higher average ticket price (US$7.85, up five per cent, from US$7.50), largely derived from the premium theatres have adopted for 3D projection.

In terms of tickets sold, there was a drop of around four per cent, to 1.28 billion. Compare that with the figure from 2002: 1.6 billion. Ticket sales in 2010 are projected to be the

third lowest of the past decade. High-profile under-achievers included Jerry Bruckheimer productions **Prince of Persia: Sands of Time** (based on the videogame) and **The Sorcerer's Apprentice** (based on Goethe, or so they claimed), the remake **Clash of the Titans**, the Tom Cruise spy caper **Knight and Day**, Peter Jackson's misjudged adaptation of **The Lovely Bones**, M Night Shyamalan's feeble live-action anime **The Last Airbender** (which made a lot but cost more), Chris Columbus's Harry Potter wannabe **Percy Jackson & the Olympians: The Lightning Thief** and the reviled **Sex and the City 2**.

You might think this litany of expensive failure would encourage a rethink in the studios'

profligate ways, but judging by next year's release slate (including such FX-heavy fare as *Thor*, *Sucker Punch*, *Captain America*, and new installments of the *Pirates of the Caribbean*, *Harry Potter*, *Transformers*, *Spider-Man* and *X-Men* franchises) it's still business as usual in Hollywood.

To return to *Avatar*, it made approximately US$500 million of its total North America box-office take (US$750 million) in 2010, making it the year's biggest hit by a wide margin. But the hope and expectation (in some quarters) that it would usher in a new era in which 3D would become the standard mode for the Hollywood blockbuster, in the way that sound, colour, or widescreen technologies revolutionised the industry in the past, remains unproven.

Tim Burton's **Alice in Wonderland**

Admittedly, the very next 3D movie off the blocks, Tim Burton's **Alice in Wonderland** (released March 5) was another smash hit, one of the biggest of the year, exceeding industry expectations, to amass US$334 million in North America (and US$690 million internationally).

Although Burton's characteristic visual extravagance disguised it, *Alice* was one of numerous films to be given a 3D retro-fit in post-production, as opposed to being shot stereoscopically with two different cameras. The practice – reminiscent of colourisation – signalled a gold-rush mentality among studio executives, and, as the year went on, incurred a backlash among critics and fans, including 3D's most vociferous champion, James

Cameron, who complained that it devalued the artistic potential of the process.

It should be noted, though, that all 3D movies released this year were concurrently released in 2D, giving customers in most parts of North America a choice. Seventy percent of the opening weekend audience for *Alice* opted for 3D. But just a month later, only 52% saw the remake of **Clash of the Titans** that way, a pattern that was echoed in the release of **The Last Airbender** (54%), **Despicable Me** (45%) and **Cats and Dogs 2** (55%). Intriguingly, two films that were specifically shot in 3D bucked that trend: **Step Up 3D** (81%) and **Piranha 3D** (95%). Both trumpeted their stereoscopic credentials in the title, and critics generally praised the inventive effects the filmmakers devised to exploit the form.

Regardless of whether movies were shot in 3D or converted later, all 3D movies are projected at less than half the luminance (brightness level) audiences are used to seeing in conventional 2D projection, and when glasses are worn to decode the image, that cuts it down to less than a third. *The Dark Knight* director Christopher Nolan cited this problem as the reason he refused to convert **Inception** to 3D. 'On a technical level it's fascinating, but on an experiential level I find the dimness of the image extremely irritating.'

The flagship 3D company IMAX uses a double projector system that mitigates most (though by no means all) of the losses, but IMAX's

Christopher Nolan's **Inception**

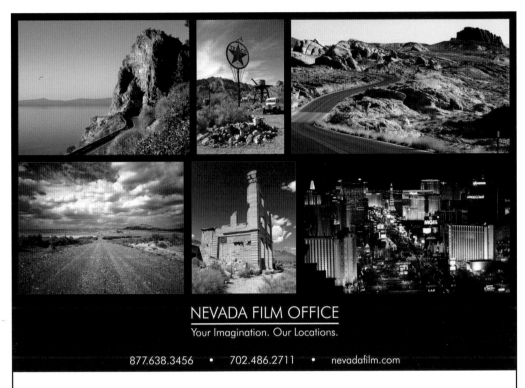

NEVADA FILM OFFICE
Your Imagination. Our Locations.

877.638.3456 • 702.486.2711 • nevadafilm.com

The Nevada Film Office (NFO) has been promoting Nevada as a film-friendly location for films, commercials, television, music videos, documentaries and other multi-media projects to the international production community for nearly 30 years. We connect productions and clients world-wide to Nevada's state-of-the-art production facilities, support services, resources and local professional crews and vendors.

The NFO provides a variety of services free of charge for hundreds of productions annually including permitting needs and requirements, research and customized location scouting tailored to specific project needs and intergovernmental coordination and liaison assistance. Customer service is at the core of our philosophy; we do our utmost to ensure that all your production needs are met with the type of hospitality that is synonymous with Nevada to make your experience as enjoyable as possible.

Our motto at the Nevada Film Office is "Your Imagination. Our Locations" as Nevada boasts a variety of unique and one-of-a-kind locations. If your next production is searching for neon and glitter, ghost towns, miles of scenic roads, majestic mountains, desert landscape or picturesque lakes, your camera will find it in Nevada. Our interactive website (nevadafilm.com) allows productions 24/7 access to hundreds of diverse location photos through our online database.

The annually published Nevada Production Directory is the number one resource tool used by industry professionals planning or conducting a shoot in Nevada. The Nevada Production Directory serves as a "yellow pages" for productions and includes a vast amount of information to obtain talent and professional crews, world-class accommodations, state-of-the-art production equipment, facilities and supplies, stages and studios and support services. In addition, the Nevada Film Office publishes "Nevada: A Visual Guide to Locations" which features the Reno/Tahoe areas, Las Vegas and Southern Nevada locales, Roads of Nevada and Nevada's Countryside to showcase the variety of locations throughout Nevada.

For a free copy of the Nevada Production Directory or visual guides, please email us at
lvnfo@nevadafilm.com

share of the market has shrunk as multiplexes raced to convert to 3D. By the end of 2010, there were nearly 2500 3D screens available to distributors across North America.

When Warner Bros abandoned plans to convert **Harry Potter and the Deathly Hallows Part One** (the penultimate entry in the series) some leapt to the conclusion that the bell tolled for 3D. But that would be premature. The costs associated with 3D versions of computer-animated features are minimal, and of the year's 15 biggest moneyspinners, half were released in stereoscopic versions.

Animation has become the most reliably lucrative of genres, and the hits piled up again this year (in order of profitability): **Toy Story 3** (Pixar/Buena Vista), **Despicable Me** (Universal), **Shrek Forever After** (Dreamworks/Paramount), **How to Train Your Dragon** (Dreamworks/Paramount), **Megamind** (Dreamworks/Paramount), and **Tangled** (Buena Vista). All made more than USD$100 million domestically – four times over in the case of *Toy Story 3*.

Lee Unkrich's **Toy Story 3**

Pixar's belated sequel – 11 years after the second installment – was also one of the most critically admired films of the year. In common with the sense of at least one of its main characters having grown up (Andy, the rarely seen child beloved by Woody and Buzz), this was the darkest and most frightening of the series.

Director Lee Unkrich (who co-directed the second *Toy Story*) fashions a brilliantly inventive and surprisingly suspenseful escape movie from the fearsome prospect of consignment to a day nursery's toddler room, funnelling the series' abiding separation anxiety into a succession of ingenious escapades, climaxing in an apocalyptic vision of the gaping inferno. (In 3D, of course.)

Iron Man 2

Of the other blockbuster hits, **Iron Man 2** was favourably reviewed by critics who appreciated its broad satire of the military-political-industrial complex and bravura turns from Robert Downey Jr, Mickey Rourke and Sam Rockwell. Rourke also featured among the has-been he-men who propelled Sylvester Stallone's lazy rehash of 1980s action flicks, **The Expendables**, to the top of the box office charts – one of a handful of mediocre mercenary tongue-in-cheek thrillers that also included **The A-Team**, **The Losers** and **Red**. Hitmen became romantic heroes in **The American** (a pretentious stab

Sylvester Stallone's **The Expendables**

at existential ennui from George Clooney and Anton Corbijn), *Knight and Day*, *Red*, and the dreadful *Killers*, while the Dreamworks trio *Shrek Forever After*, *Despicable Me* and *Megamind* all took pleasure in making heroes out of villains.

Better by far was **Salt**, with Angelina Jolie as a double agent on the run from both her US and Soviet paymasters. An absurdist action thriller, it benefited from Philip Noyce's down and dirty direction of the action.

Angelina Jolie in Philip Noyce's **Salt**

But this was kids' stuff in comparison with the summer's most cerebral sleeper, Christopher Nolan's **Inception**. The smartest CGI head trip since *The Matrix* (not saying much, admittedly), *Inception* stars Leonardo DiCaprio as Cobb, an 'excavator' who digs around in people's subconscious while they're asleep. His motivation isn't therapy but industrial espionage, and the film turns out to be a weird kind of mytho-poetic heist movie. To do the job right and penetrate multiple levels of deep sleep, Cobb requires a whole team of confederates (an architect, a burglar, a chemist…), whose jobs suggest both a criminal gang and the various departments involved in film production. Not for nothing are extras within the dream state known as 'projections' – they become hostile if they sense someone messing with their reality.

An audacious formalist who constructs his movies like a box of tricks, Nolan bends time and physics to his own ends with dazzling

ingenuity. Still, it's disappointing that each dream level plays out as a more or less straight action thriller (if they're remotely like this, Nolan's dreams must be really boring), and for all its copious layering the movie remains resolutely fixed on the surface.

Compare and contrast Leonardo DiCaprio's other dream project, Martin Scorsese's **Shutter Island**. Based on a far-fetched mystery novel by Dennis Lehane, the film worked as a full-on gothic nightmare, a pulpy reflection on the madness and violence unleashed in the mid-twentieth century, akin to Sam Fuller's delirious *Shock Corridor*. Unlike anything Scorsese has done before, the movie is seared by several horrific expressionist dream sequences that turn out to be more real than the narrative in which they are couched. The spectres of the Holocaust and the Bomb are too painful for DiCaprio's character to live with, but Scorsese implicates himself – and us, too – in the character's refuge in escapism (madness) and the ultimate refusal of reality, a lobotomy.

Martin Scorsese's **Shutter Island**

Released in February, *Shutter Island* was far too early to rank as a serious Academy Award contender in 2011, though, unusually, the 2010 Oscar went to a film released as far back as June 2009: Kathryn Bigelow's *The Hurt Locker*. Not a big box-office hit, this intense Iraq war drama found widespread support among critics and industry bodies, and in an enlarged field of ten Best Picture nominees it proved a less contentious choice than *Avatar*.

Bigelow herself became the first woman to win the Oscar for Best Direction (beating her ex-husband, James Cameron), and *The Hurt Locker* also won for best screenplay and three more categories.

Sandra Bullock was named best actress for her portrayal of a big-hearted southern matriarch in *The Blind Side* and Jeff Bridges was best actor for his alcoholic country singer Bad Blake in *Crazy Heart*.

Joel and Ethan Coen's **True Grit**

Chances are Bridges will secure a second straight nomination in 2011 for stepping into John Wayne's boots to play the one-eyed US marshal Rooster Cogburn in the Coen Brothers' remake **True Grit**. A classical western except for the prodigiously eloquent and determined teenage girl at its centre, *True Grit* finds the Coens keeping a tight rein on their sometimes snide comic inclinations and staying as close to the Charles Portis novel as they did with Cormac McCarthy's *No Country For Old Men*. It is folkloric in its hard-nosed evocation of a place and time where the prospect of sudden death is a constant factor, but where a young girl of redoubtable principle and pluck can still stir acts of remarkable self-sacrifice in even the hardest hearts.

There is a similar dynamic in **Winter's Bone**, one of the most impressive independent films of the year, a contemporary suspense drama played out in the dirt-poor Ozarks. Based on a novel by Daniel Woodrell, adapted by director Debra Granik and her partner Anne Rosellini,

Debra Granik and Anne Rosellini's **Winter's Bone**

Winter's Bone is the story of 17-year-old Ree Dolly (a breakthrough performance by Jennifer Lawrence) traversing this hardscrabble country mostly by foot, searching for her father to persuade him to meet his court date and save the farm from the bail bondsmen. It's a bleak, desolate picture of a community on the fringe of the law. Like Mattie in *True Grit*, Ree has no power here except the moral authority she insists is hers.

The other independent sleeper hit was **The Kids Are All Right**, Lisa Cholodenko's surprisingly conservative comedy about a modern lesbian family that nearly unravels when the two teenage children decide to find (and then befriend) their sperm-donor dad (Mark Ruffalo). Buoyed by expert acting, particularly from the brittle, possessive Annette Bening, who is complemented by the earthy, addle-headed Julianne Moore, the movie has warmth and wit, but loses its way in the third act as Cholodenko slams the door on Ruffalo's easygoing interloper.

Lisa Cholodenko's **The Kids Are All Right**

Derek Cianfrance supplied a more complex take on a conventional family in the heartrending independent drama **Blue Valentine**, which crosscuts between the courtship and the break-up of a young couple, impressively played by Ryan Gosling and the brilliant Michelle Williams.

Derek Cianfrance's **Blue Valentine**

Also offering insights into times of tribulation and strife was John Cameron Mitchell's surprisingly straightforward adaptation of David Lindsay-Abaire's play **Rabbit Hole**, with Nicole Kidman very moving as a bereaved mom who bonds with the teen driver who struck her toddler.

Darren Aronofsky's **Black Swan**

Still with the women, Natalie Portman produced probably the most startling, edgy performance of her career to date as Nina, a virginal, dedicated ballet dancer in Darren Aronofsky's **Black Swan**. A distaff companion piece of sorts to the director's *The Wrestler*, *Black Swan* also owes a great deal to Roman

Polanski's *Repulsion* and Michael Haneke's *The Piano Teacher*. Embracing her dark side to carry off the dual good and bad roles in *Swan Lake*, Nina dabbles in sex and drugs (including a lesbian tryst with a solicitous rival), and gradually loses her grip on reality. The movie is fantastically lurid, an exercise in pop psychology gone mad, but for high-class schlock it's hard to beat it.

If there was a male equivalent to Nina's breakdown on screen this year, it would have to be Joaquin Phoenix, playing himself in his brother-in-law Casey Affleck's vérité film, **I'm Still Here**. Ever since Phoenix's notoriously strange performance on the Letterman show in February 2009 – when he announced his retirement from acting in order to pursue a career in rap – there had been intense speculation about the star's mental health mixed with rumours that this was all a mock-doc stunt.

Casey Affleck's **I'm Still Here**

The latter turned out to be the case, though the filmmakers kept everyone guessing until a week after the film's release in September 2010, and after quite a few famous critics (among them Roger Ebert and *Entertainment Weekly's* Owen Gleiberman) had been taken in. The film included this unedifying media spectacle in its portrait of Phoenix as a cocaine-snorting egomaniac cocooned from reality by a coterie of yes men and the privileges of celebrity. It was impressive and uncompromising in its way but mostly lacked the satiric edge that Sacha Baron Cohen brought to Bruno or Steve Coogan and Rob Brydon showed playing themselves in Michael Winterbottom's faux documentary, *The Trip*.

In any case, Phoenix's phoney breakdown was trumped by leaked recordings of Mel Gibson screaming and ranting vicious abuse at his then girlfriend, Oksana Grigorieva, on several gossip websites. The sexist and racist invective persuaded his agency to sever ties with Gibson and stalled the release of Jodie Foster's film, **The Beaver**. It was meant to have been the second film in a comeback, some four years after the revelation of his anti-Semitic DUI diatribe. The first film, **Edge of Darkness**, proved to be a middling conspiracy thriller that made little impression at the box office. Gibson's reputation was so battered that cast and crew revolted when Todd Phillips toyed with the idea of handing him a cameo role in **The Hangover 2**.

Judd Apatow's **Get Him to the Greek**

It was not a stellar year for comedy, but Russell Brand and Jonah Hill made an amusing odd-couple team as a debauched rock star and his fan-boy record company minder in **Get Him to the Greek** – a spin-off from *Forgetting Sarah Marshall* and the year's only effort from the House of Apatow.

Hill was also impressive as John C Reilly's creepy filial rival for Marisa Tomei's affections in **Cyrus**, an intentionally discomforting not-so romantic comedy by Mark and Jay Duplass, indie darlings here infiltrating the mainstream.

Another indie darling, actress Greta Gerwig, also moved up an income bracket when she starred opposite Ben Stiller in **Greenberg**, Noah Baumbach's typically acute portrait of a

Matthew Vaughn's **Kick-Ass**

neurotic narcissistic under-achiever, scarcely aware that he's his own worst enemy.

In all these films, and in the subversive comic book mentality of Edgar Wright's zany **Scott Pilgrim vs the World**, and Matthew Vaughn's hyper-violent teen (and pre-teen) vigilante superhero caper, **Kick-Ass**, you sense a younger, hipper, edgier sensibility creeping into studio comedies – and not before time, judging by such formulaic fare as **The Back Up Plan**, **The Bounty Hunter** and **Date Night**. Yet, by-and-large, audiences stuck with what they knew. America may not have been quite ready for the full force of Jim Carrey's rabidly gay conman in the wacky-but-true black comedy, **I Love You Philip Morris** (the film was released in most of the world in February, but came out in December in the US under the transparent fig leaf of an improbable Oscar-campaign). A haphazard but wildly passionate effort from *Bad Santa* scribes Glenn Ficarra and John Requa, the movie felt like it pushed the representation of homosexuality several steps beyond earnest tearjerkers like *Milk* and *Brokeback Mountain*.

Amid the usual late flurry of Academy hopefuls, the clear favourites were David Fincher's **The Social Network**, David O Russell's blue-collar boxing biopic **The Fighter** (with Mark Wahlberg and Christian Bale), *Black Swan* and Danny Boyle's **127 Hours** – plus the UK production, **The King's Speech**.

There was admirable diversity about these contenders. Boyle's follow up to the Oscar-triumph of *Slumdog Millionaire* was his first American film since *The Beach* and his first shot in the US since *A Life Less Ordinary*, but you couldn't accuse him of playing safe. The true story of climber Aron Ralston, who found himself between a rock and a hard place, trapped in a Utah crevice with no prospect of rescue, *127 Hours* is a paradox: a dynamic, kinetic movie about stasis and paralysis; a sensational, exhilarating film about self-mutilation and death – which is not to deny that it's also properly harrowing. The story's built-in restrictions inspire Boyle to his giddiest heights, this is probably his best since *Trainspotting*, and James Franco's delivers one of the performances of the year as a young man forced to confront his imminent extinction.

David Fincher's **The Social Network**

The year's best films
True Grit (Ethan and Joel Coen)
Shutter Island (Martin Scorsese)
127 Hours (Danny Boyle)
The Social Network (David Fincher)
Toy Story 3 (Lee Unkrich)

Directory
All Tel/Fax numbers begin (+1)
Academy of Motion Picture Arts & Sciences, Pickford Center, 1313 North Vine St, Los Angeles, CA 90028. Tel: (310) 247 3000. Fax: 657 5431. mpogo@oscars.org. www.oscars.org.
American Film Institute/National Center for Film & Video Preservation, 2021 North Western Ave, Los Angeles, CA 90027. Tel: (1 323) 856 7600. Fax: 467 4578. info@afi.com. www.afi.com.
Directors Guild of America, 7920 Sunset Blvd, Los Angeles, CA 90046. Tel: (1 310) 289 2000. Fax: 289 2029. www.dga.org.
Independent Feature Project, 104 W 29th St, 12th Floor, New York, NY 10001. Tel: (1 212) 465 8200. Fax: 465 8525. ifpny@ifp.org. www.ifp.org.
International Documentary Association, 1201 W 5th St, Suite M320, Los Angeles, CA 90017-1461. Tel: (1 213) 534 3600. Fax: 534 3610. info@documentary.org. www.documentary.org.
Motion Picture Association of America, 15503 Ventura Blvd, Encino, CA 91436. Tel: (1 818) 995 6600. Fax: 382 1784. www.mpaa.org.

Danny Boyle's **127 Hours**

As for *The Social Network*, this enthralling account of the birth of Facebook was a masterly piece of storytelling (the exemplary script was by Aaron Sorkin, of *The West Wing* fame). Jesse Eisenberg starred as Mark Zuckerberg, in this telling a petulant misfit with a genius for programming who invents the ultimate networking site to redress the balance in a world tilted towards the pretty and the privileged. Zuckerberg comes out on top, a self-made billionaire by his mid-20s, but his success leaves him every bit as isolated as before... Friendless, in fact.

TOM CHARITY is film critic for CNN.com and Lovefilm, and a regular contributor to *Sight & Sound* and *CinemaScope*. He also pro-grammes the Vancity Theatre in Vancouver.

Uruguay Jorge Jellinek

The last two years have witnessed the consolidation of Uruguayan cinema. Steady production has seen around ten features and documentaries released each year, with the support of local film funds reducing the impact of the international financial crisis. Many of the films have picked up prizes at major international festivals, helping to promote a new generation of young filmmakers.

The Institute of Cinema and Audiovisual (ICAU) has been distributing more than US$1 million each year in promoting film production and distribution. Along with other local funds, it has stimulated the appearance of new directors and producers, emerging from the growing number of graduates from film schools.

Alvaro Brechner's **Bad Day to Go Fishing**

Highlights of the year included the surprising success of **Giant** (*Gigante*) by newcomer Adrián Biniez, an offbeat comedy about a big, shy security guard, which was awarded the Silver Bear for First Film at the Berlin Film Festival, as well as **Bad Day to Go Fishing** (*Mal día para pescar*), a colourful adaptation of Juan Carlos Onetti's short tale by Alvaro Brechner, which won prizes at Mar del

Gonzalo Arijón's **Stranded**

Plata, Varsovia, Lima and Gijón. And Gonzalo Arijón's **Stranded** (*La sociedad de la nieve*), a powerful documentary about 16 Uruguayans rescued after a plane crash in the Andes, won the Joris Ivens prize at the International Documentary Festival Amsterdam.

More films were released in 2010, mostly from new directors, although there was a steady decrease in audience attendance. Pablo Stoll's comedy, **Hiroshima**, was his first production following the death of his *Whisky* co-director, Juan Pablo Rebella. With its edgy humour and off-beat style (no dialogue but plenty of local rock music), the story of a near-autistic young musician (Juan Andrés Stoll, the director's brother) who wanders along

Pablo Stoll's **Hiroshima**

desolate beaches, it attracted divided opinions and alienated some of its limited audience. Stoll has just finished shooting a new feature, **Three** (*Tres*), about a ménage à trois, based on a script he wrote with Rebella.

With 30,000 tickets sold as the year drew to a close, experimental artist Martin Sastre's adaptation of Dani Umpi's novel, **Miss Tacuarembó**, the story of a young girl's desire to triumph as a singer while confronting prejudice in a small town, was a breakout success. With its mixture of pop art, Almodovar influences, kitsch homages to popular icons of the eighties (from *Fame* to the Venezuelan soap opera *Cristal*) and cheerful songs by popular actress Natalia Oreiro, the fitfully engaging film divided opinions and offended conservative Catholics with its irreverent references to Christian iconography.

Enrique Buchichio's **Leo's Room**

Enrique Buchichio's feature debut, **Leo's Room** (*El cuarto de Leo*) is a sober, low-key comedy about a young man struggling with his sexuality and self-esteem. Employing a controlled, but emotionally charged style, an impressive soundtrack and fine performances from a cast that included Argentinean Martín Rodríguez, it performed well to a small audience and was appreciated by critics.

Popular Uruguayan actor Daniel Hendler turned director with **Norberto's Deadline** (*Norberto apenas tarde*), a light-hearted comedy about a frustrated man who, after being laid off from his job, decides to cut the routine in his life, finding work as real estate broker, while attending an acting workshop. Middle-age crises and the peculiar world of independent theatre are combined with wry humour and enchanting performances that include Fernando Amaral and César Troncoso.

Federico Veiroj's **A Useful Life**

More experimental and risky is **A Useful Life** (*La vida útil*), the second feature by Federico Veiroj. It is an original and melancholy comedy about a forty-something programmer of a film archive who has to change his life after the institution shuts down. Classically filmed in black and white, and featuring non-professional actors, it's an endearing homage to cinema, It picked up the Best Film at the Havana Film Festival, Best Director at Valdivia and special mentions at San Sebastian and Varsovia. It was chosen to represent Uruguay at the Academy Awards and Goyas.

Of the documentaries produced over the last year, Sebastián Bednarik's **Mundialito** reveals the backdrop to the football tournament, organised by FIFA in 1980 which took place in Uruguay to celebrate the 50th anniversary of the World Cup. Well constructed, although occasionally a little derivative, it offers a mine of archive material in presenting the political, social and cultural upheavals of the time.

Diana Castro's **Seven Moments** (*Siete instantes*) also examines the military dictatorship during this period. Seven Uruguayan women that were imprisoned as political prisoners during the 1970s and

1980s are interviewed, offering an insight into decisions that changed their lives.

Federico González Rejón's entertaining **The Parsleys** (*Perejiles*) employs hidden cameras to follow a group of people who pose as press in order to gain access to exclusive events. It caused a degree of controversy with some participants threatening legal action if the film was screened, but all disputes were eventually settled.

Gustavo Hernández's exercise in terror, **The Silent House** (*La casa muda*), presented an 80-minute story of a massacre in just one single shot. It was presented in the Directors Fortnight at Cannes. It will be released locally in 2011. Also on the horizon is the promising feminist comedy, **Lean and Mean Cows** (*Flacas vacas*), by Santiago Svirsky. It presents the contradictions between three middle-aged friends who go on vacation together. And Pablo Fernández, Eduardo Piñero and Alejandro Pi attempt to break new ground with the violent drama **Reus**, which reflects on the rise of social tensions in a popular neighbourhood, where old codes are broken between local gangs and store owners, most of them Jewish, who have lived there for decades.

Currently in post-production is Daniela Speranza's long-awaited comedy **Rambleras**, topping off a superb year in Uruguayan film.

JORGE JELLINEK has been a film critic and journalist for over 20 years, contributing to newspapers, magazines and radio. He participated on the jury at many festivals, and was vice-president of the Uruguayan Critics' Association and Artistic Director of the Punta del Este Film Festival. He debuted as an actor in *A Useful Life*.

Adrián Biniez's **Giant**

The year's best films
Giant (Adrián Biniez)
Bad Day to Go Fishing (Álvaro Brechner)
Leo's Room (Enrique Buchichio)
Hiroshima (Pablo Stoll)
Mundialito (Sebastián Bednarik)

Quote of the year
'Frivolity is a part of contemporary culture and of course as contemporary artists we are working on their time.' MARTIN SASTRE *answering critics to his film* **Miss Tacuarembó**.

Directory
All Tel/Fax numbers begin (+598)
Asociación de Productores y Realizadores de Cine y Video del Uruguay (ASOPROD), Maldonado 1792, Montevideo. Tel: 418 7998. info@asoprod.org.uy. www.asoprod.org.uy.
Cinemateca Uruguaya, Lorenzo Carnelli 1311, 11200 Montevideo. Tel: 418 2460. Fax: 419 4572. cinemuy@chasque.net. www.cinemateca.org.uy.
Fondo Para el Fomento y Desarrollo de la Producción Audiovisual Nacional (FONA), Palacio Municipal, Piso 1°, Montevideo. Tel: 902 3775. fona@prensa.imm.gub.uy. www.montevideo.gub.uy/cultura/c_fona.htm.
Instituto Nacional del Audiovisual (INA), Reconquista 535, 8° Piso, 11100 Montevideo. Tel/Fax: 915 7489/916 2632. ina@mec.gub.uy. www.mec.gub.uy/ina.

Vietnam Sylvie Blum-Reid

The last year has seen significant productions domestically and films financed by Vietnamese in the Diaspora. New talents have emerged, while stars and directors of Vietnamese descent are returning to the country to make films. Audience figures are on the increase and the choice of local films cover an eclectic mix of art-house, historical drama, literary adaptation, big-budget action (kung-fu), and comedy. A significant number of these films also play on the international film festival circuit.

Bui Thac Chuyen's **Adrift**

Phuong Hoang's lavish period drama **Heroes of the Tay-Son Dynasty** (*Tay Son Hao Kiet*), about an eighteenth century peasant rebellion against Chinese troops, proves that Vietnam can produce big production films. At the same time, the art-house sector is well catered for. Bui Thac Chuyen's second feature, **Adrift** (*Choi Voi*), is an erotic drama about lesbianism and loneliness in contemporary Vietnam, presented from a female perspective. It stars Linh-Dan Pham, was scripted by Phan Dang Di and went on to win the FIPRESCI prize at the Venice Film Festival. The film is a co-production between Feature Film Studio no. 1 and Acrobates Films (France), who also financed **Bi, Don't Be Afraid!** (*Bi, Dung So,*

Bi!), Dang Di Phan's intimate portrait of a family living in Hanoi, focusing on a six-year-old boy.

Dustin N'Guyen returned to Vietnam to star in Luu Huynh's **The Legend Is Alive**, a kung-fu action film about a mentally disabled martial artist who goes on a road trip after his mother dies. The actor is also set to direct **Monk on Fire** (*Lua Phat*), which Hanoi's lifestyle magazine, *AsiaLIFE*, described as 'an Asian Western with bikes instead of horses, swords instead of guns and super-powered monks.'

Veteran filmmaker Nhat Minh Dang released **Don't Burn**, an adaptation of *Dang Thuy Tram's Diary*. The film is an anti-war drama based on the actual story of a young female doctor during the war. It was selected as Vietnam's entry for the Best Foreign Language Film category at the 2010 Academy Awards and received six awards at the eigth Golden Kite Ceremony in March.

14 days (*14 Ngay Phep*), the story of a Vietnamese expatriate who spends his vacation back in his home country, was directed and scripted by Viet-kieu director Nguyen Trong Khoa. 'We want to reveal another Vietnam, a Vietnam that is not only

Dang Di Phan's **Bi, Don't Be Afraid!**

heroic in wartime but also modern and receptive to changes in peacetime,' said Jimmy Nghiem Pham, managing director of the production company Chanh Phuong.

Clash (*Bay Rong*) by Le Thanh Son is a high-powered action film featuring a tattooed woman, Phoenix, who teams up with four men on a series of missions. It was the highest-grossing film in 2010 and was successful on general release in other countries.

The inaugural film of the Vietnam Film Festival, Nguyen Phan Quang Binh's **The Endless Field** (*Canh dong bat tan*), is a melodrama involving a rice-farmer in the Mekong Delta who falls in love with a prostitute. A very artful work, it is an adaptation of a novel by Nguyen Quoc Tu.

Dustin N'Guyen in Charlie N'Guyen's **Fool for Love**

Fool For Love (*De Mai Thinh*), directed by Charlie N'Guyen, whose direct translation is 'let's decide tomorrow', is a gay romantic comedy, an unusual contrast considering its conservative setting, which unfolds at a seaside resort and revolves around the relationship between a singer and a bathroom cleaner. It has become an unexpected local hit. Actor Dustin N'Guyen co-wrote and co-produced the film.

Director Tran Anh Hung crosses geographic, cultural and linguistic borders with an adaptation of Japanese author Haruki Murakami's novel **Norwegian Wood** (*Norumei No Mori*). Set and produced in Japan, it weaves a tragic story involving sexuality, loss and mourning among university students in the late 1960s. 2009 also witnessed the release of

Tran Anh Hung's **Norwegian Wood**

Tran's long-awaited French co-production, the neo-noir **I Come With the Rain**, starring Josh Hartnett.

A number of 'green' Vietnamese documentaries have been commissioned for 2011, aimed at encouraging aspiring filmmakers to participate in environmental issues. These will air at Hanoi's European Documentary Film Festival in June.

As 2010 came to a close, Trieu Tuan's **Journey from Shanghai** (*Vuot Qua Ben Thuong Hai*), the year's most anticipated film, opened. It retraces the journeys of Nguyen Ai Quoc, better known as Ho Chi Minh.

The year's best films
Norwegian Woods (Tran Anh Hung)
Adrift (Bui Thac Chuyen)
Bi, Don't Be Afraid (Phan Dang Di)
Don't Burn (Nhat Minh Dang)
Fool for Love (Charlie N'Guyen)

Quotes of the year
'We want to reveal another Vietnam, a Vietnam that is not only heroic in wartime but also modern and receptive to changes in peacetime.' JIMMY NGHIEM PHAM

'Vietnam is a cinematic dreamland.' JOHNNY NGUYEN

SYLVIE BLUM-REID is associate professor of French & Film at the University of Florida (Gainesville). She has published on Franco-Asian cinema.

Additional Countries

BURKINA FASO

The shooting of Missa Hébié's **While Waiting for the Vote** (*En attendant le vote*) has captured most of the attention in Burkina Faso's film world this year. Mobilising significant resources and well-known actors from the region, the production was completed in August, with a release expected some time in 2011.

Elsewhere, Aboubacar Sidnaba Zida's fifth feature, **Somzita**, attacked ungratefulness. A young man wants to marry the daughter of a rich benefactor, who took him into his home and made hin his heir. However, following the death of the elderly patriarch, the young man divorces his wife in order to enjoy the riches of his inheritance on his own.

Sarah Bouyain's **The Place in Between**

Sarah Bouyain, a Burkinabe now living in France, directed **The Place in Between** (*Notre étrangère*). Inspired by a true story, the film deals with a young woman of mixed race who, upon the death of her father, travels to Burkina Faso in search of her mother.

Sadly, Burkina Faso's most internationally renowned actor, Sotigui Kouyate, died on April 17, aged 74. His last performance, in Rachid Bouchareb's *London River*, saw him awarded the Silver Bear for Best Actor at the 2009 Berlin Film Festival.

The human rights film festival, Ciné Droit Libre, continued this year and there was also the first edition of a new festival dedicated to the African women in filmmaking.

HONORÉ ESSOH is a journalist and filmmaker who works for media outlets in West Africa. He is associate in a film production company in Ivory Coast and his first feature film, entitled *Robin Hood of the Web,* is cuurently in development.

CAMBODIA

One of the most affecting feature films ever produced about the Khmer Rouge era was made in 2009 in Cambodia and released in late 2010. Directed by former actor Chhay Bora, **Lost Loves** (*Khleat Sen Chhangay*) follows the daily life of a woman during those years, opening with her family herded into a forced-labor camp at the regime start, in 1975, and ending with her remembering, in old age, those who survived – and those who did not.

Kauv Sotheary in Chhay Bora's **Lost Loves**

The central role of Amara, a woman filled with fear and grief that she does not dare express, is brilliantly performed by Kauv Sotheary, confirming her position as one of Cambodia's leading actresses. Likewise, the film's beautiful cinematography and its bleakly realistic depiction of the Khmer Rouge's cruelties add a sense of true horror to the ruthlessness of a regime that claimed nearly two million lives in less than four years.

The film premiered during the Cambodia International Film Festival in October. Hosted by the Cambodian Ministry of Culture, the festival presented 120 features, animated films and documentaries from 30 countries. The event is intended to encourage more momentum in the Cambodian film industry – whose production schedule has been meager over the last year – and to draw Cambodians back into cinemas.

MICHELLE VACHON is a journalist based in Cambodia who mainly covers the arts, culture, and archaeology.

CAMEROON

Cameroon's cinema is dominated by documentaries, with good quality films continuing to be the privilege of foreign-based filmmakers.

Such is the case with **Manu Dibango**, which traces the extraordinary career of the popular musician. Directed by Frenchman Pascal

Jean-Marie Teno's **Sacred Places**

Vasselin, and written by Paris-based Calixthe Beyala, the cheerfulness and the charisma of Diabango's classic 1972 hit, 'Soul Makossa', is captured in this captivating portrait.

Based in the United-States, Jean-Marie Teno travelled to Burkina Faso's capital for his documentary, **Sacred Places** (*Lieux Saints*). The film looks at the problems facing film in Africa, focussing on one small cinema club, detailing the lack of venues available for people to see films.

Coming out of a new generation of filmmakers, Patrick Epape is based in Cameroon. For his latest film he followed four dancers in the Cameroonian capital for a year and half. **Life** details their daily lives, both on and off stage, capturing the spirit of their performances and the stark contrast with reality.

The film event of the year is the festival Ecrans Noirs, which ran from 29 May to 5 June. Around 20 Cameroonian documentaries and shorts screened. – *Honoré Essoh*

CHAD

A Screaming Man (*Un homme qui crie*), the fourth feature from acclaimed director Mahamat Saleh Haroun, revolves around the current civil war in Chad. Not only the highlight of the Chadian film year, it is one of the most outstanding African films of 2010. After 13 years of absence, the continent not only had a film in competition for the Golden Palm at the Cannes Film festival, but Haroun managed to win the Jury Prize.

A Screaming Man unfolds during the civil war. A former Chadian swimming champion who, to preserve his work as lifeguard in a big hotel in the capital city, resolves to sacrifice his son, sending him to war. Adam's and Abdel's relationship is the main focus of the film and, according to the director, it relates to modern day Chad: 'Between the father and the son is the transportation of memory, genes, and culture.'

Mahamat Saleh Haroun's **A Screaming Man**

The film's strength lies in the sparseness of the script, with Haroun once again employing a minimalist approach to draw the audience in to these characters' worlds, heightening the emotional engagement with them and the sacrifices that are made.

The authorities also named Haroun head of a project to establish an audiovisual training centre in the country. The creation of a national fund to support film production in Chad was also announced.

The other major figure in Chadian film, Issa Serge Coelo, continues to live in France. He is involved in the rebirth of a local cinema, organising training projects for young people and the reopening of the old venue in the capital city, with the support of the government.

AGNES THOMASI has over 15 years of experience as a media practitioner. She trained at Radio Deutsche Welle Training Centre in Koln, Germany, the International Institute of Journalism in Berlin, AACC Communication Training Centre in Nairobi and Leeds Metropolitan University in the United Kingdom.

COSTA RICA

The last year has seen the release of four films made in 2009, which were screened at international festivals before being distributed domestically.

Hilda Hidalgo's adaptation of Gabriel Garcia Marquez' novel **Love and Other Demons** (*Del amor y otros demonios*) was co-produced with Colombia. An impeccable production, the film plays with symbolism to undermine cultural stereotypes, particularly those that appear in the author's own books.

Paz Fabrega **Cold Water of the Sea** (*Agua fria de mar*), has yet to be released in Costa Rica, but was awarded the Tiger of the Festival at the Rotterdam International Film Festival, amongst many other international awards. Hernan Jimenez's debut, **A ojos cerrados**, was received well by both audiences and critics. An exploration of familial relationships, it tells the story of an entrepreneurial young businesswoman faced with the choice of accompanying her grandfather on a trip to take her recently deceased grandmother's ashes to the Caribbean, or accepting a chance of a lifetime job. The grandfather, played by a non-professional actor, is the heart of the movie. Jimenez is currently filming his follow-up, **El regreso**.

Hernan Jimenez's **A ojos cerrados**

Horror is not a particularly common genre in Costa Rica. But the last year saw two films released: Ramiro and Adrian Garcia's **The Accursed** and Miguel Gomez's **El sanatorio**. The former is based in two short stories by Joseph Conrad W. W. Jacobs. The result, though occasionally suspenseful, barely passes for horror and the special effects are rudimentary. Gomez's film is more a parody of horror films, about a group of friends making a documentary about a haunted sanitorium.

Isabel Martinez and Vicente Ferraz's **El ultimo comandante** stars Damian Alcazar as Paco Jarquin, a Sandinista commander who has chosen to forget his military past and is now the owner of a local dance school. The film received outstanding reviews, particularly for Alcazar's performance.

Next year will also see the release of Miguel Gomez's **El fin**, Oscar Castillo's **El compromiso** and work will begin on Laura Astorga's **Princesas rojas**.

There is a proposal to establish a law to promote filmmaking currently passing through Congress, as well as a project to create a film library.

MARIA LOURDES CORTÉS teaches film at the Universidad de Costa Rica and directs the Film and Television School of the Veritas University and the Cinergia audiovisual foundation. The most recent of her numerous books on Costa Rican and Central American cinema is *La pantalla rota. Cien años de cine en Centroamérica* (2005).

GABON

One of the major events this year was the shooting of Henri Joseph Koumba Bididi's **The Lion of Poubara** (*Le lion de Poubara*). Best known for 2002's *The Elephant's Balls*, Bididi's latest film is the story of a young man who wants to bring to his home a lion meant for a European zoo. It featured the famous singer and former First Lady, Patience Dabany, as well as veteran Philippe Mory and Eriq Ebouaney.

The new generation of filmmakers in Gabon continue to make progress. Such is the case for Manouchka Kelly Labouba with her humorous sophomore short, **The Liar and the Thief** (*Le menteur et le voleur*). She also helped initiate the Short Film Night of Gabon, two editions of which took place over the last year, in January and April.

Another impressive film was Antoine Abessolo Minko's 52-minute documentary, **Itchinda, or Circumcision Among the Mahongwé** (*Itchinda ou la circoncision chez les Mahongwe*). This film details the different stages of entrance into the world of adults and was one of the productions screened at the fourth edition of the Documentary Stopovers of Libreville. – *Agnes Thomasi*

GHANA

The year may have started slowly, but when it finally did pick up, no one was in doubt over the fact that the Ghanaian film industry would record a good outing in 2010. With a few key films that kept cinemas busy (as well as the home-video business solvent) and added a touch of glamour to the Ghana Movie Awards held in November, it became clear that Ghana is becoming a worthy competitor to its Anglophone neighbour, Nigeria, whose Nollywood product has dominated the African cinematic landscape for last decade.

Ghana has John Appeah to thank for the enthralling romantic drama, **Elmina**, which was premiered at the Tate Gallery in London in October 2010. The film looks set to win international awards. Produced by Revele Films, four years after *Run Baby Run* won the top prize at the 2007 Africa Film Academy Awards, *Elmina*'s strong theme of love and betrayal, as well as its powerful depiction of contemporary life in Accra, resonates strongly as a film. With a decidedly Ghanaian outlook. An international cast, including UK-based artist Douglas Fishburn, also gives the film a truly urbane profile.

A good number of the year's films sought to expand their markets by targeting both local audiences and the African Diaspora. Nana Hema Doku's **Ex-Wife**, a romantic comedy set in South-east London, shows how young Ghanaian filmmakers are using the experiences of Africans abroad to tell compelling stories. Also noteworthy is

Frank Rajah Arase's **The Game**, a sexy, contemporary drama and Phil Efe Bernard's **Betrayal**, a romantic thriller set in Ghana, which is a welcome addition to the home video market. However, Albert Mensah's **Cats and Dogs** struggled to fulfil its potential as a comical animated film for children.
– *Steve Ayorinde*

GUATEMALA

Guatemala took a significant leap in film production during 2010, with an unprecedented 12 films produced. The most successful was Julio Hernández's **Las marimbas del infierno**. A fusion of tradition and modernity, it features an old unemployed marimba player who forms a band with a young heavy metal musician. Their band allows them to escape the tedium of their everyday lives.

Rodolfo Espinoza's **Aquí me quedo** shows how civil violence even affects those living in rural areas, while Héctor Herlidan's **El profe Omar** tells the story of a technology teacher sent to a school in the countryside, where he finds himself teaching with nothing more than chalk and a blackboard. Mendel Samayoa's **La vaca** is a comedy about two women who come to blows when their lover dies, leaving them joint owners of a cow. Jimmy and Sammy Morales' **Gerardi** tells the story of Monseñor Gerardi, a supporter of the guerrillas during the civil war, who was eventually killed. **El mito del tiempo**, directed by indigenous filmmaker, Jaguar X, presents the unwritten chapters of Popol Vuh – the Mayan bible – through the eyes of a child. All these films are unique for their taking place in the rural areas of the country.

Inn urban setting, Mario Rosales' **El regreso de Lencho** tells the story of a painter, returning from New York, who wants to create a collective of artists and motivate them to live through their work. Verónica Riedel's **Cápsulas** is about a child at risk in the home of his mother and a drug dealer. The family

Enrique Pérez's **Puro Mula**

want to go to the United States but the boy's father kidnaps him in order to start a new life. In Enrique Pérez's **Puro Mula**, Joel is a young man disappointed with his life. His sister asks him to look after her child, who then goes missing, changing Joel's life forever. Leonel Ramos' **Maligno** details the investigation by a group of friends into the murder of several children, while in Rafael Tres's **Un día de Sol**, a young woman whose only passion is football faces up to pressures from a society unwilling to accept a woman taking part in what is seen as a man's sport. – *Maria Lourdes Cortés*

GUINEA

Despite a poor year, there are signs to suggest that the future looks a little brighter for filmmakers in Guinea. The only major release last year was the documentary **The Path to the Lord** (*Le Chemin vers le Seigneur*) directed by Dénis Leno. It details a popular annual Christian pilgrimage that takes place in the town of Boffa, west Guinea.

From 16 to 30 April, the first edition of the Fortnight of Guinean Film was held. As it was the first film event organised by the authorities for several years, it is hoped to raise the political will to give new impetus to the seventh art in the country.

France-based director Cheick Doucouré is preparing a documentary on past presidential elections in Guinea, while his compatriot, Cheick Fantamandy Camara, the director of *Clouds Over Conakry*, has shot some scenes of his second feature, **Morbayassa**, in Senegal during July. He will next be filming in Guinea and France. It is slated for a late 2011 release. Meanwhile, Camara is working on another feature film project, **the Miracle** (*Kabananko*), whose plot revolves around a dance company. – *Agnes Thomasi*

IRAQ

Diaspora Iraqi filmmakers who fled the country since the early days of Saddam Hussein's regime, or in the aftermath of the consecutive wars, are beginning to re-emerge on the international film scene. One of the most talented and active directors is Baghdad-born Mohamed Al-Daradji, who studied theatre directing and escaped to the Netherlands in 1995. He studied filmmaking in London and last year unveiled his latest feature, **Son of Babylon**. It has since has toured various film festivals, including Abu-Dhabi and Sundance. It eventually won the Amnesty International Film Prize and the Peace Film Award at the Berlin Film Festival.

Mohamed Al-Daradji's **Son of Babylon**

Shot on location in Iraq, it is a touching story of a young Kurdish boy traveling across Iraq with his grandmother, in search for his father, who went missing during the first Gulf War. Al-Daradji also received *Variety*'s coveted Middle East Filmmaker of the Year Award at Abu-Dhabi Film Festival, where he also presented his new documentary, **In My Mother's Arms**, which documents the fate of seven young children

about to be thrown out of their orphanage. Other documentary films looked at the state of Iraq and its people. These included Tarik Rasouli's **Iraq, Finally** and Karzan Kader's **Bekas**. – *Sherif Awad*

IVORY COAST

In terms of quantity and quality, features are lagging significantly behind documentaries in the Ivory Coast. After five years, veteran director Idriss Diabaté released **Yankel! Africa at the Workshop** (*Yankel ! L'Afrique à l'atelier*), a tribute to the painter and writer Jacques Yankel, who trained the majority of the most famous painters of the Côte d'Ivoire.

Armand 'Gauze' Gbaka-Brédé's **M'Bede or the Metamorphosis of a Reliquary** (*M'Bede ou la métamorphose d'un reliquaire*) is looks into a reliquary from Gabon bought for €2.3 million by a European billionaire. The film is a fascinating account of what happened in Gabon, France and Switzerland.

E-Burny 2002 is a slightly above average feature about the war in Côte d'Ivoire. Directed by John Clavaire Soubinan Kakou, it is about a teenager who seeks revenge following the murder of her parents during the war.

The most anticipated film of 2011 is a feature-length animated adaption of the successful comic book, 'Aya de Yopougon', by the France-based Ivorian writer, Margaret Abouet.

The country's two shorts films festivals, the International Festival of Short Film and Clap Ivoire, which unspool in April and September, once again attracted record crowds. – *Honoré Essoh*

KYRGYZSTAN

Of the two films produced in Kyrgyzstan in 2010, one became the region's biggest sensation, screening at Cannes, Locarno,

Aktan Arym Kubat's **The Light Thief**

Almaty, Pusan and other film festivals. **The Light Thief** was directed by Aktan Arym Kubat. The film's protagonist is an electrician who locals lovingly call Mister Light. He not only connects people back on to the mains when they have been cut off for not paying their bills, he brings light, love and laughter into their lives. But greed and political maneuvering threaten his way of life. This film not only reflects the situation in the country, it also brings to the surface racial tensions that have been simmering in the country for some time. In interview, Aktan Aryn Kubat said, 'It seems to me that our country needs not only energy light, but a spiritual one as well, so that the shine of it will fill up the relationships between people.'

The second film, Tynai Ibragimov's **Woman at the Stirrup**, was shot on video. It is a psychological melodrama about a married couple whose relationship is failing and results in their separation. The film is structured as a series of episodes, each replete with traditional rituals, customs and songs, enhancing the atmosphere of culture and ethnicity out of which the relationship grew.

Due to the lack of financial support, younger filmmakers could only afford to shoot short films. Over 20 were produced in the last year, some of which were screened at international festivals. They included Nargiza Mamatkulova's impressive *Earrings*.

There were three Kyrgyz projects presented in the Open Doors programme at the Locarno

Film Festival: Nurlan Asanbekov's **The Singing Grannies**, Erkin Soliev's **Princess Nazhik** and Elnura Osmonalieva's **Pasture in the Skies**. – *Gulnara Abikeyeva*

LEBANON

Last year, Lebanese cinema reached a wide exposure not only in Arab festivals, but also throughout Europe and the rest of the World. The Civil War and its aftermath, the religious and political tensions inside the country and close to its borders, are notable thematic elements in most of the films released.

Every Day is a Holiday, the feature debut of Dima El-Horr, was the first film of the year and received a positive reception at Rotterdam and Alexandria, amongst other festivals. The dreamlike story follows a trio of Arab women en route to a remote prison to visit their detained husbands, only to find themselves stranded in the desert, where they relive the memories of former times.

Abu-Dhabi Festival provided a platform for many Lebanese premieres, with two features winning major prizes. The Best Arab Film went to **Here Comes the Rain** (*Shatti Ya Dini*), with **OK, Enough, Goodbye** (*Tayeb, Khalas, Yalla*) picking up the Best Arab Film Debut.

Bahij Hojeij's **Here Comes the Rain**

In **Here Comes the Rain**, writer-director Bahij Hojeij continued to explore the mysterious kidnappings during the Lebanese civil war, where many political activists mysteriously disappeared for long periods of time. The story centers around one of them, the 50-year-old Ramez (Hassan Mrad, winner of the Best Actor at the 34th Brussels Film Festival), who, after 20 years of captivity, struggles to communicate with his wife and two children, who are now grown up. Only Zeinab (Carmen Lebbos), whose husband was also detained, appears to understand him.

Raniah Attieh and Daniel Garcia's OK, Enough, Goodbye

OK, Enough, Goodbye, which was co-written and directed by Raniah Attieh and Daniel Garcia, is an intimate story about a middle-aged Lebanese man whose childish attachment to his mother has kept him from experiencing normal relationships with friends and neighbors. The film succeeds in capturing the conservative ambiance of the small city of Tripoli, where individuals are isolated by the choices they make.

In the documentary **We Were Communists**, Maher Abi Samra revisits the Lebanese Civil War through the stories of four men from different backgrounds, who recount their experiences on the battlefield, their broken dreams and disillusionment evident throughout. Mohamed Soueid's **How Bitter My Sweet!** (*Bahebak Ya Wahsh!*) also explores Lebanese society in the aftermath of the war and the hardship of making a living in an unstable economic environment. **The Fifth Column** by Vatche Boulghourjian and **In their Blood** (*Bi Rouh bi Dam*) by Katia Jarjoura were two shorts

depicting the decent into violence and mayhem of young teens on the streets of Beirut.

In 2011, writer-director Nadine Labaki, who received international recognition for *Caramel*, will present **Where Do We Go Now?** She also co-stars in the story of a group of Lebanese women caught in the middle of religious tensions, between Christians and Muslims, in their village. – *Sherif Awad*

MALI

The last year finally saw the release of Sidi Diabaté's **Da Monzon, the Battle of Samanyana** (*Da Monzon, la bataille de Samanyana*), which was produced by the National Centre of Cinematography of Mali (CNCM). Fully funded by the government, the local blockbuster traces the life of the legendary King Da Monzon Diarra, a national hero.

The CNCM has increased its support over the last three years. It has also produced Ibrahima Toure's story of two prisoners, **Spider Webs** (*Toiles d'araignée*), in which a young woman rebels against the customs of her village and a teacher objects to the dictatorship. The film is scheduled for a 2011 release.

Awa Traoré's directorial debut, the documentary **Waliden, Child of Other People** (*Waliden, enfant d'autrui*), details through passionate and moving testimonies, the abuse suffered by children adopted through the local customs. It is an experience Traoré also suffered as a child.

Awa Traoré's **Waliden, Child of Other People**

Mauritanian director Abderrahmane Sissako, who has close ties with Mali, has taken over one of the oldest cinemas in the country. Closed for 15 years, some screenings were held in November, with the full restoration of the cinema scheduled to be completed in 2012. – *Honoré Essoh*

MAURITANIA

Local production is still dominated by documentaries, which offered up a few surprises. One of them was Cheikh N'Diaye's **The Shadow of the Marabouts** (*L'Ombre des Marabouts*), in which the director turns his camera on the world of the Marabouts, in neighboring Senegal. Through the portraits of a peasant, a hairdresser and a journalist, the film examines the development of Marabouts' fraternities in Senegalese society since French colonialisation.

Back to the Cemeteries (*Retour aux cimetières*) was another documentary that dealt with a sensitive subject – Mauritanians who were deported out of the country in the late 1980s. When these people returned, they discovered that their cemeteries had been turned into farmland. It is one of the flagship films of the fifth edition of the National Film Week, which unfolded in Nouakchott, in November, and was organised by the House of Filmmakers of Mauritania.

The other film event was the Documentary Film Festival of Kaédi, which also takes place in November. The director of the festival, now in its third edition, is Ethmane Diagana, who has also completed the 52-minute documentary, **Cinema, My Country and Myself** (*Le cinéma mon pays et moi*), which reflects on the reasons for the decline of film in Mauritania. – *Agnes Thomasi*

MONTENEGRO

Like Serbia, Montenegro sports its own homegrown video market, albeit run on a shoestring budget. Its independence from state funds enables the films produced to feature a strong satirical bite. This can be evidenced in action spoofs such as Drasko Djurovic's *Invasion of Prcevo*, in which NATO attempts to rescue an abducted American citizen from a village and country which are not on the map, or Ivan Djurovic's *The Golden Nunchuck*, featuring a martial arts master who is pursuing an evil Montenegrin king. Similarly, a popular television comedy series, *Money or Else*, directed by Milan Karadzic and airing in 2008-9, was eventually turned into a feature.

On the other hand, the state does its own bit to popularise cinema. It introduced acting and television/film directing courses in 1997 and 2003 respectively. Homegrown students should look to filmmaker Zivko Nikolic (1941–2001), active in the golden days of Montenegrin cinema, for inspiration. He dedicated his whole opus to capturing the local spirit, often with touches of surrealism and the grotesque. He will be remembered for his Mediterranean sensuality and the tasteful nudity inherent in comedies of the absurd such as *Unseen Wonder* (1984) or *The Beauty of Sin* (1986).

The portmanteau film **Love, Scars**

The first generation of graduate directors from the Faculty of Dramatic Arts in Cetinje, appeared in 2010 with the omnibus **Love, Scars** (*Ljubav, oziljci*). Four love stories, directed by Ivana Cetkovic, Milos Pusonjic, Mladen Vujacic and Branislav Milatovic, are adaptations of various literary works, from Mario Benedetti to Charles Bukowski. The film premiered at the 24th International

Film Festival in Herceg Novi. This major Montenegrin film festival is still a showcase for local projects, but it became an international event in 2007.

Several feature projects are lined up for 2011. Currently in post-production is Branko Baletic's **A Local Vampire** (*Tenac/Lokalni vampir*), a comedy about a case of vampirism in transitional Montenegro. Baletic's career in Serbia includes the acclaimed *Balkan Express*. He moved to Montenegro to become a champion of the Republic's independence, a professor of film directing (*Love, Scars* was made by his students) and chairman of Montenegrin Cinematheque. At present, he is also the most experienced filmmaker/ producer in the country. He has been active as a producer, but *A Local Vampire* is his first film in 15 years. – *Goran Gocić*

NEPAL

The last year has seen an increase in the number of films produced – almost doubling the previous year's figure – many of them digital. However, the means of exhibition remain limited and the problems of actually having films screened is likely to see few of them succeed commercially. Steps are being taken to improve this. But the quality of films also needs to improve.

Around 60 films were produced, although the returns were small. Two action-oriented love stories, Gyanendra Deuja's **Protection** (*Hifajat*) and Madan Ghimire's **Friendship** (*Dosti*) opened in April and attracted some commercial success. The first was based on women empowerment while the latter was a love story between two friends.

Manoj Pandit's **Dasdhunga**, detailing the mysterious accident that befell two popular communist leaders, Madan Bhandari and Jiba Raj Asrit, was praised for its technical merit and narrative skill, but was not liked by audiences. Likewise, **Dasgaja**, based on the

encroachment of the Nepali boarder by India, was also not to audience tastes. Sovit Basnet directed **Kanyadan**, whose story centres around the marriage of two girls, saw some return on its investment.

Popular music video director Alok Nembang's **Someone Mine** (*Kohi Mero*) unfolded against the stunning backdrop of the Mustang district, while Simos Sunuwar's **First Love** also sported a higher budget. Sadly, neither director attempted anything beyond the most rudimentary approach to their material.

Ambitious and popular director Tulasi Ghimire's **The Nation** (*Desh*) focused on escalating corruption and the lack of accountability in the state machinery. Surprisingly, the film achieved a modicum of success. By contrast, Ukesh Dahal's **Each Movements** (*Palpal*), a profile of a male prostitute, failed to make an impact.

Sabir Shrestha's **Who Stole My Heart** (*Kasle Choryo Mero Man*) was released in October. Winning over large audiences, it is a classic rich-meets-poor tale.

Of the year's documentaries, Hari Thapa's **Sherpas – The True Heroes of Mount Everest** won the Best Film Award at the Kathmandu International Film Festival. Abinash Bikram Shah's **Time is Perhap** and Manoj Raj Pandey's **Living by the River** were also released.

New talent and an increase in production does offer some hope for the future.

PRABESH SUBEDI is a freelance journalist and documentary maker. He is also the editor of the e-magazine *Filmnepal.com*.

PAKISTAN

Pakistan has been plagued with terrorism and suicide attacks for some time now. If that was not enough, 2010 saw floods never witnessed before. A large area was devastated, affecting almost two million people. Leisure, and particularly film-going, had to take a back seat. And the few of us who still wanted our kicks would either eat out or watch films via illegal telecasts on Cable or illegally imported DVDs.

Foreign films performed better than domestic fare in multiplexes in Rawalpindi, particularly with newly constructed and renovated cinemas in Lahore and Karachi. Sadly, there was a visible decline in the quality of locally produced fare.

Syed Noor and Masood Butt were the only directors to release Punjabi titles: **The Bride** (*Wohti Le Key Jani Ai*) and **Daughter** (*Lado Rani*) respectively. Pakistan-India co-production **The Heritage** (*Virsa*), directed by Pankaj Batra and filmed in Australia, was a decent romantic drama about a rich brat and a well-behaved girl. However, the film failed to find an audience. Indian actor Arya Babbar and Pakistani fashion model Mehreen Raheed played the leads.

Cinema entertainment tax is exempt in Punjab for local films, but imports were taxed at 65% of the admission price. Foreign distributors and those importing films claimed it would shut down the industry, and threatened to go to the court to address this discrimination. Justice arrived in the last week of October and the tax was withdrawn. Up to October, there were 36 Hollywood and Bollywood imports, compared to 48 for the whole of 2009. Only a handful of them made money. Most of the releases are widely available on illegal cable channels and pirated DVDs at the fraction of what you would pay to see them at the multiplexes. Thankfully, there are still diehard film fans who go to cinemas to see the latest releases.

AIJAZ GUL is a film critic and writes for Pakistani and foreign publications. He is author of four books on films and member of FIPRESCI and NETPAC. He teaches film at media institutes.

PALESTINE

Last year, the continuous struggle in Palestine affected production resources for Palestinian filmmakers living in their homeland or elsewhere, which resulted in few films being produced.

Documentaries have become a powerful tool in the hands of Palestinian filmmakers to communicate to the world their rights and stories. Among the recent documentaries shown at festivals around the world is Kamal Aljafari's **Port of Memory**, in which the writer and director tells the story of his own family, who were told to leave their own home in Ajami, Jaffa's once-active sea-front, before 1948.

Kamal Aljafari's **Port of Memory**

Raised in Abu-Dhabi and Amman, Dahna Abourahme is a Palestinian filmmaker who studied in New York, then returned to teach in Lebanon. Last year, she presented a follow-up to her first documentary *Until When*, which was about Palestinian refugees in the West Bank. In **Kingdom of Women**, Abourahme went to Ein el-Hilweh, the largest Palestinian refugee camp in South Lebanon, where women took charge of their own destiny after the detention of their men, by the Israeli army that was occupying part of South Lebanon, rolled northward into the city of Sidon, back in 1982.

Acclaimed artist and filmmaker Julian Schnabel directed **Miral**, the story of writer Rula Jebreal who was raised in an orphanage in East Jerusalem and grew up during occupation and war. As portrayed by Freida Pinto, Miral

Julian Schnabel's **Miral**

remained ignorant of the conflict unfolding outside the institution's walls until she accepted a teacher's position at a refugee camp during the Intifada. After its premiere in Venice, **Miral** was screened at three Arab festivals, in Abu-Dhabi, Carthage and Doha.

Norwegian filmmaker Vibeke Løkkeberg directed the documentary **Tears of Gaza** which details the 2009 bombing of Gaza by the Israeli military.

Julia Pacha's **Budrus**, which was executive produced by Jehane Noujaim, takes place in the film's eponymous Palestinian village, thirty-one kilometres north-west of Ramallah, which attracted the world's attention in 2003, when the Israeli government decided to build a fence that ran straight through it. As a result, the village became a site of protest. Bacha, who has followed events in Budrus over the past five years, chose to focus on the Palestinian activist, Ayed Morrar, the head of the village, and his 15-year-old daughter, Iltezam, who tried, along with the villagers and activists, to unite Fatah, Hamas and Israelis in an unarmed peaceful protest to save the village from destruction. The documentary premiered in Tribeca, New York, where it received a Special Jury Mention. – *Sherif Awad*

PERU

Two contrasting trends could be seen in Peruvian cinema over the last year. There was a considerable increase in the number

of film projects and the Consejo Nacional de Cinematografía (CONACINE) received an increased number of entries for their screenwriting competitions. On the other hand, there was a significant decrease in the audiences for local films.

Three new directors appeared on the scene, with a collection of distinctive debuts, which all played successfully at international festivals: Javier Fuentes' **Undertow** (*Contracorriente*), Héctor Gálvez's **Paradise** (*Paraíso*), and Daniel and Diego Vega's **October** (*Octubre*). *Undertow* was awarded the World Cinema Audience Award at the Sundance Film. *October* received the jury prize in Un Certain Regard at Cannes Film Festival. However, such international recognition did not help to increase the domestic box office takings. The six films were among six that attract less than 80,000 admissions, some kind of record for Peruvian cinema.

Daniel and Diego Vega's **October**

Audience scarcity accounts for the majority of Latin American films being low-budget productions. The trend remains the same: a combination of local funding, support from IBERMEDIA and European foundations, ensuring that the entire budget of a film is covered before it opens, resulting in neither profit nor losses. This is one of the major dilemmas facing a number of countries in the region, including Peru.

Paradise is a small tale set in a marginalised community in Lima, where a group of boys, their position untenable due to extreme poverty, dream about a better future. *October*, by contrast, is an ironic story about a man who suddenly finds himself saddled with a baby, which may be his. Both films are presented unsentimentally, with no driving narrative, preferring instead to observe the actions and behaviour of the characters.

Javier Fuentes' **Undertow**

Undertow focuses on a ménage à trois between a young fisherman, his wife and his lover, a painter who is ostracised by the local community and, following a fatal accident, returns to the fisherman as a ghost. Romance, mystery and social prejudices are intertwined in a story that employs melodrama and nuanced characterisation to tell its tale.

Veteran directors Francisco Lombardi and Augusto Tamayo returned with two thrillers: **She** (*Ella*) and **The Vigil** (*La vigilia*). Like his previous film, *A Naked Body*, Lombardi's focus is a female corpse. It is the silent part of a triangle made up by her husband and involuntary killer, and her lover. *The Vigil* opens with a young girl from a rough city neighbourhood breaking into the house of an ageing intellectual. The resulting action is a tense play-off between the two characters, drawing on their different backgrounds and response to situations. It is the final part of Tamayo's trilogy, which began with *The Elusive Good* and *Crossing a Shadow*, which analyses Peruvian society.

The year's weakest film was **Illary**, directed by Nilo Pereira. It attempted to grapple with the civil unrest that was prompted by the terrorist activities of the Shining Path movement in the 1980s. Unfortunately, that subject has received better treatment in other films.

Eight films are slated for release in 2011. It remains to be seen whether audiences will improve on this year and actually turn out to see them.

ISAAC LEÓN FRÍAS is a film critic and Professor of Language and Film History at the University of Lima. From 1965 to 1985 he was director of *Hablemos de Cine* magazine and from 1986 to 2001 ran Filmoteca de Lima.

SENEGAL

Music lovers will enjoy young Dyana Gaye's pleasant musical, **Saint-Louis Blues** (*Un transport en commun*). During the trip from the capital city Dakar to another town, Saint-Louis, the destinies of passengers in a taxi cross, revealing their dreams, anger and joys through a mixture of song and good humour.

Adopting a very different style, Alassane Diago's documentary, **Tears of Emigration** (*Les Larmes de l'émigration*), is the story of his village. The majority of men left for Europe,

Alassane Diago's **Tears of Emigration**

leaving their families without news. Diago's mother has awaited his father's return for 20 years, while his brother-in-law left 5 years ago. The film is a noble account of the pain these women have experienced.

Mariama Sylla Faye's **Infantryman Marc Guèye: My Quill, My Fight** (*Tirailleur Marc Guèye: ma plume, mon combat*) is another powerful documentary. It charts the unusual life of a Senegalese war veteran who talks about his daily life, memories of war and the difficulty he has had in getting his memoirs published. The struggle has lasted 37 years.

The last year saw the death, on 8 March, of documentary filmmaker Mahama Johnson Traoré, who was acclaimed for the films *Diankha-bi* and *Lambaye*. – *Honoré Essoh*

SYRIA

Although few private companies contribute to film production in Syria, in addition to the General Organisation for Cinema – the main national entity handling films and festivals – the number of features produced every year does not surpass half a dozen. Nevertheless, interest in Syrian cinema has been increasing worldwide with the rise of new filmmakers such as Hatem Ali, who directed *Endless Night*, which won the Golden Taura at Taormina in 2009, and the musical *Selena*, starring Lebanese singer Myriam Fares.

In 2010, **Once Again** (*Mara Okhra*), the feature debut of writer-director Joud Said, competed

Abdel-Latif Abdel-Hamid's **September's Rain**

at Abu-Dhabi and Cairo, as well as the Arab Film Festival in San Francisco, where it was awarded Best Film. It sheds a light on Lebanese-Syrian relations through the story of a secret affair between a married Syrian man and his beautiful Lebanese colleague.

The 18th Damascus Film Festival also saw a screening of Abdel-Latif Abdel-Hamid's **September's Rain** (*Matar Aylol*), where it received the Bronze Award. An ensemble comedy it features a family whose members are romantically entangled.

Aliaa Khachouk's **I Was Once Told**

Canadian-based, Syrian-born writer-director Aliaa Khachouk screened her feature debut, **I Was Once Told**, at the Montreal World Film Festival. The film stars Nada Houmsi as Leila, a tender woman hoping to find affection in the new world. **To Damascus with Love**, in which Mohamed Abdel-Aziz narrates a forbidden love story between a Jewish Syrian woman and a Muslim man, competed for the Muhr Award at the Dubai Film Festival. – *Sherif Awad*

UZBEKISTAN

According to statistics from an independent consulting agency, at the request of Indigo Film production company, profits resulting from investment in any film project in Uzbekistan are in the region of 176%. It is no surprise that more investors are interested in looking into the film industry.

There were around 60 features produced in 2010. The state film organization, Uzbekfilm, produced 13 of them, all of which were shot on 35mm. The remainder were produced by private studios on video. Such quality is sufficient for Uzbek exhibition, where most venues screen DVDs.

The average budget for a local film is between US$30,000 and USD$50,000, with tickets for films priced at US$1.50. If distribution of the film is successful it can earn up to US$150,000. Such was the case with Mirmaksud Akhunov's **Mister X**, recognised as a best domestic film of the year. In a twist on the Cinderella story, a young man is the main protagonist.

The main staples of Uzbek cinema are comedies and soap-style dramas. There were some exceptions. Farid Davletshin's **Tsunami-2** was a surprisingly successful one. Shot in Thailand, it tells the story of an Uzbek couple trapped when the 2004 tsunami hit the country's coastline. Featuring a significant amount of CGI, the film stands apart from other releases. There was also an attempt at fantasy with Rustam Sagdiyev's **Me is I**, in which the soul of a character killed in a car crash transfers into the body of the person who caused the accident. It's mix of comedy and drama works well throughout.

The boundary between commercial and art house releases that has been so visible in Uzbekistan film has become less distinct

Elkin Tuychiev's **Postscript**

with recent releases. Elkin Tuychiev and Ayub Shakhobiddinov have seen to this. Tuychiev's **Postscript** has been screened at festivals in Pusan, Anapa and Moscow, and tells the story of provincial TV repair man and his relationship with his younger brother. Tuychiev also released two commercial films and was recognised as the best director of 2010. Shakhobiddinov's **Late Life** tells the story of a man who believes his life to be worthless and attempts to start it all over again.

Forthcoming films include young female director Saodat Ismailova's **40 Days of Silence**. Supported by a variety of international funds, it is about a woman who, as the title suggests, chooses not to speak for a lengthy period and focuses on four women who live under one roof and look to each other for comfort and support, as they each try to overcome the obstacles in their lives.
– *Gulnara Gabikeyev*

A NEW FILM BY ANDRZEJ BARAŃSKI
FORTHCOMING IN 2011

A PRINCIPALITY

KSIĘSTWO CA 120' B/W 35MM

PRODUCED BY SKORPION ART., TVP SA – FILM AGENCY,
17, J. P. WORONICZA ST., 00-999 WARSAW, POLAND,
WWW.INTERNATIONAL.TVP.PL

Festival News

The profile of the International Film Guide increased significantly over the last year, both in the presence of the IFG Inspiration Award at the closing ceremonies of numerous festivals and via the online IFG Festival Spotlight which offers on-the-ground day to day coverage of screenings and events by our team of contributors. This included coverage of Black Nights in Estonia, BUFF in Sweden, Cape Winelands in South Africa, Cinemagic in Belfast, Cottbus in Germany, Era New Horizons in Poland, Fantasporto in Portugal, Far East Film Festival in Italy, London Turkish Film Festival, Tampere in Finland, Visions du Réel in Switzerland, Vilnius in Lithuania and Zlín in the Czech Republic. IFG contributors not only submitted daily reports of events – both public and industry – and screenings, they also wrote blogs and columns for festival newspapers and websites. Individual spotlights focussed on the work of cutting-edge production companies, studios and speciality outfits.

The IFG Inspiration Award was created to champion the work of up-and-coming directors. It is hoped that with each year and an increase in the winning entries, a global network of directors will emerge, with the IFG following each of these filmmakers' careers, focusing on new work and continuing the Guide's remit of celebrating new voices in world cinema.

The IFG Inspiration Award and online contributor coverage are elements of the various partnerships between the IFG and international film festivals, which also includes copies of the print edition for circulation to festival guests, jury members, plus directors/producers who have films in competition,

etc. Ensuring that each festival has year-round exposure, both in the annual IFG report and online, through dedicated advertising, festival reporting and related events, expands the role of the IFG, offering a more comprehensive account of each festival's identity and events throughout the year.

IFG Festival Spotlight coverage in 2010 began with Fantasporto, whose focus on the best of fantasy and horror releases unfolded amid the stunning setting of Oporto, Portugal. At the 12th edition of the Far East Film Festival, IFG contributor Nina Caplan enjoyed the blend of Italian culture and Asian film, including retrospectives of Patrick Lung Kong and the eclectic output of Shintoho Studios. Wine and film also lay at the heart of Cape Winelands, one of South Africa's premiere festivals for new and emerging talent, from home and abroad. At BUFF, children and youth correspondent Elinor Groom witnessed yet another successful edition of the celebrated Swedish children's film festival, which screened over 90 features and shorts across 5 days. For its 15th edition, Vilnius International Film Festival screened 100 plus films from over 50 countries under the banner 'Reborn at the Cinema', while Festival Director Jean Perret departed Nyon's Visions du Réel with a vital programme that underpinned the importance of documentary and non-fiction film. History, particularly Finland's rich cinematic past, was central to the Tampere International Short Film Festival, whereas the influence of East European culture around the world and the ebb and flow of migrant communities dominated one of the vital strands at Cottbus. Closer to the IFG's home, the London Turkish Film Festival highlighted the importance of Turkish film on the world stage with a selection of new films and the best releases from recent years. And as Zlín celebrated an historic 50 years, it looked back at a rich tapestry of film culture and celebrated the work of one-time Zlín resident and hugely influential animation filmmaker Karel Zeman, whose 100th birthday was in 2010. The year ended with coverage of the Black Nights Film Festival and the announcement of the European Film Awards, which ran alongside the festival. Tallinn is the 2011 European Capital of Culture and Black Nights, created and run by Tiina Lokk, is one of the many platforms that confirms the Estonian capital as a major cultural venue.

The role of the International Film Guide also expanded into education. At Cinemagic, IFG Editor Ian Haydn Smith led a two-day workshop on film journalism, one of the many workshops that Cinemagic hosts for 16 to 25-year-olds, from screenwriting masterclasses with Julian Fellowes and Ryan Rowe to understanding digital and 3D effects with some of the world's top practitioners. One of the students from the journalism workshop, Siobahn Griffin, has written a report on the importance of Cinemagic for this section.

This year-round presence of IFG contributors works to reinforce the importance of festivals, from all reaches of the globe, in engaging audiences with the latest developments in film and cross-media platforms, as well as educating new generations of cinemagoers.

An Industry Focus at Era New Horizons

In 2011, Wrocław's Era New Horizons International Film Festival will feature several events aimed at the film industry, underpinning its status as the place to be for overseas film industry delegates interested in looking for business in Poland.

Every year, Era New Horizons is visited by a wealth of industry delegates: film producers, sales agents, festival programmers, TV buyers

One of the outdoor screenings at Era New Horizons

and distributors. Era New Horizons provides a networking platform for filmmakers from Poland and abroad. It also regularly attracts programmers from festivals as diverse as Berlinale, Venice, Edinburgh, Indie Lisboa, Gothenburg, Pusan and many more.

In 2010, the festival featured the first edition of the **New Horizons Studio**, a three-day workshop intended for young Polish directors, producers, writers, composers, etc. Lecturers included experienced industry professionals such as Sandy Lieberson, Tine Klint as well as directors Jonathan Caouette and Nuri Bilge Ceylan. The next edition will also be open to a limited number of foreign participants.

In 2011, together with its partners at the Norwegian Film Institute and Music Export Norway, Era New Horizons will run a special programme of new Norwegian films and a retrospective of Anja Breien, under the heading **Norway Expanded**. In addition to the screenings, the **Polish-Norwegian Co-production Forum** will take place. Several potential co-production projects will be discussed at one-on-one meetings. There will also be a video library featuring the latest Norwegian films and panel discussions dealing with all areas of international co-production. The project will also include concerts of Norwegian musicians at the festival club and a dedicated art exhibition. The project is co-financed from the means of the Cultural Exchange Fund, which operates within the EEA Financial Mechanism and Norwegian Financial Mechanism.

The festival has also risen in stature with sales agents, becoming a strong partner for those looking for Polish distribution for their films. In 2011, after their success at last year's festival, the following films secured a Polish release including the following, which were distributed domestically by the festival: Anocha Suwichakornpong's *Mundane History*, Michelangelo Frammartino's *Le quattro volte*, Nikolay and Yelena Renard's *Mama*, Kornél Mundruczó's *Tender Son – The Frankenstein Project*, Bruno Dumont's *Hadewijch*, Cédric Dupire and Gaspard Kuentz's *We Don't Care About Music Anyway* and Gaspar Noé's *Enter the Void*.

The 11th Era New Horizons International Film Festival will take place in Wrocław between the 21-31 July, 2011. It will include retrospectives of Pinku eiga – Japanese erotic films, and showcase the works of Terry Gilliam, Bruno Dumont and Jack Smith. It will also focus on the work of Andrzej Munk, as next year will mark the 90th anniversary of his birth and 50th anniversary of his death. Munk was one of the foremost representatives of the post-war Polish Film School. His best-known films include *Eroica* and *Passenger*. And in collaboration with Rotterdam International Film Festival, there will be the programme **Red Westerns**, a review of films from Soviet Russia and the former Eastern Bloc made between 1920 and 1980.

With so many different programmes, aimed equally at the public and industry, Era New Horizons looks set to grow once again in 2011.

Cinemagic at 20

Cinemagic International Film and Television Festival for Young People celebrated its 20th anniversary in 2010. An award-winning festival, it uses film and the moving image to educate, motivate and inspire young people to broaden their horizons and use their talents for the greater good. Originating in Belfast, the festival now hosts events around the world, from England, Ireland and France to cities across the USA. As one of the participants in the film

journalism talent lab at the Belfast edition of the festival, I gained an insight into what a journalism career involves. I also interviewed Joan Burney Keatings, who has been Chief Executive of Cinemagic for the last ten years, on the highlights of this year's edition, its achievements and future hopes.

Joan reflected fondly upon the success of Cinemagic in 2010, which delivered eleven festivals around the globe, to an audience of 30,000. Joan commented on how she has been 'exceptionally humbled' by the level of industry professionals and distributors who had gone out of their way to support the organisation internationally. Her highlight of the year was the International Film Camp, which brought together five students from five international cities to Belfast for one week to make a short film. Their progress was documented on Ireland's UTV channel each night, culminating in the broadcast of the completed film.

Reflecting back upon the development of Cinemagic since taking over as Chief Executive, Joan championed the ongoing commitment of guests who continue to support the festival and praised the innovation and creativity of the young people who submit an increasing number of films to the festival each year. Describing Cinemagic as 'dynamic, hard working, creative and forward-thinking organisation that has expanded greatly worldwide,' Joan credits the success of the

Liam Neeson, Cinemagic Chief Executive Joan Burney Keatings and a group of young cinemagoers

organisation to the small team of staff who are dedicated to growing it into the largest Children's festival of its kind. She also spoke of how she welcomes with confidence challenges brought on by the expansion of Cinemagic to cities like New York and thanked the continued support and commitment of international partners.

Belfast's 2010 edition of Cinemagic ended with an awards ceremony in the city's majestic city hall. Joan appeared on stage at the end of the event to hand the Festival's Lifetime Achievement Award to Sesame Street, which was accepted by Sesame Workshop's President and Chief Executive, Gary Knell. Joan also spoke highly of her delight at the 'absolute amazing talent' of the young people who participated in the workshops, master-classes, juries and panel events; an edition that welcomed special guests such as Liam Neeson, Julian Fellowes, Patrick Bergin, Suranne Jones, casting director John Hubbard and Dreamwork Animation's Phil McNally.

On a concluding note, Joan spoke of her hopes for Cinemagic over the next few years, including 'Cinemagic USA' – a documentary to be produced by UTV in 2011. She also looked forward to continuing the success of the festivals, from securing fantastic films and world-class film industry professionals, to engaging, inspiring and bringing together many more young people from all walks of life to learn and develop skills that Joan hopes will help them believe in themselves and face the future with confidence. – *Siobhan Griffin*

The European Film Awards

The 23rd European Film Awards brought glitz and glamour to the Estonian capital of Tallinn, despite facing much adversity in the shape of inclement weather and striking Finnish cabin crews. The likes of Juliette Binoche, Wim Wenders and Bruno Ganz took their place amongst many up-and-coming stars of European Cinema for a ceremony that celebrated the rich diversity of films from the last year. The event was also a celebration of Estonia itself, arriving on the heels of the 14th Black Nights Film Festival and serving as the launch event for Tallinn's hosting of the 2011 European Capital of Culture.

Roman Polanski appearing via Skype at the 23rd European Film Awards. Photo: EFA/René Velli

Hosted by German comedy star Anke Engelke and Estonian actor Märt Avandi, it was a genuinely enjoyable celebration of the many achievements of European cinema over the course of the last year.

Samuel Maoz (European Discovery for **Lebanon***). Photo: Scanpix Baltics/Karli Saul*

The big winner was Roman Polanski, appearing via Skype (a fitting form, since it's an Estonian invention), who walked away with European Film, European Director and European Screenplay for *The Ghost Writer*. Whilst there was consternation from some quarters that the film was closer to the Hollywood fare that the EFA tries to distance itself from, there was a general air of triumph that after so much notoriety over the past year Polanski had come up trumps once again. Other big winners included *Lebanon*, whose tense, claustrophobic and deeply personal story won director Samuel Maoz the Best Newcomer Award (a prize that caused him to remark that film may be the only business in which you can be a newcomer when you're approaching 50).

Indeed the night seemed to be very much a celebration of both the old and new guard of European cinema. Young talents currently taking part in the Shooting Stars initiative (such as Agata Buzek who is attracting rave reviews for her performance in *Rewers*) took their place alongside the likes of Bruno Ganz, who received the lifetime achievement award, an opportunity for director Wim Wenders to tell the story of Ganz and Dennis Hopper fighting on the set of *The American Friend*.

As was proven by the evening, the awards, and the European Film Academy, provide an important focal point for the European film industry.
– *Laurence Boyce*

For more on the European Film Academy, go to: http://www.europeanfilmacademy.org/

Sheffield Moves to June

One of the most important events in the British film calendar, Sheffield Doc/Fest will move dates to June from 2011. Previously hosted in November, the festival will welcome directors, industry delegates and audiences to a much warmer climate in future. Steve Hewlett, Chair of the festival commented, 'Sheffield Doc/Fest has undergone something of a sea-change in the last four years since Heather Croall became Festival Director. The stats are remarkable – up from 500 delegates in 2006 to nearly 2000 in 2009 and €10.5 m of deals negotiated at MeetMarket last year. But with a pile-up of European documentary festivals in the autumn, so after much consideration we've decided to move to June. This move will allow more inventive programming, more public outreach and allow us to improve our offering, and enable us to work more effectively with other creative organisations in Sheffield. We'll also be announcing a couple of important partnerships with international documentary organisations in the coming weeks. Britain is the home of documentary film and Sheffield Doc/Fest will take its place among the best documentary festivals in the world.'

Last year's festival saw 19 world, 8 European and 45 UK premieres from 45 countries,

Sheffield Doc/Fest 2010 © pixeldavephotography.co.uk

in addition to its successful MeetMarket, which was introduced in 2006 and attracts a high number of attendees, from all areas of the film industry. Together, the events and screenings, as well as many discussions and social events, provide a platform that has made Doc/Fest one of the essential European festivals for documentary and non-fiction film. As Artistic Director Heather Croall states, 'the thing people love about Sheffield Doc/Fest is its boutique feel and the fact that it's very democratic. People come here knowing they will meet the right people, see the best new docs, and if they're in MeetMarket, make a deal. I'm very excited about moving to June – it'll bring some new and exciting developments to the festival – watch this space!'

The 2011 Sheffield Doc/Fest runs from 8-12 June. For more information, go to: www.sheffdocfest.com

Edinburgh Receives a Facelift

Following the departure of Artistic Director Hannah McGill and silence over her successor, the Edinburgh Film Festival announced a radical makeover for the June event, which will see it move away from the conventional structure of a competitive festival and more towards a curatorial programme. Instead of the one director, there will be three: Mark Cousins, who oversaw two editions of the festival in the 1990s, actress Tilda Swinton, and another former director of the festival, Lynda Myles.

Tilda Swinton and Mark Cousins who, along with a Lynda Myles, will be heading up EIFF 2011.

Cousins described the move as 'probably the most radical shakeup the festival has had'. This new direction is likely to break out of the confines of the conventional festival, employing many of the spaces used in August, when the city comes alive with its theatre, music and performances festivals, to offer audiences a potentially unique experience. Or, as Cousins describes it, 'We want this to be a kind of Meltdown [referring to the prestigious London festival that each year is curated by a major artist, from David Bowie and Ornette Coleman to Patti Smith and Nick Cave] meets the Venice Biennale'.

The festival will be produced by James Mullighan, who has successfully overseen the growth of Shooting People, a major international network for independent filmmakers, for the last few years.

The 2011 edition of the Edinburgh Film Festival runs from 15-26 June. For more information, go to: www.edfilmfest.org.uk/

*Brian Cox and director Dagur Kariu on the red carpet for **The Good Heart** at Cineworld. Photo: Edinburgh International Film Festival 2010*

Digital Festival Report

Power To the Pixel 2010

Digital Filmmaking Today:
Changing the Way Stories Are Told

The message at this year's Power to the Pixel – the annual showcase for leading filmmakers, innovators and entrepreneurs in the area of digital film – came across loud and clear. A huge paradigm shift is sweeping the world, and the way that audiences are accessing and consuming media is totally changing. For the majority of younger audiences, the change has already happened. Not only are they increasingly moving from one platform to the next in a matter of seconds, they expect their content to do the same. In this respect, they're rather more ahead of the game than the content creators; most media businesses, according to organiser Liz Rosenthal, are still using single platforms and creating linear content. If they want to continue to engage new audiences, they're going to have to shift the scope and style of their storytelling.

The goal of the 4-day event, was to demystify what's actually happening, right down to understanding the words and concepts flowing from the horses mouths of the leading practitioners in the field – transmodia, oross platform, new digital media.

One of the most interesting speakers of the day was Michel Reilhac, Executive Director of ARTE France Cinéma, who gave the keynote address. Change will only truly come, he argued, when transmedia moves 'from marketing gimmick to fully-fledged art form'. Several filmmakers who were present are

already treating it as such. Lance Weiler, for example, named by WIRED as one of '25 people helping to re-invent entertainment and change the face of Hollywood', has a new project, *HiM*, which is the first transmedia project to be supported by the Sundance film lab. He refers to himself as a 'story architect' as opposed to a filmmaker, and asks himself three questions when considering a new project. The first – what is the story I want to tell? – is pretty traditional. The second and third, however, are less orthodox, signalling the sea-change Rosenthal spoke of: how will I deliver the story, and what kind of audience participation do I want or need?

Writer Maureen McHugh (No Mimes Media), another speaker and transmedia trailblazer, defined it as an omniverous artform, absorbing platforms and 'eating us all'. But at the moment she believes it's a naïve artform (about 12 years old, she estimated, citing *The Blair Witch Project* as the starting point), for which we don't yet have the right conventions. Right now, transmedia projects are copying older artforms, such as videogames and film, but in the future creators will have to start

Maureen McHugh of No Mimes Media

defining those new conventions or become increasingly marginalised.

This shift in the mode of storytelling was evidenced in the projects pitched in The Pixel Market, a global event, where 18 cross-media projects were culled from 23 countries, 9 of them pitching to win the Arte Pixel Pitch Prize of GBP6,000. One of the general concerns raised throughout the conference was that transmedia at the moment was encouraging certain types of stories, yet the projects pitching this year ranged a wide variety of genres, from thrillers and sci-fi, to love stories, rites of passage tales and documentaries. This breadth was a sign, Reilhac argued, that the field was maturing. The winning project, *Granny's Dancing on the Table* – a coming-of-age fairytale spanning film, gaming, live events, interactive and publishing – came from Sweden's Helene Granqvist of Good Film and Hanna Sköld of Tangram Films.

But what of funding in this brave new world?

Helene Granqvist and Hanna Sköld's **Granny's Dancing on the Table**

For research and development, production or marketing? Reilhac argued that 'there is no new money, only new money that needs to be educated into new uses.' And big studios already have departments dedicated to digital content. Although they aren't ploughing anything like as much money in to their projects as their other departments, they're certainly starting to. One of the success stories, the world's first online dance adventure, *The Legion of Extraordinary Dancers*, was presented as a case study by Keith Quinn, Senior Vice President of Paramount Digital Entertainment.

Of particular use for anyone wanting to learn

The first online dance adventure, **The Legion of Extraordinary Dancers**

more about the topics discussed at the event, Power to the Pixel announced the launch of its new website, The Pixel Report. Devoted to showcasing new forms of storytelling, filmmaking and cross-media business development that is in tune with an audience-centred digital era, it's an essential tool for content creators, a resource for policy-makers and funding bodies, and a unique guide for the future of film and media. The website is edited by Liz Rosenthal and Tishna Molla, who have teamed with Michael Gubbins (previously of Screen International and Screendaily.com). More info at: www.thepixelreport.org

HANNAH PATTERSON is a freelance film journalist, commissioning editor of Kamera Books and associate editor of Kamera.co.uk. She also writes for theatre and film, and works as a documentary producer.

IFG Inspiration Award Winners

Created in 2008 in order to celebrate the work of new and promising directors, the IFG Inspiration Award is the result of IFG-Festival partnerships. It is designed to provide emerging filmmakers at the start of their careers with the opportunity to promote themselves and their work. The prize is often awarded by the main jury, or the judges of a section that focuses on first-time directors. The winning filmmakers are featured in the following year's guide and also receive coverage on the IFG website. As they progress on to their follow-up films, the IFG will continue its coverage of them, creating an international network of filmmakers.

First Squad Wins at Fantasporto

Yoshiharu Ashino's **First Squad**

Directed by Yoshiharu Ashino and based on a story by Aljosha Klimov and Misha Shprits, **First Squad** (*Fâsuto sukuwaddo*) is a fascinating blend of documentary and anime, shot through with a strong influence of Soviet constructivist design. Taking as its starting point the archival evidence of both Nazi and Soviet forces's interest in the occult during the Second World War, the film tells of a small band of Russian youths attuned to psychic spirits and who are trained in the battle against Hitler's invading forces. When her comrades are killed in an aerial attack, Nadya must travel into the underworld to bring them back, before the evil Baron Von Wolff, a mythical German warrior resurrected by Himmler, routs the Russian front line. The scene is thus set for a thrilling climax, which blends medieval swordplay with the machinery of modern warfare.

The action is intercuut with a series of interviews interviews with survivors from the war and experts in the fields of military history and tthe paranormal. The result, whether you buy into the mythmaking or just see the film as another example of ambitious animation, is a unique film, whose narrative ingenuity is matched by its strong visual style, particularly in the stunning opening sequence, which confirms Ashino as a major new talent in animation.

The Other Bank Wins at Cape Winelands

George Ovashili's **The Other Bank**

George Ovashili's **The Other Bank** continues the long tradition of anti-war films, with the impact of the Georgian-Abkhazian conflict seen from a child's point of view. Tedo Bekhauri gives a powerful central performance as a young boy who decides to set out through the devastated Georgian landscape in search of his father. Along the way, he encounters a society brutalised and worn down by conflict, but is also witness to acts of charity and kindness.

Ovashili's powerful drama is startling not only for its power, but as a bold and visionary film from a first-time filmmaker. In awarding Ovashili, who has already received prizes from festivals from around the world, the Jury commented, 'This remarkable film offers a fresh perspective on the struggle people face in countries torn apart by conflict and civil strife... *The Other Bank* is an emotionally powerful work that balances an intimate story within a large canvas to devastating effect.'

If I Want to Whistle, I Whistle Wins at Zlin

The Inspiration Award was the main prize of the European Debuts section of Zlin International Film Festival for Children and Youth hosted. The winner was Florin Serban's prison drama, **If I Want to Whistle, I Whistle**, which not only revealed a new voice in European cinema, it exemplified the essence of the European Debuts section.

Silviu has only a few weeks remaining before his release, when he is visited by his younger brother, who informs him that he is to return to

Italy with his wayward mother. Fearing for the boy's future, Silviu decides on drastic action in order to change his mother's mind. In doing so, he places his own future and those around him at risk.

With its controlled direction and performances by non-professional actors, many of whom were inmates at the time, Serban has produced a powerful portrait of institutional life, which ranks alongside the work of British

Michelangelo Frammartino's **Le Quattro Volte**

director Alan Clarke (*Scum*) and is reminiscent of the films of Luc and Jean-Pierre Dardennes in its portrayal of the brutal realities of life.

Le Quattro Volte Wins at Era New Horizons

In a festival dominated by striking and original features, the main Jury of Era New Horizons awarded the IFG Inspiration Award to Michelangelo Frammartino's **Le Quattro Volte**. A rich and lyrical film, it presents the cycle of life through four stages; the last days of an elderly man; a billy kid's short existence; a tree's final stages; and the embers of the tree, as they turn to smoke and enter the air we all breathe. Through this elliptical narrative, Frammartino draws out the humour of everyday life (aided in no small part by a dog's comic turn in one of the film"s lighter moments) and explores the nature of existence, be it human, plant or animal.

Like Frammartino's debut, *The Gift, La Quattro*

Florin Serban's **If I Want to Whistle, I Whistle**

Volte features no dialogue, relying instead on the director's skill as a visual storyteller to communicate his themes. The result is a riveting and deeply moving film, whose unwillingness to play up to any convention marks the film out as one of the year's most striking and bold works.

Tilva Rosh Wins at Cottbus

The jury at this year's Film Festival Cottbus awarded the International Film Guide Inspiration Award to Nikola Lezaic for his feature debut, **Tilva Rosh**, which examines the lives of a group of youths living in one of Serbia's most industrial towns.

A shadow of its former self, Bor was once the epicentre of the Serbian copper mining industry. It is now a depressed area, where jobs are hard to find and the local populace has

Nikola Lezaic's **Tilva Rosh**

been overlooked. Tod and Stefan spend most of their time recreating Jackass-style stunts on video (the footage was shot by Bor locals). When their old friend Dunja arrives back from France for the holidays, the two boys jostle for her attention, their determination to win her affection threatening their friendship.

An astutely observed coming-of-age film, where the young men realise that they are no longer boys and have no choice to grow up, Lezaic expertly captures the pitfalls of the adult world, where idealism and hope no longer seem to have a place.

Festival Director Profile

Olivier Père –
Locarno Film Festival

This year saw a more streamlined Locarno Film Festival, which began the tenure of newly appointed Artistic Director, Olivier Père. Formerly the head of Cannes' prestigious Directors Fortnight, the announcement of his appointment was commented on by the festival's President, Marco Solari, as a natural choice as he had 'spent years heading up a section that is closest to the nature of the Locarno Festival, which has always focused on young cinema, discovery and experimentation.'

Oliver Père's first decision was to overhaul the programme structure, placing emphasis on the two main competitive strands, the International Competition and Filmmakers of Tomorrow, each with 18 entries. This freed up the festival to 'pay attention to the identity and history of Locarno, being a place of discovery for new directors, new films.'

One of the festival's most popular features, the nightly outdoor screenings on the Piazza Grande, which play before an audience of

8,000, remained a hub for 'more mainstream and popular films, pitched at the right level for the piazza'.

Away from general audiences, the three-day event, Industry Days, was launched. It was a chance for buyers to watch films screening on the Piazza Grande and in the two competition strands in advance, as well as workshops and round-table events, organised by the festival's industry Office. It's aim, as Olivier Père commented, was to 'provide Locarno with an additional asset as a platform for professional networking and a meeting place for the independent film industry'.

The resulting festival was an outstanding success. 'We managed to breathe new life into the Festival,' commented Père, 'with a more audacious selection, eclectic choices that represent an opening to more popular genres and an even greater curiosity towards all forms of cinema.'

And what of the future? According to Père, 'Next year we'll follow this dynamic policy of the Festival del film Locarno, with the objective of consolidating its position as the essential rendezvous for worldwide independent cinema and for new, young directors… Our goals are to invite important figures in contemporary film, to develop the meeting between the public and artists, and to persuade professionals that Locarno is able to play an important role in the discovery and launching of ambitious cinematographic oeuvres. It is in this direction that we are going to pursue our work, both through international communication and the Festival's organisation, making it more welcoming and exciting.'

64°
Festival del film
Locarno
3–13 | 8 | 2011

www.pardo.ch

Main sponsors:

UBS æt MANOR° swisscom

Luciano Barisone –
Visions du Réel

Luciano Barisone has been appointed the Director of Nyon's prestigious Visions du Réel Festival of documentary and non-fiction film. Replacing Jean Perret, who had been in charge since 1995, Barisone arrives after successfully steering Florence's Festival dei Popoli since 2008. A Genoa-born journalist and film critic, he worked for a number of film festivals, including Bergamo Film Meeting, Festival du Film d'Amour of Mons, Torino Film Festival, FID Marseille, Locarno International Film Festival, Festival of La Rochelle, Venice Film Festival and DocLisboa, prior to launching Alba's Infinity Festival in 2002.

The role of documentary and non-fiction film is of central importance to cinema, as far as the new director is concerned. As he replied to a question about his thoughts on the role of documentary, 'For me [it] is cinema, nothing else: I could say, as Godard did, the truth 24 times per second. It's a look at the world, a narrative structure, a form of art. Not simply an act of information. The subject is important but not the most important thing. What is important is the way this subject is elaborated, the shape it takes at the end of a long process of observation, dealing with people and waiting for the unexpected, edited according to the an inside rhythm, a mental music, an inner sense of time and space. But cinema is not only a form. It's also something ethical, something that has to connect a personal point of view with a special respect

for the people, those who are in front of the camera but also those who will watch the films.' As for the increasing prominence of non-fiction film over the last decade, his answer is simple, it is 'a lack of imagination of fiction cinema. I think that many filmmakers are going back to the sources of cinema in order to find through the observation of the reality a sort of a new inspiration that could make up for this lack.'

As for his new role, it is a festival he has known for some time: 'Visions du Réel was the natural continuation of a professional career that was more and more deeply involved in the so called non-fiction cinema. I have known the festival since 1998, when I began to look for films in order to recommend them to other festivals or to select them for my own festival. I always considered Visions du Réel a perfect meeting point, where you could watch very good films, meet directors, producers, commissioning editors, international film sellers and buyers, and at the same time witness a very selective market place, with a good catalogue and a very good platform to pitch new projects.'

The 2011 edition will continue many of the strands that have been in place over the course of the last two decades, as well as branching out, creating a more interconnected festival and one that has strong appeal for audiences, press and industry delegates alike. His goal is 'to create a programme where the film selected could be linked all together in an organic way. I would like to have not only the best non-fiction films of this moment of the year, in world, international or European premiere, but also a sort of a net between them. My idea of the festival is a sort of living installation where the locations of the festival, the audience, the films, the filmmakers, the producers and all the other professionals could live together for a week in the most harmonious way possible.' And placing the audience at the heart of this is central to the new director's vision.

By casting a wider net, Barisone is looking to increase audience attendance and industry presence for the 17th edition, offering a mix of screenings, interviews, debates and masterclasses, that is hoped to generate the same degree of cinéphilia around documentary and non-fiction films that exists for fictional features. In addition to this, the Doc Outlook-International Market will be expanded, offering a new approach to pitching and building links between delegates from all corners of the world.

Those attending the next edition of Visions du Réel will also discover that the presence of a new director is not the only physical change. 'This year you will find quite a lot of changes. Firstly, technical changes (HD in some venues and all films will be screened with English and French subtitles), as well as changes of location. The centre of the festival will be around the Salle Communale, with a large covered area intended for catering and public meetings, with free wi-fi access. The other venues will be the multiplex Capitol, the Usine à Gaz and the Marens Theatre. The Doc Outlook-International Market will be located in the Colombière Theatre.'

In addition to the three strands that make up the **Compétition Internationale**, which features world, international and European premieres, with a special consideration given to first and second films by young directors, the festival will also feature: **Helvétiques**, which includes out-of-competition, world, international and European premieres; the best in world production premiered in Switzerland, in the **État d'esprit** section; short film premieres in **Premiers Pas**; **Atelier(s)**, which celebrates the work of important and distinctive filmmakers (in 2011, it will be Spanish filmmaker José Luis Guerin and the American filmmaker Jay Rosenblatt); and **Séances Spéciales**, which identifies the work of important young filmmakers, will highlight the work of Marilia Rocha from Brazil and Giovanni Cioni from Italy, and include focus discussions on non-

fiction film production in Colombia. A final strand, **Port Franc**, which discusses major issues of the day facing non-fiction film, will in 2011 be presented under the theme *The Trace*.

The last 16 editions of Visions du Réel have cemented its position as one of Europe's most vital platforms for documentary and non-fiction film. Beyond its role as a showcase for new films and as-yet-undiscovered talent, as well as discussions and interviews with established filmmakers, the festival has reached out to engage with issues that are not only important in the development of cinema, but in the way we live our lives. Luciano Barisone's vision of how the Visions du Réel will develop in the future guarantees that this mission will continue.

Visions du Réel 2011 takes place from 7-13 April. For more information, go to: www. visionsdureel.ch/en.

Film Festivals Calendar

January

Dhaka International Film Festival	p. 395
Future Film Festival	p. 398
Göteborg International Film Festival	p. 343
International Film Festival Rotterdam	p. 367
Palm Springs International Film Festival	p. 364
Santa Barbara International Film Festival	p. 405
Slamdance Film Festival	p. 374
Solothurn Film Festival	p. 375
Sundance Film Festival	p. 376
Trieste Film Festival	p. 409
Tromsø International Film Festival	p. 383

February

Berlin-Internationale Filmfestspiele Berlin	p. 320
Big Sky Documentary Film Festival	p. 393
Cartagena International Film Festival	p. 323
Cinequest	p. 394
Clermont-Ferrand Short Film Festival	p. 324
Fajr International Film Festival	p. 335
Fantasporto	p. 337
Glasgow Film Festival	p. 399
Hungarian Film Week	p. 401
Iranian Intl. Market for Films and TV Programmes	p. 335
Jameson Dublin International Film Festival	p. 402
Portland International Film Festival	p. 365
Victoria Independent Film & Video Festival	p. 387
ZagrebDox	p. 410

March

Anima: Brussels Animation Film Festival	p. 392
Ann Arbor Film Festival	p. 392
Bermuda International Film Festival	p. 393
Bradford International Film Festival	p. 394
Buff Film Festival	p. 321
Cape Winelands Film Festival	p. 323
Cinéma du Réel	p. 360
Cleveland International Film Festival	p. 394
Early Melons Intl. Student Film Festival	p. 395
Fribourg International Film Festival	p. 340

Guadalajara International Film Festival	p. 400
Hong Kong International Film Festival	p. 347
Intl. Film Fest. & Forum on Human Rights	p. 348
Israel Film Festival (New York)	p. 402
Málaga Film Festival	p. 357
Miami International Film Festival	p. 358
New Directors/New Films	p. 404
Palm Beach International Film Festival	p. 404
Sofia International Film Festival	p. 406
South by Southwest Film Festival	p. 375
Tampere Film Festival	p. 380
Thessaloniki Documentary Festival	p. 381
True/False Film Festival	p. 409
Vilnius International Film Festival	p. 409

April

Brussels Intl. Festival of Fantastic Film	p. 394
Buenos Aires Intl. Independent Film Fest.	p. 321
Chicago Latino Film Festival	p. 394
CPH:PIX	p. 326
Crossing Europe Film Festival Linz	p. 395
Crossroads Film Festival	p. 329
East End Film Festival (EEFF)	p. 396
European Independent Film Festival	p. 397
Far East Film Festival	p. 339
Festival International du Film de Boulogne-Billancourt	p. 397
Filmfest Dresden	p. 397
Florida Film Festival	p. 398
Full Frame Documentary Film Festival	p. 398
Glimmer: Hull Intl. Short Film Festival	p. 399
goEast Festival of Central and Eastern European Film	p. 342
Hotdocs Canadian Intl. Doc Film Festival	p. 401
Istanbul International Film Festival	p. 351
Las Palmas de Gran Canaria Intl. Film Fest.	p. 354
Mipdoc	p. 403
Visions du Réel Intl. Film Festival - Nyon	p. 360
San Sebastian Human Rights Film Festival	p. 405
San Francisco International Film Festival	p. 367
Sarasota Film Festival	p. 406
Stockholm Intl. Film Festival Junior	p. 406

Tribeca Film Festival — p. 383
USA Film Festival — p. 409
Valencia Intl. Action & Adventure Film Fest. — p. 384
Viewfinders Intl. Film Festival for Youth — p. 409
Washington, DC International Film Festival — p. 410

May

Cannes International Film Festival — p. 322
International Film Festival Innsbruck — p. 401
Israel Film Festival (Miami) — p. 402
Krakow Film Festival — p. 354
Oberhausen Intl. Short Film Festival — p. 362
Seattle International Film Festival — p. 369
Stuttgart Festival of Animated Film — p. 407
Zlin Intl. Film Festival for Children & Youth — p. 388

June

Annecy/Intl. Animated Film Festival — p. 392
Cambofest — p. 394
Cinema Jove International Film Festival — p. 394
Edinburgh International Film Festival — p. 331
Emden International Film Festival — p. 396
Filmfest München — p. 398
Huesca Film Festival — p. 401
Los Angeles Film Festival — p. 357
Midnight Sun Film Festival — p. 403
Moscow International Film Festival — p. 359
Palm Springs Intl. Festival of Short Films — p. 404
Pesaro Film Festival — p. 364
St Petersburg International Film Festival — p. 405
Shanghai International Film Festival — p. 371
Sheffield Doc/Fest — p. 372
Silverdocs: AFI/Discovery Channel Doc. Fest — p. 373
Singapore International Film Festival — p. 374
Sunny Side of the Doc — p. 407
Sydney Film Festival — p. 407
Taormina Film Festival in Sicily — p. 407
Transilvania Intl. Film Festival Cluj-Napoca — p. 409

July

Divercine — p. 395
Durban International Film Festival — p. 395
Era New Horizons Intl. Film Festival — p. 332
Guanajuato International Film Festival
    Expresión en Corto — p. 400
FID Marseille — p. 397
Galway Film Fleadh — p. 399
Giffoni Intl. Film Fest. (Giffoni Experience) — p. 342
Golden Apricot International Film Festival — p. 399
Jerusalem International Film Festival — p. 351

Karlovy Vary International Film Festival — p. 353
La Rochelle International Film Festival — p. 354
Melbourne International Film Festival — p. 358
New Zealand Intl. Film Festival (Auckland) — p. 360
New Zealand Intl. Film Festival (Wellington) — p. 360
Sarajevo Film Festival — p. 405
Vila do Conde — p. 409

August

Espoo Ciné International Film Festival — p. 334
Haugesund - Norwegian Intl. Film Festival — p. 345
Festival del film Locarno — p. 355
Montreal World Film Festival — p. 358
Odense International Film Festival — p. 363
Open Air Filmfest Weiterstadt — p. 404
Venice International Film Festival — p. 386

September

Aspen Filmfest & Shortsfest — p. 392
Atlantic Film Festival — p. 392
Bogotá Film Festival — p. 393
Boston Film Festival — p. 393
Buster Film Festival — p. 326
Edmonton International Film Festival — p. 396
Festival Intl. Du Film Francophone de Namur — p. 397
Filmfest Hamburg — p. 398
Helsinki International Film Festival -
    Love & Anarchy — p. 346
Independent Film Week — p. 348
Kaunas International Film Festival — p. 402
Lucas International Children's Film Festival — p. 403
Napa/Sonoma Wine Country Film Festival — p. 403
Netherlands Film Festival, Utrecht — p. 359
New York Film Festival — p. 404
Raindance Film Festival — p. 366
Reykjavik International Film Festival — p. 366
San Sebastian International Film Festival — p. 368
Silent Film Days in Tromsø — p. 406
Telluride Film Festival — p. 380
Toronto International Film Festival — p. 382
Vancouver International Film Festival — p. 386
Zurich Film Festival — p. 410

October

Abu Dhabi Film Festival — p. 317
American Film Festival (AFF) — p. 391
Augsburg Children's Film Festival — p. 393
Austin Film Festival & Conference — p. 319
Banff Mountain Film Festival — p. 393
Bergen International Film Festival — p. 320

Chicago International Film Festival	p. 323	St George Bank Brisbane Intl. Film Festival	p. 321
Chicago Intl. Children's Film Festival	p. 394	CPH:Dox	p. 326
Cinekid Festival	p. 324	Cairo International Film Festival	p. 322
Cyprus International Film Festival	p. 395	Cambofest	p. 394
Doclisboa	p. 395	Cinéma Tous Ecrans	p. 324
Doha Tribeca Film Festival	p. 395	Coca-Cola Cinemagic International Film	
Festival du Cinema International		and TV Festival	p. 325
en Abitibi-Temscamingue	p. 397	Cork Film Festival	p. 327
Festival du Nouveau Cinema - Montreal	p. 397	European Film Forum Scanorama	p. 396
Films from the South (FFS)	p. 398	FilmFestival Cottbus	p. 328
Ghent International Film Festival	p. 341	Festival Dei Popoli	p. 397
Fort Lauderdale International Film Festival	p. 340	Festival Des 3 Continents	p. 340
Haifa International Film Festival	p. 400	Fredrikstad Animation Festival	p. 398
Hamedan International Festival of Films		Gijón International Film Festival	p. 342
for Children and Young Adults	p. 344	Holland Animation Film Festival	p. 401
Hof International Film Festival	p. 346	Huelva Latin American Film Festival	p. 348
Hawaii International Film Festival	p. 400	International Film Festival India	p. 349
Heartland Film Festival	p. 401	Intl. Short Film Festival Winterthur	p. 350
Intl. Leipzig Fest. - Doc. & Animated Film	p. 401	Leeds International Film Festival	p. 355
Israel Film Festival (Los Angeles)	p. 402	Ljubljana International Film Festival	p. 402
Jihlava Intl. Documentary Film Festival	p. 402	London Turkish Film Festival	p. 402
BFI London Film Festival	p. 356	Intl. Filmfestival Mannheim–Heidelberg	p. 357
Mill Valley Film Festival	p. 358	Mar del Plata International Film Festival	p. 357
Molodist - Kiev International Film Festival	p. 403	Margaret Mead Film & Video Festival	p. 403
Montpellier Intl. Fest. of Mediterranean Film	p. 403	Oulu Intl. Children's & Youth Film Festival	p. 363
Mumbai Film Festival	p. 403	St Louis International Film Festival	p. 405
Philadelphia International Film Festival	p. 405	Seville European Film Festival	p. 369
Pordenone Silent Film Festival	p. 365	Starz Denver Film Festival	p. 330
Pusan International Film Festival (PIFF)	p. 366	Stockholm International Film Festival	p. 376
Ravenna Nightmare Film Festival	p. 405	Taipei Golden Horse Film Festival	p. 407
Rome International Film Festival	p. 367	Tallinn Black Nights Film Festival	p. 377
San Sebastian Horror & Fantasy Film Fest.	p. 405	Thessaloniki International Film Festival	p. 381
Sitges Intl. Fantastic Film Fest. of Catalonia	p. 374	Torino Film Festival	p. 382
Tibet Film Festival	p. 408		
Tokyo International Film Festival	p. 382		
Uppsala International Short Film Festival	p. 409		
Valladolid International Film Festival	p. 385		
Viennale - Vienna International Film Festival	p. 387		

November

American Film Market	p. 318
Amiens International Film Festival	p. 318
Amsterdam International Documentary	
Film Festival - (IDFA)	p. 319

December

Almería Intl. Short Film Festival	p. 391
Dubai International Film Festival	p. 331
Intl. Fest. of New Latin American Cinema	p. 401
International Film Festival of Kerala	p. 401
River to River: Florence Indian Film Fest.	p. 405
Third Eye Asian Film Festival	p. 407

Leading Festivals

Abu Dhabi Film Festival
October 13-22, 2011

The Abu Dhabi Film Festival (formerly the Middle East International Film Festival) was established in 2007 with the aim of helping to create a vibrant film culture throughout the region. Presented each October by the Abu Dhabi Authority for Culture and Heritage (ADACH), the Festival is committed to curating exceptional programmes to engage and educate the local community, inspire filmmakers and nurture the growth of the regional film industry. With its commitment to presenting works by Arab filmmakers in competition alongside those by major talents of world cinema, the Festival offers Abu Dhabi's diverse and enthusiastic audiences a means of engaging with their own and others' cultures through the art of cinema. At the same time, a strong focus on the bold new voices of Arab cinema connects with Abu Dhabi's role as a burgeoning cultural capital in the region and marks the Festival as a place for the world to discover and gauge the pulse of recent Arab filmmaking. *Inquiries to:* Abu Dhabi Film Festival, PO Box 2380, Abu Dhabi, UAE. Tel: (971 2) 556 4000. e: contact@adff.ae. Web: www.abudhabifilmfestival.ae.

AWARDS 2010
Narrative Feature Competition
Black Pearl Award for Best Narrative Film:
Silent Souls (Russia), Aleksei Fedorchenko.
Black Pearl Award for Best Narrative Film from the Arab World: **Here Comes the Rain** (Lebanon), Bahij Hojeij.
Black Pearl Award for Best Actor: Andrew Garfield in **Never Let Me Go** (UK/USA).
Black Pearl Award for Best Actress: Lubna Azabal in **Incendies** (Canada/France).

Peter Scarlet, Executive Director of the Abu Dhabi Film Festival

Jury Special Mention: **Carlos** (France/Germany), Olivier Assayas.
Documentary Feature Competition Black Pearl Award for Best Documentary Film: Shared by **Nostalgia for the Light** (Chile/Germany/France), Patricio Guzmán and **Pink Saris** (India/UK), Kim Longinotto.
Black Pearl Award for Best Documentary by an Arab Director or Related to Arab Culture: Shared by **Homeland** (Netherlands), George Sluizer and **We Were Communists** (France/Lebanon/United Arab Emirates), Maher Abi Samra.
Jury Special Mentions: **Tears of Gaza** (Norway), Vibeke Løkkeberg and **How Bitter My Sweet!** (Lebanon), Mohamed Soueid.
New Horizons/Afaq Jadida Competition
Best Narrative Film by a New Director: **Gesher** (Iran), Vahid Vakilifar.

Best Narrative Film by a New Director from the Arab World: **OK, Enough, Goodbye** (Lebanon/United Arab Emirates), Rania Attieh and Daniel Garcia.

Best Documentary by a New Director: Shared by **El Ambulante** (Argentina), Eduardo de la Serna, Lucas Marcheggiano and Adriana Yurcovich; **Bill Cunningham New York** (USA), Richard Press.

Best Documentary by a New Director from the Arab World: Jury Special Mention to **Living Skin** (Egypt), Fawzi Saleh.

Abu Dhabi Film Festival Audience Choice Award: **West is West** (UK), Andy De Emmony.

ADFF NETPAC Award: **Zephyr** (Turkey), Belma Bas.

Report 2010

The recently renamed Abu Dhabi Film Festival celebrated an outstanding fourth edition, featuring a selection of 171 films from 43 countries and a variety of events, which attracted tens of thousands of festival goers – marked by a 31% increase in ticket sales – and more than 1,200 film industry professionals. New to the programme for 2010 were the **Afaq Jadida (New Horizons) Competition** for first and second-time directors from around the world, and the **Emirates Competition** for short films from the UAE and other Gulf nations – a further extension of ADFF's commitment to fostering a vibrant film culture in the region. Additionally, the Festival featured a *Showcase* of outstanding recent world cinema, screened out of competition, a programme in conjunction with New York's Museum of Modern Art focusing on experimentation in Arab cinema from the 1960s to the present, and special screenings of the restored classics *Metropolis* and Charlie Chaplin's *The Circus*. The **What in the World Are We Doing to Our World?** section also returned to focus on environmental issues. An important first for ADFF this year was SANAD, a development and post–production fund, which provides talented filmmakers from the Arab world with support for feature-length documentary and narrative films. Each year, ADFF is committed to showing projects supported by SANAD and

this year marked the inaugural SANAD FilmLab, which offers SANAD grant recipients with the opportunity to participate in script writing and pitching workshops, as well as one to one meetings and training sessions with industry experts. Among the festival's many guests were Adrien Brody, Freida Pinto, Jonathan Rhys–Meyers, Julianne Moore, Khaled Abol Naga, Clive Owen, Gérard Depardieu, Om Puri, Uma Thurman, Yehia el Fakharany and Yosra. **– Utkarsh Talati**, Advertising & Media Coordinator.

American Film Market
November 2-9, 2011

The business of independent motion picture production and distribution – a truly collaborative process – reaches its peak every year at the American Film Market. Over 8,000 leaders in motion picture production and distribution – acquisition and development executives, agents, attorneys, directors, financiers, film commissioners, producers and writers – converge in Santa Monica for eight days of screenings, deal-making and hospitality. The AFM plays a vital role in global production and finance. Each year, hundreds of films are financed, packaged, licensed and green lit, sealing over $800 million in business for both completed films and those in pre-production. With the AFM-AFI FEST alliance, attendees capitalise on the only festival-market combination in North America. *Inquiries to:* 10850 Wilshire Blvd, 9th Floor, Los Angeles, CA 90024–4311, USA. Tel: (1 310) 446 1000. e: afm@ifta-online.org. Web: www.americanfilmmarket.com.

Amiens International Film Festival
November 11-20, 2011

A competitive festival in northern France for shorts, features, animation and documentaries. Also retrospectives, tributes and the 'Le monde comme il va' series, which includes works from Africa, Latin America and Asia. 'Europe, Europes' presents new works from Young European Talents (Shorts,

Documentaries and Animation). *Inquiries to:* Amiens International Film Festival, MCA, Place Léon Gontier, 80000 Amiens, France. Tel: (33 3) 2271 3570. e: contact@filmfestamiens.org. Web: www.filmfestamiens.org.

Amsterdam-International Documentary Film Festival (IDFA)
November 16-27, 2011

The world's largest documentary festival, built up over 23 years, IDFA 2010 opened with Leonard Retel Helmrich's *Position Among the Stars*, the third part of his trilogy on a family in Indonesia. Over the following 11 days, IDFA screened 304 documentaries and sold over 180,000 tickets. Aside of the regular sections, IDFA featured several competition programmes. The major winner of the 2010 festival was the opening film, *Position Among the Stars*, by Leonard Retel Helmrich, which won both the VPRO IDFA Award for Best Feature-Length Documentary and the Dioraphte IDFA Award for Dutch Documentary. In addition to the screenings, there were daily talk shows, debates and two masterclasses, by Leonard Retel Helmrich and Finnish director Pirjo Honkasalo, who was responsible for this year's Top 10. IDFA has two markets: the FORUM, a market for international co–financing; and Docs for Sale, which stimulates the sales and distribution of creative documentaries. From December 2008, Docs for Sale also boasts an online marketplace where new as well as older documentaries can be viewed all year long. Docs for Sale Online is a place where sales agents and producers can show their documentaries to potential buyers and exhibitors online, even after IDFA is over. *Inquiries to:* International Documentary Film Festival–Amsterdam, Frederiksplein 52, 1017 XN Amsterdam, Netherlands. Tel: (31 20) 627 3329. e: info@idfa.nl. Web: www.idfa.nl.

AWARDS 2010
VPRO IDFA Award for Best Feature-Length Documentary: **Position Among the Stars** (Netherlands), Leonard Retel Helmrich.
Special Jury Award: **You Don't Like the Truth**

– 4 Days Inside Guantánamo (Canada), Luc Coté and Patricio Henriquez.
NTR IDFA Award for Best Mid–Length Documentary: **People I Could Have Been and Maybe Am** (Netherlands), Boris Gerrets.
IDFA Award for First Appearance: **Kano: An American and His Harem** (the Philippines), Monster Jimenez.
Diorophte IDFA Award for Dutch Documentary: **Position Among the Stars** (Netherlands), Leonard Retel Helmrich.
Publieke Omroep IDFA Audience Award: **Waste Land** (Brazil/UK), Lucy Walker.
IDFA Award for Student Documentary: **What's in a Name** (Belgium), Eva Küpper.
Hyves IDFA DOC U Award: **Autumn Gold** (Austria/Germany), Jan Tenhaven.
IDFA Award for Best Green Screen Documentary: **Into Eternity** (Denmark/Finland/ Sweden, Michael Madsen.
Honourable Mention: **The Pipe** (Republic of Ireland), Risteard Ó Domhnaill.
IDFA DocLab Award for Digital Storytelling: **Highrise/Out My Window** (Canada), Katerina Cizek.

Austin Film Festival & Conference
October 20-27, 2011

For eighteen years, the Austin Film Festival has been dedicated to celebrating the art of storytelling through film. There are four days of panels and eight days of films and parties, with networking opportunities for filmmakers, screenwriters and film-lovers alike. The conference provides over 80 inspiring and interactive panels, round tables and 'get to know you sessions' with established screenwriters and filmmakers. The festival programme shows narrative, animation and documentary features and shorts, including premieres, advanced screenings, independent films and retrospective screenings. Film screenings are complemented by lively and informative Q&A sessions with filmmakers and cast members. *Inquiries to:* Austin Film Festival, 1801 Salina Street, Austin, TX 78702, USA. Tel: (1 512) 478 4795. e: info@austinfilmfestival. com. Web: www.austinfilmfestival.com.

Bergen International Film Festival
October 19-26, 2011

Norway's beautiful capital of the fjords launches the 12th BIFF in 2011. The festival, which is the largest of the Norwegian film festivals in terms of content, has a main International Competition of about 15 films, as well as an International Documentary Competition. There's also the prestigious Checkpoints' Award, which champions subjects related to Human Rights and is awarded to the people the winning film is portraying. The documentary section makes BIFF one of the Nordic countries' largest annual documentary events. The festival has sidebars with international art house films, a Norwegian Shorts Competition, as well as premieres of the upcoming Winter and Christmas theatrical releases, thanks to extensive collaboration with Norway's distributors. It also hosts seminars and other events. *Inquiries to:* Bergen International Film Festival, Georgernes Verft 12, NO-5011 Bergen, Norway. Tel: (47) 5530 0840. e: biff@biff.no. Web: www.biff.no.

AWARDS 2010
Jury Award-Cinema Extraordinaire Competition: **Le Quattro Volte** (Italy), Michelangelo Frammartino.
Documentary Award: **The Autobiography of Nicolae Ceausescu** (Romania), Andrej Ujica.
Checkpoints Award: **Budrus** (Israel/Palestine), Julia Bacha – The prize money goes to Mr Ayed Morrar and the villagers of Budrus, Palestine.
Filmweb's Audience Award: **World Peace and Other 4th Grade Achievements** (USA), Chris Farina.
Filmweb's Talent Award: Kedy Hassani.
Youth Documentary Award: **Bogota Change** (Colombia/Denmark), Andreas Møl Dalsgaard.
Norwegian Short Film Award: **Jenny**, Ingvild Søderlind.

Berlin-Internationale Filmfestspiele Berlin
February 10-20, 2011

Interest in the Berlinale 2010, among visitors from both the film industry and the general public, has been greater than ever: 20,000 accredited visitors from 128 countries, including 4,000 journalists, attended the 60th Berlin International Film Festival. Approximately 493,000 cinemagoers attended the festival, with around 300,000 audience tickets sold. Altogether, 403 films were shown across 955 screenings. Besides the 'regular sections' (Competition, Panorama, Forum, Generation, Perspektive Deutsches Kino and Berlinale Shorts), there was the comprehensive 'Play it again…!' retrospective and the Homage to Hanna Schygulla and Wolfgang Kohlhaase, as well as the Berlinale Special and the Culinary Cinema, almost all of which were fully booked. The European Film Market and the Co–Production Market offered a wide range of prospects for industry professionals, as the Berlinale Talent Campus did for up-and-coming filmmakers. Under Jury President Werner Herzog, Francesca Comencini, Nuruddin Farah, Cornelia Froboess, José Maria Morales, Yu Nan and Renée Zellweger brought glamour, passion and expertise to the Berlinale 2010. *Inquiries to:* Internationale Filmfestspiele Berlin, Potsdamer Str 5, D–10785 Berlin, Germany. Tel: (49 30) 259 200. e: info@berlinale.de. Web: www. berlinale.de.

Photographer: Jan Eindszus © Internationale Filmfestspiele Berlinale

AWARDS 2010
Golden Bear: **Honey** (Germany/Turkey), Semih Kaplanoglu.
Jury Grand Prix Silver Bear: **If I Want to Whistle, I Whistle** (Romania/Sweden), Florin Serban.

Silver Bear for Best Director: Roman Polanski for **The Ghost Writer** (France/Germany/UK).
Silver Bear for Best Actress: Shinobu Terajima for **Caterpillar** (Japan).
Silver Bear for Best Actor Ex Aequo: Grigori Dobrygin and Sergei Puskepalis for **How I Ended This Summer** (Russian Federation).
Golden Bear for Best Short: **Incident By A Bank** (Sweden), Ruben Östund.
Silver Bear for Best Short: **The Descent** (Israel), Shai Miedzinski.

St George Bank Brisbane International Film Festival
Early November 2011

Since its inception in 1992, more than 375,000 film-goers have immersed themselves in the BIFF experience. St George Bank BIFF has become a well-renowned Australian festival, launching films like *The Full Monty*, *The Usual Suspects*, *Doing Time for Patsy Cline*, *Feeling Sexy*, *Gettin' Square*, *In America*, *A Prairie Home Companion*, *Fay Grim*, *Where in the World is Osama bin Laden?* and *An Education*. It showcases the best in world cinema, documentaries, retrospectives, late night thrillers, animation, a short film competition and much more! *Inquiries to:* St George Bank BIFF, GPO Box 15094, Brisbane City East, Queensland 4002, Australia. Tel: (61 7) 3224 4114. e: biff@biff.com.au. Web: www.stgeorgebiff.com.au.

Buenos Aires International Independent Film Festival
April 6-17, 2011

The 13th edition of BAFICI will take place in various cinemas located in different neighbourhoods of Buenos Aires. The programme will include the world premieres of feature films from Argentina, as well as foreign shorts in the official competition, retrospectives and thematic sections. Moreover, the festival offers its attendees and participants a series of special activities that connect film with other artistic disciplines: music concerts, book presentations, free outdoor films for children

(Little Bafici) and adults, workshops and business meetings such as 'Buenos Aires Lab', 'Talent Campus' and 'Industry Office'. *Inquiries to:* Buenos Aires Festival Internacional de Cine Independiente, Avenue Roque Saenz Peña 832, 6 Piso, 1035 Capital Federal, Buenos Aires, Argentina. Tel: (54 11) 4393 4670. e: prensa@bafici.gov.ar. www.bafici.gov.ar.

AWARDS 2010
International Official Selection
Best Feature Film: **Alamar** (Mexico), Pedro González-Rubio.
Special Jury Award: **La Bocca del Lupo** (Italy), Pietro Marcello.
Distinction to Best Argentine Film: **Lo Que Más Quiero** by Delfina Castagnino.
Best Director: Corneliu Poromboiu for **Police, Adjective** (Romania).
Best Actor: Dragos Bucur for **Police, Adjective** (Romania).
Best Actress: Shared by Pilar Gamboa and María Villar in **Lo Que Más Quiero** (Argentina).

BUFF Film Festival
March 15-19, 2011

The 28th edition of the annual BUFF Film Festival will take place in Malmö, Sweden in March 2011. BUFF is screening about 100 films and the screening sections are: Best Children Film Competition, Best Youth Film Competition, Short Film Competition, New Nordic Film, Panorama, School Cinema, Shorts and Pre School Film Screenings. A

Danish director Birger Larsen receiving the Achievement Award from Daniel Sandström, editor in chief at the newspaper Sydsvenskan. Photo by Magnus Grubb.

THE 28th INTERNATIONAL CHILDREN AND
YOUNG PEOPLE'S FILM FESTIVAL IN MALMÖ

≡BUFF
FILMFESTIVAL

MARCH 15-19 2011

SCREEN
Arena for young filmmakers

BUFF:FF
Financing Forum

www.buff.se

special section of the festival is SCREEN with seminars and workshops for up-and-coming filmmakers. In 2011 we will organise the fifth edition of BUFF Financing Forum including a cross media innovation hub. *Inquiries to:* BUFF - Filmfestival, PO Box 4277, SE 203 14 Malmö, Sweden. Tel: (46 40) 239211. e: info@buff.se. Web: www.buff.se.

AWARDS 2010

City of Malmö Children's Film Award: **The Indian** (The Netherlands), Ineke Houtman.
Youth People's Jury Award: **LOL – Laughing Out Loud** (France), Lisa Azuelos.
Swedish Church Award: **Vegas** (Norway), Gunnar Vikene.
County Council of Skåne Short Film Award: **The Mouse** (Denmark), Pil Maria Gunnarsson.
Sydsvenskan and BUFF Honorary Award: Birger Larsen, Director (Denmark).

Report 2010

BUFF 2010 screened 98 films. Among the feature length films, we had world premieres of *My Good Enemy* (Denmark), *When We Own the World* (Germany) and *Me and My*

Umbrella (Brazil). We presented work-in-progress sessions with upcoming films such as *A Thousand Times Stronger* and *The Great Bear*. BUFF Financing Forum (BUFF:FF) selected 20 projects that were presented during the festival. BUFF:FF also hosted the 2nd KIDS–Regio Forum. As part of SCREEN we arranged the Kino Kabaret with people from 13 countries making films together over 48 hours. **– Daniel Lundquist**, Festival Coordinator.

Cairo International Film Festival
End November/early December 2011

The festival is organised by the General Union of Arab Artists and is the oldest film festival in the Middle East, with the aim of promoting the Egyptian, Arab and African film industry. Competitions for feature films, feature digital films and Arab films. *Inquiries to:* Cairo International Film Festival, 17 Kasr el Nile St, Cairo, Egypt. Tel: (20 2) 2392 3562. e: info@cairofilmfest.com. Web: www.cairofilmfest.com.

Cannes International Film Festival
May 11-22, 2011

Cannes remains the world's leading festival and the best known, attracting key films, personalities and industry professionals. The official selection includes the Competition, films out of competition, special screenings, 'Un Certain Regard', short films in competition, Cinéfondation and Cannes Classics (created 2004). The Marché du Film, with facilities improved and extended since 2000 (Producers network, Short Film Corner), is part of the official organisation. *Inquiries to:* Festival de Cannes, 3, rue Amélie 75007 Paris, France. Tel: (33 1) 5359 6100. e: festival@festival-cannes.fr. Web: www.festival-cannes.com.

AWARDS 2010

Palme d'Or Feature Film: **Uncle Boonmee Who Can Recall His Past Lives** (France/Germany/Spain/Thailand/UK), Apichatpong Weerasethakul.

Apichatpong Weerasethakul, whose film **Uncle Boonmee Who Can Recall His Past Lives** *was awarded the Palme d'Or at the 2010 Cannes Film Festival.*

Grand Prix: **Of Gods and Men** (France), Xavier Beauvois.
Best Director: Mathieu Amalric for **On Tour** (France).
Best Screenplay: Lee Chang-dong for **Poetry** (South Korea).
Best Actress: Juliette Binoche for **Certified Copy** (France/Italy).
Best Actor: Javier Bardem for **Biutful** (Mexico/Spain) and Elio Germano for **Our Life** (France/Italy).
Jury Prize: **A Screaming Man** (Belgium/Chad/France), Mahamat-Saleh Haroun.
Palme d'Or Short Film: **Barking Island** (France), Serge Avedikian.
Jury Prize Short Film: **Bathing Micky** (Denmark/Sweden), Frida Kempff.

Cape Winelands Film Festival
March 16-26, 2011

The Cape Winelands Film Festival (CWFF) is one of the largest film events on the African continent. Since the first edition, it has significantly grown in size and international participation. The 2011 edition will feature more than 300 screenings at Oude Libertas open air amphitheatre in the scenic Winelands district of Stellenbosch, as well as in the historic independent art cinema of the Labia Theatre in the beautiful city centre of Cape Town. The main objective of the CWFF is to provide a window on world cinemas. The festival also aims to build a rich film culture among South African audiences by celebrating great achievements of the past. The major theme of the 2011 edition will be on reconciliation by celebrating similarities between cultures, breaking down stereotypes and enhancing tolerance towards different viewpoints and perspectives. Highlights include a strong Eastern European and Middle Eastern, as well as Brazilian, focus. *Inquiries to:* Leon van der Merwe, Festival Director, Cape Winelands Film Festival, 1 Waterkant, 52 Arum Road, Bloubergrant, Cape Town 7441, South Africa. Tel: (27 21) 556 3204. e: films_for_africa@ telkomsa.net. Web: http://films-for-africa.co.za.

Cartagena International Film Festival
February 24-March 3, 2011

As the oldest Film Festival in America, Cartagena de Indias has proved that it's been the best platform for the promotion and exhibition of national and international films, where filmmakers have gained worldwide attention and recognition. The city, besides being an architectural masterpiece and one of the most attractive cultural & tourism destinations in the Caribbean, is the perfect gateway for the discovery of Ibero-American talent and in experiencing successful audiovisual projects by the film industry's special members. More than 8,500 films and over two million spectators have made FICCI a delightful experience. *Inquiries to:* Cartagena International Film Festival, Centro, Calle San Juan de Dios, Baluarte San Francisco Javier, Cartagena, Colombia. Tel: (57 5) 660 1037 or 664 2345. e: gerencia@ficcifestival. com, comercial@ficcifestival.com. Web: www. ficcifestival.com.

Chicago International Film Festival
October 6-20, 2011

The Chicago International Film Festival is among the oldest competitive events in North America. It spotlights the latest work by established international directors as well as newcomers. Now in its 47th year, the Festival annually presents more than 175 films from over 45 countries. Films exhibited in our competitions are the defining core of the Festival (International Feature Film, New

Directors, Docufest, and Short Subject). In addition to these, there are programmes that showcase new trends in international and independent filmmaking (World Cinema and After Dark) and that highlight the work of under-represented filmmakers and alternative viewpoints (Black Perspectives, Cinema of the Americas, ReelWomen and OUTrageous). The Festival bestows its highest honour, the Gold Hugo, on the best feature in the International Competition, with separate prizes for new directors, documentaries, and shorts. *Inquiries to:* Chicago International Film Festival, 30 E Adams St, Suite 800, Chicago, IL 60603, USA. Tel: (1 312) 683 0121. e: info@chicagofilmfestival.com. Web: www.chicagofilmfestival.com.

AWARDS 2010
International Feature Film Competition
Gold Hugo for Best Film: **How I Ended the Summer** (Russia), Alexei Popogrobsky.
Silver Hugo Special Jury Award: **We Are What We Are** (Mexico), Jorge Michel Grau and **A Somewhat Gentle Man** (Norway), Hans Petter Moland.
Silver Hugo for Best Actress: Liana Liberato for **Trust** (USA).
Silver Hugo for Best Actor: Youssouf Djaoro for **A Screaming Man** (Belgium/Chad/France).
Silver Hugo for Best Ensemble: Antonio Gasalla and Graciela Borges for **Brother and Sister** (Argentina).
Silver Hugo for Best Screenplay: Mahamat-Saleh Haroun for **A Screaming Man** (Belgium/Chad/France).
Gold Plaque: Márta Mészáros in recognition of her long and distinguished career in the international cinema on the occasion of **Last Report On Anna** (Hungary).
Silver Plaque: **The Matchmaker** (Israel), Avi Nesher for the lighthearted but touching way it describes a coming of age in an Israel torn between memory and desire.

Cinekid Festival
October 12-21, 2011

Cinekid Festival is an annual Film, Television and New Media Festival for Children held in Amsterdam, the Netherlands. Every year, more than 50,000 children are given an opportunity to attend one or more of the 500 media productions that Cinekid presents: feature films, children's documentaries, short films, animations, TV series and single plays, cross-media productions, interactive installations, and set-ups and workshops. The main festival is held in Amsterdam, but approximately 30 satellite festivals are held in cities all over the Netherlands. Cinekid for Professionals is the place to be for anybody involved with children and media. Readings; seminars; a chance to meet fellow professionals; viewings of the best and latest international productions – plus all the information about them; an opportunity to be kept up to date with the very latest developments and trends: at Cinekid for Professionals it's all possible. *Inquiries to:* Cinekid Festival, Korte Leidsedwarsstraat 12, 1017 RC Amsterdam, Netherlands. Tel: (31 20) 531 7890. e: info@cinekid.nl. Web: www.cinekid.nl.

Cinéma Tous Ecrans
November 1-7, 2011

Cinéma Tous Ecrans (Cinema for any screen) is an international film festival focusing on fiction films produced for cinema, TV, the web, cell phones and urban screens. The only one of its kind in Switzerland, the festival celebrates the evolution of cinema, welcoming films which are presented on a variety of different screens, but have equal artistic worth, using visual media formats from the past, present and future. *Inquiries to:* Claudia Durgnat, Director, Cinéma Tous Ecrans, Maison des Arts du Grütli, 16 rue Général Dufour, CP 5730, CH-1211 Geneva 11, Switzerland. Tel: (41 22) 809 6918. e: info@cinema-tous-ecrans.ch. Web: www.cinema-tous-ecrans.ch.

Clermont–Ferrand Short Film Festival
February 4-12, 2011

International, National and 'Lab' competitions for 35mm films and digital works on DigiBeta and Beta SP, all completed after July 1, 2009, of 40 minutes or less. All the entries will be listed in the Market catalogue. Many other side programmes (retrospectives and panoramas such as 'Moroccan Retrospective' and 'Zombies, Vampires and Other Undead' in 2010). The 32nd edition attracted more than 144,000 admissions and welcomed 3,000 professionals. *Inquiries to:* Clermont-Ferrand Short Film Festival, La Jetée, 6 Place Michel–de L'Hospital 63058 Clermont–Ferrand Cedex 1, France. Tel: (33 473) 916 573. e: info@clermont-filmfest.com. Web: www.clermont-filmfest.com.

AWARDS 2010
Grand Prix
International: **Blue Sofa** (Italy), Pippo Delbono, Giuseppe Baresi and Lara Fremder.
National: **Dónde Está Kim Basinger?** (Argentina/France), Edouard Deluc.
Lab: **Petite Anatomie de L'Image** (Belgium), Olivier Smolders.
Audience Prize
International: **Sinna Mann** (Norway), Anita Killi.
National: **Comme Le Temps Passe** (France), Cathy Verne.
Lab: **Photograph of Jesus** (UK), Laurie Hill.

Coca–Cola Cinemagic International Film & Television Festival for Young People
November 17-December 2, 2011

The largest film festival for young people in the UK and Ireland runs an action packed programme of fascinating events. Film and TV enthusiasts have a wealth of screenings, masterclasses with film and television industry guests, workshops for schools, a young film jury and Q&As to choose from. All of these aim to inspire, entertain, motivate and create opportunities for young people aged from 4 to 25. Young people aged 16 to 25 who are interested in finding out more about working in the media industry can do just that via the 'Talent Lab' event. The Cinemagic Outreach and Education department works throughout the year with school and youth groups across Northern Ireland, offering a packed programme of exciting and hands-on educational opportunities for teachers and students, ranging from careers events to production training and from film criticism to media literacy workshops with top industry professionals. *Inquiries to:* Coca-Cola Cinemagic International Film & Television Festival, 49 Botanic Ave, Belfast, BT7 1JL, Northern Ireland. Tel: (44 28) 9031 1900. e: info@cinemagic.org.uk. Web: www.cinemagic.org.uk.

AWARDS 2010
Best Short Film as voted for by a Children's Jury: **Le Silence Sous l'Ecorce**, (France), Joanna Lurie.
Best Feature Film as voted for by a Children's Jury: **From Time To Time** (UK), Julian Fellowes.
Best Short Film as voted for by a Teenage Jury: **Canary** (UK), Oliver Hudson.
Best Feature Film as voted for by a Teenage Jury: **Boy** (New Zealand), Taika Waititi.
Cinemagic Young Filmmaker Awards: Victoria Park Primary School, Birmingham, for **Aztec Gold**, in the Under 15 year old category; Daniel Allen for **Education for Leisure** in the 15–17 year old category; William McGregor for **Who's Afraid of the Water Sprite** in the 18–25 year old category; **Andrew Barry for The Snatchers** in the Best Script category; Will Maloney for **Diamond White Love** for the Best Community film; and William McGregor for **The Little** in the Innovation category.
After School Film Club of the Year: Harberton School, Belfast. Special commendations went to Nazareth House Primary School and De La Salle High School.
Talent Lab Awards
Most Promising Actor in the Hubbard Acting Masterclass: Joanne Gallagher.
Most Promising Screenwriter in the Julian Fellowes Masterclass: Jordan Dunbar.
Most Promising Actor in the Patrick Bergin and Sile Bermingham Masterclass: Cal Hunter.
Most Promising Scriptwriter in the Ryan Rowe Masterclass: Jonathan Moreland.
Most Promising Make–up Artist for Film and TV in the Maria Moore Masterclass: Caroline Daye.

TVP
TELEWIZJA POLSKA

Siobhan Griffin, winner of the Most Promising Journalist Award, with Erica Roseingrave of Coca-Cola and IFG Editor Ian Haydn Smith, at Cinemagic's Gala Awards Ceremony in Belfast City Hall. Photo by Aaron McCracken/Harrison Photography.

Most Promising Film Producer in the Causeway Pictures Masterclass: David McAlister.
Most Promising Film Journalist in the Ian Haydn Smith Masterclass: Siobhan Griffin.
Most Promising Broadcaster in the Marc Mallett Masterclass: Bridgid Moore.
Most Promising Screenwriter in the Ben Schiffer Masterclass: Ross McLean.
UTV Arts & Entertainment TV Presenting Award: Cathryn Corr.
UTV News & Current Affairs TV Presenting Award: Alan Fenton.

Report 2010
A host of industry professionals including Oscar-winning screenwriter Julian Fellowes; President and Chief Executive of Sesame Workshop, Gary Knell; actor Patrick Bergin and DreamWorks Animation's Phil McNally joined 400 guests at a Gala Awards Ceremony, hosted by UTV's Marc Mallett, in Belfast City

Hall, to celebrate the successes of the 20th anniversary festival. After 17 days action packed with film screenings, workshops, masterclasses, and industry discussions, the festival culminated with a celebration for young people, showcasing and awarding their talent, and looking back at the successes of the last 20 years of Cinemagic. A special award was presented to Gary Knell, President and Chief Executive of Sesame Workshop, for a Lifetime Contribution to Children's Television and Julian Fellowes, creator of recent ITV hit period drama series, *Downtown Abbey*, received the award for Best Feature Film for a Children's Audience as chosen by a young people's jury, for 'From Time to Time', which had its Northern Ireland premiere at the Festival. Arts and Culture Minister Nelson McCausland who attended the awards ceremony congratulated the festival organisers, saying 'Cinemagic Festival which is celebrating its 20th year is now the largest children and young people's film event in the UK and the Republic of Ireland. Through this festival, Cinemagic continues to inspire young people to find something exciting, create something new and do something different and I applaud the Festival for their work in inspiring the next generation of filmmakers.' – **Claire Baxter**, Press & Marketing Officer.

Copenhagen Film Festivals
CPH:PIX April 14-May 1, 2011
BUSTER September 15-25, 2011
CPH:DOX November 3-12, 2011

Copenhagen Film Festivals is the Danish capital's festival powerhouse with the country's three major international film events, which together attract more than 120,000 admissions a year. CPH PIX – the new feature (fiction) film festival was launched in 2009; BUSTER – the international film festival for children and youth was launched in 2000; CPH:DOX – the international documentary film festival was launched in 2004. *Inquiries to:* Tagensvej 85F, DK–2200 Copenhagen N, Denmark. Tel: (45) 3312 0005. e: info@cphpix. dk, buster@buster.dk, info@cphdox.dk. Web: www.cphfilmfestivals.dk.

AWARDS 2010
CPH PIX
New Talent Grand PIX: **Amer** (Belgium),
Hélène Cattet and Bruno Forzani.
Politiken Audience Award: **Ajami** (Israel)
Scandar Copti and Yaron Shani.
BUSTER
Best BUSTER (Children's Jury): **The**
Crocodiles (Germany), Christian Ditter.
Best Film For Children (International Jury):
EEP! (The Netherlands), Ellen Smith.
Best Film For Youth (Youth Jury): **Vegas**
(Norway), Gunnar Vikene.
CPH:DOX
DOX:AWARD: **Le Quattro Volte** (Italy),
Michelangelo Frammartino.
NEW: VISION Award: **In Free Fall** (Germany),
Hito Steyerl.
Politiken's Audience Award: **Lost Inside**
A Dream – A Story of Dizzy Mizz Lizzy
(Denmark), Theis Molin.

Cork Film Festival
November 6-13, 2011

Cork Film Festival is one of Ireland's most
important cultural events and, entering its
56th year, is its longest running film festival.
There is a strong aesthetic drive to the festival,
which includes a comprehensive look at World
Cinema, a Documentary Panorama, a platform
for new Irish cinema and programmes devoted
to new and innovative explorations in cinema.
In particular, the festival celebrates the art
of the short film, with a programme of over
45 short films. The Short Film Competition
includes awards for Best International Short,

The Cork audience goes 3D for **The Moomins Comet Chase.**

Best European Short and Best Irish Short.
The festival's 'Explorations' strand includes
retrospectives, programmes of experimental
work and 'live cinema'). *Inquiries to:* Cork
Film Festival, Emmet House, Emmet Place,
Cork, Ireland. Tel: (353 21) 427 1711. e: info@
corkfilmfest.org. Web: www.corkfilmfest.org.

AWARDS 2010
Best Irish Short: **Pentecost**, Peter McDonald.
Claire Lynch Award for Best First-Time Irish
Director: **Small Change**, Cathy Brady.
Best International Short: **Baby** (UK), Daniel
Mulloy.
Cork Short Film Nominee for the European
Film Awards: **Incident By A Bank** (Sweden),
Ruben Ostlund.
Audience Award for Best International Short:
Miss Remarkable and Her Career (Denmark/
Ireland/Sweden), Joanna Rubin Dranger.
Audience Award for Best Irish Short: **Passing**,
David Freyne.
Award of the Festival for Best Short: **Holding**
Still (Germany), Florian Riegel.

The producer of the Best International Short Film, Ohna Falby with International Jury members; Tony Donoghue (Filmmaker, Ireland), Ahmet Boyacioglu (Filmmaker, Turkey) and Alessandro Marcionni (Locarno Film Festival, Switzerland)

Outlook Award for Best LGBT Short: **Blokes**, Marialy Rivas Chile.
'Made In Cork' Award for Best Short: **Kettle**, Brian Power.

Report 2010
The 55th edition of the Cork Film Festival attracted over 23,000 admissions to a wide-ranging programme of screenings, talks, masterclasses and special events. Guests included legendary star Maureen O'Hara for the premiere of a new documentary by Sé Merry Doyle, *Dreaming The Quiet Man*. British director Julien Temple gave the Directors' Masterclass and many international filmmakers attended, including Frédéric Pelle (premiering his first feature, *Elsewhere*) documentarist Pip Chodorov, artist Paki Smith and Ohna Falby of Sister Films in London, the producer of Daniel Mulloy's award-winning short film *Baby*. The festival devoted a special focus to Portuguese short filmmaking with guests from the Agencia Curtas Metragens (celebrating 10 years) and Indielisboa Film Festival. **– Sean Kelly**, Festival Manager.

FilmFestival Cottbus:
Festival of East European Cinema
November 1–6, 2011

Celebrating its 20th anniversary in 2010, FilmFestival Cottbus has developed into the world's leading festival of East European cinema. Each year in November, it presents a representative survey of contemporary feature films and shorts from the Central and Eastern European region. While the programme centres around the feature film competition, different sections are dedicated to National Hits, Spectrum – different artistic approaches, Retrospectives or Children's and Youth film. A Focus every year casts a spotlight upon a special region. With almost 19,000 visitors in 2010 and a total prize value of €82,200, the festival attracts actors and producers, as well as many visitors from the region, who also gather at the Cottbus receptions in Berlin, Karlovy Vary, Wroclaw and Sarajevo.

AWARDS 2010
Feature Film Competition
LUBINA for Best Film: **White White World** (Germany/Serbia/Sweden), Oleg Novković.
LUBINA for Best Director: Ágnes Kocsis for **Adrienn Pàl** (Austria/France/Hungary/The Netherlands).
LUBINA for Outstanding Actress: Eva Gabor for **Adrienn Pàl** (Austria/France/Hungary/The Netherlands).
LUBINA for Outstanding Actor: Taavi Eelmaa for **The Temptation of St Tony** (Estonia).
IFG Inspiration Award: **Tilva Roš** (Serbia), Nikola Ležaić.
Short Feature Competition
Main Prize: **Sea of Desires** (Russia), Shota Gamisonia.
Special Prize: **Music in the Blood** (France/ Romania), Alexandru Mavrodineau.
From Cottbus to Cinema – Distributon Support Prize for a Festival Film: The Prize will be awarded during the reception of the FilmFestival Cottbus on the occasion of the Berlinale 2011.
Promotion prize of the GWFF: Anastasia Posnova (Russia).
Promotion prize of the DEFA Foundation: Yael Reuveny (Israel).
Prize for Best Debut Film: **Another Sky** (Russia), Dmitriy Mamuliya.
Audience Award: **The Light Thief** (France/ Germany/ Kyrgyzstan/ The Netherlands), Aktan Arym Kubat.

FIPRESCI: **Another Sky** (Russia), Dmitriy Mamuliya.
Prize of the Ecumenical Jury: **Adrienn Pàl** (Austria/France/Hungary/The Netherlands), Ágnes Kocsis.
Don Quijote–Prize:
Dialogue Prize for Intercultural Communication: **Vespa** (Hungary), Diana Groó.
Cottbus Discovery Award: **Tales of the Defeated** (Germany/Israel), Yael Reuveny.

Report 2010

With a multifaceted programme, as comprehensive and international as never before, as well as awards endowments reaching a new record high (of now altogether €82,200), the 20th jubilee year proved to be a magnet for audiences and a favoured meeting point for the industry from East and West alike. For the first time, the Focus 'globalEAST' traced the Eastern European influences in contemporary cinema around the world in a transcontinental analysis spanning from Brazil to Bollywood, from the United States to Israel. Amongst the numerous international guests was Sylvia Kristel, who celebrated a remarkable comeback in the Croatian-French co-production, *2 Sunny Days*. In addition to the already well-established Russian Day, Polish Horizons (in cooperation with ERA New Horizons, Wroclaw) and the newly established U18 – German-Polish Youth Film Competition for the first time appeared as independent sections. The Academy Award nominees from Israel, Poland and Russia experienced their first German premiere as did all entries in the feature film competition. The main award

The opening ceremony of the festival is annually held at the Staatstheater Cottbus. Photographer: Copyright: pool production/Thomas Goethe

winner of this competition *White, White World* one of the numerous projects successfully pitched at the East–West co–production market Connecting Cottbus, which took place for the 12th time already. **– Roland Rust**, Festival Director.

Crossroads Film Festival
April 1-3, 2011

The Crossroads Film Festival is the premiere film festival in central Mississippi, celebrating its twelfth anniversary in 2011. Founded in 1999 in the capital city of Jackson – known as 'The Crossroads of the South' – the festival was designed as a place where the strands and influences of art, theme, and culture come together. Every year the event endeavours to celebrate film, music, and food, along with the great culture and heritage of Mississippi. The festival provides a cross-cultural backdrop of screenings, concerts and receptions, as well as workshops and forums. Over the years, the

festival has celebrated filmmakers with ties to Mississippi, beginning with Robert Altman in its premiere year and including Morgan Freeman, resident Joey Lauren Adams, and Vicksburg local, Charles Burnett. Crossroads is a top Mississippi stop for many films made in the state: *Prom Night in Mississippi, Ballast, Big Bad Love, O Brother, Where Art Thou?, The Rising Place, I'll Fly Away, Cries of Silence, Red Dirt* and *Blossom Time* among them. *Inquiries to:* Crossroads Film Festival, PO Box 22604, Jackson, MS 39225, USA. Tel: (1 601) 510 9148. e: info@crossroadsfilmfestival.com. Web: www.crossroadsfilmfestival.com.

AWARDS 2010
Feature Narrative: **The Last Confession of Alexander Pearce** (Australia),Michael James Rowland.
Feature Documentary: **A Village Called Versailles** (USA),S Leo Chiang.
Short Documentary: **I Am a Man: From Memphis, A Lesson in Life** (USA), Jonathan Epstein.
Short Narrative: **The Big Bends** (USA), Jason Marlow.
Student: **We Are All Here** (USA),Yonghwa Choi.
Animated: **Alma** (Spain), Rodrigo Blaas.
Experimental: **Insurgency of Ambition** (USA), Anya Belkina.
Local Music Video: **After the Fall** (USA), Rob Piantanida.
Adam Ford Youth Filmmaking: **A Soldier in Skirts** (USA), Sarah Bailin and Emma Bailin;

*Mississippi filmmakers during Q & A at 2010 festival, from L to R, Front Porch Dance Company (**Dealing**), Joe York with the mic (**Smokes & Ears**), Jason Marlow (**The Big Bends**), Chris Spear (**Shock**), actor Mario, producers James and Heather Matthews (**When Cotton Blossoms**). Photo: Kip Caven*

Volunteers at the 2010 festival. Photo: Kip Caven

Crippled (South Korea), Ien Chi.
The Ruma (MS Made Film): **Smokes & Ears** (USA), Joe York.
Programmer's Choice Award: **Brutal Beauty** (USA), Chip Mabry.
Audience Choice Award: **Citizen Architect: Samuel Mockbee and the Spirit of the Rural Studio** (USA), Sam Wainwright Douglas.
Transformative Film: **Rebuilding Hope** (USA),Jen Marlowe.

Report 2010
The 2010 festival screened nearly 120 films, representing Australia, Spain, South Korea, Canada, Germany, the Netherlands, United Kingdom, China, Mexico, Japan, and USA. The festival featured a 10th anniversary screening of *O Brother, Where Art Thou?*, award-winning film *Stingray Sam*, the films of Hayao Miyazaki, and presented an innovative workshop on motion-tracked virtual cameras. The Jury included members from National Black Programming Consortium, Barefoot Workshops, SoAL Film Festival, Filmmakers Alliance and other industry professionals. The board of directors created the Transformative Film Award to honor a project that has ability to transform attitudes, lives and, ultimately, history. This award will be given annually.
– **Nina Parikh**.

Starz Denver Film Festival
November 2011

The Starz Denver Film Festival presents more than 200 films from around the world and plays host to over 150 filmmakers. Including new international features, cutting-edge independent fiction and non-fiction works, shorts and a variety of special programmes, the Starz Denver Film Festival also features the best in student work with the inclusion of the First Look Student Film section. SDFF pays tribute to established film artists with retrospective screenings of their works. Entry fee: $40 ($20 for students). The Denver Film Society also programmes the Starz FilmCenter, Colorado's only cinematheque, daily throughout the year. *Inquiries to:* Denver Film Society at the Starz FilmCenter, 900 Auraria Parkway, Denver, Colorado 80204, USA. Tel: (1 303) 595 3456. e: dfs@ denverfilm.org. Web: www.denverfilm.org.

Dubai International Film Festival
Mid December 2011

The Dubai International Film Festival (DIFF), the leading Festival in the Middle East, Africa and near Asia, was launched in 2004 with the theme of 'Bridging Cultures/Meeting Minds'. DIFF reflects Dubai's cosmopolitan and multicultural character and its mission to promote global understanding and intercultural dialogue. The festival showcases a wide selection of features, shorts and documentaries from around the world, in and out of competition. The Festival continues to act as a platform for showcasing excellence in Arab cinema and contributing to the development and growth of the regional industry and talent. The Muhr Awards for Excellence in Arab Cinema, initiated in 2006, gained a sibling prize in 2008, the Muhr Asia Africa Competition, with an aim to recognising filmmakers originating from these markets. In 2010, the Festival introduced a new competition component: the Muhr Emirati Awards, focusing on UAE talent. The Muhr Awards champion emerging and established filmmakers and encourage creativity from Asia, Africa and the region. In 2010, the Festival also debuted the Dubai Film Market, the most comprehensive film market in the Arab world and a multi-faceted initiative that works 'from script to

screen', covering every aspect of cinema from conceptualisation to distribution. The Dubai Film Market will house the Dubai Film Connection, the Festival's successful co-production market; the Dubai Film Forum, its popular hub for talent development, funding, workshops and networking; Enjaaz, the dedicated post-production support programme; and Dubai Filmmart, specialising in content trade, acquisition and distribution. As the only gateway of its kind between the major film centres of Europe and South East Asia, the Dubai Film Market will represent and further the interest of the more than 70 nations in the wider region. The 2010 Festival built on the success of previous years, with a roster of 157 films from 57 nations including 41 world premieres and 13 international premieres; an influx of A-list talent from Europe, the Americas, the Middle East and Asia; and a thriving industry operation. *Inquiries to:* Dubai Media City, PO Box 53777, Dubai, United Arab Emirates. Tel: (971 4) 391 3378. e: diffinfo@dubaimediacity.ae. Web: www.dubaifilmfest.com.

Edinburgh International Film Festival
June 15–26, 2011

EIFF has developed into a crucial business hub for the UK and international film industry, a key attraction for Edinburgh, and one of the world's best-loved audience festivals. With an emphasis upon new talent, discovery and innovation, EIFF's vibrant programme of films and events combines a commitment to audience edification and pleasure with a strong ongoing stake in the development the UK and Scottish film industries. *Inquiries to:* Edinburgh International Film Festival, 88 Lothian Rd, Edinburgh EH3 9BZ, Scotland. Tel: (44 131) 228 4051. e: info@edfilmfest.org.uk. Web: www.edfilmfest.org.uk.

AWARDS 2010
Michael Powell Award for Best New British Feature: **Skeletons** (UK), Nick Whitfield.
Standard Life Audience Award: **Get Low** (USA), Aaron Schneider.

PPG Award for Best Performance in a British Feature Film: David Thewlis for **Mr Nice** (UK).
Moët New Director's Award: Gareth Edwards for **Monsters** (UK).
Projector.tv Best New International Feature: **The Dry Land** (USA), Ryan Piers Williams.
Best Feature Documentary Award: **The Oath** (USA), Laura Poitras.
UK Film Council Award for Best British Short Film: **Baby** (UK), Daniel Mulloy.
McLaren Award for Best New British Animation in Partnership with BBC Film Network: **Stanley Pickle** (UK), Victoria Mather.
In association with European Film Academy – Short Film Nominee Edinburgh for the European Film Awards: **Maria's Way** (UK), Anne Milne.
Best International Short Film Award sponsored by Steedman & Company: **Rita** (Italy), Fabio Grassadonia and Antonio Piazza.
Short Scottish Documentary Award Supported by Baillie Gifford: **Maria's Way** (UK), Anne Milne.

Report 2010

The Festival was another fantastic success with great audience figures and a superb programme of films and associated events. In 2010 Premieres included the UK Premiere of Sylvain Chomet's *The Illusionist*, a Special 3D Gala Preview of *Toy Story 3*, plus a special Gala Screening of *The Man Who Would Be King* to celebrate Sir Sean Connery's 80th year and his dedicated support of EIFF as Patron since 1992. **– Ross Wilson**, Head of Marketing.

Era New Horizons International Film Festival

July 21–31, 2011

Era New Horizons International Film Festival is the largest film festival in Poland and regarded as one of the most important film events in Central Europe, visited each year by an increasing number of cinema lovers from Poland and abroad. Era New Horizons presents films that go beyond the borders of conventional cinema. Its main objective is to present uncompromising, innovative and

Artistic Director, Joanna Lapinska with the Hungarian director Kornel Mundruczo. Photo by T Rykaczewski.

original cinema from all over the world. The festival's name suggests an exploration of new horizons in film language, expressions and storytelling. The festival belongs to the elite group of festivals accredited by FIAPF – the International Federation of Film Producers Associations. *Inquiries to:* Era New Horizons International Film Festival, 1 Zamenhofa Street, 00-153 Warsaw, Poland. Tel: (48 22) 530 6640. e: festival@enh.pl. Web: www.enh.pl.

AWARDS 2010

New Horizons International Competition Grand Prix: **Mundane History** (Thailand), Anocha Suwichakornpong.
FIPRESCI Jury Prize: **Mama** (Russia), Nikolay and Yelena Renard.
Audience Prize: **Le Quattro Volte** (Germany/Italy/Switzerland), Michelangelo Frammartino.
IFG Inspiration Award: **Le Quattro Volte** (Germany/Italy/Switzerland), Michelangelo Frammartino.

The festival organizer, New Horizons Association guarantees all three winning films distribution in Poland.

Films on Art International Competition
Best Film Award: **We Don't Care about Music Anyway** (France/Netherlands/UK), Cédric Dupire and Gaspard Kuentz. This title is also guaranteed distribution in Poland.
Jury Special Mention: **Over Your Cities Grass Will Grow** (Belgium/Germany/The Netherlands), Sophie Fiennes.
New Polish Films Competition
Wrocław Film Award Founded by the President of the City: **Made in Poland** by Przemyslaw Wojcieszek.
Best New Director Prize: **Ewa** (Poland), Adam Sikora and Ingmar Villqist.

Report 2010
For its 10th edition, the festival presented over 500 films from 50 countries, including 240 features, bringing over 530 screenings to festival audiences and visiting industry guests. The festival's audience reached

Festival Director, Roman Gutek with the Grand Prix winner, Anocha Suwichakornpong. Photo by T Rykaczewski.

122,500 people. Films in competition, country focuses, director retrospectives and New Horizons Studio highlighted the festival's 2010 platform. The festival organisers presented opportunities for audiences to discover emerging filmmakers from around the world, while savouring the classic work of established film artists. During the 2010 edition, five competitions were held. Festival's flagship – NEW HORIZONS

International Competition; FILMS ON ART International Competition, NEW POLISH FILMS Competition, European Short Films and Polish Short Films Competition. The prizes awarded valued over 70,000 Euros. Film awarded in the NEW HORIZONS International Competition and FILMS ON ART competition are guaranteed distribution in Poland and will be released in theatres in the first half of 2011 and on DVD in May 2011. For the first time in 2010, the FIPRESCI Jury awarded Prize of the International Film Critics (FIPRESCI Prize). This year's festival featured the first edition of the NEW HORIZONS Studio. The three-day workshop was intended for young professionals in the film industry from Poland. Their lecturers included the American director Jonathan Caouette and the Turkish master Nuri Bilge Ceylan. Xavier Beauvois' *Of Gods and Men* and Gaspar Noé's *Enter the Void* opened the festival, while Francis Ford Coppola's *Tetro* was the closing film. The festival paid tribute to the French New Wave master Jean-Luc Godard, who turned 80 in December 2010. Over 100 of Godard's films were shown in this full retrospective. New cinema of Turkey was profiled at this year's festival. The directors whose films were shown in this category began their careers in the 1990s and have since become successful at many European festivals. The festival audiences had the privilege to see the Wojciech Jerzy Has retrospective that coincided with the tenth anniversary of Has' death. The Quay Brothers, best known for their stop-motion animation, presented a full retrospective of their works. It included interpretations of Has' films. The 10th Era New Horizons International Film Festival hosted over 250 foreign guests, among them 160 film industry professionals. 650 Polish guests were present, including 280 industry professionals. 315 journalists from Poland and abroad were accredited to the festival. Among the festival guests there were the directors: Jonathan Caouette, Yeşim Ustaoğlu, Petr Zelenka, Kornél Mundruczó, Stig Björkman, Petter Mettler, the Quay Brothers, Anocha Suwichakornpong, Philippe Mora, Nuri Bilge Ceylan, Jasmila Žbanić,

Laura Mulvey. In addition to film screenings, this year's festival hosted many other artistic events. For example, Mike Patton performed his Mondo Cane album on the opening night of the festival on Wroclaw's Wyspa Slodowa. This musical project consists of Patton's covers of popular Italian songs from the 1950s and 1960s. This concert was the first in his European tour. Equally significant was the only Polish showing of the world-renowned Dutch composer Michel van der Aa's film opera, *The Book of Disquiet*. The narrator was Klaus Maria Brandauer and the opera featured the Portuguese singer Ana Moura and the German orchestra musikFabrik. The festival audiences had the privilege to see the first monographic exhibit related to Wojciech Jerzy Has, which complemented a film retrospective of Has' work. In cooperation with the Ha!art publishers, the film festival has published several books devoted to all the subjects of this year's retrospectives as well as new Turkish film and surrealism in Polish cinema. – **Agnieszka Wolak**, PR Director.

Espoo Ciné International Film Festival
August 19–28, 2011

Espoo Ciné has established itself as the annual showcase of contemporary European, primarily long feature, cinema in Finland. The 22nd Espoo Ciné festival will take place in Espoo, Finland 19–28 August. The traditional section should appeal to every film buff in Finland, and the growing fantasy selection should attract those hungry for stimulation of the imagination. Annual special programmes present, for example, French and Spanish gems, films from Eastern Europe, documentaries, gay films and US indies, not to forget the best of contemporary Finnish cinema, outdoor screenings, retrospectives, sneak previews, seminars and distinguished guests. Estimated amount of screenings: 150–200. Estimated attendance: 27,000. For entry regulations see the website. *Inquiries to:* Espoo Ciné, PO Box 95, FI–02101 Espoo, Finland. Tel: (358 9) 466 599. e: office@ espoocine.fi. Web: www.espoocine.fi.

Fajr International Film Festival
February 5–15, 2011
Iranian International Market for Films and TV Programmes
February 4–8, 2011

In the international programme of the festival, there are three different competitive sections: International Competition, Competition of Spiritual Cinema (emphasising cinema's role as a rich medium for the expression of the essence of religious faith) and Competition of Asian Cinema (organised with the aim of promoting film art and industry in Asian countries). The non–competitive sections include Festival of Festivals' (a selection of outstanding films presented at other international festivals), 'Special Screenings' (films of documentary or narrative content which introduce cinema or cultural developments in certain geographical regions), retrospectives, etc. Coinciding with the international programme, the Iranian Film Market (IFM) provides not only a friendly atmosphere for cutting deals, but also a unique showcase for new Iranian productions with English subtitles or simultaneous translation, premiered for the international participants. In the national programme, there are different competitive sections as well. Director: Mahdi Masoud Shahi. *Inquiries to:* Fajr International Film Festival, No. 13, 2nd Floor, Delbar Alley, Toos St, Valiye Asr Ave, Tehran 19617–44973, Iran. Tel: (98 21) 2273 5090/4801. Fax: 2273 4801. e: office@fajrfestival.ir. Web: www. fajrfestival.ir.

AWARDS 2010
International Competition:
Best Film: **Ward No. 6** (Russia), Karen Shakhnazarov.
Special Jury Prize: **The World Is Big and Salvation Lurks Around the Corner** (Bulgaria/Germany/Hungary/Slovenia), Stephan Komandarev.
Best Director: Adrian Biniez for **Gigante** (Argentina/Germany/Spain/Uruguay).
Best Script: **As the Colour of Purple** (Iran), Ebrahim Hatamikia.

February 4th to 8th, 2011 / Tehran

iifm

2011

14TH

IRANIAN INTERNATIONAL

MARKET

FOR
Films and TV Programs

Organized by:
Institute of Film Festivals
Farabi Cinema Foundation

13, Delbar Alley, Toos St., Valiye Asr Ave.,Tehran 19617, Iran.
Tel: +98 (21) 22741252-4, 22734939
Fax: +98 (21) 22734953
E-mail: fcf1@dpi.net.ir

Best Actor: Vladimir Ilyin for **Ward No. 6** (Russia).

Best Artistic Achievement: **Pain** (Turkey), Cemal San.

Best Short Film: **Ahmad's Garden** (Australia), Aaron Wilson.

Best Short Animation (Jointly): **Young Man & the Crafty Tailor** (Iran), Rashin Kheiriyeh and The Wolf and the Sheep (Iran), Mohammad Ali Soleimanzadeh.

Competition of Spiritual Cinema:

Best Film: **Letters to Father Jacob** (Finland), Klaus Haro.

Special Jury Prize: **Castaway on the Moon** (South Korea), Lee Hae–jun.

Best Director: **Vision** (Germany), Margarethe Von Trotta.

Best Script: **Thomas** (Finland), Mikka Soini.

Competition of Asian Cinema:

Best Film: **True Noon** (Tajikistan), Nosir Saidov.

Best Director: Nosir Saidov for **True Noon** (Tajikistan).

Best Script: **The Equation of Love and Death** (China), Cao Baoping.

Asian Film Jury and writer of True Noon during the closing ceremony

Special Jury Prize: **Farewell, Gulsary!** (Kazakhstan), Ardak Amirkulov.

Audience Award: **Evening of the 10th Day** (Iran), Maojtaba Raie.

Interfaith Award: **Gold & Copper** (Iran), Haomayoun As'adian.

Report 2010

In Fajr 2010, the jury members included such international figures as Olivia Stewart (UK/Producer), Naum Kleiman (Russia/Film

29th Fajr International Film Festival

February 5th/15th 2011 Tehran-Iran

Organized by:
Institute of Film Festivals
13, Delbar Alley, Toos St., Valiye Asr Ave., Tehran 19617 Iran.
Tel:+98 21 22741250-1/+98 21 22735090
Fax:+98 21 22734801
E-mail:office@fajrfestival.ir

Historian), Ramesh Sippy (India/Director), Riri Riza (Indonesia/Director), Isabel Pisano (Spain/Writer), Murali Nair (India/Director), Hulya Ucansu (Turkey/Film Critic), Carlos Padron (Cuba/Actor) etc. A sidebar section was devoted to 'The Cinema of Oppression'. The screening of unseen productions from previous years in the national sections was one of the most outstanding features in this edition. One of these titles, **A**s the Color of Purple was named the best film in the national competition. **– Amir Esfandiari**, Head of International Affairs.

Fantasporto
February 24–March 3, 2012

The 32nd edition of Fantasporto – Oporto International Film Festival takes place in several theatres of Oporto, mostly at the Rivoli – Teatro Municipal, Teatro Sá da Bandeira and Warner Lusomundo Theatres. Apart from the Competitive Sections (Fantasy, Directors Week, Orient Express) the Festival will also include the traditional sections 'Panorama of the Portuguese Cinema', 'Anima–te' for younger audiences, 'Première' for previews and vintage features and 'Love Connection' section. The Retrospectives will include a focus on an emergent cinematography, on a classical name and others dedicated to the special guests of the edition. The festival closes, as every year, with the famous Vampires Ball. Director: Mário Dorminsky. *Inquiries to:* Fantasporto, Rua Anibal Cunha 84, Sala 1.6, 4050–048 Porto, Portugal. Tel: (35 1) 222 058 819 e: info@fantasporto.com. Web: www.fantasporto.com.

AWARDS 2010
International Jury Fantasy
Best Film Award Grand Prix Fantasporto:
Heartless (UK), Phillip Ridley.
Jury's Special Award/Award Super Bock:
Deliver Us From Evil (Denmark/Norway/Sweden), Ole Bornedal.
Best Direction: **Heartless** (UK), Phillip Ridley.
Best Actor: Jim Sturgess for **Heartless** (UK).
Best Actress: Neve McIntosh for **Salvage** (UK).

The lobby of the Rivoli Theatre, with robots, fantasy decoration and a crowd waiting for the new screening. (30th Fantasporto 2010).

Best Screenplay: Arnaud Bordas, Yannick Dahan, Stéphanie Moissakis and Benjamin Rocher for **La Horde** (France).
Best Special Effects or Cinematography: Yannick Dahan and Benjamin Rocher for **La Horde** (France).
Best Short Film: **La Carte** (France), Stefan le Lay.
Special Mention of the Jury: **Valhalla Rising** (Denmark/UK), Nicholas Winding Refn and **Embargo** (Portugal), António Ferreira.
20th Director's Week
Best Film Award/Manoel de Oliveira Award: **Fish Tank** (UK), Andrea Arnold.
Jury's Special Award: **Ward Number 6** (Russia), Karen Shakhnazarov.
Best Director: Pater Sparrow for **1** (Hungary).
Best Screenplay: Andrea Arnold for **Fish Tank** (UK).
Best Actor: Zóltan Mucsi for **1** (Hungary).
Best Actress: Elena Anaya for **Hierro** (Spain).
Orient Express Awards
Best Film Award: **Thirst** (South Korea), Chan–wook Park.
Special Award Orient Express: **A Frozen Flower** (South Korea), Yoo Ha.
Critics Award: **TMA** (Czech Republic), Juraj Horz.
Audience Award: **Solomon Kane** (USA), Michael J Basset.
Homage of the Year: French Cinema for its contribution to European Cinema.
Career Awards: Samuel Hadida (Producer, France), Colin Arthur (Make–Up & Special Effects Specialist, USA) and Luís Galvão Teles (Director, Portugal).
International Film Guide Inspiration Award: **First Squad** (Canada/Japan/Russia), Yoshiharu Ashino.

TVP
TELEWIZJA POLSKA

Report 2010

2010 saw the 30th edition of Fantasporto, which is Portugal's leading festival. Great Britain, France, South Korea and Denmark were the winners. Other highlights included special programmes, such as 'Robotics', with a film and lecture programme, including demonstrations by top scientists in co-operation with Spanish and Portuguese Universities, and 'Special Effects' in the presence of Colin Arthur, make-up artist on *2001: A Space Odyssey*. All of which enhanced the celebration of 30 years of a festival like no other in Portugal's city of Port wine. The Opening Night screened the premiere of *Solomon Kane* in the presence of its director, Michael Basset, and its producer, Samuel Hadida (also honoured in this edition) and the Closing Ceremony showed *The Crazies* by Breck Eisner. The festival had 92% of seats occupied in three screening theatres, with a total of 1,200 seats. In total 60,000 spectators attended the festival. A unique event in Portugal and a big party for cinema fans from all over the world. Around 270 guests (directors, producers and actors, distributors and sales agents) and over 300 media representatives attended the 30th edition. Fantasporto 2010 presented over 400 features and short films produced by, among others, 5 American major companies and the biggest European producers, with the help of over 300 producers and sales agents from around the world. *Heartless* by Philip Ridley was the winner of the 30th edition of Fantasporto, an award received by the director himself. Already championed by the festival for *Reflecting Skin*

Colin Arthur, make-up artist and workshop director, shows the head of an ape, one of the few surviving props of **2001: A Space Odyssey**, in the Closing ceremony of the 30th Fantasporto 2010. Photo by José Maria Contell.

and *The Passion of Darkly Noon*, Ridley not only won the Best Film Award in the main category, Grand Prix Fantasporto 2010, his film also picked up Best Actor and Best Screenplay. Another British film, Andrea Arnold's *Fish Tank*, received the Manoel de Oliveira Best Film Award in the Directors Week. The story of a vampire priest, *Thirst* by Park Chan–Wook from South Korea, won the Orient Express Award in the Asian films category. The Special award of the Main Competition Jury went to Danish director Ole Bornedal with *Deliver us From Evil*. France scored with the Best Screenplay and Best Special Effects awards for *La Horde* by Yannick Dahan. The Portuguese film, *Embargo*, by Antonio Ferreira, won a special mention for its screenplay. The Directors Week also saw Russian Karen Shakhnazarov's adaptation of a Anton Chekhov story, *Ward Number 6*, win the Special Jury prize.
– **Mário Dorminsky**, Festival Director.

Far East Film Festival
April 29-May 7, 2011

Born in 1998, the Far East Film Festival is the most highly anticipated annual event in **Udine**. A popular festival, *a celebration of cinema* that blends quality and entertainment in equal measure, it has carved a truly unique place for itself by presenting International and European Premieres from Japan, China, Hong Kong, Thailand, Philippines, Indonesia, Malaysia, South Korea, Taiwan, Vietnam and Singapore. With attendance figures of over 50,000 people, Far East Film has seen, year after year, an increase in interest from the international, national, and local public, including in excess of one thousand accreditation requests from journalists and buyers from Europe, Asia and America, all of whom are now loyal FEFF fans! Far East Film is now considered the most important showcase for Asian cinema in Europe. *Inquiries to:* Centro Espressioni Cinematografiche, Via Villalta 24, 33100 Udine, Italy. Tel: (39 04) 3229 9545. e: fareastfilm@cecudine.org, Web: www.fareastfilm.com.

AWARDS 2010
(The Festival doesn't have a jury so all the awards are voted for by the audience. The Audience Awards are voted for by the regular audience as well as by the White Dragon Accreditation Holders. The Black Dragon Awards are voted for by the Black Dragon Accreditation holders who support the Festival by paying a higher price for their accreditation. The Myfilms Award is voted for by the users of the Myfilms website.)

Patrick Lung Kong and His Wife together with Pang Ho-Cheung and his wife the producer Subi Liang. Photo by Paolo Jacob

Audience Award First Prize: **Castaway on the Moon** (South Korea), Lee Hey–jun.
Audience Award Second Prize: **Accidental Kidnapper** (Japan), Hideo Sakaki.
Audience Award Third Prize: **The Dreamer** (Indonesia), Riri Riza.
Black Dragon Award First Prize: **Castaway On The Moon** (South Korea), Lee Hey–jun.
Black Dragon Award Second Prize: **City Of Life And Death** (China), Lu Chuan.
Black Dragon Award Third Prize: **Accidental Kidnapper** (Japan), Hideo Sakaki.
Myfilms Award: **Bandage** (Japan), Takeshi Kobayashi.

Report 2010
Far East Film Festival surpassed the threshold of 50,000 spectators, coming from 12 different countries. The audience arrived in Udine for all the premieres presented in the competition section but also for the two retrospectives (one about Patrick Lung Kong, the other about Shintoho films) and the panel discussions held every afternoon by cinema experts. FEFF12 was

APRIL 29th
MAY 7th
2011
Udine, Italy
www.fareastfilm.com

THE FILM FESTIVAL FOR POPULAR ASIAN CINEMA
FEFF13
UDINE FAR EAST FILM

a record-breaking edition, not only because of the extraordinary programme, formed largely by previews of major new titles, but also for its excellent quality, from the top talent of new Asian cinema. **– Linda Carello**, Executive Manager.

Patrick Lung Kong in the theatre during our opening night. He was presenting at FEFF the World premiere of Dream Home. Photo by Paolo Jacob

Festival Des 3 Continents
November 23-30, 2011

The only annual competitive (with fiction and documentary) festival in the world for films that originate solely from Africa, Asia, and Latin and Black America. It's one of the few festivals where genuine discoveries may still be made. From Hou Hsiao–hsien and Abbas Kiarostami in the 1980s, to Darejan Omirbaev and Jia zang Ke more recently, yet-to-be-discovered greats have been screened and acknowledged in Nantes. For more than 30 years, F3C has also charted the film history of the southern countries through retrospectives (genres, countries, actors and actresses), screening more than 1,200 films and bringing to light an unrecognised part of the world's cinematographic heritage. The Produire Au Sud workshop created in 2000 in Nantes, takes place during the Festival of 3 Continents in order to support the creation of a network of young producers from Asia, Africa and Latin America and lay the foundations for lasting cooperation between European film professionals and emerging professionals from the South. *Inquiries to:* Festival des 3 Continents, BP 43302, 44033 Nantes Cedex 1, France. Tel: (33 2) 4069 7414. e: festival@3continents.com. Web: www.3continents.com.

Fort Lauderdale International Film Festival
Late October/early November 2011

The festival features more than 200 films from around the globe with screenings in Miami, Palm Beach and Fort Lauderdale. Awards include Best Film, Best Foreign-Language Film, Best American Indie, Best Director, Actor, Screenplay, Best Florida Film and Kodak Student prizes for Narrative (over 20 minutes), Short Narrative (20 minutes or under), Documentary and Experimental. *Inquiries to:* The Fort Lauderdale International Film Festival, 1314 East Las Olas Blvd, Suite 007, Fort Lauderdale, FL 33301, USA. Tel: (1 954) 760 9898. e: info@fliff.com. Web: www.fliff.com.

Fribourg International Film Festival
March 19-26, 2011

The festival promotes and supports independent cinema and young filmmakers from Asia, South America and Africa. The core of the festival is the high level competition of feature-length fiction and documentary films, which attracts every year audacious, artistic and visionary films. This official selection is enhanced by a short film programme. Furthermore, special sections and retrospectives offer the possibility of going deeper into a cinematographic topic, genre or period. *Inquiries to:* Fribourg International Film Festival, Ancienne Gare, Case Postale 550, CH–1701 Fribourg, Switzerland. Tel: (41 26) 347 4200. e: info@fiff.ch. Web: www.fiff.ch.

AWARDS 2010
Grand Prix Le Regard d'Or: **The Other Bank** (Georgia/Kazakhstan), George Ovashvili.
Talent Tape Award: **Tehroun** (Iran), Nader T Homayoun.
Special Jury Award: **Norteado** (Mexico/Spain), Rigoberto Perezcano.
Audience Award: **The Other Bank** (Georgia/Kazakhstan), George Ovashvili.
Ecumenical Jury Award: **Lola** (Philippines), Brillante Mendoza.
FIPRESCI Jury Award: **Border** (Armenia/Netherlands), Harutyan Khachatryan.

IFFS Jury 'Don Quijote Award': **Lola**
(Philippines), Brillante Mendoza.
Ex–Change Award: **El Vuelco Del Cangrejo**
(Colombia), Oscar Ruiz Navia.

Ghent International Film Festival
October 11-22, 2011

Belgium's most prominent annual film event,
which attracts an attendance of 132,000
plus and is selected by Variety as one of
the 50 'must attend' festivals due to its
unique focus on film music. This competitive
festival awards grants worth up to $60,000
and screens around 100 features and 50
shorts, most without a Benelux distributor.
Besides the official competition focusing
on the impact of music on film, the festival
includes the following sections: Festival
Previews (World, European, Benelux or Belgian
premières), World Cinema (films from all
over the world, mainly without a distributor),
retrospectives, a programme of media art,
film music concerts, seminars and a tribute
to an important international film maker.
The festival's Joseph Plateau Awards are the
highest honours in Benelux. Presented for
the first time in 2001, the festival also hands
out the World Soundtrack Awards, judged by
some 270 international composers. Every
year in October, the Ghent Film Festival is
the meeting point for film music composers
and fans worldwide. *Inquiries to:* Ghent
International Film Festival, 40B Leeuwstraat,
B–9000 Ghent, Belgium. Tel. (32 9) 242 8060.
e: info@filmfestival.be. Web: www.filmfestival.
be. and www.worldsoundtrackacademy.com.

AWARDS 2010
International Competition:
Grand Prix for Best Film: **Die Fremde**
(Germany), Feo Aladag.
George Delerue Award for Best Music: **The
Housemaid** (South Korea), Im Sangsoo.
Special Mention for Best Actor: **Dragomir Mrsic
in Snabba Cash** (Sweden), Daniel Espinosa.
Special Mention for Best Actress: Maryam
Zaree in **Shahada** (Germany), Burhan Qurbani.
Special Joseph Plateau Honorary Award:
Catherine Deneuve.
Special Joseph Plateau Honorary Award: Paul
Greengrass.
Port of Ghent Public Choice Award: **Die
Fremde** (Germany), Feo Aladag.
Canvas Audience Award: **Submarino**
(Denmark/Sweden), Thomas Vinterberg.
Explore Award: **Pure** (Sweden), Lisa Langseth.
Prix EFA Ghent: **Berik** (Denmark), Daniel
Joseph Borgman.
*National Lottery Award for Best Belgian
Student Short:* **Marie** (Belgium), Jozefien
Scheepers.
Special Mention: **Astaghfiro** (Belgium), Adil El
Arbi and Bilall Fallah.

Report 2010
Some 13 films competed in the international
competition with the jury comprised of
Els Dottermans, Agnes Kocsis, Wolfgang
Kohlhaase, Goran Paskaljevic, Jan Verheyen
and Jean–Paul Wall. The festival hosted 4
premieres of Belgian films: *Smoorverliefd*, *Little
Baby Jesus of Flandr*, *Pulsar* and *22nd of May*.
Striking festival previews: Mike Leigh's *Another
Year*, Saverio Costanzo's *The Solitude of Prime*

Festival director Jacques Dubrulle, director François Ozon and actress Catherine Deneuve at the 2010 Ghent Film Festival. Photographer: Luk Monsaert.

Numbers, Gregg Araki's *Kaboom*, François Ozon's *Potiche*, Thomas Vinterberg's *Submarino* and Woody Allen's *You Will Meet A Tall Dark Stranger*. Memorable guests included Catherine Deneuve, François Ozon and Paul Greengrass. Other festival activities: the exhibition 'Jacques Tati: Deux Temps, Trois Mouvements', a tribute concert to five-time Oscar winner John Barry and the 10th edition of the World Soundtrack Awards. Special guests were Gabriel Yared, Angelo Badalamenti, Howard Shore, Craig Armstrong, Stephen Warbeck, Gustavo Santaolalla, Bruno Coulais, Frédéric Devreese, Alberto Iglesias and Elliot Goldenthal. **– Tom Heirbaut**, Press & Industry.

Giffoni International Film Festival (Giffoni Experience)
July 12-23, 2011

Located in Giffoni Valle Piana, a small town about 40 minutes from Naples, the Giffoni International Film Festival for Children and Young People was founded in 1971 by Claudio Gubitosi, to promote films for youthful audiences and families. It now includes five competitive sections: Elements +6 (animated and fiction feature length films and short films that tell fantastic stories, juried by 500 children aged six to nine); Elements +10 (animated and fiction feature length films and short films, mainly fantasy and adventure, juried by 500 children aged 10 to 12); Generator +13 sees 450 teenagers (aged 13 to 15) assessing features and shorts about the pre–adolescent

world; Generator +16 has 400 jurors (aged 16 to 19) and takes a curious look at cinema for young people. Troubled Gaze has 100 jurors (from 19 years old) and is the section which explores the relationship between sons and parents. *Inquiries to:* Giffoni Film Festival, Cittadella del Cinema, Via Aldo Moro 4, 84095 Giffoni Valle Piana, Salerno, Italy. Tel: (39 089) 802 3001. e: info@giffoniff.it. Web: www.giffoniff.it.

Gijón International Film Festival
End November 2011

One of Spain's oldest festivals (49th edition in 2011), Gijón is now at the peak of its popularity. Having firmly established itself as a barometer of new film trends worldwide, it draws a large and enthusiastic public. Gijón has built on its niche as a festival for young people, programming innovative and independent films made by and for the young, including retrospectives, panoramas, exhibitions and concerts. Alongside the lively Official Section, sidebars celebrate directors who have forged new paths in film making. *Inquiries to:* Gijón International Film Festival, PO Box 76, 33201 Gijon, Spain. Tel: (34 98) 518 2940. e: info@gijonfilmfestival.com. Web: www.gijonfilmfestival.com.

goEast Festival of Central and Eastern European Film
April 6–12, 2011

goEast has been celebrating and promoting the diversity of Central and Eastern European Film since 2001. Presented by the German Film Institute – DIF, goEast presents films made by our Eastern neighbours to an interested audience, at the same time exploring the wider cultural landscape and providing a specialist forum for dialogue between East and West. The festival centres on films otherwise seldom screened in Germany, on the promotion of young filmmakers from East and West, and on cultural dialogue. Rapidly changing developments – not just in Central and Eastern Europe – raise important questions and give rise to debates in which European identities can be experienced directly. News travelled fast about the ambitious goEast programme and the special atmosphere offered by attractive locations such as the Caligari festival cinema. Over the years, goEast has established its place on the domestic and international cultural calendar, as evidenced by the international guests and wide general audience who flock to Wiesbaden each spring for the festival and its films. The festival hosts FIPRESCI Jury. Deadline: 31st December 2010. *Inquiries to:* Deutsches Filminstitut – DIF, goEast Film Festival, Schaumainkai 41, 60596 Frankfurt M, Germany. Tel: (49 11) 236 843–0. e:info@filmfestival–goeast.de. Web: www. filmfestival–goeast.de.

AWARDS 2010

The Škoda Award for Best Film – the 'Golden Lily': **Street Days** (Georgia), Levan Koguashvili. *Award of the City of Wiesbaden for Best Director:* József Pacskovszky for **Days of Desire** (Hungary). *Documentary Award – 'Remembrance and Future':* **Oy Mama** (Israel), Orna Ben Dor and Noa Maiman. *Award of the Federal Foreign Office:* **How I Ended This Summer** (Russia), Alexey Popogrebskiy. *goEast Reinhard Kämpf Memorial Prize:* **Osadne** (Czech Republic/ Slovakia), Marko Škop.

GoEast Jury and Award Winners at the Closing Ceremony in the Caligari FilmBühne (left to right): József Berger, Franziska Petri, Maciej Karpiński, Andrej Plachov, Boris Mitić, Rok Biček, Noa Maiman, József Pacskovszky, Alexej Popogrebski, Levan Koguashvili. Photographer: Bozica Babic

Report 2010

For the third time at the goEast Film Festival, the Robert Bosch Foundation awarded their Co-Production Prize for young German and Eastern European Filmmakers. Three projects were chosen and supported with a total sum of €194,300. The Awards Ceremony in Caligari FilmBühne on 27 April 2010 was a fitting climax to the tenth edition of goEast. After the closing reception traditionally held in Wiesbaden city hall, the party began at Kulturpalast. For seven days, Wiesbaden was immersed in the glow of cinematic discoveries, stimulating encounters, moments of emotion and excitement. The Festival Jury, presided over by Andrej Plachov, awarded to films from Georgia, Hungary, Israel and Russia four prizes worth €29,500 in total. More than 120 full-length and short films, distributed over four festival cinemas, viewed by over 9,000 visitors – an impressive resumé for the tenth edition of goEast, which further included the Homage to Otar Iosseliani, the symposium 'Liberating Laughter – A Short History of Eastern European Screen Humour', the Students' Competition and varied programme of accompanying events. For the third time at the goEast Film Festival, the Robert Bosch Foundation awarded their Co-Production Prize for young German and Eastern European Filmmakers. Three projects were chosen and supported with a total sum of €207,400. – **Stefan Adrian**, Festival Manager.

Göteborg International Film Festival
January 28-February 7, 2011

Now in its 34th year, Göteborg International Film Festival is one of Europe's key film events. With a large international programme and a special focus on Nordic films, including the Nordic Competition, GIFFF is Scandinavia's most important film festival. International seminars, masterclasses and the market place Nordic Film Market attract buyers and festival programmers to the newest Scandinavian films. The 30th jubilee, in 2007, introduced a new international competition – The Ingmar Bergman International Debut Award (TIBIDA). Some 1,800 professionals attend and more than 124,000 tickets are sold to 450 films from around 70 countries. *Inquiries to:* Göteborg International Film Festival, Olof Palmes Plats 1, S– 413 04 Göteborg, Sweden. Tel: (46 31) 339 3000. e: info@giff.se. Web: www.giff.se.

AWARDS 2010

Dragon Award Best Nordic Film: **R** (Denmark), Tobias Lindholm and Michael Noer.
The Nordic Film Award – Audience Choice: **The Angel** (Norway), Margreth Olin.
The Ingmar Bergman International Debut Award: **Can Go Through Skin** (The Netherlands), Esther Rots.
Dragon Award Best Swedish Documentary: **Familia** (Sweden), Mikael Wiström and Alberto Herskovitz.
Dragon Award New Talent: **Oh, Holy Night** (Sweden), Niklas Andersson.
Dragon Award Best Feature Film – Audience Choice: **The Topp Twins: Untouchable Girls** (New Zealand), Leanne Pooley.
The Synch Leader – Best Swedish Short: **Nudist** (Sweden), My Sandström.
Best Swedish Shor – Audience Choice: **Nudist** (Sweden), My Sandström and Tussilago (Sweden), Jonas Odell.
The Church of Sweden Film Award for Best Swedish Film: **Sebbe** (Sweden), Babak Najafi.
The FIPRESCI Award: **R** (Denmark), Tobias Lindholm and Michael Noer.
The Kodak Nordic Vision Award: **The Good Heart** (Denmark/Germany/Iceland), Rasmus Videbæk.
The Lorens Award: **Metropia** (Sweden), Kristina Åberg.
Nordic Film Music Prize: **Letters to Father Jacob** (Finland), Dani Strömbäck.

Hamedan International Festival of Films for Children and Young Adults
2011 Festival date to be announced

The International Festival of Films for Children and Young Adults includes different competitive sections: the International Competition of Short and Feature Films and International Competition of Short and Feature Animated Works. Three international juries judge the films: International Jury, International Youth Jury and CIFEJ Jury. Also there are some non–competitive sections, such as out of competition, special screenings, tributes and retrospectives. In the national section, new Iranian children films and videos are screened in the competitive sections. *Inquiries to:* Organisation of International Festivals, 13, 2nd Floor, Delbar Alley, Toos Street, Valiye Asr Avenue, Tehran, 19617–44973, Iran. Tel: (98 21) 2274 1250/1251. Fax: (98 21) 2273 480. e: office@icff.ir. Web: www.icff.ir.

AWARDS 2010
International Sections
International Competition of Animated Works
Golden Butterfly Award for the Best Short Film Director: Philip Hunt for **Lost And Found** (UK).
Golden Butterfly Award for the Best Short Film: **The Farmer And The Robot** (Iran), Abdollah Alimorad.
Golden Butterfly Award for the Best Feature Film Director: Eduardo Schuldt for **The Dolphin: Story Of A Dreamer** (UK).
Golden Butterfly Award for Special Jury Prize: Farshad Shafi'ie for **Mohammad Zackaryia** (Iran).
Golden Butterfly Award for the Best Feature Film: **The Jasmine Birds** (Syria), Sulafa Hijazi.

International Young Jury on stage.

International Competition of Live–action Works
Golden Butterfly Award for the Best Short Film
Director: Nuno Rocha for **3×3** (Portugal).
Golden Butterfly Award for Special Jury Prize:
Hanna Bergholm for **Gorilla** (Finland).
Golden Butterfly Award for the Best Short
Film: **Football Field** (Iran), Jalal Nassiri Hanis.
Golden Butterfly Award for the Best Asian
Feature Film: **The Homeless Student** (Japan),
Tomoyuki Furuyama.
Golden Butterfly Award for the Best Creative
Technical or Artistic Achievements: Baris
Ozbicer, Director of Photography on **Honey**
(Germany/Turkey).
Golden Butterfly Award for the Best Young
Performer: Sae Ron Kim for **A Brand New Life**
(France/South Korea).

Haugesund –
Norwegian International Film Festival
New Nordic Films: August 17-20, 2011
The Amanda Awards Ceremony:
August 20, 2011
The Norwegian International Film Festival:
August 17-26, 2011

Film Festival
Situated at the west coast of Norway, our
charming festival, often called the 'Nordic
Cannes', is a gateway to the Norwegian film
and cinema industry. With Liv Ullmann as
Honorary President, The Norwegian Film
Festival ensembles the complete Norwegian
film industry and press corps participating
in red carpet screenings, festival parties and
events along with our most famous actors and
actresses.

The **Amanda** Awards ceremony – the
Norwegian 'Oscar' – will celebrate the
previous year's Norwegian film production
during a live TV show.
The New Nordic Films Market attracts
film professionals from all over the world.
The market programme consists of films
at three different levels in the production
phase; screening of the best completed
Nordic films from 2011, a showcase for
works in progress of upcoming films and a
successful co-production and film financing
forum. Festival Director: Gunnar Johan Løvvik.
Programme Director: Håkon Skogrand.
Honorary President: Liv Ullmann. *Inquiries to:*
Norwegian International Film Festival, PO Box
145, N-5501 Haugesund, Norway. Tel: (47 52)
743 370. e: info@filmfestivalen.no. Web: www.
filmfestivalen.no.

AWARDS 2010
The Norwegian Film Critics Award: **Submarino**
(Denmark/Sweden), Thomas Vinterberg.
The Ray of Sunshine: **Another Year** (UK), Mike
Leigh.
Audience Award: **The Hedgehog** (France/Italy),
Mona Achache.
Andreas Award: **Of Gods and Men** (France),
Xavier Beauvois.
Honorary Award: Swedish actress Lena
Endre was presented with the Norwegian
International Film Festival's and Liv Ullmann's
Honorary Award.

Report 2010
The 38th Norwegian International Film
Festival's official opening film was Maria

Director Maria Sødahl (left) with actresses Lena Endre and Line Verndal on the red carpet before the 2010 festival's official opening with **Limbo***. Photographer: Helge Hansen*

Sødahl's debut film *Limbo*, and the official closing was marked with Stefan Faldbakken's *The Writing on the Wall*. A total of 113 films were screened during the festival with 80% of these being European productions. Some 1,591 professionals visited the festival. The festival's Nordic section, New Nordic Films, saw a record attendance with a participation of 366 professionals from 25 nations. Among the festival guests were Brian Cox, Stephen Rea, Michael Cera, Edgar Wright, Lena Endre and Nick Moran. **– Nina Mari Bræin**, Head of Press.

Helsinki International Film Festival – Love & Anarchy
September 15-25, 2011

The largest film festival in Finland, which achieved a record breaking attendance in 2010 of over 53,000 admissions. Organised annually since 1988, the festival has found its place as the top venue for the new and the alternative in cinema and in popular culture. The festival has a memorable subtitle, 'Love & Anarchy', adopted from a Lina Wertmüller film from the 70's. The subtitle Love & Anarchy has turned into a trademark of cutting edge films over the years: films with a spark of something different, fearlessly plunging into unexplored frontiers. The winner of the Finnkino Prize voted for by the audience gets distribution by the leading operator of multiplex theatres Finnkino with the winner in 2010 being the Japanese animation film *Summer Wars* directed by Mamoru Hosoda.

Inquiries to: Helsinki International Film Festival, Mannerheimintie 22-24, PO Box 889, FI-00101 Helsinki, Finland. Tel: (358 9) 6843 5230. e: office@hiff.fi. Web: www.hiff.fi.

Hof International Film Festival/ Internationale Hofer Filmtage
October 25-30, 2011

The Hof International Film Festival – often nicknamed 'The German Telluride' – was founded in the northern Bavarian town of Hof in 1968 by current festival director Heinz Badewitz and several up-and-coming filmmakers of the day (Wim Wenders, Volker Schloendorff, Werner Herzog and Rainer Werner Fassbinder among them) and has since gone on to become one of the most important film festivals in Germany, concentrating both on German films by the new filmmaking generation and on independent films from abroad. Another kingpin are the retrospectives that so far were dedicated to directors as varied as Monte Hellman, Mike Leigh, Lee Grant, John Sayles, Brian de Palma, Peter Jackson, Roger Corman, John Cassavetes, Costa Gavras, Wayne Wang and Bob Rafelson. It's a festival that attracts not only cinema goers and critics, but also producers, distributors and the media – not to forget the filmmakers themselves. *Inquiries to:* Hof International Film Festival, Altstadt 8, D-95028 Hof, Germany. Fax: (49) 9281 18816. e: info@hofer-filmtage.de. Web: www.hofer-filmtage.com.

Festival Director, Heinz Badewitz, and the director Bob Rafelson, subject of the Hof retrospective, before the screening of **Five Easy Pieces** *in the biggest festival cinema.*

Report 2010

In celebration of 40 years of *Five Easy Pieces*, starring a young Jack Nicholson and Karen Black, the Hof IFF invited American 'indie' legend Bob Rafelson to the Hof IFF. Over the course of his retrospective, he presented ten of his films. In all, 115 films were screened at the fest's latest edition, 68 of which were full-length films, 20 films were documentaries and 41 were international productions. As for prizes – traditionally not awarded by the festival itself, since all films are judged to be of equal importance and quality: The City of Hof Award is given by the City of Hof to a German director or actor close to the festival and Hof and is chosen by the City of Hof and festival director, Heinz Badewitz; the award – a porcelain sculpture created locally – went to director Caroline Link. The Young German Cinema Award is awarded by Bavaria Film, Bavarian Broadcasting (BR) and HypoVereinsbank for an outstanding artistic performance in a German language film screened in Hof and is given to a young person in any production category (excluding directors and actors). The award

includes prize money of €10,000. It went to film editor Marty Schenk of Ayşe Polat's *Luk's Luck* and to Peter Aufderhaar for music and sound design in Dennis Todorovic's *Sasa*. The Eastman Award for Young Talents is awarded by Kodak Germany and includes €4,000's worth of film stock; it is given to a young German director whose film screened at the festival. It went to Florian Cossen for *The Days I Was Not Born*. – **Rainer Huebsch**.

Hong Kong International Film Festival
March 20-April 5, 2011

The Hong Kong International Film Festival (HKIFF) is one of Asia's most reputable platforms for filmmakers, film professionals and filmgoers from all over the world to launch new works and experience outstanding films. Screening over 290 titles from more than 50 countries in 11 major cultural venues across the territory, the Festival is Hong Kong's largest cultural event that reaches an audience of over 600,000 including 5,000 business executives who attend the Hong Kong Film and Television

Market (FILMART), a concurrent event of the HKIFF. Committed to discovering new talent, the Festival premieres the breadth of Chinese cinema and showcases Asian talents. As a lifestyle event, festival-goers can enjoy world-class films, attend seminars hosted by leading filmmakers from around the world, visit film exhibitions, join celebration parties, and more. The Festival draws extensive media coverage from over 560 global press members and continues to grow in vital importance as the premier platform to launch films to Asia. *Inquiries to:* Hong Kong International Film Festival Office, 21/F, Millennium City 3, 370 Kwun Tong Road, Kowloon, Hong Kong. Tel: (852) 2970 3300. e: info@hkiff.org.hk. Web: www.hkiff.org.hk.

Huelva Latin American Film Festival
November 2011

The Latin American Film Festival in Huelva, which celebrates its 37th edition in 2011, is one of the most important cinematographic contests of its kind. The most outstanding films from both shores of the Atlantic get together in the third week of November in Huelva, in one of the main Latin American cultural events. Due to its international vocation, the Latin American Film Festival in Huelva aims to open the European film market to upcoming talented young people from the Latin American sector, and also hosts the Latin American Co-Production Forum, where outstanding producers, directors and distributors meet. The best film is awarded the Golden Colombus. *Inquiries to:* Casa Colon, Plaza del Punto s/n, 21003 Huelva, Spain. Tel: (34 95) 921 0170. e: festival@festicinehuelva.com. Web: www.festicinehuelva.com.

Independent Film Week
September 2011

Independent Film Week is the oldest and largest forum in the US for the discovery of new projects in development and new voices on the independent film scene. It is qualitatively and quantitatively the best and biggest opportunity in the nation for an independent filmmaker to find a funder or producer. Annually, IFP invites approximately 125 new works–in–development. Projects are accepted into one of three sections: Emerging Narrative, No Borders International co-Production Market, and Spotlight on Documentaries. A wide range of industry decision-makers make Independent Film Week their annual meeting point in New York to discover new documentaries and narrative feature projects. Strategically positioned between the Toronto and New York Film Festivals, it is an efficient week for meetings, screenings and re-connecting with colleagues. *Inquiries to:* Independent Film Week, 68 Jay Street Room 425 Brooklyn, NY 11201, USA. Tel: (1 212) 465 8200. Web: www.independentfilmweek.com.

International Film Festival and Forum on Human Rights (FIFDH)
March 4-13, 2011

The inspiration and impetus behind the International Film Festival and Forum on Human Rights (FIFDH) came from Human Rights defenders, filmmakers, representatives from the media and the University of Geneva. The FIFDH coincides with the UN Human Rights Council and is a platform for all public and private actors defending human dignity. The festival is an International Forum on Human Rights that informs and denounces violations wherever they take place. Situated in the heart of Geneva, the International Capital for Human Rights, the festival also serves as a go-between for all human rights activists. For one week, it offers debates, original film screenings and solidarity initiatives. With its concept *'a film, a subject, a debate'*, the aim of the FIFDH is to denounce attacks on human dignity and to raise public awareness through films and debates in the presence of filmmakers, defenders of human rights and recognised specialists. *Inquiries to:* Leo Kaneman and Yaël Reinharz Hazan, Directors, FIFDH Maison des Arts du Grütli, 16 rue Général Dufour, CP 5251 CH 1211 Geneva 11,

Switzerland. Tel: (41 22) 809 6900. e: contact@fifdh.ch. Web: www.fifdh.ch.

AWARDS 2010

Grand Prix FIFDH: ex aequo **Burma VJ – Reporting From A Closed Country** (Denmark/Germany), Anders Høgsbro Østergaard and **Dirty Paradise** (Switzerland), Daniel Schweizer.
Barbara Hendricks Foundation for Peace and Reconciliation Award: **Children of War** (Uganda), Bryan Single.
OMCT Award: **Nino's Place** (France), Aude Leo Rapin and Adrien Selbert.
Youth Jury Award: **Burma VJ – Reporting From A Closed Country** (Denmark/Germany), Anders Høgsbro Østergaard.

Report 2010

Once again, the International Film Festival and Forum on Human Rights (FIFDH) in Geneva raised awareness through its concept *'a film, a subject, a debate'*, on the struggle for human rights worldwide. By the time this year's

edition ended, more than 18,000 festivalgoers had attended the films and participated in the accompanying debates. The festival was organised around 12 topics, of which 'Solidarity with the People of Iran', 'Respect for the Roma', 'Indigenous Populations Sacrified', 'Russia: Freedom to Remain Silent', 'Burma: Elections under Surveillance', 'Trafficking of Women', 'Human Rights: The Chinese Puzzle', 'No Peace Without Justice?', 'Islam in Europe', 'Depenalisation of Homosexuality', 'In the Backstage of the International Criminal Tribunal for the former Yugoslavia' among others, provoked enormous interest and involvement. Among the festival's 80 guests, Juliette Binoche, Abderrahmane Sissako, The 'Yes Man' Andy Bichelbaum, Robert Badinter, Caroline Fourest, Manfred Nowak, were some of the high-profile personalities who attracted large crowds keen to debate crucial civil-society issues with them – precisely the kind of exchange needed if people are to mobilise in support of human rights victims and further the cause of human rights. The 2010 jury comprised: French Writer Jean-Marie Gustave Le Clézio, Iranian Actress Golshifteh Farahani, French Filmmaker Tony Gatlif, Pakistani Human Rights Lawyer Hina Jilani, and UN Special Envoy for Aid in Pakistan Jean-Maurice Ripert.
– **Jeffrey Hodgson**, Administrator.

International Film Festival of India
Late November/early December 2011

Annual, government-funded event recognised by FIAPF and held in Goa under the aegis of India's Ministry of Information and Broadcasting. Comprehensive 'Cinema

Actress Juliette Binoche, at a Human Rights Special Event for Cinemas in Africa, at the FIFDH. Photo: Miguel Bueno

of the World' section, foreign and Indian retrospectives and a film market, plus a valuable panorama of the year's best Indian films, subtitled in English. *Inquiries to:* The Directorate of Film Festivals, Sirifort Cultural Complex, August Kranti Marg, New Delhi 110049, India. Tel: (91 11) 2649 9398. e: dir. dff@nic.in. Web: www.iffi.nic.in.

The International Short Film Festival Winterthur
November 9-13, 2011

The International Short Film Festival Winterthur is Switzerland's most significant short film event. The festival takes place each year in November and attracts over 14,500 spectators. It is a popular audience event and an important platform for European short films and filmmakers. During five days, over 200 films are shown from all over the world. The core of the festival is the International and National Competition, where the latest short film productions contend with each other for prizes worth 46,000 CHF (€34,700). In addition, the festival offers a rich and varied supporting programme that includes thematic film programmes, panel discussions, special events and concerts. At the Swiss Film School Day and the Producers' Day, filmmakers can meet important contacts from the film industry and participate at special industry events. *Inquiries to:* International Short Film Festival Winterthur, Steiggasse 2, Postfach, CH-8402 Winterthur, Switzerland. Tel: (41 52) 212 1166. e: info@kurzfilmtage.ch. Web: www.kurzfilmtage.ch.

Festival audience 2010. Photographer: Eddymotion.ch

15th International SHORT FILM FESTIVAL WINTERTHUR 9–13 November 2011

www.kurzfilmtage.ch

Zürcher Kantonalbank

AWARDS 2010
Grand Prize of the International Competition: **The External World** (Germany), David O'Reilly.
Promotional Award of the International Competition: **Deafness** (Ukraine), Myroslav Slaboshpytskiy.
Prize for the Best Swiss Film: **Stick Climbing** (Austria/Switzerland), Daniel Zimmermann.
Swiss Cinematography Award: Yuri Lennon's **Landing on Alpha 46** (Switzerland), Pascal Walder.
Audience Price: **Heimatland** (Switzerland), Loretta Arnold, Andrea Schneider, Marius Portmann and Fabio Friedli.
Shortrun Award: **Baggern** (Switzerland), Corina Schwingruber.

Report 2010
The festival team is happy to be able to look back at yet another highly successful festival. More than 14,500 spectators visited the International Short Film Festival Winterthur from Wednesday to Sunday, allowing the festival to record yet another increase in attendance figures. Many screenings were sold out. The largest audience magnets were the International and Swiss Competition programmes. A particular highlight was the zombie and trash night on Saturday, which also sold out. The events hosted for the industry were once again a great success, above all the Producers' Day, where over 800 entries were recorded at the various events. The members of this year's jury included Balz Bachmann (composer), Catherine Colas (programme editor of short and medium-length films at ZDF/ARTE), Sergio Fant (short film programmer for the Orizzonti sidebar of the Venice Film Festival), Ardiouma Soma (Director of the African Film Library of Ouagadougou, Responsible for selecting and programming films at FESPACO), Jeanne Waltz (chief stage

designer, scriptwriter and director). **– Delphine Lyner**, Executive Director.

Istanbul International Film Festival
April 2-17, 2011

The only film festival that takes place on two continents, the Istanbul International Film Festival boasts the largest attendance in Turkey with 150,000 in 2010. In its 30th edition, the Festival will be organising two parallel photography exhibitions, and featuring a special section curated by the Turkish Film Critics Association in its programme. The festival will also include a section that assembles prominent examples of video art from the past 30 years. The 2011 edition will feature the sixth of its industry events, Meetings on the Bridge, and the fourth of its award-giving feature film development workshops. The Festival programme focuses on features dealing with the arts and the artist, or literary adaptations in its main competition, the Golden Tulip: selections from world festivals, with other thematic sections such as, 'The World of Animation', 'Mined Zone', 'Women's Films', 'Documentary Time', 'Human Rights in Cinema' with the Council of Europe Film Award – FACE, 'Young Masters' and a competitive showcase of Turkish cinema with emphasis on new talents and innovative approaches. The deadline for submissions is December 31, 2010. *Inquiries to:* Ms Azize Tan, Istanbul Foundation for Culture and Arts, Sadi Konuralp 5, Sishane 34433, Istanbul, Turkey. T: (90 212) 334 0720. e: film.fest@iksv.org. Web: www.iksv.org/film/english.

AWARDS 2010
International Competition
Golden Tulip: **The Misfortunates** (Belgium), Felix Van Groeningen.
Special Prize of the Jury: Sandrine Kiberlain in **Mademoiselle Chambon** (France), Stéphane Brizé.
FIPRESCI Prize: **Mademoiselle Chambon** (France), Stéphane Brizé.
FACE Award: **Ajami** (Israel–Germany), Scandar Copti and Yaron Shani.

FACE Award Special Prize of the Jury: **The Day God Walked Away** (France–Belgium), Philippe van Leeuw.
People's Choice Awards: **I Killed My Mother** (France), Xavier Dolan.
National Competition
Special Prize of the Jury: **Bal/Honey** (Germany/Turkey), Semih Kaplanoğlu.
FIPRESCI Prize: **Vavien** (Turkey), Yağmur Taylan and Durul Taylan.
Golden Tulip: **Vavien** (Turkey), Yağmur Taylan and Durul Taylan.
Best Turkish Director of the Year: Miraz Bezar for **Min Dît – Ben Gördüm/The Children of Diyarbakir**.
Best Actress: Şenay Orak for **Min Dît – Ben Gördüm/The Children Of Diyarbakır**.
Best Actor: Tansu Biçer for **Beş Şehir/Five Cities**.
Best Screenplay: Engin Günaydin for **Vavien**.
Best Director of Photography: Bariş Özbiçer for **Bal/Honey**.
Best Music: Mustafa Biber for **Min Dît – Ben Gördüm/The Children Of Diyarbakır**.
People's Choice Awards: **Bal/Honey** (Germany/Turkey), Semih Kaplanoğlu.
Meetings On The Bridge
Feature Film Project Development Workshop Award: Orhan Eskiköy and Zeynel Dogan for **Babamin Sesi/Voice of My Father**.
CNC Award: Emre Yeksan and Emrah Serbes for **Ust Kattaki Terörist/Terrorist Upstairs**.

Jerusalem International Film Festival
July 7-16, 2011

Celebrating its 28th Anniversary this year, the Jerusalem International Film Festival, Israel's most prestigious cinematic event, offers an alternative Middle East headline – that those of all faiths, ethnicities, and political positions have the opportunity to sit side-by-side in the shadow of the silver screen – to be moved, to share discourse and yes, to hope. Our Opening Gala event attracts over 6,000 spectators, under the stars, in the shadow of the ancient Jerusalem Walls. During the festival over 70,000 people increase their awareness of contemporary world cinema.

The festival's programme will present 150 films in a wide spectrum of themes and categories focusing on the Best of International Cinema; Best of New Israeli Cinema; Human Rights and Social Justice. Other categories include: Documentaries; Animation; Jewish Themes; Retrospectives; Avant Garde; Restorations; Television; Special Tributes and Classics. The festival has become the largest local market for international films where distributors from all over the world have the opportunity to bring the finest of World Cinema to the growing and increasingly influential Israeli Audience. Israeli filmmakers have the world première of their films at the Festival, knowing that a strong local reaction is tantamount to a new Israeli film's success througout Europe and the world. International distributors increasingly look to the Festival as a guide to new Israeli film, knowing that success in Jerusalem means a success world-wide. The festival offers dozens of professional events and seminars designed to promote and assist local filmmakers and to connect Israel to the European and International Industry. The festival has not only become the harbinger and launching point for new and cutting edge Israeli Cinema, but also an active and proud promoter. Past examples include, 'The Jerusalem Pitch Point'. For the 5th consecutive year, the festival has been a meeting place for Israeli filmmakers and producers with key members of the European and International film industry, whose aim is to encourage and promote co–productions with Europe, and beyond, of Israeli feature films. Submission deadline: April 1, 2011. *Inquiries*

to: Jerusalem Film Festival, Hebron Road 11, Jerusalem 91083, Israel. Tel: (972 2) 565 4333. e: daniel@jff.org.il. Web: www.jff.org.il.

AWARDS 2010
The Haggiag Award for Best Full-Length Feature Film: **Intimate Grammar**, Nir Bergman.
The Van Leer Award for Best First/Second Feature Film: **The Wanderer**, Avishai Sivan.
The JCC US Marketing and Distribution Award for Israeli Feature Films: **Infiltration**, Marek Rozenbaum, Itai Tamir, Michael Rozenbaum, Sophie Dulac, and Michel Zana.
The Gottlieb Award for Best Screenplay in a Full–Length Feature: Yossi Madmoni, Ari Folman, Ori Inbar, and Doron Tsabari for **Revolution 101**.
The Haggiag Family Award for Best Actress: Hila Fledman, Efrat Ben Zur, Alit Kreis and Gal Salomon for **And On The Third Day**.
The Haggiag Family Award for Best Actor: Assaf Ben Shimon for **Infiltration**.
The Haggiag Family Award for Editing: Ami Tir and Maor Keshet for **Revolution 101**.
The Haggiag Family Award for Music: Assaf Tager for **Andante**.
The Van Leer Award for Cinematography in a Full-Length Film: Shai Goldman for **The Wanderer**.
The Van Leer Award for Best Documentary: **A Film Unfinished**, Yael Hersonski.
The Best Director of a Documentary Film Award: Eran Paz for **Jeremiah**.
The Adélie Hoffenberg Award for Independent Israeli Short Film: **Yellow Mums**, Firas Khoury.
The Van Leer Award for Best Short Narrative Film: **First Aid**, Yarden Karmin.
Awards for Israeli Drama in Memory of Anat Pirchi
Best Drama: Nina Menkes for **Dissolution**.
Honourable Mention: Anton Chikishev for **Ivan**.
Best Animation: Michal Abulafia and Moran Somer for **Miracle Lady**.
'In the Spirit of Freedom' Awards in Memory of Wim van Leer
Nathan Cummings Foundation Award: Olivier Masser-Depasse for **Illégal** (Belgium/France/Luxembourg).

Jean Reno at Jerusalem International Film Festival. Photo: Nir Shanani.

28ᵗʰ JERUSALEM FILM FESTIVAL

Founder: Lia van Leer

July 7-16, 2011

Honourable Mention: Tony Gatlif for **Korkoro** (France).

Films for a Change Award: Lixin Fan for **Last Train Home** (Canada/China).

Honourable Mention: Netta Loevy for **World Class Kids** (Israel).

Vivian Ostrovsky Award: Rob Lemkin and Thet Sambath for **Enemies of the People** (Cambodia/UK).

Honourable Mention: Julia Bacha, Ronit Avni and Rula Salameh for **Budrus** (Israel/Palestine/USA).

The Jewish Experience Awards

Lia Award: Todd Solondz for **Life During Wartime** (USA).

Honourable Mention: Jacob Tierney for **The Trotsky** (Canada).

Avner Shalev Yad Vashem Chairman's Award: Fabienne Rousso–Lenoir for **Cabaret Berlin** (France/Germany).

Honourable Mention: Claude Lanzmann for **Le Rapport Karski** (France).

Forum for the Preservation of Audio–Visual Memory Award: **A Film Unfinished** (Israel), Yael Hersonski.

Special Mention: **Stalin Thought of You** (Netherlands/Russia), Kevin McNeer.

The Jerusalem Foundation Award for Experimental Films & Video Works

First Prize: **Poetry Meant to Kill**, Nadav Bin–Nun.

Second Prize: **Autobody**, Tali Keren.

The Wim van Leer Award for High School Students: **Puddle**, Oded Rimon from the Nissui School, Jerusalem.

Karlovy Vary International Film Festival
July 1-9, 2011

Founded in 1946, Karlovy Vary is one of the most important film events in Central and Eastern Europe. It includes the Official Selection – Competition, Documentary Films in Competition, East of the West – Films in Competition and other programme sections which give the unique chance to see new film production from all around the world. Film Entry deadline: April 1, 2011. *Inquiries to:* Film Servis Festival Karlovy Vary, Panská 1, CZ 110 00 Prague 1, Czech Republic. Tel: (420 2) 2141 1011. e: program@kviff.com. Web: www.kviff.com.

AWARDS 2010

Grand Prix– Crystal Globe: **The Mosquito Net** (Spain), Agustí Vila.

Special Jury Prize: **Kooky** (Czech Republic/Denmark), Jan Svěrák.

Best Director: Rajko Grlić for **Just Between Us** (Croatia/Serbia/Slovenia).

Best Actress: Anaïs Demoustier for **Sweet Evil** (France), Olivier Coussemacq.

Best Actor: Mateusz Kościukiewicz and Filip Garbacz for **Mother Teresa of Cats** (Poland).

Special Mention: **Another Sky** (Russia), Dmitri Mamulia and **There Are Things You Don't Know** (Iran), Fardin Saheb Zamani.

Best Documentary Film Under 30 Minutes: **The River** (Lithuania), Julia Gruodienė and Rimantas Gruodis.

Best Documentary Film Over 30 Minutes: **Familia** (Sweden), Mikael Wiström and Alberto Herskovits.

Special Jury Mention: **Tinar** (Iran), Mahdi Moniri.

East of the West Award: **Aurora** (Romania/France/Germany/Romania/Switzerland), Cristi Puiu.

Special Mention: **The Temptation of St. Tony** (Estonia/Finland/Sweden), Veiko Õunpuu.

Crystal Globe for Outstanding Artistic Contribution to World Cinema: Nikita Mikhalkov (Russia) and Juraj Herz (Czech Republic).

Festival President's Award: Jude Law (UK).

Audience Award: **Oldboys** (Denmark), Nikolaj Steen.

Krakow Film Festival
May 23-29, 2011

Krakow Film Festival is devoted to documentary, short and animated films. One of the oldest film events in Europe, the festival celebrates its 51st anniversary in 2011. Over the years, the Festival has gained many distinguished friends – here remarkable documentary filmmakers like Krzysztof Kieslowski, Andrzej Fidyk and Marcel Łozinski made their debut; here Pier Paolo Pasolini, Werner Herzog, Mike Leigh, Kenneth Branagh and Oscar winners Jan Sverak and Zbigniew Rybczynski presented their films. Every year KFF hosts over 500 accredited guests – filmmakers, journalists, festival representatives and around 17,000 viewers. The festival is divided into 3 sections: International Documentary Film Competition (new), International Short Film Competition and the National Competition. The diverse programme also includes retrospectives, thematic cycles and masters' screenings. The festival is accompanied by the Krakow Film Market and Dragon Forum (pitching) – a magnet bringing many film professionals to Krakow. *Inquiries to:* Krakow Film Festival, Ul Basztowa 15/8A, 31–143 Krakow, Poland. Tel: (48 12) 294 6945. e: info@kff.com.pl. Web: www.kff.com.pl.

AWARDS 2010
Feature Length Documentary Competition 30 to 60 minutes category – The Golden Horn: **Sanya and Sparrow** (Russia), Andriej Griazew. *Feature Length Documentary Competition Over 60s minute category – The Golden Horn:* **Beyond This Place** (Switzerland), Kaleo La Belle. *International Short Film Competition – The Golden Dragon:* **Out of Reach** (Poland), Jakub Sto ek. *National Competition – The Golden Hobby – Horse:* **Warsaw Available**, Karolina Bielawska and Julia Ruszkiewicz. *The EFA Nomination Krakow 2010:* **Tussilago** (Sweden), Jonas Odell. *Dragon of Dragons Special Prize for Lifetime Achievement:* Jonas Medas.

La Rochelle International Film Festival
July 1-10, 2011

Our world-renowned Festival is non-competitive and features more than 250 original and new releases from all over the world to a large audience (78,150 in 2010) of very enthusiastic film buffs. The festival includes tributes to contemporary directors or actors, often in their presence (last year: Sergey Dvortsevoy (Kazakhstan), Pierre Etaix (France), Peter Liechti (Switzerland), Lucian Pintilie (Poland), Ghassan Salhab (Lebanon). A panorama of Indian cinema; retrospectives devoted to the work of past filmmakers (last year: Elia Kazan and Greta Garbo); Here and There, a selection of unreleased films from all over the world; From Yesterday till Today, premieres of rare films restored and re-edited; Carpets, Cushions and Video, video works projected on the ceiling above spectators who are lying down; Films for Children. The festival ends with an all night programme of five films, followed by breakfast in cafés overlooking the old port. *Inquiries to:* La Rochelle International Film Festival, 16 rue Saint Sabin, 75011 Paris, France. Tel: (33 1) 4806 1666. e: info@festival–larochelle.org. Web: www.festival–larochelle.org. Director: Mrs Prune Engler; Artistic Director: Mrs Sylvie Pras; Managing Director: Mr Arnaud Dumatin.

Las Palmas de Gran Canaria International Film Festival
April 1-9, 2011

The festival is proud of its role as a defender of creative and independent productions from outside the mainstream. There are two main competitive sections: the Official Section, including arthouse feature films and short films unreleased in Spain, and the New Directors Section. The main awards are the Golden Lady Harimaguada and the Silver Lady Harimaguada. They both have monetary prizes and are split into three parts relating to the director, the firm responsible for producing the film and the Spanish distributor… if this exists! Another important prize is the Best New

Director Award, for which there is also a cash prize. *Inquiries to:* Las Palmas de Gran Canaria International Film Festival, León y Castillo 322, 4ª Planta, 35007 Las Palmas de Gran Canaria. Tel: (34 928) 446 833. e: coordinacion@festivalcinelaspalmas.com or programacion@festivalcinelaspalmas.com. Web: www.festivalcinelaspalmas.com.

Leeds International Film Festival
November 3-20, 2011

Presented by Leeds City Council, the Leeds International Film Festival is the largest regional Film Festival in the United Kingdom and will celebrate its 25th Anniversary in 2011. The Film Festival programme will feature Official Selection, Cinema Versa, Fanomenon, Thought Bubble, Short Film City and Cherry Kino. In addition, Leeds Film organises year-round exhibition with partner organisations in the city, education programmes and delivers the Leeds Young People's Film Festival. *Inquiries to:* Leeds International Film Festival, The Town Hall, The Headrow, Leeds, LS1 3AD, UK. Tel: (44 113) 247 8398. e: leedsfilmfestpr@gmail.com. Web: www.leedsfilm.com.

Festival del film Locarno
August 3-13, 2011

Founded in 1946, located right in the heart of Europe in a Swiss-Italian town on Lake Maggiore, the Festival del film Locarno is one of the world's top film events, offering a panoramic view of the full range of current cinematic expression. With its three competitive sections, Concorso internazionale (International Competition), Concorso Cineasti del presente (Filmmakers of the Present) Concorso Pardi di domani (Leopards of Tomorrow), the Festival takes stock of new approaches and perspectives in filmmaking; throughout its 63 years history, Locarno has often discovered or confirmed the reputation directors who now enjoy widespread recognition. The Festival also provides a showcase for major new films from around the world: every night the famous open

John C Reilly. © Festival del film Locarno / Ti-Press - Putzu

air screenings offer prestigious premieres to an audience up to 8,000 people in the extraordinary setting of Piazza Grande. The Festival del film Locarno has also established itself in recent years as an important industry showcase for auteur filmmaking, a perfect networking opportunity for distributors, buyers and producers from all countries with over 3,000 film professionals and 900 journalists attending – together with 150,000 filmgoers. *Inquiries to:* Festival del film Locarno, Via Ciseri 23, CH–6601 Locarno, Switzerland. Artistic Director: Olivier Père. Tel: (41 91) 756 2121. e: info@pardo.ch. Web: www.pardo.ch.

AWARDS 2010
Concorso internazionale
Pardo d'oro (Golden Leopard): **Winter Vacation** (China), LI Hongqi.
Premio speciale della giuria (Special Jury Prize): **Morgen** (France/Hungary/Romania), Marian Crisan.
Pardo per la migliore regia (Best Director): Denis Côté for **Curling** (Canada).
Pardo per la miglior interpretazione femminile (Best Actress): Jasna Duricic in **White White World** (Germany/Serbia/Sweden).
Pardo per la miglior interpretazione maschile (Best Actor): Emmanuel Bilodeau in **Curling** (Canada).
Concorso Cineasti del presente
Pardo d'oro – Premio George Foundation (Golden Leopard): **Paraboles** (France), Emmanuelle Demoris.
Premio speciale della giuria CINÉ CINÉMA (Special CINÉ CINÉMA Jury Prize): **Foreign**

Parts (France/USA), Verena Paravel and JP Sniadecki.

Special Mention: **Ivory Tower** (Canada/France), Adam Traynor.

Opera prima

Pardo per la migliore opera prima (Best First Feature): **Foreign Parts** (France/USA), Verena Paravel and JP Sniadecki.

Special Mention: **Aardvark** (Argentina/USA), Kitao Sakurai.

Other Awards

Prix du Public UBS (Audience Awards): **The Human Resources Manager** (France/Germany/Israel), Eran Riklis.

Variety Piazza Grande Award: **Rare Exports: A Christmas Tale** (Finland/France/Norway/Sweden), Jalmari Helander.

Report 2010

Highlights of the 63rd Festival, the first edition led by Olivier Père, included: the retrospective on Ernst Lubitsch; major names in world cinema in conversation with festivalgoers at the Forum, from Chinese director Jia Zhang–ke and Swiss filmmaker Alain Tanner (Pardo d'onore Swisscom, Leopard of Honour), to Israeli producer Menahem Golan (Premio Raimondo Rezzonico per il Miglior Produttore Indipendente, Best Indie Producer Award), plus French actress Chiara Mastroianni (Excellence Award Moët & Chandon); or the Open Doors co-production lab for new projects by a dozen of filmmakers from Central Asia. **– Alessia Botani**, Head of Editorial Content.

BFI London Film Festival
October 2011

The UK's largest and most prestigious public film festival presented at the BFI Southbank, West End venues, and at cinemas throughout the capital. The programme comprises around 200 features and documentaries as well as showcasing over 100 short films. There is a British section and a very strong international selection from Asia, Africa, Europe, Latin America, US independents and experimental and avant–garde work. More than 1,600 UK and international press and industry representatives attend and there is a buyers/sellers liaison office. *Inquiries to:* Emilie Arnold, London Film Festival, BFI Southbank, Belvedere Road, South Bank, London SE1 8XT, UK. Tel: (44 20) 7815 1305. e: emilie.arnold@bfi.org.uk. Web: www.bfi.org.uk/lff.

AWARDS 2010
Star of London

Best Film: **How I Ended This Summer** (Russia), Alexei Popogrebsky.

Best British Newcomer: **The Arbor** (UK), Clio Barnard.

The Sutherland Trophy Winner: **The Arbor** (UK), Clio Barnard.

The BFI London Film Festival Grierson Award: **Armadillo** (Denmark), Janus Metz.

BFI Fellowship: Danny Boyle.

Report 2010

The 54th BFI London Film Festival screened a total of 197 features and 105 shorts, including 18 World, 23 International and 28 European premieres, many presented by cast members and filmmakers. Amongst others, directors Danny Boyle, Mike Leigh, Mark

*Closing Night Gala, **127 Hours**, from left, Aron Ralston, Danny Boyle and James Franco.*

Romanek, Julian Schnabel and Apichatpong Weerasethakul took the opporunity to present their latest works in London. The Festival's events included Masterclasses by Alejandro González Iñárritu, Lisa Cholodenko, Olivier Assayas and Peter Mullan, and Screen Talks by Darren Aronofsky and Mark Romanek. Another highlight was the industry keynote speech by Ken Loach, which launched the extensive 2010 industry programme. Jury members of this year's four awards categories included: Gabriel Byrne, Patricia Clakson, John Hillcoat, Rebecca O'Brien, Sandy Powell, Olivia Williams and Michael Winterbottom. **–Tim Platt**, Festival Marketing Manager.

Los Angeles Film Festival
June 16-26, 2011

Now in its seventeenth year, the Los Angeles Film Festival is widely recognised as a world-class event, showcasing the best in new American and international cinema and providing the film-loving public with access to some of the most critically acclaimed filmmakers, film industry professionals, and emerging talent from around the world. The Festival features unique signature programmes including the Filmmaker Retreat, Ford Amphitheatre Outdoor Screenings, Poolside Chats, and more. Additionally, the Festival screens short films created by high school students and has a special section devoted to music videos. Over 200 features, shorts, and music videos, representing more than 40 countries, make up the main body of the Festival. *Inquiries to:* Los Angeles Film Festival, 9911 W Pico Blvd, Los Angeles, CA 90035, USA. Tel: (1 310) 432 1200. e: lafilmfest@filmindependent.org. Web: www.lafilmfest.com.

Málaga Film Festival
March 26–April 2, 2011

The Malaga Film Festival, together with the Goya prizes, have grown to become the two key appointments for the whole audiovisual sector of Spanish Cinema. A festival that brings together all the industry professionals both to present their films and to debate questions affecting the audiovisual sector. *Inquiries to:* Malaga Film Festival, Calle Ramos Marin 2, 29012 Malaga, Spain. Tel: (34 95) 222 8242. e: info@festivaldemalaga.com. Web: www.festivaldemalaga.com.

International Filmfestival Mannheim-Heidelberg
November 2011

The festival of independent new film artists presents around 40 international new feature films in two main sections, International Competition and International Discoveries. Our films are genuine premieres as we do not screen any films that have already been screened at other festivals such as Cannes, Berlin, Venice, Locarno, or at any German festival. The selection process is a radical one: they have to be really outstanding new arthouse films by new directors. The newly-born MANNHEIM MEETING PLACE is a new project of the International Filmfestival Mannheim-Heidelberg aiming at supporting outstanding film projects concerning distribution or co-production. The focus will be on the improvement of market opportunities of completed arthouse films. Furthermore, selected producers are invited to become potential co–producers of new film projects. More than 60,000 filmgoers and 1,000 film professionals attend. *Inquiries to:* Dr Michael Koetz, International Filmfestival Mannheim–Heidelberg, Collini–Center, Galerie, D-68161 Mannheim, Germany. Tel: (49 621) 102 943. e: info@iffmh.de. Web: www.iffmh.de.

Mar del Plata International Film Festival
Mid November 2011

The festival is the only A-grade film festival in Latin America with an Official Competition, usually comprising around 15 films, generally two from Argentina. Other sections include Latin American Films, Out of Competition, Point of View, Near Darkness, Soundsystem, Heterodoxy, Documentary Frame, Argentine

Showcase, Memory in Motion and The Inner Look. *Inquiries to:* Mar del Plata International Film Festival, Hipólito Yrigoyen 1225 (C1085ABO), Buenos Aires, Argentina. Tel: (54 11) 4383 5115. e: info@ mardelplatafilmfest. com. Web: www.mardelplatafilmfest.com.

Melbourne International Film Festival
July 21–August 7, 2011

MIFF is unequivocally regarded as the most significant film event in Australia. It has the largest and most diverse programme of screenings and special events in the country, in addition to the largest audience. There is also growing international regard for MIFF as a film market place, with a steady increase in sales agents attending. The longest-running festival in the southern hemisphere showing more than 400 features, shorts, documentaries and new media works, presented in five venues. *Inquiries to:* MIFF, PO Box 4982, Melbourne 3001, Victoria, Australia. Tel: (61 3) 8660 4888. e: miff@melbournefilmfestival. com.au. Web: www.melbournefilmfestival. com.au.

Miami International Film Festival
March 4-13, 2011

The Festival, presented by Miami Dade College, is considered one of the best Ibero-centric film festivals in the U.S. It is designed to introduce the finest selection of current films and filmmakers to South Florida's residents and visitors. The Festival encompasses international film screenings, gala premieres, REEL seminars and the Miami Film Society, which offers Members an inclusive and rewarding range of year-round activities that investigate and celebrate the artistry and innovation of the world's most imaginative cinematic visionaries. *Inquiries to:* Miami International Film Festival, 25 NE 2nd Street, Suite 5518, Miami, Florida 33132, USA. Tel: (1 305) 237 3456. e: info@miamifilmfestival.com. Web: www. miamifilmfestival.com.

AWARDS 2010
World Cinema Competition Knight Grand Jury Prize: **Lola** (France/Philippines), Brillante Mendoza.
Ibero-American Competition Knight Grand Jury Prize: **To the Sea**, (Mexico), Pedro González-Rubio.
Dox Competition Grand Jury Prize: **Sins of My Father**, (Argentina/Colombia), Nicolas Entel.
Shorts Competition Grand Jury Prize: **Believe** (UK), Paul Wright.
Cutting the Edge Competition: **Pepperminta** (Austria /Switzerland), Pipilotti Rist.
The Fipresci Prize: **Judge**, (China), Liu Jie.

Mill Valley Film Festival
October 2011

Known as a filmmakers' festival, the Festival offers a high profile, prestigious, non-competitive and welcoming environment perfect for celebrating the best in independent and world cinema. MVFF presents over 200 films from 50 countries featuring a wide variety of high calibre international programming, in beautiful Marin County, just across the Golden Gate Bridge. Celebrating its 34th year in 2011, the festival includes the innovative Children's Film Fest, celebrity tributes, seminars and special events. *Inquiries to:* Mill Valley Film Festival/California Film Institute, 1001 Lootens Place, Suite 220, San Rafael, CA 94901, USA. Tel: (1 415) 383 5256. e: mvff@cafilm.org. Web: www.mvff.com.

Montreal World Film Festival
August 25-September 5, 2011

The goal of the festival is to encourage cultural diversity and understanding between nations, to foster the cinema of all continents by stimulating the development of quality cinema, to promote filmmakers and innovative works, to discover and encourage new talents, and to promote meetings between cinema professionals from around the world. Apart from the 'Official Competition' and the 'First Films Competition', the festival presents 'Hors Concours' (World Greats), a 'Focus on World

Cinema' and 'Documentaries of the World', plus tributes to established filmmakers and a section dedicated to Canadian student films. *Inquiries to:* Montreal World Film Festival 1432 de Bleury St, Montreal, Quebec, Canada H3A 2J1. Tel: (1 514) 848 3883 e. info@ffm-montreal.org. Web: www.ffm-montreal.org.

Moscow International Film Festival
June 2011

The large competition remains international in scope and genres, covering Europe and the CIS, South East Asia, Latin and North America. The Media-Forum (panorama and competition) is devoted to experimental films and video art. There is also a wide panorama of recent Russian films, and a special documentary cinema programme, 'Free Thought'. In addition, the festival included the programmes 'Asian Extreme', 'Focus on Chile', '8 1/2 films', 'Russian Trace', 'Socialist Avant– Gardizm', 'New Wave Forever', Tchekhov's Motives and retrospectives of Claude Chabrol, Luc Besson and Sergio Leone. The festival also runs the Industry Co–Production Forum. *Inquiries to:* Moscow International Film Festival, Sadovnicheskaya ulitsa, 72–2, Moscow 115035, Russia. Tel: (7 495) 725 2622. e: info@moscowfilmfestival.ru. Web: www.moscowfilmfestival.ru.

AWARDS 2010
Golden George Film Award: **Hermano** (Venezuela), Marcel Rasqiun.
Silver George Film Award: **Der Albaner** (Albania/Germany), Johannes Naber.
Silver George Film Award for the Best Direction: **Rozyczka** (Poland), Jan Kidawa–Blonski.
Silver George Film Award for the Best Actor: Nik Xhelilaj for **Der Albaner** (Albania/Germany),
Silver George Film Award for the best actress: Vilma Cibulkova for **Zemský Ráj To Na Pohled** (Czech Republic).
Silver George Film Award for the Best Film of the Perspectives Competition: **Rewers** (Poland), Borys Lankosz.
Special Prize for Outstanding Contribution To

World Cinema: Claude le Louch (France).
Special Prize for Outstanding Achievement In The Career of Acting And Devotion To The Principles Of K Stanislavsky's School: Emmanuelle Béart (France).

Netherlands Film Festival, Utrecht
September 21-30, 2011

Since 1981, The Netherlands Film Festival (NFF) has presented the latest crop of Dutch feature films, documentaries, short films and television films to the Dutch public, as well as an audience of international and Dutch-based professionals. Many of these productions are world premieres, of which a selection compete for the grand prize of Dutch cinema, the Golden Calf for Best Film. During the festival, each film genre is allotted its own special day. Retrospectives and special programmes offer audiences a chance to review films from previous years. Furthermore the festival screens films made by talented young filmmakers from the Dutch audio-visual institutes as well as short and long films from neighbouring Flanders. Interviews, workshops, parties and exhibitions make the festival complete – a unique platform that highlights the very best of Dutch cinema. The Holland Film Meeting (HFM) is a sidebar of the Netherlands Film Festival that provides a series of business-oriented events for the international professionals in attendance. The HFM consists of the Benelux Screenings, the Netherlands Production Platform (NPP), professional workshops and panels, the Variety Cinema Militants Programme and the Binger-Screen International Interview. *Inquiries to:* Netherlands Film Festival, PO Box 1581, 3500 BN Utrecht, Netherlands. Tel: (31 30) 230 3800. e: info@filmfestival.nl. Web: www.filmfestival.nl.

NETHERLANDS FILM FESTIVAL 21 SEP- 30 SEP 2011 UTRECHT

24RD HOLLAND FILM MEETING, SEP 22 – SEP 26, 2011
THE ANNUAL GET-TOGETHER OF DUTCH AND FOREIGN FILM PROFESSIONALS
FOR MORE INFORMATION: WWW.FILMFESTIVAL.NL

Golden Calf winners 2010: Barry Atsma (Best Actor) & Carice van Houten (Best Actress). Photo: Felix Kalkman

AWARDS 2010

Country of Origin for all shown:
The Netherlands
Best Short Film: **Broken Moon**, Arno Dierickx.
Best Short Documentary: **Weapon of War**, Ilse van Velzen and Femke van Velzen.
Best Full-Length Documentary: **Farewell**, Ditteke Mensink.
Best TV Drama: **Finnemans**, Thomas Korthals Altes.
Best Production Design: **Happily Ever After**, Vincent de Pater.
Best Camera: **R U There**, Lennert Hillege.
Best Sound Design: **R U There**, Peter Warnier.
Best Editing: **Tirza**, Job ter Burg.
Best Music: **C'est Déjà l'été**, Ernst Reijseger.
Best Male Supporting Role: **Her Majesty**, Jeroen Willems.
Best Female Supporting Role: **Joy**, Coosje Smid.
Best Actor: **Stricken**, Barry Atsma.
Best Actress: **Happy Housewife**, Carice van Houten.
Best Screenplay: **Joy**, Helena van der Meulen.
Best Director: **Tirza**, Rudolf van den Berg.
Best Full-Length Feature Film: **Joy**, Frans van Gestel, Jeroen Beker, Arnold Heslenfeld and IDTV Film.
Special Jury Award: **Happily Ever After**, Cast.
Film 1 Audience Award: **Happily Ever After**, Pieter Kramer.
Dutch Film Critics Award: **Dusk**, Hanro Smitsman.

Report 2010

This year the Netherlands Film Festival celebrated its 30th birthday: Celebrate the Dutch Film! During this year's event there was a great emphasis placed on acting and a retrospective view on Dutch film of the past 30 years and the reflection on today's society. Rudolf van den Berg's *Tirza* opened the Festival and the Golden Calves were awarded during the Dutch Film Gala, which concluded the Festival. The Festival pulled in a record number of 154,000 visitors. The Netherlands Online Film Festival (NOFF), NFF TV (YouTube) and the NFF website attracted 3 million visitors. **– Marieke Saly**.

New Zealand International Film Festival

Auckland July 2011
Wellington End July 2011

Since 2009, both the Auckland International Film Festival and the Wellington Film Festival have dropped their individual identities to become known as the New Zealand International Film Festival. The Festival provides a non-competitive New Zealand premiere showcase and welcomes many international filmmakers and musicians. Highlights of its programme, brimming with animation, arthouse, documentaries and retrospective programmes, tour to a further 14 New Zealand centres. Festival Director: Bill Gosden. *Inquiries to:* New Zealand International Film Festivals, Box 9544, Marion Square, Wellington 6141, New Zealand. Tel: (64 4) 385 0162. e: festival@nzff.co.nz. Web: www.nzff.co.nz.

Visions du Réel, International Film Festival – Nyon

April 7-13, 2011

Visions du Réel is a unique international Festival providing an overview of the best of cinema du réel, with films challenging the usual boundaries of genre, made by independent filmmakers and producers taking risks in radical aesthetical choices, with strong writing and new forms of storytelling. As part of Visions du Réel, Doc Outlook-International Market features Pitching Sessions, Market Screenings and Panels that attract 710

VISIONS DU RÉEL
INTERNATIONAL FILM FESTIVAL
DOC OUTLOOK-INTERNATIONAL MARKET
NYON, 7-13 APRIL 2011

THE FINE FESTIVAL IN THE HEART OF EUROPE WITH ITS FAMOUS
SECTIONS OPEN TO THE SUPERB DIVERSITY OF FILMS DU RÉEL...
THE MARKET WITH A PREMIUM SELECTION, COPRODUCTION MEETINGS,
PACE MAKER FOR TENDENCIES IN NEW MEDIA...

NYON: THE SPRING OF FESTIVALS!

ENTRY FORMS AND REGULATIONS
WWW.VISIONSDUREEL.CH

Deadlines for entries Festival: 15 October 2010 and 15 December 2010
Deadline for Market: 1 March 2011

Schweizerische Eidgenossenschaft   Bundesamt für Kultur BAK
Confédération suisse   Office fédéral de la culture OFC
Confederazione Svizzera
Confederaziun svizra   Direktion für Entwicklung und Zusammenarbeit DEZA
                                     Direction du développement et de la coopération DDC

MEDIA   SRG SSR idée suisse

PARTNER
OF
DOC
ALLIANCE

professionals from 33 countriies across the world, even with the eruptions of that blasted Icelandic volcano! With the departure of Jean Perret and Gabriela Bussmann, the Festival enters a new era under the aegis of Luciano Barisone. Entry deadlines: Festival: 15 December 2010. Market: 1 March 2011. *Inquiries to:* Visions du Réel, 18 Rue Juste-Olivier, CH-1260 Nyon, Switzerland. Tel: (41 22) 365 4455. e: docnyon@visionsdureel.ch. Web: www.visionsdureel.ch.

AWARDS 2010

International Competition
Grand Prix La Poste Suisse Visions du Réel:
Into Eternity (Denmark/Finland), Michael Madsen.
Prix SRG SSR Idée Suisse: **Sainte Anne, Hopital Psychiatrique** (France), Ilan Klipper and **Something About Georgia** (France), Nino Kirtadzé.
Audience Prize: **Salaam Isfahan** (Belgium/Iran), Sanaz Azari.
Young Audience Prize of the Société des Hôteliers de la Côte: **Le Plein Pays** (France), Antoine Boutet.
Special Mention: **Aisheen (Still Alive in Gaza)** (Qatar/Switzerland), Nicolas Wadimoff.
Inter-religious Jury Prize: **Steam of Life** (Finland/Sweden), Joonas Berghäll and Mika Hotakainen.
Regards Neufs
Prix de le Canton Vaud: **Alda** (Czech Republic), Viera Cákanyová and **La Cuerda Floja** (Mexico), Nuria Ibáñez Castañeda.
Special Mention: **Nargis, When Time Stopped Breathing** (Germany).

Gabriela Bussmann and Jean Perret at the closing night of the 16th edition of Visions du Réel. Photo: Michel Perret © for Visions du Réel

Cinéma Suisse
Prize of the George Foundation for the Best Film Newcomer: **Goodnight Nobody** (Germany/Switzerland), Jacqueline Zünd.
Prize of Suissimage and the Société Suisse des Auteurs SSA: **Beyond This Place** (Germany/Switzerland), Kaleo La Belle.
Prize Télévision Suisse Romande 'Perspective d'un doc': **Guerrilla Gardening ou la reconquête des villes** (Switzerland), Nicolas Humbert
Prize Loterie Romande Vaud et Genève (First Steps): **Cotonov Vanished** (Switzerland), Andreas Fontana.
From All Sections
Prize Buyens-Chagoll: **Aisheen (Still Alive in Gaza)** (Qatar/Switzerland), Nicolas Wadimoff.

Report 2010

What a fine selection in 2010, with 166 films from 31 countries. A large number of visitors, as well as professionals from a wide range of backgrounds, were delighted with this great diversity of genres, scenarios, opinions and visions, which have been the hallmark of the Festival for 16 years. Nyon was again the capital of this branch of film, with 47 works receiving their world premiere and 36 their European premiere. The place to be with Alan Berliner and Wu Wenguang in the 'Ateliers', Iran, China, EURODOC, ARTE-SRG SSR idée suisse, Doc Alliance in 'Séances spéciales', Tracey Emin in Reprocessing Reality, and then Lou Reed himself, not forgetting the rappers of *Aisheen (Still Alive in Gaza)* in a two-way link-up from Gaza; and the Doc Outlook-International Market and its co-production meetings at the summit. – **Brigitte Morgenthaler**, Communication & Partnerships.

Oberhausen
International Short Film Festival
May 5-10, 2011

The International Short Film Festival Oberhausen, one of the leading short film festivals in the world, is known for its open attitude towards short formats and its focus on experimental works. The traditional competitions – International, German, Children's Shorts and Music Video – provide an extensive overview of current international short film and video production, and a fifth competition for regional films (NRW Competition) was introduced in 2009. The 2010 curated programme, From The Deep, presented a rare look at early film prior to 1918, revealing rarely seen artefacts and continuing Oberhausen's exploration of the issue of the presentation of artistic films. Oberhausen also continued its PODIUM series of lively and very well attended discussions. Retrospectives of the works of Swedish avant-garde pioneer Gunvor Nelson and the young Indian director Amit Dutta were among the other highlights of the festival. Deadline for entries: 15 January 2011. Entry forms and regulations can be downloaded at www. kurzfilmtage.de from October 2010. Festival Director: Dr Lars Henrik Gass. *Inquiries to:* Oberhausen International Short Film Festival, Grillostrasse 34, D-46045 Oberhausen, Germany. Tel: (49 208) 825 2652. e: info@ kurzfilmtage.de. Web: www.kurzfilmtage.de.

Odense International Film Festival
August 22-28, 2011

Denmark's only international short film festival invites the best international unusual short films with original and imaginative content. Besides screenings of more than 200 National and International short films and Danish documentaries, Odense Film Festival offers a number of exciting retrospective programmes and viewing of all competition films in the Video Bar. The festival hosts a range of seminars for film professionals, librarians and teachers, educates children and youth in the field of forceful, alternative film experiences and is a meeting place for international film directors and other film professionals in the field of short films and documentaries. *Inquiries to:* Odense International Film Festival, Kulturmaskinen, Farvergården 7, DK-5100 Odense C, Denmark. Tel: (45) 6551 2821. e: filmfestival@odense.dk. Web: www.filmfestival.dk.

Oulu International Children's and Youth Film Festival
November 21-27, 2011

Annual festival with a competition for feature films for children and youth, it screens recent titles and retrospectives. Oulu is set in northern Finland, on the coast of the Gulf of Bothnia. *Inquiries to:* Oulu International Children's and Youth Film Festival, Hallituskatu 7, FI-90100 Oulu, Finland. Tel: (358 8) 881 1293. e: eszter.vuojala@oufilmcenter.fi. Web: www. oulunelokuvakeskus.fi/lef.

AWARDS 2010
Kaleva Award: **The Crocodiles Strike Back** (Germany), Christian Ditter.
CIFEJ-Prize: **Super Brother** (Denmark), Birger Larsen.
The Church Media Foundation's Prize: **Look At Me** (Finland), Iiris Härmä.
The Northern Film and Media Foundation POEM's Little Bear Award: Mari Rantasila.

Report 2010
The festival was a success with over 16,000 admissions. There were 11 films in competition. The other sections were Kaleidoscope, Growing Pains (Youth Section),

Film Director Mari Rantasila with children. Photo: Emilia Ponkala.

Finnish Survey, Documentary and Short Films. The focus was on Italian children's films and on Italian animator Enzo D'Alò. The Guest of Honour was Finnish director and scriptwriter Marjut Komulainen. An exhibition entitled Dante in Comics, a Youth Concert and a Creative Class Seminar enriched the programme. **– Eszter Vuojala**, Festival Director.

Festival guests. Photo: Emilia Ponkala..

Palm Springs International Film Festival
January 6-17, 2011

Palm Springs, celebrating its 22nd edition in 2011, is one of the largest film festivals in the US, hosting 130,000 attendees for a line-up of over 189 films at the 2010 event. Special sections of the festival have included Cine Latino, New Voices/New Visions, Gala Screenings, Awards Buzz (Best Foreign Language Oscar Submissions), World Cinema Now, Modern Masters and the True Stories documentary section. The festival includes a Black Tie Awards Gala on January 8, 2011 – 2010 honorees included Morgan Freeman, Helen Mirren, Jason Reitman, Quentin Tarantino, Jeff Bridges, Anna Kendrick, Mariah Carey, and Jeremy Renner. *Inquiries to:* Darryl MacDonald, 1700 E Tahquitz Canyon Way, Suite 3, Palm Springs, CA 92262, USA. Tel: (1 760) 322 2930. e: info@psfilmfest.org. Web: www.psfilmfest.org.

AWARDS 2010
Mercedes-Benz Audience Award for Best Narrative Feature: **The Girl with the Dragon Tattoo** (Denmark/Germany/Sweden), Niels Arden Oplev.

Audience Award for Best Documentary Feature: **The Most Dangerous Man in America: Daniel Ellsberg and the Pentagon Papers** (USA), Judith Erlich and Rick Goldsmith.
FIPRESCI Award for Best Foreign Language Film: **Involuntary** (Sweden), Ruben Östlund.
FIPRESCI Award Best Actor: Tedo Bekhauri for **The Other Bank** (Georgia/Kazakhstan), George Ovashvili.
FIPRESCI Award Best Actress: Anne Dorval for **I Killed My Mother** (Canada), Xavier Dolan.
New Voices/New Visions Award: **A Brand New Life** (France/South Korea), Ounie Lecomte.
John Schlesinger Award for Outstanding First Feature: **Eyes Wide Open** (Israel), Haim Tabakman.
Bridging the Borders Award: **Letters to Father Jacob** (Finland), Klaus Härö.

Pesaro Film Festival
June 19-27, 2011

The Mostra Internazionale del Nuovo Cinema/Pesaro Film Festival was founded in Pesaro in 1965 by Bruno Torri and Lino Miccichè, and since 2000 has been directed by Giovanni Spagnoletti. The Pesaro Film Festival, in addition to being known for the dynamic and original documentation it offers, is synonymous with discoveries, with showcasing emerging cinematographers, with re-readings and 'Special Events'. *Inquiries to:* Mostra Internazionale del Nuovo Cinema/Pesaro Film Festival, Via Emilio Faà di Bruno 67, 00195 Rome, Italy. Tel: (39 06) 445 6643/491156. e: info@pesarofilmfest.it. Web: www.pesarofilmfest.it.

AWARDS 2010
New Cinema Competition: **Eighteen** (South Korea), Jang Kun-jae.
Amnesty Italia/Cinema and Human Rights: ex aequo **Plennyy/Captive** (Russia), Aleksey Uchitel and **Budrus** (Israel/Palestine/USA), Julia Bacha.
Pesaro Cinemagiovane: **Kislorod/Oxygen** (Russia), Ivan Vyrypayev.
Special Mention: **Miyoko** (Japan), Yoshifumi Tsubota.

Public's Award: **Travelling with Pets** (Russia), Vera Storozheva.

Pordenone Silent Film Festival
October 1-8, 2011

The world's first and largest festival dedicated to silent cinema, now celebrating its 30th year. The event sees archivists, historians, scholars, collectors and enthusiasts from around the world arriving for the event, along with cinema students chosen to attend the internationally recognised 'Collegium'. Year-by-year, the festival consistently succeeds in rediscovering lost masterpieces from the silent years, all accompanied by original live music. Festival Director: David Robinson. *Inquiries to:* Le Giornate del Cinema Muto c/o La Cineteca del Friuli, Palazzo Gurisatti, via Bini 50, 33013 Gemona (UD), Italy. Tel: (39) 0432 980458. e: info.gcm@cinetecadelfriuli.org. Web: www. giornatedelcinemamuto.it.

Director David Robinson amuses festival attendants with a far too long list of thanks. Photo by Paolo Jacob.

Report 2010
Highlights of the 2010 festival include the international premiere of John Ford's comedy *Upstream*, long believed to be lost and recently repatriated from the New Zealand Film Archive thanks to the National Film Preservation Foundation; MoMA's new colour copy of Douglas Fairbanks' *Robin Hood*; and orchestral shows such as Keaton's *The Navigator* accompanied by the improvisational European Silent Screen Virtuosi, and a special performance of *Wings*, with score by Carl Davis. Two major retrospectives offered the opportunity to rediscover, respectively, the surviving silent films of three 'Shochiku Masters', Kiyohiko Ushihara, Yasujiro Shimazu and Hiroshi Shimizu, and three great personalities of Soviet cinema, Abram Room, Mikhail Kalatozov and Lev Push. Sir Jeremy Isaacs, a champion of the renaissance for live accompaniment to silent films, delivered to great acclaim the annual Jonathan Dennis Memorial Lecture. – **Giuliana Puppin**, Press.

Portland International Film Festival
February 10-26, 2011

Portland International Film Festival will be an invitational event presenting more than 100 films from 30 plus countries to 35,000 people from throughout the Northwest. Along with new international features, documentaries and shorts, the festival will feature showcases surveying Hispanic film and literature, Pacific Rim cinema and many of the year's foreign-

TVP
TELEWIZJA POLSKA

An audience at the 33rd Portland International Film Festival. Photo by Jason E. Kaplan

language Oscar submissions. *Inquiries to:* Northwest Film Center, 1219 SW Park Ave, Portland, OR 97205, USA. Tel: (1 503) 221 1156. e: info@nwfilm.org. Web: www.nwfilm.org.

Pusan International Film Festival (PIFF)
October 2011

PIFF is known as the most energetic film festival in the world and has become the largest film festival in Asia. Films must have been produced within one year of the festival and subtitled in English. PIFF screens over 350 films from over 70 countries of which around 140 are world and international premieres; also, retrospectives, special programmes in focus, seminars and masterclasses. In addition, its project market – Pusan Promotion Plan (PPP) – has been a platform for moving Asian film projects forward in the international marketplace, along with its own talent campus, Asian Film Academy (AFA), offering various filmmaking programmes for young talent from all over Asia. *Inquiries to:* 1st Floor, 6 Tongui-dong, Jongno-gu, Seoul 110-040, Korea. Tel: (82 2) 3675 5097. e: publicity@piff. org. Web: www.piff.org.

Raindance Film Festival
September 28-October 9, 2011

Raindance is the largest independent film festival in the UK and aims to reflect the cultural, visual and narrative diversity of international independent filmmaking, specialising in first time filmmakers. The

festival screens around 100 feature films and 150 shorts, as well as hosting a broad range of workshops, masterclasses and workshops. *Inquiries to:* Festival Producer, Raindance Film Festival, 81 Berwick St, London, W1F 8TW, UK. Tel: (44 20) 7287 3833. e: festival@ raindance.co.uk. Web: www.raindance.org.

Reykjavík International Film Festival
September 22-October 2, 2011

The festival is one of the most exciting film events in Northern Europe, as well as Iceland's major annual film event. The main purpose of the festival is to offer a wide selection of alternative, independent cinema. The festival's intention is to provide cultural diversity, to provoke the public's interest in independent cinema, to impart film's social importance and to provoke discussions. The festival emphasises the relation between film and other art forms with art exhibitions, concerts etc. The festival's main award, The Discovery of the Year (the Golden Puffin Award) is dedicated to new filmmakers. *Inquiries to:* Reykjavík International Film Festival, Fríkirkjuvegur 1, 101 Reykjavík, Iceland. Tel: (354) 411 7055. Web: www.riff.is.

AWARDS 2010
The Golden Puffin, Discovery Award: **Le Quattro Volte** (Germany/Italy/Switzerland), Michaelangelo Frammartino.
FIPRESCI Award: **Le Quattro Volte** (Germany/ Italy/Switzerland), Michaelangelo Frammartino.
The Church of Iceland Award: **Tomorrow** (France/Hungary/Romania), Marian Crisan.

The swimming pool cinema where Billy Wilder's **Some Like It Hot** *was screened.*

Reykjavík International Film Festival
Sept. 22 - Oct. 2 **2011**

→ **riff.is**

RIFF Audience Award: **Littlerock** (USA), Mike Ott.
RIFF Environmental Award: **Earth Keepers** (Canada), Sylvie von Brabant.
The Golden Egg, RIFF 2010 Talent Laboratory Award: **The Passenger** (Faroe Islands), Sakaris Fridi Stora.

International Rome Film Festival
October 28-November 5, 2011

The city of Rome provides a magnificent backdrop to the festival with the Auditorium Parco della Musica and the Cinema Village being the main nerve centre. The festival offers films, retrospectives, meetings and major international stars, which attracts film lovers as well as being a great event for all those who work in cinema, exhibit cinema and tell us stories through cinema. The festival has now established itself as a truly unique occasion, with people flocking to events, exhibitions, encounters and screenings, offering proof of a great passion and interest in culture. The Business Street, a five-day long Roman film market for accredited professionals, provides a setting for producers, distributors and all film professionals to meet, debate, share their experiences and do business with a special focus on Europe. *Inquiries to:* International Rome Film Festival, Viale Pietro De Coubertin 10, 00196 Rome, Italy. Tel: (39 06) 4040 1900. e: press.international@romacinemafest.org. Web: www.romacinemafest.org.

AWARDS 2010
Golden Marco Aurelio Jury Award Best Film:
Kill Me Please (Belgium), Olias Barco.

Silver Marco Aurelio Award Best Actress: The entire female cast of **The Good Herbs** (Mexico).
Silver Marco Aurelio Award Best Actor: Toni Servillo for **Una Vita Tranquilla** (France/Germany/Italy).

International Film Festival Rotterdam
January 26-February 6, 2011

With its adventurous, original and distinctive programming, Rotterdam highlights new directors and new directions in contemporary world cinema, exemplified by its Tiger Awards Competition for first and second features; the annual showcase of films from developing countries that have been supported by the festival's Hubert Bals Fund; CineMart, the international co-production market developed to nurture the financing and production of new cinema. *Inquiries to:* International Film Festival Rotterdam, PO Box 21696, 3001 AR Rotterdam, Netherlands. Tel: (31 10) 890 9090. e: tiger@filmfestivalrotterdam.com. Web: www.filmfestivalrotterdam.com. www.cinemareloaded.com and www.youtube.com/iffrotterdam.

AWARDS 2010
VPRO Tiger Awards: **Agua Fría de Mar** (Costa Rica/France/Mexico/Netherlands/Spain), Paz Fábrega and **Mundane History** (Thailand), Anocha Suwichakornpong and **Alamar** (Mexico), Pedro Gonzalez-Rubio.
Tiger Awards for Short Film: **Wei Wen** (China), Ying Liang and **Atlantiques** (France/Senegal), Mati Diop and **Wednesday Morning Two A.M.** (USA), Lewis Klahr.

San Francisco International Film Festival
April 21-May 5, 2011

The longest running film festival in the Americas, in its 54th year, SFIFF continues to grow in importance and popularity. It presents more than 200 international features and shorts, and plays host to more than 80,000 film lovers and hundreds of filmmakers, journalists and film industry professionals, throwing sensational parties, celebrating Bay Area film culture and showcasing new technologies. Around $100,000 is awarded annually through special awards including the New Directors Award, the Golden Gate Awards and the FIPRESCI Prize. *Inquiries to:* San Francisco International Film Festival, Programming Dept, San Francisco International Film Festival, 39 Mesa St, Suite 110, The Presidio, San Francisco, CA 94129, USA. Tel: (1 415) 561 5014. e: achang@sffs.org. Web: www.sffs.org.

AWARDS 2010

New Directors Award: **Alamar** (Mexico) Pedro González-Rubio.
FIPRESCI Prize: **Frontier Blues**, (Iran/Italy/UK) Babak Jalali.
Golden Gate Awards
Investigative Documentary: **Last Train Home** (Canada/China) Lixin Fan.
Documentary Feature: **Pianomania** (Austria/Germany) Lilian Franck and Robert Cibis.
Bay Area Documentary Feature: **Presumed Guilty** (Mexico) Roberto Hernández and Geoffrey Smith.
Documentary Short: **The Shutdown** (Scotland) Adam Stafford.
Bay Area Short, First prize: **Embrace of the Irrational** (USA) Jonn Herschend.
Bay Area Short, Second prize: **Leonardo** (USA) Jim Capobianco.
Narrative Short: **The Armoire** (Canada) Jamie Travis.
Animated Short: **Tussilago** (Sweden) Jonas Odell.
New Visions: **Release** (USA) Bill Morrison.
Work for Kids and Families: **Leonardo** (USA) Jim Capobianco.
Work for Kids and Families Honourable Mention: **The Mouse That Soared** (USA) Kyle Bell.
Youth Work: **Moon Shoes** (USA) Joel Vanzeventer.
Youth Work Honourable Mention: **Alisha** (USA) Daniel Citron.
Audience Award for Best Narrative Feature: **Winter's Bone** (USA) Debra Granik.
Audience Award for Best Documentary Feature: **Budrus** (Israel) Julia Bacha.

San Sebastian International Film Festival
September 17-25, 2011

Held in an elegant Basque seaside city known for its superb gastronomy and beautiful beaches, the San Sebastian Film Festival remains the Spanish speaking world's most important event in terms of glamour, competition, facilities, partying, number of screenings and attendance (1,866 production and distribution firms, government agencies and festival representatives from 53 countries, and 1,053 journalists from 36 countries). Events include the Official Competitive section, Zabaltegi, with its €90,000 cash award, Kutxa-New Directors for first or second long features in Zabaltegi – New Directors or the Official Section, Horizontes Latinos with its 35,000 Euro cash award and meticulous retrospectives. In partnership with the Rencontres Cinémas Amérique Latine in Toulouse, the Films in Progress industry platform aims to aid the completion of Latin American projects. Cinema in Motion 6 is rendezvous at which to discover projects by filmmakers from from Magreb and Portuguese-speaking African countries and developing Arab countries, presented only to professionals in partnership with Amiens Film Festival and Fribourg Film Festival. *Inquiries to:* San Sebastian International Film Festival, Apartado de Correos 397, 20080 Donostia, San Sebastian 20080, Spain. Tel: (34 943) 481 212. e: ssiff@sansebastianfestival.com. Web: www. sansebastianfestival.com.

AWARDS 2010

Official Selection
Golden Shell for Best Film: **Neds** (France/Italy/UK), Peter Mullan.
Special Jury Prize: **Misterios de Lisboa** (Spain), Raul Ruiz.
Silver Shell for Best Actress: Nora Navas for **Pa Negre** (Spain).
Silver Shell for Best Actor: Connor McCarron for **Neds** (France/Italy/UK).
Jury Award for Best Cinematography: Jimmy Gimferrer for **Aita** (Spain).

Jury Award for Best Screenplay: Bent Hamer for **Home For Christmas** (Germany/Norway/Sweden).

Seattle International Film Festival
May 19-June 12, 2011

The largest film festival in the US, SIFF presents more than 250 features, 50 documentaries, and 100 shorts annually. There are cash prizes for the internationally juried New Directors Showcase and Documentary Competition, and for Short Films in the categories of Live Action, Documentary, and Animation. Festival sections include: Alternate Cinema, Face the Music, FutureWave, Films4Familes, Contemporary World Cinema, Emerging Masters, Documentary Films, Tributes and Archival Films. *Inquiries to:* Seattle International Film Festival, 400 Ninth Avenue North, Seattle, WA 98109, USA. Tel: (1 206) 464 5830. e: info@siff.net. Web: www.siff.net.

AWARDS 2010
New Directors Showcase
Grand Jury Prize: **The Reverse** (Poland), Borys Lankosz.
Special Jury Mentions: **Turistas** (Chile), Alicia Scherson and **Gravity** (Germany), Maximilian Erlenwein.
Documentary Competition
Grand Jury Prize: **Marwencol** (USA), Jeff Malmberg.
FIPRESCI Award for Best American Film
FIPRESCI Award: **Night Catches Us** (USA), Tanya Hamilton.
Special Jury Mention: Jenna Fischer for **A Little Help** (USA).
Short Awards
Narrative Grand Jury Prize: **Little Accidents** (USA), Sara Colangelo.
Documentary Grand Jury Prize: **White Lines And The Fever: The Death of DJ Junebug** (USA), Travis Senger.
Animation Grand Jury Prize: **The Wonder Hospital** (USA), Beomsik Shim.
Special Jury Mention for Short Animation: **Cherry On The Cake** (United Kingdom), Hyebin Lee.

Futurewave
WaveMaker: **Remember** (USA), Scott Calvert.
Special Jury Award: **Celina's Story** (USA), Celina Chadwick and Alisha (USA), Daniel Citron.
FutureWave Shorts Audience Award: **Remember** (USA), Scott Calvert.
Youth Jury Award for Best FutureWave Feature: **ReGENERATION** (USA), Philip Montgomery.
Youth Jury Award for Best Films4Families Feature: **From Time to Time** (UK), Julian Fellowes.
FutureWave Online Audience Award powered by IndieFlix: **Shawn Harris: Personal Trainer** (USA), Tyler Silver and Simon Turkel.
Golden Space Needle Audience Awards
Best Film: **The Hedgehog** (France), Mona Achache.
Best Documentary: **Ginny Ruffner: A Not So Still Life** (USA), Karen Stanton and **Waste Land** (UK), Lucy Walker.
Best Short Film: **Ormie** (Canada), Rob Silvestri.
Best Director: Debra Granik for **Winter's Bone** (USA).
Best Actor: Luis Tosar for **Cell 211** (Spain).
Best Actress: Jennifer Lawrence for **Winter's Bone** (USA).
Lena Sharpe Award for Persistence of Vision, Presented by Women in Film/Seattle: **The Topp Twins: Untouchable Girls** (New Zealand), Leanne Pooley.

Seville European Film Festival
November 4-12, 2011

Seville European Film Festival is well established as a showcase for recent high-quality, but not always high-profile, European films. Already attracting an impressive critical mass of European industry figures, Seville attaches several new building blocks each year and succeeds in growing, both in size and stature with each edition. As a result of the festival's international success, the European Film Academy (EFA) will hold its European Film Awards nominations announcement here until at least 2012. The Festival also has the support of the main European fund for aiding

TELEWIZJA POLSKA

co-production, Eurimages. Along with the official selection and parallel programmes, the Festival continues to strengthen as a meeting place for industry professionals. *Inquiries to:* Seville European Film Festival. Avenida del Cid 1, Pabellón de Portugal, 41004 Seville, Spain. Tel: (34 955) 115 586. e: info@festivaldesevilla. com. Web: www.festivaldesevilla.com.

AWARDS 2010

Stephen Frears at SEFF10 Credit: Lolo Vasco/SEFF'10

Golden Giraldillo Official Section: **Son of Babylon** (Egypt/France/Iraq/Netherlands/ Palestine/UAE/UK), Mohamed Al-Daradji.
Silver Giraldillo Official Section: **Black Field** (Greece), Vardis Marinakis.
Special Jury Award: **Tender Son** (Austria/ Germany/Hungary), Kornél Mundruczó.
Best Direction Award: **In a Better World** (Denmark), Susanne Bier.
Best Actress Award: (Ex Aequo) Samira Maas for **Joy** (Netherlands) and Sofia Georgovassili for **Black Field** (Greece).
Best Actor Award: Rhys Ifans for **Mr Nice** (Spain/UK).
Best Script Award: **In a Better World** (Denmark), Susanne Bier and Anders Thomas Jensen.
Best Director of Photography Award: Mátyás Erdély for **Tender Son** (Austria/Germany/ Hungary).
Special Mention: **Joy** (Netherlands), Mijke de Jong and **Naufragio** (Spain), Pedro Aguilera.
Golden Giraldillo to the Best Documentary Film: **Last Chapter: Goodbye Nicaragua** (Spain/Sweden), Peter Torbiornsson.
Special Mention: **Farewell** (Netherlands), Ditteke Mensink.

Eurimages Award: **The Front Line** (Belgium/ Italy), Renato De María.
Audience Choice Award: **Tamara Drewe** (UK), Stephen Frears.
Silver Giraldillo Award for Best Direction of a First Feature Film (First Films First): **Gigola** (France), Laure Charpentier.
Campus Jury Award: **Son of Babylon** (Egypt/ France/Iraq/Netherlands/Palestine/UAE/UK), Mohamed Al-Daradji.
Asecan Award (Film Writers Association of Andalusia): **Silent Souls** (Russia), Aleksei Fedorchenko.
International Honorary Award: Stephen Frears.
SEFF Tribute Award: Joris Ivens and Marceline Loridan-Ivens.
Tribute Life Achievement Award: Vicente Aranda.
SEFF/SILE Industry Award: Claudia Landsberger.
City Of Seville Award: Carlos Saura.
RTVA Career Award: Antonio Banderas.

SEVILLA FESTIVAL FESTIVAL **DE CINE EUROPEO** **SEFF'11** 4 - 12 NOV

European Film Awards Nominations
Seville, 5th November 2011

Un proyecto de
NODO
AYUNTAMIENTO DE SEVILLA
ICAS, SEVILLA INSTITUTO DE LA CULTURA Y LAS ARTES
Organiza
Andalucía FilmCommission

www.festivaldesevilla.com

Report 2010

The festival's seventh edition featured more than 180 feature length productions, documentaries and short films – an increase on previous years – produced from 38 different countries, attracting more than 74,000 spectators. The main awards include financial support for distribution (up to 50,000 euros), in order to promote a film's opening on the commercial circuit. The country focus this last edition was the Netherlands. The section 'Wild Tulips', backed by Netherlands' Eye Film Institute, showcased recent Dutch films – the largest screening of Dutch films at a festival. The event paid tribute to Dutch pioneer documentary filmmaker Joris Ivens. His widow, Marceline Loridan-Ivens, attended Seville and taught a masterclass at the Festival Campus programme. Claudia Landsberger, head of the Holland Film Institute, was recognised with the Industry Award. The European Film Academy (EFA) held once more the ceremony for announcing the European Film Awards nominations in Seville as part of the Festival, in the frame of the agreement in force until 2012, which also enables the festival to screen a selection of the films competing for the awards, as well as short films nominated. SEFF 2010 renewed an agreement with the main European fund for aiding co-productions, Eurimages, whose executive director, Roberto Olla, participated in activities at the Festival, including coordinating a roundtable discussion about international film financing. In the 'Eurodoc' section, Lorenz Knauer's environmental film, *Jane's Journey*, received its European premiere, which was attended by Jane Goodall. The Festival's prizewinner was *Last Chapter, Goodbye Nicaragua* by Swedish director Peter Torbiorsson, which received its international premiere here. In a further departure, a new sidebar, 'First Films First', featured directorial debuts such as Greek filmmaker Vardis Marinakis' Ottoman Empire-set period drama *Black Field* and Hattie Dalton's Edinburgh closer *Third Star*. SEFF 2010 gained a greater Spanish flavour, showcasing European co-productions with popular Spanish actors.

While maintaining its status as a favoured meeting point for the European film industry, the Seville European Film Festival has strengthened its commitment to Spain's film sector. **– Alejandro Blesa**, Relaciones Externas.

Shanghai International Film Festival
June 11-19, 2011

If there is golden time in the history of China's film industry, it is now. SIFF, as China's only A-category international film festival, is playing a bigger role in connecting China and the rest of the world, and providing everyone with a chance to do something good. SIFF is mainly composed of the competition section (Jin Jue Award, Asian New Talent Award and Shorts Award), SIFF Mart (Film Market, China Film Pitch and Catch, Co-production Film Pitch and Catch), SIFFORUM and Film Panorama. Sign-up to enter your films or projects, or book a place in the market at www.siff.com to join the world's biggest market of Chinese film and discovered the abundant resources of talent, storytelling, facilities and box-office potential. *Inquiries to:* Shanghai International Film Festival, 11F, B, STV Mansions, 298 Wei Hai Road, Shanghai 200041, China. Tel: (86 21) 6253 7115. Web: www.siff.com.

AWARDS 2010
Jin Jue Awards
Best Feature Film: **Kiss Me Again** (Italy), Gabriele Muccino.
Jury Grand Prix: **Deep In The Clouds** (China), Jie Liu.
Best Director: Jie Liu for **Deep In The Clouds** (China).
Best Actor: Christian Ulmen for **Wedding Fever In Campobello** (Germany/Italy).
Best Actress: Vittoria Puccini for **Kiss Me Again** (Italy).
Best Screenplay: Gabriele Muccino for **Kiss Me Again** (Italy).
Best Cinematography: Christopher Doyle for **Ondine** (Ireland).
Best Music: Giong Lim for **Deep In The Clouds** (China).

Sheffield Doc/Fest
June 8-12, 2011

For five days, Sheffield Doc/Fest brings the international documentary family together to celebrate the art and business of documentary making. Combining a film festival, industry sessions and market activity, the Festival offers pitching opportunities, controversial discussion panels and in-depth filmmaker masterclasses, as well as a wealth of inspirational documentary films from across the globe. The Festival opens with the Crossover Summit, the place to learn about new models of funding, production and distribution across the digital landscape. Around 140 documentary films are screened, mainly from a call for entries made in November. Over 50 debates, discussions, case studies, interviews and masterclasses are presented and there are a number of well-attended social and networking events. The MeetMarket takes place over two days of the Festival. It is a highly effective initiative; pre-scheduled one-on-one meetings where TV commissioning editors, executive producers, distributors and other financiers meet with independent producers and filmmakers to discuss documentary projects in development that are seeking international financing. The

Sheffield Youth Jury Award winner director Laura Fairrie (middle) for **The Battle for Barking** *at the BT Vision Doc/Fest Awards Ceremony. From left to right: Hussain Currimbhoy (Doc/Fest Film Programmer), 2010 Youth Jury: Funsho M. Parrott, Ben Melbourne, Laurence Senior, Laura Fairrie (winner), Georgina Thomas, Hannah Woodhead, Liam Thornton; Heather Croall (Festival Director) and Hardeep Singh Kohli (comedian/ writer/ broadcaster and documentary maker). Photos copyright of Jacqui Bellamy, Pixelwitch Pictures pixelwitchpictures@gmail.com*

film programme is also open to the public. Previously held in November, Doc/Fest has now moved to the summer with the 18th Sheffield Doc/Fest taking place from 8-12 June 2011. *Inquiries to:* Sheffield Doc/Fest, The Workstation, 15 Paternoster Row, Sheffield, S1 2BX, UK. Tel: (44 114) 276 5141. e: info@sidf.co.uk. Web: www.sheffdocfest.com.

AWARDS 2010
Special Jury Award: **Pink Saris** (UK, Kim Longinotto.
The BT Vision Sheffield Innovation Award: **The Arbor** (UK), Clio Barnard.
Sheffield Youth Jury Award: **The Battle for Barking** (UK), Laura Fairrie.
Sheffield Green Award: **Rainmakers** (Netherlands), Floris-Jan van Luyn.
Sheffield Student Doc Award: **No Easy Time** (UK), Will Woodward.
The Sheffield Doc/Fest Audience Award: **Father, Son and the Holy War** (India, 1995), Anand Patwardhan and **Scenes from a Teenage Killing** (UK), Morgan Matthews.
Sheffield Inspiration Award: Kim Longinotto. The Award celebrates a figure in the industry who has championed documentary and helped get great work into the public eye. The 2010 award winner was acclaimed British documentary filmmaker Kim Longinotto, director of Cannes and Sundance award-winning films *Sisters in Law*, *Rough Aunties* and *Pink Saris* which won the Special Jury Award. Longinotto is one of the pre-eminent filmmakers working in both broadcast and theatrical documentary today, widely revered for her incisive, compassionate portraits of female oppression and injustice.

Report 2010
The 17th Sheffield Doc/Fest, which attracted record numbers, opened with the UK premiere of *Joan Rivers: A Piece of Work*. The film's award-winning directors Ricki Stern and Annie Sundberg accompanied the great comic icon in a live Q&A session. Rolf Harris was also in attendance for the screening of *Arena: Rolf Harris Paints His Dream* by multi award-winning director Vikram Jayanti. The success

Joan Rivers with Heather Croall, Festival Director. Photos copyright of Jacqui Bellamy, Pixelwitch Pictures pixelwitchpictures@gmail.com

of Mark Cousins' new special film strand celebrating one of India's most enduring filmmakers Anand Patwardhan was evident – *Father, Son and Holy War* won the Audience Award 2010, with *Scenes from a Teenage Killing* directed by Morgan Matthews. Doc/Fest's Film Programmer Hussain Currimbhoy commented of the winning films: 'Both films are about violence in society and their ties to masculinity so I can't think of a more

relevant set of films to be giving our prize to at this particular moment in time.' – **Annabel Bennett**, Marketing and Development Manager.

SILVERDOCS: AFI/Discovery Channel Documentary Festival
June 20-26, 2011

SilverDocs encompasses a seven-day international film festival and five-day concurrent conference that promotes documentary film as a leading art form. SilverDocs takes place at the AFI Silver Theatre, one of the premiere exhibition spaces in the country, and the top art-house cinema in the Washington, DC region. Anchored in the US capital, where important global and national issues are the daily business, SilverDocs is marked by its relevance, broad intellectual range, and wide public appeal. Among its numerous special programmes is the Charles Guggenheim Symposium, which in 2010, honored legendary film director Frederick

Wiseman. Past recipients include Albert Maysles, Spike Lee, Martin Scorcese, Barbara Kopple and Jonathan Demme. *Inquiries to:* AFI Silver Theatre and Cultural Center, 8633 Colesville Road, Silver Spring, MD 20910, USA. Tel: (1 301) 495 6720. e: info@silverdocs.com Web: www.silverdocs.com.

AWARDS 2010

Sterling US Feature Award: **I Love You, Mommy** (USA), Stephanie Wang-Breal.
Sterling World Feature Award: **The Woman With the 5 Elephants** (Switzerland), Vadim Jendreyko.
Sterling Short Award: **This Chair Is Not Met** (UK), Andy Taylor Smith.
Cinematic Vision Award: **Marwencol** (USA), Jeff Malmberg and **Witness-Budrus** (Israel/Palestine/USA), Julia Bacha.
Writers Guild of America Documentary Screenplay Award: **A Film Unfinished** (Germany/Israel), Yael Hersonski.
Feature Audience Award: **Men Who Swim** (Italy/Sweden/UK), Dylan Williams.
Short Audience Award: **Bye Bye Now** (UK), Aideen O'Sullivan and Ross Whitaker.

Singapore International Film Festival
June 14-26, 2011

The largest international film festival in Singapore, SIFF has become significant in the Singapore arts landscape because of its dynamic film programming and commitment to the development of film culture and local cinema. The Festival screens over 200 films annually, from all genres, with a focus on groundbreaking Asian cinema. Under the umbrella of the Silver Screen Awards, SIFF recognizes excellence in Asian cinema with its 3 awards categories – Asian Film Competition, Singapore Short Film Competition and the Singapore Film Awards introduced in 2009. *Inquiries to:* Singapore International Film Festival, 554 Havelock Road, Suite 02-00A Ganges Centre, Singapore 169639, Singapore. Tel: (65) 6738 7567. e: filmfest@pacific.net.sg. Web: www.filmfest.org.sg.

Sitges International Fantastic Film Festival of Catalonia
October 2011

Sitges is one of the leading fantasy film festivals and offers a stimulating universe of encounters, exhibitions, presentations and screenings of fantasy films from all over the world. It is an essential rendezvous for film lovers and audiences eager to come into contact with new tendencies and technologies applied to film and the audiovisual world. *Inquiries to:* Sitges Festival Internacional de Cinema Fantastic de Catalunya, Calle Davallada 12, 3rd Floor, CP:08870 Sitges, Barcelona, Spain. Tel: (34 93) 894 9990. e: festival@cinemasitges.com. Web: www.cinemasitges.com.

Slamdance Film Festival
January 21-27, 2011

The festival is organised and programmed exclusively by filmmakers for filmmakers, and the sole aim is to nurture, support and showcase truly independent works. In doing so, Slamdance has established a unique reputation for premiering new films by first-time writers and directors working within the creative confines of limited budgets. This Academy qualifier also attracts and launches established artists, with world-class alumni including Steven Soderbergh, Christopher Nolan, Marc Forster and Jared Hess. The Festival has helped hundreds of films find distribution, including *The King of Kong, Weirdsville, Mad Hot Ballroom* and the breakout *Paranormal Activity.* Organised by filmmakers for filmmakers, Slamdance adamantly supports self-governance amongst independents and exists to deliver what filmmakers go to festivals for – a chance to show their work and a launching point for their careers. *Inquiries to:* Slamdance Inc, 5634 Melrose Ave, Los Angeles, California 90038, USA. Tel: (1 323) 466 1786. e: programming@slamdance. Web: www.slamdance.com.

Solothurn Film Festival
January 20-27, 2011

Since 1964, the Solothurn Film Festival has presented an overview of the previous year's output of Swiss filmmaking. Solothurn is a popular meeting place for the film and media industry as well as the broad public. Apart from the main focus on current national film productions of all genres and lengths, which includes many premieres of new Swiss films, the festival programme also includes a retrospective of a prominent filmmaker or actor, the music-clip section 'sound&stories' and the 'Invitation' section with a selection of films produced in countries bordering Switzerland. Young talent can be discovered in the film school section. The screenings are accompanied by a variety of daily round-table discussions, talk shows, film industry meetings, master classes and seminars. Outside of the official programme, Solothurn hosts the Swiss Film Academy's announcement of the nominees for the Swiss Film Prize 'Quartz' during the 'Night of the Nominations' in the middle of the festival. *Inquiries to:* Solothurn Film Festival, PO Box 1564, CH-4502 Solothurn, Switzerland. Tel: (41 32) 625 8080. : 623 6410. e: info@solothurnerfilmtage.ch. Web: www. solothurnerfilmtage.ch.

Report 2010
The 45th Solothurn Film Festival, held in January 2010, hosted around 1,200 professionals, and over 51,000 cinemagoers

Festival goers enjoying one of the screenings

46th Solothurn Film Festival
20 – 27 January 2011   www.solothurnfilmfestival.ch

enjoyed 300 films in different programme sections. The festival programme highlighted the thematic and stylistic spectrum of Swiss filmmaking, with works ranging from the political documentary *Dharavi, Slum for Sale* by Lutz Konermann, to the comedy *Champions* by Riccardo Signorell, and socio-critical films such as *La guerre est finie* by Mitko Panov. The festival lived up to its reputation as the showcase of Swiss film productions. Film talks, special programmes and controversial discussions about film politics formed the frame of the festival. The retrospective, called 'Rencontre', was devoted to the Swiss film music composer Niki Reiser, who works with directors such as Dani Levy, Doris Dörrie, Tom Tykwer and Caroline Link, and who has won the German Film Award several times. The winner of the best music-clip was 'One Up Down Left Right' by Mike Rath and Jonas Meyer, which won both the audience and the jury awards. The jury prize 'Prix de Soleure', which is endowed with CHF 60,000, was awarded to Nicola Bellucci for his documentary *Nel Giardino Dei Suoni*, which is a touching, poetic exploration of the relationship of mind, body and sound. The Public Award went to the Film *Bödälä – Dance the Rhythm* by Gitta Gsell. **Ivo Kummer**, Festival Director.

South by Southwest Film Festival
March 11 19, 2011

The festival explores all aspects of the art and business of independent filmmaking. The Conference hosts a five-day adventure in the latest filmmaking trends and new technology, featuring distinguished speakers and mentors. The internationally acclaimed festival boasts some of the most wide-ranging programming of any US event of its kind, from provocative documentaries to subversive Hollywood comedies, with a special focus on emerging talents. *Inquiries to:* South by Southwest Film Festival, Box 4999, Austin, TX 78765, USA. Tel: (1 512) 467 7979. e: sxsw@sxsw.com. Web: http://sxsw.com.

Stockholm International Film Festival
November 16-27, 2011

The Stockholm International Film Festival, which this year launches its 22nd festival, is one of Europe's leading cinematic events. The festival's focus is the new and cutting-edge and the competitive section is exclusive for directors making their first, second or third feature film. The festival presents over 180 films from 50 different countries and annually welcomes 130,000 visitors and 1,000 accredited journalists and industry officials, as well as around a hundred directors, actors and producers. The festival is recognised by FIAPF and hosts a FIPRESCI jury, and is also a member of the European Coordination of Film Festivals. In 2009, it started a Festival on Demand service where ten films from the official programme received their premiere On Demand (through Telia Digital-tv) and were made available throughout Sweden. Distinguished guests over the years include Gus Van Sant, Susan Sarandon, Wong Kar Wai, David Lynch, Lauren Bacall, Quentin Tarantino, Dennis Hopper, Roman Polanski, Ang Lee, David Cronenberg and Charlotte Rampling. *Inquiries to:* Stockholm International Film Festival, PO Box 3136, S-103 62 Stockholm, Sweden. Tel: (46 8) 677 5000. e: info@stockholmfilmfestival.se. Web: www.stockholmfilmfestival.se.

Sundance Film Festival
January 19-29, 2011

Long known as a celebration of the new and unexpected, the Sundance Film Festival puts forward the best in independent film from the US and around the world. For ten days in January, audiences in darkened theatres will discover the 125 feature films and 80 shorts that festival programmers have scoured the world to find. The critically acclaimed festival presents features and documentaries from the US and around the world, and competition films are combined with nightly premieres of works by veteran film artists for a programme that inspires, challenges, delights, startles and moves. Archival gems by early independent filmmakers, animation of every kind, cutting edge experimental works, midnight cult films, and a jam-packed schedule of panel discussions at Prospector Theatre, Filmmaker Lodge and New Frontier on Park, live shows at the Music Café and a host of spirited parties and events up and down historic Main Street, make for a complete film experience that celebrates the art and community of independent filmmaking. Continuing the tradition of sharing the festival with online audiences, www.sundance.org/festival takes both original content and the nuts and bolts of festival going beyond the streets of Park City. With short films from the festival, filmmaker interviews, and breaking news, combined with film listings, box office information and travel tips, Sundance Film Festival Online is a single online source for experiencing the Sundance Film Festival both on the web and on the ground. *Inquiries to:* John Cooper, Director, Festival Programming Department, Sundance Institute, 8530 Wilshire Blvd, 3rd Floor, Beverly Hills, CA 90211-3114, USA. Tel: (1 310) 360 1981. e: institute@sundance.org. Web: www.sundance.org.

AWARDS 2010
Grand Jury Prize, Documentary: **Restrepo** (USA), Sebastian Junger and Tim Hetherington.
Grand Jury Prize, Dramatic: **Winter's Bone** (USA), Debra Granik.
World Cinema Jury Prize, Documentary: **The Red Chapel** (Denmark), Mads Brügger.
World Cinema Jury Prize, Dramatic: **Animal Kingdom** (Australia), David Michôd.
World Cinema Audience Award, Documentary: **Wasteland** (UK), Lucy Walker.
World Cinema Audience Award, Dramatic: **Contracorriente** (Colombia/France/Germany/Peru), Javier Fuentes-León.

Best of NEXT Presented by YouTube:
Homewrecker (USA), Todd Barnes and Brad
Barnes.
World Cinema Directing Award, Documentary:
Space Tourists (Switzerland), Christian Frei.
World Cinema Directing Award, Dramatic:
Southern District (Bolivia), Juan Carlos Valdivia.
Waldo Salt Screenwriting Award: **Winter's
Bone** (USA), Debra Granik.
World Cinema Screenwriting Award: **Southern
District** (Bolivia), Juan Carlos Valdivia.
World Cinema Documentary Editing Award:
A Film Unfinished (Germany/Israel), Yael
Hersonski.
*World Cinema Cinematography Award,
Documentary:* **His & Hers** (Ireland), Ken
Wardrop.
*World Cinema Cinematography Award,
Dramatic:* **The Man Next Door** (Argentina),
Mariano Cohn and Gastón Duprat.
International Jury Prize in Short Filmmaking:
The Six Dollar Fifty Man (New Zealand), Mark
Albiston and Louis Sutherland.
*World Cinema Documentary Special Jury
Prize:* **Enemies of the People** (Cambodia/UK),
Rob Lemkin and Thet Sambath.
*World Dramatic Special Jury Prize for Breakout
Performance:* Tatiana Maslany in **Grown Up
Film Star** (Canada).

Tallinn Black Nights Film Festival (PÖFF)
PÖFF Main Programme November
24-December 4, 2011
Children and Youth Film Festival Just Film:
November 18-27, 2011
Animation Film Festival Animated Dreams:
November 18-22, 2011
Student and Short Film Festival Sleepwalkers:
November 19-23, 2011
Nokia Mobile Phone Film Festival MOFF:
September 1-December 3, 2011
Baltic Event co-production market:
November 28-30, 2011
Black Market Industry Screenings:
November 30-December 3, 2011

In 2011, the Tallinn Black Nights Film Festival
(founded in 1997) will celebrate its 15th
edition. The festival had more than 65,000

*December 3rd, Closing Ceremony of the 2010 Tallinn Black Nights Film
Festival (PÖFF), Sergei Loznitsa, director of the feature film* **My Joy**
*(Germany-Ukraine-Netherlands) and members of the International
Competition Programme EurAsia Jury (from left) Csaba Kéel, Piret
Tibbo-Hudgins, Intishal al Timimi, Fatemeh Simin Motamed-Arya,
David Willis, head of the PÖFF Tiina Lokk, Deputy Mayor at
Foundation Tallinn 2011 Jaanus Mutli. Photo: Rivo Sarapik*

admissions during 2010 and together with
the Baltic Event and Black Market Industry
Screenings it welcomed over 450 foreign
guests from 45 countries. The 14th edition
of the festival screened over 680 films from
86 countries, 264 of them full length, across
a total of 770 screenings which were held
during the festival (this includes screenings
in other cities). PÖFF, recognised by FIAPF,
is a unique event that combines a feature
film festival with sub-festivals, a film industry
gathering called the Baltic Event and Black
Market Industry Screenings. The PÖFF
main programme has three international
competitions – EurAsia, Tridens Baltic feature
film competition and competition of North
American indie films – along with Panorama,
Forum and several special programmes. All
competing films are judged by international
and local juries including FIPRESCI jury that
awards the best Baltic films. The Student and
Short Film Festival, 'Sleepwalkers', includes
an international competition for student
films – fiction, documentary or animation
films; national competition of Estonian short
films, and various special programmes. The
Animation Film Festival, 'Animated Dreams',
holds an international competition of shorts.
Its non-competitive programmes include a
retrospective of a filmmaker and focus on a
country. The Children and Youth Film Festival,
'Just Film', includes the competition of

December 3rd, Closing Ceremony of the 2010 Tallinn Black Nights Film Festival (PÖFF), Veiko Õunpuu, director of the feature film **The Temptation of St. Tony** *(Estonia-Sweden-Finland). Photo: Rivo Sarapik*

children and youth films, and non-competitive programmes. The Nokia Mobile Film Festival MOFF organises a competition of short films made with mobile phones. The Baltic Event film and co-production market screens the latest feature films from the Baltic countries, along with a co-production market for projects from the Baltic countries, Central and Eastern Europe, Russia and Scandinavia. The Black Market Industry Screenings focus on new films from the neighbouring regions and smaller film industry countries: Baltics, Central and Eastern European countries, Nordic countries, Russia and Central-Asian countries like Georgia, Ukraine, Romania, Armenia, Kazakhstan, Uzbekistan, Kyrgyztan, Tadjikistan. In addition to these, the literary rights market, 'Books To Films', presents film literature from Estonia, Latvia, Lithuania, Nordic countries, Russia and other neigbouring countries to possible producers and filmmakers who are looking for new material. This year's special focus was on Russian cinema, with a special roundtable discussion called 'Industry Day', which discussed co-production, financing and film distribution issues in contemporary Russia. Some of the most important figures in the Russian film industry attended, including Sergei Selyanov from CTB Film Company. The goal is to enhance audio-visual co-operation on both sides of the Eastern border of the EU and Nordic countries, and to give filmmakers visibility and access to the bigger audiovisual markets around the world. In 2010, a new business platform, 'Black Market Online', was

launched. A business-to-business environment, Black Market Online allows film professionals to watch films online and access additional information including film industry contacts, country overviews about film industries, new coming-soon and lineups and new films from the North East European regions. During 2010, the European Film Awards ceremony came to Tallinn and was the cornerstone and launch pad of Tallinn's year as European Culture Capital in 2011. *Inquiries to:* Tallinn Black Nights Film Festival (PÖFF), Telliskivi 60A, 10412 Tallinn, Estonia. Tel: (372) 631 4640. e: poff@poff.ee. Web: www.poff.ee.

AWARDS 2010
International competition programme EurAsia
Grand Prix: **My Joy** (Germany/The Netherlands/Ukraine), Sergei Loznitsa.
Best Director: Chris Kraus for **The Poll Diaries** (Austria/Estonia/Germany).
Best Actor: Mikael Persbrandt for **In A Better World** (Denmark/Sweden).
Best Actress: Katja Küttner for **Priness** (Finland).
Best Cinematographer: Mikhail Krichman for **Silent Souls** (Russia).
Special Jury Prize: **Son of Babylon** (Egypt/France/Iraq/The Netherlands/Palestine/United Arab Emirates/UK), Mohamed Al-Daradji.
Tridens Baltic Competition Best Film: **Eastern Drift** (France/Lithuania/Russia), Sharunas Bartas.
Scottish Leader Estonian Film Award: **The Temptation of St Tony** (Estonia/Finland/Sweden), Veiko Õunpuu.

December 3rd, Closing Ceremony of the 2010 Tallinn Black Nights Film Festival (PÖFF), Chris Kraus, director of the feature film **The Poll Diaries** *(Germany-Austria-Estonia). Photo: Rivo Sarapik*

FIPRESCI Award for Best Baltic Film: **The Temptation of St Tony** (Estonia/Finland/Sweden), Veiko Õunpuu.
Best North American Independent Film: **Incendies** (Canada/France), Denis Villeneuve.
FICC Jury Don Quijote Award: **3 Seasons In Hell** (Czech Republic/Germany/Slovakia), Tomáš Mašin.
NETPAC Jury Award: **Peepli Live** (India), Anusha Rizvi and **The Light Thief** (France/Germany/Kyrgyzstan/The Netherlands), Aktan Arym Kubat.
Audience Award: **Toilet** (Japan), Naoko Ogigami.
Lifetime Achievement Award: Actor and musician Vesa-Matti Loiri.

Report 2010

The 14th Black Nights Film Festival was the most successful edition yet. Popular films included Danny Boyle's *127 Hours*, *My Joy* (with director Sergei Loznitsa in attendance) and Estonia's own *The Temptation of St Tony*. There were also retrospectives focusing on Finnish cinema and the Czech New Wave. Guests included legendary Finnish comedy actor and Lifetime Achievement Award recipient Vesa-Matti Loiri and renowned American director Jeff Lipsky. The Student and short film festival showcased numerous international and national shorts, with workshops that included an examination of 3D cinema, run with the aid of the European Film Academy. There was also a special programme of shorts from the Argentina Film School and a section in which the Tampere International Short Film Festival screened some of the very best shorts from Finland.

Just Film celebrated its 10th birthday by screening the Estonian premiere of *Harry Potter and the Deathly Hallows: Part 1*. Other highlights included the international premiere of *Ways To Live Forever*, a film based on Sally Nicholls' award winning children's book, *Dog Pound*, a tough and powerful drama about life in a detention centre for young criminals, and the quirky teen drama *Youth In Revolt*. Opening with the world premiere of the Estonian animated film, *Sky Song*, Animated Dreams cemented its reputation as the most important festival in of its kind in the Baltic region. The international competition showcased some of the finest global animated shorts selected from more than 400 entries, alongside features such as *The Illusionist*. The lecture programme, 'Keyframes', focused on 'Animated Documentaries' with lectures by luminaries such as Andy Glynne, the director of 'Animated Minds', a series of films dealing with mental illness. Focusing upon films from Latvia, Lithuania and Estonia, the Baltic Event co-production market presented 12 projects from the Baltic countries, Scandinavia, Russia and Central and Eastern Europe, whilst the new initiative, 'Baltic Event for East', presented four projects from the Ukraine and Russia. The Black Market Industry Screenings introduced films from the Baltic regions, Finland, Russia, Kazakhstan, Uzbekistan, Azerbaijan, Georgia, Baltics, Russia, Central-Asia and South-Caucus. Filmmakers from the regions were on hand to present their new films and works-in-progress, whilst distributors presented their own line-ups. Black Market Online allows film professionals to watch films online and access

additional information, including film industry contacts, country overviews about film industries and new films from the North East European region. **– Laurence Boyce**, Festival Programmer.

Tampere Film Festival
March 9-13, 2011

The Festival is the oldest and the largest short film festival in Northern Europe and celebrates its 41st Anniversary in 2011. The festival programme consists of the International and Finnish short film competitions and the special thematic programme. It is famous for its excellent and innovative programming, magnificent festival atmosphere and, of course, the Finnish Sauna Party. Besides the 120 screenings, the festival is packed with various seminars, panel discussions and meetings for film professionals and enthusiasts. The Festival promotes up-and-coming filmmakers – it is an event to find future masters of cinema. The high-quality Film Market has over 4,000 titles from all over the world. The special thematic programmes for the 41st edition include the highlights of Chinese and Romanian short film, horror short films and animation retrospectives by Paul Bush, Jonas Odell and Tatu Pohjavirta. This year's Canon of Short Film presents masters of modern animation. The Canon of Short Film is a project carried out by 8 major short film festivals. The aim is to collect, discuss and screen the best and most influential short films of all times. Videotivoli, the international event for films made by children and young people, offers a colourful section of genres and cinematic means of expression, with topics ranging from fairy tales and fantasies to serious life experiences and global issues. *Inquiries to:* Tampere Film Festival, PO Box 305, FI-33101 Tampere, Finland. Tel: (358 3) 223 5681. e: office@tamperefilmfestival.fi. Web: www.tamperefilmfestival.fi.

AWARDS 2010
International Competition
Grand Prix: **Lumikko** (Finland), Miia Tervo.

Best Animation: **I know You** (Austria, Germany), Gudrun Krebitz.
Best Fiction: **Somumjarn Tiang naa noi koi rak** (Thailand), Wichanon.
Best Documentary ex aequo: Philip Widman's **Destination Finale** (Germany) and *The Darkness of Day* (USA), Jay Rosenblatt.
EFA Nominee Tampere: **Lumikko** (Finland), Miia Tervo.
Audience Award: **Wagah** (India), Supriyo Sen.

Telluride Film Festival
September 2-5, 2011

Four days of film heaven are found each Labour Day weekend when passionate film lovers ascend to the high Colorado mountain village of Telluride, where the tradition is to keep the programme a secret until opening day. Audiences discover new narrative and documentary features, with directors, actors and writers in attendance. The Festival also showcases rare archival restorations, silent films with live scores, short film programmes, special events and tributes. The 37th Festival Silver Medallion honorees were Claudia Cardinale, Colin Firth and Peter Weir. Previous tributes have included: director Margarethe von Trotta and actors Anouk Aimee and Viggo Mortensen in 2009; actress Jean Simmons, directors David Fincher and Jan Troell in 2008; actor Daniel Day Lewis, composer Michel Legrand and Indian director Shyam Benegal in 2007. A Special Medal went to UCLA Film & Television Archive. Jan-Christopher Horak presented examples of the Archive's work plus Stanton Kaye's *Brandy In the Wilderness* and *Chicago*, with the Mont Alto Motion Picture Orchestra performing their score. This year's Guest Director, author Michael Ondaatje, presented a selection of six archival prints of rarely-seen gems. Recent guest directors have included Alexander Payne and Slavoj Zizek. The 'Pordenone Presents' selection was Mario Camerini's *Rotaie* with Judith Rosenberg performing her original score. Richard Leacock and Sami van Ingen presented Robert Flaherty's restored sound version of *Moana*. Serge Bromberg brought his 'Retour de

Geoffrey Rush and Tom Hooper. Photo: Arun Nevader.

Flamme 3D' show. The Festival also featured a Spotlight on Armenia's Harutyun Khachatryan featuring several of his poetic documentaries. A selection of Berlin and Cannes highlights joined a lineup of discoveries including *Chico and Rita*, *Oka! Amerikee*, *The First Film*, *The King's Speech*, *The Way Back*, *Precious Life*, *Incendies*, *The First Grader*, *Tabloid*, *A Letter to Elia*, *Carlos*, *Happy People*, *Never Let Me Go*, plus sneak previews of *127 Hours* and *The Black Swan*. The Backlot continued a tradition of focusing on films and the arts with thirteen documentaries about Jack Cardiff, Ingmar Bergman, Daniel Schmid, Philip Lopate, Mikhail Kalatozov, Jacques Tati, Hollywood studios, bluegrass music, Richard Leacock, Louis Sarno and Ion B. The 2010 poster artist was Pixar's Oscar-winning director Ralph Eggleston. Each year there are intimate conversations, seminars in the park and a lively student program, all book-ended by the Opening Night Feed and the Labour Day Picnic. Screened in nine venues including the Abel Gance Outdoor Cinema, the festival presentations meet the highest technical standards. Telluride is a non-competitive, non-profit festival. Complete past programmes and information about entering features and shorts, programmes for high school and college students and video highlights can be found on the festival's website. *Inquiries to:* Telluride Film Festival, 800 Jones Street, Berkeley, CA 94710 USA. Tel: (1 510) 665 9494. e: mail@telluridefilmfestival.org. Web: www. telluridefilmfestival.org.

Thessaloniki International Film Festival
November 4-13, 2011
Thessaloniki Documentary Festival
March 11-20, 2011

In its 52nd year, the oldest and the most important film event in South-East Europe targeted a new generation of filmmakers as well as independent films by established directors. The International Competition (for first or second features) awarded the Golden Alexander (€20,000) to Bogdan George Apetri for *Outbound* (Austria/Romania) and the Silver Alexander (€10,000) to Athina Rachel Tsangari for *Attenberg* (Greece). Other sections include Balkan Survey, the informative section Independence Days, the thematic section Focus, Greek Films, retrospectives, plus master classes, galas and exhibitions. As always, the festival's market, Agora, acted as an umbrella service for film professionals who benefited from the services of the Balkan Script Development Fund, Crossroads Co-production Forum, Agora Film Market and Salonica Studio Student Workshops. The Thessaloniki Documentary Festival – Images of the 21st Century is Greece's major annual non-fiction film event. Its sections include 'Views of the World' (subjects of social interest), 'Portraits – Human Journeys' (highlighting the human contribution to cultural, social and historical developments) and 'Recording of Memory' (facts and testimony of social and historic origin). The festival also hosts the third largest documentary market in Europe, the Thessaloniki DocMarket. *Inquiries to:* Thessaloniki International Film Festival, 9 Alexandras Ave, 114 73 Athens, Greece. Tel: (30 210) 870 6000. e: info@filmfestival.gr. Web: www.filmfestival.gr. Festivals Director: Dimitri Eipides. Inquiries to: Thessaloniki Documentary Festival (contact details as above).

AWARDS 2010
Thessaloniki International Film Festival
Golden Alexander: **Outbound** (Austria/ Romania), Bogdan George Apetri.
Silver Alexander: **Attenberg** (Greece), Athina Rachel Tsangari.

Bronze Alexander: **Jean Gentil** (Dominican Republic/Germany/Mexico), Laura Amelia Guzman and Israel Cardenas.
Best Director Award: Marian Crisan for **Morgen** (France/Hungary/Romania).
Best Screenplay Award: Marek Lechki for **Erratum** (Poland).
Best Actress Award: Ana Ularu for **Outbound** (Austria/Romania).
Best Actor Award ex aequo: Andras Hathazi and Yilmax Yalcin for **Morgen** (France/Hungary/Romania).
Artistic Achievement Award: **Zephyr** (Turkey), Belma Bas.

AWARDS 2010
Thessaloniki Documentary Festival – Images of the 21st Century
Hellenic Red Cross Audience Award for a Greek film over 45 minutes: **Gaza We Are Coming** (Greece), Yorgos Avgeropoulos and Ioannis Karypidis.
Hellenic Red Cross Audience Award for a foreign film over 45 minutes: **Eyes Wide Open-Exploring Today's South America** (Uruguay), Gonzalo Arijon.
Hellenic Red Cross Audience Award for a Greek film under 45 minutes: **Active Member** (Greece), Lefteris Fylaktos.
Hellenic Red Cross Audience Award for a foreign film under 45 minutes: **Odysseas** (Greece), Vahagn Karapetyan.

Tokyo International Film Festival
October 22-30, 2011

Over the nine days of the Festival, films from a variety of genres will be shown in several intriguing sections: *'Competition'*, which selects the 'Tokyo Sakura Grand Prix' from a carefully chosen ensemble of premiere films directed by both talented first-timers and recognized directors; *'Special Screenings'*, which premieres highly entertaining films prior to their public release in Japan; *'Winds of Asia – Middle East'*, which boasts the largest number of films and audience in all of the TIFF screenings; *'Japanese Eyes'*, which showcases a broad range of independent Japanese films for the worldwide audience; and *'natural TIFF'* highlights films with theme of the 'coexistence of mankind and nature'. TIFFCOM, an entertainment content business market affiliated with TIFF, is expanding every year to establish its position as one of the major business opportunities in Asia. *Inquiries to:* Unijapan/TIFF Office, 5F Tsukiji Yasuda Building, 2-15-14 Tsukiji Chuo-ku, Tokyo 104-0045, Japan. Tel: (81 3) 3524 1081. e: tiff-pr@tiff-jp.net. Web: www.tiff-jp.net.

Torino Film Festival
November 2011

Torino Film Festival is one of Europe's most important cinematographic events and is known for its discoveries as well as its unique retrospectives. The festival constitutes a meeting point for contemporary international cinema and pays particular attention to emerging cinemas and filmmakers and promotes awareness of new directors whose work is marked by strong formal and stylistic research. Its programme includes competitive sections for international features, Italian and international documentaries and Italian shorts, as well as spotlights and premieres. *Inquiries to:* Torino Film Festival, Via Montebello 15, 10124 Torino, Italy. Tel: (39 011) 813 8811. e: info@torinofilmfest.org. Web: www.torinofilmfest.org.

Toronto International Film Festival
September 8-18, 2011

The Toronto International Film Festival presents one of the world's largest annual showcases of Canadian film with the Canada First!, Short Cuts Canada and Canadian Open Vault programmes. The festival screens over 300 films from more than 60 countries and attracts thousands of Canadian and international industry delegates as well as over 1,000 international media. The Festival consistently strives to set the standard for excellence in film programming with audiences shown the work of emerging talent and masters of the cinema craft from around the world. As always, the Festival remains committed to supporting Canadian filmmakers and has been a platform for Canada's artists. In 2010, TIFF opened TIFF Bell Lightbox, a breathtaking five-storey complex located in downtown Toronto that provides a permanent home for film lovers to celebrate cinema from around the world. *Inquiries to:* Toronto International Film Festival, Reitman Square, 350 King Street West, Toronto, Ontario, M5V 3X5 Canada. Tel: (1 416) 599 3499. e: proffice@tiff.net. Web: www.tiff.net.

AWARDS 2010

Best Canadian Short Film: **Les Fleurs de l'âge**, Vincent Biron.
SKYY Vodka Award for Best Canadian First Feature Film: **The High Cost of Living**, Deborah Chow.
The City of Toronto Award for Best Canadian Feature Film: **Incendies**, Denis Villeneuve.
The Prize of the International Critics (FIPRESCI Prize) for the Discovery Programme: **Beautiful Boy** (USA), Shawn Ku.
The Prize of the International Critics (FIPRESCI Prize) for Special Presentations: **L'Amour Fou** (France), Pierre Thoretton.
The Cadillac People's Choice Award: **The King's Speech** (Australia/UK), Tom Hooper.
The Cadillac People's Choice Midnight Madness Award: **Stake Land** (USA), Jim Mickle.
The Cadillac People's Choice Documentary Award: Force of Nature: **The David Suzuki Film** (Canada), Sturla Gunnarsson.

Tribeca Film Festival
April 20-May 1, 2011

The Tribeca Film Festival was founded in 2002 by Robert De Niro, Jane Rosenthal and Craig Hatkoff to spur the economic and cultural revitalisation of Lower Manhattan through an annual celebration of film, music and culture. The Festival's mission is to help filmmakers reach the broadest possible audience, enable the international film community and general public to experience the power of cinema and promote New York City as a major filmmaking centre. Since its founding, the Festival has at-

tracted over 2.6 million attendees from the US and abroad and has generated over $600 million in economic activity for New York City. The Festival is anchored in Tribeca with additional venues throughout Manhattan and includes film screenings, special events, concerts, a family street fair, and 'Tribeca Talks' panel discussions. *Inquiries to:* Tribeca Film Festival, 375 Greenwich St, New York, NY 10013, USA. Tel: (1 212) 941 2400. e: festival@tribecafilm-festival.org. Web: www.tribecafilm.org.

AWARDS 2010

The Founders Award for Best Narrative Feature: **When We Leave (Die Fremde)** (Germany), Feo Aladag.
Best New Narrative Filmmaker: Kim Chapiron for **Dog Pound** (France).
Best Documentary Feature: **Monica & David** (USA), Alexandra Codina.
Best New Documentary Filmmaker: Clio Barnard for **The Arbor** (UK).
Best Actress in a Narrative Feature: Sibel Kekilli for **When We Leave (Die Fremde)** (Germany).
Best Actor in a Narrative Feature: Eric Elmosnino for **Gainsbourg, Je t'Aime...Moi Non Plus** (France).
Best New York Narrative: **Monogamy** (USA), Dana Adam Shapiro.
Best New York Documentary: **The Woodmans** (China/Italy/USA), C Scott Willis.
Heineken Audience Award: **RUSH: Beyond the Lighted Stage** (Canada), Scot McFadyen and Sam Dunn.
Best Narrative Short: **Father Christmas Doesn't Come Here** (South Africa), Bekhi Sibiya.
Best Documentary Short: **White Lines & The Fever: The Death of DJ Junebug** (USA), Travis Senger.
Student Visionary Award: **some boys don't leave** (USA), Maggie Kiley.

Tromsø International Film Festival
January 18-22, 2012

Norway's largest film festival for the audience with more than 50,000 admissions in six days, Tromsø International Film Festival presents cutting edge international art house cinema, screening more than 180 titles. This includes a feature competition and several exciting sidebars, among them 'Films from the North', with new shorts and docs from arctic Scandinavia, Canada and Russia. The festival is also an important meeting place for industry professionals. *Inquiries to:* Tromsø International Film Festival, PO Box 285, N-9253 Tromsø, Norway. Tel: (47) 7775 3090. e: info@tiff.no. Web: www.tiff.no.

AWARDS 2010

Aurora Prize: **The Door** (Germany), Anno Saul.
Norwegian Peace Film Award: **The Other Bank** (Georgia/Kazakhstan), George Ovashvili
FIPRESCI Prize: **10 to 11** (Turkey), Pelin Esmer.
Don Quijote: **Whisper In The Wind** (Iraq), Shahram Alidi.
Tromsø Palm: **Exhaling Music** (Norway), Trond Eliassen.
Silver Audience Award: **For A Moment, Freedom** (Austria/France/Turkey), Arash T Riahi.

Report 2010

The Russian feel-good musical *Hipsters,* by Valery Todorovsky, kicked off the 20th edition of Tromsø International Film Festival this year, which was extended by an extra day to mark its special anniversary. The festival's main prize, the **Aurora** was awarded to Anno Saul's *The Door* (Germany), starring Danish leading man Mads Mikkelsen. Tromsø's main square was once again transformed into an open air cinema with a big snow screen that besides featuring daily family programmes,

The people of Tromsø gathered at the town square to watch **Nanook of the North** *with live soundtrack.*

was the venue for a packed screening of Robert J Flaherty's silent classic documentary *Nanook of the North*, accompanied live by Swedish composer/musician Matti Bye and his ensemble. **– Håvard Stangnes**, Head of Communications.

Valencia International Action and Adventure Film Festival
April 8-16, 2011

Valencia International Action and Adventure Film Festival aims to present itself as an international showcase of the greatest action films. It also pays tribute to the most successful action and adventure films of all time, through retrospectives of renowned artists who made these films an essential element in the development of the film industry. In the 30th anniversary edition, which took place in 2009, Salomon Castiel took the role of director of Valencia's Mostra which was devoted to Mediterranean cinema. In 2010,

FROZEN LAND / MOVING PICTURES

22nd TROMSØ INTERNATIONAL FILM FESTIVAL
JANUARY 18–22, 2012

the Festival changed its main subject and celebrated a new edition under the name of Valencia International Action and Adventure Film Festival. At the same time, the festival scheduled an overview of films that provide a cultural bridge between the peoples of the Mediterranean region. *Inquiries to:* Fundación Municipal de Cine, Plaza de la Almoina 4, Puertas 1,2 and 3, 46003 Valencia, Spain. Tel: (34 96) 392 1506. e: info@mostravalencia.com. Web: www.mostravalencia.org.

Valladolid International Film Festival
October 22-29, 2011

One of Spain's key events, the festival spotlights the latest work by established directors and newcomers. It features competitions for features, shorts and documentaries and also offers retrospectives, a selection of recent Spanish productions and a congress of new Spanish directors. *Inquiries to:* Valladolid International Film Festival Office, Teatro Calderón, Calle Leopoldo Cano, s/n 4ª Planta, 47003 Valladolid, Spain. Tel: (34 983) 426 460. e:festvalladolid@seminci.com. Web: www.seminci.com.

AWARDS 2010
International Jury Awards
Golden Spike for Feature Film ex aequo:
Certified Copy (Iran), Abbas Kiarostami and **No Return** (Argentina/Spain) Miguel Cohan.
Silver Spike for Feature Film: **The Mosquito Net** (Spain), Agustí Vila.
Special Jury Prize: **On The Path** (Austria/Bosnia & Herzegovina/Croatia/Germany), Jasmila Zbanic.
Pilar Miró Prize for Best New Director: Miguel Cohan for **No Return** (Argentina/Spain).
Best Actress: Emma Suárez for **The Mosquito Net** (Spain).
Best Actor: Jesper Christensen for **A Family** (Denmark).
FIPRESCI Award: **No Return** (Argentina/Spain), Miguel Cohan.
Miguel Delibes Award for Best Screenplay: Denis Villeneuve and Valérie Beaugrand-Champagne for **Incendies**.
Best Director of Photography Award: Nagao Nakashima for **The Fourth Portrait** (Taiwan).
Best Original Music: Cyrin Morin for **The Human Resources Manager** (France/Germany/Israel).
Cultural Diversity Award: **Even The Rain** (France/Mexico/Spain), Iciar Bollain.
FIPRESCI Award: **No Return** (Argentina/Spain), Miguel Cohan.
Golden Spike for Short Film: **To Kill a Bumblebee** (Israel), Tal Granit and Sharon Maymon.
Silver Spike for Short Film: **Érintés** (Hungary), Ferenc Cakó.
Best European Short: **Little Children, Big Words** (Sweden), Lisa James Larsson.
Meeting Point Section Best Feature: **Sebbe** (Sweden), Babak Najafi.
Meeting Point Section Best Short: **The Cage** (Romania/Netherlands), Adrian Sitaru.
Meeting Point Section Best Spanish Short: **A or B**, Leticia Dolera.
Best Documentary: Voices Unbound: **The Story of the Freedom Writers**, (USA), Daniel Anker.

Vancouver International Film Festival
September 29-October 14, 2011

The Vancouver International Film Festival
is among the largest film festivals in North
America and one of the largest cultural
events in Canada. VIFF is a microcosm of its
home city: cosmopolitan, innovative, friendly,
culturally complex and very accessible. The
festival shows over 600 screenings of more
than 350 films from 80 countries with around
150,000 people attending. Founded in 1982,
the festival's mandate is to encourage the
understanding of other nations through the art
of cinema, to foster the art of cinema, and to
stimulate the motion picture industry in British
Columbia and Canada. Specialities include East
Asia, Nonfiction Features, and films related
to arts, music, Africa and the environment.
Inquiries to: VIFF, 1181 Seymour St, Vancouver,
British Columbia, Canada V6B 3M7. Tel: (1 604)
685 0260. e: viff@viff.org. Web: www.viff.org.

Venice International Film Festival
August 31-September 10, 2011

The Venice Film Festival offers an overview
of world cinema, in a spirit of freedom and
tolerance, under Marco Müller's directorship.
The Festival includes competitive and out-
of-competition sections, in addition to
retrospectives, tributes, and exquisite art
exhibitions around downtown Venice. The
official line-up of the 68th edition will be
announced in a press conference that will take
place in Rome at the end of July 2011. *Inquiries
to:* La Biennale di Venezia, Mostra Internazionale
d'Arte Cinematografica. San Marco 1364/A,
Ca' Giustinian, 30124 Venice, Italy. Tel (39 041)
521 8711. e: foreignpress@labiennale.org. Web:
www.labiennale.org/en/cinema.

AWARDS 2010
VENEZIA 67 Section
Golden Lion for Best Film: **Somewhere** (USA)
Sofia Coppola.
Silver Lion for Best Director: Álex de la Iglesia
for **Balada Triste de Trompeta** (France/Spain).
Special Jury Prize: **Essential Killing** (Hungary/

Sofia Coppola, left, with the stars of **Somewhere**, *Elle Fanning and
Stephen Dorff at the 2010 Venice Film Festival. Photo: Giorgio Zucchiatti*

Ireland/Norway/Poland) Jerzy Skolimowski.
Coppa Volpi for Best Actor: Vincent Gallo for
Essential Killing (Hungary/Ireland/Norway/
Poland).
Coppa Volpi for Best Actress: Ariane Labed for
Attenberg (Greece).
*Marcello Mastroianni Award for Best New
Young Actor or Actress:* Mila Kunis for **Black
Swan** (USA).
Osella for Best Cinematography: Mikhail
Krichman for **Silent Souls** (Russia).
Osella for Best Screenplay: Álex de la Iglesia
for **Balada Triste de Trompeta** (France/Spain).
Special Lion: Monte Hellman.
ORIZZONTI Section
Award for Full-length Film: **Verano de Goliat**
(Canada/Mexico) Nicolás Pereda.
Special Jury Prize for Full-length Film: **The
Forgotten Space** (Austria/Netherlands) Nöel
Burch and Allan Sekula.
Award for Medium-Length Film: **Out** (Israel)
Roee Rosen.
Award for Short Film: **Coming Attractions**
(Austria) Peter Tscherkassky.
Special Mention: **Jean Gentil** (Dominican
Republic/Germany/Mexico) Laura Amelia
Guzmán and Israel Cárdenas.
Controcampo Italiano Award: **20 Sigarette**
(Italy) Aureliano Amadei.
Special Mention: Vinicio Marchioni for **20
Sigarette** (Italy).
Lion of the Future – 'Luigi de Laurentiis' Venice

Award for a Debut Film: **Majority** (Turkey) Seren Yüce.
Golden Lion for Lifetime Achievement: John Woo.

Report 2010

The 67th Venice International Film Festival held at Venice Lido has the aim of raising awareness and promoting all the various aspects of international cinema in a spirit of freedom and tolerance. Marco Müller, who directed the 67th edition, has been heading the Festival since 2004. The screenings schedule included 11 days, from 1st to 11th September, with five International Juries assigned the official awards of the Festival. The Golden Lion for Best Film was awarded to *Somewhere.* The Jury for this award was chaired by Quentin Tarantino. **– Giovanni Alberti**, Press Department.

Victoria Independent Film & Video Festival

February 3-12, 2012

No matter if it is controversial cinema, Oscar-winning drama, provocative documentary or the list of special guests attending the Victoria Film Festival, this romp though the world of film is the event you don't want to miss! With historic architecture and fabulous vistas, downtown streets are lined with theatres, shops, museums and cafes that provide the perfect backdrop for the home of the boutique schmooze. The Festival screens 150 films at four downtown venues. As Vancouver Island's biggest and longest running film festival it's the place to see the best of independent cinema in one of the top destinations in the world, according to Condé Nast. A great package at the legendary Fairmont Empress is available. The 17th Annual Victoria Film Festival presents the most exclusive industry event of the year. SpringBoard features masterclasses along with talks by the top young filmmakers of the day. Online registration and information can be found at www.victoriafilmfestival. com. *Inquiries to:* Victoria Film Festival, 1215 Blanshard St, Victoria, British Columbia, V8W 3J4 Canada. Tel: (1 250) 389 0444. : 389 0406.

e: festival@victoriafilmfestival.com Web:www. victoriafilmfestival.com.

AWARDS 2010

Best Feature Film: **Defendor** (Ontario), Peter Stebbings.
Best Canadian Feature: **Shine of Rainbows** (British Columbia/Ireland), Vic Sarin.
Canwest Award for Best Documentary: **Last Train Home** (Quebec/China), Lixin Fan.
Best Short Animation: **The Empress** (Alberta), Lyle Pisio.
Best Short Award: **Armoire** (Ontario), Jamie Travis.
Audience Favourite Award: **The Yes Men Fix the World** (USA), Andy Bichlbaum, Mike Bonanno and Kurt Engfehr.

VIENNALE –
Vienna International Film Festival
October 20-November 2, 2011

The Viennale is Austria's most important international film event, as well as one of the oldest and best-known festivals in the German-speaking world. It takes place every October at beautiful cinemas in Vienna's historic centre, providing a festival with an international orientation and a distinctive urban flair. A high percentage of the approximately 96,000 visitors to the festival are made up of a decidedly young audience. In its main programme, the Viennale shows a carefully picked selection of new films from all over the globe as well as new films from Austria. The choice of films offers a cross section of bold filmmaking that stands apart from the aesthetics of mainstream conventionality and is politically relevant. Aside from its focus on the newest feature films of every genre and structural form imaginable, the festival pays particular attention to documentary films and international short films, as well as experimental and crossover works. The Viennale receives regular international acclaim for its annual organisation of a large-scale historic retrospective in collaboration with the Austrian Film Museum, its numerous special programmes, as well as for its tributes and homages dedicated to prominent personalities and institutions in international filmmaking. *Inquiries to:* Viennale, Siebensterngasse 2, 1070 Vienna, Austria. Tel: (43 1) 526 5947. office@ viennale.at. Web: www.viennale.at.

Report 2010

To some a surprise, the most striking success of this year's Viennale was the tribute that the festival dedicated to American writer and director Larry Cohen, whose presence at a lot of his films' screenings was a huge benefit. A great discovery to many people in Vienna was the oeuvre of Canadien filmmaker Denis Côté, whose first ever 'retrospective' took place here. Lou Reed's arrival in Vienna for the screening of his first film, *Red Shirley*, generated immense interest with the public and the press, while the extended short film programme turned out to be a secret success. John Turturro, Olivier Assayas, Mike Leigh, Marco Bellocchio and Apichatpong Weerasethakul were among the most notable guests at this year's festival. **– Fredi Themel**, Head of Press Department.

Viennale opening 2010: Apichatpong Weerasethakul, Viennale director Hans Hurch, Xavier Maly (actor; **Des hommes et des dieux***) in front of the Gartenbaukino, October 21, 2010. Photo: Viennale/Robert Newald*

Zlín International Film Festival for Children and Youth
May 29-June 5, 2011

The Zlín Film Festival is the world's oldest and largest festival of its kind. The festival's core is its international competitions: feature films for children, feature films for youth, animated films for children, and European debuts. The main

prize of Zlín's festival is the Golden Slipper. Aside from the competitions, the programme is made up of many non-competitive sections. Among the most significant were the presentations of films from European countries. In 2011, the focus will be on Italian cinema. The 51st Zlín Film Festival will also observe the 110th anniversary of Walt Disney's birth. Among the most notable supporting events are the mini-salon of artistically rendered film clapperboards, the international festival of ethical advertising, 'The Rainbow Marble', and a retrospective of the international festival of student films, 'Zlín Dog'. The non-competitive informative section will feature many full-length films, short animations and documentaries. A rich supporting programme full of entertainment for the youngest audience will also be offered throughout the festival week. **Rainbow Marble** is an international advertising festival that is part of the Zlín Film Festival whose creativity is complemented by a focus on the ethical dimensions of advertising. We value a responsible approach toward commercial communications and we point out the necessity for 'rediscovering' the advertising code of ethics. Aside from the ethical advertising competition, the festival also includes a technical conference – the only one in the entire Czech Republic to tackle the issue of media education. We're also preparing many interesting lectures for the conference Rainbow Marble (June 1-2, 2011). **Zlín Dog** is one of the most important international festivals of student films in the Czech Republic (certainly the most significant as far as focusing on animation and production from students of the Visegrad countries is concerned). The 8th year of the festival will focus on active participation by film students and meetings with prominent personalities. This international student film festival will offer four days of the world's best student films – in the competitive categories of traditional animation, computer and combined animation, feature and documentary films from the Visegrad countries. This year will start off with many famous film personalities from Zlín's studios. A presentation of the

Christopher Lee. Photo: Copyright 2010 Filmfest, s.r.o.

latest technology – 3D and mapping – is also sure to be a hit (March 1-4, 2011). *Inquiries to:* FILMFEST s.r.o., Filmová 174, CZ-76179 Zlín, Czech Republic, Tel: (420) 577 592275. e: festival@zlinfest.cz. Web: www.zlinfest.cz.

AWARDS 2010
International Expert Jury for Feature Films
Golden Slipper for Best Feature Film for Children: **The Magic Tree** (Poland), Andrzej Maleszka.
Golden Slipper for the Best Feature Film for Youth: **Sebbe** (Sweden), Babak Najafi.
The City of Zlín Award – Special Recognition for a Feature Film for Children: **The Crocodiles** (Germany), Christian Ditter.
The Miloš Macourek Award – Special Recognition for a Feature Film for Youth: **Dear Lemon Lima** (USA), Suzi Yoonessi.
International Jury for Animated Films
Golden Slipper for Best Animated Film: **Lost and Found** (UK), Philip Hunt.
The Hermína Týrlová Award for Young Artists Aged Under 35: **The Employment** (Argentina), Santiago Bou Grasso.

International Expert Jury for the European Debuts Competition
The Europe Award: **If I Want to Whistle, I Whistle** (Romania), Florin Serban.
Special Jury Award: **Silent Voices** (France), Léa Fehner.
International Expert Jury for Feature Films of the Visegrad Countries
The Czech Minister of Culture Award: **Mall Girls** (Poland), Katarzyna Roslaniec.
FICC Jury
The Don Quixote Award: **Karla and Jonas** (Denmark), Charlotte Sachs Bostrup.
Special FICC Jury Award: **The Indian** (The Netherlands), Ineke Houtman.
Ecumenical Jury Award for Children: **The Indian** (The Netherlands), Ineke Houtman.
The Ecumenical Jury Award for Youth: **Sebbe** (Sweden), Babak Najafi.
International Children's Jury for Feature Films for Children
Main Prize of the Children's Jury for Best Feature Film for Children: **Echoes of the Rainbow** (China/Hong Kong), Alex Law.
International Children's Jury for Feature Films for Youth
Main Prize of the Children's Jury for Best Feature Film for Youth: **The Crocodiles** (Germany), Christian Ditter.

Audience Community
The Golden Apple for the Most Successful Feature Film: **Storm** (Denmark), Giacomo Campeotto.
The Golden Apple for Most Successful Animated Film: **Hip.Hop.Hippityhop** (Germany), Ralf Kukula.
Recognition for Lifetime Achievement in Film-Making for Children and Youth: Zdenek Sverák.

Report 2010
The 50th Zlín Film Festival was a celebration of Czech and Slovak film works and their creators. Attendance at projections was 35,000 (70,000 including attendance at the supporting events of the programme). The biggest stars of this year's Zlín Film Festival included world-renowned British actor Sir Christopher Lee and talented British actress Jodie Whittaker. Audiences were delighted with the appearance of Scott Rosenbaum at a screening of his film, *The Perfect Age of Rock 'n' Roll*, being gicen its Czech première atthe festival. Jury members for feature films included Benjamin Ribout and Scott Rosenbaum; for animated films Arto Louis Eriksen and Jan Tománek; and legendary director Dušan Hanák presided over the European debuts competition. – **Martin Pášma**, PR and Press Services

Festivals and Markets of Note

Almería International Short Film Festival, Diputación de Almería, Area de Cultura, Calle Navarro Rodrigo 17, 04001 Almeria, Spain. Tel: (34 950) 211 100 e: info@almeriaencorto.es. Web: www.almeriaencorto.net. *(Competition for international shorts with professional meetings and complementary cultural activities – Early Dec.)*

american film festival
october 2011
wrocław, poland

www.americanfilmfestival.pl

American Film Festival (AFF), Zamenhofa 1, 00-153 Warsaw, Poland. Tel: (48 22) 530 6656. e: aff@snh.org.pl. Web: www.americanfilmfestival. pl. *(The American Film Festival, the first film event in Central Europe solely devoted to the works of contemporary and classic American cinema, takes place in the cultural heritage city of Wroclaw, Poland. The event is organised by the* New Horizons Association, *which also presents the* Era New Horizons International Film Festival *(www.enh.pl) in the city of Wroclaw. The festival allows Polish audiences to become acquainted with independent contemporary American cinema, with presentations of the latest films from both established directors and up-and-coming talents. In this way, it hopes to present the diverse culture and political/social realities of the United States in a fuller way than has ever been tried before. The festival has among its many goals the desire to break through the stereotype of American cinema as strictly big-budget, star-driven international product. It presents contemporary independent productions in two major competitive sections: SPECTRUM,*

*a panorama section of contemporary American cinema, focusing on artists in mid-career and those making significant directorial debuts; and AMERICAN DOCS, a programme of compelling and award-winning documentaries from the film festival circuit. While the main focus is on contemporary films, the festival will also devote itself to an educational initiative to revive classic American films and showcase lesser-known film auteurs with comprehensive retrospectives of their works. 'We want to bring the best quality American films from the past and the present to Poland with this initiative', Festival Director Roman Gutek declared. The first edition of the AFF in 2010 was a resounding hit with audiences and local media. The festival screened close to 100 films, many of which were sell-outs for the enthusiastic audience of cinema lovers. Over 25,000 spectators participated in the festival's inaugural run, where 46 of the titles presented during 5 festival days were Polish premieres and 12 were screened for the first time in Europe. 'Spark of Being', a found footage film by celebrated avant-garde filmmaker Bill Morrison also had its World Premiere here. Twenty indie features were screened in competition (**Spectrum**), with hits from Cannes, Sundance, South by Southwest and Tribeca FF, including Vincent D'Onofrio's* Don't Go in the Woods *and Tim Rutili's* All My Friends Are Funeral Singers. **American Docs**,

Bill Morrison had the international premiere of his latest film, **Spark of Being**, *at the first American Film Festival. Photo by M.Kulczynski*

documentary section included And Everything Is Going Fine, Steven Soderbergh's study of the life and death of performance artist Spalding Gray, and Michael Moore's Capitalism: A Love Story. Aside from the American independent features and documentaries in competition, the festival presented a programme of avant-garde films entitled **On the Edge** and a selection of out-of-competition films in the **Highlights** section, introducing the biggest American indie films of the year, including Greenberg, Kaboom, The Killer Inside Me and Please Give. While the accent was definitely on new work, the festival also presented a host of retrospective programmes as part of its goal of educating the public about the American independent film scene. Chief among these was a complete retrospective of the films of pioneering indie director John Cassavetes. Another highlight was the **Decade of Independents** section, a survey of important works of the past decade. The programme also included classic Hollywood films in the **Play It Again, Sam** section. Directors in attendance included Michael Mohan (One Too Many Mornings), Alex Mar (American Mystic), Paul Gordon (The Happy Poet), Olivier Lécot (A NY Thing), Chuck Workman (Visionaries), Tyler Measom and Jennilyn Merten (Sons of Perdition), Tim Rutili (All My Friends Are Funeral Singers), Alistair Banks Griffin (Two Gates of Sleep), and Bill Morrison (Spark of Being). Other featured film artists include screenwriter Samuel Gray Anderson (Lucky Life) and screenwriter/producer Catherine Di Napoli (Untitled). Awards in 2010: Best Narrative Feature Audience Award (and cash prize of $10,000): Winter's Bone, directed by Debra Granik. Best Documentary Features Audience Award (and $5,000): The Two Escobars, the feature debut of Jeff and Michael Zimbalist. Artistic director: Urszula Śniegowska – October.)

Anima: Brussels Animation Film Festival, Folioscope, Ave de Stalingrad 52, B-1000 Brussels, Belgium. Tel: (32 2) 534 4125. e: info@folioscope.be. Web: www.animatv. be. (Celebrating its 30th Anniversary in 2011, the festival will screen over 100 films in the international competition (shorts and features, commercials, music videos), retrospectives,

exhibitions, lessons, workshops for the kids, the Futuranima professional days, round-table discussions, numerous guests and film concerts make Brussels an international appointment not to be ignored. It's also the place to find out about Belgian animation, with a national competition and screenings in panorama – March 4-13, 2011.)

Ann Arbor Film Festival, PO Box 8232, Ann Arbor, MI 48107, USA. Tel: (1 734) 995 5356. e: info@aafilmfest.org. Web: www.aafilmfest. org. (Cutting-edge, high calibre and artist-made films are showcased in the longest-running independent and experimental film festival in North America. All lengths and genres of film are screened, including experimental, animation, documentary, music video and narrative, from all over the world – March 22-27, 2011.)

Annecy/International Animation Film Festival and International Animation Film Market (MIFA), CITA, c/o Conservatoire d'Art et d'Histoire, 18 Avenue du Trésum, BP 399, 74013 Annecy Cedex, France. Tel: (33 4) 5010 0900. e: info@citia.org. Web: www.annecy.org. (Discover the best in contemporary creation and the talents of tomorrow during the International Animation Film Festival, the most important appointment with animation in the world. The MIFA is the animation industry's foremost showcase in terms of co-producing, purchasing, selling, financing and distributing animation content for all broadcasting platforms – Festival: June 6-11, 2011; MIFA: June 8-10, 2011.)

Aspen Filmfest & Shortsfest, 110 E Hallam, Ste 102, Aspen, CO 81611, USA. Tel: (1 970) 925 6882. e: info@aspenfilm.org. Web: www.aspenfilm.org. (Shortsfest: Short subject competition showcasing the great filmmakers of tomorrow and introducing a rich variety of current productions from around the world – April 5-10 2011; Filmfest: Feature-length invitational which champions independent film at its eclectic, thoughtful, and often inspiring best – Sept 21-26, 2011.)

Atlantic Film Festival, 1601 South Park St, Halifax, NS, B3J 2L2, Canada. Tel: (1 902) 422 3456. e: festival@atlanticfilm.com. Web: www.

atlanticfilm.com. (The Festival screens some of the best International, Canadian and Atlantic Canadian films. Our programmers scour the world for unique films for an Atlantic Canadian film festival audience, whether it's inspiring documentaries, off-beat Film Noir, beautifully-crafted animation or the latest Hollywood has to offer. In addition to screening films from around the world, the Festival offers opportunities to unlock the doors and bridge the gap between music and film, the Music & Image Conference provides musicians and filmmakers alike with an engaging educational and networking opportunity to help bring together these two, very connected industries. Strategic Partners, an International Film, TV and Multiplatform co-production market, kicks off the Atlantic Film Festival, running Sept 15-18. As one of the world's pre-eminent co-production markets, Strategic Partners brings top national & international industry players together to discover and develop compelling projects, create long-term relationships and make investment happen – all set against the backdrop of the vibrant coastal city of Halifax, Nova Scotia – Sept 15-24, 2011.)

Augsburg Children's Film Festival, Filmtage Augsburg, Schroeckstrasse 8, 86152 Augsburg, Germany. Tel: (49 821) 158 083. e: filmbuero@t-online.de. Web: www.filmtage-augsburg.de. (International features for children – Oct.)

Banff Mountain Film Festival, Mountain Culture at The Banff Centre, Box 1020, 107 Tunnel Mountain Drive, Banff, AB, T1L 1H5, Canada. Tel: (1 403) 762 6675. e: banffmountainfilms@banffcentre.ca. Web: www.banffcentre.ca/mountainculture. (International competition for films and videos related to mountains and the spirit of adventure; Aug 3 deadline for entries – Oct 29-Nov 6, 2011.)

Bermuda International Film Festival, Broadway House, PO Box HM 2963, Hamilton HM MX, Bermuda. Tel: (441) 293 3456. e: info@biff.bm. Web: www.biff.bm. (The festival features the best of independent film from around the world in three competition categories: features, documentaries and shorts. Q&A sessions with

directors, the festival's popular lunchtime 'Chats with…' sessions and, of course, parties, give filmgoers and filmmakers a chance to mingle in an intimate and relaxed setting. A competition victory earns each film's director an invitation to sit on the festival jury the following year. Submission deadline: 1 October – March 18-24, 2011.)

Big Sky Documentary Film Festival, 131 South Higgins Ave, Suite 3-6, Missoula, Montana 59802, USA. Tel: (1 406) 541 3456. e: info@bigskyfilmfest.org. Web: www.bigskyfilmfest.org. (The festival will screen more than 100 films, including world and US premieres, classics, rare and experimental works on Montana's largest screen at the historic Wilma Theatre in downtown Missoula, Montana. In addition to ten days of screenings, the event will feature many public and VIP events including panel discussions, galas, receptions and networking round-tables. The competitive event is open to non-fiction films and videos of all genres, subject matter, lengths and production dates. Awards and cash prizes will be given for Best Documentary Feature (over 50 minutes), Best Documentary Short (15-50 minutes), Best Mini-Doc (under 15 minutes) and best documentary about the American West (the Big Sky Award) – Feb 11-20, 2011.)

Bogota Film Festival, Residencias Tequendama, Centro Internacional Tequendama, Cra 10 Suite 27-51 Of 325, Bogotá, Colombia. Tel: (57 1) 341 7562. e: prensa@bogocine.com. Web: www.bogocine.com. (International competitive section, National Competitive section and side bars. Features, animation, shorts, documentary – Late Sept/early Oct.)

Boston Film Festival, 126 South St, Rockport, MA 01966, USA. Tel: (1 617) 523 8388. e: press@bostonfilmfestival.org. Web: www.bostonfilmfestival.org. (Showcasing a selection of feature films, documentaries and shorts. Filmmakers, actors and supporters have the opportunity to network at various events and a variety of awards are given annually. Q&A sessions with directors and actors follow every screening giving filmgoers a first hand access to the filmmaking process – Sept.)

Bradford International Film Festival, National Media Museum, Bradford, BD1 1NQ, UK. Artistic Director: Tony Earnshaw. Tel: (44 1274) 203317. e: tony.earnshaw@nationalmediamuseum.org.uk. Web: www.bradfordfilmfestival.org.uk. (*Bradford has become a byword for exciting, adventurous programming – a showcase for the new, the ground-breaking, the unusual and the obscure – March 17-27, 2011.*)

Brussels International Festival of Fantastic Film, 8 Rue de la Comtesse de Flandre 1020 Brussels, Belgium. Tel: (32 2) 201 1713. e: info@bifff.net. Web: www.bifff.net. (*Competitive international and European selection for shorts and features – April 7-19, 2011.*)

Cambofest, PO Box 707, 12000 Phnom Penh, Cambodia. Tel: (855 12) 194 2702. e: info@cambofest.com. Web: www.cambofest.com. (*Independent, grass-roots Film, Video and Animation – June and Nov.*)

Chicago International Children's Film Festival, Facets Multimedia Inc, 1517 W Fullerton, Chicago, IL 60614, USA. Tel: (1 773) 281 9075. e: kidsfest@facets.org. Web: www.cicff.org. (*North America's largest and most celebrated film festival devoted to films for and by children, featuring over 250 of the best films and videos from over 40 countries. More than 100 filmmakers, media professionals & celebrities attend the festival to lead interactive workshops with children – Oct.*)

Chicago Latino Film Festival, International Latino Cultural Center of Chicago, 676 North La Salle St, Suite 520, Chicago, IL 60654, USA. Tel: (1 312) 431 1330. e: info@latinoculturalcenter.org. Web: www.latinoculturalcenter.org. (*The Festival is non-competitive, except for the coveted Audience Choice Award, where more than 35,000 filmgoers have the opportunity to vote for their favourite film from over 100 films featured. The festival promotes awareness of Latino culture through a wide variety of art forms and education including film, music, dance, visual arts, comedy and theatre – April 1-14, 2011.*)

Cinéma du Réel, BPI Centre Georges Pompidou, 25 rue du Renard, 75197 Paris Cedex 04, France. Tel: (33 1) 4478 4516. Web: www.cinemadureel.org. (*Since 1978, the Cinéma du Réel international documentary film festival has been an outstanding international meeting point, where public and professionals discover the films of experienced directors as well as new talents, the history of documentary cinema as well as contemporary works. The festival programmes around 100 films for its various sections, screened at the Centre Pompidou, the Centre Wallonie-Bruxelles, the MK2 Beaubourg film theatre, the Paris City Hall and several other theatres in the Ile-de-France area. Submissions open in September for films with a 2010 copyright; deadline Nov 15th – March 24-April 3, 2011.*)

Cinema Jove International Film Festival, La Safor 10-5, 46015 Valencia, Spain. Tel: (34 96) 331 1047. e: info@cinemajove.com. Web: www.cinemajove.com. (*Promotes the work of young filmmakers and has two competitive sections: feature films screened for the first time in Spain and another for the best shorts on the international scene. These constitute the thrust of a programme that also embraces tributes to veteran filmmakers, young 'cult film' directors, exhibitions and professional meeting points – Mid June.*)

Cinequest, PO Box 720040, San Jose, CA 95172-0040, USA. Tel: (1 408) 295 3378. e: contact@cinequest.org. Web: www.cinequest.org. (*The festival remains one of the last strongholds for the discovery of new and emerging film artists and presents a dynamic event of 200 international films with over 400 film artists, technologists, and professionals from 34 countries in attendance – Feb 22-March 6, 2011.*)

Cleveland International Film Festival, 2510 Market Ave, Cleveland, OH 44113-3434, USA. Tel: (1 216) 623 3456. e: marshall@clevelandfilm.org. Web: www.clevelandfilm.org. (*Ohio's premiere film event features more than 150 feature films and more than 150 shorts, originating from close to 80 countries. Visiting filmmakers, panel discussions, and student screenings are all CIFF highlights. Organised by the Cleveland Film Society whose aim is to help the world discover* the power of the film arts to educate, entertain and celebrate the human experience – March 24-April 3, 2011.)

Crossing Europe Film Festival Linz, Graben 30, 4020 Linz, Austria. Tel: (43 732) 785700. info@crossingeurope.at. Web: www.crossingeurope.at. (The European Competition showcases young European cinema dealing with contemporary subjects and is open to a director's first or second films. The European Panorama is non-competitive and includes features that have been highly acclaimed and distinguished with awards at international festivals. Since 2010 the festival established a new competitive section with European documentaries. The festival grants a central place to the diversity and richness of the cultural distinctiveness of young European cinema. Apart from the competitions, the festival offers a full programme of tributes to outstanding film directors; film evenings centring on music and youth cultures, working worlds, plus much more – April 12-17, 2011.)

Cyprus International Film Festival, PO Box 70, Anapafseos & Anonymou, Agioi Theodoroi, Corinthia, Greece. Tel: (357) 9979 8112. Web: www.cyprusfilmfestival.org. (The festival offers new and upcoming directors the opportunity to showcase their talent in front of a jury of internationally acclaimed cinema experts, directors and actors. Animation, feature films, music videos, short films and video art – Oct.)

Dhaka International Film Festival, c/o Rainbow Film Society, BS Bhaban, Level 3, Room 105, 75 Science Laboratory Rd, Dhaka-1205, Bangladesh. Tel: (88 2) 862 1062. e: ahmedshovan@yahoo.com. Web: www.dhakafilmfest.org. (The festival will screen approximately 150 films from more than 40 countries. There is a competitive section for Asian cinema and categories include: Retrospective, Tributes, Cinema of the World, Children's Film, Focus, Bangladesh Panorama, Women Filmmakers, Independent Films Section and Spiritual Films Section – Jan 13-21, 2012.)

Divercine, Canelones 2226 Apt 102, Casilla de Correo 5023, 11200 Montevideo, Uruguay. Tel: (59

82) 401 9882. e: ricardocasasb@gmail.com. Web: www.divercine.com.uy. (International festival showcasing films for Children and Youth – July.)

Doclisboa, Largo da Madalena 1, 1°, 1100-317 Lisbon, Portugal. Tel: (351 21) 8 883 093. e: doclisboa@doclisboa.org. Web: www.doclisboa.org. (Competitive with the international section featuring a selection of some of the best documentaries from around the world, produced last season (2010-11). Some have already won awards and received critical acclaim, for others it will be their first screening – Oct 20-30, 2011.)

Doha Tribeca Film Festival, Web: www.dohatribecafilm.com. (The Festival will include a wide range of programming and include approximately 30 feature films, highlighting internationally acclaimed Arab films, plus the best of Hollywood, Bollywood, family films, documentaries, animation and world cinema. The films are screened at Doha's celebrated Museum of Islamic Art and in cinemas across Doha and other choice venues around Doha. While uniquely Qatari in its identity, the festival is modelled on the success of Tribeca Film Festival's dedication to engaging the local community and helping to promote and support filmmaking talent – late Oct)

Durban International Film Festival, Centre for Creative Arts, University of KwaZulu-Natal, Durban 4041, South Africa. Tel: (27 31) 260 2506. e: cca@ukzn.ac.za. Web: www.cca.ukzn.ac.za. (Daring, innovative and controversial films and filmmakers from around the world will take the spotlight at the 32nd Durban International Film Festival. The festival programmers have scoured the globe for films that excite, thrill, raise awareness and provoke. These films will be presented in over 200 screenings at venues across Durban and in surrounding communities. Alongside the screenings of films, the festival offers an extensive workshop and seminar programme, as well as training and industry events – July 21-31, 2011.)

Early Melons International Student Film Festival, Tupolevova 18, 85101 Bratislava, Slovakia. Tel: (421 9) 1093 8268. e: info@

earlymelons.com. Web: www.earlymelons.com. *(The Festival is a young artistic event, dedicated to different aspects of student cinematography. It is focused on recent European film production, with a special focus on V4 countries production. The basic aim of the festival is to become a free platform for people who desire to understand the world through film, video-art and photography. The Festival contributes to the popularity of student cinematography among the Slovak audience and is composed of several sections: international competition (the international jury will award the best films in the categories of Best Fiction, Best Animation, Best Documentary and Grand Prix), international video-art competition, Slovak competition, profiles of jury members, profiles of European film schools and student film festivals, workshops supervised by film professionals connected with student film production, masterclasses and others – March 16-20, 2011.)*

East End Film Festival (EEFF), The Brady Arts Centre, 192-196 Hanbury St, London, E1 5HU, UK. Tel: (+44) 020 7364 7917. e: film@eastendfilmfestival.com. Web: www. eastendfilmfestival.com. *(In 2011, The East End Film Festival will return for its 10th anniversary edition, spanning 6 days and nights, across numerous cinemas and music venues in London's East End. The EEFF programme reflects the multi-cultural make-up of East London, with a strong emphasis on local, grassroots film exhibition showcasing alongside the 'new wave' of British, Asian and Eastern European cinema, blended with an innovative mix of video art, music and cross-platform live events. EEFF aims to champion work that transcends political, cultural and artistic boundaries, to provide a platform for undiscovered talent and serve the diverse local communities in the most exciting artistic hub in Europe – London's East End. In 2010, EEFF screened over 200 films hosted in 29 different venues attracting an audience of over 30,000 people. Film award categories include: Audience Award, Best UK Short Film, Best Documentary Feature, Best UK First Feature and Best International First Feature – April 27-May 2, 2011.)*

Edmonton International Film Festival, Edmonton International Film Society, Suite 201, 10816A-82 Ave, Edmonton, Alberta, T6E 2B3, Canada. Tel: (1 780) 423 0844. e: info@edmontonfilmfest.com. Web: www. edmontonfilmfest.com. *(The festival screens cinematic gems of all genres from around the globe and celebrates the unique voices in filmmaking such as directors, writers and producers. Our schedule includes 55 feature-length slots, and 110 short films programmed into feature-length packages. All films screened at EIFF must be Edmonton premieres – Sept 23-Oct 1, 2011.)*

Emden International Film Festival, An der Berufschule 3, 26721 Emden, Germany. Tel: (49) 4921 9155-31. e: filmfest@vhs-emden.de. Web: www.filmfest-emden.de. *(The main focus is on current film productions from North Western Europe. Due to its extensive programme of new British and Irish films, the festival has also come to be regarded as a showcase for these productions in Germany. With over 100 films on 7 screens it is primarily a major audience festival for its 22,000 or so visitors and has developed into a meeting place for numerous representatives of the German and North-West European film industry – June 15-22, 2011.)*

European Film Forum Scanorama, Ozo Strasse 4, Vilnius 08200, Lithuania. Tel: (370 5) 276 0367. e: info@kino.lt . Web: www.scanorama. lt. *(The festival screens a variety of genres including features, documentaries, shorts and experimental films from new and emerging talents that represent contemporary European film. From its beginning as a Nordic Film Forum crossing Lithuania from its capital Vilnius, central Kaunas to the coast Klaipeda, Scanorama has become a successful film festival, embracing cinematographic achievements from the very South to the very North of Europe. Each year Scanorama also welcomes audiovisual professionals to the annual workshop, 'Go Young Generation'. Filmmakers from all over Europe give lectures to young professionals from the Baltic States, exchanging ideas and looking for ways to make films together – Nov 10-27, 2011.)*

European Independent Film Festival (ÉCU), 108 Rue Damremont, Paris 75018, France. e: info@ ecufilmfestival.com. Web: www.ecufilmfestival. com. *(ÉCU is one of Europe's premier events for independent filmmakers and their audiences. The Official Selection will showcase the best independent films from around the World. The festival is a unique and interactive experience, offering attendees the chance to participate in professional filmmaking workshops, Q&A sessions with the directors, music events and after-parties – April 1-3, 2011.)*

FID Marseille, 14 Allée Léon Gambetta, 13001 Marseille, France. Tel: (33 4) 9504 4490 e: welcome@fidmarseille.org. Web: www. fidmarseille.org. *(The festival presents about 170 films, mostly international premieres, in a rich programme made up of the official selection: (international competition, national competition, competition of first films plus parallel screens, round tables, etc. – early July.)*

Festival Dei Popoli, Borgo Pinti 82 Rosso, 50121 Firenze, Italy. Tel: (39 055) 244 778. e: festival-deipopoli@festivaldeipopoli.191.it. Web: www. festivaldeipopoli.org. *(International documentary film festival focusing on social, anthropological, historical and political issues. It includes the following sections: Official Selection, Italian Pan-orama, tributes/retrospectives, seminars, panel discussions, special events – mid Nov.)*

Festival du Cinema International en Abitibi-Temiscamingue, 215 Mercier Ave, Rouyn-Noranda, Quebec J9X 5WB, Canada. Tel: (1 819) 762 6212. e: info@festivalcinema.ca. Web: www. festivalcinema.ca. *(The Festival presents nearly 150 International shorts, medium and full-length features; animation, documentary and fiction from more than 30 countries – Oct 29-Nov 3, 2011.)*

Festival du Nouveau Cinema – Montreal, 3805 Boulevard St-Laurent, Montreal, Quebec, Canada H2W 1X9. Tel: (1 514) 282 0004. e: info@ nouveaucinema.ca. Web: www.nouveaucinema. ca. *(Highlights the development of new trends in cinema and new media, providing a showcase for new, original works, particularly in the fields of independent cinema and digital creation. The festival welcomes Quebec, Canadian and international artists in a convivial atmosphere that prizes public and professional exchange. Official competition: Golden SheWolf – QUEBECOR with $15,000 for the Best Feature – Oct 12-23, 2011.)*

Festival International du Film de Boulogne-Billancourt, Neo Festivals de Cinema, 23 Avenue Sainte Foy, 92200 Neuilly, France. Tel: (33 6) 8038 8980. e: caroline.mitchell@neofestivals.com. Web: www.neofestivals.com. *(The festival presents some 20 feature films and documentaries, in and out of competition. Films that offer a positive look at our world, films that confront life with a smile, films that help us imagine the very best is possible. Comedies, romantic comedies, inspirational stories, films that put forward an optimistic view. The Competition presents 6 feature films, premiering in France and produced within 2 years of the Festival. Films from every genre and every continent, cultural and artistic diversity being one of the primary goals of this Festival. Films in competition will be screened, in 35mm or Beta Digital, at the Cinéma Pathé in Boulogne-Billancourt – April 1-4, 2011.)*

Festival International du Film Francophone de Namur, 175, Rue des Brasseurs, 5000 Namur, Belgium Tel: (32 81) 241 236. e: info@fiff.be. Web: www.fiff.be. *(The festival promotes French-speaking film and tries, for this purpose, to gather in Namur all the directors, producers, screenwriters, actors, distributors and industry figures involved in French-speaking cinematographic creation. It is really a place of thinking and discussion by means of conferences and professional meetings. The Festival also contributes to the education and the training of young people, offering teaching activities and personal spaces. The Bayards reward the happy prizes winner for the various competitions: feature films, short films and debuts – Sept 30-Oct 7, 2011.)*

Filmfest Dresden – International Short Film Festival, Alaunstrasse 62, D-01099, Dresden, Germany. Tel: (49 351) 829 470. e: info@filmfest-dresden.de. Web: www.filmfest-dresden.de. *(Filmfest Dresden is an international short film festival and includes short animated and fiction films as well as documentary and experimental films. Founded in 1989, it has developed into a major short film festival in Germany and hosts one of the best-funded short film competitions across Europe. The main sections of the festival are the International and the National Competitions. These are accompanied by various other thematic events. The festival also organises workshops and seminars for young filmmakers. Visitors, the press and film producers also use the festival as a meeting place and to exchange opinions and discuss new ideas – April 12-17, 2011.)*

Filmfest Hamburg, Steintorweg 4, 20099 Hamburg, Germany. Tel: (49 40) 3991 9000-0. e: info@filmfesthamburg.de. Web: www. filmfesthamburg.de. *(Under the direction of Albert Wiederspiel, the renowned film festival takes place every year in the fall. Around 130 international films are screened, as German or world premieres, in the following sections: Agenda, Eurovisuell, Voila!, Vitrina, Nordlichter, Deluxe, TV Films in Cinema and Michel Children's and Youth Filmfest. The many facets of the programme range from cinematically highbrow art house films to innovative mainstream cinema. The Douglas Sirk Award honours outstanding contributions to film culture and business. Filmfest Hamburg also sees itself as a platform for cultural exchange and dialogue: in past years, the festival has, among others, shed light more on productions from Asia (from Iran to Japan and Korea) and Europe (from the UK and Scandinavia to France, Spain and Eastern Europe) – Late Sept/ early Oct.)*

Filmfest München, Sonnenstr 21, D-80331, Munich, Germany. Tel: (49 89) 381 9040. e: info@ filmfest-muenchen.de. Web: www.filmfest-muenchen.de. *(Germany's largest summer festival, screening over 200 films from more than 40 countries – June 24-July 2, 2011.)*

Films from the South (FFS), Dronningensgt. 16, N-0152 Oslo, Norway. Tel: (47 22) 8224 80/81/82.

e: info@filmfrasor.no. Web: www.filmfrasor. no. *(A unique international film festival based in the capital of Norway. Since 1991, the festival has presented the best films and filmmakers from Asia, Africa and Latin America to a diverse audience. Each year approximately 100 feature films and documentaries are screened, over ten festival days and 230 screenings – Oct.)*

Florida Film Festival, Enzian Theatre, 1300 South Orlando Ave, Maitland, Florida 32751, USA. Tel: (1 407) 644 5625 x 327. Web: www. floridafilmfestival.com. *(Showcases cutting-edge American independent and international film, plus educational forums, glamorous parties and other special events – April 8-17, 2011.)*

Fredrikstad Animation Festival, PO Box 1405, N-1602 Fredrikstad, Norway. Tel: (47) 4024 9364. e: mail@animationfestival.no. Web: www. animationfestival.no. *(Competitive festival organised by the Norwegian Animation Forum which showcases Nordic, Baltic and international animation including retrospectives and workshops – Nov 9-13, 2011.)*

Full Frame Documentary Film Festival, 324 Blackwell St, Suite 500, Washington Bldg, Bay 5, Durham, NC 27701, USA. Tel: (1 919) 687 4100. e: info@fullframefest.org. Web: www.fullframefest. org. *(Each spring Full Frame welcomes filmmakers and film lovers from around the world to historic downtown Durham, North Carolina for a four-day, morning to midnight array of over 100 films as well as discussions, panels, and southern hospitality. Set within a four-block radius, the intimate festival landscape fosters community and conversation between filmmakers, film professionals and the public – April 14-17, 2011.)*

Future Film Festival, Via Pietralata, 65/2, 40122 Bologna, Italy. Tel: (39 051) 296 0672. e: ffinfo@futurefilmfestival.org. Web: www. futurefilmfestival.org. *(The festival is dedicated to animation and special effects and highlights the changes in digital imaginary and analyses the evolution of cinema and animation. It hosts panels, international previews, special events and workshops – Jan.)*

GET THE COMPLETE PICTURE!
23rd GALWAY FILM FLEADH
5-10 JULY 2011
WWW.GALWAYFILMFLEADH.COM

Galway Film Fleadh, 36D Merchants Dock, Merchants Road, Galway City, Ireland. Tel: (353 91) 562 200. e: info@galwayfilmfleadh. com. Web: www.galwayfilmfleadh.com. ('The Galway Film Fleadh is a wonderful event. Might rain. Doesn't matter!' – Anthony Minghella. The Galway Film Fleadh screens the best of New Irish Films, Feature Documentaries and World Cinema. It also platforms excellence in filmmaking, with retrospectives, public interviews, tributes and masterclasses. (Stephen Daldry, Sir Ronald Harwood, Brendan Gleeson, Anjelica Huston Christopher Hampton, Michael Fassbender, Ted Hope, Peter O' Toole, Jessica Lange, Kathy Bates, Robert Towne, Paul Schrader, Mira Nair, Patricia Clarkson, Abbas Kiarostami, Paolo Taviani and many more). In addition, the Galway Film Fair, a transatlantic bridge for the European Film and Television Industry, hosts 600 one-on-one meetings for producers with projects and invited film financiers, seminars, networking breakfasts and other industry events – July 5-10, 2011.)

Audiences and Industry gather for another screening at the Galway Film Fleadh

Glasgow Film Festival, 12 Rose St, Glasgow G3 6RB, UK. Tel: (44 141) 352 8613. e: info@ glasgowfilmfestival.org.uk. Web: www. glasgowfilmfestival.org.uk. (The festival is now the third largest film festival in the UK. It is 11 days of great films, guests, events and parties, catering to an audience of more than 30,000 people across 17 key city centre venues. The festival welcomes features, shorts and work in all genres, and is committed to supporting Scottish talent and providing audiences with the opportunity to see the best of world cinema – Feb 17-27, 2011.)

Glimmer: Hull International Short Film Festival, Suite 12 Danish Buildings, 44-46 High St, Hull, HU1 1PS, UK. Tel: (44) 01482 381512. e:office@hullfilm.co.uk. Web: www.hullfilm.co.uk. (Dedicated to showcasing the very best short films from across the world, of any genre that run up to a maximum of 45 minutes and were made after 1st January 2009. The wide and diverse selection of films include dramas, documentaries, artist's film, video and animation with over 200 films screened. Attended by special guests from the film world and with a host of great events for everyone to enjoy. Numerous competitions, masterclasses, and special programmes – April 22-24, 2011.)

Golden Apricot International Film Festival, 3 Moskovyan St, 0001 Yerevan, Armenia. Tel: (374) 1052 1042. e: info@gaiff.am. Web: www. gaiff.am. (The festival takes place in the capital of Armenia, Yerevan, at the foot of biblical Mount Ararat. The theme of the festival is 'Crossroads of Cultures and Civilization' and the aim is to build cultural bridges and foster dialogue in this very complex corner of the planet. Established in 2004, it has fast become a premier destination in the region for filmmakers of all genres, particularly those advancing universal values of peace, cultural harmony and mutual understanding. As one journalist wrote, the festival became a pleasant place for elite film meetings: 'Classics of the art house films can be understood: a fantastic country with such ancient history, dramatic presence and future perspective, naturally, interests any

artist'. Internationally acclaimed filmmaker Atom Egoyan (Canada) is President of the Festival and noted filmmaker Harutyun Khachatryan (Armenia) is the Director. The festival includes two main competition sections: International Competition (Feature and Documentary) and Armenian Panorama National Competition. One Grand Prize 'Golden Apricot', and one Special Prize, 'Silver Apricot', are awarded in each category. Other festival sections are: Directors Across Borders Regional Competition, retrospectives, master-classes etc. – July 10-17, 2011.)

Atom Egoyan, Claudia Cardinale, Harutyun Khachatryan at a special evening dedicated to the actress.

Guadalajara International Film Festival,

Nebulosa 2916, Colonia Jardines del Bosque, Guadalajara, Jalisco, Mexico. Tel: (52 33) 3121 7461. e: info@festivalcinedgl.udg.mx. Web: www. guadalajaracinemafest.com. *(Recent Mexican and Ibero-American film productions of quality, increasing the awareness of the world film industry by screening the work of noteworthy Ibero-American film directors and presenting other remarkable and innovative films by new filmmakers – March 25-April 1, 2011.)*

Guanajuato International Film Festival

Expresión en Corto, Fabrica La Aurora, Local 5-B, Col. Aurora San Miguel de Allende, Gto. México C.P. 37700. Tel: (52 415) 152 7264. e: info@expresionencorto.com. Web: www. expresionencorto.com. *(Hosted since 1997 in two beautiful colonial-era World Heritage Sites, San Miguel de Allende and Guanajuato Capital, this massive festival occupies the final 10 days of July and receives over 2,400 submissions from more than 90 countries in its international competition. It screens over 400 films and presents a variety of conferences, workshops and tributes to both nationally and internationally renowned filmmakers. Among its many activities, the festival annually welcomes the Cinéfondation Residence laureates during its MexiCannes Summer Residence Programme and holds a 48-Hour Collegiate Production Rally. The festival also hosts an International Pitching Market which brings together international producers, distributors and diverse film financing institutions from around the world, who are interested in co-producing the top Mexican feature-length projects currently in development – July 22-31, 2011.)*

Haifa International Film Festival, 142 Hanassi Ave, Haifa 34 633, Israel. Tel: (972 4) 8353 515. e: film@haifaff.co.il. Web: www.haifaff.co.il. *(The festival attracts an ever-growing audience of over 60,000 spectators along with hundreds of Israeli and foreign professionals from the film and television industries. Some 180,000 people take part in the activities of the festival, including the outdoor events, screenings, workshops. During the festival around 150 new films from the best and most recent international productions are premiered with some 220 screenings in seven theatres: feature films, documentaries, animation, short films, retrospectives and tributes – Oct 13-19, 2011.)*

Hawaii International Film Festival, 680 Iwilei Rd, Suite 100, Honolulu, Hawaii 96813, USA. Tel: (1 808) 792 1577. e: info@hiff.org. Web: www. hiff.org. *(Established in 1981, the festival seeks to promote cultural understanding between the peoples of Asia, the Pacific and North America through the medium of film. The Festival screens* an average of 150 features, documentaries and film shorts and also conducts seminars and workshops – Mid to Late Oct.)

Heartland Film Festival, 200 S Meridian, Suite 220, Indianapolis, Indiana 46225-1076, USA. Tel: (1 317) 464 9405. e: info@heartlandfilmfestival.org. Web: www.heartlandfilmfestival.org. *(The festival screens independent films from around the world and presents US$150,000 in cash prizes and Crystal Heart Awards to the Festival's top-judged submissions, including Best Dramatic Feature, Best Documentary Feature and Best Short Film. The festival comprises student and professional films, a variety of special events and a one-of-a-kind experience in one of the Midwest's most inviting cities – Oct 13-22, 2011.)*

Holland Animation Film Festival, Hoogt 4, 3512 GW Utrecht, Netherlands. Tel: (31 30) 233 1733. e: info@haff.nl. Web: www.haff.awn. nl. *(International competitions for independent and applied animation; special programmes, retrospectives, student films, exhibitions – Nov.)*

Hot Docs Canadian International Documentary Festival, 110 Spadina Ave, Suite 333, Toronto, Ontario, M5V 2K4, Canada. Tel: (1 416) 203 2155. e: info@hotdocs.ca. Web: www.hotdocs. ca. *(North America's largest documentary festival, conference and market, which presents a selection of more than 150 cutting-edge documentaries from Canada and around the globe. Through its industry programmes, Hot Docs also provides a full range of professional development, market and networking opportunities for documentary professionals April 28-May 8, 2011.)*

Huesca Film Festival, Avenida del Parque 1,2, 22002 Huesca, Spain. Tel: (34 974) 212 582. e: info@huesca-filmfestival.com. Web: www.huesca-filmfestival.com. *(Well-established shorts festival with official competitive sections composed of the Iberoamerican, International Shorts and European Documentary contests. The winners receive the Award Danzante and the winners of the Award Danzante in the Iberoamerican and International contest automatically qualify to*

enter the Short Films category of the Academy of Motion Picture Arts and Sciences in Hollywood for the concurrent season – June 3-11, 2011.)

Hungarian Film Week, Magyar Filmunió, Városligeti, Fasor 38, 1068 Budapest, Hungary. Tel: (36 1) 351 7760. e: filmunio@filmunio.hu. Web: www.hungarianfilmweek.com. *(Well-established regular showcase presenting the former year's Hungarian film production to local and foreign professionals as well as to the Hungarian public. The event attracts internationally acclaimed journalists and critics, festival directors and programmers, producers and distributors. Competitive, with Hungarian features, documentaries and short films – Feb 1-8, 2011.)*

International Festival of New Latin American Cinema, Calle 2, Number 411 Entre 17 & 19 Vedado, Havana 10400, Cuba. Tel: (53 7) 552 841. Web: www.habanafilmfestival.com. *(The festival screens animation, documentary and fiction films made in the preceding year – Dec.)*

International Film Festival Innsbruck, Museumstrasse 31, A-6020 Innsbruck, Austria. Tel: (43 512) 5785 0014. e: info@iffi.at. Web: www.iffi.at. Director: Helmut Groschup. *(Films about Africa, Latin America and Asia. Competitive – May 31-June 5, 2011.)*

International Film Festival of Kerala, Mani Bhavan, Sasthamangalam, Trivandum, Kerala 695010, India. Tel: (91 471) 231 0323. Web: www.iffk.keralafilm.com. *(The festival boasts an extremely popular competition section for films produced or co-produced in Asia, Africa and Latin America within the last year of the festival cycle. The usual sections include world cinema, documentaries (in film formats), short fiction (in film formats), retrospectives, homages and tributes – Dec.)*

International Leipzig Festival for Documentary and Animated Film, Grosse Fleischergasse 11, 04109 Leipzig, Germany. Tel: (49 341) 308 640. e: info@dok-leipzig.de. Web: www.dok-leipzig. de. *(The festival screens the best, most exciting,* *moving and artistically outstanding animated and documentary films from more than 50 countries. Competitive – Oct 17-23, 2011.)*

Israel Film Festival, Israfest Foundation, 6404 Wilshire Blvd, Suite 1240, Los Angeles, CA 90048, USA. Tel: (1 323) 966 4166. e: meir@israelfilmfestival.org. Web: www.israelfilmfestival.com. *(The festival's aim is to showcase Israel's thriving film and television industry, providing an intercultural exchange that advances tolerance and understanding and enriches America's vision of Israel's impressive social and cultural diversity. It screens feature films, documentaries, television dramas and short films and has become one of the nation's leading foreign film festivals and the largest showcase for Israeli films in the United States, as well as a launching pad for several notable US premieres – 2011 dates: Oct 20-Nov 3 Los Angeles; March 31-April 14 New York; May 11-19 Miami.)*

Jameson Dublin International Film Festival, 50 Upper Mount St, Dublin 2, Ireland. Tel: (353 1) 662 4260. e: info@jdiff.com. Web: www.jdiff.com. *(One of Ireland's premiere feature film festivals, aimed squarely at the cinema-going public and presenting over 120 films from around the world. Irish Film Talent is celebrated as an integral part of the JDIFF programme each year by presenting Irish film in all its forms, from archival and documentary to the very latest Irish feature films from first time directors – Feb 17-27, 2011.)*

Jihlava International Documentary Film Festival, Jana Masaryka 16, PO Box 33, 58601 Jihlava, Czech Republic. Tel: (420 7) 7410 1656. e: office@dokument-festival.cz. Web: www.dokument-festival.cz. *(The festival shows work from around the world with screenings followed by after-film talks, plus an accompanying programme of workshops, panel discussions, theatre, authors' readings, concerts, and exhibitions. The festival has four competitive sections: Opus Bunum for world documentaries of innovative themes and high aesthetic quality; Between the Seas presents high quality films from the countries of Central and Eastern Europe; Czech Joy surveys the newest Czech filmmaking; and the Fascinations section*

focuses on experimental documentary. The festival is accompanied by one of the leading events of the year for film professionals: The East European Forum – an encounter between Eastern European documentary filmmakers with producers from prominent European TV stations. In addition, we also collaborate with the market of documentary film from Central and Eastern Europe: East Silver – Oct.)

Kaunas International Film Festival, Antanavos G. 2-31, LT-46280 Kaunas, Lithuania. Tel: (370) 6550 6559. e: info@kinofestivalis.lt. Web: www.kinofestivalis.lt. *(Kaunas Iinternational Film Festival is one of Lithuania's most appreciated film festivals and the main film event in Kaunas, the country's second largest city. The main priority of the festival is a combination of the artistic and social statements in film. In the Wide Angle section the festival presents internationally acclaimed films that reflect modern tendencies. The Identity section shows films with different angles on social issues, where identity in a global context is examined. Kaunas IFF is the only film festival in the region to present a special section on music films with Music Moves the World and films about art in the All the Muses section. These are the three main programmes in the festival, with additional retrospective and themed sections that change each year. Screening in Kaunas and Vilnius – Sept 27-Oct 9, 2011.)*

London Turkish Film Festival, 52B Beatty Rd, London, N16 8EB. Tel: (44 20) 7503 3584. e: vedide@ltff.org.uk. Web: www.ltff.org.uk. *(The growth of London's annual showcase for Turkish films has mirrored the increasing international standing of Turkish cinema over the last fifteen years, with more showings and events in more venues across the capital. The LTFF Golden Wings Awards include the groundbreaking Digital Distribution Award, a €30,000 UK and Ireland cinema exhibition contract, alongside The People's Choice Award and The Lifetime Achievement Award – Nov.)*

Ljubljana International Film Festival, Cankarjev Dom, Prešernova Cesta 010, 1000 Ljubljana, Slovenia. Tel: (386 1) 241 7147. Web: http://

en.liffe.si. *(The festival provides an overview of contemporary world film production and shows over 90 feature films and 15 shorts films in more than 250 screenings. It also includes a film workshop, multi-media interactive projects, exhibition and other events. Competitive – Nov.)*

Lucas International Children's Film Festival, c/o Deutsches Filmmuseum, Schaumainkai 41, 60596 Frankfurt/Main, Germany. Tel: (49 69) 9612 20670. e: info@ lucasfilmfestival.de. Web: www. lucasfilmfestival.de. *(Germany's oldest children's film festival, which is dedicated to showing independent films from all over the world for children aged from four to twelve – Sept 4-11, 2011.)*

Margaret Mead Film & Video Festival, American Museum of Natural History, Central Park, West & 79th St, New York, NY 10024-5192, USA. Tel: (1 212) 769 5000. e: meadfest@amnh.org. Web: www.amnh.org/mead. *(The longest running premiere showcase for International documentaries in the United States, encompassing a broad spectrum of work, from indigenous community media to experimental non-fiction – Mid-Nov.)*

Midnight Sun Film Festival, Kansanopistontie 5, 99600 Sodankylä, Finland. Tel: (358 16) 614 522. e: office@msfilmfestival.fi. Web: www. msfilmfestival.fi. *(The festival is one of the most unique in the world, with internationally renowned film directors, young directors and an international audience meeting under the midnight sun, in the relaxed and informal 'spirit of Sodankylä'. The festival is informally divided in three sections: films by the most famous film directors of all time, pearls of the new cinema and silent films with live music – June 15-19, 2011.)*

Mipdoc, 11 rue du Colonel Pierre Avia, BP 572, 75726 Paris Cedex 15, France. Tel: (33 1) 4190 4580. e: info.miptv@reedmidem.com. Web: www.miptv.com. *(Specialist international screening marketplace and conference for documentaries – April 2-3, 2011.)*

Molodist International Film Festival (Kiev), 6 Saksahanskoho St, Kiev 01033, Ukraine. Tel:

(380 44) 461 9803. e: so_happy@molodist.com or program@molodist.com. Web: www.molodist. com. *(FIAPF accredited specialised international film festival of director's first films. The festival's main goal is to discover new young filmmakers from around the world. The competition programme consists of student films, first short film (animation, documentary, fiction film) and first full-length fiction film. Programme director: Denis Nikitenko – Oct 22-30, 2011.)*

Montpellier International Festival of Mediterranean Film (Cinemed), 78 Ave du Pirée, 34000 Montpellier, France. Tel: (33 4) 9913 7373. e:info@cinemed.tm.fr. Web: www. cinemed.tm.fr. *(The best recent production with more than 120 films previously unscreened films in the official selection and more than €100,000 worth of prizes in cash, aid and services for the winners in the various competitions. Comprising features, shorts, documentaries and experimental films – Late Oct.)*

Mumbai Film Festival, Mumbai Academy of The Moving Image (MAMI), B 111, Crystal Plaza, New Link Rd, Andheri (W), Mumbai 400 053, India. Tel: (91 22) 4106 8223. e: press@mumbaifilmfest. com. Web: www.mumbaifilmfest.com. *(The only independent film festival in India, divided into five sections: International Competition for the First Feature Films of Directors, World Cinema, Indian Showcase, Mumbai Dimensions and Retrospectives – end Oct.)*

Napa Sonoma Wine Country Film Festival, PO Box 303, Glen Ellen, CA 95442, USA. Tel: (1 707) 935 3456. e: wcfilmtest@aol.com. Web: www. wcff.us. *(World cinema, culture and conscience gather in the heart of California's premium wine region, Napa and Sonoma Valleys just 50 miles north of the Golden Gate Bridge. Films are screened during the day in select theatres and at night under the stars in spectacular vineyard settings. The festival is gently paced, mainly non-competitive and accepts features, documentaries, shorts, and animation. All genres are welcome. Programme categories are: World Cinema, US Cinema, EcoCinema (environment), Arts in Film and Cinema of Conscience (social issues) – September).*

New Directors/New Films, Film Society of Lincoln Center, 165 West 65th Street, 4th Floor, New York, NY 10023, USA. Tel: (1 212) 875 5610. e: festival@filmlinc.com. Web: www.filmlinc.com. *(One of the premiere international showcases for the work of emerging filmmakers. It is a non-competitive festival with no separate categories and no prizes awarded. Feature films and shorts are chosen according to quality from all categories: animated, experimental, documentary, dramatic etc. – March 25-April 5, 2011.)*

New York Film Festival, Film Society of Lincoln Center, 165 West 65th Street, 4th Floor, New York, NY 10023-6595, USA. Tel: (1 212) 875 5610. e: festival@filmlinc.com. Web: www.filmlinc.com. *(The festival shows new works by directors from around the world, featuring inspiring and provocative cinema by emerging talents and first-rank international artists, whose films are often recognised as contemporary classics – late Sept-early Oct.)*

Open Air Filmfest Weiterstadt, PO Box 1164, D-64320 Weiterstadt, Germany. Tel: (49 61) 501 2185. e: filmfest@weiterstadt.de. Web: www.filmfest-weiterstadt.de. *(Mainly short films of all genres, formats and lengths although the programme has been extended to include feature films and documentaries. Attending filmmakers may camp in the forest, next to the festival area. Competitive, May 15 deadline for entries – Aug 11-15, 2011.)*

Palm Beach International Film Festival, 289 Via Naranjas, Royal Palm Plaza, Suite 48, Boca Raton, Florida 33432, USA. Tel: (1 561) 362 0003.

e: info@pbifilmfest.org. Web: www.pbifilmfest.org. *(The Festival is committed to supporting emerging filmmakers of today and tomorrow, and screens independent features, shorts and documentaries from around the world. Competitive – March 23-31, 2011.)*

Palm Springs International Festival of Short Films & Film Market, 1700 E Tahquitz Canyon Way, Suite 3, Palm Springs, CA 92262, USA. Tel: (1 760) 322 2930. e: info@psfilmfest.org. Web: www.psfilmfest.org. *(Competitive shorts festival and market. Student, animation, documentary, live action and international competition with Audience and Juried Awards. Seminars and workshops – June.)*

Pan-Asia Film Festival, Asia House, 63 Cavendish St, London W1G 7LP, UK, Tel: (44 20) 7307 5430. e: enquiries@asiahouse.co.uk. Web: www.asiahouse.org. *(The festival is presented by Asia House, the UK's leading pan-Asian cultural organisation. It aims to celebrate the best in new Asian cinema, bringing together some of the freshest, emerging talent from Asia alongside work by established filmmakers, reflecting the vibrancy and energy in Asian filmmaking today. The festival supports the Asia House mission of contributing to the understanding and knowledge of the countries and cultures of Asia in the UK. It is the only festival of its kind in the UK, offering London audiences the opportunity to engage in Asian cinema from the whole of the continent – from the Persian Gulf to the Pacific, providing a platform for promoting Asian cinema in the UK. Pan-Asia Film Festival forms part of Asia House's year-round cultural programme, which has a* reputation for high quality talks, discussions, performance and film covering the arts, culture and current affairs of Asia. Asia House also runs the only fest in the UK dedicated to writing about Asia, the Asia House festival of Asian Literature. The third edition of the Pan-Asia Film Festival will be held in London – March 2011).

Philadelphia Film Festival, Philadelphia Film Society, 1600 North 5th Street, Philadelphia, PA 19122, USA. Tel: (1 267) 239 2941. e: info@filmadelphia.org. Web: www.filmadelphia.com. *(The festival screens over 100 International and USA features, documentaries, shorts and animation from 25 countries to an audience of over 30,000. Usually held in Spring, the festival moved to Autumn in order to programme from a much wider and excellent selection of films, following their debuts at Cannes, Toronto, Venice etc. – Mid Oct.)*

Ravenna Nightmare Film Festival, Via Mura di Porta Serrata 13, 48100 Ravenna, Italy. Tel: (39 05) 4468 4242. e: ravennanightmare@gmail.com. Web: www.ravennanightmare.it. *(The festival revolves around Halloween weekend and features horror and fantastic film. The main event of the festival is the International Competition for features, which usually admits around 10-12 feature films, all of which are national premieres. Also features a number of special events out of competition, retrospectives, parties, music, and literature events featuring important writers of the horror genre – late Oct.)*

River to River: Florence Indian Film Festival, Piazza Santo Spirito 1, 50125 Firenze, Italy. Tel: (39 055) 286 929. Web: www.rivertoriver.it. *(The Festival had its first edition in October 2001 at the Rondò di Bacco Theatre of Palazzo Pitti in Florence, Italy. The aim of River to River is to promote only films from and about India, and it is the first Festival of this kind in the world – Dec.)*

St Louis International Film Festival, 3547 Olive St, St Louis, MO 63103-1014, USA. Tel: (1 314) 289 4150. e: mailroom@cinemastlouis.org. Web: www.cinemastlouis.org. *(SLIFF showcases the best in cutting-edge features and shorts from around the globe. The majority of the more than 300 films screened, many of them critically lauded award-winners, will receive their only St Louis exposure at the festival. Competitive – Nov.)*

St Petersburg International Film Festival, 10 Kamennostrovsky Ave, St Petersburg 197101, Russia. Tel: (7 812) 237 0072. e: info@filmfest.ru. Web: www.filmfest.ru. *(Non-competitive, showcasing the best films from around the world – June.)*

San Sebastian Horror and Fantasy Film Festival, Reina Regente 8, 20003 Donostia-San Sebastian, Spain. Tel: (34 943) 481 197. e: cinema_cinema@donostia.org. Web: www.sansebastianhorrorfestival.com. *(Cult, cutting-edge horror fantasy festival; short film and feature competition – Late Oct/early Nov.)*

San Sebastian Human Rights Film Festival, Donostia Kultura, Plaza de la Constitucion 1, 20003 Donostia-San Sebastian, Spain. Tel: (34 943) 481 471. e: cinederechoshumanos@donostia.org. Web: www.cineyderechoshumanos.com. *(Short films and features about human rights – April 8-15, 2011.)*

Santa Barbara International Film Festival, 1528 Chapala St 203, Santa Barbara, CA 93101, USA. Tel: (1 805) 963 0023. e:info@sbfilmfestival.org. Web: www.sbfilmfestival.org. *(Celebrating its 25th Anniversary in 2010 the festival screens over 250 international films and will host a plethora of parties, making it a spectacular entertainment experience – Jan 27-Feb 6, 2011.)*

Sarajevo Film Festival, Zelenih beretki 12/1, 71000 Sarajevo, Bosnia and Herzegovina. Tel: (387 33) 209 411. e: press@sff.ba. Web: www.sff.ba. *(The festival presents a wide selection of both competitive and non-competitive films. The main focus is the region of Southeast Europe (Albania, Austria, Bosnia and Herzegovina, Bulgaria, Croatia, Cyprus, Greece, Hungary, Macedonia, Malta, Montenegro, Romania, Serbia, Slovenia, Turkey) with filmmakers from this region competing in the Feature, Short and Documentary film sections. The festival aims to present important*

TELEWIZJA POLSKA

and innovative films of high artistic value made throughout the world – July 22-30, 2011.)

Sarasota Film Festival, 1991 Main St, Main Plaza, Sarasota, Florida 34236, USA. Tel: (1 941) 364 9514. e: kathy@sarasotafilmfestival.com. Web: www.sarasotafilmfestival.com. *(Independent films and events in a beautiful location; hospitable, inquisitive audiences plus a well-organised and publicised programme – April 8-17, 2011.)*

Silent Film Days in Tromsø, PO Box, 285, N-9253 Tromsø, Norway. Tel: (47) 7775 3090. e: info@tiff.no. Web: www.verdensteatret.no/ stumfilmdager. *(The programme encompasses not only the great classics of silent film, but also many hidden treasures recovered from national and international archives – presented here to a new audience. All films are screened with live music, composed and performed by international artists. The style of music ranges from the classical piano or organ accompaniment of the silent film tradition to jazz, rock and electronic music. The fifth edition of Silent Film Days in 2010 featured the city's own Tromsø Chamber Orchestra in collaboration with German composer and conductor Günter A Buchwald, performing to the Russian/American double comedy feature* Chess Fever *(V Pudovkin) and* Double Whoopee *(L Foster). Another festival highlight was F W Murnau's classic,* Nosferatu, *reawakened by a massive soundtrack by doom metal band* River to Aintry *in front of a packed theatre at Verdensteatret, which is Tromsø's original cinema, opened in 1916. Other performers included MoMA in-house silent film pianist Ben Model, the renowned Swedish silent film music composer*

River to Aintry performing to FW Murnau's Nosferatu. *Photo: Håvard Stangnes*

Matti Bye with his ensemble, and Norwegian/ Russian electronic act Gaute Barlindhaug, Nasra Ali Omar and Victor Shubin – Sept 8-11, 2011.)

Sofia International Film Festival, 1 Bulgaria Sq, Sofia 1463, Bulgaria. Tel: (359 2) 952 6467. e: office@sofiaiff.com. Web: www.siff.bg. *(Competitive festival showcasing new Bulgarian and Balkan films to international audiences. It includes the following sections: Official programme (international competition for 1st or 2nd features and special screenings), documentary programme (competition), Bulgarian feature films, Balkan films showcase, European screen, World screen, Bulgarian shorts competition, Shorts, retrospectives, tributes and special events. Sofia Meetings: Co-production Market for 1st, 2nd or 3d features of the director takes place March 10-13, 2011. Festival: March 4-20, 2011.)*

Stockholm International Film Festival Junior, PO Box 3136, S-103 62 Stockholm, Sweden. Tel: (46 8) 677 5000. e: info@stockholmfilmfestival.

Silent Film Days in Tromsø

September 8-11, 2011

se. Web: www.stockholmfilmfestival.se. *(The Junior festival is one of the leading film festivals for children in Sweden. The festival screens about 25 films and invites filmmakers from all over the world to meet the young audience in Stockholm. Junior is also involved in getting youngsters to make their own film and arranges filmmaking workshops and the national short film competition 1 minute film for everyone between 6-16 years of age. In 2010 the 11th festival welcomed 17,000 visitors – April 11-16, 2011.)*

Stuttgart Festival of Animated Film (ITFS), Film-und Medienfestival GmbH, Schlosstrasse 84, 70176 Stuttgart, Germany. Tel: (49 711) 925 460. e: kontakt@festival-gmbh.de. Web: www. itfs.de. *(One of the largest events for animated film worldwide. The festival showcases a diverse range of animated film starting with artistic short films, through TV series and children's films and rounded off with feature-length animation. The festival focuses particularly on supporting talented young filmmakers with a special sponsorship award and the Young Animation competition – May 3-8, 2011.)*

Sunny Side of the Doc, Résidence le Gabut Bâtiment E, 16 rue de l'Aimable Nanette, 17000 La Rochelle, France. Tel: (33 5) 4655 7979. e: info@sunnysideofthedoc.com. Web: www.sun-nysideofthedoc.com. *(International documentary market and essential rendezvous point for documentary filmmakers – June 21-24, 2011.)*

Sydney Film Festival, PO Box 96, Strawberry Hills, NSW 2012, Australia. Tel: (61 2) 9318 0999. e: info@sff.org.au. Web: www.sydneyfilmfestival. org. *(The Sydney Film Festival is one of the longest running events of its kind in the world. Each year the festival brings the best new films from around the world to audiences in Sydney. As well as brand new features from over 40 countries, we screen short films, Australian features, documentaries and archive titles, many of which are recently restored. The festival hosts a number of awards to recognise excellence in filmmaking, including the Dendy Awards for Australian Short Films, (which are Academy Award eligible), the FOXTEL Australian Documentary*

Awards and the Official Competition, which celebrates 'courageous and audacious filmmaking'. When the festival is over, we run the Travelling Film Festival, taking mini-festivals to 15 venues across regional NSW, the Northern Territory and rural Queensland – June 8-19, 2011.)

Taipei Golden Horse Film Festival, e: info@ goldenhorse.org.tw. Web: www.goldenhorse.org. tw. *(The most prominent annual film festival in Taiwan, comprised of two parts. The Golden Horse Awards Competition encourages the development of Chinese-language films. The international programme is intended to introduce excellent films from around the world to Taiwanese audiences in order to stimulate an exchange of ideas and inspire creativity – Late Nov/early Dec.)*

Taormina Film Fest in Sicily, Corso Umberto 19, 98039 Taormina Messina, Italy. Tel Rome office: (39 064) 86808 e: communications@ taorminafilmfest.it. Web: www. taorminafilmfest. it. *(With the aim of offering festival access to audiences around Sicily, finding extra screening space for its shows, increasing its impact in Sicily, offering a wide range of media stories and increasing tourism in the entire region, from 2009 the festival changed its name to become the Taormina Film Fest in Sicily. In addition to sharing Taormina's films and entertaining many of its actors, directors and journalists, each of the new locations around the island participate in the eight-day festival with their own exclusive film programme. The festival has a strong identity as a Mediterranean festival with strong ties to the US and world cinema and has chosen to remain a boutique showcase for a limited number of highly-selected films from the most recent production – June.)*

Third Eye Asian Film Festival, Asian Film Foundation, Rajkamal Studio, Parel, Mumbai 400012, India. Tel: (91 22) 2413 7791. e: affmumbai@gmail.com. Web: www.affmumbai. com. *(The Third Eye Asian Film Festival was established in 2002 by the then Mayor of Mumbai, Kiran Shantaram. The main objective of the Festival is to promote Asian Cinema, presented by Asian Film Foundation, a registered organisation*

TVP
TELEWIZJA POLSKA

Third ◉ Eye

Asian Film Festivel
Mumbai
Dec.22- Dec. 29, 2011

Read about competions

www.affmumbai.com

supported by state Government of Maharashtra. Mumbai has a big film industry. However in India only Hollywood & Bollywood films are released in the theatre. No Asian Film receive any theatrical release. That is why the prime objective is to promote Asian Cinema. Asian countries share cultural similarities and common socio-economic situations. The Third Eye Asian Film Festival was established to create awareness about each other amongst Asian countries with cinema as a common bond, bringing people together and fostering understanding between cultures.

Members and guests at the opening Ceremony.

2011 will mark the 10th edition of the Third Eye Asian Film Festival and it will be celebrated on a grand scale. To attract the college students, the dates of the festival have been shifted from October to December and will be held during the Christmas holidays. The list of awards given in the 9th Third Eye Asian Film Festival by the International Jury: Debut/Second Feature Film Competition Best Film Award was shared by Son of Babylon (Iraq), directed by Mohamed Al Daradji and Judge (China), directed by Liu Jie. In the Short Film Fiction Competition, the Best Short Film Fiction Award was shared by Majid in China (China), directed by Xu Zheng and Diploma (Israel), directed by Yaelle Kayam. The Special Jury Award was given to The Bitter End of Coffee (Iran), directed by Mortaza Akoochekian, with a Special Mention to Masala Mama (Singapore), directed by Michael Kam. The Netpac Award Winner was Judge (China), directed by Liu Jie. Chairman: Kiran Shantaram. Festival Director: Sudhir Nandgaonkar – Dec 22-29, 2011).

Tibet Film Festival, 154D St Paul's Rd, London N1 2LL, UK. Tel: (44) 07876 796735. e: tibetfilmfest@day-for-night.org. Web: www. day-for-night.org/tibetfilmfestival. (The Tibet Film Festival brings together inspiring films on Tibet and Tibetan culture, whilst also looking at neighbouring regions and shared cultural, geographical and historical links. In particular, the festival seeks to stimulate broader discussions on human rights, conflict, freedom and cultural identity. Whilst the focus is on the most recent films on Tibet-related subjects, the festival has also become known for its offshoot visual arts, poetry and music events. Based in London, the festival tours the UK each year and has also toured to other international venues in Copenhagen and Seoul. A year-round programme of screenings and events is also held. It is the first major international festival of its kind, providing a platform for young and emerging Tibetan filmmakers, offering audiences rare opportunities to engage in a wide range of films that may otherwise not achieve theatrical releases. A catalogue from past festivals and other Tibet related material is available to festivals, venues, NGOs and educational institutions. Tibet Film Festival is organised by London-based organisation, Day for Night, which works to promote accessibility and diversity in visual culture. The 4th edition of the festival will take place in Autumn 2011).

Transilvania International Film Festival Cluj-Napoca (TIFF), Popa Soare 52, Sector 2, 023984 Bucharest, Romania. Tel: (40) 21 326 6480. e:info@ tiff.ro. Web: www.tiff.ro. *(Founded in 2002, TIFF has grown rapidly to be the most important film-related event in Romania and one of the most spectacular annual events in the region. Over the years, TIFF has invited, as recipients of the Lifetime Achievement Award or special guests of the event, important figures from world cinema, including Wim Wenders, Claudia Cardinale, Catherine Deneuve, Julie Delpy, Fanny Ardant, Michael Radford, Annie Girardot, Udo Kier, Vanessa Redgrave, Nicolas Roeg and Franco Nero. In 2010, over 55,000 people attended the screenings in the thirteen venues of Cluj Napoca, eager not to miss over 240 features and short films presented in the Competitive and Showcase sections. Having become a traditional premiere hub for domestic features, which are now landmarks of the evolution of the so-called Romanian New Wave, TIFF has also developed a market of Romanian work-in-progress fiction and documentary feature projects, scheduled as part of Romanian Days, which takes place during the festival – Cluj June 3-12, 2011, Sibiu June 15-19, 2011.)*

Trieste Film Festival, Via Donota 1, 34121 Trieste, Italy. Tel: (39 040) 347 6076. e: info@ alpeadriacinema.it. Web: www.alpeadriacinema. it. *(The leading festival in Italy showcasing Central and Eastern European Cinema – Jan 20-27, 2011.)*

True/False Film Festival, 5 South Ninth St, Columbia, Missouri 65201, USA. Tel: (1 573) 442 8783. e: info@truefalse.org. Web: www. truefalse.org. *(International documentary festival screening some 50 films and including two shorts programmes – March 3-6, 2011.)*

Uppsala International Short Film Festival, PO Box 2104, SE-750 02 Uppsala, Sweden. Tel: (46 18) 120 025. e: info@shortfilmfestival.com. Web:

www.shortfilmfestival.com. *(Sweden's premiere arena for short film, having attained both national recognition of the Swedish Film Institute and genuine international renown. In addition, the festival is the most important international cultural event in Uppsala. Every year the festival shows more than 300 short films in five different sections, exploring the diversity and richness of the short film – from new film to retrospective programmes, from fiction, documentary and experimental film to animation. Competitive – Oct 24-30, 2011.)*

USA Film Festival, 6116 N Central Expressway, Suite 105, Dallas, Texas 75206, USA. Tel: (1 214) 821 6300. e: usafilmfestival@aol.com. Web: www.usafilmfestival.com. *(The festival features the best new American and foreign films, the Academy qualifying National Short Film and Video Competition and special tributes – April.)*

ViewFinders International Film Festival for Youth, PO Box 36139, Halifax, NS, B3J 3S9, Canada. Tel: (1 902) 422 3456. e: festival@ atlanticfilm.com. Web: www.atlanticfilm.com. *(ViewFinders is a five-day celebration of film, video and media, geared towards youth, ages 3-18. The festival includes a comprehensive school programme complete with a guide for educators, as well as evening and weekend screenings and events for families and young adults. ViewFinders features films from around the world and includes a selection of films made by children and youth – April 12-16, 2011.)*

Vila do Conde, Auditório Municipal, Praça da República, 4480-715 Vila do Conde, Portugal. Tel: (351 252) 646 516. e: info@curtas.pt. Web: www. curtasmetragens.pt. *(National and International shorts competitions with special programme and retrospectives – July 9-17, 2011.)*

Vilnius International Film Festival (Kino Pavasaris), Gediminas Ave 50, Vilnius 01110, Lithuania. Tel: (370) 5249 7221. e: info@ kinopavasaris.lt. Web: www.kinopavasaris. lt. *(Vilnius International Film Festival (Vilnius IFF) 'Kino Pavasaris' is the biggest and most important cinema event in Lithuania. Since 1995, the festival has earned its reputation*

The Mayor of Vilnius hosts a reception at the Town Hall. Featured are the jury (left to right, Nick Holdsworth, Tatyana Liutayeva, Vilius Navickas, Nikolai Nikitin, Antoine Simkine, Peter Suschitzky) of 15th Vilnius International Film Festival. Photo: Aurimas Zdanavicius

for screening new films of the highest quality newest, carefully picked from the world's best festivals, where they are awarded prizes by both the audience and film critics. Serious discussion, visits by widely-respected Lithuanian and international filmmakers, events for industry guests, and social and educational projects play an essential part of the festival, as do the many parties. Vilnius IFF also brings together a wide range of film festival representatives to the annual 'Central and Eastern European International Film Festivals Forum'. Every year the festival presents more than 100 films, which are divided into a number of programmes. In 2010 more than 54,000 people attended the screenings. In 2011, the 16th edition of Vilnius IFF is once again proud to present the competition programme 'New Europe – New Names', which was first introduced in 2009 and has now become a popular fixture at the festival. The best debut films from Eastern and Central Europe are in competition for 'The Best Film'

Award, chosen by an International Jury of leading film professionals – March 17-31, 2011.)

Washington, DC International Film Festival (Filmfest DC), PO Box 5571, Washington, DC 20009, USA. Tel: (1 202) 717 0700. e: filmfestdc@filmfestdc.org. Web: www.dciff.org. *(Competitive festival celebrating the best in world cinema from over 30 countries – April.)*

ZagrebDox, Factum Centre for Drama Art, Nova Ves 18/3, 10 000 Zagreb, Croatia. Tel: (385 1) 485 4821. e: info@zagrebdox.net. Web: www.zagrebdox.net. *(International and competitive documentary film festival – Feb 28-March 7, 2011.)*

Zurich Film Festival, Bederstrasse 51, 8002 Zurich, Switzerland. Tel: (41 44) 286 6000. e: info@zurichfilmfestival.org. Web: www.zurichfilmfestival.org. *(The festival presents film premieres from all over the world, offers cinematic treats to a fascinated national and international audience, and facilitates direct on-the-spot exchanges with filmmakers. The International Competition forms the core of the festival. The competition will present films by young, aspiring filmmakers who will compete for the Golden Eye with their first, second or third films. All competition films are world, European or Swiss premieres. Films will be screened in the following three categories: International Feature Film Competition, German-Language Feature Film Competition, International Documentary Film Competition. With numerous events and parties complementing the cinema programme, the festival offers an ideal platform for networking and exchanging ideas – Sept 22-Oct 2, 2011.)*

Index to Advertisers

Abu Dhabi Film Commission — 60
Al Arabia Cinema — 121
American Film Festival — 391
Artefact Films — 57, 98, 297
Barcelona-Catalunya Film Commission — 237
British Film Institute — 41
BUFF Film Festival — 322
Cineuropa — 10, 103
Cork Film Festival — 327
FilmFestival Cottbus — 329
Czech Film Center — 109
DB Cine — 268
Dolby Laboratories, Inc — back cover
Egyptian Media Production City Co. — 119
Era New Horizons International Film Festival — 333
Estonian Film Foundation — 125
European Film Awards — 302
Fajr International Film Festival — 336
Fantasporto — 338
Far East Film Festival — 339
Farabi Cinema Foundation — 161
Filmgate — 9
Film I Väst — 32
Film Riga — 179, 180
Galway Film Fleadh — 399
Ghent International Film Festival — 341
goEast Festival of Central and Eastern
    European Film — 343
Golden Apricot International Film Festival — 400
Haguesund - Norwegian International
    Film Festival — 345
Hof International Film Festival — 123, 347
Icelandic Film Centre — 152
International Film Festival & Forum
    on Human Rights (FIFDH) — 349
International Short Film Festival Winterthur — 350

Iranian International Market for Film
    and TV Programmes — 335
Jerusalem International Film Festival — 353
Locarno International Film Festival — 2, 311
London Book Fair — 3
Malta Film Commission — 185
Ministry of Education and Culture of Cyprus,
    Cultural Dept. — 107
Mississippi Film Office — 269
Moroccan Cinematographic Center — 190
Netherlands Film Festival — 359
Nevada Film Office — 271
Visions du Réel, International Film Festival -
    Nyon — 361
Oulu International Children's and Youth
    Film Festival — 363
Pordenone Silent Film Festival — 365
Portland International Film Festival — 365
Reykjavík International Film Festival — 367
Samefive — 6, 390
Second Run DVD — 27, 254
Seville European Film Festival — 370
Sheffield Doc/Fest — 373
Silent Film Days in Tromso — 406
Soho House Berlin — 139
Solothurn Film Festival — 375
Swiss Films — 245, 247
Tallinn Black Nights Film Festival (PÖFF) — 379
Third Eye Asian Film Festival — 408
Tromsø International Film Festival — 384
Telewizja Polska S.A. — 207, 298
Valladolid International Film Festival — 385
Viennale - Vienna International Film Festival — 77, 388
Vilnius International Film Festival
    'Kino Pavasaris' — 401
Whistling Woods International — 4, 40